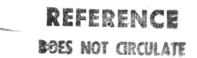

REFERENCE
DOES NOT CIRCULATE

MAR 0 2 2006

SO-ANP-397

3 1192 01309 8932

R 790.2092 C767 v. 66

Contemporary theatre, film,
and television.

Contemporary Theatre, Film and Television

ISSN 0749-064X

Contemporary Theatre, Film and Television

A Biographical Guide Featuring Performers,
Directors, Writers, Producers, Designers, Managers,
Choreographers, Technicians, Composers, Executives,
Dancers, and Critics in the United States, Canada,
Great Britain and the World

Thomas Riggs, Editor

Volume 66

Includes Cumulative Index Containing References to
Who's Who in the Theatre and *Who Was Who in the Theatre*

EVANSTON PUBLIC LIBRARY
1703 ORRINGTON AVENUE
EVANSTON, ILLINOIS 60201

Detroit • New York • San Francisco • San Diego • New Haven, Conn. • Waterville, Maine • London • Munich

Contemporary Theatre, Film & Television, Vol. 66

Editor
Thomas Riggs

CTFT Staff
Mariko Fujinaka, Janice Jorgensen, Candice Mancini, Annette Petrusso, Susan Risland, Lisa Sherwin, Arlene True, Pam Zuber

Project Editor
Joseph Palmisano

Editorial Support Services
Ryan Cartmill

Composition and Electronic Capture
Carolyn A. Roney

Manufacturing
Drew Kalasky

© 2006 Thomson Gale, a part of the Thomson Corporation.

Thomson and Star Logo are trademarks and Gale is a registered trademark used herein under license.

For more information, contact
Thomson Gale
27500 Drake Rd.
Farmington Hills, MI 48331-3535
Or you can visit our internet site at
http://www.gale.com

ALL RIGHTS RESERVED
No part of this work covered by the copyright herein may be reproduced or used in any form or by any means—graphic, electronic, or mechanical, including photocopying, recording, taping, Web distribution, or information storage retrieval systems—without the written permission of the publisher.

This publication is a creative work fully protected by all applicable copyright laws, as well as by misappropriation, trade secret, unfair competition, and other applicable laws. The authors and editors of this work have added value to the underlying factual material herein through one or more of the following: unique and original selection, coordination, expression, arrangement, and classification of the information.

For permission to use material from the product, submit your request via the Web at http://www.gale-edit.com/permissions, or you may download our Permissions Request form and submit your request by fax or mail to:

Permissions Department
Thomson Gale
27500 Drake Rd.
Farmington Hills, MI 48331-3535
Permissions Hotline:
248-699-8006 or 800-877-4253, ext. 8006
Fax 248-699-8074 or 800-762-4058

Since this page cannot legibly accommodate all copyright notices, the acknowledgments constitute an extension of the copyright notice.

While every effort has been made to secure permission to reprint material and to ensure the reliability of the information presented in this publication, Thomson Gale neither guarantees the accuracy of the data contained herein nor assumes any responsibility for errors, omissions or discrepancies. Thomson Gale accepts no payment for listing; and inclusion in the publication of any organization, agency, institution, publication, service, or individual does not imply endorsment of the editors or publisher. Errors brought to the attention of the publisher and verified to the satisfaction of the publisher will be corrected in future editions.

LIBRARY OF CONGRESS CATALOG CARD NUMBER 84-649371

ISBN 0-7876-9039-2
ISSN 0749-064X

Printed in the United States of America
10 9 8 7 6 5 4 3 2 1

Contents

Preface

Provides Broad, Single-Source Coverage in the Entertainment Field

Contemporary Theatre, Film and Television (CTFT) is a biographical reference series designed to provide students, educators, researchers, librarians, and general readers with information on a wide range of entertainment figures. Unlike single-volume reference works that focus on a limited number of artists or on a specific segment of the entertainment field, *CTFT* is an ongoing publication that includes entries on individuals active in the theatre, film, and television industries. Before the publication of *CTFT*, information-seekers had no choice but to consult several different sources in order to locate the in-depth biographical and credit data that makes *CTFT's* one-stop coverage the most comprehensive available about the lives and work of performing arts professionals.

Scope

CTFT covers not only performers, directors, writers, and producers, but also behind-the-scenes specialists such as designers, managers, choreographers, technicians, composers, executives, dancers, and critics from the United States, Canada, Great Britain, and the world. With 225 entries in *CTFT 66*, the series now provides biographies on approximately 19,798 people involved in all aspects of theatre, film, and television.

CTFT gives primary emphasis to people who are currently active. New entries are prepared on major stars as well as those who are just beginning to win acclaim for their work. *CTFT* also includes entries on personalities who have died but whose work commands lasting interest.

Compilation Methods

CTFT editors identify candidates for inclusion in the series by consulting biographical dictionaries, industry directories, entertainment annuals, trade and general interest periodicals, newspapers, and online databases. Additionally, the editors of *CTFT* maintain regular contact with industry advisors and professionals who routinely suggest new candidates for inclusion in the series. Entries are compiled from published biographical sources which are believed to be reliable, but have not been verified for this edition by the listee or their agents.

Revised Entries

To ensure *CTFT's* timeliness and comprehensiveness, entries from previous volumes, as well as from Gale's *Who's Who in the Theatre*, are updated for individuals who have been active enough to require revision of their earlier biographies. Such individuals will merit revised entries as often as there is substantial new information to provide. Obituary notices for deceased entertainment personalities already listed in *CTFT* are also published.

Accessible Format Makes Data Easy to Locate

CTFT entries, modeled after those in Gale's highly regarded *Contemporary Authors* series, are written in a clear, readable style designed to help users focus quickly on specific facts. The following is a summary of the information found in *CTFT* sketches:

- *ENTRY HEADING:* the form of the name by which the listee is best known.

- *PERSONAL:* full or original name; dates and places of birth and death; family data; colleges attended, degrees earned, and professional training; political and religious affiliations when known; avocational interests.

- *ADDRESSES:* home, office, agent, publicist and/or manager addresses.

- *CAREER:* tagline indicating principal areas of entertainment work; resume of career positions and other vocational achievements; military service.

- *MEMBER:* memberships and offices held in professional, union, civic, and social organizations.

- *AWARDS, HONORS:* theatre, film, and television awards and nominations; literary and civic awards; honorary degrees.

- *CREDITS:* comprehensive title-by-title listings of theatre, film, and television appearance and work credits, including roles and production data as well as debut and genre information.

- *RECORDINGS:* album, single song, video, and taped reading releases; recording labels and dates when available.

- *WRITINGS:* title-by-title listing of plays, screenplays, scripts, and musical compositions along with production information; books, including autobiographies, and other publications.

- *ADAPTATIONS:* a list of films, plays, and other media which have been adapted from the listee's work.

- *SIDELIGHTS:* favorite roles; portions of agent- prepared biographies or personal statements from the listee when available.

- *OTHER SOURCES:* books, periodicals, and internet sites where interviews or feature stories can be found.

Access Thousands of Entries Using *CTFT*'s Cumulative Index

Each volume of *CTFT* contains a cumulative index to the entire series. As an added feature, this index also includes references to all seventeen editions of *Who's Who in the Theatre* and to the four-volume compilation *Who Was Who in the Theatre.*

Available in Electronic Format

Online. Recent volumes of *CTFT* are available online as part of the Gale Biographies (GALBIO) database accessible through LEXIS-NEXIS. For more information, contact LEXIS-NEXIS, P.O. Box 933, Dayton, OH 45401-0933; phone (937) 865-6800, toll-free: 800-543-6862.

Suggestions Are Welcome

Contemporary Theatre, Film and Television is intended to serve as a useful reference tool for a wide audience, so comments about any aspect of this work are encouraged. Suggestions of entertainment professionals to include in future volumes are also welcome. Send comments and suggestions to: The Editor, *Contemporary Theatre, Film and Television*, Thomson Gale, 27500 Drake Rd., Farmington Hills, MI 48331-3535; or feel free to call toll-free at 1-800-877-GALE.

Contemporary Theatre, Film and Television

ADCOCK, Danny 1948–

PERSONAL

Born 1948, in Sydney, New South Wales, Australia.

Career: Actor.

CREDITS

Film Appearances:

Policeman, *The Cars That Ate Paris* (also known as *Cars* and *Cars That Eat People*), Paramount, 1974.

Trooper Hayes, *Lost in the Wild* (also known as *Barney*), 1976.

Bus driver, *The Earthling,* 1980.

Thomas, *Kitty and the Bagman,* Paramount, 1982.

Jingles, *On the Run,* United Artists, 1982.

Brown, *We of the Never Never,* Triumph Releasing, 1982.

John Meadows, *Early Frost,* 1982.

Ray, *Fran,* 1985.

Mitchell, *Quigley Down Under,* Metro–Goldwyn–Mayer/United Artists, 1990.

James Dean, *Resistance,* Angelika, 1992.

ASIO detective, *Joey,* 1997.

Ispector Higgs, *Get Rich Quick,* Vivo Films, 2004.

Bilko, *A Family Legacy* (short film), 2005.

Television Appearances; Movies:

ASIO agent, *Deadline,* Nine Network, 1982.

Cody: A Family Affair, Seven Network, 1994.

Athol Callaghan, *Halifax f.p.: Swimming with Sharks,* 1999.

Studds, *Airtight,* UPN, 1999.

Television Appearances; Series:

P.O. "Buffer" Johnston, *Patrol Boat,* Australian Broadcasting Corporation, 1979.

Duncan Adams, *Arcade,* Ten Network, 1980.

The Coral Island, ITV, 1981.

The Bush Gang, Australian Broadcasting Corporation, 1981.

Geoff Carlson, a recurring role, *Prisoner,* Ten Network, 1982–83.

Joe Parker, *Sons and Daughters,* Seven Network, 1982.

Firefighter Danny "Nugget" Hunt, *Fire,* 1995–96.

Barry Baxter, a recurring role, *Blue Heelers,* Seven Network, 2004.

Television Appearances; Miniseries:

Lloyd Ross, *True Believers,* Australian Broadcasting Corporation, 1988.

Television Appearances; Episodic:

Donald, "North of the Headland," *Riptide,* Seven Network, 1969.

Don Reilly, "Once a Killer," *Homicide,* Seven Network, 1970.

Des Giles, "Patterson's Curse," *Homicide,* Seven Network, 1970.

Les Baker, "Twenty Six Hours," *Matlock Police,* Ten Network, 1971.

Bob Miller, "The Acquittal," *Homicide,* Seven Network, 1971.

Thomas, "Heroes' Day," *Matlock Police,* Ten Network, 1971.

Stevens, "No Short Cuts," *Division 4,* Nine Network, 1971.

Kevin O'Brien, "Millbank Nugget," *Matlock Police,* Ten Network, 1971.

Radio operator, "The Trader," *Spyforce,* Nine Network, 1971.

Nipper Cameron, "Bent Law," *Division 4,* Nine Network, 1971.

Woodsie, "A Continental Gentleman," *Division 4,* Nine Network, 1972.

"Blue" Fisher, "Anti–Gravity," *Homicide,* Seven Network, 1972.

Tony Carr, "Boney Meets the Daybreak Killer," *Boney,* Seven Network, 1972.

Len Barker, "If Marie Dies, the World Stops," *Matlock Police,* Ten Network, 1972.

KennyHudson, "Senior Stewart," *Division 4,* Nine Network, 1972.

Jeff Miller, "Skeleton Key," *Homicide,* Seven Network, 1973.

Mike Chapman, "Collision Course," *Matlock Police,* Ten Network, 1973.

"The Monkey Game," *Division 4,* Nine Network, 1973.

Neil Freeman, "I Killed Amanda Clarke," *Homicide,* Seven Network, 1973.

Alex Andrews, "Sky High," *Matlock Police,* Ten Network, 1973.

Harry Fisher, "There's Going to Be a War," *Ryan,* 1974.

Jimmy Logan, "Have a Good Weekend," *Matlock Police,* Ten Network, 1975.

Frank Gardiner, "Big Fish, Small Fry," *Division 4,* Nine Network, 1975.

Dave Coburn, "Outside Chance," *Homicide,* Seven Network, 1976.

"Final Curtain," *King's Men,* Nine Network, 1976.

Ben Salter, "Mrs. Peter Ramsay," *Young Ramsay,* Seven Network, 1978.

"Smoke out at Wombat Crescent," *Kingswood Country,* Seven Network, 1981.

Detective Donnolly, "I Know Where She's Gone: Parts 1 & 2," *A Country Practice,* Seven Network, 1982.

Graham Randall, "The Reckoning: Parts 1 & 2," *A Country Practice,* Seven Network, 1983.

Tommy Ambrose, "From This Day Forward: Parts 1 & 2," *A Country Practice,* Seven Network, 1983.

Charlie Simmons, *E Street,* Ten Network, 1991.

Antec Strzelecki, "Family: Parts 1 & 2," *A Country Practice,* Seven Network, 1992.

Jarrod Banks, "High Country Justice," *Snowy River: The McGregor Saga,* Nine Network and The Family Channel, 1995.

Gordon Macleay, *Home and Away,* Seven Network, 1998.

Rhys "Kegs" Keagan, "Blood Relations," *Water Rats,* Nine Network, 1999.

T'raltixx, "Crackers Don't Matter," *Farscape,* Sci–Fi Channel, 2000.

Alan Slater, "All the Sons and Daughters," *All Saints,* Seven Network, 2001.

Co–Kura Strappa, "Losing Time," *Farscape,* Sci–Fi Channel, 2001.

Co–Kura Strappa, "Incubator," *Farscape,* Sci–Fi Channel, 2001.

Co–Kura Strappa, "Into the Lion's Den: Parts 1 & 2," *Farscape,* Sci–Fi Channel, 2001.

Damien Broadbent, "Cops and Robbers," *Stingers,* 2004.

ADDY, Mark 1964(?)–

PERSONAL

Born January 14, 1964 (some sources cite 1963), in York, England; married Kelly (a bar manager); children: Ruby. *Education:* Attended Royal Academy of Dramatic Art, London.

Addresses: *Agent*—International Creative Management, 8942 Wilshire Blvd., Beverly Hills, CA 90211. *Publicist*– I/D Public Relations, 8409 Santa Monica Blvd., West Hollywood, CA 90069.

Career: Actor. Also worked as a stand–up comedian.

Awards, Honors: Screen Actors Guild Award (with others), outstanding performance by a cast, MTV Movie Awards nomination (with others), best dance sequence, Golden Satellite Award nomination, best performance by an actor in a supporting role in a motion picture—comedy or musical, Film Award nomination, best performance by an actor in a supporting role, British Academy of Film and Television Arts, 1998, all for *The Full Monty;* Young Artist Award nomination (with Jami Gertz), most popular mom & pop in a television series, 2004, for *Still Standing.*

CREDITS

Film Appearances:

Sam, *Dark Romances Vol. 2* (also known as *Dark Romances Vol. 2: Bleeding Hearts*), 1990.

Dave Althorpe, *The Full Monty,* Fox Searchlight Pictures, 1997.

Malcolm, *Married 2 Malcolm,* 1998.

Mac MacArther, *Jack Frost* (also known as *Frost*), Embassy, 1998.

Frank, *The Last Yellow,* Universal, 1999.

Andy, *The Announcement,* 2000.

Fred Flintstone, *The Flintstones in Viva Rock Vegas,* Universal, 2000.

Tournaments: A Cross between Pro Football and Stock Car Racing (documentary short film), Columbia TriStar, 2001.

Roland, *A Knight's Tale,* Sony Pictures Releasing, 2001.

The Rock Music Scene in 1370 (documentary short film), Columbia TriStar, 2001.

Heath Ledger Profile (documentary short film), Columbia TriStar, 2001.

Cisco, *Down to Earth* (also known as *Einmal Himmel und zurueck*), Paramount, 2001.

David Filby, *The Time Machine,* Warner Bros., 2002.

Ron, *Heartlands,* Miramax, 2002.
Father Thomas Garrett, *The Order* (also known as *The Sin Eater* and *Sin Eater—Die Seele des Boesen*), Twentieth Century–Fox, 2003.
Steamer Captain, *Around the World in 80 Days,* Buena Vista, 2004.

Television Appearances; Movies:
Phil Mycroft, *The Heart Surgeon,* BBC, 1997.
Ass, *The Flint Street Nativity,* ITV, 1999.

Television Appearances; Series:
Detective Constable Gary Boyle, *The Thin Blue Line,* 1996.
Ken Sunnyside, *The Sunnyside Farm,* 1997.
Nigel Conway, *Too Much Sun,* BBC, 2000.
Bill Miller, *Still Standing,* CBS, 2002—.

Television Appearances; Pilots:
Macrobius, *Earth Scum,* ABC, 1998.

Television Appearances; Miniseries:
Detective Constable Sherrington, *Band of Gold,* HBO, 1995.

Television Appearances; Episodic:
Mal Prentis, "The Big Squeeze," *A Very Peculiar Practice,* BBC, 1988.
Mal Prentis, "Death of a University," *A Very Peculiar Practice,* BBC, 1988.
"England Show II: Wastin' the Company's Money," *Married ... with Children,* Fox, 1992.
PC, "Unknown Soldier," *Between the Lines,* 1994.
Alec Kitson, "A Normal Life," *Peak Practice,* ITV, 1995.
Norman Greengrass, "Domestic," *Heartbeat,* ITV, 1995.
Detective Constable Newley, *Ghostbusters of East Finchley,* BBC, 1995.
Norman Greengrass, "Old Colonials," *Heartbeat,* ITV, 1996.
Himself, "The Dog and Pony Show," *The Drew Carey Show,* 1997.
"A Knight's Tale," *HBO First Look,* HBO, 2001.
On–Air with Ryan Seacrest, syndicated, 2004.
The Wayne Brady Show, syndicated, 2004.
The View, ABC, 2005.

Television Appearances; Specials:
The Making of "A Knight's Tale" (documentary), HBO, 2001.
Presenter, *The 29th Annual People's Choice Award,* CBS, 2003.
Presenter, *The 30th Annual People's Choice Award,* CBS, 2004.

Stage Appearances:
Appeared as Bottom, *A Midsummer Night's Dream.*

OTHER SOURCES

Periodicals:
Flicks, February, 1999, p. 42.

AIKEN, Liam 1990–

PERSONAL

Full name, Liam Patraic Aiken; born January 7, 1990, in New York, NY; son of Bill (a producer; died) and Moya Aiken.

Addresses: *Contact*—Abraham's Artists, 9200 Sunset Blvd., Suite 1130, Los Angeles, CA 90069.

Career: Actor. Appeared in a television commercial for Ford Windstar.

Awards, Honors: Young Artist Award, best performance in a feature film, 1999, for *Stepmom;* Young Artist Award nomination, best performance in a feature film, 2003, for *Road to Perdition;* Young Artist Award nomination, best performance in a feature film, 2004, for *Good Boy!;* Young Artist Award nomination, best performance in a feature film, Broadcast Film Critics Association Award nomination, best young actor, 2005, for *Lemony Snicket's "A Series of Unfortunate Events."*

CREDITS

Film Appearances:
Ned, *Henry Fool,* Sony Pictures Classics, 1997.
Ben Harrison, *Stepmom,* Columbia TriStar, 1998.
Nathan, *The Object of My Affection,* 1998.
Emmett Wilder, *The Rising Place,* 1999.
Emanuele Gallmann at age 7, *I Dreamed of Africa,* 2000.
Abner, *Sweet November,* 2001.
Sweet November: From the Heart (short film), 2001.
Emmett, Virginia's son, *The Rising Place,* Warner Bros., 2001.
Peter Sullivan, *Road to Perdition,* Twentieth Century–Fox, 2002.
Owen Baker, *Good Boy!,* Metro–Goldwyn–Meyer, 2003.
Klaus Baudelaire, *Lemony Snicket's "A Series of Unfortunate Events,"* Paramount, 2004.

Television Appearances; Movies:
Kid, *Montana* (also known as *Nothing Personal*), HBO, 1998.

Television Appearances; Specials:
The 76th Annual Academy Awards, ABC, 2004.
The 10th Annual Critics' Choice Awards, The WB, 2005.

Television Appearances; Episodic:
Jack Erickson, "Disappeared," *Law & Order,* NBC, 1998.
"I Dreamed of Africa," *HBO First Look,* HBO, 2000.
Robbie Bishop, "Bright Boy," *Law & Order: Criminal Intent,* NBC, 2002.
Today, NBC, 2003, 2004.
The Oprah Winfrey Show, syndicated, 2004.

Stage Appearances:
Bobby Helmer, *A Doll's House,* Belasco Theatre, New York City, 1997.

RECORDINGS

Video Games:
(In archive footage) Voice of Klaus Baudelaire, *Lemony Snicket's "A Series of Unfortunate Events,"* 2004.

OTHER SOURCES

Periodicals:
New York Daily News, December 23, 2004.
New York Magazine, December 13, 2004.

ALBERT, Edward 1951–
   (Edward Laurence Albert, Edward Lawrence Albert, Edward Albert, Jr.)

PERSONAL

Full name, Edward Laurence Albert, Jr.; born February 20, 1951, in Los Angeles, CA; son of Eddie (an actor; full name, Edward Laurence Albert) and Margo (an actress, singer, and dancer; full name, Maria Margarita Guadalupe Bolado Castilla y O'Donnell) Albert; married Kate Woodville, 1978; children: Thais Carmen Woodville. *Education:* Attended the University of California, Los Angeles, and the University of Oxford; studied acting in Stratford–upon–Avon, England. *Avocational Interests:* Ranching and raising horses, raising organic fruits and vegetables.

Addresses: *Agent*—Wallis Agency, 4444 Riverside Dr., Suite 105, Burbank, CA 91505.

Career: Actor and producer. Musician and composer. Also worked as a photographer, poet, and freelance writer; photography exhibited in Los Angeles, CA.

Awards, Honors: Golden Globe Award nomination, best actor in a musical or comedy, and Golden Globe Award, most promising new comer, 1973, for *Butterflies Are Free;* received a Palisades Award and Harriet Hugo Award for his poetry.

CREDITS

Television Appearances; Series:
Quisto Champion, *The Yellow Rose,* NBC, 1983–84.
Jeff Wainwright, *Falcon Crest,* CBS, 1986.
Elliot Burch, *Beauty and the Beast,* 1987–90.
California, 1997.
Dr. Bennett Devlin, *Port Charles,* ABC, 1997–99.
Voice of Rafe, *Invasion America* (animated), The WB, 1998.
(As Edward Laurence Albert) Mr. Collins, *Power Rangers Time Force,* Fox, 2001.

Television Appearances; Miniseries:
Sebastian, "Gli antenati," *Alle origini della mafia* (also known as *Roots of the Mafia*), 1976.
Lewis Barry, *Black Beauty,* NBC, 1978.
Ron "Dal" Dalrymple, *The Last Convertible,* NBC, 1979.

Television Appearances; Movies:
Edward Van Bohlen, *Killer Bees,* ABC, 1974.
James Radney, *Death Cruise,* ABC, 1974.
Paul Matthews, *The Millionaire,* 1978.
Tom Buchanan, *Silent Victory: The Kitty O'Neil Story,* CBS, 1979.
Phil Wharton, Kennedy Committee investigator, *Blood Feud,* syndicated, 1983.
Dan, *The Girl from Mars,* The Family Channel, 1991.
Charles Stella, *Body Language,* USA Network, 1992.
Star Witness, 1995.
Captain Gray, *Space Marines,* Showtime, 1996.
(As Edward Laurence Albert) Ned Shelly, *Seduced by a Thief,* Lifetime, 2001.
Alex Wheeler, *No Regrets,* Lifetime, 2003.

Television Appearances; Specials:
Battle of the Network Stars XV, ABC, 1983.
Bill Watson, "Daddy Can't Read," *ABC Afterschool Special,* ABC, 1988.

Television Appearances; Episodic:
"Eddie Albert," *This Is Your Life,* 1958.

"A Terribly Strange Bed," *Great Mysteries* (also known as *Orson Welles' "Great Mysteries"*), syndicated, 1973.

Johnny Kinglsey McLean, "Blood of the Dragon: Parts 1 & 2," *Kung Fu*, ABC, 1974.

Edward Milland, "Nightmare," *The Rookies*, ABC, 1975.

Thor Halverson, "A Life in the Balance," *Medical Story*, NBC, 1975.

Clay Peters, "The Test of Brotherhood," *Police Story*, NBC, 1976.

(As Edward Lawrence Albert) Lee Marx, "The Adventure of Caesar's Last Sleep," *Ellery Queen*, NBC, 1976.

Billy, "Bought and Paid For," *Police Story*, 1976.

The Mike Douglas Show, 1977.

Doug Warren, "The Little People," *The Love Boat*, ABC, 1978.

Joey Green, "The Hero," *The Littlest Hobo*, CTV and syndicated, 1981.

Carl, "Bank Job," *Today's F.B.I.*, ABC, 1982.

Sam, "In the Bag," *Tales of the Unexpected*, 1982.

Tony Holiday, "Hit, Run, and Homicide," *Murder, She Wrote*, CBS, 1984.

"Man at the Window," *The Hitchhiker*, HBO, 1985.

Oliver Alden, "Deadly Connection," *The New Mike Hammer* (also known as *Mike Hammer*), CBS, 1987.

Lester Farnum, "North of the Border," *Houston Knights*, CBS, 1987.

"The Added Starter," *Midnight Caller*, 1991.

Drew Dobson, "Dapper Drew," *FBI: The Untold Stories*, 1991.

"Birthright," *Paradise*, 1991.

Charlie Harper, "Nearest and Dearest," *Bodies of Evidence*, 1992.

Tio Mendoza, "Scorpio Lover," *Silk Stalkings*, CBS and USA Network, 1992.

"Das Boat House," *Civil Wars*, ABC, 1992.

Lamar, "Legacy," *In the Heat of the Night*, CBS, 1993.

(As Edward Laurence Albert) Zayra, "A Man Alone," *Star Trek: Deep Space Nine*, syndicated, 1993.

"Hello and Goodbye," *L.A. Law*, NBC, 1993.

Frank Haskall, "Treasure of the Ages," *Time Trax*, syndicated, 1993.

(As Edward Albert, Jr.) Quinn, "Incorrect Dosage," *Dark Justice*, 1993.

Dr. William Burke, "Where the Heart Is: Parts 1 & 2," *Dr. Quinn, Medicine Woman*, CBS, 1994.

Dr. William Burke, "Ready or Not," *Dr. Quinn, Medicine Woman*, CBS, 1995.

Voice of the Silver Surfer/Norrin Radd, "Doomsday," *The Fantastic Four* (animated; also known as *The Marvel Action Hour: The Fantastic Four*), syndicated, 1996.

(As Edward Laurence Albert) Voice of Matt Murdock/Daredevil, "Sins of the Fathers Chapter 6: Framed," *Spider-Man* (animated), syndicated, 1996.

(As Edward Laurence Albert) Voice of Matt Murdock/Daredevil, "Sins of the Fathers Chapter 7: The Man without Fear," *Spider-Man* (animated), syndicated, 1996.

Kidnapper, "Cyclone," *Walker, Texas Ranger*, CBS, 1996.

Arthur DeRhodes, "Doppelganger," *Profiler*, NBC, 1997.

Dr. William Burke, "Colleen's Paper," *Dr. Quinn, Medicine Woman*, CBS, 1997.

Dan Singleton, "Vanishing Act," *The Sentinel*, UPN, 1997.

Voice of the sheriff, "The Jersey Devil," *Extreme Ghostbusters* (animated), syndicated, 1997.

Robert Janson, "Ghost Story," *High Tide*, 1997.

"The Heart of the Elephant: Part 1," *Conan*, 1997.

Diamond Dave, "You Bet Your Family," *Sabrina, the Teenage Witch*, ABC, 1998.

Charles Gandy, "Angel of Mercy," *Nash Bridges*, CBS, 1998.

"Gone Fishin'," *Mike Hammer, Private Eye*, syndicated, 1998.

Deputy Chief Bain, "End Game," *Martial Law*, CBS, 1999.

"Simple Wooden Boxes," *Chicken Soup for the Soul*, PAX, 1999.

Beck, "Off with Her Head," *She Spies*, syndicated, 2003.

Also appeared as French soldier Luc in *Hawkeye*, syndicated.

Television Appearances; Pilots:
Paul Matthews, *The Millionaire* (also known as *The New Millionaire*), CBS, 1978.

Television Appearances; Other:
Host of *Different Point of View*, *On Call*, and *Viva*.

Film Appearances:
George Mellish, *The Fool Killer* (also known as *Violent Journey* and *El asesino de tontos*), Allied Artists, 1965.

Don Baker, *Butterflies Are Free*, Columbia, 1972.

Peter Latham, *Forty Carats* (also known as *40 Carats*), Columbia, 1973.

Lieutenant Tom Garth, *Midway* (also known as *The Battle of Midway*), Universal, 1976.

Jerry, *Un taxi mauve* (also known as *The Purple Taxi* and *Un taxi color malva*), Parafrance, 1977.

Ross Pine, *The Domino Principle* (also known as *The Domino Killings* and *El domino principe*), Avco–Embassy, 1977.

Nico Tomasis, *The Greek Tycoon*, Universal, 1978.

Jeff, *The Squeeze* (also known as *Diamond Thieves, The Heist, Controrapina, Der Diamantencoup, Gretchko, Rip Off—The Diamond Connection, L'ultimo colpo,* and *The Rip-Off*), Maverick, 1978.

Brian, *When Time Ran Out* (also known as *The Day the World Ended* and *Earth's Final Fury*), Warner Bros., 1980.

Cabren, *Galaxy of Terror* (also known as *An Infinity of Terror, Mindwarp, Mindwarp: An Infinity of Terror, Planet of Horrors,* and *Quest*), New World Pictures, 1981.

Michael Rogan, *A Time to Die* (also known as *Seven Graves for Rogan*), Almi, 1982.

Wash Gillespie, *Butterfly,* Analysis, 1982.

Ted, *The House Where Evil Dwells,* Metro–Goldwyn–Mayer, 1982.

Veliki transport (also known as *Heroes*), 1983.

Tom, *Ellie,* Film Ventures, 1984.

"Tag" Taggar, *Getting Even* (also known as *Hostage: Dallas*), American Distribution Group, 1986.

Captain Danny Jackson, *Terminal Entry,* Celebrity Home Entertainment, 1986.

Danny Warren, *The Underachievers* (also known as *Night School*), Lightning, 1988.

Commander Merrill, *The Rescue,* Buena Vista, 1988.

Jason Marks, *Distortions,* Cori/Academy Entertainment, 1988.

Eddie Powers, *Accidents,* Trans–World Entertainment, 1988.

Dana Lund, *Mind Games,* Metro–Goldwyn–Mayer/United Artists, 1989.

Harry "Punchy" Moses, *Fist Fighter* (also known as *Peleador a puno libro, A puno libro,* and *A puno limpio*), LIVE Home Video, 1989.

Colonel Lavara, *Wild Zone* (also known as *Okavango*), Columbia/TriStar Home Video, 1989.

Filipe Soto, *Exiled in America,* Prism Entertainment, 1990.

Kurt Williams, *Out of Sight, Out of Mind* (also known as *Out of Sight, Out of her Mind* and *Sight Unseen*), 1990.

Mr. C, *Shootfighter: Fight to the Death* (also known as *Shootfighter*), 1992.

Broken Trust, Monarch Home Video, 1993.

Jeffrey West, *The Ice Runner,* Borde Releasing, 1993.

Decklin, *Red Sun Rising,* 1993.

(As Edward Albert, Jr.) Chief of examiners, *Hard Drive* (also known as *Enter Deliah*), Triboro Entertainment Group, 1994.

(As Edward Albert, Jr.) Barry Carlisle, *Guarding Tess,* TriStar, 1994.

(As Edward Albert, Jr.) Remy Grilland, *Demon Keeper,* New Horizons Home Video, 1994.

Richard, *Sexual Malice,* A–pix Entertainment, 1994.

Howard, *Sorceress* (also known as *Temptress II*), Triboro Entertainment Group, 1994.

The Royal Affair, 1995.

Max Simpson, *The Secret Agent Club,* Cabin Fever Entertainment, 1996.

Frank Rebbins, *Kid Cop,* Image Organization/Brainstorm Media, 1996.

Voice of Daredevil, *Spider–Man: Sins of the Fathers* (animated), 1996.

USMA West Point, 1998.

(As Edward Albert, Jr.) Himself, *Some Nudity Required* (documentary), Only Child, 1998.

Athos, *The Man in the Iron Mask,* Invisible Film Studio/The Fastest Cheapest Best Film Corporation, 1998.

(As Edward Laurence Albert) *Unbowed,* 2000.

U.S. Deputy Marshal Coburn, *Stageghost* (also known as *Stage Ghost*), Alpha, 2000.

(In archive footage) Ensign Thomas Garth, *The Making of "Midway,"* Universal Studios Home Video, 2001.

(As Edward Laurence Albert) Mr. Collins, *Power Rangers Time Force—Quantum Ranger: Clash for Control,* 2001.

(As Edward Laurence Albert) Mr. Collins, *Power Rangers Time Force—Photo Finish,* 2001.

Darksuit, *Mimic 2,* Miramax, 2001.

Mayor Phillips, *Ablaze,* New City Releasing, 2001.

(As Eddie Albert, Jr.) Senator Richards, *Extreme Honor* (also known as *Last Line of Defence 2*), Dreamfactory, 2001.

(As Edward Albert, Jr.) *Remembering Roman Holiday,* Paramount, 2002.

(As Edward Laurence Albert) Mr. Collins, *Power Rangers Time Force: The End of Time,* 2002.

(As Edward Laurence Albert) Mr. Collins, *Power Rangers Time Force: Dawn of Destiny,* 2002.

King Otto/Ridgewell, *A Light in the Forest,* RGH/Lions Share, 2002.

Marc Neihauser, *Fighting Words,* Fighting Words Productions, 2003.

Captian, *Sea of Fear,* Even Keel, 2004.

Alfred, *A–List,* Infin, 2004.

Martin Harris, *The Work and the Glory,* Excel, 2004.

Radio Appearances:
Performed with his father in radio broadcasts.

Stage Appearances:
Mr. McGee, *Very Warm for May,* Carnegie Hall/Weill Hall, New York City, 1994.

Very Truly Yours, Tiffany Theater, 1998.

Naylor, *Cesar and Ruben,* El Portal Theatre, Hollywood, CA, 2003.

Appeared as Don, *Terribly Strange Bed,* London; as Fortinbras, *Hamlet,* Mark Taper Forum, Los Angeles; and as Jim O'Connor, *The Glass Menagerie,* Manhattan Theater Club, New York City; also appeared in *Our Town* and *Room Service.*

ALDA, Alan 1936–

PERSONAL

Original name, Alphonso Joseph D'Abruzzo; born January 28, 1936, in New York, NY; son of Alphonso Giovanni Giuseppe Roberto (an actor and singer under stage name Robert Alda) and Joan (maiden name, Browne) D'Abruzzo; married Arlene Weiss (a teacher, photographer, and musician), March 15, 1957; children: Eve, Elizabeth, Beatrice. *Education:* Fordham University, B.S., 1956; studied at Cleveland Playhouse; attended Paul Sills's Improvisational Workshop at Second City, New York City, 1963.

Addresses: *Agent*—United Talent Agency, 9560 Wilshire Blvd., Suite 500, Beverly Hills, CA 90212. *Contact*—c/o Martin Bergman Productions, 641 Lexington Ave., New York, NY 10022.

Career: Actor, writer, producer, and director. Performed Abbott–and–Costello–style sketches with father at the Hollywood Canteen, 1945. Appeared in the improvisational revues *Compass,* Yachtsman Hotel, Hyannis, MA, 1962, and *Second City,* Second City at Square East, New York City, 1963. Worked as a teacher at Compass School of Improvisation, New York City, 1963. National Commission on the Observance of International Women's Year, presidential appointee, 1976; National ERA Countdown Campaign, cochairperson, 1982. Was a televison spokesman for both IBM and Atari Personal Computers. Trustee of Museum of Broadcasting, 1985, and Rockefeller Foundation, 1989. *Military Service:* U.S. Army Reserve; became second lieutenant.

Member: Screen Actors Guild, Directors Guild of America, Writers Guild of America, American Federation of Television and Radio Artists, Actors Equity Association.

Awards, Honors: All for *M*A*S*H:* Emmy Award nominations, best actor in a comedy series, 1973, 1974, 1975, 1976, 1977, 1978, 1979, 1980, 1981, and 1983; Golden Globe Award nomination, best TV actor—musical/comedy, 1973, 1974, 1977, 1978, and 1979; People's Choice Award, favorite male television performer, 1975; Emmy Awards, best actor in a comedy series, 1974 and 1982; Emmy Award, actor of the year in a series, 1974; Golden Globe Awards, best actor in a series—musical/comedy, 1975, 1976, 1980, 1981, 1982, and 1983; Humanitas Prize, 30 minute category, Human Family Educational & Cultural Institute, 1980; Emmy Award nominations, best director of a comedy series, 1975, for episode "Bulletin Board," 1976, for "The Kids," 1979, for "Dear Sis," 1980, for "Dreams," 1981, for "The Life You Save," 1982, for "Where There's a Will, There's a War," and 1983, for "Goodbye, Farewell and Amen"; Outstanding Directorial Achievement Awards for Television Comedy, Directors Guild of America, 1976, for episode "Dear Sigmund," 1981, for "The Life You Save," and 1982, for "Where There's a Will, There's a War"; Emmy Awards, best director of a comedy series, 1977, for episode "Dear Sigmund," and 1978 (with Burt Metcalfe), for "Comrades in Arms—Part I"; Emmy Award nominations, best writing in a comedy

series, 1977, for episode "Dear Sigmund," 1978, for "Fallen Idol," and 1982, for "Follies of the Living, Concerns of the Dead"; Writers Guild of America Award, 1977; Emmy Award, best writing for a comedy or comedy–variety or music series, 1979, for episode "Inga"; Humanitas Award for writing. Ford Foundation grant; *Theatre World* award, 1963, for *Fair Game for Lovers;* Antoinette Perry Award nomination, best actor in a musical, 1967, for *The Apple Tree;* Golden Globe nomination, most promising newcomer—male, 1969, for *Paper Lion;* Emmy Award nomination, best actor in a drama special, 1974, for *6 Rms Riv Vu;* Golden Apple Star of the Year, Hollywood Women's Press Club, 1974 and 1979; honorary degrees, Fordham University, 1978, Drew University, 1979, Columbia University, 1979, Connecticut College, 1980, and Kenyon College, 1982; Emmy Award nomination, best actor in a drama or comedy special, 1978, for *Kill Me If You Can;* Golden Globe nomination, best motion picture actor musical/comedy, 1979, for *Same Time, Next Year;* People's Choice Awards, best male performer on television, Procter & Gamble Productions, 1979, 1980, 1981, and 1982; Marquee Award, best actor, American Movie Awards, 1980, for *The Seduction of Joe Tynan;* People's Choice Awards, all–around favorite male entertainer, 1980 and 1981; Hasty Pudding Man of the Year, Hasty Pudding Theatricals, 1980; NATO Star of the Year, 1981; Golden Globe Award nomination, best motion picture actor comedy/musical, Writers Guild of America Award nomination, best comedy written directly for the screen, Marquee Award, favorite star—male, American Movie Awards, 1982; Golden Globe Award nomination, best screenplay—motion picture and best motion picture actor, 1982, for *The Four Seasons;* Bodil Award, best American film, Bodil Festival, 1982, for *The Four Seasons;* D. W. Griffith Award, and New York Film Critics Association Award, best supporting actor, National Board of Review Award, best supporting actor, 1989, for *Crimes and Misdemeanors;* Film Award nomination, best actor in a supporting role, British Academy of Film and Television Arts, 1991, for *Crimes and Misdemeanors;* Antoinette Perry Award nomination, best performance by a leading actor in a play, 1992, for *Jake's Women;* Emmy Award nomination, best supporting actor in a special, 1993, for *And the Band Played On;* inducted into Television Academy Hall of Fame, 1994; Golden Globe Award nomination, best actor in a miniseries or movie made for television, 1995, for *White Mile;* Emmy Award nomination, outstanding guest actor, 2000, for *ER;* Valentine Davies Award, Writers Guild of America, 2000; Emmy Award nomination, outstanding supporting actor, 2001, Screen Actors Guild Award nomination, outstanding performance by a male actor, 2002, for *Club Land;* Academy Award nomination, best performance by an actor in a supporting role, Film Award nomination, best performance by an actor, British Academy of Film and Television Arts, Screen Actors Guild Award nomination (with others), outstanding performance by a cast, 2005 for *The Aviator.*

CREDITS

Television Appearances; Series:
Secret File, U.S.A., 1955.
That Was the Week That Was, NBC, 1964.
(Uncredited) *What's My Line?,* syndicated, 1968.
Story Theatre, 1971.
Captain Benjamin Franklin "Hawkeye" Pierce, *M*A*S*H,* CBS, 1972–83.
Jack Burroughs, *The Four Seasons,* CBS, 1984.
Host and narrator, *Scientific American Frontiers,* PBS, 1993–97.
Dr. Gabriel Lawrence, a recurring role, *ER,* NBC, 1999.
Host, *The Museum of Television and Radio: Influences,* Bravo, 2000.
Senator Arnold Vinick, *The West Wing,* NBC, 2004—.

Television Appearances; Movies:
Marshall Barnett, *Playmates,* ABC, 1972.
Jonathan Paige, *Truman Capote's "The Glass House"* (also known as *The Glass House*), CBS, 1972.
Sheriff Dan Barnes, *Isn't It Shocking?,* ABC, 1973.
Paul Friedman, *6 Rms Riv Vu,* 1974.
Caryl W. Chessman, *Kill Me If You Can,* NBC, 1977.
Captain Benjamin Franklin 'Hawkeye' Pierce, *M*A*S*H: Goodbye, Farewell and Amen,* CBS, 1983.
Dr. Robert Gallo, *And the Band Played On,* HBO, 1993.
Dan Cutler, *White Mile,* HBO, 1994.
Jake, *Neil Simon's "Jake's Women"* (also known as *Jake's Women*), CBS, 1996.
Willie Walters, *Club Land,* Showtime, 2001.
Ernie Goodman, *The Killing Yard,* Showtime, 2001.

Television Appearances; Specials:
Hotel 90, CBS, 1973.
Lily, CBS, 1973.
Marlo Thomas and Friends in Free to Be ... You and Me, ABC, 1974.
Annie and the Hoods, ABC, 1974.
Cohost, *CBS: On the Air,* CBS, 1978.
*Making M*A*S*H,* PBS, 1981.
Scared Sexless (also known as *Report on America: Scared Sexless*), NBC, 1987.
The All–Star Salute to Our Troops, CBS, 1991.
*Memories of M*A*S*H,* CBS, 1991.
Host, *One on One: Classic Television Interviews,* CBS, 1993.
Host, *About All You Can Eat* (documentary), PBS, 1994.
The Kennedy Center Honors: A Celebration of the Performing Arts, CBS, 1994.
Interviewee, *Woody Allen: A to Z,* TCM, 1997.
Interviewee, *Alan Alda: More Than Mr. Nice Guy,* Arts and Entertainment, 1997.
Interviewee, *CBS: The First 50 Years,* CBS, 1998.
*M*A*S*H, Tootsie & God: A Tribute to Larry Gelbart,* PBS, 1998.

The Italian Americans II: A Beautiful Song, PBS, 1998.
The Great American History Quiz, History Channel, 1999.
Interviewee, *Intimate Portrait: Marlo Thomas* (documentary), Lifetime, 2000.
Interviewee, *The 70s: The Decade That Changed Television* (documentary), ABC, 2000.
Interviewee, *Television: The First 50 Years* (documentary), PBS, 2001.
Interviewee, *Intimate Portrait: Rita Moreno* (documentary), Lifetime, 2001.
*M*A*S*H: TV Tales* (documentary), E! Entertainment Television, 2002.
*M*A*S*H: 30th Anniversary Reunion,* Fox, 2002.
TV Guide 50 Best Shows of All Time: A 50th Anniversary Celebration, ABC, 2002.
Presenter, *CBS at 75: A Primetime Celebration,* CBS, 2003.
Interviewee, *100 Years of Hope and Humor,* NBC, 2003.
Mouthing Off: 51 Greatest Smartasses, 2004.
Emmy's Great Moments (also known as *TV Land Presents: Emmy's Greatest Moments*), TV Land, 2004.

Television Appearances; Awards Presentations:
Presenter, *The 19th Annual Tony Awards,* 1965.
Presenter, *The 28th Annual Primetime Emmy Awards,* ABC, 1976.
Host, *The 30th Annual Primetime Emmy Awards,* CBS, 1978.
Cohost, *The 58th Annual Academy Awards Presentation,* ABC, 1986.
The 3rd Annual American Comedy Awards, ABC, 1989.
Presenter, *The 46th Annual Tony Awards,* CBS, 1992.
Presenter, *The 46th Annual Primetime Emmy Awards,* ABC, 1994.
The 10th Annual Television Academy Hall of Fame, The Disney Channel, 1994.
Presenter, *The 48th Annual Tony Awards,* CBS, 1994.
Presenter, *The 51st Annual Golden Globe Awards,* TBS, 1994.
Presenter, *The Walt Disney Company Presents the American Teacher Awards,* The Disney Channel, 1994.
The Television Academy Hall of Fame (also known as *The Academy of Television Arts and Sciences's Hall of Fame*), NBC, 1995.
The 77th Annual Academy Awards, ABC, 2005.

Television Appearances; Episodic:
Carlisle Thompson III, "Bilko, the Art Lover," *The Phil Silvers Show,* CBS, 1957.
Dr. Glazer, "Soda Pop and Paper Flags," *Route 66,* CBS, 1962.
Dr. John Griffin, "Many a Sullivan," *The Nurses,* CBS, 1963.

Dr. John Griffin, "Night Sounds," *The Nurses,* CBS, 1963.

The Shari Lewis Show, NBC, 1963.

Freddie Wilcox, "The Sinner," *East Side, West Side,* CBS, 1963.

Nick Staphos, "Picture Me a Murder," *Trials of O'Brien,* CBS, 1965.

Clay, "Six Months to Mars," *Coronet Blue,* 1967.

Frank St. John, "Higher and Higher," *Premiere,* 1968.

The David Frost Revue, syndicated, 1971.

The Carol Burnett Show, CBS, 1974.

Reflections on the Silver Screen with Professor Richard Brown, 1990.

The Rosie O'Donnell Show, syndicated, 1997, 1998.

Late Night with Conan O'Brien, NBC, 1998.

Interviewee, *Inside the Actors Studio,* 2000.

Travis Smiley, PBS, 2004.

The Tony Danza Show, syndicated, 2004.

"The Aviator," *History vs. Hollywood,* History Channel, 2004.

The Tonight Show with Jay Leno, NBC, 2005.

The Late Late Show with Craig Ferguson, CBS, 2005.

Showbiz Tonight, CNN, 2005.

The View, ABC, 2005.

The Charlie Rose Show, PBS, 2005.

"Found," *Getaway,* Nine Network, 2005.

Also appeared as a guest in *Memory Lane, The Match Game,* NBC, and the *Today Show,* NBC.

Television Appearances; Pilots:

Arnold Barker, *Where's Everett?,* CBS, 1966.

Frank St. John, *Higher and Higher, Attorneys at Law,* CBS, 1968.

Jack Burroughs, *The Four Seasons,* 1984.

Television Appearances; Other:

The Tree and the Cross, ABC, 1964.

Out of the Flying Pan, National Educational Television (now PBS), 1966.

It's Almost Like Being, National Educational Television, 1966.

Television Work; Series:

(With Marc Merson) Executive producer, (with Allan Katz and Don Reo) producer, and creator, *We'll Get By,* CBS, 1975.

(With Martin Bregman) Executive producer and creator, *The Four Seasons,* CBS, 1984.

Television Director; Specials:

Director, *M*A*S*H: 30th Anniversary Reunion,* Fox, 2002.

Television Director; Movies:

*M*A*S*H: Goodbye, Farewell and Amen,* CBS, 1983.

Television Work; Episodic:

(With others) Director, *M*A*S*H* (including the episodes "Bulletin Board," "The Kids," "Dear Sigmund," "Dear Sis," "Comrades in Arms—Part I," "Dreams," "The Life You Save," "Where There's a Will, There's a War," and "Goodbye, Farewell and Amen"), CBS, between 1972–83.

Television Work; Pilots:

Director and creator, *Hickey vs. Anybody,* NBC, 1976.

(With Marc Merson) Producer, *Susan and Sam,* NBC, 1977.

Film Appearances:

Charley Cotchipee, *Gone Are the Days* (also known as *The Man from C.O.T.T.O.N.* and *Purlie Victorious*), Hammer, 1963.

George Plimpton, *Paper Lion,* United Artists, 1968.

Lieutenant (Junior Grade) Morton Krim, *The Extraordinary Seaman,* Metro–Goldwyn–Mayer, 1969.

Delano, *Jenny* (also known as *And Jenny Makes Three*), Cinerama, 1969.

John J. "Son" Martin, *The Moonshine War,* Metro–Goldwyn–Mayer, 1970.

Myles Clarkson, *The Mephisto Waltz,* Twentieth Century–Fox, 1971.

Major Evelyn Ritchie, *To Kill a Clown,* Twentieth Century–Fox, 1972.

Bill Warren, *California Suite* (also known as *Neil Simon's "California Suite"*), Columbia, 1978.

George Peters, *Same Time, Next Year,* Universal, 1978.

Title role, *The Seduction of Joe Tynan,* Universal, 1979.

Jack Burroughs, *The Four Seasons,* Universal, 1981.

Michael Burgess, *Sweet Liberty,* Universal, 1986.

Steve Giardino, *A New Life,* Paramount, 1988.

Lester, *Crimes and Misdemeanors,* Orion, 1989.

Eddie Hopper, *Betsy's Wedding,* Touchstone/Buena Vista, 1990.

Leo Green, *Whispers in the Dark,* Paramount, 1992.

Ted, *Manhattan Murder Mystery* (also known as *The Dancing Shiva Couple Next Door*), TriStar, 1993.

President, *Canadian Bacon,* Gramercy Pictures, 1995.

Bob, *Everyone Says I Love You* (also known as *Woody Allen Fall Project*), Miramax, 1996.

Richard Schlicting, *Flirting with Disaster,* Miramax, 1996.

National Security Advisor Alvin Jordan, *Murder at 1600* (also known as *Executive Privilege* and *Murder at 1600 Pennsylvania Avenue*), Warner Bros., 1997.

Kevin Hollander, *Mad City,* Warner Bros., 1997.

Sidney Miller, *The Object of My Affection,* Twentieth Century–Fox, 1998.

Keepers of the Frame (documentary), 1998.

Dan Wanamaker, *What Women Want,* Paramount, 2000.

Senator Ralph Owen Brewster, *The Aviator,* Miramax, 2004.

Film Director:

The Four Seasons, Universal, 1981.

Sweet Liberty, Universal, 1986.

A New Life, Paramount, 1988.

Betsy's Wedding, Touchstone/Buena Vista, 1990.

Stage Appearances:

Jack Chesney, *Charley's Aunt,* Barnesville, PA, 1953.

Leo Davis, *Room Service,* Teatro del Eliseo, Rome, 1955.

Understudy for the role of Clarence "Lefty" McShane, *The Hot Corner,* John Golden Theatre, New York City, 1956.

Billy Tuck, *Nature's Way,* Valley Playhouse, Chagrin Falls, OH, 1958.

The Book of Job, Cleveland Playhouse, Cleveland, OH, 1958–59.

David Williams, *Who Was That Lady I Saw You With?,* Cleveland Playhouse, 1958–59.

Monique, Cleveland Playhouse, 1958–59.

Toni, *To Dorothy, a Son,* Cleveland Playhouse, 1958–59.

Telephone man, *Only in America,* Cort Theatre, New York City, 1959.

Sky Masterson, *Guys and Dolls,* Grand Theatre, Sullivan, IL, 1959.

Title role, *Li'l Abner,* Grand Theatre, 1960.

Darwin's Theories, Madison Avenue Playhouse, New York City, 1960.

David, *The Woman with Red Hair,* Teatro dei Servi, Rome, 1961.

Fleider, and understudy for the title role, *Anatol,* Boston Arts Center, Boston, MA, 1961.

Fergie Howard, *Golden Fleecing,* Southbury Playhouse, CT, 1961.

Charley Cotchipee, *Purlie Victorious,* Cort Theatre, 1961, then Longacre Theatre, New York City, 1961–62.

Howard Mayer, *A Whisper in God's Ear,* Cricket Theatre, New York City, 1962.

Benny Bennington, *Fair Game for Lovers,* Cort Theatre, 1963.

Dr. Gilbert, *Cafe Crown,* Martin Beck Theatre, New York City, 1964.

Mike Mitchell, *Sunday in New York,* Bucks County Playhouse, New Hope, PA, 1964.

F. Sherman, *The Owl and the Pussycat,* American National Theatre and Academy (ANTA) Theatre, New York City, 1964–65.

Adam, "The Diary of Adam and Eve," Captain Sanjar, "The Lady or the Tiger?," and Flip, The Prince, Charming, "Passionella," in *The Apple Tree* (triple–bill), Shubert Theatre, New York City, 1966–67.

There's a Girl in My Soup, Playhouse–on–the–Mall, Paramus, NJ, 1968.

Stage manager, *Our Town,* Shaftesbury Theatre, London, 1991.

Jake, *Jake's Women,* Neil Simon Theatre, New York City, 1992, then Center Theatre Group, Ahmanson Theatre/James A. Doolittle Theatre, Los Angeles, 1992–93.

Marc, *Art,* Royale Theatre, New York City, 1998.

Richard Feynman, *QED,* Vivian Beaumont Theatre, New York City, 2001–2002.

The Play What I Wrote, Lyceum Theatre, New York City, 2003.

Shelly Levene, *Glengarry Glen Ross,* Royale Theatre, New York City, 2005, then Bernard B. Jacobs Theatre, 2005.

Also appeared in stock productions as Wade in *Roger the Sixth,* Artie in *Compulsion,* Irwin Trowbridge in *Three Men on a Horse,* and Horace in *The Little Foxes,* all 1957.

Major Tours:

Willie Alvarez, *Memo,* U.S. cities, 1963.

Francis X. Dignan, *King of Hearts,* U.S. cities, 1963.

Woodrow O'Malley, *Watch the Birdie!,* U.S. cities, 1964.

Stage Director:

The Midnight Ride of Alvin Blum, Westport Country Playhouse, CT, 1966, then Playhouse–on–the–Mall, 1966.

WRITINGS

Screenplays:

The Seduction of Joe Tynan, Universal, 1979.

The Four Seasons, Universal, 1981.

Sweet Liberty, Universal, 1986.

A New Life, Paramount, 1988.

Betsy's Wedding, Touchstone/Buena Vista, 1990.

Television Movies:

*M*A*S*H: Goodbye, Farewell and Amen,* CBS, 1983.

Television Episodes:

(With others) *M*A*S*H* (including the episodes "Dear Sigmund," "Fallen Idol," "Follies of the Living, Concerns of the Dead," and "Inga") CBS, 1972–83.

Television Specials:

*M*A*S*H: 30th Anniversary Reunion,* Fox, 2002.

Television Series:

(With Allan Katz, Susan Silver, and Peter Meyerson) *We'll Get By,* CBS, 1975.

(With others) *The Four Seasons* (based on his screenplay of the same title), CBS, 1984.

Television Pilots:
We'll Get By, CBS, 1974.
Hickey vs. Anybody, NBC, 1976.
Susan and Sam, NBC, 1977.

Stage Sketches:
Darwin's Theories (musical revue), produced at Madison Avenue Playhouse, 1960.

Other:
Co–author of dictionary *The Language of Show Biz.* Contributor to periodicals, including *Ms., TV Guide,* and *Redbook.*

RECORDINGS

Albums:
(With Marlo Thomas and others) *Free to Be ... You and Me,* Bell Records, 1973.

Other albums include *The Apple Tree* (original cast recording), Columbia Records.

OTHER SOURCES

Books:
Strait, Raymond, *Alan Alda: A Biography,* St. Martin's, 1983.

Periodicals:
American Film, April, 1981.
New York Times, April 19, 1981; May 18, 1994.
People, June 15, 1981.
The Washington Post, August 23, 2004.
TV Guide, October 23, 1999, pp. 34–36.

ANTHONY, Marc 1968–

PERSONAL

Original name, Marco Antonio Muniz; born September 16, 1968, in New York, NY; son of Felipe (a hospital lunchroom worker and musician) and Guillermina (a housewife) Muniz; married Dayanara Torres Delgado (a model), May 9, 2000 (divorced, 2004); married Jennifer Lopez (an actress, singer), June 5, 2004; children: (with ex–girlfriend) Arianna, (first marriage) Cristian, Ryan.

Addresses: *Office*—Marc Anthony Productions, 1385 York Ave., Suite 6F, New York, NY 10021. *Agent*—William Morris Agency, 1325 Avenue of the Americas, New York, NY 10019; Creative Artists Agency, 9830 Wilshire Blvd., CA 90212. *Manager*—Casablanca Records, 8255 Sunset Blvd., Los Angeles, CA 90046.

Career: Singer and actor. Began his musical career in his early teens, providing the background vocals for commercial jingles; wrote songs and performed as backup singer for Sa–Fire; also sang backup for the groups Menudo and Latin Rascals; appeared in television commercials for Coca Cola, 1998, RADD, 2001, and the "I Love New York" Tourism Committee, 2002; appeared in print ads, including American Dairy Farmers and Milk Processors, 2000.

Awards, Honors: *Billboard* Award, best new artist of the year, 1994; Tu Musica Award, best tropical album of the year, and Grammy Award nomination, tropical album of the year, National Academy of Recording Arts and Sciences, for *Todo a su tiempo;* Lo Nuestro Award, Ace Award, and Diplo Award, in Puerto Rico, 1994, all for *Otra nota;* ALMA Award (with Tina Arena), outstanding performance of a song, 1999, for *The Mask of Zorro;* Grammy Award, best tropical Latin album, 1999, for *Contra la corriente;* Grammy Award nomination, best male pop performance, 2000, for *I Need to Know;* ASCAP Award, most performed songs from motion pictures, ASCAP Film and Television Music Awards, and Blockbuster Entertainment Award nomination, favorite song from a movie, 2001, for *Runaway Bride;* ALMA Award nomination, outstanding actor, 2002, for *In the Time of the Butterflies;* ALMA Award, outstanding performance in a special, 2002, for *Christmas in Rockefeller Center;* American Music Award, favorite Latin artist, 2004; Grammy Award, best Latin pop album, 2005, for *Amar sin mentiras.*

CREDITS

Film Appearances:
Flaco, *East Side Story,* 1988.
Latin band at disco, *Carlito's Way,* 1993.
Marine guard, *Natural Causes,* 1994.
Himself, *Familia RMM combinacion perfecta* (documentary), RMM Records, 1994.
Himself, *Los mejores videos de India & Marc Anthony* (documentary short film), Sony Music Video, 1995.
Agent Ray, *Hackers,* Derio, 1995.
Cristiano, *Big Night,* Samuel Goldwyn, 1996.
Juan Lacas, *The Substitute,* Orion, 1996.
Himself, *I Am, from Cuban Son to Salsa,* 1997.
Himself, *RMM 10th Anniversary Collection VOL. 1,* RMM Records, 1997.
Himself, *RMM 10th Anniversary Collection VOL. 3,* RMM Records, 1997.
Himself, *The 22nd New York Salsa Festival* (also known as *Ralph Mercado Presents ... The 22nd New York Salsa Festival*), 1997.

Himself, *Romance del cumbanchero* (documentary; also known as *Romance del cumbanchero: La musica de Rafael Hernández*), Banco Popular, 1998.

Con la musica por dentro, 1999.

Noel, *Bringing out the Dead,* Paramount, 1999.

Jennifer Lopez: Feelin' So Good, 2000.

Guittara mia (documentary), Banco Popular, 2000.

Himself, *Raices* (documentary), Banco Popular, 2001.

Samuel, *Man on Fire,* Twentieth Century–Fox, 2004.

Himself, *Vengeance Is Mine: Reinventing "Man on Fire"* (documentary), Twentieth Century–Fox Home Entertainment, 2005.

Television Appearances; Movies:

Lio, *In the Time of the Butterflies* (also known as *En el tiempo de las mariposas*), Showtime, 2001.

Television Appearances; Specials:

71st Annual Macy's Thanksgiving Day Parade, 1997.

A Rosie Christmas, CBS, 1999.

The Americanos Concert, PBS, 1999.

Mi Gente! My People! (documentary), 1999.

The Latin Beat (documentary), ABC, 1999.

Interviewee, *Grammy Countdown,* CBS, 2000.

Marc Anthony: The Concert from Madison Square Garden, HBO, 2000.

Gloria Estefan, Caribbean Soul: The Atlantis Concert (also known as *Gloria Estefan: Live in Atlantis*), CBS, 2000.

Christmas in Rockefeller Center, NBC, 2000.

Christmas in Washington, TNT, 2000.

Sports Illustrated's Sportsman of the Year 2000, CBS, 2000.

Voice of Mario, *The Robinita Hood: An Animated Special from the "Happily Ever After: Fairy Tales for Every Child" Series* (animated), HBO, 2000.

Holiday Music Spectacular from Miami Beach 2000, Fox, 2000.

For VH1 Save the Music Foundation, VH1, 2001.

Rock and Roll Hall of Fame and Museum: 16th Annual Induction Ceremony, VH1, 2001.

Interviewee, *Tito Puente: The King of Latin Music* (documentary), PBS, 2001.

Come Together: A Night for John Lennon's Words and Music, TNT and The WB, 2001.

VH1 Divas Live: The One and Only Aretha Franklin, VH1, 2001.

Judge, *Miss Universe,* CBS, 2001.

Michael Jackson: 30th Anniversary Celebration, CBS, 2001.

Christmas in Rockefeller Center, NBC, 2001.

InStyle Celebrities at Home, NBC, 2001.

Miss Universe Pageant, CBS, 2002.

The Victoria's Secret Fashion Show, CBS, 2002.

Harry for the Holidays, NBC, 2003.

The Making of "Man on Fire" (documentary), 2004.

Television Appearances; Awards Presentations:

The 1999 ALMA Awards, 1999.

The 42nd Annual Grammy Awards, 2000.

2000 Blockbuster Entertainment Awards, Fox, 2000.

The 6th Annual Blockbuster Entertainment Awards, Fox, 2000.

The 2nd Annual Latin Grammy Awards, 2001.

Presenter, *The 28th Annual American Music Awards,* ABC, 2001.

The 3rd Annual Latin Grammy Awards, CBS, 2002.

Presenter, *The 45th Annual Grammy Awards,* CBS, 2003.

World Music Awards 2004, ABC, 2004.

The 32nd Annual American Music Awards, ABC, 2004.

Presenter, *The 2004 MTV Video Music Awards,* MTV, 2004.

The 47th Annual Grammy Awards, CBS, 2005.

Television Appearances; Episodic:

Saturday Night Live, NBC, 1999.

Mad TV, Fox, 2000.

The Tonight Show with Jay Leno, NBC, 2001 and 2002.

(In archive footage) "La verdad sobre el divorcio de Marc Anthony y Dayanara," *El show de Cristina,* 2004.

(In archive footage) "Bombazos y Exclusivas," *El show de Cristina,* 2004.

"Man on Fire," *HBO First Look,* HBO, 2004.

(In archive footage) "Bodas Recientes," *Que bodas!,* 2004.

Inside the Actors Studio, Bravo, 2004.

Stage Appearances:

Salvador Algron, *The Capeman,* Marquis Theatre, New York City, 1998.

RECORDINGS

Albums:

When the Night Is Over, Atlantic, 1991.

Otra nota, Soho Latino/RMM, 1992.

Todo a su tiempo, Soho Latino/RMM, 1995.

Asi como hoy, 1996.

Contra la corriente, RMM, 1997.

Marc Anthony, Columbia, 1999.

I Need to Know, Columbia, 1999.

Desde un principio: From the Beginning, Sony Discos Inc., 1999.

When I Dream at Night, Sony International, 2000.

Unauthorized, Peter Pan, 2000.

You Sang to Me, Sony International, 2000.

Libre, Sony, 2001.

Mended, Columbia, 2002.

I Need You, Sony International, 2002.

Tragedy, Sony International, 2002.

I've Got You, Sony, 2002.

Everything You Do, Sony International, 2003.

Exitos eternos, Universal Latino, 2003.
The Hits, 2004.
Valio la pena, Sony International, 2004.
Amar sin mentiras, Sony Discos Inc., 2004.

WRITINGS

Songs:

Wrote songs, including "You Said You Love Me" and "I Better Be the Only One" for Latin singer Sa–Fire; wrote songs for pop band Menudo.

OTHER SOURCES

Books:

Contemporary Hispanic Biography, Volume 3, Gale, 2003.
Contemporary Musicians, Volume 33, Gale, 2002.
Johns, Michael Anne, *Marc Anthony,* Andrews McMeel Publishing, 2000.

Periodicals:

Billboard, December 20, 1997, p. 1.
Entertainment Weekly, October 8, 1999, p. 32.
Interview, February, 1999, p. 84.
People Weekly, December 13, 1999, p. 185.

Electronic:

Marc Anthony Official Site, http://www.marchanthonyonline.com/, July 13, 2005.

ARMSTRONG, Samaire 1980 1980–

PERSONAL

Given name is pronounced Sah–mee–rah; full name, Samaire Rhys Armstrong; born October 31, 1980, in Tokyo, Japan. *Education:* Attended University of Arizona and (briefly) Parsons School of Design. *Avocational Interests:* Judo, fencing.

Addresses: *Agent*—Mike Jelline, International Creative Management, 8942 Wilshire Blvd., Beverly Hills, CA 90211. *Manager*—Loch Powell, Leverage Management, 3030 Pennsylvania Ave., Santa Monica, CA 90404. *Publicist*—Mia Hansen, Aquarius Public Relations, 7700 Sunset Blvd., Suite 100, Los Angeles, CA 90046.

Career: Actress. Creator of the fashion clothing label Naru.

CREDITS

Film Appearances:
Kara Fratelli, *Not Another Teen Movie* (also known as *Sex Academy*), Columbia, 2001.
Sophie, *Would I Lie to You?,* 2002.
Josie, *DarkWolf,* Twentieth Century–Fox, 2003.
Maggie, *Just My Luck,* Twentieth Century–Fox, 2005.
Abigail, *Stay Alive,* Spyglass Entertainment/Wonderlens/Endgame Entertainment/Wonderland Sound and Vision, 2005.
Jenny, *Rise,* Senator International, 2005.

Television Appearances; Series:
Anna Stern, a recurring role, *The O.C.,* Fox, 2003–2004.
Emily, a recurring role, *Entourage,* HBO, 2004–2005.

Television Appearances; Episodic:
Meredith, "Taboo or Not Taboo," *Party of Five,* Fox, 2000.
Laurie, "Smooching and Mooching," *Freaks and Geeks,* NBC, 2000.
Laurie, "Discos and Dragons," *Freaks and Geeks,* NBC, 2000.
Brittany, "When Good Ideas Go Bad," *That's Life,* CBS, 2000.
Tasha, "Sailing Away," *ER,* NBC, 2001.
Angie Becker, "Look Closer," *Judging Amy,* CBS, 2001.
Natalie Gordon, "Lord of the Flies," *The X–Files,* Fox, 2001.
Guest, *The Sharon Osbourne Show,* syndicated, 2004.
Guest, *Last Call with Carson Daly,* NBC, 2004.
Guest, *On–Air with Ryan Seacrest,* syndicated, 2004.
Christine, "You're Buggin' Me," *NYPD Blue,* ABC, 2004.

Television Appearances; Pilots:
Carly Wilson (some sources cite Katja), *111 Gramercy Park,* ABC, 2003.

Television Appearances; Specials:
2003 MTV Movie Awards, MTV, 2002.
101 Most Unforgettable SNL Moments, E! Entertainment Television, 2004.

RECORDINGS

Videos:

Appeared as Penny in the music video "Penny & Me" by Hanson, and in the music video "Bad Day" by Daniel Powter.

OTHER SOURCES

Periodicals:

Entertainment Weekly, December 17, 2004, p. 35; January 14, 2005, p. 18.

Lemonade, September, 2003, pp. 60–61.
TV Guide, February 14, 2004, p. 20.

ARNOLD, Tichina 1971–
(Tichina R. Arnold)

PERSONAL

Born June 28, 1971, in New York, NY; married Tajuan Brewster (an Olympic boxer). *Education:* Attended High School of Music and Art, New York, NY.

Addresses: *Contact*—York & Harper, 7364 1/2 Melrose, Los Angeles, CA 90046.

Career: Actress and singer.

Awards, Honors: Emmy Award nomination, outstanding ingenue in a daytime drama series, 1988, Soap Opera Digest Award nomination, outstanding female newcomer: daytime, 1989, for *Ryan's Hope;* Image Award, best supporting actress in a comedy series, National Association for the Advancement of Colored People, 1996, for *Martin.*

CREDITS

Television Appearances; Series:
Zena Brown, *Ryan's Hope,* ABC, 1987–89.
Sharla Valentine, *All My Children,* ABC, 1988–89.
Pamela "Pam" James, *Martin,* Fox, 1992–97.
Nicole Barnes, a recurring role, *One on One,* UPN, 2001–2003.
Rochelle, *Everybody Hates Chris,* UPN, 2005.

Television Appearances; Episodic:
(As Tichina R. Arnold) Delores, "Theo's Women," *The Cosby Show,* NBC, 1989.
Leona, "Out of the Half–Light," *Law & Order,* NBC, 1990.
Host, *Soul Train,* 1994.
Carla, "Soul Mate to Cellmate," *The Jamie Foxx Show,* The WB, 1998.
"Ghost Town," *Pacific Blue,* USA Network, 1999.
Mrs. Murphy, "Norm vs. the Boxer," *The Norm Show,* ABC, 1999.
"He's All Crass, She's All Class!," *Rendez–View,* 2001.
Adina, "Past Imperfect," *Soul Food,* Showtime, 2002.
"Martin Lawrence: Comic Trip," *Biography,* Arts and Entertainment, 2002.
"Martin Lawrence," *E! True Hollywood Story,* 2003.
Nicole, "Hi Mom," *Eve,* 2003.

Punk'd, MTV, 2004.
Kiara, "Thanksgiving," *Listen Up,* CBS, 2004.
Nicole Barnes, "Cap and Frown," *One on One,* UPN, 2005.

Television Appearances; Movies:
Mary, *The Brass Ring,* 1983.
Pesty, *The House of Dies Drear,* PBS, 1984.
Susie, *Perfect Prey* (also known as *When the Bough Breaks II*), HBO, 1998.

Television Appearances; Specials:
GED—Get It!, PBS, 1993.
Circus of the Stars Goes to Disneyland, CBS, 1994.
Competitor, *Superstar American Gladiators,* ABC, 1995.
Interviewee, *Intimate Portrait: Tisha Campbell–Martin* (documentary), Lifetime, 2003.

Television Appearances; Awards Presentations:
The 14th Annual Daytime Emmy Awards, ABC, 1987.
Song performer, *The 17th Annual Daytime Emmy Awards,* ABC, 1990.
Soul Train Lady of Soul Awards, syndicated, 1996.
The 10th Annual Soul Train Music Awards, WB, 1996.

Film Appearances:
Crystal, *Little Shop of Horrors,* Warner Bros., 1986.
Evelyn Ruth, *Starlight: A Musical Movie,* 1988.
Vera Cook, *How I Got into College,* Twentieth Century–Fox, 1989.
Ticket seller, *Scenes from a Mall,* Buena Vista, 1991.
Tracy, *Fakin' Da Funk,* 1997.
A Luv Tale, 1999.
Robber, *Dancing in September,* Warner Home Video, 2000.
Ritha, *Big Momma's House* (also known as *Big Mamas Haus*), Twentieth Century–Fox, 2000.
Aisha, *Civil Brand,* Lions Gate Films, 2002.
Ray Goods, *Yo Alien,* Daughters 2 Feed, 2002.
Desiree, *On the One,* Cataland, 2004.
Getting Played, 2005.

Also appeared in *Cuttin' Da' Mustard.*

Stage Appearances:
(New York City stage debut) *The Me Nobody Knows,* Billie Holiday Theatre, New York City, 1982.

Appeared in *Little Shop of Horrors,* New York City; *The Haggadah,* Joseph Papp Theatre, New York City; *Topsy Turvy,* New York City; *Really Rosie,* Music Hall, Detroit, MI.

Major Tours:
Appeared in *The Buddy Holly Story,* U.S. cities.

ASHMORE, Aaron 1979–

PERSONAL

Full name, Aaron Robert Ashmore; born October 7, 1979, in Richmond, British Columbia, Canada; son of Rick and Linda Ashmore; twin brother of Shawn (an actor).

Addresses: *Contact*—K. G. Talent, 55A Sumach St., Toronto, Ontario M5A 3J6, Canada.

Career: Actor.

Awards, Honors: Gemini Award nomination, best performance in a children's or youth program or series, Academy of Canadian Cinema and Television, 1995; New York International Independent Film & Video Festival Award, best actor, 2002; Saturn Award nomination, Cinescape genre face of the future, Academy of Science Fiction, Horror, and Fantasy Films, 2003; Teen Choice Award nomination (with Anna Paquin), choice chemistry, 2003; MTV Movie Award nomination, best kiss (with Anna Paquin) and MTV Movie Award, breakthrough male, 2004.

CREDITS

Film Appearances:
Student in pageant, *Married to It,* 1991.
Bobby Christianson, *The Safety of Objects,* IFC Films, 2001.
Dwayne, *Treed Murray* (also known as *Entre l'arbre et l'ecorce* and *Get Down*), Alliance Atlantis, 2001.
Matt "Hutch" Hutchinson, *The Skulls II,* Universal, 2002.
Eric/Lou Woods, *My Brother's Keeper* (also known as *Le sang du frere*), Little Ricky, 2004.
Bobby, *Safe,* Shoes Full of Feet, 2004.

Television Appearances; Movies:
Young Byron Spencer, *Gross Misconduct,* CBC, 1993.
Luke Lawson, *Crime in Connecticut: The Story of Alex Kelly* (also known as *Le retour d'Alex Kelly*), CBS, 1999.
Bob Bartram, *Love Letters,* ABC, 1999.
Charlie, *Run the Wild Fields,* Showtime, 2000.
Second son, *Blackout,* CBS, 2001.
Chris Welsh, *The Familiar Stranger* (also known as *My Husband's Double Life*), Lifetime, 2001.
Jason, *Dying to Dance,* NBC, 2001.
Ted, *Charms for the Easy Life,* Lifetime, 2002.
John Boyajian, *A Christmas Visitor,* Hallmark Channel, 2002.

Randy Kehler, *The Pentagon Papers,* F/X, 2003.
Marc Hall, *Prom Queen: The Marc Hall Story* (also known as *Prom Queen*), 2004.
Tyler, *Brave New Girl,* 2004.
Chad, *A Separate Peace,* Showtime, 2004.
Corporal Randy Taylor, *A Bear Named Winnie,* CBC, 2004.

Television Appearances; Episodic:
Billy, "The Tale of the 13th Floor," *Are You Afraid of the Dark?,* Nickelodeon, 1993.
Teenager, "Juliet Is Bleeding," *Due South,* CBS and CTV, 1996.
Ax Double, "The Capture: Part 2," *Animorphs,* Nickelodeon, 1999.
Robert, "Something to Prove," *The Famous Jett Jackson,* The Disney Channel, 2000.
Jake, "The Tale of the Lunar Locusts," *Are You Afraid of the Dark?,* Nickelodeon, 2000.
Neil Hudson, "Time to Be Heroes," *La Femme Nikita,* USA Network, 2000.
Young Paul, "Grandma's Shoes," *Twice in a Lifetime,* PAX and CTV, 2000.
Trevor Gordon, "Tree Hugger," *The Eleventh Hour,* CTV, 2002.
Troy Vandegraff, "Credit Where Credit's Due," *Veronica Mars,* UPN, 2004.
Troy Vandegraff, "Meet John Smith," *Veronica Mars,* UPN, 2004.
Troy Vandegraff, "The Wrath of Con," *Veronica Mars,* UPN, 2004.
Troy Vandegraff, "You Think You Know Somebody!," *Veronica Mars,* UPN, 2004.
Trevor, "365 Days," *The West Wing,* NBC, 2005.
Taz Thomas, "Kettle Black," *The Eleventh Hour,* CTV, 2005.
Trevor, "King Corn," *The West Wing,* NBC, 2005.

ASNER, Jules 1968–

PERSONAL

Original name, Julie White; born February 14, 1968, in Tempe, AZ; daughter of Lee (a furniture saleswoman); married Matthew Asner, 1992 (divorced, 1996); married Steven Soderbergh (a director), May 10, 2003. *Education:* University of California, Los Angeles, degree in political science and journalism.

Addresses: *Agent*—William Morris Agency, 13625 Avenue of the Americas, New York, NY 10019.

Career: Actress and journalist. Previously worked as an entertainment reporter for *Good Morning England,* HCTV, Reuters Television, *The Entertainment Show,* and

Extra; contributor to *Buzz* magazine; appeared in a television commercial for Kentucky Fried Chicken, 2003; also worked as a model.

CREDITS

Television Appearances; Series:
Host, *Wild On ... ,* E! Entertainment Television, 1997–99.
Guest host, *E! Goes to Cannes!,* E! Entertainment Television, 1999.
Co–anchor, *E! News Daily,* E! Entertainment Television, 1999–2002.
Host, *Revealed with Jules Asner,* E! Entertainment Television, 2001—.
Host, *Life & Style,* syndicated, 2004–2005.

Television Appearances; Specials:
Host, *Entertainers '97,* E! Entertainment Television, 1997.
Host, *Live Primetime Emmy Nominations,* E! Entertainment Television, 1999.
Host, *Countdown to the Primetime Emmys,* E! Entertainment Television, 1999.
Anchor, *Countdown to the Academy Awards,* E! Entertainment Television, 1999.
Host, *The Stars Come Out: The GLAAD Awards,* E! Entertainment Television, 2000.
Host, *Primetime Emmy Awards Post–Show,* E! Entertainment Television, 2000.
Host, *Primetime Emmy Award Nominations,* E! Entertainment Television, 2000.
Anchor, *E! Live Academy Award Nominations,* E! Entertainment Television, 2000.
Host, *Live by Request: K. D. Lang,* E! Entertainment Television, 2000.
Anchor, *Live 2001 Primetime Emmy Awards Post Show,* E! Entertainment Television, 2001.
Host, *Inside the Academy Awards,* E! Entertainment Television, 2001.
Host, *Hollywood Unites: An E! News Special,* E! Entertainment Television, 2001.
Host, *Heatwave,* E! Entertainment Television, 2001.
Host, *E! News Daily: Everything Emmy,* E! Entertainment Television, 2001.
Host, *Countdown to the Red Carpet: The 2001 Academy Awards,* E! Entertainment Television, 2001.
Host, *All about Ally* (documentary), E! Entertainment Television, 2001.
Host, *2001 Golden Globes Post–Show,* E! Entertainment Television, 2001.
Presenter, *2001 ALMA Awards,* ABC, 2001.
Anchor, *Live Post Show: The 2002 Academy Awards,* E! Entertainment Television, 2002.
Host, *Live from the Red Carpet: The 2002 SAG Awards,* E! Entertainment Television, 2002.
Host, *The 2002 Golden Globe Awards Live Post Show,* E! Entertainment Television, 2002.

Host, *Live by Request: Blondie,* Arts and Entertainment, 2004.
Host, *A&E's Live by Request: Kenny Chesney,* Arts and Entertainment, 2004.

Television Appearances; Movies:
Best Actress, E! Entertainment Television, 2000.

Television Appearances; Episodic:
"Re–Enter the Dragon," *Action,* syndicated, 1999.
"Blowhard," *Action,* syndicated, 1999.

Also appeared in *Bob Patterson,* ABC; *Sidewalks Entertainment.*

Television Appearances; Pilots:
Host, *Assignment E!,* E! Entertainment Television, 2002.

Television Director; Series:
Hard Copy, 1989.

Film Appearances:
Jay and Silent Bob Strike Back, Dimension Films, 2001.

AVARY, Roger 1965–
   (Roger Roberts Avary, Yrava Regor)

PERSONAL

Original name, Franklin Brauner; born August 23, 1965, in Flin Flon, Manitoba, Canada; son of Edwin Roberts and Brigitte (maiden name, Bruninghaus) Avary; married; wife's name, Gretchen; children: Gala Blue. *Education:* Art Center College of Design, Pasadena, CA, 1987.

Addresses: *Agent*—Creative Artists Agency, 9830 Wilshire Blvd., Beverly Hills, CA 90212–1804.

Career: Writer, director, producer, and cinematographer. Worked as a writer and director for D'Arcy, Masius, Benton & Bowles (an advertising agency), Los Angeles, CA, 1989–90, and J. Walter Thompson (an advertising agency), Los Angeles, CA, beginning in 1990; previously worked as a clerk at Video Archive, Manhattan Beach, CA.

Awards, Honors: Los Angeles Film Critics Association Award (with David Webb Peoples), best screenplay, 1992, for *Unforgiven;* Best Film Award and Critics

Award, Mystfest, 1994, International Fantasy Film Award nomination, best film, Fantasporto, 1995, all for *Killing Zoe;* New York Film Critics Circle Award (with Quentin Tarantino), best screenplay, Los Angeles Film Critics Association Award (with Tarantino), best screenplay, Boston Society of Film Critics Award (with Tarantino), best screenplay, 1994, Academy Award (with Tarantino), best screenplay written directly for the screen, Film Award (with Tarantino), best screenplay—original, British Academy of Film and Television Arts, Chicago Film Critics Association Award(with Tarantino), best screenplay, Independent Spirit Award (with Tarantino), best screenplay, 1995, all for *Pulp Fiction.*

CREDITS

Film Work:
Director and producer, *The Worm Turns,* 1983.
Production assistant, *Maximum Potential* (also known as *Dolph Lundgreen: Maximum Potential*), 1987.
Cinematographer, *My Best Friend's Birthday,* 1987.
(As Roger Roberts Avary) Director, *Killing Zoe,* October Films, 1994.
Executive producer, *Boogie Boy,* Sterling, 1998.
Executive producer, *The Last Man,* 2000.
Director and executive producer, *The Rules of Attraction* (also known as *Die Regeln des Spiels*), Lions Gate Films, 2002.
Director, producer, cinematographer, and editor, *Glitterati,* Roger Avary, 2004.
Director, *Glamorama,* Lions Gate Films, 2005.

Film Appearances:
(As Yrava Regor) 13th Morningside Volunteer Infantryman, *Phantasm IV: Oblivion* (also known as *Phantasm IV, Phantasm IV: Infinity,* and *Phantasm: oblIVion*), 1998.
Fraklin Brauner, *Standing Still,* Rice/Walters, 2004.

Television Work; Movies:
Executive producer and director, *Mr. Stitch,* Sci–Fi Channel, 1996.

Television Producer; Pilots:
Odd Jobs, NBC, 1997.

Television Appearances; Specials:
The 67th Annual Academy Awards, ABC, 1995.

Television Appearances; Episodic:
Appeared in "The Rules of Attraction," *Anatomy of a Scene,* Sundance Channel.

RECORDINGS

Music Videos:
Director, "The Whole World Lost Its Head," *The Go Go's,* 1994.

WRITINGS

Screenplays:
The Worm Turns, 1983.
99 Days, 1991.
(With Mario Puzo) *The Lorch Team,* 1992.
(And creator, with Quentin Tarantino) Background dialogue, *Reservoir Dogs,* Miramax, 1992.
(Uncredited) *True Romance* (also known as *Breakaway*), Warner Bros., 1993.
(As Roger Roberts Avary) *Killing Zoe,* October Films, 1994.
(With Tarantino) *Pulp Fiction,* Miramax, 1994.
(Uncredited) *Crying Freeman,* 1995.
Hatchetman, 1995.
(Uncredited) *RPM,* 1998.
The Rules of Attraction (adaptation of the novel of the same title by Brett Easton Ellis; also known as *Die Regeln des Spiels*), Lions Gate Films, 2002.
Glitterati, Roger Avary, 2004.
Glamorama (adaptation of the novel by Ellis), Lions Gate Films, 2005.
Rewrite, *Lords of Dogtown,* Sony Pictures Releasing, 2005.

Television Movies:
Mr. Stitch, Sci–Fi Channel, 1996.

Television Pilots:
Odd Jobs, NBC, 1997.

Children's Fiction:
Marshall's Dreams, 1991.

OTHER SOURCES

Periodicals:
The Washington Post, October 12, 2002, pp. C1 and C3.

B

BAKER, Ian 1947–

PERSONAL

Born 1947, in Melbourne, Victoria, Australia. *Education:* Attended Swinburne College of Advanced Education (now Victorian College of the Arts).

Addresses: *Agent*—Hilary McQuaide, Skouras Agency, 1149 Third St., 3rd Floor, Santa Monica, CA 90403.

Career: Cinematographer. Film House, worked as camera operator for commercials; photographer, 1977—.

Awards, Honors: Australian Film Institute Award, best cinematography, 1976, for *The Devil's Playground;* Australian Film Institute Award nomination, best cinematography, 1978, for *The Chant of Jimmie Blacksmith;* Australian Film Institute Award, Film Critics Circle of Australia Award, and If Award, all best cinematography, 2003, for *Japanese Story.*

CREDITS

Film Cinematographer:
"The Priest," *Libido,* BEF Film Distributors, 1973.
The Devil's Playground, 1976, EMC/International Film Exchange, 1981.
The Chant of Jimmie Blacksmith, Hoyts Distribution, 1978, New Yorker Films, 1980.
Barbarosa, Universal, 1982.
The Clinic, Roadshow Film Distributors, 1982.
Iceman, Universal, 1984.
Plenty, Twentieth Century–Fox, 1985.
Roxanne, Columbia, 1987.

A Cry in the Dark (also known as *Evil Angels*), Warner Bros., 1988.
The Punisher, New World, 1989.
Everybody Wins, Orion, 1990.
The Russia House, Metro–Goldwyn–Mayer, 1990.
Mr. Baseball, Universal, 1992.
Six Degrees of Separation, Metro–Goldwyn–Mayer, 1993.
I.Q., Paramount, 1994.
The Chamber, Universal, 1996.
Fierce Creatures, MCA/Universal, 1997.
Queen of the Damned (also known as *Anne Rice's "Queen of the Damned"*), Warner Bros., 2002.
It Runs in the Family, Metro–Goldwyn–Mayer, 2003.
Japanese Story, Samuel Goldwyn Films, 2003.

Television Cinematographer; Miniseries:
The Last Frontier, CBS, 1986.

BALASKI, Belinda 1947–

PERSONAL

Born December 8, 1947, in Inglewood, CA.

Career: Actress. BB's Kids (acting workshop for children), teacher of commercial and theatrical workshops.

Member: Academy of Motion Picture Arts and Sciences, Actors' Equity Association.

Awards, Honors: Los Angeles Drama Critics Circle Award, for *Bus Stop;* Robbie Awards for *Dark at the Top of the Stairs* and *Picnic.*

CREDITS

Film Appearances:

Mary, *Black Eye,* Warner Bros., 1974.

Essie Beaumont, *Bobbie Jo and the Outlaw,* American International Pictures, 1976.

Rita, *The Food of the Gods* (also known as *H. G. Wells' "Food of the Gods"*), American International Pictures, 1976.

Maryann, *Cannonball* (also known as *Carquake*), New World, 1976.

Getting It Over With (short film), 1977.

Till Death, Cougar Films, 1978.

Betsy, *Piranha,* New World, 1978.

Terry Fisher, *The Howling,* Avco Embassy, 1981.

Mrs. Joe Harris, *Gremlins,* Warner Bros., 1984.

Bernice Pitnik, "Critic's Corner" and "Roast Your Loved One" segments, *Amazon Women on the Moon* (also known as *Cheeseburger Film Sandwich*), MCA/Universal, 1987.

Movie theater mom, *Gremlins 2: The New Batch,* Warner Bros., 1990.

Stan's mom, *Matinee,* Universal, 1993.

Rita, *American Perfekt,* Keystone Releasing, 1998.

Neighbor, *Small Soldiers,* DreamWorks/Red Feather Photoplays, 1998.

Lois, *Santa Monica Boulevard,* Millennium Independents/Quickstar Productions, 2001.

Vampire mother, *The Vampire Hunters Club,* Doodle Barnett Productions/Irena Belle Films, 2001.

Also appeared in the films *Goodnight Moon; Next Time I Fall in Love; Rachel & Marla; Two Way Street;* and *Windows.*

Film Work:

Special vocal effects artist, *Explorers,* Paramount, 1985.

Television Appearances; Movies:

Janet Willimer, *Locusts,* ABC, 1974.

The Werewolf of Woodstock, ABC, 1975.

Ginger, *Force Five* (also known as *Final Tactic*), CBS, 1975.

Jenny Storm, *Death Scream* (also known as *Streetkill* and *The Woman Who Cried Murder*), ABC, 1975.

Ann, *Having Babies II,* ABC, 1977.

Lynn Hollister, *Mrs. R's Daughter,* NBC, 1979.

Anatomy of an Illness, CBS, 1984.

Terry, *Deadly Care,* CBS, 1987.

Nell, *Proud Men,* ABC, 1987.

Mrs. Nicholson, *Runaway Daughters,* Showtime, 1994.

The graphic designer, *The Second Civil War,* HBO, 1997.

Barterer's wife, *The Warlord: Battle for the Galaxy* (also known as *The Osiris Chronicles*), UPN, 1998.

Appeared in the movie *Halfway to Danger,* ABC.

Television Appearances; Specials:

Cindy Britton, *The Runaways,* ABC, 1974.

Terry Fisher (in archive footage), *Making a Monster Movie: Inside "The Howling,"* 1981.

Margaret Landry, *Henry Hamilton Graduate Ghost,* ABC, 1984.

Are You My Mother?, ABC, 1986.

Helen Green, *My Dissident Mom,* CBS, 1987.

Dr. Shallman, *America Behind Closed Doors,* CBS, 1992.

Television Appearances; Miniseries:

Principal, *Seduced by Madness: The Diane Borchardt Story* (also known as *Seduced by Madness*), NBC, 1996.

Television Appearances; Episodic:

Obie Graff, "Requiem for a Lost Son," *The Cowboys,* ABC, 1974.

"Ragtime Billy Peaches," *Baretta,* ABC, 1975.

Judy Collins, "A Coven of Killers," *S.W.A.T.,* ABC, 1975.

Medical examiner Ginny Simpson, "The Velvet Jungle," *Starsky and Hutch,* ABC, 1977.

Arla, "An Act of Love," *The Fantastic Journey,* NBC, 1977.

Sue Cantrell, "Angels on the Run," *Charlie's Angels,* ABC, 1978.

Missy, "The Innocent," *How the West Was Won,* ABC, 1979.

Lucille, "The Visitor," *Vega$,* ABC, 1979.

"Labor Pains," *The A–Team,* NBC, 1983.

Lois, "Death Watch," *Matt Houston,* ABC, 1985.

Judy, "Fire Man," *Hunter,* NBC, 1985.

Darlene Cooper, "Family Forecast," *Simon & Simon,* CBS, 1986.

"Artful Dodging," *Our House,* NBC, 1988.

Dr. Stephanie Ambrose, "Dinner at Eight," *Falcon Crest,* CBS, 1989.

Dr. Stephanie Ambrose, "Uneasy Allies," *Falcon Crest,* CBS, 1989.

Dr. Stephanie Ambrose, "Enquiring Minds," *Falcon Crest,* CBS, 1989.

Scrub nurse, "The Medical Mystery," *Father Dowling Mysteries,* ABC, 1990.

Winifred Swanson, "Foreverware," *Eerie, Indiana,* NBC, 1991.

"Operation Lemonade," *FBI: The Untold Stories,* ABC, 1992.

Mother, "The Hole in the Head Gang," *Eerie, Indiana,* NBC, 1992.

Worried mother, "Shark's Cove," *Baywatch,* syndicated, 1992.

Cleo Jennings, "Sail Away," *Baywatch,* syndicated, 1996.

Appeared as Phyllis Cleary in an episode of *Reasonable Doubts;* also appeared in episodes of *Divorce Court, Hard Copy, Hotel, Santa Barbara, Sierra, True Confessions,* and *Unsolved Mysteries.*

Stage Appearances:

Appeared as Elma, *Bus Stop,* Met Theatre; as Reenie, *Dark at the Top of the Stairs,* Met Theatre; as Jill, *The Fox,* Back Alley Theatre; in *A Good Look at Bondy Kern,* Bucks County, PA; as girl, *Infancy and Childhood,* Old Globe Theatre, San Diego, CA; as Wendy, *Peter Pan,* Starlight Opera, San Diego; as Millie, *Picnic,* Met Theatre; and as Joanne, *Vanities,* Albuquerque, NM.

RECORDINGS

Videos:

Unleashing the Beast: Making "The Howling," Metro–Goldwyn–Mayer/United Artists Home Entertainment, 2003.

Welcome to Werewolfland, Kinowelt Home Entertainment, 2004.

BARNES, Art
    See MUMY, Bill

BARRETT, Brendon Ryan 1986–

PERSONAL

Born August 5, 1986, in Roseville, Sacramento, CA; father, a veterinarian; mother, a veterinarian; brother of Caitlin Barrett (an actress). *Education:* Studied at Off–Broadway Dance Academy, Folsom, CA. *Avocational Interests:* Drawing cartoon characters.

Addresses: *Agent*—Stone Manners Talent and Literary Agency, 6500 Wilshire Blvd., Suite 550, Los Angeles, CA 90048.

Career: Actor and dancer. Appeared in television commercials, print advertisements, and industrial films.

Awards, Honors: Winner of International Model and Talent Competition, 1995; Young Artist Award nomination, best leading young actor in a television movie, pilot, miniseries, or series, 1999, for *Logan's War: Bound by Honor.*

CREDITS

Television Appearances; Series:

Andy Weber, *Soul Man,* ABC, 1997.

Television Appearances; Movies:

Johnny Sapp, *Stolen Innocence,* CBS, 1995.

Andy Wilson, *The Shadow Men,* HBO, 1998.

Logan Fallon at age ten, *Logan's War: Bound by Honor,* CBS, 1998.

Voice of Casper, *Casper's Haunted Christmas* (animated; also known as *Le noel hante de Casper*), USA Network, 2000.

Television Appearances; Episodic:

Cameron Mancuso, "Only Connect," *Touched by an Angel,* CBS, 1998.

Stan, "Caroline and the Horny Kid," *Caroline in the City,* NBC, 1999.

Ethan Killion, "The Odd Couples," *Two of a Kind,* ABC, 1999.

Ethan Killion, "The Goodbye Girl," *Two of a Kind,* ABC, 1999.

Jason, "Big Dougie," *The King of Queens,* CBS, 2000.

Television Appearances; Pilots:

Fuddy's son, *What's Up, Peter Fuddy?,* Fox, 2001.

Film Appearances:

Chris Carson, *Casper: A Spirited Beginning,* Twentieth Century–Fox Home Entertainment, 1997.

Taylor, *Durango Kids,* PorchLight Entertainment, 1999.

Young Ryan, *Boys and Girls,* Alliance Atlantis Communications, 2000.

Troy, *Lloyd* (also known as *Lloyd: The Ugly Kid* and *The Ugly Kid*), SoHo Entertainment, 2001.

Stage Appearances:

An American Divorce, 1996.

Fritz, *The Nutcracker,* Sacramento Ballet, Sacramento, CA, 1996.

Moment to Moment, 1996.

BARUCHEL, Jay 1982–

PERSONAL

Full name, Jonathan Adam Saunders Baruchel (some sources cite Jay Martin Baruchel); born 1982, in Ottawa, Ontario, Canada; son of Serge (an antiques dealer) and Robyne (a freelance writer) Baruchel. *Education:* Attended Fine Arts Core Education School, Montreal, Quebec, Canada.

Addresses: *Agent*—Creative Artist Agency, 9830 Wilshire Blvd., Beverly Hills, CA 90212. *Manager*—Rozon/Mercer Management, 201 North Robertson, Beverly Hills, CA 90211. *Publicist*—Baker/Winokur/Ryder, 9100 Wilshire Blvd., 6th Floor, West Tower, Beverly Hills, CA 90212.

Career: Actor. Drummer in the rock group Martin.

CREDITS

Television Appearances; Series:
Ross, *Are You Afraid of the Dark?*, Nickelodeon, c. 1995.
Thomas Thompson, *My Hometown*, YTV, 1996.
Host, *Popular Mechanics For Kids*, syndicated, 1997–98.
Steven Karp, *Undeclared*, Fox, 2001.
Winston Stone, *The Stones*, CBS, 2004.
Skip Ross, *Just Legal*, The WB, 2005.

Television Appearances; Pilots:
Jimmy Fleming, *Matthew Blackheart: Monster Smasher*, syndicated, 2002.
Kelvin, *The Robinson Brothers*, Fox, 2004.
Skip Ross, *Just Legal*, The WB, 2005.

Television Appearances; Episodic:
Beanpole, *The Worst Witch*, ITV1, 1998.

Film Appearances:
Supporting actor, *Who Gets the House?* (also known as *Qui garde la maison?*), 1999.
Vic Munoz, *Almost Famous* (also known as *Untitled: Almost Famous the Bootleg Cut*), Columbia TriStar, 2000.
Harry, *The Rules of Attraction* (also known as *Die Regeln des Spiel*), Lions Gate, 2002.
Jeremy Curran, *Nemesis Game*, Lions Gate Films, 2003.
Danger Barch, *Million Dollar Baby*, Warner Bros., 2004.
Title role, *I Am Reed Fish*, 2005.

Film Work:
Director, producer, cinematographer, editor, and special effects, *Edgar and Jane* (short film), Eden Arts, 2002.

WRITINGS

Screenplays:
Edgar and Jane (short film), Eden Arts, 2002.

OTHER SOURCES

Periodicals:
Interview, February, 2005, p. 66.
People Weekly, November 12, 2001, p. 93.

BATINKOFF, Randall 1968–

PERSONAL

Born October 16, 1968, in Monticello, NY. *Education:* Brown University, B.A., international relations.

Addresses: *Agent*—Paradigm, 10100 Santa Monica Blvd., #2500, Los Angeles, CA 90067; The Gersh Agency, 232 N. Canon Dr., Beverly Hills, CA 90210.

Career: Actor. Appeared in television commercials.

CREDITS

Film Appearances:
Tim, *Streetwalkin'* (also known as *City Streets* and *Cookie*), Paramount, 1985.
Stan Bobrucz, *For Keeps* (also known as *Maybe Baby*), RKO, 1988.
Jeffrey, *Buffy the Vampire Slayer*, Fox, 1992.
Rip Van Kelt, *School Ties*, Paramount, 1992.
Howard the mail carrier, *The Joke*, 1992.
Reg Goldman, *The Player*, 1992.
Chad Shadowhill, *Higher Learning*, Izaro Films, 1995.
Peter, *Walking and Talking*, Miramax, 1996.
Carol's date, *As Good As It Gets*, Columbia Tristar, 1997.
CTN junior executive, *Mad City*, Warner Bros., 1997.
Ken, *The Peacemaker*, DreamWorks, 1997.
Rand, *The Curve* (also known as *Dead Man's Curve*), Trimark Pictures, 1998.
Sugar: The Fall of the West (also known as *Sugar*), 1999.
Jimmy Rapture, *Rockin' Good Times*, 1999.
Bradbury, *Let the Devil Wear Black*, Trimark Pictures, 1999.
Jamie, *The Last Marshal*, Big Picture Entertainment Group, 1999.
Terry Cowens, *Along for the Ride*, 1999.
Gardner, *Just Sue Me*, 2000.
Lawrence, *Free*, 2001.
Sam, *The Month of August*, Angelic Entertainment, 2002.
Beau Stoddard, *Detonator*, Cinetel Films, 2003.
I Love Your Work, 2003.
Paulie, *April's Shower*, Regent Releasing, 2003.
Nick, *Walking on the Sky*, 2004.
Jim, *True Love*, Antic Pictures, 2004.
Nathan Collins, *Blue Demon*, 2004.
Max Sherman, *Love Hollywood Style*, 2005.
Sergeant Frank Mills, *Venice Underground*, 2005.
Scott Davis, *Touched*, 2005.
Jeff, *Fear Itself*, 2005.

Television Appearances; Movies:

David Harding, *The Stepford Children*, NBC, 1987.

Johnny Perfect, *Heartwood*, The Family Channel, 1998.

Title role, *Hefner: Unauthorized* (also known as *Hugh Hefner: The True Story*), USA Network, 1999.

Television Appearances; Pilots:

Paul Margolin, *One More Try*, CBS, 1982.

Reverend David Grantland, *Christy*, ABC, 1994.

Television Appearances; Series:

Terence Dean, *Better Days*, 1986.

Reverend David Grantland, *Christy* (also known as *Catherine Marshall's "Christy"*), ABC, 1994–95.

Everett Moreland, *Relativity*, ABC, 1996–97.

Television Appearances; Episodic:

Calvin Chillcut, "Finger of God," *Touched by an Angel*, CBS, 2000.

James Green, "Learning to Fly," *She Spies*, syndicated, 2003.

Ex–boyfriend, "Rap Sheet," *CSI: Miami*, CBS, 2004.

BLACK, Michael Ian 1971–
(Michael Black, Michael Schwartz)

PERSONAL

Original name, Michael Ian Schwartz; born August 12, 1971, in Chicago, IL; raised in Hillsborough, NJ; son of Robert (an executive) and Jill (a store owner) Schwartz; married Martha Hagen, 1998; children: Elijah, Ruth. *Education:* Attended New York University. *Religion:* Jewish.

Addresses: *Agent*—United Talent Agency, 9560 Wilshire Blvd., Suite 500, Beverly Hills, CA 90212. *Manager*—Ted Schachter, Schachter Management, 1157 South Beverly Dr., 2nd Floor, Los Angeles, CA 90035.

Career: Actor, writer, director, producer, and comedian. The State (also known as the New Group and The State: Full–Frontal Comedy), performer, beginning 1988; Stella (comedy trio), comedian, appearing at comedy clubs, beginning 1997. Cable News Network, political and topical commentator; voice for commercials, including voice of sock puppet for Pets.com website, 1999.

CREDITS

Television Appearances; Series:

Multiple roles, *You Wrote It, You Watch It*, 1992.

Member of ensemble, *The State*, MTV, 1993.

Johnny Bluejeans, *Viva Variety*, Comedy Central, 1996.

Multiple roles, *Random Play*, VH1, 1999.

Philip "Phil" Washington Stubbs, *Ed* (also known as *Stuckeyville*), NBC, 2000–2004.

Host, *Late Friday*, NBC, 2001.

Host, *Spy TV*, NBC, 2001.

Michael, *Stella*, Comedy Central, 2005.

Television Appearances; Miniseries:

Interviewee, *I Love the '80s*, VH1, 2002.

Interviewee, *I Love the '70s*, VH1, 2003.

Interviewee, *I Love the '80s Strikes Back*, VH1, 2003.

Interviewee, *I Love the '90s*, VH1, 2004.

Interviewee, *I Love the '90s: Part Deux*, VH1, 2005.

Television Appearances; Specials:

The State's 43rd Annual Halloween Special, CBS, 1995.

(As Michael Black) Johnny Bluejeans, *The Viva in Vegas Special*, Comedy Central, 1998.

Host, *IFP Gotham Awards 2003* (also known as *The 13th Annual IFP Gotham Awards*), Bravo, 2003.

Interviewee, *VH1 Big in '03*, VH1, 2003.

TV Road Trip: Los Angeles, Travel Channel, 2003.

Host, *Reel Comedy: Stuck on You*, Comedy Central, 2003.

NBC's Funniest Out–takes #2, NBC, 2003.

Spinal Tap Goes to 20, Independent Film Channel, 2004.

Interviewee, *Boomer Nation*, Arts and Entertainment, 2004.

Television Appearances; Other:

Stephen Hawking, "In the Woods" segments, *The Bogus Witch Project* (movie), 2000.

Hey, Neighbor (pilot), Fox, 2000.

Voice of Zak the dog, *Dog Days* (pilot), NBC, 2000.

Television Appearances; Episodic:

Joey Diaz, "Rockin' Robin," *NYPD Blue*, ABC, 1994.

Luc, *Spin City*, ABC, 1998.

Himself, *Pyramid*, syndicated, 2002, 2003.

Guest, *The Michael Essany Show*, E! Entertainment Television, 2003.

Voice of second Al Foster, *Crank Yankers*, Comedy Central, 2003.

Kevin the sex offender, "Clementine's Pregnant," *Reno 911!*, Comedy Central, 2003.

Michael, *Crank Yankers*, Comedy Central, 2003.

Himself, "Tournament 1, Game 3," *Celebrity Poker Showdown*, Bravo, 2003.

Himself, "Tournament 2, Game 3," *Celebrity Poker Showdown*, Bravo, 2004.

Himself, "Tournament 2, Championship," *Celebrity Poker Showdown*, Bravo, 2004.

Chris, "More FBI Help," *Reno 911!*, Comedy Central, 2004.

Guest host, *The Late Late Show with Craig Kilborn,* CBS, 2004.

Voice of Dr. Ian Black, "Vehicular Manslaughter," *Tom Goes to the Mayor,* Cartoon Network, 2005.

Guest, *Late Show with David Letterman,* CBS, 2005.

Also voice for *Camp Chaos Presents VH1 Illustrated,* VH1; narrator, *TNN's Lifegame,* The Nashville Network.

Television Work; Series:

Producer, *Viva Variety,* Comedy Central, 1996.

Creator and executive producer, *Stella,* Comedy Central, 2005.

Television Creator; Other:

The State's 43rd Annual Halloween Special, CBS, 1995.

Every Week (pilot), VH1, 2000.

(And executive producer) *Hey, Neighbor,* Fox, 2000.

Film Appearances:

(As Michael Schwartz) Party attendee, *I'm Your Man,* Interfilm Technologies, 1992.

Martin Huber (narrator), *Big Helium Dog,* Rayisdead Co./View Askew Productions, 1999.

McKinley, *Wet Hot American Summer,* USA Films, 2001.

Ed, *The Baxter,* IFC Films, 2005.

Christopher, *Partners,* 2005.

Expiration Date, Roadkill Productions, 2005.

RECORDINGS

Videos:

Male student, *Cults: Saying No under Pressure,* 1991.

Michael (also director and writer), *Stella Shorts 1998–2002,* 2002.

Albums:

Recorded a comedy album with The State, Warner Bros.

WRITINGS

Television Series:

You Wrote It, You Watch It, 1992.

The State, MTV, 1993.

Viva Variety, Comedy Central, 1996.

Random Play, VH1, 1999.

Stella, Comedy Central, 2005.

Television Scripts; Other:

The State's 43rd Annual Halloween Special, CBS, 1995.

Hey, Neighbor (pilot), Fox, 2000.

Film Scripts:

(As Michael Schwartz) *I'm Your Man,* Interfilm Technologies, 1992.

Other:

Coauthor of a book *State by State with The State.* Author of "Michael Ian Black Is a Very Famous Celebrity," a column for the online edition of *McSweeney's,*1997.

OTHER SOURCES

Electronic:

Stella Comedy Group, http://www.stellacomedy.com, August 29, 2005.

BRAFF, Zach 1975–

PERSONAL

Full name, Zachary I. Braff; born April 6, 1975, in South Orange, NJ; son of Hal (an attorney and professor) and Anne (a psychologist) Braff; brother of Joshua Braff (a novelist) and Adam J. Braff (a writer and producer). *Education:* Northwestern University, B.F.A., 1997.

Addresses: *Agent*—Josh Lieberman, Creative Artists Agency, 9830 Wilshire Blvd., Beverly Hills, CA 90212. *Manager*—Sandra Chang, Industry Entertainment, 955 South Carrillo Dr., 3rd Floor, Los Angeles, CA 90048.

Career: Actor, director, writer, and producer. Music producer, including music for the soundtrack album *Garden State,* 2004; director of music videos, including "Superman" by Lazlo Bane, 2002, and "Chariot" by Gavin DeGraw, 2005. Appeared in the public service announcement series *The More You Know,* NBC; voice for commercials for Cottonelle paper products, 2003. Formerly worked as a waiter.

Member: Phi Kappa Phi.

Awards, Honors: Teen Choice Award nominations, choice television actor in a comedy, 2002, 2003, 2004, 2005, Golden Satellite Award, International Press Academy, best actor in a comedy or musical series, Golden Globe Award nomination, best actor in a musical or comedy television series, and Emmy Award nomination, outstanding lead actor in a comedy series, 2005, all for *Scrubs;* Hollywood Discovery Award, Hollywood Film Festival, breakthrough directing, 2004; National Board of Review Award, best debut director, nomination for Grand Jury Prize, Sundance Film Festival, dramatic category, Chicago Film Critics Association Award, best new director, Phoenix Film Critics Society Award, breakout of the year behind the camera, and Pauline Kael Breakout Award, Florida Film Critics Circle, 2004, Independent Spirit Award, Independent Features Project/West, best first feature (with others), Independent Spirit Award nomination, best first screenplay, Screen Award nomination, Writers Guild of America, best original screenplay, Empire Award nomination, best newcomer, Online Film Critics Society Award, best breakthrough filmmaker, and Online Film Critics Society Award nominations, best breakthrough performance and best original screenplay, Teen Choice Award nominations, choice movie actor in a drama, choice movie blush scene, choice male movie breakout performance, and choice movie "liplock" and choice movie love scene (both with Natalie Portman), and MTV Movie Award nominations, breakthrough male and best kiss (with Portman), 2005, all for *Garden State;* Grammy Award, National Academy of Recording Arts and Sciences, best compilation soundtrack for a motion picture, television, or other visual media (with others), 2005, for *Garden State.*

CREDITS

Film Appearances:

Nick Lipton, *Manhattan Murder Mystery,* TriStar, 1993.
Wesley, *Getting to Know You* (also known as *Getting to Know All about You*), Sundance Channel, 1999.
Dean, *Endsville,* Stick Figure Productions, 2000.
Fred, *Blue Moon,* Castle Hill/Curb Entertainment, 2000.
Benji, *The Broken Hearts Club: A Romantic Comedy,* Screen Gems, 2000.
Andrew Largeman, *Garden State,* Fox Searchlight, 2004.
Himself, *The Misbehavers* (documentary), NightHawk Studios, 2004.
Voice of Chicken Little, *Chicken Little* (animated), Buena Vista, 2005.
Michael, *The Last Kiss,* DreamWorks, 2005.

Film Director:

Lionel on a Sunday (short film), Studio 22 Productions, 1997.
Garden State, Fox Searchlight, 2004.

Television Appearances; Series:

Dr. John "J. D." Dorian, *Scrubs,* NBC, beginning 2001.

Television Appearances; Specials:

Tony/Tammy, "My Summer as a Girl," *CBS Schoolbreak Special,* CBS, 1994.
Scrubs: The Outtake Show, NBC, 2003.
Himself, *I'm Still Here: Real Diaries of Young People Who Lived During the Holocaust,* MTV, 2005.

Television Appearances; Episodic:

David Cummings, "Dawn Saves the Trees," *The Baby-Sitters Club,* HBO, c. 2000.
Voice of X-Stream Mike, "Election Blu-Galoo," *Clone High,* MTV, 2002.
Voice of Paul Revere, "A.D.D.: The Last 'D' Is for Disorder," *Clone High,* MTV, 2002.
Phillip Litt, "Spring Breakout," *Arrested Development,* Fox, 2005.

Television Appearances; Movies:

Himself, *It's a Very Merry Muppet Christmas Movie,* NBC, 2002.

Television Guest Appearances; Episodic:

The Late Late Show with Craig Kilborn, CBS, 2001, 2004.
Jimmy Kimmel Live, ABC, 2004.
"Garden State," *Anatomy of a Scene,* Sundance Channel, 2004.
Live with Regis and Kelly, syndicated, 2004.
Rove Live, 10 Network (Australia), 2004.
The Panel, 10 Network, 2004.
Ellen: The Ellen DeGeneres Show, syndicated, 2004.
Punk'd, MTV, 2005.
The View, ABC, 2005.

Television Appearances; Awards Presentations:

Presenter, *The 56th Annual Primetime Emmy Awards,* ABC, 2004.
Presenter, *The 10th Annual Screen Actors Guild Awards,* TNT, 2004.
The 62nd Annual Golden Globe Awards, NBC, 2005.
The 20th IFP Independent Spirit Awards, Independent Film Channel and Bravo, 2005.

Television Appearances; Pilots:

Nobody's Watching, The WB, 2005.

Television Director; Episodic:

"My Last Chance," *Scrubs,* NBC, c. 2004.
"My Best Laid Plans," *Scrubs,* NBC, c. 2004.

Stage Appearances:

Fleance and young Siward, *Macbeth,* New York Shakespeare Festival, Martinson Hall, Public Theatre, New York City, 1998.
Sebastian, *Twelfth Night,* New York Shakespeare Festival, Delacorte Theatre, Public Theatre, New York City, 2002.

RECORDINGS

Videos:

The Making of "Garden State," Twentieth Century-Fox Home Entertainment, 2004.

WRITINGS

Screenplays:
Garden State, Fox Searchlight, 2004.

OTHER SOURCES

Books:
Newsmakers, Issue 2, Thomson Gale, 2005.

Periodicals:
Entertainment Weekly, November 23, 2001, p. 35; September 13, 2002, p. 86; August 6, 2004, p. 52.
Los Angeles Times, August 2, 2004.
New Jersey Monthly, August, 2004, p. 70.
New York Times, July 25, 2004.
People Weekly, August 30, 2004.
TV Guide, March 6, 2004, pp. 34–35.
Washington Post, August 1, 2004, pp. N1, N7.

Electronic:
Spliced Online, http://www.splicedonline.com, July 1, 2004.

Other:
Fresh Air from WHYY (radio series), National Public Radio, October 4, 2004.

BROYLES William, Jr. 1944–
      (William Broyles)

PERSONAL

Full name, William Dodson Broyles, Jr.; born October 8, 1944, in Houston, TX; son of William Dodson and Elizabeth (maiden name, Bills) Broyles; married Sybil Newman (an art director), August 15, 1973 (marriage ended); married Linda Purl (an actress; divorced); married, wife's name Andrea (an artist). *Education:* Rice University, B.A., 1966; Oxford University, M.A., 1968.

Addresses: *Agent*—Creative Artists Agency, 9830 Wilshire Blvd., Beverly Hills, CA 90212.

Career: Writer and actor. U.S. Naval Academy, Annapolis, MD, instructor in philosophy, 1970–71; assistant superintendent of school in Houston, TX, 1971–72; *Texas Monthly,* Austin, founding editor, beginning 1972; *Texas Monthly Press,* editor, beginning 1975; *Newsweek,* editor in chief, 1982–84; *California,*

past editor. *Military service:* U.S. Marine Corps, fighter pilot, 1969–71; served in Vietnam; became captain; received Bronze Star.

Member: Texas Institute of Letters.

Awards, Honors: Four National Magazine Awards for *Texas Monthly;* Golden Globe Award, best television drama series (with others), 1990, for *China Beach;* ShoWest Award, National Association of Theatre Owners, screenwriter of the year, 2001; Fennecus Award nomination, best adapted screenplay, and Apex Award nomination, best adapted dramatic screenplay, both 1995, and Academy Award nomination and Screen Award nomination, Writers Guild of America, both best adapted screenplay (with Al Reinert), 1996, all for *Apollo 13;* inducted into Texas Film Hall of Fame, 2002.

CREDITS

Television Creator and Executive Producer; Series:
(With others) *China Beach,* ABC, 1988–91.
Under Cover, ABC, 1991.
Spy Games, ABC, 1991.

Television Executive Producer; Movies:
Before the Storm, ABC, 1991.

Television Appearances; Specials:
Interviewee, *Faces of the Enemy,* PBS, 1987.

Television Appearances; Episodic:
Himself, "Cast Away," *HBO First Look,* HBO, 2000.

RECORDINGS

Video Games:
Voice of Jonas Fearwitt, *Dust: A Tale of the Wired West* (video game), 1995.
Wilson: The Life and Death of a Hollywood Extra, 2001.
Stop: Surviving as a Cast Away, 2001.
The Making of "Cast Away," 2001.

WRITINGS

Screenplays:
Apollo 13, MCA/Universal, 1995, released as *Apollo 13: The IMAX Experience,* 2002.
(As William Broyles) *Entrapment* (also known as *Verlockende falle*), Twentieth Century–Fox, 1999.

Cast Away, Twentieth Century–Fox, 2000, published as *Cast Away: The Shooting Script,* Newmarket Press, 2001.

Planet of the Apes, Twentieth Century–Fox, 2001, published by Newmarket Pictorial Moviebooks, 2001.

Unfaithful (also known as *Infidele* and *Untreu*), Twentieth Century–Fox, 2002.

The Polar Express (animated; also released as *The Polar Express: An IMAX 3D Experience*), Warner Bros., 2004.

Jarhead, Universal, 2005.

Television Series:
China Beach, ABC, 1988.

Television Miniseries:
(With Al Reinert) *J.F.K.: Reckless Youth,* NBC, 1993.

Television Pilots:
Under Cover, ABC, 1991.

Television Episodes:
Spy Games, ABC, 1991.

Other:
Brother in Arms: A Journey from War to Peace (memoir), Avon, 1987.

(Editor, with Chris Van Allsburg and Robert Zemeckis) *All Aboard the Polar Express: The Movie* (board book), Houghton Mifflin, 2004.

(With Van Allsburg, Zemeckis, Melissa Morgan, and Heidi Cho) *The Polar Express the Movie: Keepsake Memory Book,* Houghton Mifflin, 2004.

(With Van Allsburg, Zemeckis, and Tracey West) *The Magic Journey,* Houghton Mifflin, 2004.

Contributor to periodicals, including *Atlantic Monthly, Columbia Journalism Review, Esquire, Playboy,* and *U.S. News and World Report.*

OTHER SOURCES

Books:
Broyles, William Jr., *Brother in Arms: A Journey from War to Peace,* Avon, 1987.

BRULE, Robin

PERSONAL

Born in Ottawa, Ontario, Canada. *Education:* Attended Canterbury School of the Arts, George Brown College, and Actor's Network.

Career: Actress.

CREDITS

Television Appearances; Series:
Ellen Fisher, *Flash Forward,* ABC, 1996.

Sophie, *When Husbands Cheat,* Lifetime, 1998.

Christy Dyer, *Caracara* (also known as *The Last Witness*), HBO, 1999.

Angie Hart, *The City* (also known as *Deep in the City*), CTV (Canada), 1999.

Mara, *An American in Canada* (also known as *Frostbite*), CBC (Canada), 2002.

Tracey, *The Shields Stories* (also known as *Dolls, Dolls, Dolls, Dolls*), W Network, 2004.

Sophie, *Metropia,* Omni Network, 2004.

Also appeared in the series *Straight Up,* PBS.

Television Appearances; Movies:
Lucille–Ann, *Talk to Me,* ABC, 1996.

Cloe (some sources cite Dana Ballard), *Ultimate Deception* (also known as *Ultimate Betrayal*), USA Network, 1999.

Angie Hart, *The City,* CTV (Canada), 1999.

Debbie Morin, *The Wandering Soul Murders* (also known as *Criminal Instinct: The Wandering Soul Murders* and *Sur les traces de Littleflower*), Lifetime, 2001.

Michelle Barker, *A Mother's Fight for Justice* (also known as *Crash Course*), Lifetime, 2001.

Ginny, *Sanctuary* (also known as *Nora Roberts' "Sanctuary"*), CBS, 2001.

Natalie Behrens, *Killer Instinct: From the Files of Agent Candice DeLong,* Lifetime, 2003.

Stephanie Comfort, *Cool Money,* USA Network, 2005.

Television Appearances; Episodic:
Leah, "Dining Club," *Ready or Not,* Showtime, 1996.

Andrea Best, "Second Sight/Chocolate Soldier," *PSI Factor: Chronicles of the Paranormal,* syndicated, 1997.

Rachel Lindsey, "A Friend in Need," *Traders,* Global (Canada), 1998.

Rachel Lindsey, "Six Degrees of Duplicity," *Traders,* Global, 1998.

Rachel Lindsey, "Reap the Whirlwind," *Traders,* Global, 1998.

Rachel Lindsey, "The Last Good Deal," *Traders,* Global, 1999.

Sister Louise, "Prostitutes for Jesus," *Puppets Who Kill,* Comedy Central, 2004.

Stephanie, "Steph's Life," *Bliss,* Showtime, 2004.

This Is Wonderland, 2005.

Appeared as Tanya Zane in an episode of *Kevin Hill,* UPN; and as Leah, "Warts and All," *Ready or Not,* Showtime.

Television Appearances; Pilots:
Muriel, *Nothing Too Good for a Cowboy,* CBC (Canada), 1998.

Film Appearances:
Second intern, *Three to Tango,* Warner Bros., 1999.
Louise, *Gossip,* Warner Bros., 2000.
Jenn, *Girls Who Say Yes* (short film), 2000.
Tracey, *The Harp* (short film), 2005.

Stage Appearances:
Appeared in productions of *The Dining Room, The Gingerbread Lady, A Midsummer Night's Dream,* and *Under Milkwood.*

BULLOCK, Donna 1955–

PERSONAL

Born December 11, 1955, in Dallas, TX; daughter of Jack (a real estate agent) and Shirley Ann (a secretary; maiden name, Black) Bullock; married Sherman Howard (an actor). *Education:* Attended Southern Methodist University, 1979. *Religion:* Episcopal.

Addresses: *Agent*—Leverton/Sames Associates, 1650 Broadway, New York, NY 10019; House of Representatives, 400 S. Beverly Dr., Suite 101, Beverly Hills, CA 90212.

Career: Actress. Contestant in pageants, such as Miss Teen America.

Member: Actors' Equity Association, American Federation of Television and Radio Artists, New York Arts Group.

Awards, Honors: Obie Award (with others), 1983, for *Top Girls.*

CREDITS

Stage Appearances:
Heaven Can Wait, Kenley Players, Warren, OH, 1977.
Katie Yoder, *Plain and Fancy,* Equity Library Theatre, New York City, 1980.
Member of the ensemble, *Noel,* Goodspeed Opera House, East Haddam, CT, 1980.
Jenny, *Portrait of Jenny,* Henry Street Settlement Theatre, New York City, 1982.
Liz, *Billy Liar,* Westside Mainstage, New York City, 1982.
Raven, *The Evangelist,* Wonderhorse Theatre, 1982.
Fiona Kelly, *Shot thru the Heart,* Birmingham Theatre, Birmingham, MI, 1983.
Jeanine, Win, and a waitress, *Top Girls,* New York Shakespeare Festival, Public Theatre, New York City, 1983.
Nancy, *Stem of a Briar,* Kenyon Festival, Gambier, OH, 1983.
The Dining Room, Plaza Theatre, Dallas, TX, 1983–84.
Catherine Simms, *The Foreigner,* Astor Palace Theatre, New York City, 1984–85.
Holly Burrell, *Foxfire,* Ahmanson Theatre, Los Angeles, 1985–86.
Bobbi/Gabby, *City of Angels,* Virginia Theatre, New York City, 1990–92.
Jenny Brinker, *Allegro,* City Center Theatre, New York City, 1994.
Mother, *Ragtime,* Ford Center for the Performing Arts, 1997–98.
Lucy, *A Class Act,* Ambassador Theatre, New York City, 2000–2001, then Pasadena Playhouse, Pasadena, CA, 2002.
Beatrice, *Much Ado about Nothing,* F. M. Kirby Shakespeare Theatre, Madison, NJ, 2003.

Also appeared in *Sweet Bird of Youth.*

Major Tours:
Jenny, *The Umbrellas of Cherbourg,* West coast cities, 1980.
A Christmas Carol, U.S. cities, including Baltimore, MD, and New Orleans, LA, 1981–82.
Sally Smith, *Me and My Girl,* U.S. cities, 1988–89.

Television Appearances; Series:
Maggie Clemons, *Against the Grain,* NBC, 1993–94.

Also appeared as Kim McGuire, *All My Children,* ABC.

Television Appearances; Movies:
Amy, *Breaking Through* (also known as *After the Silence*), ABC, 1996.
Val Williams, *The Accident: A Moment of Truth Movie* (also known as *The Accident* and *An Innocent Heart*), NBC, 1997.
Tracy Rose, *Columbo: A Trace of Murder,* ABC, 1997.
Julia Sinclair, *A Vow to Cherish,* CBS, 1999.

Television Appearances; Pilots:
Patsy, *Hearts Island,* 1985.
Marcy Roberts, *Real Life,* CBS, 1988.
Bonnie, *Guys Like Us,* ABC, 1996.

Television Appearances; Episodic:
Connie, "Digger's Daughter," *Dallas,* CBS, 1978.
Connie, "The Lesson," *Dallas,* CBS, 1978.
Connie, "Spy in the House," *Dallas,* CBS, 1978.
Linda, "Parlour Floor Front," *Tales from the Darkside,* syndicated, 1985.
Sandy Keegan, "Everything You've Always Wanted to Know about Teenagers (But Were Afraid to Ask)," *TV 101,* 1988.
Sandy Keegan, "Home," *TV 101,* 1988.
Sandy Keegan, "On the Road," *TV 101,* 1989.
Sandy Keegan, "First Love: Part 2," *TV 101,* 1989.
Laura Downing, "Sugar and Spice, Malice and Vice," *Murder, She Wrote,* CBS, 1992.
Josie, "Chemical Reactions," *Sisters,* NBC, 1993.
Sydney (some sources say Anita), "Tough Love," *Touched by an Angel,* CBS, 1994.
Beth Crane, "Father," *Nowhere Man,* UPN, 1995.
Karen Anderson, "Winning," *The Client* (also known as *John Grisham's "The Client"*), CBS, 1995.
Nancy Pierson, "Deadly Dose," *Matlock,* ABC, 1995.
District attorney Barbara Lewis, "Peter's Excellent Adventure," *Melrose Place,* Fox, 1996.
Adair Peck, "Three Dates and a Breakup: Parts 1 & 2" *Frasier,* NBC, 1997.
"The Hurricaine," *The Cape,* 1997.
Mrs. Beth Scarborough, "Confession," *Diagnosis Murder,* CBS, 2001.
Pamela Jenkins, "Crush," *Smallville,* The WB, 2002.
Stacey, "Forever Young," *Touched by an Angel,* CBS, 2002.
Lillian Dorning, "Need to Know," *JAG,* CBS, 2002.
Karen Pepper, "Making Love Work," *Six Feet Under,* HBO, 2003.
Barbara Woodard, "The Other Side of Caution," *The Lyon's Den,* NBC, 2003.
Mrs. Cummings, "Love Kills," *She Spies,* syndicated, 2003.
Penny Hannaway, "Swimming," *The Guardian,* CBS, 2003.
Therapist, "A Couple of Choices," *Medium,* NBC and CTV, 2005.

Also appeared as Alyssa Meadows, *Sweet Justice;* Karen Rogoff, *Family Law,* CBS; in *The Division,* Lifetime.

Film Appearances:
Psychiatrist, *Chameleon,* WarnerVision, 1995.
Deputy press secretary Melanie Mitchell, *Air Force One* (also known as *AFO*), Columbia, 1997.
Amy Mann, *Debating Robert Lee,* 2004.
Mrs. Kidman, *The Girl Next Door,* Twentieth Century–Fox, 2004.

RECORDINGS

Video Games:
Voice of Aunt Josephine, *Lemony Snicket's "A Series of Unfortunate Events,"* Activision, 2004.

BUONO, Cara 1974–

PERSONAL

Born March 1, 1974, in New York, NY. *Education:* Columbia University, B.A., English and political science, c. 1992.

Addresses: *Agent*—Gersh Agency, 130 W. 42nd St., New York, NY 10036; United Talent Agency, 9560 Wilshire Blvd., Suite 500, Beverly Hills, CA 90212. *Contact*—Cunningham Escott Dipene, 10635 Santa Monica Blvd., Suite 130, Los Angeles, CA 90025. *Manager*—Handprint Entertainment, 1100 Glendon Ave., Ste. 1000, Los Angeles, CA.

Career: Actress, screenwriter, and director.

CREDITS

Film Appearances:
Dawn, *Gladiator,* Columbia, 1992.
Judy Dobson, *Waterland,* Fine Line, 1992.
A Dog Race in Alaska, 1993.
Teresa Salazar, Nacho's daughter, *The Cowboy Way,* Universal, 1994.
Kate, *Kicking and Screaming,* Warner Bros., 1995.
Esther Lesser, *Killer: A Journal of Murder* (also known as *The Killer*), First Independent Films, 1996.
Toni–Ann Antonelli, *Made Men,* 1996.
Rachel, *River Red,* Castle Hill, 1997.
Virginia Clemens, *Man of the Century,* Fine Line, 1998.
Julie, *Next Stop, Wonderland,* Miramax, 1998.
(Uncredited) Molly, *Lulu on the Bridge,* 1998.
Claire Suarez, *Attention Shoppers,* Paramount, 1999.
Janis, *Chutney Popcorn,* Pryor Cashman Sherman & Flynn, 1999.
Nina Cohen, *Two Ninas,* Castle Hill, 1999.
Bette, *Happy Accidents,* IFC Films, 1999.
Christina Painter, *Takedown* (also known as *Track Down*), Dimension Films, 2000.
Edith Banner, *Hulk,* United International, 2003.
Joanne Schwartzbaum, *From Other Worlds,* Belladonna, 2004.

Film Director:
Baggage (short film), 1997.

Television Appearances; Movies:
(Uncredited) *In the Line of Duty: Ambush in Waco,* NBC, 1993.
Tracy Lien, *Victim of Love: The Shannon Mohr Story* (also known as *Crimes of Passion: Victim of Love*), NBC, 1993.

Young Gerry Cummins, *Deep in My Heart,* CBS, 1999.
Sherry Donato, *In a Class of His Own,* Showtime, 1999.

Television Appearances; Series:
Grace Foster, *Third Watch,* NBC, 2004–2005.

Television Appearances; Episodic:
Diane Lowe, "Cool Winter Blues," *I'll Fly Away,* 1992.
Diane Lowe, "The Way Things Are," *I'll Fly Away,* 1992.
Diane Lowe, "Slow Coming Dark," *I'll Fly Away,* 1992.
Rose Polito, "The Hopeless Romantic," *Tribeca,* 1992.
Shelly Taggert, "Girlfriends," *Law & Order,* NBC, 1995.
Connie, "A Time to Kill," *New York Undercover,* 1995.
Alice Simonelli, "Punk," *Law & Order,* NBC, 1998.
Carly Hanson, "Intentions," *Family Law,* CBS, 2001.
Charlotte Fielding, "Phantom," *Law & Order: Criminal Intent,* NBC, 2002.
Eric's girlfriend, "Chasing the Bus," *CSI: Crime Scene Investigation* (also known as *C.S.I.*), CBS, 2002.
Bettina Martinelli, "That Voodoo That You Do," *Queens Supreme,* CBS, 2002.
Michelle, "The Love Bandit," *Miss Match,* NBC, 2003.

Also appeared as Samantha, *Sesame Street,* PBS; Christie, *The Single Guy,* NBC.

Television Appearances; Pilots:
Linda, *Lowell Ganz/Babaloo Mandel Project,* ABC, 2000.

Television Appearances; Specials:
Abby Morris, *Abby, My Love,* (also known as *Schoolbreak Special: Abby, My Love*), CBS, 1991.

Stage Appearances:
Understudy for the role of Evelyn Foreman, *The Tenth Man,* Vivian Beaumont Theatre, New York City, 1989–90.
Katie Taylor, *Some Americans Abroad,* Vivian Beaumont Theatre, New York City, 1990.
Rosa Delle Rose, *The Rose Tattoo,* Circle in the Square Theatre, New York City, 1995.
Mary Scaccia, *Good Thing,* Theater at St. Clement's Church, New York City, 2001–2002.

RECORDINGS

Video Games:
Voice of Sarah, *Mafia,* Take 2 Interactive, 2002.

WRITINGS

Screenplays:
Baggage (short film), 1997.
(With Brad Anderson) *When the Cat's Away,* 2001.

BURDITT, Jack

PERSONAL

Married Amy; children: Becky, Katie, another daughter, one son.

Addresses: *Agent*—Endeavor, 9601 Wilshire Blvd., 3rd Floor, Beverly Hills, CA 90210.

Career: Writer and producer. *The Signal* (newspaper), Santa Clarita Valley, CA, columnist, c. 1992–2000; NBC Studios, development deal, 2000—.

Awards, Honors: Writers Guild of America Award nomination (TV), episodic comedy, 1996, for *Mad about You;* Emmy Awards (with others), outstanding individual achievement in writing for a comedy series and outstanding comedy series, 1996, both for *Frasier.*

CREDITS

Television Work; Series:
Coproducer and story editor, *Frasier,* NBC, 1993.
Supervising producer, *Ink,* CBS, 1996.
Co–executive producer, *Just Shoot Me,* NBC, 1997.
Consulting producer, *The Mike O'Malley Show,* NBC, 1999.
Executive producer and creator, *DAG,* NBC, 2000.
Consulting producer, *Inside Schwartz,* NBC, 2001.
Producer and consulting producer, *Watching Ellie,* NBC, 2002.
Executive producer, *I'm with Her,* ABC, 2003.
Consultant, *Luis,* Fox, 2003.

Also worked as executive producer and creator, *Deal.*

Television Work; Pilots:
Executive producer, *Just Married,* NBC, 2000.
Executive producer, *Deal,* NBC, 2005.
Executive producer, *Full Nest,* ABC, 2005.

WRITINGS

Television Episodes:
"The Unplanned Child," *Mad about You,* NBC, 1993.
(With Jeffrey Lane) "Disorientation," *Mad about You,* NBC, 1994.
"Home," *Mad about You,* NBC, 1994.
"Our Fifteen Minutes," *Mad about You,* NBC, 1995.
(With Lane) "Up in Smoke: Part 2," *Mad about You,* NBC, 1995.

"The Friend," *Frasier,* NBC, 1996.

(With others), "Moon Dance," *Frasier,* NBC, 1996.

"High Crane Drifter," *Frasier,* NBC, 1996.

"Getting over the Hemp," *Ink,* CBS, 1996.

"United We Fall," *Ink,* CBS, 1996.

"Life without Mikey," *Ink,* CBS, 1997.

(With Stephen Nathan) "Going to the Dogs," *Ink,* CBS, 1997.

"La cage," *Just Shoot Me,* NBC, 1997.

"Pass the Salt," *Just Shoot Me,* NBC, 1998.

(With Pam Brady) "Eve of Destruction," *Just Shoot Me,* NBC, 1998.

"Nina Sees Red: Parts 1 & 2," *Just Shoot Me,* NBC, 1999.

"Softball," *Just Shoot Me,* NBC, 1999.

(With Mike Reynolds) "Hello Goodbye," *Just Shoot Me,* NBC, 1999.

(With Andy Gordon and Eileen Conn) *DAG,* NBC, 2000–2001.

"Roommates," *Inside Schwartz,* NBC, 2001.

"Aftershocks," *Watching Ellie,* NBC, 2002.

I'm With Her, ABC, 2003–2004.

Television Stories; Episodic:

"Deconstructive Criticism," *Mad about You,* NBC, 1993.

Television Pilots:

(With Andy Gordon and Eileen Conn) *DAG,* NBC, 2000.

Just Married, NBC, 2000.

Deal, NBC, 2005.

Full Nest, ABC, 2005.

BURTON, Hilarie 1982–

PERSONAL

Born July 1, 1982, in Loudoun County, VA. *Education:* Attended New York University and Fordham University.

Addresses: *Agent*—Endeavor, 9601 Wilshire Blvd., 3rd Floor, Beverly Hills, CA 90210.

Career: Actress.

Awards, Honors: Teen Choice Award nominations, choice breakout television actress in a drama or action adventure and choice female breakout television star, both 2004, for *One Tree Hill.*

CREDITS

Television Appearances; Series:

Herself, *Total Request Live* (also known as *Total Request with Carson Daly* and *TRL*), MTV, 2000—.

Host, *Beat Seekers* (also known as *MTV Hits*), MTV, 2002.

Peyton Sawyer, *One Tree Hill,* The WB, 2003.

Television Appearances; Specials:

Cohost, *MTV Does Miami,* MTV, 2003.

Host, *The Real World Las Vegas Reunion* (also known as *7 the Hard Way: The Real World Las Vegas Reunion*), MTV, 2003.

Host, *Sorority Life Reunion,* 2003.

MTV's New Year's Eve 2004, MTV, 2003.

Host, *Spring Break Celebrity Fantasies,* MTV, 2004.

Television Appearances; Episodic:

Female "VJ", "100 Light Years from Home," *Dawson's Creek,* The WB, 2002.

Host, *Pepsi Smash,* The WB, 2003.

Guest cohost, *The View,* ABC, 2003.

Guest, *Late Show with David Letterman,* 2003.

Unscripted, HBO, 2005.

Television Appearances; Miniseries:

Interviewee, *The 100 Scariest Movie Moments,* Bravo, 2004.

Radio Appearances:

Host of the syndicated radio series *W.O.B.U.*

BURTON, Kate 1957–

PERSONAL

Full name, Katherine Burton; born September 10, 1957, in Geneva, Switzerland; daughter of Richard (an actor) and Sybil (a producer; maiden name, Williams) Burton; married Michael Ritchie (a stage director), 1984; children: Morgan, Charlotte. *Education:* Brown University, B.A., 1979; Yale University, M.F.A., 1982. *Politics:* Democrat.

Addresses: *Agent*—The Gersh Agency, 232 North Canon Dr., Beverly Hills, CA 90210.

Career: Actress. Tony Administration Committee, member.

Awards, Honors: *Theatre World* Award, 1983, for *Present Laughter, Alice in Wonderland,* and *Winners;* Daytime Emmy Award, outstanding performer in a children's special, 1996, for *Notes for My Daughter;* Joe. A. Callaway Award, Actors' Equity Foundation, 2001, Antoinette Perry Award nomination, best actress in a play, 2002, Outer Critics Circle Award nomination, all for *Hedda Gabler;* Antoinette Perry Award nomination, best featured actress in a play, 2002, for *The Elephant Man.*

CREDITS

Film Appearances:

(Uncredited) Serving maid, *Anne of the Thousand Days* (also known as *Anne of a Thousand Days*), Universal, 1969.

Joan "J. J." Caucus, Jr., *Doonesbury: A Broadway Musical* (also known as *Doonesbury: A Musical Comedy* and *Doonesbury: A New Musical*), 1983.

Margo Litzenberger, *Big Trouble in Little China* (also known as *John Carpenter's "Big Trouble in Little China"*), Twentieth Century–Fox, 1986.

Mrs. Burns, *Life with Mikey* (also known as *Give Me a Break*), Buena Vista, 1993.

Helen Blathwaite, *August,* Samuel Goldwyn Company, 1996.

Woman in bed, *The First Wives Club,* Paramount, 1996.

Looking for Richard (documentary), Twentieth Century–Fox, 1996.

Dorothy Franklin, *The Ice Storm,* Fox Searchlight Pictures, 1997.

Cheryl, *Celebrity,* Miramax, 1998.

Rest home sister, *The Opportunists,* First Look Pictures Releasing, 2000.

Tracy, *Unfaithful* (also known as *Infidele* and *Untreu*), Twentieth Century–Fox, 2002.

Carla Cronin, *Swimfan* (also known as *Swimf@n* and *Tell Me You Love Me*), Twentieth Century–Fox, 2002.

Martha, *The Paper Mache Chase* (short), 2003.

Sherry Baby, 2004.

Stay, Twentieth Century–Fox, 2005.

Marcia, *Some Kind of Heaven,* 2005.

Voice of Night, *The Story of a Mother,* 2006.

Television Appearances; Series:

Anne Kramer, *Home Fires,* NBC, 1992.

Fran Richardson, *Monty,* Fox, 1994.

Assistant district attorney Susan Alexander, *The Practice,* ABC, 1997, 2000, 2001, 2004.

Television Appearances; Miniseries:

Vanessa Ogden, *Ellis Island,* CBS, 1984.

Agatha Bradford, *Evergreen,* NBC, 1985.

Host, *The Hanging Gale,* Bravo, 1999.

Cindy Whiting, *Empire Falls,* HBO, 2005.

Television Appearances; Movies:

Ophelia, *Uncle Tom's Cabin,* Showtime, 1987.

Deborah, *Love Matters,* Showtime, 1993.

Katherine Donohue, *Mistrial,* HBO, 1996.

Sara Miller, *Obsessed,* Lifetime, 2002.

Connie Posey, *The Diary of Ellen Rimbauer,* ABC, 2003.

Television Appearances; Specials:

Alice, "Alice in Wonderland," *Great Performances,* PBS, 1983.

Agnes O'Neill, "Journey into Genius" (also known as "Eugene O'Neill: Journey into Genius"), *American Playhouse,* PBS, 1988.

"Richard Burton: In from the Cold," *Great Performances,* PBS, 1989.

Brenda Gardner, "Notes for My Daughter," *ABC Afterschool Specials,* ABC, 1995.

Voice, "Buckminster Fuller: Thinking Out Loud," *American Masters,* PBS, 1996.

Abigail, "Ellen Foster," *Hallmark Hall of Fame,* CBS, 1997.

Voice, *Blood Money: Switzerland's Nazi Gold* (documentary), Arts and Entertainment, 1997.

Richard Burton: Taylor–Made for Stardom (documentary), Arts and Entertainment, 2002.

Intimate Portrait: Jane Kaczmarek (documentary), Lifetime, 2002.

Narrator, *The Incredible Human Body* (documentary), PBS, 2002.

Herself, *Intimate Portrait: Elizabeth Taylor* (documentary), Lifetime, 2002.

Presenter, *The 59th Annual Tony Awards,* CBS, 2005.

Television Appearances; Pilots:

Assistant district attorney Susan Alexander, *The Practice,* ABC, 1997.

Television Appearances; Episodic:

Randy Lofficier, "If You Knew Sammy," *Spenser: For Hire,* ABC, 1987.

Randy Lofficier, "Play It Again, Sammy," *Spenser: For Hire,* ABC, 1988.

Sister Bettina, "Sisters of Mercy," *Law and Order,* NBC, 1991.

Susan Lowenberg Jones, "Keeping Up with the Joneses," *Brooklyn Bridge,* CBS, 1993.

Sheila Byrne, "My Brother's Keeper," *100 Centre Street,* Arts and Entertainment, 2001.

Attorney Erica Gardner, "Armed Forces," *Law & Order,* NBC, 2001.

Stephanie Uffland, "The Pardoner's Tale," *Law & Order: Criminal Intent,* NBC, 2001.

Attorney Erica Gardner, "Darwinian," *Law & Order,* NBC, 2004.

Sarah Brainerd, "Slow News Day," *The West Wing,* NBC, 2004.

Erica Gardner, "Cut," *Law & Order,* NBC, 2004.

Dr. Sheri Jordan, "Silent Era," *Judging Amy,* CBS, 2005.

Dr. Ellis Grey, "A Hard Day's Night," *Grey's Anatomy,* ABC, 2005.

Dr. Ellis Grey, "No Man's Land," *Grey's Anatomy,* ABC, 2005.

Dr. Ellis Grey, "Shake Your Groove Thing," *Grey's Anatomy,* ABC, 2005.

Stage Appearances:

(New York debut) Daphne, *Present Laughter,* Circle in the Square, New York City, 1982.

Alice, *Alice in Wonderland,* Virginia Theatre, New York City, 1983.

May, *Winners,* Roundabout Theatre, New York City, 1983.

J. J., *Doonesbury,* Biltmore Theatre, New York City, 1983.

Eva, *The Accrington Pals,* Hudson Guild Theatre, New York City, 1984.

Pegeen, *The Playboy of the Western World,* Roundabout Theatre, 1985.

The Plough and the Stars, Roundabout Theatre, 1985.

Alexandra, *On the Verge; or, The Geography of Yearning,* Hartford Stage Company, Hartford, CT, 1985–86.

The Three Sisters, Hartman Theatre, Stamford, CT, 1985–86.

Sasha, *Wild Honey,* Virginia Theatre, 1986–87.

Isabella, *Measure for Measure,* Mitzi E. Newhouse Theatre, New York City, 1989.

Betty McNeil, *Some Americans Abroad,* Vivian Beaumont Theatre, New York City, 1990.

Alice, *Aristocrats,* Huntington Theatre Company, Boston, MA, 1990–91.

Julie, *Jake's Woman,* Neil Simon Theatre, New York City, 1992, then Center Theatre Group, James A. Doolittle Theatre, Los Angeles, CA, 1992–93.

Lauren, Grace, and Annie, *London Suite,* Union Square Theatre, New York City, 1995.

Sarah, *Company,* Criterion Theatre, Center Stage Right, New York City, 1995.

Arcadia, Los Angeles, CA, 1997.

Lyssa Dent Hughes, *An American Daughter,* Cort Theatre, New York City, 1997.

Mrs. Molly Burton, *The Matchmaker,* Adams Memorial Theater Main Stage, Williamstown, MA, 1998.

Agnes, *Lake Hollywood,* Signature Theatre Company, New York City, 1999.

Daisy Connolly, *Give Me Your Answer, Do!,* Gramercy Theatre, New York City, 1999–2000.

The Beauty Queen of Lenane, Walter Kerr Theatre, New York City, 1999, then Waterford, Ireland, 2000.

Title role, *Hedda Gabler,* Huntington Theatre Company, Boston, MA, 2000–2001, then Ambassador Theatre, New York City, 2001–2002.

Pinhead/Mrs. Kendal, *The Elephant Man,* Royale Theatre, New York City, 2002.

Anna, *Boston Marriage,* Joseph Papp Public Theatre, New York City, 2002.

Three Sisters, Playhouse Theatre, London, 2003.

The Water's Edge, Nikos Stage, Williamstown Theatre Festival, Williamstown, MA, 2004.

Constance Middleton, *The Constant Wife,* American Airlines Theatre, New York City, 2005.

The Rage of Achilles, 92nd Street Y, New York City, 2005.

Also appeared in *Romeo and Juliet,* Off–Broadway production.

RECORDINGS

Taped Readings:

Loves Music, Loves to Dance, 1991.

Patricia Cornwell's "All That Remains," HarperCollins, 1992.

Anne Lamott's "Crooked Little Heart," Random Audio, 1997.

Barbara Taylor Bradford's "The Triumph of Katie Byrne," BDD Audio, 2002.

Georgia Byng's Molly Moon's "Incredible Book of Hypnotism," Harper Children's Audio, 2003.

Patricia Cornwell's "Portrait of a Killer: Jack the Ripper," Putnam Berkley Audio, 2003.

OTHER SOURCES

Periodicals:

People Weekly, October 15, 2001, p. 139.

Playbill, October 31, 2001, pp. 22, 24.

C

CAPLAN, Twink

PERSONAL

Born in Pittsburgh, PA. *Education:* Studied ballet.

Addresses: *Manager*—Richard Murphy, Melanie Greene Management and Productions, 425 North Robertson Dr., Los Angeles, CA 90048.

Career: Actress and producer. Columbia Pictures, worked as development executive; Heckling/Caplan (production company), partner with Amy Heckerling. Worked as radio talk show host in Pennsylvania; appeared in commercials. Formerly danced with Nicholas Petrov Ballet Groups; once employed by Bob Dylan's Rolling Thunder Revue; also worked for *Women's Wear Daily,* New York City.

CREDITS

Film Appearances:

Miriam, *Shame, Shame on the Bixby Boys,* Sebastian International Pictures, 1978.

Melinda, *Falling in Love Again* (also known as *In Love*), International Picture Show, 1980.

Marsha, *Underground Aces,* Filmways, 1981.

Cigarette girl, *Under the Rainbow,* Warner Bros., 1981.

Bank customer, *Pennies from Heaven,* Metro–Goldwyn–Mayer, 1981.

Talking Walls (also known as *Motel Vacancy*), New World, 1987.

Nosy neighbor, *The New Homeowner's Guide to Happiness,* 1988.

Jenny, *The Boy from Hell* (also known as *Bloodspell*), Forum Home Video, 1988.

Rona, *Look Who's Talking* (also known as *Daddy's Home*), Columbia TriStar, 1989.

Diedre, *Pucker Up and Bark like a Dog,* Fries Entertainment, 1990.

Jenny, *Night Angel* (also known as *Hellborn*), Fries Entertainment, 1990.

Rona, *Look Who's Talking Too,* TriStar, 1990.

Marianne, *Little Sister* (also known as *Mister Sister*), 1992.

Crying woman, *The Pickle,* Columbia, 1993.

Miss Geist, *Clueless* (also known as *I Was a Teenage Teenager* and *No Worries*), Paramount, 1995.

Crying flower customer, *A Night at the Roxbury,* Paramount, 1998.

Chelsea Myers, *Billboard Dad,* Warner Home Video, 1998.

Gena, *Loser* (also known as *The Loser*), Columbia, 2000.

Suzanne, *Crazy as Hell,* DEJ Productions, 2002.

Mrs. Goldberg, *Winter Break* (also known as *Snow Job*), Universal Studios Home Video, 2003.

Peaches Gilroy, *The Hand Job,* Ballistic Media Group, 2005.

Film Work:

Associate producer, *Clueless* (also known as *I Was a Teenage Teenager* and *No Worries*), Paramount, 1995.

Producer, *Loser* (also known as *The Loser*), Columbia, 2000.

Television Appearances; Series:

Miss Geist, *Clueless,* ABC, 1996–97.

Performed as go–go dancer for *The Clark Race Show.*

Television Appearances; Movies:

First hooker, *Murder Can Hurt You,* ABC, 1980.

Zoe, *Perfect People,* ABC, 1988.

Television Appearances; Episodic:

Pregnant girl, "When It's Hot, It's Hot," *Private Benjamin*, CBS, 1982.

"Hour Three," *Bare Essence*, NBC, 1983.

Linda Barry, "Barry vs. Barry," *Divorce Court*, syndicated, 1986.

Cinnamon, "Of Human Bondage," *Valerie*, NBC, 1986.

Joann, "Walk on the Mild Side," *Who's the Boss?*, ABC, 1987.

"TV George," *Mr. Belvedere*, ABC, 1987.

Joujou, "Goldilocks and the Three Barristers," *L.A. Law*, NBC, 1987.

USO singer, "Rockets Red Glare," *Still the Beaver*, WTBS, 1988.

Hannah, "Thou Shalt Not ... —February 2, 1974," *Quantum Leap*, NBC, 1989.

Ellen Bloom, "Uptown Anne Marie," *My Talk Show*, syndicated, 1990.

Woman interviewer, "Chris the Escort," *Get a Life*, Fox, 1991.

The judge, "Two Men and a Baby Pig," *Cousin Skeeter*, Nickelodeon, 1999.

Madeline Chessly, "Friends," *Vengeance Unlimited*, ABC, 1999.

Carol Flankenship, "Miss Pretty," *Just Shoot Me!*, NBC, 1999.

Mother, "Death Benefits," *George Burns Comedy Week*, CBS, 2000.

"Lydia and the Professor," *That's Life*, CBS, 2000.

Bridget, "The Ring Cycle," *Frasier*, NBC, 2002.

Appeared as "Slipperee" woman in an episode of *Sister, Sister*.

Television Appearances; Pilots:

Woman, *London and Davis in New York*, CBS, 1984.

Home economics teacher, *Fast Times*, CBS, 1986.

Television Appearances; Specials:

Interviewee, *Clueless: The E! True Hollywood Story*, E! Entertainment Television, 2001.

Television Work; Series:

Co-executive producer, *Clueless*, ABC, beginning 1996.

Television Work; Pilots:

Co-executive producer of *Nineteen* and *Forever Young*.

Stage Appearances:

Coming to Terms, Nightflight Theatre, 1982.

CARNER, Charles Robert 1957–
(Charles Carner, Charlie Carner)

PERSONAL

Born April 30, 1957, in Chicago, IL; son of Charles Robert, Sr. and Barbara (maiden name, Shields; later surname Traeger) Carner; married Debra Sharkey (an actress and writer); children: Michael, Grace Noelle. *Education:* Columbia College, Chicago, IL, B.A., 1978. *Religion:* Roman Catholic.

Addresses: *Office*—South Side Films, 26039 Mulholland Highway, Calabasas, CA 91302. *Agent*—Creative Artists Agency, 9830 Wilshire Blvd., Beverly Hills, CA 90212.

Career: Writer, director, and producer. Tony Bill Productions, Venice, CA, story editor, 1979–81; Fred Weintraub Productions, Beverly Hills, CA, screenwriter, 1981–82; Catalina Production Group, Sherman Oaks, CA, screenwriter, 1983–84; Trian Productions, Los Angeles, screenwriter, 1984–85; TriStar Productions, Los Angeles, screenwriter and director, 1985–89; South Side Films, Calabasas, CA, writer; V.P. Merchandising, Anderson, AL, cofounder, 1996. Holy Cross Family Ministries, member of board of directors; past member of executive committee, U.S. Catholic Conference, Catholics in Media, and City of Angels Film Festival.

Member: Writers Guild of America, National Rifle Association (life member), Sierra Club (life member).

Awards, Honors: Best student film award, Chicago International Film Festival, 1978, for *Assassins*; Bronze Wrangler Award, Western Heritage Awards, outstanding television feature film (with others), 2002, for *Crossfire Trail*.

CREDITS

Television Director; Movies:

(As Charlie Carner) *A Killer Among Friends* (also known as *Friends to the End*), CBS, 1992.

One Woman's Courage, NBC, 1994.

Vanishing Point, Fox, 1997.

(And producer) *The Fixer*, Showtime, 1998.

Who Killed Atlanta's Children? (also known as *Echo of Murder*), Showtime, 2000.

(And executive producer) *Christmas Rush* (also known as *Breakaway*), TBS, 2002.

(And executive producer) *Red Water,* TBS, 2003.
Judas, ABC, 2004.

Television Director; Episodic:

"The Silent Treatment," *Reasonable Doubts,* NBC, 1991.
"Framed," *The Untouchables,* syndicated, 1993.

Television Appearances; Movies:

(As Charles Carner) First reporter, *The Fixer,* Showtime, 1998.

Film Work:

Associate producer, *Blind Fury,* TriStar, 1989.

Director of the student film *Assassins.*

WRITINGS

Screenplays:

Gymkata, Metro–Goldwyn–Mayer, 1985.
Let's Get Harry (also known as *The Rescue*), TriStar, 1986.
Blind Fury (also based on story by Carner), TriStar, 1989.

Television Movies:

Seduced, CBS, 1985.
Eyes of a Witness, CBS, 1991.
(As Charlie Carner; with others) *A Killer Among Friends* (also known as *Friends to the End*), CBS, 1992.
Vanishing Point, Fox, 1997.
The Fixer, Showtime, 1998.
Who Killed Atlanta's Children? (also known as *Echo of Murder*), Showtime, 2000.
Crossfire Trail (also known as *Louis L'Amour's "Crossfire Trail"*), TNT, 2001.
Christmas Rush (also known as *Breakaway*), TBS, 2002.

Television Episodes:

"The Leopard," *Midnight Caller,* NBC, 1991.
"Framed," *The Untouchables,* syndicated, 1993.

Also author of "The Hostage Game," an episode of *Midnight Caller,* NBC.

CASADOS, Eloy
(Eloy P. Casados, Eloy Phil Casados, Phil Casados)

PERSONAL

Born in Long Beach, CA.

Career: Actor.

CREDITS

Film Appearances:

(As Eloy Phil Casados) Charlie, boy in jail cell, *Pieces of Dreams,* United Artists, 1970.
(As Phil Casados) *Mustang,* 1973.
Hugo, *Walk Proud,* Universal, 1979.
Prairie Fox, *Sacred Ground,* Pacific International, 1983.
(As Eloy Phil Casados) Pedro, *Under Fire,* Orion, 1983.
Alvarez, *Cloak & Dagger,* Universal, 1984.
Tom–Tom (Daniel Whitefeather) *Down and Out in Beverly Hills,* Buena Vista, 1986.
Squanto, *New World,* 1986.
Carlos, *The Best of Times,* Universal, 1986.
Chavez, *Hollywood Vice Squad* (also known as *The Boulevard*), Concorde, 1986.
First thug, *Born in East L.A.,* Universal, 1987.
Antoine, *Blaze,* Warner Bros., 1989.
Ruiz Sanchez, *A Climate for Killing* (also known as *A Row of Crows*), CIC Video, 1991.
Jose, *Harley Davidson and the Marlboro Man,* United International, 1991.
Tony Orlando, *The Linguini Incident,* Academy Entertainment, 1991.
Tony Stucci, *White Men Can't Jump,* Twentieth Century–Fox, 1992.
Hank Tucker, *Skeeter,* New Line Cinema, 1993.
Louis Prima, *Cobb,* Warner Bros., 1994.
First sheriff, *Nature of the Beast* (also known as *Bad Company* and *The Hatchet Man*), New Line Cinema, 1995.
Vince's trainer, *Play It to the Bone* (also known as *Play It*), Buena Vista, 1999.
Antonio, *Girl's Best Friend,* 2001.
Rico, *Dark Blue,* United Artists, 2002.
Detective Eddie Cruz, *Hollywood Homicide,* Revolution, 2003.
Homeless Native American, *D–War* (also known as *Dragon Wars*), Younggu–Art, 2005.

Television Appearances; Movies:

(As Eloy Phil Casados) Ishi as an adult, *Ishi: The Last of His Tribe,* History Channel, 1978.
Dwight Willits, *Amber Waves,* ABC, 1980.
(As Eloy Phil Casados) Ron, *Freedom,* ABC, 1981.
Feather Earrings, *The Legend of Walks Far Woman,* NBC, 1982.
Gregorio, *The Alamo: Thirteen Days to Glory,* 1987.
Ground crewman, *Steal the Sky,* HBO, 1988.
Stones for Ibarra, CBS, 1988.
To Heal a Nation, NBC, 1988.
Thin man, *Prime Target,* NBC, 1989.
Dominguez, *Bloodlines: Murder in the Family,* NBC, 1993.
Albert, *Grand Avenue,* HBO, 1996.
Lieutenant Tony Grenaldi, *Murder Live!,* NBC, 1997.
Mexican doctor, *Epoch,* Sci–Fi Channel, 2000.

Television Appearances; Series:
(As Eloy Phil Casados) Tsiskawa, *Young Dan'l Boone*, 1977.

Television Appearances; Miniseries:
Ektor, *The Big One: The Great Los Angeles Earthquake* (also known as *The Great Los Angeles Earthquake*), NBC, 1990.
Trial: The Price of Passion, NBC, 1992.

Television Appearances; Pilots:
(As Eloy Phil Casados) *Panic in Echo Park*, NBC, 1977.
"Mirrors: Parts 1 and 2," *Houston Knights*, CBS, 1987.
Ortega, *Bar Girls*, CBS, 1990.
Human Target, 1992.

Television Appearances; Episodic:
Spanish Officer, "The Rose and the Gun," *The Blue Knight*, CBS, 1976.
(As Eloy Phil Casados) Rudy Cortes, "Jury Duty: Part 2," *Family*, 1976.
(As Eloy P. Casados) Frank, "Kindred Spirits," *The Incredible Hulk*, CBS, 1979.
"The Virgin and the Turkey," *Hill Street Blues*, NBC, 1985.
Raoul, "Knight Flight to Freedom," *Knight Rider*, NBC, 1986.
Manolo Sanchez, "Come and Get It," *Hill Street Blues*, NBC, 1986.
"Hot Pursuit: Part 2," *Hunter*, NBC, 1987.
Smith, "The Big Kiss," *Northern Exposure*, CBS, 1991.
Joe Valentine, "Guess Who's Coming to Dinner?," *Hudson Street*, CBS, 1995.
Manager, "If You're Going to Talk the Talk," *Murphy Brown*, CBS, 1996.
Sheriff Sam Coyote, "Plague," *Walker, Texas Ranger*, CBS, 1996.
Maximo Ortiz, "Inside Out," *Nash Bridges*, CBS, 1997.
Sheriff Sam Coyote, "Lucas: Part 2," *Walker, Texas Ranger*, CBS, 1997.
Sheriff Sam Coyote, "Tribe," *Walker, Texas Ranger*, CBS, 1998.
Sheriff Sam Coyote, "War Cry," *Walker, Texas Ranger*, CBS, 1998.
Voice of Enrique, "Death of a Propane Salesman: Part 2," *King of the Hill* (animated), Fox, 1998.
"Happy Hank's Giving," *King of the Hill* (animated), Fox, 1999.
Voice of Enrique, "Hank's Bad Hair Day," *King of the Hill* (animated), Fox, 2000.
Diego, "In–Laws, Outlaws," *NYPD Blue*, ABC, 2001.

Also appeared as Louis Hodapp, *High Incident*, ABC; Clement, *Nothing Sacred*, ABC; *American Family*, PBS.

RECORDINGS

Video Games:
Voice of John Jackson, *Code Blue*, Legacy International, 2000.

CHAMBERS, Justin 1970–
(Justin W. Chambers)

PERSONAL

Born July 11, 1970, in Springfield, OH; son of John (a deputy police officer) and Pam (a deputy police officer) Chambers; married, wife's name Keisha (a model agency booker); children: Isabella, Maya and Keisha (twins), Eva, Jackson. *Education:* Studied at H.B. Studios and Ron Stetson Studios.

Addresses: *Agent*—Warren Zavala, Gersh Agency, 232 North Canon Dr., Beverly Hills, CA 90210. *Manager*—Sandra Chang, Industry Entertainment, 955 South Carrillo Dr., 3rd Floor, Los Angeles, CA 90048.

Career: Actor. Appeared in stage productions in the 1990s; model, including work in television commercials and print advertisements for Calvin Klein fragrances.

CREDITS

Television Appearances; Series:
Nicholas "Nick" Terry Hudson, *Another World* (also known as *Another World: Bay City*), NBC, 1995.
Caleb Haskell, *Four Corners*, CBS, 1998.
Chris Lassing, *Cold Case*, CBS, 2003.
Dr. Alex Karev, *Grey's Anatomy*, ABC, 2005.

Television Appearances; Movies:
George, "Harvest of Fire," *Hallmark Hall of Fame*, CBS, 1996.
Cole Clayborne, "Rose Hill," *Hallmark Hall of Fame*, CBS, 1997.
Rick, *Hysterical Blindness*, HBO, 2002.

Television Appearances; Miniseries:
Adult Hocking Linthorne, *Seasons of Love*, CBS, 1999.

Television Appearances; Episodic:
Officer Nick Caso, "Unis," *New York Undercover*, Fox, 1996.
Rick, "Stones," *Swift Justice*, UPN, 1996.

Television Appearances; Pilots:
Allies, CBS, 1999.
Charles Brody, *The Secret Service*, ABC, 2004.

Film Appearances:
Trey Tobelseted, *Liberty Heights*, Warner Bros., 1999.

Massimo Lenzetti, *The Wedding Planner* (also known as *Wedding Planner—verliebt, verlobt, verplant*), Sony Pictures Entertainment, 2001.

D'Artagnan, *The Musketeer,* Universal, 2001.

Ryan, *Leo,* Vortex Films, 2002.

German soldier, *For Which It Stands* (short film), University of Southern California, 2003.

Sergeant Matt Parish, *In Control of All Things,* Shadow Machine Films, 2004.

Rhett Butler, *Southern Belles,* Southern Belles LLC, 2005.

RECORDINGS

Videos:

Appeared in the music video "Under the Table and Dreaming" by Dave Matthews Band.

OTHER SOURCES

Periodicals:

Us Weekly, February 19, 2001, p. 20.

CHAPMAN, Sean

PERSONAL

Born in Germany.

Career: Actor.

CREDITS

Film Appearances:

Rodney, *Leidenschaftliche Bluemchen* (also known as *Boarding School, Passion Flower Hotel, Preppy School Girls,* and *Virgin Campus*), Atlantic, 1978.

Sam Diggins, *Party Party,* Twentieth Century–Fox, 1982.

Buchanan, *Underworld* (also known as *Transmutations*), 1985.

Captain Lyndhurst, *The Fourth Protocol,* Lorimar, 1987.

Frank Cotton, *Hellraiser* (also known as *Clive Barker's "Hellraiser"*), New World, 1987.

Mark, *Eat the Rich,* New Line Cinema, 1987.

Bob Harper, *For Queen and Country,* Atlantic Releasing Corporation, 1988.

Frank Cotton, *Hellbound: Hellraiser II* (also known as *Hellraiser II*), New World, 1988.

Arthur Smith, *Tangier Cop* (also known as *Heartbreak City*), 1997.

Rupert, *The Sea Change* (also known as *Cambio de rumbo*), 1998.

Paul, *Seven Days to Live* (also known as *Du lebst noch 7 Tage, Seven D,* and *7 Days to Live*), 2000.

Bent cop, *Gangster No. 1* (also known as *Gangster Nr. 1*), Columbia TriStar, 2000.

Edward Dmytryk, *One of the Hollywood Ten* (also known as *Punto de Mira*), 2000.

Television Appearances; Movies:

Platoon commander, *Contact,* BBC, 1985.

Tom Riley, *The Black and Blue Lamp,* BBC, 1988.

Danny, *A Master of Marionettes,* 1989.

Jean, *A Woman at War,* 1991.

Franky, *Hero of the Hour,* 2000.

Brigadier MacLellan, *Sunday,* Channel 4, 2002.

Larry Quartermain, *Entrusted,* 2003.

Television Appearances; Series:

Ben Ellington, *Ellington,* YTV, 1996.

James Strickland, *Peak Practice,* ITV, 2001–2002.

Television Appearances; Miniseries:

Graham Richards, *Trial & Retribution V,* 2002.

DCI Frank Lane, *The Commander: Virus,* ITV, 2005.

Television Appearances; Specials:

James, *Scum,* BBC, 1977.

Barry Giller, *Made in Britain* (also known as *Tales Out of School: Made in Britain*), CTV, 1982.

Mark, *Mirrorball,* BBC and BBC America, 2000.

Television Appearances; Pilots:

Peter Tracey, *K–9 and Company,* BBC, 1981.

Television Appearances; Episodic:

Coleman, "The Acorn Syndrome," *The Professionals,* 1980.

Mayhew, "The Evil That Men Do," *Bergerac,* BBC1, 1991.

Sante, "The End," *Absolutely Fabulous,* BBC, 1994.

Cousin Cockshaw, "Special," *French and Saunders,* BBC, 1994.

Jon Lester, "When Opportunity Knocks," *The Bill,* ITV1, 1995.

John Bonetti, "All for Love," *Wycliffe,* ITV, 1995.

Cousin Cockshaw, "The Quick and the Dead," *French and Saunders,* BBC, 1996.

William/Edmond, "The Raven in the Foregate," *Cadfael 3,* ITV and PBS, 1998.

Marilyn Monroe, *Emmerdale Farm,* YTV, 1999.

DCI Ian Norton, "Two below Zero," *Silent Witness,* BBC, 2001.

Alex Robinson, "Class Act," *Heartbeat,* ITV, 2002.

Alex Robinson, "Caught in the Headlights," *Heartbeat,* ITV, 2002.

Ethan Issacs, "Bent Moon on the Rise," *Murphy's Law,* BBC, 2004.

Jimmy Kirby, "Second Sight," *Midsomer Murders,* ITV and Arts and Entertainment, 2005.
Carl, "Sins of the Father," *The Royal,* ITV, 2005.
Ray Spitz, Jr., *New Tricks,* BBC, 2005.

Stage Appearances:
Robert, *Certain Young Men,* Almeida Theater, London, 1999.

RECORDINGS

Video Games:
Battle Engine Aquila, Infogrames, 2003.

CHATELAIN, Christine

PERSONAL

Career: Actress.

CREDITS

Film Appearances:
Zoie, *Late Night Sessions,* Asylum, 1999.
Blake Dreyer, *Final Destination,* New Line Cinema, 2000.
Kaitlin, *Seeking Winonas,* Belial Productions/Rushlight Entertainment, 2001.
Sexy waitress, *3000 Miles to Graceland,* Warner Bros., 2001.
Andie, *40 Days and 40 Nights* (also known as *40 jours et 40 nuits*), Miramax, 2002.
Tonya, *Stark Raving Mad,* Newmarket Capital Group, 2002.
Mitzi Cole, *Intern Academy* (also known as *Whitecoats*), TVA Films, 2004.

Television Appearances; Series:
Taylor, *The Collector,* 2004.

Television Appearances; Movies:
Ellen, *For Hope,* ABC, 1996.
Monica, *Don't Look behind You,* Fox Family Channel, 1999.

Television Appearances; Episodic:
Devia, "When in Rome ... ," *Breaker High,* UPN, 1997.
Young Max's mother, "Heat," *Dark Angel,* Fox, 2000.
Young Max's mother, "C.R.E.A.M.," *Dark Angel,* Fox, 2000.

Moreena, "Prime Location," *The Immortal,* syndicated, 2000.
Jenny Tergeson, "The Last Dance," *Mysterious Ways,* PAX, 2001.
Allie Prescott, "House of Shadows," *Beyond Belief: Fact or Fiction,* Fox, 2002.
"Bet Your Life," *Just Cause,* PAX, 2002.
Nicole, "Cabin Pressure," *The Dead Zone,* USA Network, 2003.
Cavava, "The Spider's Stratagem," *Andromeda* (also known as *Gene Roddenberry's "Andromeda"*), syndicated, 2004.

Also appeared in *Glory Days,* The WB; and as Lorelei, *2gether: The Series,* MTV.

Television Appearances; Other:
Farrah, "Disco Inferno," *Strange Frequency* (pilot), VH1, 2001.
Brenda, *Out of Order* (miniseries), Showtime, 2003.

CHEPOVETSKY, Dmitry
(Dmitri Chepovetsky)

PERSONAL

Born in Lvov, U.S.S.R. (now Ukraine).

Career: Actor.

CREDITS

Film Appearances:
Eton, *Saving Grace,* Saving Grace Productions, 1998.
Angel, *I'll Be Home for Christmas,* Buena Vista, 1998.
Technician, *Mission to Mars* (also known as *M2M*), Buena Vista, 2000.
Dashing prince, *Cinderella: Single Again,* Shocking Buckwheat Pictures, 2000.
Dr. Welby, *Chain of Fools,* Warner Bros., 2000.
Spencer, *Dark Water,* Simpatico Pictures, 2001.
Sergei, *K–19: The Widowmaker* (also known as *K*19: The Widowmaker* and *K–19: Terreur sous la mer*), Paramount, 2002.
Bartender, *The Safety of Objects,* 2001, IFC Films, 2003.

Television Appearances; Series:
Jeff, a recurring role, *Higher Ground,* Fox Family Channel, 2000.
Bob Melnikov, *ReGenesis,* The Movie Network (Canada), 2004.

Television Appearances; Miniseries:

Third NEST man, *Atomic Train,* NBC, 1999.

Haven, CBS, 2001.

(As Dmitri Chepovetsky) Fatelov, *Master Spy: The Robert Hanssen Story,* CBS, 2002.

Television Appearances; Movies:

Ben, *Sweet Dreams,* NBC, 1996.

Kaysat controller, *Max Q* (also known as *Max Q: Emergency Landing*), ABC, 1998.

Ron Dusak, *The Familiar Stranger* (also known as *My Husband's Double Life*), Lifetime, 2001.

Courtyard guard, *Spinning Boris,* Showtime, 2003.

Television Appearances; Episodic:

British soldier, "Amnesty," *Hawkeye,* syndicated, 1995.

Lieutenant Richard Harper, "Dod Kalm," *The X–Files,* Fox, 1995.

Claude, "No Sell–out," *Madison,* Global (Canada), 1996.

Account manager, "Blinded by the Son," *Strange Luck,* Fox, 1996.

First government man (some sources cite role of young Bill Mulder), "Apocrypha," *The X–Files,* Fox, 1996.

Supervisor, "Folie a Deux," *The X–Files,* Fox, 1998.

Keith Harmon, "Marcey Bennett," *Cold Squad,* CTV (Canada), 1998.

Sergei, "Evil Eye," *F/X: The Series,* 1998.

Cal Hamilton, "Y2K: Total System Failure," *The Net,* USA Network, 1999.

Rick Feldman, "Murder 101," *The Sentinel,* UPN, 1999.

Boris, "Small Victories," *Stargate SG–1,* Showtime and syndicated, 2000.

"TKO," *Hollywood Off–Ramp,* E! Entertainment Television, 2000.

Derrick Larch, "Twin," *So Weird,* The Disney Channel, 2000.

"Dr. Tara," *Blue Murder,* Global, 2001.

Sergei, "The Body Shop," *Sue Thomas: F.B.Eye,* PAX, 2004.

Russian soldier, "Full Alert," *Stargate SG–1,* Sci–Fi Channel and syndicated, 2005.

Appeared as David Brokerman in an episode of *The Marshal,* ABC.

Stage Appearances:

Brother Luc, *Orphan Muses,* Firehall Theatre, Burnaby, British Columbia, Canada, 1996.

(Compared to This) Hell Will Be Sweet, Factory Theatre, Toronto, Ontario, Canada, 1997.

Kuzma Nikolayevich Heerin, *The Festivities,* Rushin Productions, 2000.

Jonathan, *Slip Knot,* Factory Theatre, 2002.

Michael, *The Danish Play,* Extra Space, Tarragon Theatre, Toronto, 2002.

Joseph, *Remnants,* Tarragon Theatre, 2003.

Maverick, *Top Gun! The Musical,* Factory Theatre, 2003.

Ivan the Terrible (title role), *The Trials of John Demjanjuk: A Holocaust Cabaret,* Theatre Asylum, Studio Theatre, Harbourfront Centre, Toronto, 2004.

Also appeared in a production of *Zadie's Shoes.*

CHER 1946–

(Sonny and Cher)

PERSONAL

Full name, Cherilyn Sarkisian LaPierre; born May 20, 1946, in El Centro, CA; daughter of John Sarkisian (a truck driver) and Georgia Holt (a model and actress; original name, Jackie Jean Crouch); adopted daughter of Gilbert LaPiere (a banker); half–sister of Georganne LaPiere (an actress); married Sonny Bono (a singer, restaurateur, and politician), October 27, 1964 (some sources say 1969; divorced, May 1975 [some sources say February 20, 1974]); married Gregg Allman (a musician), June 1975 (divorced); children: (first marriage) Chastity Bono (an activist); (second marriage) Elijah Blue Allman (a musician). *Education:* Studied drama with Jeff Corey.

Addresses: *Agent*—International Creative Management, 8942 Wilshire Blvd., Beverly Hills, CA 90211. *Office*—Bill Sammeth Organization, P.O. Box 960, Beverly Hills, CA 90213–0960; Reprise Records, 3000 Wilshire Blvd., Burbank, CA 91505–4694. *Manager*—Lindsay Scott Management, 8899 Beverly Blvd., Ste. 600, Los Angeles, CA 90048. *Publicist*—Warner Bros. Records, 75 Rockefeller Center, New York, NY 10019.

Career: Actress, producer, director, and singer. Backup singer for the musical groups the Crystals and the Ronettes; performer and recording artist with Sonny Bono as Caesar and Cleo, then as Sonny and Cher, beginning in 1964; member of the rock band Black Rose, c. 1979–80; nightclub performer in Las Vegas, NV, and Atlantic City, NJ. Head of Isis Productions, an independent film company; founder of Sanctuary, a catalog sales company, 1994; creator of an Internet catalog at Cher.com, 1999. Also appeared in commercials and infomercials.

Awards, Honors: Grammy Award nomination, best female pop vocal, National Academy of Recording Arts and Sciences, 1971, for "Gypsies, Tramps, and Thieves"; Emmy Award nominations, outstanding single variety or musical program, 1972, and outstanding variety musical series, 1972, 1973, and 1974, and Golden

Globe Award, best actress in a television comedy or musical, 1974, all for *The Sonny and Cher Comedy Hour;* Emmy Award nomination, outstanding comedy, variety or music series, 1975, for *Cher;* Golden Globe Award nomination, best actress in a supporting role, 1983, for *Come Back to the Five and Dime, Jimmy Dean, Jimmy Dean;* Golden Globe Award, best actress in a supporting role in a motion picture, Academy Award nomination, best supporting actress, 1983, Film Award nomination, best supporting actress, British Academy of Film and Television Arts, 1985, for *Silkwood;* Palm d'Or, best actress, Cannes International Film Festival, 1985, Golden Globe Award nomination, best performance by an actress in a supporting role, 1986, for *Mask;* Hasty Pudding Woman of the Year, Hasty Pudding Theatricals, Harvard University, 1985; Academy Award, best actress, Golden Globe Award, best actress in a motion picture comedy or musical, 1987, David di Donatello Award, best foreign actress, Silver Ribbon Award, best actress, Italian National Syndicate of Film Journalists, 1988, and Film Award nomination, best actress, British Academy of Film and Television Arts, 1989, all for *Moonstruck;* Golden Globe Award nomination, best performance by an actress in a supporting role in a series, miniseries, or motion picture, Golden Satellite Award nomination, best performance by an actress in a supporting role, 1997, for *If These Walls Could Talk;* Vanguard Award, GLAAD Media Awards, 1998; Star on the Walk of Fame (with Sonny Bono), 1998; Fashion Award, 18th Annual American Fashion Awards, 1999; Legend Award, World Music Awards, 1999; platinum and gold record awards, Recording Industry Association of America; Emmy Award nomination, outstanding individual performance, 2000, for *Cher: Live in Concert from Las Vegas;* Lucy Award (with others), Women in Film Lucy Awards, 2000; Emmy Award nomination, outstanding variety, music or comedy special, 2003, for *Cher: The Farewell Tour.*

CREDITS

Film Appearances:
Herself, *Wild on the Beach* (also known as *Beach House Party*), Twentieth Century–Fox, 1965.
Herself, *Good Times* (also known as *Sonny & Cher in Good Times*), Columbia, 1967.
Title role, *Chastity,* American International Pictures, 1969.
Sissy, *Come Back to the Five and Dime, Jimmy Dean, Jimmy Dean,* Cinecom International, 1982.
Dolly Pelliker, *Silkwood,* Twentieth Century–Fox, 1983.
Florence "Rusty" Dennis, *Mask* (also known as *Peter Bogdanovich's "Mask"*), Universal, 1985.
Kathleen Riley, *Suspect,* TriStar, 1987.
Alexandra Medford, *The Witches of Eastwick,* Warner Bros., 1987.
Loretta Castorini, *Moonstruck,* Metro–Goldwyn–Mayer/ United Artists, 1987.

Rachel Flax, *Mermaids,* Orion, 1990.
Herself, *The Player,* Fine Line, 1992.
Herself, *Ready to Wear* (also known as *Pret–a–Porter*), Miramax, 1994.
Margaret O'Donnell, *Faithful,* New Line Cinema, 1996.
Elsa Morganthal Strauss–Armistan, *Tea with Mussolini* (also known as *Un te con Mussolini*), Metro–Goldwyn–Mayer, 1999.
Mayor of the Sunset Strip, Samuel Goldwyn, 2002.

Television Appearances; Series:
(With Sonny Bono as Sonny and Cher) Host, *The Sonny and Cher Comedy Hour,* CBS, 1971–74.
Host, *Cher,* CBS, 1975–76.
(With Sonny Bono as Sonny and Cher) Host, *The Sonny and Cher Show,* CBS, 1976–77.
Parabens, 1993.

Television Appearances; Movies:
Club Rhino, 1990.
Dr. Beth Thompson, "1996," *If These Walls Could Talk,* HBO, 1996.

Television Appearances; Specials:
Sonny & Cher: Nitty Gritty Hour, 1970.
Third wife, *The First Nine Months Are the Hardest,* NBC, 1971.
How to Handle a Woman, NBC, 1972.
The Flip Wilson Special, NBC, 1975.
Host, *Cher ... Special,* ABC, 1978.
Host, *Cher and Other Fantasies,* NBC, 1979.
Night of 100 Stars, ABC, 1982.
Host, *Cher—A Celebration at Caesar's Palace,* Showtime, 1983.
The Barbara Walters Special, ABC, 1985, 1988.
Bugs Bunny/Looney Tunes All–Star 50th Anniversary, 1986.
(In archive footage) *The Muppets: A Celebration of 30 Years,* 1986.
Superstars and Their Moms, ABC, 1987.
Pee–Wee's Playhouse Christmas Special (also known as *Christmas at Pee Wee's Playhouse* and *Pee–Wee Herman's Christmas Special*), CBS, 1988.
Comic Relief III, HBO, 1989.
An Evening with Bette, Cher, Goldie, Meryl, Olivia, Lily, and Robin, ABC, 1990.
(Uncredited; in archive footage) *Superstar: The Life and Times of Andy Warhol,* 1990.
Cher ... at the Mirage, CBS, 1991.
Host, *Cher's Video Canteen,* 1991.
Host, *Coca–Cola Pop Music Backstage Pass to Summer,* 1991.
Host, *MTV's 10th Anniversary Special,* MTV, 1991.
Dame Edna's Hollywood, NBC, 1991.
In a New Light, ABC, 1992.
The Grand Opening of Euro Disney, CBS, 1992.
Tina Turner: Going Home, The Disney Channel, 1993.

What Is This Thing Called Love? (also known as *The Barbara Walters Special*), ABC, 1993.

(In archive footage) *Victor Borges Tivoli 150 aar,* 1993.

(In archive footage) *Rowan & Martin's Laugh–In: 25th Anniversary Reunion,* 1993.

The Atlantic Records Story, 1994.

Comic Relief: Behind the Nose, BBC, 1995.

Happy Birthday Elizabeth—A Celebration of Life, ABC, 1997.

(Uncredited) Herself, *An Audience with Elton John,* ITV, 1997.

AFI's 100 Years ... 100 Movies, CBS, 1998 and 1999.

Host, *Sonny and Me: Cher Remembers,* CBS, 1998.

(In archive footage) *A Really Big Show: Ed Sullivan's 50th Anniversary,* 1998.

The X–Files Movie Special, Fox, 1998.

(In archive footage; with Sonny Bono) *Detroit Rock City,* 1999.

Super Bowl XXXIII, ABC, 1999.

Cher: Live in Concert at the MGM Grand in Las Vegas (also known as *Cher: Live in Concert from Las Vegas*), HBO, 1999.

VH1 Divas Live '99, VH1, 1999.

Hollywood Animal Crusaders (documentary), Animal Planet, 1999.

Interviewee, *100 Greatest Dance Songs,* VH1, 2000.

Rock to Erase MS, VH1, 2001.

I Love Lucy's 50th Anniversary Special, CBS, 2001.

The Royal Variety Performance 2001, ITV, 2001.

48 edicion de los premios Ondas, 2001.

National Lottery Christmas Cracker (also known as *Dale's National Lottery Christmas Cracker*), 2001.

Still Cher (documentary), BBC, 2002.

MTV Icon: Aerosmith (documentary), MTV, 2002.

Elvis Lives, NBC, 2002.

Judi Dench: A BAFTA Tribute, BBC, 2002.

American Bandstand's 50th Anniversary Celebration, ABC, 2002.

VH1 Divas Las Vegas, VH1, 2002.

Hollywood Salutes Nicolas Cage: An American Cinematheque Tribute, TNT, 2002.

Inside TV Land: Style and Fashion (documentary), TV Land, 2003.

50 Sexiest Video Moments, VH1, 2003.

Cher: The Farewell Tour, NBC, 2003.

101 Most Shocking Moments in Entertainment, E! Entertainment Television, 2003.

Cher: The E! True Hollywood Story (documentary), E! Entertainment Television, 2003.

Reel Comedy Stuck On You, Comedy Central, 2003.

The Eurovision Song Contest Semi Final, 2004.

ABBA: Our Last Video Ever (also known as *The Last Video*), 2004.

The Eurovision Song Contest, 2004.

(In archive footage) *101 Biggest Celebrity Oops,* E! Entertainment Television, 2004.

Introducing Graham Norton, Comedy Central, 2004.

Dick Clark's New Year's Primetime Rockin' Eve 2005, ABC, 2004.

Television Appearances; Miniseries:

(In archive footage) *Retrosexual: The 80's* (documentary), VH1, 2004.

Television Appearances; Awards Presentations:

Copresenter, *The 45th Annual Academy Awards,* NBC, 1973.

The 16th Annual Grammy Awards, CBS, 1974.

The 46th Annual Academy Awards, NBC, 1974.

The 55th Annual Academy Awards Presentation, ABC, 1983.

The 56th Annual Academy Awards Presentation, ABC, 1984.

Presenter, *The 58th Annual Academy Awards Presentation,* ABC, 1986.

MTV 1988 Video Music Awards, MTV, 1988.

The 60th Annual Academy Awards Presentation, ABC, 1988.

MTV 1989 Video Music Awards, MTV, 1989.

The 61st Annual Academy Awards Presentation, ABC, 1989.

Presenter, *MTV 1991 Video Music Awards,* MTV, 1991.

The 1991 Billboard Music Awards, 1991.

The American Film Institute Salute to Jack Nicholson, CBS, 1994.

The 1998 Billboard Music Awards, 1998.

The 70th Annual Academy Awards, ABC, 1998.

Honoree, *The 18th Annual American Fashion Awards,* 1999.

Honoree, *The 1999 World Music Awards,* 1999.

The 26th Annual American Music Awards, 1999.

The BRIT Awards '99, 1999.

Presenter, *The 52nd Annual Primetime Emmy Awards,* ABC, 2000.

The 72nd Annual Academy Awards Presentation, ABC, 2000.

The 29th Annual American Music Awards, ABC, 2002.

The 2002 Billboard Music Awards, Fox, 2002.

Television Appearances; Pilots:

Tom Snyder's Celebrity Spotlight, NBC, 1980.

Television Appearances; Episodic:

Where the Action Is, 1965.

(As Sonny and Cher) *Top of the Pops,* BBC, 1965, 1966.

Herself, "The Puzzler Is Coming," *Batman,* ABC, 1966.

Herself, "The Duo Is Slumming," *Batman,* ABC, 1966.

(As Sonny and Cher) *Beat–Club,* 1966, 1967.

The Andy Williams Show, NBC, 1967.

Ramona, "The Hot Number Affair," *The Man from U.N.C.L.E.,* NBC, 1967.

Rowan & Martin's Laugh–In, NBC, 1968, 1969.

The Dick Cavett Show, 1970.

"Love and the Sack," *Love, American Style,* ABC, 1971.

Voice of herself, "The Secret of Shark Island," *The New Scooby–Doo Movies* (animated), 1972.

The Carol Burnett Show, 1975.

The Tonight Show Starring Johnny Carson, NBC, 1975, 1977, 1979, 1981, 1983, 1985.

Omnibus, 1980.

Late Night with David Letterman, NBC, 1986, 1987.

Saturday Night Live, NBC, 1987, 1992.

Top of the Pops, 1987, 1991, 1992, 1995, 1996, 1998, 1999, 2001.

Voice of herself, "Here's to Good Friends," *Roseanne,* ABC, 1988.

Herself, *The Howard Stern Show,* 1991.

Herself, *Dame Edna's Hollywood,* 1991.

Los domingos por Norma, 1992.

"El lejano Oeste," *Un, dos, tres ... responda otra vez,* 1993.

"Cerrado por vacaciones," *Un, dos, tres ... responda otra vez,* 1993.

Herself, *Don't Forget Your Toothbrush,* Channel 4, 1994.

Clive Anderson Talks Back, Channel 4, 1995.

(Two episodes) *TFI Friday,* Channel 4, 1996.

The RuPaul Show, VH1, 1996.

Herself, *Live and Kicking,* BBC, 1996, 1999.

The Rosie O'Donnell Show, syndicated, 1996, 1998.

Behind the Music, VH1, 1997.

The National Lottery Stars, 1999.

"Gypsies, Tramps and Weed," *Will & Grace,* NBC, 2000.

"Wetten, dass ... ? Aus Erfurt," *Wetten, dass ... ?,* 2001.

GMTV, ITV, 2001.

Parkinson, BBC, 2001.

So Graham Norton, Channel 4, 2001.

The Oprah Winfrey Show, syndicated, 2002.

"A.I.: Artificial Insemination," *Will & Grace,* NBC, 2002.

Access Hollywood, syndicated, 2002.

"Cyndi Lauper," *Behind the Music,* VH1, 2002.

NFL Monday Night Football, ABC, 2002.

Entertainment Tonight, syndicated, 2003.

Celebrities Uncensored, E! Entertainment Television, 2003.

Tinseltown TV, International Channel, 2004.

Pulse, Fox, 2004.

Rove Live, Ten Network, 2004.

Larry King Live, CNN, 2004.

Appeared in *Hullabaloo,* NBC; Also appeared in episodes of *Beavis and Butthead,* MTV; *The Glen Campbell Goodtime Hour,* CBS; *The Hollywood Palace,* ABC; and *The Merv Griffin Show,* NBC, syndicated, and CBS.

Television Work; Movies:

Director of "1996" segment, *If These Walls Could Talk,* HBO, 1996.

Television Work; Specials:

Executive producer, *Sonny & Me: Cher Remembers,* CBS, 1998.

Executive producer, *Cher: The Farewell Tour,* NBC, 2003.

Other Television Work:

Executive producer, *Oak Ridge,* 1998.

Stage Appearances:

Come Back to the Five and Dime, Jimmy Dean, Jimmy Dean, Martin Beck Theatre, New York City, 1982.

RECORDINGS

Albums:

All I Really Want to Do, Imperial, 1965.

Sonny Side of Cher, Imperial, 1966.

With Love, Imperial, 1966.

Cher, Imperial, 1967.

Backstage, Imperial, 1968.

Golden Greats, 1968.

3614 Jackson Highway, Atco, 1969.

Cher Sings the Hits, 1971.

Gypsys, Tramps & Thieves, Universal Special Products, 1971.

Cher's Greatest Hits, 1972.

Cher Superpak, Vol. 1, 1972.

Cher Superpak, Vol. 2, 1972.

Cher, Kapp, 1972.

Foxy Lady, MCA, 1972.

Hits of Cher, United Artists, 1972.

Bittersweet White Light, MCA, 1973.

Dark Lady, MCA, 1974.

Half Breed, MCA, 1974.

Very Best, 1974.

The Very Best of Cher, Vol. 2, 1975.

Stars, Warner Bros., 1975.

Greatest Hits, MCA, 1975.

I'd Rather Believe in You, Warner Bros., 1977.

Cherished, Warner Bros., 1977.

Two the Hard Way, Allman & Woman, 1977.

Take Me Home, Casablanca, 1978.

This Is Cher, Sunset, 1978.

Prisoner, Casablanca, 1979.

Take Me Home, Universal Special Products, 1979.

Best of Cher, Vol. 1, 1981.

Best of Cher, Vol. 2, 1981.

I Paralyze, Varese Vintage, 1982.

Golden Greats, 1985.

The Best of Cher, EMI America, 1987.

Cher, Geffen, 1988.

Heart of Stone, Geffen, 1989.

Outrageous, Special Music, 1989.

The Ugly Duckling, Windham Hill, 1990.

Best of Cher, EMI America, 1991.

Love Hurts, Geffen, 1991.

Bang Bang and Other Hits, Capitol, 1992.

All I Really Want to Do/The Sonny Side of Cher, EMI Legends, 1992.

Greatest Hits: 1965–1992, Geffen Records, 1993.

Greatest Hits, Import, 1993.

Take Me Home/Prisoner, Alex, 1994.

It's a Man's World, Warner Bros., 1996.

Cher: The Casablanca Years, PolyGram, 1996.
The Long and Winding Road, Ariola Express, 1996.
You Better Sit Down Kids, Disky, 1996.
Gypsys, Tramps & Thieves: 25 Great Songs, Movie Play, 1997.
Believe, Warner Bros., 1998.
Original Hits, Disky, 1998.
Cher with Sonny, Entertainers, 1998.
Greatest Hits, 1999.
Bittersweet: Love Songs Collection, MCA Records, 1999.
Believe, Import, 1999.
If I Could Turn Back Time: Cher's Greatest Hits, Geffen, 1999.
Take Me Home, 1999.
Sunny, Magic, 1999.
Bang Bang: The Early Years, Capitol/EMI Records, 1999.
Black Rose, EMI, 1999.
All or Nothing, WEA International, 1999.
Greatest Hits, WEA/Universal, 1999.
Cher Favorites, Intercontinental, 1999.
Not.Com.mercial, 2000.
Story, EMI Plus, 2000.
20th Century Masters—The Millennium Collection: The Best of Cher, MCA Records, 2000.
Millennium Edition, Universal International, 2000.
Best of Cher, Columbia, 2000.
Maximum Cher, Griffin Music, 2000.
The Way of Love: The Cher Collection, MCA Records, 2000.
Behind the Door: 1964–1974, Raven Records, 2000.
Greatest Hits, Vol. 1, Fuel, 2000.
Holdin' Out for Love, Import, 2001.
Living Proof, WEA International, 2001.
Essential Collection, Hip–O Records, 2001.
Believe, WEA International, 2001.
Living Proof, WEA International, 2002.
Absolutely the Best, Vol. 1, Fuel 2000 Records, 2002.
Blue, Universal International, 2003.
The Very Best of Cher, Warner Bros. Records, 2003.
Live: The Farewell Tour, Warner Bros. Records, 2003.
The Very Best of Cher—Special Edition, Warner Bros. Records, 2003.
20th Century Masters—The Millennium Collection: The Best of Cher, Vol. 2, Hip–O Records, 2004.
The Very Best of Cher—Bonus Tracks, Warner Strategic Marketing, 2005.
All I Really Want to Do/The Sonny Side of Cher, Beat Goes On, 2005.

Albums; With Sonny Bono as Sonny and Cher:
Look at Us, Atco, 1965.
Baby Don't Go, Reprise, 1965.
Wondrous World, Atco, 1966.
In Case You're in Love, Atlantic, 1967.
Good Times, Atlantic, 1967.
The Best of Sonny and Cher, Atlantic, 1968.
Sonny & Cher Live, Kapp, 1969.
The Nitty Gritty Hour, View Video, 1970.

All I Ever Need Is You, Kapp, 1971.
Live in Las Vegas, MCA, 1974.
Mama Was a Rock 'n' Roll Singer, 1974.
Greatest Hits, MCA, 1975.
The Beat Goes On, Atco, 1975.
At Their Best, 1989.
I Got You Babe, Rhino Records, 1993.
The Beat Goes ON: The Best of Sonny & Cher, Rhino Records, 1993.
You Better Sit Down Kids, Great Hits, 1996.
All I Ever Need: The Kapp/MCA Anthology, MCA Records, 1996.
I Got You Babe & Other Hits, Flashback Records, 1997.
Sonny & Cher Greatest Hits, 1998.
The Singles+, BR Music, 2000.
The Essentials, Rhino Records, 2002.

Recorded *Live, The Two of Us, Atlantic Singles,* Rhino; singles with Sonny Bono include "Baby Don't Go," "The Beat Goes On," "I Got You Babe," and "You Better Sit Down Kids."

Albums; With Others:
(With Gregg Allman) *Allman and Woman: Two the Hard Way,* Warner Bros., 1976.
(With Black Rose) *Black Rose,* Casablanca, 1980.
(With others) *For Our Children Too!,* Wea/Atlantic/Rhino, 1996.

Also recorded the single (with Peter Cetera) "After All" (theme song from the film *Chances Are*), 1989.

Videos:
(With Sonny Bono as Sonny and Cher) *Sonny and Cher: Nitty Gritty Hour,* 1970.
Storyteller, *Rabbit Ears: The Ugly Duckling,* 1985.
Michael Jackson: The Legend Continues, 1988.
Cherfitness: A New Attitude, 1991.
Cherfitness: Body Confidence, 1992.
Oscar's Greatest Moments, 1992.
Cher: Extravaganza—Live at the Mirage, 1992.
(With Sonny Bono as Sonny and Cher) *Flashbacks 2: Pop Parade,* 1994.
Tina Turner: Celebrate Live (also known as *Happy Birthday Tina!*), 1999.
Cher: Live in Concert, 1999.
Reflections on "The X–Files," 2004.
The Very Best of Cher: The Video Hits Collection, 2004.

Also appeared in music videos, including (with Peter Cetera) "After All."

Video Director:
The Very Best of Cher: The Video Hits Collection, 2004.

Video Games:
Voice of Isadora, *Nine,* 1996.

WRITINGS

Nonfiction:
(With Robert Haas) *Forever Fit: The Lifetime Plan for Health, Beauty, and Fitness,* Bantam, 1991.
(With Andrew Ennis and Joan Nielsen) *Cooking for Cher,* Simon & Schuster, 1997.
The First Time (autobiography), Simon & Schuster, 1998.

Videos:
The Very Best of Cher: The Video Hits Collection, 2004.

OTHER SOURCES

Books:
Contemporary Musicians, Volume 35, Gale, 2002.
Goodall, Nigel, *Cher in Her Own Words,* Omnibus Press, 1992.
Jacobs, Linda, *Cher: Simply Cher,* EMC Corp., 1975.
Petrucelli, Rita, *Cher: Singer and Actress,* illustrated by Luciano Lazzarino, Rourke Enterprises, 1989.
Taraborrelli, J. Randy, *Cher: A Biography,* St. Martin's Press, 1986.

Periodicals:
Billboard, September 18, 1999, p. 134.
Entertainment Weekly, May 31, 1996, p. 22; February 5, 1999, p. S7; April 23, 1999, pp. 16–21; November 1, 1999, p. 116.
Interview, October, 1994, p. 172; December, 1998, pp. 94–99.
Ladies Home Journal, November, 1996, p. 178; July, 1999, p. 42.
New York Times, March 20, 1988.
People Weekly, January 21, 1991; May 25, 1998, p. 84; November 22, 1999, pp. 10–11.
Premier, February, 1988.
Rolling Stone, April 15, 1999, p. 45.
TV Guide, May 16, 1998, pp. 28–30, 33.
Women's Wear Daily, September 13, 1999, p. 94S.

CHINLUND, Nick 1961–
(Nicholas Chinlund)

PERSONAL

Born November 18, 1961, in New York, NY. *Education:* Brown University, degree in history.

Addresses: *Agent*—Paradigm, 360 N. Crescent Dr., Beverly Hills, CA 90210. *Manager*—Davien Littlefield Management, 939 8th Ave., Suite 609, New York, NY 10019.

Career: Actor and producer. Worked at Williamstown Theater Festival, 1988–89; performed voice work in a television commercial for Tums.

CREDITS

Film Appearances:
(As Nicholas Chinlund) Hugo, *The Ambulance,* 1990.
Hatchett, *Lethal Weapon 3,* Warner Bros., 1992.
Deputy Tomay, *Army of One* (also known as *Joshua Tree*), 1993.
Pinkerton Detective O'Brady, *Bad Girls,* Twentieth Century–Fox, 1994.
Jeremy Avery, *Unveiled,* Twentieth Century–Fox Video, 1994.
Calderon, *Eraser,* IRS Releasing, 1996.
Lex, *A Brother's Kiss,* First Look Pictures Releasing, 1996.
Bob Morgan, *Mr. Magoo,* Buena Vista, 1997.
William "Billy Bedlam" Bedford, *Con Air,* Metro–Goldwyn–Mayer/Pathe, 1997.
Iggy, *Frogs for Snakes,* The Shooting Gallery International, 1998.
Mitch, *Chutney Popcorn,* Pryor Cashman Sherman & Flynn, 1999.
Lee, *Something Sweet,* 2000.
Himself, *The Kid* (also known as *Disney's "The Kid"*), Buena Vista, 2000.
Salesman, *Auggie Rose* (also known as *Beyond Suspicion*), Twentieth Century–Fox, 2000.
Mike Murphy, *Once in the Life,* Lions Gate Films, 2000.
Tim, *Training Day,* Warner Bros., 2001.
Matthew Starr, *Amy's Orgasm* (also known as *Amy's O* and *Why Love Doesn't Work*), Magic Lamp Releasing, 2001.
Chief, *Below,* Dimension Films, 2002.
100 Mile Rule, Velocity, 2002.
Michael "Slo" Slowenski, *Tears of the Sun,* Columbia, 2003.
Father 2, *Bun–Bun,* Talantis, 2003.
Journey to Safety: Making "Tears of the Sun," Columbia TriStar, 2003.
Title role, *Goodnight, Joseph Parker,* Kubla Khan, 2004.
Toombs, *The Chronicles of Riddick* (also known as *The Chronicles of Riddick: The Director's Cut*), United International, 2004.
Voice of Toombs, *The Chronicles of Riddick: Dark Fury,* Universal, 2004.
Daxus, *Ultraviolet,* Columbia TriStar, 2005.
McGivens, *The Legend of Zorro,* Columbia, 2005.

Film Work:
Associate producer, *A Brother's Kiss,* First Look Pictures Releasing, 1996.

Television Appearances; Movies:
Commander, *Daybreak*, HBO, 1993.
Dr. Ted Meeks, *Reform School Girl*, Showtime, 1994.
Nick Parma, *Letter to My Killer*, USA Network, 1995.
Dr. Jake Sandler, *Resurrection*, HBO, 1999.

Television Appearances; Miniseries:
Frederick Remington, *Rough Riders*, TNT, 1997.

Television Appearances; Episodic:
"Auto Erotica," *Zalman King's "Red Shoe Diaries"* (also known as *Red Shoe Diaries*), Showtime, 1992.
Weldon Small, "You Bet Your Life," *NYPD Blue*, ABC, 1994.
Voice of Chopshop, "SWAT Kats Unplugged," *Swat Kats: The Radical Squadron*, 1994.
Voice of Dr. Lieter Greenbox, "Unlikely Alloys," *Swat Kats: The Radical Squadron*, 1994.
Donald Addie Pfaster, "Irresistible," *The X–Files*, Fox, 1995.
Voice of Temple, "Race against Danger," *The Real Adventures of Jonny Quest*, 1996.
Late Show with David Letterman, CBS, 1997.
(Uncredited) Detective Tancredi, "Anywhere But Here," *Third Watch*, NBC, 1999.
(Uncredited) Detective Tancredi, "Responsible Parties," *Third Watch*, NBC, 1999.
(Uncredited) Detective Tancredi, "Impulse," *Third Watch*, NBC, 1999.
"First Love: Parts 1 & 2," *Cracker*, Arts and Entertainment, 1999.
Donald Addie Pfaster, "Orison," *The X–Files*, Fox, 2000.
Detective Tancredi, "Alone in a Crowd," *Third Watch*, NBC, 2000.
Detective Tancredi, "32 Bullets and a Broken Heart," *Third Watch*, NBC, 2000.
Daniel Hartman, "Do the Right Thing," *Providence*, NBC, 2000.
(Uncredited) Detective Tancredi, "The Lost," *Third Watch*, NBC, 2000.
Ian Jack, "The Lorelais' First Day at Chilton," *Gilmore Girls*, The WB, 2000.
Peck, "Endurance," *Law & Order*, NBC, 2000.
Jeff Briggs/Jim Briggs, "Sleight–of–Hand," *Diagnosis Murder*, CBS, 2000.
Major Ellis, "Listening to Fear," *Buffy the Vampire Slayer*, The WB, 2000.
Major Ellis, "Into the Woods," *Buffy the Vampire Slayer*, The WB, 2000.
Donny Hennessy, "Strapped," *The Fugitive*, CBS, 2001.
Donny Hennessy, "Jenny," *The Fugitive*, CBS, 2001.
McNeely, "6 Hours," *Walker, Texas Ranger*, CBS, 2001.
Mickey Rutlege/Apollo, "You've Got Male," *CSI: Crime Scene Investigation* (also known as *C.S.I.*), CBS, 2001.
Matthew Linwood Brodus, "Execution," *Law & Order: Special Victims Unit* (also known as *Law & Order: SVU*), NBC, 2002.

(Uncredited) Chief Doug Smith, "Christopher," *The Sopranos*, HBO, 2002.
Neil Ryder, "Open Heart," *MDs*, ABC, 2002.
Frank Elliott, "Embedded," *Law & Order*, NBC, 2003.
Detective Sullivan, "Impossible," *Desperate Housewives*, ABC, 2005.
Detective Sullivan, "Live Alone and Like It," *Desperate Housewives*, ABC, 2005.

CHINYAMURINDI, Michael

PERSONAL

Full name, Michael N. Chinyamurindi. *Education:* Earned M.F.A. degree.

Career: Actor.

CREDITS

Film Appearances:
Solomon, *Bopha!*, Paramount, 1993.
Claude from Mombasa, *Congo*, Paramount, 1995.
Leroy, *Skyscraper*, PM Entertainment Group, 1997.
(Uncredited) Waiter, *The Lost World: Jurassic Park*, MCA/Universal, 1997.
N'Dugo, *George of the Jungle*, Buena Vista, 1997.
Dr. Jacob Netanyel, *Guardian*, Helkon Filmverleih, 2000.
African leader, *Megiddo: The Omega Code 2* (also known as *Megiddo*), Gener8Xion Entertainment, 2001.
Lebo Manaka, *Ubuntu's Wounds* (short film), Home Box Office, 2002.
Voice, *The Wild Thornberrys Movie* (animated), Paramount, 2002.
Volinka, *Gate to Heaven* (also known as *Tor zum Himmel*), Bavaria Film International, 2003.

Television Appearances; Series:
Isaac, a recurring role, *The Young and the Restless*, CBS, 2002.

Television Appearances; Movies:
First prisoner, *Mandela*, HBO, 1987.
Dr. Isiohoro, *Special Report: Journey to Mars*, CBS, 1996.

Television Appearances; Episodic:
Mlungisi, "A Miracle Happens Here," *ER*, NBC, 1995.
Masai father, "Out of Africa," *Chicago Hope*, CBS, 1996.

Second Nigerian, "What a Dump!," *NYPD Blue*, ABC, 1997.

Djohar, "Hired Guns," *Soldier of Fortune, Inc.* (also known as *Special Ops Force*), syndicated, 1998.

Hailu Kebede, "Weaver of Hate," *NYPD Blue*, ABC, 1998.

Joseph Kingibe, "Bloodlust," *Profiler*, NBC, 1998.

Colonel Shohala, "Embassy," *JAG*, CBS, 1998.

Dr. Solomon Merkmallen, "Biogenesis," *The X–Files*, Fox, 1999.

Nimbala's translator, "In This White House," *The West Wing*, NBC, 2000.

Ashet, "Long Day's Journey," *Angel*, The WB, 2003.

Abraham Duc, "Sixteen Going On Seventeen," *Judging Amy*, CBS, 2003.

Kisangani, *ER*, NBC, 2003.

Doctor/God, "No Bad Guy," *Joan of Arcadia*, CBS, 2004.

Doctor/God, "Silence," *Joan of Arcadia*, CBS, 2004.

Doctor/God, "Friday Night," *Joan of Arcadia*, CBS, 2004.

RECORDINGS

Video Games:

Voices, *Gladius*, Lucasfilm, 2003.

Voices of Jamel–Udeen, Lambert, and Barney, *The Chronicles of Riddick: Escape from Butcher Bay*, Vivendi Universal Games, 2004.

CHISHOLM, Anthony
(Tony Chisholm)

PERSONAL

Addresses: *Agent*—Artists Agency, 10100 Santa Monica Blvd., Suite 305, Los Angeles, CA 90067.

Career: Actor. Geva Theatre, Rochester, NY, member of company, 1999–2000.

CREDITS

Stage Appearances:

Snow, *Ice Bridge*, Joseph Papp Public Theatre, New York City, 1984.

Habu, *Tracers*, Joseph Papp Public Theatre, 1985.

Wolf, *Two Trains Running*, Walter Kerr Theatre, New York City, 1992.

Fielding, *Jitney*, Geva Theatre, Rochester, NY, 1999–2000, then Second Stage Theatre, New York City, 2000.

Solly Two Kings, *Gem of the Ocean*, Center Theater Group, Mark Taper Forum, Los Angeles, 2003, then Walter Kerr Theatre, 2004.

Appeared in *Black Visions*, Public Theatre, New York City; *The Coming of the Hurricane*, Crossroads Theatre Company; *Day of Absence* and *Les Blancs*, both Center Stage Theatre; *Driving Miss Daisy*, Portland Stage Company; *I Am a Man*, Goodman Theatre, Chicago, IL; *I Just Stopped By to See the Man*, Steppenwolf, Chicago; *Ma Rainey's Black Bottom*, Denver Center, Cleveland Playhouse; *Fences*, Indiana Repertory; *King Lear*, New York Shakespeare Festival, Delacorte Theatre in the Park, New York City; *The Mighty Gents*, off–Broadway production; *Of Mice and Men*, Geva Theatre; *The Talented*, Manhattan Theatre Club, New York City; *Tracers*, New York Shakespeare Festival, then Royal Court Theatre, London, and Seymour Centre, Sydney, Australia; also appeared in *Back in the World* and in productions at Cincinnati Playhouse.

Major Tours:

Performed in touring productions of *Ain't Supposed to Die a Natural Death*, *Fences*, *Jitney*, *Ma Rainey's Black Bottom*, *No Place to Be Somebody*, and *Two Trains Running*.

Film Appearances:

Up Tight!, 1968.

Third cowboy, *Putney Swope*, Cinema V, 1969.

Black plainclothes man, *Cotton Comes to Harlem*, 1970.

(As Tony Chisholm) *Death of a Prophet*, 1981.

Dillon, *Let's Get Bizzee*, Xenon Entertainment Group, 1996.

A Dozen Kliks, 1998.

Langhorne, *Beloved*, Universal, 1998.

Floyd, *Bought & Sold* (also known as *A Jersey Tale*), Artisan, 2003.

Space cowboy, *Alone* (short film), Gregory Orr, 2004.

Pastor, *Coalition*, 2004.

Geechee man, *Dream Street*, Lonette, 2005.

Television Appearances; Series:

Burr Redding, *Oz*, HBO, 2001–2003.

Television Appearances; Specials:

Servant to Cornwall, *King Lear*, 1974.

Ned, *Sojourner*, CBS, 1975.

Television Appearances; Movies:

Paul Marsden, *Murder in Black and White*, 1990.

Also appeared in *Vietnam War Stories*.

Television Appearances; Episodic:

Freddy Wells, "Unis," *New York Undercover*, Fox, 1996.

Eric, "Adam 55–3," *Third Watch*, NBC, 2001.

Wally Zane, "Zero Tolerance," *100 Centre Street*, Arts and Entertainment, 2002.

Leroy Russell, "Execution," *Law & Order: Special Victims Unit* (also known as *Law & Order: SVU*), NBC, 2002.

Big Elwood, "Songs in the Night," *Hack*, CBS, 2002.

Big Elwood, "Black Eye," *Hack*, CBS, 2003.

Frederick Speed, "Under Color of Law," *The Handler*, CBS, 2003.

CLAVELL, Kira

PERSONAL

Addresses: *Agent*—Murray Gibson, Characters Talent Agency, 150 Carlton St., 2nd Floor, Toronto, Ontario, Canada M5A 2K1.

Career: Actress and model.

Awards, Honors: Canadian Comedy Award nomination, "pretty funny" female performance in a film, 2003, for *Rub & Tug.*

CREDITS

Television Appearances; Movies:

Erica, *The Stepsister*, USA Network, 1997.

Connie, *Dr. Jekyll & Mr. Hyde* (also known as *The Prophesy of the Tiger*), syndicated, 1999.

Cynthia, *Sealed With a Kiss* (also known as *First Comes Love*), CBS, 1999.

Summer princess, *Snow Queen*, Hallmark Channel, 2002.

The queen, *Cool Money*, USA Network, 2005.

Television Appearances; Episodic:

Coyantu, "Little Tin God," *Highlander* (also known as *Highlander: The Series*), syndicated, 1996.

"From Honey, With Love," *Honey, I Shrunk the Kids: The TV Show*, syndicated, 1998.

Vam Mi, "Unchain My Heart: Parts 1–4," *Ninja Turtles: The Next Mutation*, 1998.

Jasmine Kwong, "Time to Be Heroes," *La Femme Nikita*, USA Network, 2000.

Emma Laybourne, "The Breach," *Secret Agent Man*, UPN, 2000.

Vashista, "Demons of the Night: Parts 1 & 2," *The Immortal*, syndicated, 2000.

Jasmine Kwong, "A Girl Who Wasn't There," *La Femme Nikita*, USA Network, 2001.

Jasmine Kwong, "All the World's a Stage," *La Femme Nikita*, USA Network, 2001.

Jasmine Kwong, "The Evil that Men Do," *La Femme Nikita*, USA Network, 2001.

Vashista, "Kiyomi," *The Immortal*, syndicated, 2001.

Terry the TechnoSexual, "Ghoul Whipped," *The 5th Quadrant*, 2002.

Kathryn Chao, "Lama Hunt," *Just Cause*, PAX, 2002.

"Memento Mori," *Adventure Inc.*, syndicated, 2002.

Lyn Sing, "A Modern Mata Hari," *The Eleventh Hour*, CTV (Canada), 2003.

Renata, "Born to Kill," *Street Time*, Showtime, 2003.

Yuki Makito, "Upgrade," *Jake 2.0*, UPN, 2004.

Amaterasu, "New Order: Parts 1 & 2," *Stargate SG–1*, Sci–Fi Channel and syndicated, 2004.

Appeared as Lisa in an episode of *Platinum*, UPN.

Television Appearances; Other:

Medusa, *Voyage of the Unicorn* (miniseries), Odyssey Channel, 2001.

Veronica, *The Defectors* (also known as *Crime School*), 2001.

Film Appearances:

Cindy, *Rub & Tug* (also known as *Les masseuses*), Velocity Home Entertainment, 2002.

Liberty, *House of the Dead* (also known as *House of the dead: Le jeu ne fait que commencer*), Artisan Entertainment, 2003.

Young woman, *My Baby's Daddy*, Miramax, 2004.

Mercedes, *The Last Hit*, Norstar Entertainment, 2005.

RECORDINGS

Videos:

Behind the House: Anatomy of the Zombie Movement, Artisan Entertainment, 2004.

Voices of Raene and Moiri, *Myst IV: Revelation* (video game), Ubi Soft Entertainment, 2004.

OTHER SOURCES

Periodicals:

FilmForce IGN, October 7, 2003, p. 1.

TV Zone, November, 2000, pp. 48–52.

COVE, Martin
See KOVE, Martin

CURTIS, Cliff 1968–
(Clifford Curtis)

PERSONAL

Born July 27, 1968, in Rotorua, Aotearoa, New Zealand. *Education:* Studied acting at the New Zealand Drama School and Teatro Dmitri Scoula in Switzerland.

Addresses: *Agent*—Abrams Artists & Associates, 9200 West Sunset Blvd., #1125, West Hollywood, CA, 10001.

Career: Actor.

Awards, Honors: Film Award, best supporting actor, New Zealand Film and TV Awards, 1993, for *Desperate Remedies;* Film Award nomination, New Zealand Film and TV Awards, for *Once Were Warriors;* Film Award, best actor, New Zealand Film and TV Awards, 2000, for *Jubilee;* Film Award, best supporting actor, New Zealand Film and TV Awards, 2003, for *Whale Rider.*

CREDITS

Film Appearances:
Fraser, *Desperate Remedies,* Miramax, 1993.
Mana, *The Piano* (also known as *La lecon de piano*), Miramax, 1993.
Bully, *Once Were Warriors,* Fine Line, 1994.
Short Ears, *Rapa Nui,* Warner Bros., 1994.
Kahu & Maia, 1994.
Mananui, 1996.
Zeke, *Chicken,* 1996.
Mamooli, *Deep Rising* (also known as *The Greed*), Buena Vista, 1998.
Kip, *Six Days, Seven Nights* (also known as *6 Days 7 Nights*), Buena Vista, 1998.
Hiko, *Virus,* 1999.
Amir Abdulah, *Three Kings,* Warner Bros., 1999.
Cy Coates, *Bringing out the Dead,* 1999.
Virus: Ghost in the Machine (documentary short film), 1999.
(As Clifford Curtis) Sheikh Fadlallah, *The Insider,* Buena Vista, 1999.
Billy Williams, *Jubilee,* South Pacific, 2000.
On the Set of Three Kings (documentary), 2000.
Billy Williams, *The Making of "Jubilee"* (documentary), 2000.
Pablo Escobar, *Blow,* New Line Cinema, 2001.
Smiley, *Training Day,* Warner Bros., 2001.
The evil but handsome prince Khalid, *The Majestic,* Warner Bros., 2001.

Claudio Perrini, *Collateral Damage,* Warner Bros., 2002.
Porourangi, *Whale Rider* (also known as *Te kaike tohora*), RCV, 2002.
Frank Herrera, *Runaway Jury,* Twentieth Century–Fox, 2003.
Inspector Franklin, *Fracture,* Polyphony, 2004.
Mort Whitman, *Spooked,* Arkles, 2004.
Pizza delivery man, *Heinous Crime* (short film), 2004.
River Queen, Endgame, 2005.
The Fountain, Warner Bros., 2005.

Television Appearances; Movies:
Nessus, *Hercules in the Underworld,* syndicated, 1994.
Father Tahere, *The Chosen,* 1998.
Mike Camello, *Point of Origin* (also known as *In the Heat of Fire*), HBO, 2002.

Television Appearances; Specials:
The Making of "Whale Rider" (documentary), 2003.

Television Appearances; Episodic:
Nemis, "As Darkness Falls," *Hercules: The Legendary Journeys,* 1995.
Daniel Freeman, *City Life,* 1996.

Television Appearances; Miniseries:
Adam Kadyrov, *Traffic* (also known as *Traffic: The Miniseries*), USA Network, 2004.

CURTIS, Simon 1960–

PERSONAL

Born March 11, 1960, in London, England; married Elizabeth McGovern, December 12, 1992; children: two.

Addresses: *Agent*—International Creative Management, 40 West 57th St., New York, NY 10019.

Career: Producer and director.

Awards, Honors: TV Award nomination (with others), best single drama, British Academy of Film and Television Arts, 1992, for *The Trials of Oz;* TV Award nomination (with others), best single drama, British Academy of Film and Television Arts, 1993, for *A Doll's House.*

CREDITS

Film Executive Producer:
Edward II, Fine Line, 1991.

Twelfth Night: Or What You Will (also known as *Twelfth Night*), 1996.
The Designated Mourner, 1997.
Mrs. Dalloway (also known as *Virginia Woolf's "Mrs. Dalloway"*), First Look Pictures Releasing, 1997.
Via Dolorosa, 1999.

Television Producer; Movies:
The Trials of Oz, 1991.
Absolute Hell, BBC, 1991.
Old Times, BBC2, 1991, then Bravo, 1993.
Tales from Hollywood, PBS and BBC, 1992.
The Deep Blue Sea, 1994.
The Changeling, Bravo, 1994.
The Colour of Justice, 1999.

Television Executive Producer; Movies:
Killing Me Softly, 1995.
After Miss Julie (also known as *Performance: After Miss Julie*), BBC2, 1995.
The Tribe, BBC, 1998.
The American, PBS, 2001.
Carrie's War, BBC, 2004.
Pride, Arts and Entertainment, 2004.

Television Director; Movies:
Old Times, BBC2, 1991, then Bravo, 1993.
The Changeling, Bravo and BBC, 1994.
The Student Prince (also known as *The Prince of Hearts*), BBC and PBS, 1997.
My Summer with Des, BBC, 1998.
Man and Boy, 2002.
The American Woman, BBC, 2005.
Twenty Thousand Streets under the Sky, BBC and BBC America, 2005.

Television Director; Specials:
Nona, BBC, 1991.
The Mother (also known as *Great Performances: The Mother* and *Paddy Chayefsky's "The Mother"*), PBS and BBC, 1994.
"Royalty," The Best of Tracey Takes On..., 1996.

Television Producer; Specials:
Uncle Vanya, PBS and BBC, 1991.
A Doll's House, PBS and BBC, 1992.
Top Girls, BBC and Arts and Entertainment, 1992.
The Maitlands (also known as *Playhouse: The Maitlands*), PBS and BBC, 1993.
Hedda Gabler, PBS and BBC, 1993.
Suddenly, Last Summer, PBS and BBC, 1993.
Message for Posterity (also known as *Performance: Message for Posterity*), BBC2, 1994.
Shadow of a Gunman (also known as *Performance: Shadow of a Gunman*), BBC, 1995.

Television Executive Producer; Specials:
Broken Glass, PBS and BBC, 1996.
King Lear, PBS and BBC2, 1998.
Shooting the Past, BBC, 1999.
Justifying War: Scenes From the Hutton Enquiry, BBC4, 2004.

Television Director; Miniseries:
David Copperfield, BBC, 1999, then PBS, 2000.
The Sins, BBC America, 2000.

Television Appearances; Episodic:
Breakfast, BBC, 2005.

D

DANIELS, Jake
    See **MARTIN, Dan**

DAVID, Keith 1956(?)–

PERSONAL

Full name, Keith David Williams; born June 4, 1956 (some sources say May 8, 1954), in New York, NY; son of Lester and Delores (maiden name, Dickenson) Williams; married Margit Edwards, September 22, 1990 (divorced). *Education:* High School of Performing Arts, graduated, 1973; Juilliard School, B.F.A., 1979; studied acting at the Edith Skinner Institute and with the La Mama Repertory Company.

Addresses: Agent—Abrams Artists Agency, 9200 Sunset Blvd., 11th Floor, Los Angeles, CA 90069; Innovative Artists, 1505 10th St., Santa Monica, CA 90401. *Manager*—Sneak Preview Entertainment, 6705 Sunset Blvd., 2nd Floor, Hollywood, CA 90028.

Career: Actor and producer. Skinner Institute for Speech, certified instructor, 1982–?; Roar of the Lion, Inc., Los Angeles, CA, president, 1990–?; appeared in television commercials for Wisk Laundry Detergent, 2001, Chevrolet, 2001, U.S. Navy, 2001, UPS, 2002, AT&T, 2002, X–box, 2002—, BMW, 2003, and U.S. Navy Recruiting, 2003–04; provides voice for many commercials for TNT and TBS.

Member: Screen Actors Guild, Actors' Equity Association, American Federation of Television and Radio Artists.

Awards, Honors: Image Award nomination, National Association for the Advancement of Colored People (NAACP), 1982, for *The Thing;* Sinclair Bayfield Award, Actors' Equity Association, best Shakespearean performance, 1989, for *Coriolanus;* Antoinette Perry Award nomination, best supporting actor in a musical, 1992, for *Jelly's Last Jam;* NAACP Theatre Award, best actor, 1996, for *Seven Guitars;* Daytime Emmy Award nomination, outstanding performer in a children's special, 1999, for *The Tiger Woods Story;* Emmy Award nomination (with others), outstanding nonfiction series, 2001, for *Jazz.*

CREDITS

Film Appearances:
(Uncredited) Club patron, *Disco Godfather* (also known as *Avenging Disco Godfather* and *Avenging Godfather*), Active Home Video, 1979.
Childs, *The Thing* (also known as *John Carpenter's "The Thing"*), Universal, 1982.
King, *Platoon,* Orion, 1986.
Alphonso, *Hot Pursuit* (also known as *Perscucion intensa*), Paramount, 1987.
Buster Franklin, *Bird,* Warner Bros., 1988.
Frank, *They Live* (also known as *John Carpenter's "They Live"* and *They Live!*), Universal, 1988.
Embassy gate captain, *Braddock: Missing in Action III* (also known as *Braddock: An American M.I.A., Missing in Action III* and *Braddock: Missing in Action*), Cannon Releasing, 1988.
Maurice, *Off Limits* (also known as *Saigon*), Twentieth Century–Fox, 1988.
Teagarden, *Stars and Bars,* Columbia, 1988.
Ernie Bass, *Road House,* Metro–Goldwyn–Mayer/ United Artists, 1989.
Powerhouse, *Always,* Universal, 1990.
Will, *Hallelujah Anyhow,* 1990.
Max, *Marked for Death* (also known as *Screwface*), Twentieth Century–Fox, 1990.
Louis Fedders, *Men at Work,* Triumph Releasing, 1990.
Loach, *The Two Jakes,* Paramount, 1990.
(English version) Voice of Mama, *Sazan aizu* (animated; also known as *3x3 Eyes* and *Sazan Eyes*), 1991.

Luther Jerome, *Article 99,* Orion, 1992.

Detective Huggins, *Final Analysis,* Warner Bros., 1992.

Tommy Lang, *Caged Fear,* New Line Home Video, 1992.

Harry Young, *Desperate Motive* (also known as *Distant Cousins*), New Line Cinema, 1993.

Roger, *Reality Bites,* Universal, 1994.

Alex Holland, *Robert A. Heinlein's "The Puppet Masters"* (also known as *The Puppet Masters*), Buena Vista, 1994.

Bone Babancourt, *Temptation,* Live Home Video, 1994.

Mace, *Raw Justice,* Republic Pictures, 1994.

Jack Parkman, *Major League II,* Warner Bros., 1994.

Voice of Goliath, *Gargoyles: The Heroes Awaken* (animated), Buena Vista, 1994.

Kansas, *Notes in a Minor Key* (short film), Buena Vista, 1994.

Sergeant Cantrell, *The Quick and the Dead,* TriStar, 1995.

Kirby, *Dead Presidents,* Buena Vista, 1995.

Jackie, *Blue in the Face* (also known as *Brooklyn Boogie*), Miramax, 1995.

Andre the Giant, *Clockers,* Universal, 1995.

Voice of narrator, *Yellowstone: Realm of the Coyote* (documentary), 1995.

Stylist #1, *Loose Women,* 1996.

The priest, *The Grave,* New City Releasing, 1996.

Martin, *An Eye for an Eye,* Paramount, 1996.

Hurst, *Larger than Life,* Metro–Goldwyn–Mayer/United Artists, 1996.

Larry, *Never Met Picasso,* Turbulent Arts, 1996.

Homeless John, *Johns,* First Look Pictures Releasing, 1996.

Leo Richards, gang leader, *Flipping,* Dove International, 1997.

Police Lieutenant Ed Fox, *Volcano,* Twentieth Century–Fox, 1997.

Voice of Apollo the Sun God, *Hercules* (animated), Buena Vista, 1997.

(English version) Voice of Okkoto, *Mononoke–hime* (animated; also known as *Princess Mononoke*), Miramax, 1997.

Lamar, *Executive Target,* New City Releasing, 1997.

Voice of Goliath, *Gargoyles: The Hunted* (animated), 1998.

Voice of Goliath, *Gargoyles: The Force of Goliath* (animated), 1998.

Voice of Goliath, *Gargoyles: Deeds of Deception* (animated), 1998.

Voice of Goliath, *Gargoyles: Brothers Betrayed* (animated), 1998.

Lieutenant General Kimsey, *Armageddon,* Buena Vista, 1998.

Charlie Jensen, *There's Something about Mary* (also known as *There's Something More about Mary*), Twentieth Century–Fox, 1998.

Detective Davis, *Dark Summer* (also known as *Innocents*), Deal, 1999.

Voice of Spawn, *Spawn 3: Ultimate Battle* (animated), 1999.

Abu "Imam" al–Walid, *Pitch Black* (also known as *The Chronicles of Riddick: Pitch Black*), USA Films, 2000.

Moses Whitecotten, *Where the Heart Is,* Twentieth Century–Fox, 2000.

Big Tim, *Requiem for a Dream* (also known as *Delusion Over Addiction*), Artisan Entertainment, 2000.

Lindell, *The Replacements,* Warner Bros., 2000.

The king, *G Spots?* (short film), 2001.

Voice of council member #1, *Final Fantasy: The Spirits Within* (animated; also known as *Fainaru fantaji*), Columbia, 2001.

Matador, *Home Invaders,* Castle Hill, 2001.

Detective Lunt, *Novocaine,* Artisan Entertainment, 2001.

Mervin, *Hung–Up* (short film), 2002.

The sheriff, *29 Palms,* Artisan Entertainment, 2002.

Lester Wallace, *Barbershop,* Metro–Goldwyn–Mayer, 2002.

CIA director, *Agent Cody Banks* (also known as *L'agent Cody Banks*), Metro–Goldwyn–Mayer, 2003.

Bernard Cooper, *Head of State,* DreamWorks Distribution, 2003.

(English version) Voice of Preast, *Kaena: La prophetie* (animated; also known as *Kaena: The Prophecy*), Samuel Goldwyn Films, 2003.

Leon, *Hollywood Homicide,* Columbia, 2003.

CIA director, *Agent Cody Banks 2: Destination London,* Metro–Goldwyn–Mayer, 2004.

Abu "Imam" al–Walid, *The Chronicles of Riddick* (also known as *The Chronicles of Riddick: The Director's Cut*), Universal, 2004.

Voice of Abu "Imam" al–Walid, *The Chronicles of Riddick: Dark Fury* (animated short film), Universal Home Video, 2004.

Narrator, *Creature Feature: 50 Years of the Gill–Man* (documentary), 2004.

Narrator, *Beef 2,* 2004.

Lieutenant Dixon, *Crash,* Lions Gate Films, 2004.

Father, *Mr. & Mrs. Smith,* Twentieth Century–Fox, 2005.

The Transporter 2, Twentieth Century–Fox, 2005.

Coach, *The OH in Ohio,* 2005.

Spain, *Dirty,* 2005.

Minister, *The Sensei,* 2005.

Black Theater Today: 2005 (documentary), 2005.

Film Producer:

Creature Feature: 50 Years of the Gill–Man (documentary), 2004.

Television Appearances; Series:

Keith the Southwood carpenter, *Mister Rogers' Neighborhood,* PBS, 1983–85.

Voice of Minos, *Aladdin* (animated; also known as *Disney's "Aladdin"*), CBS, 1994.

Voices of Goliath, Officer Morgan, and Thailog, *Gargoyles* (animated), syndicated, 1994.

Voice of Goliath, *Gargoyles: The Goliath Chronicles* (animated), ABC, 1996.

Voice of Spawn, *Spawn* (animated; also known as *Todd McFarlane's "Spawn"*), HBO, 1997.

Voice of Mufasa, *House of Mouse* (animated), ABC, 2001.

Lieutenant Williams, *The Job,* ABC, 2001.

Voice, *PBS Hollywood Presents,* PBS, 2001.

Announcer, *In the Jury Room,* ABC, 2004.

Clarence, *The Big House,* ABC, 2004.

Narrator, *City Confidential,* Arts and Entertainment, 2004—.

Judge, *Ultimate Film Fanatic,* Independent Film Channel, 2005.

Television Appearances; Miniseries:
Roots: The Next Generations, ABC, 1979.

Voice, *Not for Ourselves Alone: The Story of Elizabeth Cady Stanton & Susan B. Anthony* (documentary), PBS, 1999.

Voice, *New York: A Documentary Film* (documentary; also known as *American Experience: New York—A Documentary Film*), PBS, 1999.

Narrator, *Jazz* (documentary), PBS, 2001.

Himself, *I Love the '90s* (documentary), VH1, 2004.

Television Appearances; Movies:
Chorus, *The Pirates of Penzance,* 1980.

Abe Nicholson, *Ladykillers,* ABC, 1988.

Martin Stover, *Murder in Black and White* (also known as *Janek: Cause of Death*), CBS, 1990.

Noah Owens, *Nails,* Showtime, 1992.

Lovecraft, *The Last Outlaw,* HBO, 1993.

John Paul Rivers, "There Are No Children Here," *ABC Theater,* ABC, 1993.

Warren Taft, *Vanishing Point,* Fox, 1997.

Algric Bartles, *Murder, She Wrote: South by Southwest,* CBS, 1997.

Herbet Muhammad, *Don King: Only in America,* HBO, 1997.

Earl Woods, *The Tiger Woods Story,* Showtime, 1998.

FBI Director Richard Long, *A.T.F.,* ABC, 1999.

Gunnery Sargent Brinkloff, *Semper Fi,* NBC, 2001.

Detective Charles Desett, *Pretty When You Cry,* HBO, 2001.

Also appeared in *Christmas in Tattertown.*

Television Appearances; Specials:
"Jammin': Jelly Roll Morton on Broadway," *Great Performances,* PBS, 1992.

Big Willie Thornton, "Hallelujah," *American Playhouse,* PBS, 1993.

Narrator, "Jewels of the Caribbean Sea," *National Geographic Specials,* PBS, 1994.

Narrator, "Lions of Darkness," *Into Africa* (documentary), TBS, 1994.

Narrator, *Wildlife Warriors* (documentary), NBC, 1996.

Narrator, *Discovery Channel Eco–Challenge* (documentary), The Discovery Channel, 1998.

Narrator, *Walking with Giants: The Grizzlies of Siberia* (documentary), PBS, 1999.

Voice, *Not For Ourselves Alone: The Story of Elizabeth Cady Stanton & Susan B. Anthony* (documentary), PBS, 1999.

Narrator, *Arnold Schwarzenegger: Hollywood Hero* (documentary), The Learning Channel, 1999.

Narrator, *Jackals of the African Crater* (documentary), PBS, 2000.

Narrator, *Silent Service* (documentary), History Channel, 2001.

Narrator, *Golden Seals of the Skeleton Closet* (documentary), PBS, 2001.

Narrator, *Boxing: In and Out of the Ring* (documentary), Arts and Entertainment, 2001.

Narrator, *Mark Twain* (documentary), PBS, 2001.

Narrator, *Mole People: Life in the World Below* (documentary), The Discovery Channel, 2002.

Narrator, *Egypt's Golden Empire* (documentary), PBS, 2002.

Narrator, *Comic Book Superheroes Unmasked* (documentary), History Channel, 2003.

Narrator, *Horatio's Drive: America's First Road Trip* (documentary), PBS, 2003.

Narrator, *Tomb Raider: Robbing the Dead* (documentary), History Channel, 2004.

Narrator, *Unforgivable Blackness: The Rise and Fall of Jack Johnson* (documentary), PBS, 2004.

Narrator, *The Last Stand of the Great Bear* (documentary), 2004.

Television Appearances; Pilots:
U.S. attorney, *The Adversaries,* NBC, 1998.

Miss Miami, NBC, 2002.

Dope, NBC, 2002.

Television Appearances; Episodic:
Roman Criston, "Sea of Fire," *The Equalizer,* CBS, 1988.

Jesse Turner, "Vendetta," *A Man Called Hawk,* ABC, 1989.

King Oliver, "Young Indiana Jones and the Mystery of the Blues," *The Young Indiana Jones Chronicles,* ABC, 1993.

Voice of himself, "Following the Drinking Gourd," *Rainbow Reading,* PBS, 1993.

Narrator, "Lions of Darkness," a segment of "Into Africa," *National Geographic Explorer,* TBS, 1994.

Voice of Black Panther and T'Challa, "Prey of the Black Panther," *The Fantastic Four* (animated), syndicated, 1995.

Reverend Harris, "A Time of Faith: Parts 1 & 2," *New York Undercover,* Fox, 1996.

Voice of Apollo, "Hercules and the Apollo Mission," *Hercules* (animated), syndicated, 1998.

Ian Merit, "Abandon," *The Outer Limits,* Showtime and syndicated, 2000.

Robertson, "Bronx Cheer," *Law & Order,* NBC, 2001.

Paradise, "I Know Why the Caged Rhino Sings," *Going to California,* Showtime, 2001.

Voice, "Tarzan and the Enemy Within," *The Legend of Tarzan* (animated), UPN and syndicated, 2001.

Voice, "Tarzan and the Caged Fury," *The Legend of Tarzan* (animated), UPN and syndicated, 2001.

Voice, "Tarzan and Tublat's Revenge," *The Legend of Tarzan* (animated), UPN and syndicated, 2001.

Himself, "Charlie Sheen," *Revealed with Jules Asner,* E! Entertainment Television, 2002.

Cecil Pickett, "Standards and Practices," *Arli$$,* HBO, 2002.

Matt Phelps, "Random Acts of Violence," *CSI: Crime Scene Investigation* (also known as *C.S.I.*), CBS, 2003.

Voice of Despero, "Hearts and Minds: Parts 1 & 2," *Justice League* (animated), Cartoon Network, 2003.

Voice of Atlas, "Only Human," *Teen Titans* (animated), Cartoon Network, 2004.

Himself, *The Wayne Brady Show,* syndicated, 2004.

Himself, *The Sharon Osbourne Show,* syndicated, 2004.

Voice of Guardian of the Trees, "The Quest," *Teen Titans* (animated), Cartoon Network, 2005.

Lloyd Mackie, "Winning a Battle, Losing the War," *Grey's Anatomy,* ABC, 2005.

Also appeared as Lou, "Honor," *Tribeca,* Fox; voice of Black Panther, *Marvel Action Hour: Iron Man* (animated); voice of Agent Mosely, *Spider–Man: The Animated Series* (animated).

Stage Appearances:

(Stage debut) Understudy for title role, *Othello,* New York Shakespeare Festival, Delacorte Theatre, New York City, 1979.

Coriolanus, New York Shakespeare Festival, Delacorte Theatre, 1979.

Mother Courage and Her Children, Center Stage, Baltimore, MD, 1979.

The Haggadah: A Passover Cantata, New York Shakespeare Festival, Public Theatre, New York City, 1980.

Pirate, policeman, and understudy for Pirate King, *The Pirates of Penzance,* Delacorte Theatre, 1980–81.

Pozzo, *Waiting for Godot,* Public Theatre, New York City, 1981.

Theseus and Oberon, *A Midsummer Night's Dream,* New York Shakespeare Festival, Public Theatre, 1981.

Mahalia, Hartman Theatre, Stamford, CT, 1981.

Alec Wilder: Clues to a Life, Vineyard Theatre, New York City, 1982.

Earl Dancer and narrator, *Miss Waters, to You,* AMAS Repertory Theatre, New York City, 1982.

The Fantasticks, Meadow Brook Theatre, Rochester, MI, 1983.

Macbeth, *The Threepenny Opera,* Alliance Theatre Company, Atlanta, GA, 1984.

Colline, *La Boheme,* New York Shakespeare Festival, Public Theatre, 1984.

A Map of the World, New York Shakespeare Festival, Public Theatre, 1985.

Blue Heaven, *Ceremonies in Dark Old Men,* Ford's Theatre, Washington, DC, then Negro Ensemble Company, New York City, both 1985.

Dr. Mo, *The Tale of Madame Zora,* Ensemble Studio Theatre, New York City, 1986.

Ben, *Africanis Instructus,* St. Clement's Church Theatre, New York City, 1986.

Shakespeare on Broadway for the Schools, New York Shakespeare Festival, Belasco Theatre, New York City, 1986.

Fragments of a Greek Trilogy, La Mama Experimental Theatre Club, New York City, 1987.

Tullus Aufidius, *Coriolanus,* New York Shakespeare Festival, Anspacher Theatre, Public Theatre, New York City, 1988.

Aaron, the Moor, *Titus Andronicus,* New York Shakespeare Festival, Delacorte Theatre, 1989.

Chimney man, *Jelly's Last Jam,* Center Theatre Group, Mark Taper Forum, Los Angeles Music Center, Los Angeles, 1990–91, then Virginia Theatre, New York City, 1992.

Morton, With Salt, Mark Taper Forum, Los Angeles Music Center, 1991.

Boesman, *Boesman and Lena,* Manhattan Theatre Club Stage I, New York City, 1992.

Judge Brack, *Hedda Gabler,* Roundabout Theatre, New York City, 1994.

Cole, Henry Fonda Theatre, Los Angeles, 1994.

Royd Barton, *Seven Guitars,* Walter Kerr Theatre, New York City, 1996.

Leontes, *The Winter's Tale,* Delacorte Theatre, 2000.

Macbeth, Scottsdale Center for the Arts, Scottsdale, AZ, 2000.

Kit Marlowe, Joseph Papp Public Theatre, New York City, 2000.

Title role, *Othello,* Joseph Papp Public Theatre, 2001.

Nativity: A Life Story, United Palace Theatre, New York City, 2002, 2003.

Master Harold ... and the boys, Skirball Cultural Center, Los Angeles, 2004.

Michael, *The Fourposter,* Contemporary Theatre Company, Wilmington, DE, 2005.

Desire Under the Elms, The Vineyard Theatre, New York City, 2005.

The Rage of Achilles, 92nd Street Y, New York City, 2005.

Also appeared *A Midsummer Night's Dream,* San Diego Repertory Theatre, San Diego, CA; and *The Lady from Dubuque.*

RECORDINGS

Taped Readings:
Along Came a Spider, 1993.

Video Games:
Voice of Decker, *Fallout: A Post–Nuclear Role–Playing Game* (also known as *Fallout*), Interplay Productions, 1997.
Voice of Vhailor, *Planescape: Torment,* 1999.
Voice of Lord Vekk, *Lords of Everquest,* Sony Online Entertainment, 2003.
Voice of Arbiter, *Halo 2,* 2004.

OTHER SOURCES

Books:
Contemporary Black Biography, Volume 27, Gale Group, 2001.

Periodicals:
Essence, May, 1992, p. 52.

DAVIS, Bill
See DAVIS, William B.

DAVIS, Bud
(Bud George Davis, George Bud Davis, Bud George)

PERSONAL

Career: Stunt coordinator and actor. Worked as commercial stunt coordinator for Mattel Toys, Busch beer, and automotive manufacturers GMAC, Ford, and Nissan. Stunt performer for numerous films; also works as second unit director, assistant director, second unit cinematographer, and special effects technician.

CREDITS

Film Stunt Coordinator:
Winterhawk, Howco International Pictures, 1975.
The Town that Dreaded Sundown, American International Pictures, 1976.
Grayeagle, 1977.
Superstition (also known as *The Witch*), Almi Pictures, 1982.
Miracles, Orion, 1984.

Wisdom, Twentieth Century–Fox, 1986.
Manhunter (also known as *Red Dragon: The Pursuit of Hannibal Lecter*), De Laurentiis Entertainment Group, 1986.
Black Moon Rising, New World, 1986.
King Kong Lives, De Laurentiis Entertainment Group, 1986.
Who's That Girl?, 1987.
(Uncredited) *Nowhere to Hide,* New Century Vista, 1987.
(Uncredited) *Malone,* Orion, 1987.
Child's Play, United Artists, 1988.
War Party, 1988.
(As Bud George Davis) *Men at Work,* Triumph Releasing, 1990.
Chattahoochee, Hemdale, 1990.
Navy SEALS, Orion, 1990.
(Uncredited) *Switch* (also known as *Blake Edwards' "Switch"*), Warner Bros., 1991.
(As George Bud Davis) *Deadlock* (also known as *Wedlock*), Media Home Entertainment, 1991.
HouseSitter, Universal, 1992.
Dark Horse, Live Entertainment, 1992.
Sliver (also known as *Sliver—Gier der augen*), Paramount, 1993.
So I Married an Axe Murderer, TriStar, 1993.
Wayne's World 2, Paramount, 1993.
The Temp, Paramount, 1993.
Forrest Gump, Paramount, 1994.
Wagons East, TriStar, 1994.
Star Trek: Generations (also known as *Star Trek 7*), Paramount, 1994.
(As George Bud Davis) *Clifford,* Orion, 1994.
Across the Moon, Hemdale, 1994.
Larger than Life, United Artists, 1996.
Thinner (also known as *Stephen King's "Thinner"*), Paramount, 1996.
Blood and Wine, Twentieth Century–Fox, 1997.
Austin Powers: International Man of Mystery, New Line Cinema, 1997.
Contact, Warner Bros., 1997.
Mad City, Warner Bros., 1997.
Letters from a Killer, 1998.
The Visitor, 1998.
Austin Powers: The Spy Who Shagged Me (also known as *Austin Powers 2: The Spy Who Shagged Me*), New Line Cinema, 1999.
Bowfinger, MCA/Universal, 1999.
Cast Away, Twentieth Century–Fox, 2000.
The Score, Paramount, 2001.
Just Visiting (also known as *Les visiteurs en Amerique*), Buena Vista, 2001.
Hart's War, Metro–Goldwyn–Mayer, 2002.
Unstoppable, Coast Productions, 2004.
D–War (also known as *Dragon Wars*), Younggu–Art Movies, 2005.

Film Appearances:
Chauffeur, *Dixie Dynamite,* Dimension Films, 1976.

The phantom killer, *The Town that Dreaded Sundown,* American International Pictures, 1976.

Hollywood stuntman, *Death Threat,* 1976.

Major Blackburn, *The Shadow of Chikara* (also known as *The Battle of Virgil Cane, The Curse of Demon Mountain, Demon Mountain, Diamons Mountain, Shadow Mountain, Thunder Mountain,* and *Wishbone Cutter*), New World, 1978.

Putzpuller official, *Jekyll and Hyde ... Together Again,* Paramount, 1982.

Voice of Dirge, *Transformers: The Movie* (also known as *Matrix Forever* and *Transformers*), De Laurentiis Entertainment Group, 1986.

Stan, *House of the Rising Sun,* 1987.

Cessna passenger, *War Party,* 1989.

Attendant, *Chattahoochee,* 1990.

Desperado leader, *Wagons East!,* TriStar, 1994.

Fuel truck driver, *Unstoppable,* 2004.

Television Stunt Coordinator; Series:

Fame, NBC, 1982.

Automan, ABC, 1983.

The Twilight Zone, CBS, 1985.

Aaron's Way, NBC, 1988.

DEA, Fox, 1990.

Strange Luck, Fox, 1995–96.

Television Stunt Coordinator; Miniseries:

Mr. Horn, CBS, 1979.

George Wallace, TNT, 1997.

Television Stunt Coordinator; Movies:

High Mountain Rangers, CBS, 1987.

L.A. Takedown (also known as *L.A. Crimewave* and *Made in L.A.*), NBC, 1989.

A Quiet Little Neighborhood, a Perfect Little Murder (also known as *Darling, Let's Kill the Neighbors, Honey, Let's Kill the Neighbors,* and *A Perfect Little Murder*), NBC, 1990.

In the Line of Duty: A Cop for the Killing (also known as *A Cop for the Killing* and *In the Line of Duty: Blood Brothers*), NBC, 1990.

The Stranger Within, CBS, 1990.

Writer's Block, USA Network, 1991.

(Uncredited) *Red Shoe Diaries* (also known as *Red Shoe Diaries the Movie* and *Wild Orchid III: Red Shoe Diaries*), Showtime, 1992.

T Bone N Weasel, TNT, 1992.

Against the Wall, HBO, 1994.

Andersonville, TNT, 1996.

Television Stunt Coordinator; Episodic:

"King of the Road," *Two-Fisted Tales,* Fox, 1991.

Television Stunt Coordinator; Other:

The Servants of Twilight (special; also known as *Dean R. Koontz's "The Servants of Twilight"*), CBS, 1991.

The Owl (pilot), CBS, 1991.

Path to War, 2002.

Television Appearances; Series:

Voices of Dirge, Metroplex, Predaking, and others, *Transformers* (also known as *Super God Robot Force, Transformer 2010, Transformers: Generation 1,* and *Tatakae! Cho robot seimeitai Transformer*), syndicated, 1984.

Television Appearances; Movies:

Rudy, *Nowhere to Hide* (also known as *Fatal Chase*), 1977.

Bud, *Against the Wall,* HBO, 1994.

Delaney, *Andersonville,* TNT, 1996.

Television Appearances; Episodic:

(As Bud George) Dickie Vardeman, "The Search," *Cimarron Strip,* 1967.

Vic, "Head over Heels," *CHiPs,* 1982.

Sieger, "Staying Alive While Running a High Flashdance Fever," *Automan,* 1983.

Voice, "The Birth of the Constitution," *This Is America, Charlie Brown,* 1988.

Assassin, "Sins of the Father," *Star Trek: The Next Generation,* 1990.

RECORDINGS

Videos:

Worked as a stunt coordinator for music videos by De-Barge, Meat Loaf, Ray Parker, Jr., Ratt, and Twisted Star.

DAVIS, Matthew 1978–
(Matt Davis)

PERSONAL

Born May 8, 1978, in Salt Lake City, UT. *Education:* Attended the University of Utah; studied acting at the American Academy of Dramatic Arts.

Addresses: *Agent*—International Creative Management, 8942 Wilshire Blvd., Beverly Hills, CA 90211. *Manager*—Barnes, Morris, Klein, Mark, Yorn & Levine, 1424 Second Street, 3rd Floor, Santa Monica, CA 90401; McKeon–Valeo–Myones Management, 9150 Wilshire Blvd., Suite 102, Beverly Hills, CA 90212. *Publicist*—Platform Public Relations, 2666 N. Beachwood Dr., Los Angeles, CA 90068.

Career: Actor. Previously worked as a pizza delivery person.

CREDITS

Film Appearances:

Private Jim Paxton, *Tigerland,* Twentieth Century–Fox, 2000.

Travis/Trevor, *Urban Legends: Final Cut* (also known as *Legendes urbaines 2, Legendes urbaines: La suite,* and *Leyendas urbanas: Corte final*), Columbia, 2000.

(As Matt Davis) Joe, *Pearl Harbor* (also known as *Pearl Harbour*), Buena Vista, 2001.

Warner Huntington III, *Legally Blonde,* Metro–Goldwyn–Mayer, 2001.

Matt Tollman, *Blue Crush,* Universal, 2002.

(As Matt Davis) Ensign Douglas O'dell, *Below,* Miramax, 2002.

Donald, *Seeing Other People,* Lantern Lane, 2004.

(As Matt Davis) Harrison French, *Shadow of Fear,* Nu Image, 2004.

(As Matt Davis) Mark, *Heights,* Sony Pictures Classics, 2005.

Sean, *Into the Sun,* Screen Gems, 2005.

Sebastian, *Bloodrayne,* Fantastic Films International, 2005.

Television Appearances; Movies:

Jimbo, *Lone Star State of Mind* (also known as *Coyboys and Idiots* and *Road to Hell*), Starz!, 2002.

Television Appearances; Specials:

Interviewee, *Sizzlin' Sixteen 2001,* E! Network, 2001.

Television Appearances; Pilots:

Adam, *What about Brian?,* ABC, 2005.

DAVIS, William B. 1938–
(Bill Davis, William Davis)

PERSONAL

Full name, William Bruce Davis; born January, 1938, in Toronto, Ontario, Canada; father, an attorney; mother, a psychologist; married (divorced); children: two. *Education:* University of Toronto, B.A., philosophy, 1959; attended the London Academy of Music and Dramatic Art. *Avocational Interests:* Waterskiing, downhill skiing.

Addresses: *Agent*—c/o 100 West Pender, 9th Floor, Vancouver, British Columbia V6B 1R8, Canada.

Career: Actor and writer. William Davis Centre for Actors' Study, Vancouver, British Columbia, Canada, owner, director, and teacher; member of the National

Theatre, London, England, 1965–66; former artistic director of the National Theatre School of Canada, English acting program. A Canadian national water–skiing champion; Canadian Cancer Society, spokesperson.

Awards, Honors: Screen Actors Guild Award nominations (with others), outstanding performance by an ensemble, 1997, 1998 and 1999, for *The X–Files;* Best Actor Award, Nickel Independent Film and Video Festival, 2002, for *Polished.*

CREDITS

Television Appearances; Series:

CGB Spender (also known as cigarette smoking man, smoking man, and cancer man), a recurring role, *The X–Files,* Fox, 1994–2000, 2002.

Dr. Edward A. Esseff, *Body & Soul,* PAX, 2002.

Godfrey Shepcote, *The Murdoch Mysteries,* 2004.

Dr. Carlisle Wainwright, *Robson Arms,* CTV, 2005.

Television Appearances; Miniseries:

Mr. Gedreau, *Stephen King's "It"* (also known as *It*), ABC, 1990.

Dean Swinton, *Kingdom Hospital* (also known as *Stephen King's "Kingdom Hospital"*), ABC, 2004.

Television Appearances; Movies:

Ted, *The Cuckoo Bird,* CBC, 1985.

Lawyer, *Deadly Deception,* CBS, 1987.

(As Bill Davis) Dr. Sam Easton, *The Little Match Girl,* NBC, 1987.

Heath Harris, *Matinee* (also known as *Midnight Matinee*), 1988.

Dr. Reynolds, *Anything to Survive,* ABC, 1990.

(Uncredited) Lawyer, *Omen IV: The Awakening,* Fox, 1991.

Marvin Parkins, *Diagnosis Murder* (also known as *A Diagnosis of Murder*), CBS, 1992.

Vern, *Heart of a Child,* NBC, 1994.

Huddleston, *Don't Talk to Strangers* (also known as *Dangerous Pursuit*), USA Network, 1994.

Captain Dick Roth, *Beyond Suspicion,* 1994.

Gene Reuschel, *Circumstances Unknown,* USA Network, 1995.

Group leader, *Dangerous Intentions,* CBS, 1995.

Dr. Alexander, *When the Vows Break* (also known as *Courting Justice*), Lifetime, 1995.

Teacher, *The Limbic Region,* Showtime, 1996.

Dr. Norman Ellis, *Voyage of Terror* (also known as *The Fourth Horseman*), The Family Channel, 1998.

Detective Inspector, *Murder Most Likely,* CTV, 1999, then TNT, 2000.

Ed, *Killing Moon,* 2000.

Dr. Hardwin, *Becoming Dick,* E! Entertainment Television, 2000.

Dr. Sam Verbush, *Damaged Care,* Showtime, 2002.

Father Michael, *Saint Sinner* (also known as *Clive Barker's "Saint Sinner"*), Sci–Fi Channel, 2002.

100 Days in the Jungle, 2002.

Tyson's boss, *Word of Honor,* TNT, 2003.

District Attorney Alex Myerson, *The Cradle Will Fall,* PAX and CanWest, 2004.

Television Appearances; Specials:

Inside the X–Files, Fox, 1998.

Cigarette smoking man, *The X–Files Movies Special* (documentary), Fox, 1998.

Host, *Smoking: Why Can't I Quit?,* CanWest, 2000.

Television Appearances; Episodic:

Man on the phone, "Half Wits/Save the World Parade," *SCTV Channel,* 1984.

Dave Douglas, "Trial Balloon," *The Beachcombers,* CBC, 1986.

High school teacher, "Mean Streets and Pastel Houses," *21 Jump Street,* Fox, 1987.

F.I.R.M. official, "Stavograd: Parts 1 & 2," *Airwolf,* CBS, 1987.

"Rogue Warrior," *Airwolf,* CBS, 1987.

"The Key," *Airwolf,* CBS, 1987.

Arvin, "Judgment," *Captain Power and the Soldiers of the Future,* 1988.

Curant, "The Merchant of Death," *Wiseguy,* CBS, 1988.

Mr. Wickenton, "Champagne High," *21 Jump Street,* Fox, 1988.

Inspector #2, "People Do It All the Time," *Wiseguy,* CBS, 1989.

Judge, "Crossfire," *21 Jump Street,* Fox, 1991.

Judge, "Trail of Tears," *MacGyver,* ABC, 1991.

(As William Davis) Badgely, "Homecoming," *Street Justice,* syndicated, 1992.

Doctor, "Sanctuary for a Child," *Nightmare Cafe,* NBC, 1992.

Inspector Neilsen, "Out of the Blue," *North of 60,* CBC, 1993.

Ed, "The Conversion," *The Outer Limits,* Showtime and syndicated, 1995.

Professor Myman, "Eggheads," *Sliders,* Fox, 1995.

John Wymer, "Out of Body," *The Outer Limits,* Showtime and syndicated, 1996.

Dr. Bill Nigel, "Do Not Go Gently," *Poltergeist: The Legacy,* Showtime and syndicated, 1996.

Sir Arthur Conan Doyle, "The Truth Is in Here," *Mentors,* 1999.

"Checkmate," *First Wave,* Sci–Fi Channel, 2001.

Dr. Biemler, "World's Within," *The Outer Limits,* Showtime and syndicated, 2001.

Head priest, "The Oracle," *MythQuest,* PBS and CBC, 2001.

Professor Logitch, "Pitiless as the Sun," *Andromeda,* syndicated, 2001.

Mayor Tate, "Ryan," *Smallville,* The WB, 2002.

Tate, "Relic," *Smallville,* The WB, 2003.

Tilt, ESPN, 2005.

Television Appearances; Pilots:

CGB Spender (also known as cigarette smoking man, smoking man, and cancer man), *The X–Files,* Fox, 1993.

Film Appearances:

(As William Davis) Ambulance driver, *Dead Zone,* Paramount, 1983.

(As William Davis) University dean, *Head Office,* TriStar, 1986.

Drug doctor, *Look Who's Talking* (also known as *Daddy's Home*), TriStar, 1989.

Doctor Atkins, *The Hitman,* Cannon, 1991.

Cigarette smoking man, *The X–Files: The Unopened File,* 1996.

Dr. Smoot, *Unforgettable,* Metro–Goldwyn–Mayer/ United Artists, 1996.

Mr. Drazien, *The Last Tzaddik,* 1998.

Henderson, *Perpetrators of the Crime,* 1998.

Cigarette smoking man, *The X–Files* (also known as *Aux frontieres du reel*), 1998.

Voice of Palmer, *Broken Saints,* Budget Monks, 2001.

Agent Frank Gruning, *The Proposal,* Buena Vista Home Video, 2001.

Russell, *Out of Line,* First Look, 2001.

Dr. Parish, *Mindstorm* (also known as *Le projet Mindstorm*), ImageWorks, 2001.

Tye Crow, *Anthrax,* Eagle, 2001.

Philip, *Polished,* Veni Vidi Vici, 2002.

Deputy Director Edwards, *Aftermath,* Christal, 2002.

Old Soul, *Arbor Vitae,* Stage 18, 2003.

Doc Jenkins, *Snakehead Terror,* Cinetel, 2004.

Finance Minister, *Lyon King,* Phalanx, 2004.

Alphonse David, *Goose!,* Odeon, 2004.

The X–Files: The Making of "The Truth," 2004.

Max Rules, Jumpshot, 2005.

Stage Appearances:

Niels Bohr, *Copenhagen,* Montreal, Quebec, Canada, 2003.

Appeared as Wilson, *Back to Beulah;* Harry, *On the Job;* Jefry, *Two for the See Saw;* Puppet Master, *The Puppet Master;* George, *Chapter Two;* Tony Orr, *Emma Orr.*

RECORDINGS

Video Games:

Voice of cigarette smoking man, *The X–Files Game,* 1998.

(As William Davis) Voice of Colonel Whitely, *The Thing,* Universal Interactive, 2002.

Voice of cigarette smoking man, *The X–Files: Resist or Serve,* 2004.

WRITINGS

Television Episodes:
"En Ami," *The X–Files,* Fox, 2000.

OTHER SOURCES

Periodicals:
Entertainment Weekly, February 9, 1996, p. 22.
Maclean's, July 6, 1998, p. 54.
People Weekly, November 25, 1996, p. 67.
Saturday Night, May, 1998, p. 11.

DAWSON, Rosario 1979–

PERSONAL

Born May 9, 1979, in New York, NY; daughter of Isabel (a professional vocalist) Dawson; father, a construction worker.

Addresses: *Agent*—International Creative Management, 8942 Wilshire Blvd., Beverly Hill, CA 90211. *Lawyer*—Bloom Hergott Deimer Rosenthal La Violette, 150 South Rodeo Dr., 3rd Floor, Beverly Hills, CA 90212; Lichter, Grossman, Nichols, Adler & Goodman, 9200 Sunset Blvd., Suite 1200, Los Angeles, CA 90069. *Manager*—Untitled Entertainment, 331 North Maple Dr., 2nd Floor, Beverly Hills, CA 90210.

Career: Actress.

Awards, Honors: Black Reel Award nomination, theatrical—best actress, Image Award nomination, outstanding actress in a motion picture, National Association for the Advancement of Colored People, 2000, for *Light It Up;* Teen Choice Award nomination, choice breakout performance, 2001; Black Reel Award nomination, theatrical—best supporting actress, 2003, for *25th Hour;* Rising Star Award, American Black Film Festival, 2004.

CREDITS

Film Appearances:
Ruby, *Kids,* Lions Gate Films, 1995.
Girls Night Out, 1997.
Lala Bonilla, *He Got Game,* Buena Vista, 1998.
Marisol Hidalgo, *Side Streets,* Cargo, 1998.
Stephanie Williams, *Light It Up,* Twentieth Century–Fox, 1999.

Lana, *Down to You,* Miramax, 2000.
Valerie Brown, *Josie and the Pussycats,* MCA/Universal, 2001.
Maria Codesco, *Sidewalks of New York,* Buena Vista, 2001.
Dee, *Trigger Happy,* Independent, 2001.
Audrey, *Chelsea Walls* (also known as *Chelsea Hotel*), Lions Gate Films, 2001.
Veronica, *King of the Jungle,* Urbanworld, 2001.
Anna, *Love in the Time of Money,* ThinkFilm, 2002.
Grace Quinonez, *Ash Wednesday,* Good Machine International, 2002.
Alisa, *The First $20 Million Is Always the Hardest,* Twentieth Century–Fox, 2002.
Laura Vasquez, *Men in Black II* (also known as *MIB 2* and *MIIB*), Columbia, 2002.
Dina Lake, *The Adventures of Pluto Nash* (also known as *Pluto Nash*), Warner Bros., 2002.
Naturelle Riviera, *25th Hour,* Buena Vista, 2002.
Martine, *This Girl's Life,* New World, 2003.
Andy Fox, *Shattered Glass,* Lions Gate Films, 2003.
World VDAY (also known as *Until the Violence Stops*), Iron Films, 2003.
Spike Lee's '25th Hour': The Evolution of an American Filmmaker, Touchstone, 2003.
Mariana, *The Rundown* (also known as *Welcome to the Jungle*), Universal, 2003.
Roxane, *Alexander,* Warner Bros., 2004.
Tina Santiago, *This Revolution,* Artists/Media, 2005.
Gail, *Sin City* (also known as *Frank Miller's "Sin City"*), Miramax, 2005.
Debbie, *The Devil's Rejects,* Lions Gate Films, 2005.
Mimi Marquez, *Rent,* Sony, 2005.

Also appeared as Anna, *The End of Love.*

Television Appearances; Specials:
The Source Hip–Hop Music Awards, UPN, 1999.
The 31st Annual NAACP Image Awards, Fox, 2000.
Backstage Pass (also known as *The Making of "Josie and the Pussycats"*), 2001.
AFI's 100 Years ... 100 Passions, CBS, 2002.
The Second Annual Vibe Awards, UPN, 2004.
Presenter, *2004 IFP/Independent Spirit Awards,* Bravo, 2004.
Presenter, *The 11th Annual Screen Actors Guild Awards,* TNT, 2005.

Television Appearances; Episodic:
"Sidewalks of New York," *Anatomy of a Scene,* Sundance Channel, 2001.
The Tonight Show with Jay Leno, NBC, 2001, 2002, 2005.
The Late Late Show with Craig Kilborn, CBS, 2002.
Punk'd, MTV, 2003.
The Wayne Brady Show, syndicated, 2003.
Late Night with Conan O'Brien, NBC, 2003, 2004.

"Tournament 2, Game 1," *Celebrity Poker Showdown,* Bravo, 2004.
"Tournament 2 Championship," *Celebrity Poker Showdown,* Bravo, 2004.
"Alexander," *HBO First Look,* HBO, 2004.
Late Show with David Letterman, 2004.
The View, ABC, 2004.
Live with Regis and Kelly, syndicated, 2004, 2005.
The Tony Danza Show, NBC, 2004.

RECORDINGS

Songs; Contributor:
Provided spoken vocals on "Rosario," which appeared on *1999: The New Master* by Prince; provided voice work on "She Lives in My Lap," which appeared on *Speakerboxxx/The Love Below* by Outkast.

Music Videos:
Appeared in "Out of Control" by the Chemical Brothers; "Frontin'" by Pharrell Williams, 2003; "Miss You" by Aaliyah.

OTHER SOURCES

Periodicals:
Interview, November, 2004, p. 106.
Movieline's Hollywood Life, February, 2005, pp. 44–49, 92.

---

de LINT, Derek 1950–

PERSONAL

Original name, Dick Hein de Lint; born July 17, 1950, in The Hague, Netherlands; married Dorith Jesserun; children: Jerome, Mick, Oscar. *Education:* Went to art school in the Netherlands.

Addresses: *Contact*—Trilogy Entertainment, 2450 Broadway St., Suite 675, Santa Monica, CA 90404. *Manager*–FKA Atlas Entertainment, 6100 Wilshire Blvd., Suite 1170, Los Angeles, CA 90069.

Career: Actor and director. Nederlands Film Festival, 1985, member of jury; 1995 Flanders International Film Festival, Ghent, member of jury. Appeared in a television commercial for modus.de.

CREDITS

Film Appearances:
Propagandeman 1, *Barocco,* 1976.
Mark, *Blindgangers* (also known as *Blind Spot*), 1977.
Alex, *Soldaat van Oranje* (also known as *Soldier of Orange* and *Survival Run*), 1977.
Theo van Delft, *Dag Dokter* (also known as *Inheritance*), 1978.
Erik van Poelgeest, *Kort Amerikaans,* 1979.
De Grens, 1979.
Dat moet toch kunnen, 1979.
Crew Cut, 1980.
Lieutenant Steiner, *The Lucky Star* (also known as *La belle etoile*), 1980.
Vriend Marij, *Come–Back,* 1981.
Ritsaart, *Van de koele meren des doods* (also known as *Hedwig: The Quiet Lakes*), 1982.
Jack de Graaf, *Een zaak van leven of dood,* 1983.
Paul de Wit/Nathan Blum, *Bastille,* 1984.
Handsome traveler, *Mata Hari,* 1985.
Anton Steenwijk, *De Aanslag* (also known as *The Assault*), 1986.
Jan Clopatz, *Three Men and a Baby,* Buena Vista, 1987.
Chris Brine, *Mascara* (also known as *Make–up for Murder*), Warner Bros., 1987.
Philippe, *Dagboek van een oude dwaas* (also known as *Diary of a Mad Old Man*), 1987.
Franz, *The Unbearable Lightness of Being,* Orion, 1988.
Pierre Abelard, *Stealing Heaven,* 1988.
Inni Wintrop, *Rituelen* (also known as *Rituals*), 1988.
Bertrand de Roujay, *The Free Frenchman,* Central Films, 1989.
Peter, *Die Sonne ueber dem Dschungel,* 1992.
Peter Koudbier, *Angie,* 1993.
Alex Witsen, *Affair Play,* 1995.
Bob Hooke, Sara's father, *Lang leve de koningin* (also known as *Long Live the Queen*), 1995.
Bertus, *All Men Are Mortal,* 1995.
Theo Van Sertema, *Deep Impact,* Paramount, 1998.
The Artist's Circle (short film), AtomFilms, 2000.
Karl Jorgensen, *Soul Assassin,* Universal, 2001.
Alessandro Cenci, *Superstition,* Sunrise, 2001.
Mr. Bancroft, *Tom & Thomas,* Buena Vista International, 2002.
Vlad, *The Big Charade* (short film), 2003.

Television Appearances; Series:
Dolly Dots, 1983.
Karel, *Herenstraat 10,* 1983.
Eric Hoogland, *Dossier Verhulst,* 1986.
Dr. Bernard, *China Beach,* 1989–90.
Derek Rayne, *Poltergeist: The Legacy,* Showtime and syndicated, 1996–98, then Sci–Fi Channel, 1999.

Television Appearances; Movies:
Uit de wereld van Guy de Maupassant: De vlieg, 1978.
Rob, *Slippers,* 1985.
Abramov, *The Endless Game,* 1990.
Lothar de la Rey, *Mountain of Diamonds* (also known as *Burning Shore, Gluehender Himmel, La montagna dei diamanti,* and *La montagne de diamants*), 1991.

Jacob Razak, *Pointman,* syndicated, 1994.

Dr. Estes, *A Perry Mason Mystery: The Case of the Lethal Lifestyle,* NBC, 1994.

Dirk Petersen, *The Little Riders,* The Disney Channel, 1996.

Television Appearances; Miniseries:

Hendrik van Frankrijk, *Willem van Oranje,* 1983.

Dr. Thost, *The Great Escape II: The Untold Story,* 1988.

Gus Morgan, *Burning Bridges,* 1990.

Paul Rodier, *Judith Krantz's "Secrets"* (also known as *Secrets*), 1992.

Charles Deveraux, *Barbara Taylor Bradford's "Remember"* (also known as *Remember*), 1993.

Roberto Rannaldi, *The Man Who Made Husbands Jealous,* 1997.

Prime Minister Staal, *Mevrouw de Minister,* 2002.

Preacher Hobbes, *Into the West,* TNT, 2005.

Television Appearances; Episodic:

"A Liver Runs through It," *Civil Wars,* 1993.

Serge de Chanal, "Serge the Concierge," *NYPD Blue,* ABC, 1994.

Centurion, "Star Crossed," *The Outer Limits,* Showtime and syndicated, 1999.

Carl, "Breaking Point," *The Outer Limits,* Showtime and syndicated, 2000.

PRF leader Gerard Cuvee, "Passage: Part 2," *Alias,* ABC, 2002.

Head gray man, "Reunion," *Veritas: The Quest,* ABC, 2003.

Georges van Baaren, "De cock en de moord met een swing," *Baantjer,* 2003.

Dr. Stephen Bauer, "Left for Dead," *Navy NCIS: Naval Criminal Investigative Service* (also known as *NCIS*), CBS, 2004.

Manfredi Ferrer, "Lap Dance," *The L Word,* Showtime, 2005.

Television Director; Episodic:

"The Portents," *Poltergeist: The Legacy,* Showtime and syndicated, 1999.

Stage Appearances:

Appeared in *Rocky Horror Picture Show.*

DERN, Laura 1967–

PERSONAL

Full name, Laura Elizabeth Dern; born February 10, 1967, in Santa Monica, CA; daughter of Bruce Dern (an actor) and Diane Ladd (an actress); granddaughter of Mary Lanier (an actress); godchild of Shelley Winters (an actress); companion of Ben Harper (a musician); children: (with Harper) Ellery Walker, Jaya. *Education:* Attended University of Southern California and University of California, Los Angeles; studied acting at Lee Strasberg Theatre Institute, Royal Academy of Dramatic Art, and the Tracy Roberts Workshop; studied with Peggy Feury and Sandra Seacat; attended Harvard Workshop.

Addresses: *Agent*—Creative Artists Agency, 9830 Wilshire Blvd., Beverly Hills, CA 90212. *Manager*—Untitled Entertainment, 331 North Maple Dr., Second Floor, Beverly Hills, CA 90210. *Publicist*—Wolf/Kasteler/Van Iden and Associates Public Relations, 335 North Maple Dr., Suite 351, Beverly Hills, CA 90210. *Contact*—c/o 2401 Main St., Santa Monica, CA 90405.

Career: Actress, producer, and director.

Awards, Honors: Miss Golden Globe, 1982; New Generation Award, Los Angeles Film Critics Association, 1985, for *Smooth Talk* and *Mask;* Independent Spirit Award nomination, best female lead, Independent Features Project/West, 1986, for *Smooth Talk;* Independent Spirit Award nomination, best female lead, 1987, for *Blue Velvet;* Montreal World Festival Award, best actress, 1991, Academy Award nomination, best actress, and Golden Globe Award nomination, best performance by an actress in a motion picture—drama, both 1992, all for *Rambling Rose;* Emmy Award nomination, outstanding lead actress in a miniseries or a special, 1992, and Golden Globe Award, best performance by an actress in a miniseries or motion picture made for television, 1993, both for *Afterburn;* Emmy Award nomination, outstanding guest actress in a drama series, 1994, for *Fallen Angels;* Saturn Award nomination, best actress, Academy of Science Fiction, Fantasy & Horror Films, 1994, for *Jurassic Park;* Montreal World Festival Award, best actress, 1996, for *Citizen Ruth;* Emmy Award nomination, outstanding guest actress in a comedy series, 1997, for *Ellen;* Golden Satellite Award nomination, best performance by an actress in a miniseries or motion picture made for television, International Press Academy, 1997, for *The Siege at Ruby Ridge;* Golden Globe Award nomination, best performance by an actress in a miniseries or motion picture made for television, 1999, for *The Baby Dance;* Tribute to Independent Vision Award, Sundance Film Festival, 1999; Boston Society of Film Critics Award, best supporting actress, 2004, for *We Don't Live Here Anymore.*

CREDITS

Film Appearances:

(Uncredited) Sharon Anne (Maggie's daughter), *White Lightning* (also known as *McKlusky*), United Artists, 1973.

(Uncredited) Girl eating ice cream cone, *Alice Doesn't Live Here Anymore,* Warner Bros., 1975.

Debbie, *Foxes,* United Artists, 1980.

Jessica McNeil, *Ladies and Gentlemen: The Fabulous Stains* (also known as *All Washed Up*), Paramount, 1982.

Diane, *Teachers,* Metro–Goldwyn–Mayer/United Artists, 1984.

Connie, *Smooth Talk,* Spectrafilm, 1985.

Diana, *Mask* (also known as *Peter Bogdanovich's "Mask"*), Universal, 1985.

Sandy Williams, *Blue Velvet,* Di Laurentiis Entertainment Group, 1986.

Sister, Sister, New World Entertainment/Odyssey Entertainment, 1987.

Kathleen Robinson, *Fat Man and Little Boy* (also known as *Shadowmakers*), Paramount, 1988.

Claire Clairmont, *Haunted Summer,* 1988, Cannon, 1989.

Lula Pace Fortune, *Wild at Heart,* Samuel Goldwyn, 1990.

Rose, *Rambling Rose,* New Line Cinema, 1991.

Dr. Ellie Sattler, *Jurassic Park* (also known as *JP*), Universal, 1993.

(Uncredited) Herself, *The Last Party* (documentary), LIVE Entertainment, 1993.

Sally Gerber, *A Perfect World,* Warner Bros., 1993.

Ruth Stoops, *Citizen Ruth* (also known as *Meet Ruth Stoops*), Miramax, 1996.

Miss Freida Riley, *October Sky,* Universal, 1999.

Peggy, *Dr. T and the Women,* Artisan Entertainment, 2000.

Dr. Ellie Sattler, *Jurassic Park III* (also known as *JPIII*), MCA/Universal, 2001.

Gertrude "Gert" Hart, *Focus,* Paramount Classics, 2001.

Jean Noble, *Novocaine,* Artisan Entertainment, 2001.

Randy Carpenter, *I Am Sam,* New Line Cinema, 2001.

Ruby Montgomery, *Daddy and Them,* Miramax, 2001.

Herself, *Mysteries of Love* (documentary), Metro–Goldwyn–Mayer/United Artists Home Entertainment, 2002.

Herself, *Searching for Debra Winger* (documentary), Lions Gate Films, 2002.

Terry Linden, *We Don't Live Here Anymore,* Warner Bros., 2004.

Dortha Schaefer, *The Prize Winner of Defiance Ohio* (also known as *The Prize Winner of Defiance, Ohio: How My Mother Raised 10 Kids on 25 Words or Less*), DreamWorks, 2005.

Mother, *The Girl Who Loved Tom Gordon,* Lions Gate Films, 2005.

Pam, *Happy Endings,* Lions Gate Films, 2005.

Inland Empire, Studio Canal, 2005.

Rene, *Lonely Hearts,* Millennium Films/Emmett/Furla Films, 2006.

Television Appearances; Miniseries:

Vicki Weaver, *The Siege at Ruby Ridge* (also known as *Every Knee Shall Bow: The Siege at Ruby Ridge* and *Ruby Ridge: An American Tragedy*), CBS, 1996.

Television Appearances; Movies:

Audrey Constantine, *Happy Endings,* NBC, 1983.

Crissy, *The Three Wishes of Billy Grier,* 1984.

Rebecca, *The Strange Case of Dr. Jekyll and Mr. Hyde,* 1989.

Nightmare Classics, 1989.

Mrs. Harduvel, *Afterburn,* HBO, 1992.

Helen McNulty, *Down Came a Blackbird* (also known as *Ramirez*), Showtime, 1995.

Voice of adult Bone, *Bastard out of Carolina,* Showtime, 1996.

Wanda LeFauve, *The Baby Dance,* Showtime, 1998.

Sister Pauline Quinn, *Within These Walls,* Lifetime, 2001.

Linda Peeno, *Damaged Care,* Showtime, 2002.

Television Appearances; Specials:

Heartbroken woman, *Industrial Symphony No. 1: The Dream of the Broken Hearted,* 1990.

Herself, *Jonathon Ross Presents for One Week Only: David Lynch,* 1990.

Rock the Vote, Fox, 1992.

Voice of Amelia Earhart, *A Century of Women* (documentary; also known as *A Family of Women*), TBS, 1994.

AFI's 100 Years ... 100 Movies, CBS, 1998.

The Real Ellen Story, Bravo, 1998.

Warner Bros. Story: No Guts, No Glory: 75 Years of Laughter (documentary), TNT, 1998.

Warner Bros. Story: No Guts, No Glory: 75 Years of Stars (documentary), TNT, 1998.

Berry Thompson, "A Season for Miracles," *Hallmark Hall of Fame,* CBS, 1999.

Herself, *AFI's 100 Years ... 100 Stars,* CBS, 1999.

Fall In Love with a Stranger, PAX TV, 1999.

Equality Rocks, VH1, 2000.

Herself, *The Making of "Ladies and Gentlemen, the Fabulous Stains"* (documentary; also known as *"Ladies and Gentlemen, the Fabulous Stains": Behind the Movie*), Independent Film Channel, 2004.

Television Appearances; Awards Presentations:

(Uncredited) Presenter, *The 1987 IFP/West Independent Spirit Awards,* Independent Film Channel, 1987.

(Uncredited) Herself, *The 64th Annual Academy Awards,* ABC, 1992.

The 18th Annual People's Choice Awards, 1992.

Presenter, *The 66th Annual Academy Awards,* ABC, 1994.

The 51st Annual Golden Globe Awards, TBS, 1994.

Fourth Annual Environmental Media Awards, TBS, 1994.

The 66th Annual Academy Awards Presentation, ABC, 1994.

The American Film Institute Salute to Steven Spielberg (also known as *The 23rd American Film Institute Life Achievement Award: A Salute to Steven Spielberg*), NBC, 1995.

Family Film Awards, CBS, 1996.

The Blockbuster Entertainment Awards, UPN, 1997.

The 54th Annual Golden Globe Awards, NBC, 1997.

Herself, *The 71st Annual Academy Awards,* ABC, 1999.

Hollywood Salutes Jodie Foster: An American Cinematheque Tribute, TNT, 1999.

Presenter, *The 2004 IFP/West Independent Spirit Awards,* Independent Film Channel, 2004.

Television Appearances; Episodic:

The Secret Storm, CBS, c. 1972.

"Gotham Swansong," *Shannon,* CBS, 1981.

Rebecca Laymon, "The Strange Case of Dr. Jekyll and Mr. Hyde," *Nightmare Classics,* Showtime, 1989.

Narrator, "The Song of Sacajawea," *American Heroes & Legends* (animated), 1992.

Annie Ainsley, "Murder, Obliquely," *Fallen Angels* (also known as *Perfect Crimes* and *Sydney Pollack's "Fallen Angels"*), Showtime, 1993.

Herself, *The Late Show with David Letterman,* CBS, 1993, 1995, 1996.

(Uncredited) Herself, *Saturday Night Live* (also known as *NBC's Saturday Night, Saturday Night,* and *SNL*), NBC, 1993.

Storytime, PBS, 1994.

Guest caller June, "Sleeping with the Enemy," *Frasier,* NBC, 1995.

Herself, *The Rosie O'Donnell Show,* syndicated, 1996.

Herself, "Death," *Dennis Miller Live,* HBO, 1997.

Susan, "The Puppy Episode: Parts 1 & 2," *Ellen* (also known as *These Friends of Mine*), ABC, 1997.

Herself, "I Buried Sid," *The Larry Sanders,* HBO, 1998.

Herself, *The Martin Short Show,* syndicated, 1999.

Intimate Portrait: Kelly Preston (documentary), Lifetime, 1999.

Intimate Portrait: Laura Dern (documentary), Lifetime, 1999.

Intimate Portrait: Mary Steenburgen (documentary), Lifetime, 1999.

Herself, "Shelley Winters—Full Disclosure," *Biography* (also known as *A&E Biography: Shelley Winters—Full Disclosure*), Arts and Entertainment, 2001.

Voice of serving wench, "Joust Like a Woman," *King of the Hill* (animated), Fox, 2002.

United States Poet Laureate Tabatha Fortis, "The U.S. Poet Laureate," *The West Wing,* NBC, 2002.

Voice of Katherine, "Patch Boomhauer," *King of the Hill* (animated), Fox, 2003.

Herself, *Intimate Portrait: Rosanna Arquette* (documentary), Lifetime, 2003.

Herself, *Dinner for Five,* Independent Film Channel, 2004.

Herself, *Ellen: The Ellen DeGeneres Show* (also known as *Ellen* and *The Ellen DeGeneres Show*), syndicated, 2004.

Appeared in "The Films of Clint Eastwood," "The Films of David Lynch," and "The Films of Steven Spielberg," all episodes of *The Directors,* Encore.

Television Work:

Director, *The Gift* (short special), Showtime, 1994.

Executive producer, *Down Came a Blackbird* (movie; also known as *Ramirez*), Showtime, 1995.

Coproducer, *Damaged Care* (movie), Showtime, 2002.

Stage Appearances:

Charlene Loody, *The Palace of Amateurs,* Minetta Lane Theatre, New York City, 1988.

Brooklyn Laundry, 1988.

Appeared in *Hamlet* and *A Midsummer Night's Dream.*

RECORDINGS

Videos:

Herself, *Beyond Jurassic Park* (documentary), Universal Studios Home Video, 2001.

Herself, *Becoming Sam* (short documentary), New Line Home Video, 2002.

OTHER SOURCES

Books:

Newsmakers 1992, Issue Cumulation, Gale, 1992.

Periodicals:

American Film, October, 1989, p. 46; July, 1991.

Cosmopolitan, July, 1991.

Interview, March, 1986, p. 146; September, 1990, p. 118; August, 2004, pp. 52–54.

Mademoiselle, November, 1989.

Movieline's Hollywood Life, July, 2004, pp. 58–61, 92.

Newsweek, September 15, 1986; August 27, 1990; September 23, 1991.

New York, September 30, 1991.

New Yorker, September 22, 1986.

New York Times, May 4, 1986.

Now, August 19, 2004.

People Weekly, April 29, 1985, p. 107; September 22, 1986; March 19, 1990; August 27, 1990; October 8, 1990, p. 59; October 7, 1991; November 26, 2001, p. 186; February 4, 2002, pp. 103–107.

Premiere, September, 1990, p. 86; January, 1991.

Radio Times, March 30, 1996, pp. 16–18.

Rolling Stone, October 23, 1986; September 6, 1990; October 3, 1991; October 17, 1991.

Starlog, August, 1993.

Time, May 26, 1986; September 22, 1986; August 20, 1990; January 6, 1992.

DEVARONA, Joanna
    See KERNS, Joanna

DINKLAGE, Peter 1969–

PERSONAL

Born June 11, 1969, in Morristown, NJ; father, an insurance salesman; mother, a music teacher. *Education:* Bennington College, B.A. (Libby Zion Award for Dramatic Excellence), drama, 1991; studied at the Royal Academy of Dramatic Arts, London, and Welsh School of Music and Drama, Cardiff, Wales.

Addresses: *Manager*—Turnpike Entertainment, 422 Smithwood Dr., Suite B, Beverly Hills, CA 90212. *Agent*—SMS Talent Inc., 8730 W. Sunset Blvd., Suite 440, West Hollywood, CA 90069.

Career: Actor and writer.

Awards, Honors: Best Actor Award, Ourense Independent Film Festival, Online Film Critics Society Award nomination, best breakthrough performance, 2003, Independent Spirit Award nomination, best male lead, Chlotrudis Award nomination, best actor, Screen Actors Guild Award nominations, outstanding performance by a cast (with others) and outstanding performance by a male actor in a leading role, 2004, for *The Station Agent;* Special Achievement Award, outstanding talent, Golden Satellite Awards, 2004.

CREDITS

Film Appearances:
Tito, *Living in Oblivion,* Columbia TriStar, 1995.
(Uncredited) Building manager, *Bullet,* New Line Cinema, 1996.
Leflore, *Safe Men,* October, 1998.
Roy, *Pigeonholed,* Worldwide Entertainment, 1999.
Harry Appleton, *Never Again,* Dream Entertainment, 2001.
Frank, *Human Nature,* Fine Line, 2001.
Binky, *13 Moons,* Lot 47 Films, 2002.
Dink, *Just a Kiss,* Paramount Classics, 2002.
Mike Kirkwood, *Fortunes,* Golden Fried, 2002.
Finbar McBride, *The Station Agent,* Miramax, 2003.
Maurice, *Tiptoes* (also known as *Tiny Tiptoes*), Reality Check, 2003.
Miles Finch, *Elf,* New Line Cinema, 2003.
Lindo, *Jail Bait,* Red Mountain, 2004.
Sterno, *Surviving Eden,* Cineville Inc., 2004.
Benson, *The Baxter,* IFC Films, 2005.
Sam Norton, *Little Fugitive,* Ruby Slipper, 2005.
Ben Klandis, *Find Me Guilty,* Crossroads, 2005.

Television Appearances; Specials:
Presenter, *The 9th Annual Critics' Choice Awards,* E! Entertainment Television, 2004.
Presenter, *The 56th Annual Writers Guild Awards,* Starz!, 2004.
Presenter, *The 10th Annual Screen Actors Guild Awards,* TNT, 2004.
The 2004 IFP/West Independent Spirit Awards, 2004.

Television Appearances; Episodic:
Little person, "Junk Bonds," *The $treet,* Fox, 2000.
Drug dealer, "The Long Guns," *Third Watch,* NBC, 2002.
The Tonight Show with Jay Leno, NBC, 2003.
Elliot Rosen, "Not in My Dress You Won't," *I'm with Her,* ABC, 2004.
Elliot Rosen, "Winner & Losers & Whiners & Boozers: Part 1," *I'm with Her,* ABC, 2004.
Elliot Rosen, "Drama Queen," *I'm with Her,* ABC, 2004.
Dinner for Five, Independent Film Channel, 2004.
Dr. Belber, "A Little Problem," *Life As We Know It,* ABC, 2005.
Dr. Belber, "Breaking Away," *Life As We Know It,* ABC, 2005.

Television Appearances; Pilots:
Threshold, CBS, 2005.
Bob Hart, *Testing Bob,* ABC, 2005.

Stage Appearances:
Poona the Fuckdog and Other Stories for Children, Ohio Theater, New York City, 1999.
I Wanna Be Adored, Red Line Theatre, New York City, 2000.
Imperfect Love, Red Line Theatre, 2000.
Rex, *Evolution,* Bleecker Street Theatre, New York City, 2002.
Title role, *Richard III,* Joseph Papp Public Theater/ Martinson Hall, New York City, 2004.
Theater of the New Ear, Royal Festival Hall, London, 2005.

Also appeared in *Heartpiece, The Author's Voice, Landscape of the Body,* and *Video Priests,* all Bennington College, VT; as Tom Thumb, *The Killing Act,* off-Broadway production; in *Marking* and *A Doll's House,* both New York City productions; in *Hollywood, A Misty Christmas,* and *Saint Stanislaus Outside the House,* all off-Broadway productions.

WRITINGS

Plays:
Frog, produced 1990.

OTHER SOURCES

Periodicals:

Entertainment Weekly, August 22, 2003, p. 61; December 12, 2003, p. 34.

The Washington Post, October 18, 2003.

DOOLEY, Paul 1928–

PERSONAL

Original name, Paul Brown; born February 22, 1928, in Parkersburg, WV; son of Peter James (a factory worker) and Ruth Irene (a homemaker; maiden name, Barringer) Brown; married Donna Lee Wasser, September 19, 1958 (divorced); married Winifred Holzman (a writer and actress), November 18, 1984; children: (first marriage) Robin, Adam, Peter; (second marriage) Savannah. *Education:* West Virginia University, B.A., speech and drama, 1952.

Addresses: *Agent*—Agency for the Performing Arts, 9000 Sunset Blvd., Suite 1200, Los Angeles, CA 90069.

Career: Actor and writer. Worked as a magician and a clown; cartoonist for a newspaper in Parkersburg, WV; owner of All over Creation. *Military service:* U.S. Navy, 1946–48.

Member: Actors' Equity Association, Screen Actors Guild, American Federation of Television and Radio Artists.

Awards, Honors: National Board of Review Award and D. W. Griffith Award, both best supporting actor, 1979, for *Breaking Away;* Emmy Award nomination, outstanding guest actor in a comedy series, 1994, for *Dream On;* Emmy Award nomination, outstanding guest actor in a comedy series, 2000, for *The Practice.*

CREDITS

Film Appearances:

Ted K. Worrie, *The Parisienne and the Prudes,* 1964.

Television reporter, *What's So Bad about Feeling Good?,* Universal, 1968.

Day porter, *The Out of Towners,* Paramount, 1970.

Statue of Liberty guard, *Up the Sandbox,* National General, 1972.

Gravy Train, Columbia, 1974.

Death Wish, Paramount, 1974.

Salesman, *Fore Play* (also known as *Foreplay* and *The President's Women*), Cinema National, 1975.

Hyannisport announcer, *Slap Shot,* Universal, 1977.

Voice of Gazooks, *Raggedy Ann and Andy* (animated), Twentieth Century–Fox, 1977.

Snooks Brenner, *A Wedding,* Twentieth Century–Fox, 1978.

Alex Theodopoulos, *A Perfect Couple,* Twentieth Century–Fox, 1979.

Simon Peterfreund, *Rich Kids,* United Artists, 1979.

Ray Stohler, *Breaking Away* (also known as *Bambino*), Twentieth Century–Fox, 1979.

Wimpy, *Popeye,* Paramount, 1980.

Kurt, *Paternity,* Paramount, 1981.

Joe Hiatt, *Endangered Species,* Metro–Goldwyn–Mayer/United Artists, 1982.

Hugh Kendall, *Kiss Me Goodbye,* Twentieth Century–Fox, 1982.

Dr. Gil Gainey, *Health* (also known as *H.E.A.L.T.H.*), Twentieth Century–Fox, 1982.

Claude Elsinore, *Strange Brew* (also known as *The Adventures of Bob and Doug McKenzie*), Metro–Goldwyn–Mayer/United Artists, 1983.

Dr. Ted, *Going Berserk,* Universal, 1983.

Jim Baker, *Sixteen Candles,* Universal, 1984.

Noozel, *Big Trouble,* Columbia, 1986.

(Scenes deleted) Patrick Martin, *Little Shop of Horrors,* Universal, 1986.

Roy Crane, *Monster in the Closet,* Troma, 1987.

Father Freddie, *Last Rites,* Metro–Goldwyn–Mayer/United Artists, 1988.

Randall Schwab, *O. C. and Stiggs,* Metro–Goldwyn–Mayer, 1988.

FBI director Donald R. Stark, *Flashback,* Paramount, 1990.

Owen Chase, *Shakes the Clown,* IRS Releasing, 1992.

Himself, *The Player,* Fine Line, 1992.

Big Chuck, *My Boyfriend's Back* (also known as *Johnny Zombie*), Buena Vista, 1993.

Tupperware salesperson, *A Dangerous Woman,* Gramercy, 1993.

Peebo, *The Traveling Poet* (short film), Elliottland Productions/Worldwide Pants, 1993.

Ed Dutton, *The Underneath* (also known as *Present Tense*), Gramercy, 1995.

Pollo, *God's Lonely Man,* Cinequanon Pictures International, 1996.

UFO abductee, *Waiting for Guffman,* Sony Pictures Classics, 1996.

Normand Pasco, *Qiana,* 1996.

Bud Chapman, *Clockwatchers,* BMG Independents, 1997.

Leo, *Loved,* MDP Worldwide, 1997.

Father Norton, *Telling Lies in America,* Banner Entertainment, 1997.

Jack Albert, *Error in Judgment,* 1998.

Earl Schimmel, *I'll Remember April,* Regent Entertainment, 1999.

Walter, *Runaway Bride,* Paramount, 1999.

Judge, *Happy, Texas,* Miramax, 1999.

Walter, *Guinevere,* Miramax, 1999.
Mayor Don Vaughn, *Madison,* Metro–Goldwyn–Mayer, 2000.
Hank, *Rennie's Landing* (also known as *Stealing Time*), Manga, 2001.
Dad, *The Perfect You* (also known as *Crazy Little Thing*), Thompson, 2002.
Chief Charlie Nyback, *Insomnia,* Crotalus, 2003.
Barney Whitmore, *Lake Desire,* 2003.
George Menschell, *A Mighty Wind,* Warner Bros., 2003.
Warden, *Nobody Knows Anything!,* Stargazer, 2003.
Reverend Ben Goodwin, *Employee of the Month,* Bull's Eye, 2004.
Pop Hemple, *Adventures in Homeschooling,* 5K Films, 2004.
The Making of "Invasion of the Freedom Snatchers," Behind the Scenes, 2004.
Grandpa Donald, *Come Away Home,* American Family Movies, 2005.
Dirty Love, 2005.

Television Appearances; Series:
The Dom DeLuise Show, 1968.
Dick Hale, *Coming of Age,* CBS, 1988–89.
First Gus Stemple, *Mad about You,* 1992–93.
Mickey Tupper, Martin's father, *Dream On,* HBO, 1992–94.
John Shirley, *Grace under Fire* (also known as *Grace under Pressure*), ABC, 1994–96.
Judge Philip Swackheim, a recurring role, *The Practice,* ABC, 1999.

Television Appearances; Miniseries:
William Burns, *The Murder of Mary Phagan* (also known as *The Ballad of Mary Phagan*), NBC, 1988.
Robert "Bud" McFarlane, *Guts and Glory: The Rise and Fall of Oliver North,* CBS, 1989.
Herb Tolliver, *Armistead Maupin's "Tales of the City"* (also known as *Tales of the City*), Channel Four, 1994, broadcast on *American Playhouse,* PBS, 1994.

Television Appearances; Movies:
Ames Prescott, *See China and Die* (also known as *Momma the Detective*), 1980.
The Day the Senior Class Got Married, 1985.
Gilbert "Gil" Hutchinson, *Lip Service,* 1988.
Ben McKenna, *When He's Not a Stranger* (also known as *Someone You Know*), CBS, 1989.
Doc, *Guess Who's Coming for Christmas?* (also known as *George Walters Will Be Away for the Holidays* and *UFO Cafe*), NBC, 1990.
Willy Bailey, *The Court–Martial of Jackie Robinson,* TNT, 1990.
Hal Roach, *White Hot: The Mysterious Murder of Thelma Todd* (also known as *Hot Toddy*), NBC, 1991.

Twittenham, "Frogs!," *WonderWorks Family Movie,* PBS, 1992.
Assistant district attorney Robert Norell, *Perry Mason: The Case of the Heartbroken Bride* (also known as *Perry Mason: The Case of the Bad Blood Wedding*), NBC, 1992.
Sid Wiggins, "Cooperstown," *TNT Screenworks,* TNT, 1993.
Richard Becker, *Mother of the Bride,* CBS, 1993.
Andy Milligan, "Traveler's Rest," *Showtime 30–Minute Movie,* Showtime, 1993.
Jim (one source says John) Anderson, "State of Emergency" (also known as "Slow Bleed"), *HBO Showcase,* HBO, 1994.
Emmett David, *Out There,* Showtime, 1995.
Senator Thatch, "The Computer Wore Tennis Shoes," *Disney Family Films* (also known as *The ABC Family Movie*), ABC, 1995.
Jerry Briggs, *Evolver,* Sci–Fi Channel, 1996.
"Angels in the Endzone," *Disney Family Films,* ABC, 1997.
George, *Comfort and Joy,* Lifetime, 2003.
Dean Duaney, *Tracey Ullman in the Trailer Tales,* HBO, 2003.

Television Appearances; Specials:
Let's Celebrate, 1972.
Detective, *The Shady Hill Kidnapping* (also known as *American Playhouse: The Shady Hill Kidnapping*), 1982.
Dick Albright, *The Firm,* 1983.
Don Liddle, *Steel Collar Man,* 1985.
Host in Detroit, Michigan, *The CBS All–American Thanksgiving Day Parade,* 1988.
Superman's 50th Birthday: A Celebration of the Man of Steel, CBS, 1988.
Casey Bengal, *Mathnet: The Case of the Unnatural,* PBS, 1992.
Interviewee, *Sixteen Candles: The E! True Hollywood Story* (documentary), E! Entertainment, 2001.
Tracey Ullman in the Trailer Tales, HBO, 2003.

Television Appearances; Episodic:
Welty, "No Hiding Place," *East Side/West Side,* 1963.
Comedian, *Toast of the Town,* 1964.
R. W. Wheeler, "Conflict of Interests," *The Defenders,* 1964.
Hanlon, "The Greatest Spy on Earth," *Get Smart,* NBC, 1966.
Television man, "Oedipus Hex," *Bewitched,* ABC, 1966.
Photographer, "A Punt, A Pass, and a Player," *Hallmark Hall of Fame,* 1968.
"Flanagan's Wake," *The Corner Bar,* 1972.
Miller, "Rumpelstiltskin," *Faerie Tale Theatre,* Showtime, 1982.
Father, "Hansel and Gretel," *Faerie Tale Theatre,* Showtime, 1982.

Bryce Taylor, "Resurrection," *Spenser: For Hire,* ABC, 1985.

Isaac Q. Newton, "Love, Rose," *The Golden Girls,* NBC, 1986.

Chester, "The Old Soft Shoe," *Tales from the Darkside,* 1986.

Whizzer, "I've Got a New Attitude," *Alf,* NBC, 1987.

George Corliss, "Empty Nests," *The Golden Girls,* NBC, 1987.

Whizzer, "Something's Wrong with Me," *Alf,* NBC, 1987.

Whizzer, "Break Up to Make Up," *Alf,* NBC, 1989.

Horace Van Dam, "A Father and Son Reunion," *Coach,* ABC, 1990.

Bob Spano, "The Go Between," *thirtysomething,* ABC, 1990.

Bob Spano, "Samurai Ad Man," *thirtysomething,* ABC, 1990.

Jack, "My Dinner with Jack and Delores," *Sunday Dinner,* 1991.

Casey Bengal, *Square One TV,* 1991.

Pops, "Soccer," *The Wonder Years,* 1991.

Mr. Adult in the Grungies sketch, "Episode with Rob Morrow," *The Ben Stiller Show* (also known as *The Best Man*), Fox, 1992.

Voice of Father Michael Stromwell, "It's Never Too Late," *Batman: The Animated Series* (animated), Fox, 1992.

The professor, *The Ben Stiller Show* (also known as *The Best Man*), Fox, 1992.

"Ninety–Five in the Shade," *The Boys,* 1993.

Karl Bulleri, "Safe Sex," *L.A. Law,* NBC, 1993.

"Forever Ambergris," *Tales from the Crypt,* HBO, 1993.

Walter McTeague, "Over the Rainbow," *Chicago Hope,* CBS, 1994.

Erin "The Bargain" Baron, "Bombshell," *Sisters,* NBC, 1994.

Chuck Wood, "Father Figures," *My So–Called Life,* ABC, 1994.

Chuck Wood, "Self–Esteem," *My So–Called Life,* ABC, 1994.

Enabran Tain, "The Wire," *Star Trek: Deep Space Nine,* syndicated, 1994.

Enabran Tain, "Improbable Cause," *Star Trek: Deep Space Nine,* syndicated, 1995.

Enabran Tain, "The Die Is Cast," *Star Trek: Deep Space Nine,* syndicated, 1995.

Thomas Kelsey, "Lobster Diary," *Ellen* (also known as *These Friends of Mine*), ABC, 1995.

Henry Lewis, "And Baby Makes Two," *ER* (also known as *Emergency Room*), NBC, 1995.

Henry Lewis, "The Secret Sharer," *ER* (also known as *Emergency Room*), NBC, 1995.

Henry Lewis, "Fire in the Belly," *ER* (also known as *Emergency Room*), NBC, 1996.

Joe Bangs, "The Well–Worn Lock," *Millennium,* Fox, 1996.

Voice characterization, "Dammit, Hollywood," *Duckman* (animated), USA Network, 1997.

Enabran Tain, "In Purgatory's Shadow," *Star Trek: Deep Space Nine,* syndicated, 1997.

Ralphie, "A Doll's Story," *Sabrina, the Teenage Witch,* ABC, 1997.

Judge Harper, "Dharma and Greg on a Hot Tin Roof," *Dharma and Greg,* ABC, 1998.

Agent Ivan Hamel, "Marriage," *Tracey Takes On ... ,* HBO, 1998.

"Passed Imperfect," *Sleepwalkers,* 1998.

Cop, "Lies," *Tracey Takes On ... ,* HBO, 1999.

Cheryl's dad, "Beloved Aunt," *Curb Your Enthusiasm,* HBO, 2000.

Nicholas Emblume, "Reasons to Believe," *Ally McBeal,* Fox, 2001.

Bill Ridley, "Saved by the Bell," *Providence,* NBC, 2001.

Bill, "Photo Finish," *The Geena Davis Show,* ABC, 2001.

Father, "Jeff," *Kate Brasher,* CBS, 2001.

Father Conlin, "The Time/Sex Continuum," *Jack & Jill,* The WB, 2001.

Dante Cicollo, "Undercover," *The Huntress,* USA Network, 2001.

Les Cresswell, "The Awful Truth," *Once and Again,* ABC, 2001.

Les Cresswell, "Destiny Turns on the Radio," *Once and Again,* ABC, 2001.

Cheryl's dad, "The Baptism," *Curb Your Enthusiasm,* HBO, 2001.

Cheryl's dad, "Shaq," *Curb Your Enthusiasm,* HBO, 2001.

Les Cresswell, "Pictures," *Once and Again,* ABC, 2001.

Les Cresswell, "The Gay–Straight Alliance," *Once and Again,* ABC, 2002.

Les Cresswell, "Experience Is the Teacher," *Once and Again,* ABC, 2002.

Les Cresswell, "Chance of a Lifetime," *Once and Again,* ABC, 2002.

Cheryl's dad, "Mary, Joseph and Larry," *Curb Your Enthusiasm,* HBO, 2002.

Cheryl's dad, "The Grand Opening," *Curb Your Enthusiasm,* HBO, 2002.

Stan Coffman, "Cherry Red," *Law & Order: Criminal Intent,* NBC, 2003.

Hospital administrator, "What's Love Got to Do with It?," *Becker,* CBS, 2003.

Henry Lewis, "Blood Relations," *ER,* NBC, 2004.

Buddy Ween, "Getting Off," *CSI: Crime Scene Investigation* (also known as *C.S.I.*), CBS, 2004.

Cheryl's dad, "The Survivor," *Curb Your Enthusiasm,* HBO, 2004.

Also appeared in episodes of *The Boys,* CBS; *The Mommies,* NBC.

Television Appearances; Pilots:
Don Liddle, *The Steel Collar Man,* CBS, 1985.
Touch 'Em All McCall, NBC, 2003.

Stage Appearances:

The butler, *Holiday,* Mt. Gretna, PA, 1951.

Elwood P. Dowd, *Harvey,* Jackson, WY, 1954.

Walt Dreary, *The Threepenny Opera,* 1954.

When the Owl Screams, 1963.

To the Water Tower, 1963.

Speed/Felix, *The Odd Couple,* Plymouth Theatre, New York City, 1969.

Adaptation/Next, 1969–70.

The White House Murder Case, Circle in the Square, New York City, 1970.

Jules Feiffer's Hold Me!, American Place Theatre, New York City, 1977.

The Amazin' Casey Stengel, American Place Theatre, 1981.

Sills and Company, Lamb's Theatre, New York City, 1986.

Carl Bolton, *Morning's at Seven,* Ahmanson Theatre, Los Angeles, 2002.

Tall Tales, Colony Theatre, Burbank, CA, 2003.

Appeared in *Dr. Willy Nilly, Fallout, 'Toinette.*

WRITINGS

Screenplays:

(With Robert Altman and Frank Barhyte) *Health* (also known as *H.E.A.L.T.H.*), Twentieth Century–Fox, 1982.

Teleplays; Series:

The Electric Company, PBS, 1971.

Take Five, 1976–77.

E-F

ECKHART, Aaron 1968–

PERSONAL

Born March 12, 1968, in Cupertino, CA; father, a computer executive; mother, a children's book author. *Education:* Brigham Young University, B.F.A., 1994. *Religion:* Mormon.

Addresses: *Agent*—Creative Artists Agency, 9830 Wilshire Blvd., Beverly Hills, CA 90212.

Career: Actor. Appeared in ad for Miller beer; also worked as a bus driver, construction worker, bartender, and waiter.

Awards, Honors: Independent Spirit Award, best debut performance, Special Achievement Award, Golden Satellite Awards, outstanding new talent, 1998, both for *In the Company of Men.*

CREDITS

Film Appearances:
Ken Reynolds, *Slaughter of the Innocents,* 1994.
Chad, *In the Company of Men* (also known as *En compagnie des hommes*), Sony Pictures Classics, 1997.
Nick, *Thursday,* Legacy Releasing, 1998.
Barry, *Your Friends & Neighbors,* Gramercy, 1998.
Nick Crozier, *Any Given Sunday,* Warner Bros., 1999.
Buck McKay, *Molly,* Metro–Goldwyn–Mayer/United Artists, 1999.
George, *Erin Brockovich,* Universal, 2000.
The Pledge, 2000.
Del Sizemore, *Nurse Betty* (also known as *Nurse Betty—Gefahrliche traume*), USA Films, 2000.

Man, *Tumble* (short), 2000.
Stan Krolak, *The Pledge,* Warner Bros., 2001.
Roland Michell, *Possession,* Warner Bros., 2002.
Dr. Josh Keyes, *The Core* (also known as *Core*), Paramount, 2003.
Brake Baldwin, *The Missing,* Sony Pictures Entertainment, 2003.
James Rethrick, *Paycheck,* Paramount, 2003.
Thomas Mackelway, *Suspect Zero* (also known as *Suspect 0*), Paramount, 2004.
Himself, *New Frontiers: Making "The Missing"* (documentary short), Columbia TriStar Home Entertainment, 2004.
Nick Naylor, *Thank You for Smoking,* ContentFilm International, 2005.
Zach Riley, *Neverwas,* Senator Films, 2005.
Thomas, *Conversations with Other Women,* Fabrication Films, 2005.
Sargent Leland "Lee" Blanchard, *The Black Dahlia,* Universal, 2006.

Film Work:
Co–producer, *Neverwas,* 2005.

Television Appearances; Movies:
Dwayne, *Double Jeopardy,* Showtime, 1992.

Television Appearances; Specials:
Samson, *Ancient Secrets of the Bible, Part II* (documentary), CBS, 1993.
Himself, *Remembering the Future: Paycheck & the Worlds of Philip K. Dick* (documentary), 2004.
Himself, *From Hong Kong to Hollywood: The Making of John Woo* (documentary), 2004.

Television Appearances; Episodic:
Beverly Hills, 90210, Fox, 1992.
Darryl, *Crossroads,* Arts and Entertainment, 1992.
Townsend, *Aliens in the Family,* ABC, 1996.
Frank, "Miss Right Now," *Frasier,* NBC, 2004.

Frank, "And Frasier Makes Three," *Frasier,* NBC, 2004.
Himself, *T4,* Channel 4, 2004.
Himself, *The Daily Show,* Comedy Central, 2004.

Stage Appearances:
The Mercy Seat, Acorn Theater, New York City, 2002–2003.
Oleanna, Garrick Theatre, London, 2004.

OTHER SOURCES

Periodicals:
Interview, September, 1998, p. 154; February, 1999, p. 88.
Parade Magazine, August 11, 2002, p. 14.
People Weekly, September 9, 2002, p. 81.

ENGEL, Stephen

PERSONAL

Married. *Education:* Graduated from Tufts and New York University Law School. *Religion:* Jewish. *Avocational Interests:* Sports.

Addresses: *Agent*—Creative Artists Agency, 9830 Wilshire Blvd., Beverly Hills, CA 90212.

Career: Writer, producer, show creator, and director. Previously worked as a lawyer.

Awards, Honors: CableAce Award nomination (with others), comedy series, 1995, for *Dream On.*

CREDITS

Television Work; Series:
Consulting producer, *Mad about You,* NBC, 1992.
Coproducer, *Family Album,* CBS, 1993.
Co–executive producer and story editor, *Dream On,* HBO, 1994–96.
Co–executive producer, *Just Shoot Me!,* NBC, 1997.
Executive producer, *Alright Already,* The WB, 1997.
Coordinating producer and additional cinematography, *Going Places,* PBS, 1997.
Executive producer and creator, *Work with Me,* CBS, 1999.
Executive producer and creator, *Inside Schwartz,* NBC, 2001.

Production staff, *Last Comic Standing: The Search for the Funniest Person in America,* NBC and Comedy Central, 2003.
Executive producer, show runner, and creator, *The Big House,* ABC, 2004.
Consulting producer, *Quintuplets,* Fox, 2004.

Television Work; Specials:
Production executive (Engel Bros Media), *Mysteries of Deep Space* (documentary), PBS, 1997.
Executive producer, *Lost Warriors of the Clouds* (documentary), Discovery, 1998.
Segment executive producer, "Cannibals," *Secrets of the Dead* (documentary), PBS, 2000.
Executive producer, *Adrenaline Science: Lethal Predators* (documentary), The Learning Channel, 2001.

Television Work; Pilots:
Executive producer, *Sunshine State,* Fox, 2003.

Television Work; Episodic:
Producer, "Sydney," *Going Places,* PBS, 1997.
Segment director, "London," *Going Places,* PBS, 1997.

Also directed episodes of *Dream On,* HBO.

WRITINGS

Television Pilots:
Work with Me, 1999.
Inside Schwartz, NBC, 2001.

Television Episodes:
(With others) "Madonna and Child Reunion," *Home Fires,* 1992.
"No Deposit, No Return," *Dream On,* HBO, 1992.
"The Undergraduate," *Dream On,* HBO, 1992.
"The French Conception," *Dream On,* HBO, 1993.
"Depth Be Not Proud," *Dream On,* HBO, 1993.
"Reach out and Touch Yourself," *Dream On,* HBO, 1993.
"Guardian Anger," *Family Album,* CBS, 1993.
"Winter, Spring, Summer or Fall, All You Gotta Do Is Call ... ," *Family Album,* CBS, 1993.
"Blinded by the Cheese," *Dream On,* HBO, 1994.
"The Taking of Pablum 5–2–3: Parts 1 & 2," *Dream On,* HBO, 1994.
"Hey Diddle Diddle," *Dream On,* HBO, 1996.
"Finale with a Vengeance: Part 2," *Dream On,* HBO, 1996.
Going Places, PBS, 1997.
"Nina's Birthday," *Just Shoot Me,* NBC, 1997.
"How the Finch Stole Christmas," *Just Shoot Me,* NBC, 1998.

(With Carol Leifer) "Again with the Billionaire," *Alright Already,* 1998.

(With Leifer) "Again with the Hockey Player: Part 2," *Alright Already,* 1998.

Work with Me, CBS, 1999.

"Let's Go to the Videotape," *Inside Schwartz,* NBC, 2001.

"Hart Transplant," *The Big House,* 2004.

Quintuplets, Fox, 2004.

Television Episode; Stories:

Dream On, HBO, 1992–96.

(With Carol Leifer) "Again with the White House," *Alright Already,* 1998.

OTHER SOURCES

Periodicals:

Jewish Journal of Greater Los Angeles, September 7, 2001.

FARIS, Anna 1976–

PERSONAL

Full name, Anna Kay Faris; born November 29, 1976, in Baltimore, MD; daughter of Jack and Karen Faris; married Ben Indra (an actor), June 3, 2004. *Education:* University of Washington, B.A., English literature, 1999.

Addresses: *Agent*—The Gersh Agency, 232 North Canon Dr., Beverly Hills, CA. *Lawyer*—Sloane, Offer, Weber and Dern, 9601 Wilshire Blvd., Suite 735, Beverly Hills, CA 90210. *Publicist*—Insignia Public Relations and Media Strategies, 9255 Sunset Blvd., Suite 920, Los Angeles, CA 90069.

Career: Actress.

Awards, Honors: MTV Movie Award nominations, best kiss (with Jon Abrahams) and breakthrough female performance, 2001, for *Scary Movie.*

CREDITS

Film Appearances:

Dithy, *Eden,* Legacy, 1996.

Jannelle Bay, *Lovers Lane* (also known as *I'm Still Waiting for You*), First Look, 1999.

Cindy Campbell, *Scary Movie,* Dimension Films, 2000.

Cindy Campbell, *Scary Movie 2* (also known as *Scarier Movie*), Miramax, 2001.

Polly, *May,* Lions Gate Films, 2002.

April Thomas, *The Hot Chick,* Buena Vista, 2002.

Justine, *Winter Break* (also known as *Snow Job*), Universal Studios Home Video, 2003.

Kelly, *Lost in Translation,* United International, 2003.

Cindy Campbell, *Scary Movie 3,* Dimension Films, 2003.

Jane Connelly, *Spelling Bee,* The Great Wazu, 2004.

Making 'Scary Movie 3', Dimension Home Video, 2004.

Bell, *Southern Belles,* Southern Belles LLC, 2005.

Serena, *Waiting ... ,* Lions Gate Films, 2005.

Jemima, *Brokeback Mountain,* Focus Features, 2005.

Also appeared in *Saphron Burrows* (short film).

Television Appearances; Movies:

Liz, *Deception: A Mother's Secret* (also known as *Tell Me No Lies*), NBC, 1991.

Television Appearances; Episodic:

Film '72, 2000.

The Big Breakfast, Channel 4, 2001.

The Late Late Show with Craig Kilborn, 2001.

Voice of Lisa, "Fun with Jane and Jane," *King of the Hill* (animated), Fox, 2002.

The New Tom Green Show, MTV, 2003.

Jimmy Kimmel Live, ABC, 2003.

The Wayne Brady Show, syndicated, 2003.

Total Request Live, MTV, 2003.

Erica, "The One with the Birth Mother," *Friends,* NBC, 2004.

Erica, "The One Where Joey Speaks French," *Friends,* NBC, 2004.

Mad TV, Fox, 2004.

Voice of stoned hippie chick/teen girl hippie, "Phish and Wildlife," *King of the Hill* (animated), Fox, 2004.

Erica, "The One with Rachel's Going Away Party" (also known as "The One Where Rachel Goes to Paris"), *Friends,* NBC, 2004.

Erica, "The Last One: Part 1," *Friends,* NBC, 2004.

Television Appearances; Pilots:

Dog Days, NBC, 2000.

Sarah, *Blue Skies,* NBC, 2005.

FUNK, Dan 1953–
(Daniel E. Funk)

PERSONAL

Born October 7, 1953, in Cleveland, OH.

Addresses: *Agent*—William Morris Agency, 151 El Camino Dr., Beverly Hills, CA 90212.

Career: Producer, director, and writer.

CREDITS

Television Executive Producer; Series:
E! on O.J., E! Entertainment Television, 1995.
World Gone Wild, Fox Family, 1998.
Headliners & Legends with Matt Lauer, NBC, 1998.
Rockin' Bowl, TNN, 2000.
The Other Half, syndicated, 2001.
Livin' Large, syndicated, 2002.
Cut to the Chase, TBS, 2004.

Television Work; Series:
Co–executive producer, *Star Search,* syndicated, 1983.
Producer, *Hollywood Reporter,* syndicated, 1985.
Producer, *Flip!,* CBS, 1988.
Creator, *The Other Half,* syndicated, 2001.
Live producer, *Cupid,* ABC, 2003.
Co–executive producer, *Extreme Reunion,* NBC, 2004.
Co–executive producer, *Fire Me ... Please,* CBS, 2005.

Television Executive Producer; Movies:
What about You, 1996.

Television Executive Producer; Miniseries:
Spotlight with Phyllis George, TNN, 1995.

Television Coproducer; Specials:
Fantasies, ABC, 1991.

Television Producer; Specials:
Super Model Search: Look of the Year, ABC, 1988.
The Valvoline National Driving Test, CBS, 1989.
Best Catches, CBS, 1989.
The American Red Cross Emergency Test, ABC, 1990.
The 2nd Annual Valvoline National Driving Test, CBS, 1990.
A User's Guide to Planet Earth: The American Environment Test, ABC, 1991.

Television Executive Producer; Specials:
The Tube Test, ABC, 1990.
Tube Test Two, ABC, 1991.
The American Memory Test, CBS, 1992.
The Ultimate Driving Challenge, CBS, 1992.
A Healthy Challenge: The National Nutrition Test, Lifetime, 1993.
Miss America: Their Untold Stories (documentary), NBC, 1994.
Miss America: Beyond the Crown (documentary), NBC, 1994.
In a Split Second, NBC, 1994.
After the Headlines (documentary), NBC, 1994.
America's Junior Miss Pageant, NBC, 1994.

Where Are They Now?, CBS, 1995.
The Ultimate TV Trivia Challenge, ABC, 1995.
Happy New Year, America (also known as *Happy New Year, America—1996*), CBS, 1995.
Ladies' Home Journal's Most Fascinating Women of '96, CBS, 1996 *Very Personal with Naomi Judd,* The Family Channel, 1996.
Where Are They Now? Part 2, CBS, 1996.
Very Personal with Naomi Judd, The Family Channel, 1996.
From the Moon to Mars (documentary), The Family Channel, 1996.
Ladies' Home Journal's Most Fascinating Women of '97, CBS, 1997.
American Originals, 1997.
Where Are They Now?, CBS, 1997.
Most Fascinating Women of 1998, CBS, 1998.
The 47th Annual Miss USA Pageant, CBS, 1998.
(Blanki & Bodi) *The National Hate Test,* USA Network, 1998.
Ladies' Home Journal's Most Fascinating Women of '98, CBS, 1998.
The 47th Miss Universe Pageant, CBS, 1998.
The 1998 Miss Teen USA Pageant, CBS, 1998.
Miss Universe Pageant (also known as *The 48th Annual Miss Universe Pageant*), CBS, 1999.
The 1999 Miss Teen USA Pageant, CBS, 1999.
The Ultimate Auction, Fox, 2000.
Ladies' Home Journal's Most Fascinating Women of '99, CBS, 2000.
Miss USA Pageant (also known as *The 49th Annual Miss USA Pageant*), CBS, 2000.
The 2000 Miss Teen USA Pageant, CBS, 2000.
Miss Universe Pageant (also known as *The 49th Annual Miss Universe Pageant*), CBS, 2000.
Ladies' Home Journal's Most Fascinating Women to Watch, CBS, 2001.

Televisions Director; Specials:
The Valvoline National Driving Test, CBS, 1989.
Best Catches, CBS, 1989.
The Tube Test, ABC, 1990.
The American Red Cross Emergency Test, ABC, 1990.
The 2nd Annual Valvoline National Driving Test, CBS, 1990.
A User's Guide to Planet Earth: The American Environment Test, ABC, 1991.
Tube Test Two, ABC, 1991.
Fantasies, ABC, 1991.
The American Memory Test, CBS, 1992.
The Ultimate Driving Challenge, CBS, 1992.
The American Memory Test, CBS, 1992.
In a Split Second, NBC, 1994.
Miss America: Their Untold Stories (documentary), NBC, 1994.
Miss America: Beyond the Crown (documentary), NBC, 1994.
In a Split Second, NBC, 1994.
After the Headlines (documentary), NBC, 1994.

Where Are They Now?, CBS, 1995.
Where Are They Now? Part 2, CBS, 1996.
Ladies' Home Journal's Most Fascinating Women of '96, CBS, 1996.*Where Are They Now?,* CBS, 1997.
Ladies' Home Journal's Most Fascinating Women of '97, CBS, 1997.
Ladies' Home Journal's Most Fascinating Women of '98, CBS, 1998.
Ladies' Home Journal's Most Fascinating Women of '99, CBS, 2000.
Miss USA Pageant (also known as *The 49th Annual Miss USA Pageant*), CBS, 2000.
The 2000 Miss Teen USA Pageant, CBS, 2000.
Miss Universe Pageant (also known as *The 49th Annual Miss Universe Pageant*), CBS, 2000.

Televise Segment Director; Specials:

99 Ways to Attract the Right Man, ABC, 1985.

Television Segment Director; Pilots:

People Do the Craziest Things, ABC, 1984.

Television Director; Episodic:

Extreme Reunion, NBC, 2004.
Fire Me ... Please, CBS, 2005.

Directed *The Tomorrow Show* (also known as *Tomorrow* and *Tomorrow Coast to Coast*), NBC; *Good Morning America,* ABC; *Entertainment Tonight* (also known as *E.T., ET Weekend, Entertainment This Week,* and *This Week in Entertainment*), syndicated; *Television: Inside and Out,* NBC; *People Do the Craziest Things,* ABC;

Flip!, CBS; *Fame, Fortune & Romance,* ABC; *Hollywood Reporter,* syndicated.

WRITINGS

Television Specials:

The Valvoline National Driving Test, CBS, 1989.
The Tube Test, ABC, 1990.
The American Red Cross Emergency Test, ABC, 1990.
The 2nd Annual Valvoline National Driving Test, ABC, 1990.
The American Memory Test, CBS, 1991.
The Ultimate Driving Challenge, CBS, 1993.
Miss America: Their Untold Stories (documentary), NBC, 1993.
Miss America: Beyond the Crown (documentary), NBC, 1994.
In a Split Second, NBC, 1994.
Where Are They Now?, CBS, 1995.
Where Are They Now? Part 2, CBS, 1996.
Ladies' Home Journal's Most Fascinating Women of '96, CBS, 1996.
Where Are They Now?, CBS, 1997.
Ladies' Home Journal's Most Fascinating Women of '97, CBS, 1997.
Ladies' Home Journal's Most Fascinating Women of '98, CBS, 1998.
Ladies' Home Journal's Most Fascinating Women of '99, CBS, 2000.
Ladies' Home Journal's Most Fascinating Women to Watch, CBS, 2001.

Television Episodes:

The Other Half, syndicated, 2001.

G

GEORGE, Bud
  See DAVIS, Bud

GLEESON, Brendan 1955(?)–

PERSONAL

Born November 9, 1955 (some sources cite 1956), in Belfast, Northern Ireland (some sources cite Dublin, Ireland); married Mary, 1982; children: four. *Education:* Attended National University of Ireland, University College, Dublin; trained at Royal Academy of Dramatic Art, London. *Religion:* Roman Catholicism. *Avocational Interests:* Playing the violin.

Addresses: *Manager*—Joan Scott, Joan Scott Management, 888 Seventh Ave., 35th Floor, New York, NY 10106 (some sources cite 12 West 72nd St., Suite 10D, New York, NY 10023).

Career: Actor. Street musician, c. 1970s; performer with the Abbey Theatre and the Dublin Shakespeare Theatre Festival, both Dublin, Ireland, and the Royal Shakespeare Company, Stratford–upon–Avon, England; Passion Machine (theatre company), director and writer. Also a teacher of English and Gaelic.

Awards, Honors: Boston Society of Film Critics Award, best actor, 1998, for *The General* and *I Went Down;* Irish Film and Television Award, best actor, London Critics Circle Film Award, British actor of the year, and Golden Satellite Award nomination, best actor in a motion picture—drama, International Press Academy, all 1999, for *The General;* Irish Film and Television Award nomination, best actor in a feature film, 2003, for *Wild about Harry.*

CREDITS

Film Appearances:
Quarryman, *The Field,* Avenue Entertainment, 1990.
Inspector Bolger, *Into the West,* Miramax, 1992.
Jim, *The Bargain Shop,* 1992.
Josie Conneely, *Conneely's Choice,* 1992.
Social club police officer, *Far and Away,* Universal, 1992.
M.A.N.: Matrix Adjusted Normal, 1992.
Hamish Campbell, *Braveheart,* Twentieth Century–Fox, 1995.
The Life of Reilly, 1995.
Ginger, *Trojan Eddie,* Castle Hill, 1996.
Liam Tobin, *Michael Collins,* Warner Bros., 1996.
Barney Mooney, *Angela Mooney Dies Again* (also known as *Angela Mooney*), 1997.
Bunny Kelly, *I Went Down,* Artisan Entertainment, 1997.
Father Bubbles, *The Butcher Boy,* Warner Bros., 1997.
John Harte, *Before I Sleep,* 1997.
Richard, *The Break* (also known as *A Further Gesture* and *Das Letzte Attentat*), Castle Hill, 1997.
Stubbs, *Turbulence,* Metro–Goldwyn–Mayer/United Artists, 1997.
Messaggi quasi segreti, 1997.
Garda Jim in 1939, *This Is My Father* (also known as *L'histoire de mon pere*), Sony Pictures Classics, 1998.
Martin Cahill (title role), *The General* (also known as *I Once Had a Life*), Sony Pictures Classics, 1998.
Title role, *Sweety Barrett* (also known as *The Tale of Sweety Barrett*), Handmade Films, 1998.
Jim Menries, *My Life So Far,* Miramax, 1999.
Sheriff Hank Keough, *Lake Placid* (also known as *Lac Placid*), Twentieth Century–Fox, 1999.
Harry McKee, *Wild about Harry,* Winchester Films, 2000.
John C. McCloy, *Mission: Impossible II* (also known as *M:I–2*), Paramount, 2000.
Marc Stevenson, *Harrison's Flowers* (also known as *Les fleurs d'Harrison*), Universal Focus, 2000.

"Simple" Simon McCurdie, *Saltwater,* Buena Vista Ireland, 2000.

Lord Johnson–Johnson, *Artificial Intelligence: AI* (also known as *AI Artificial Intelligence*), Warner Bros., 2001.

Michelangelo "Mickie" Abraxas, *The Tailor of Panama,* Columbia/Sony Pictures Entertainment, 2001.

Caca Milis (short film), Igloo Films, 2001.

J. J. Biker, 2001.

Frank, *28 Days Later...* (also known as *28 jours plus tard*), Twentieth Century–Fox, 2002.

Walter "Monk" McGinn, *Gangs of New York,* Miramax, 2002.

Jack Van Meter, *Dark Blue,* Metro–Goldwyn–Mayer/United Artists, 2003.

Stobrod Thewes, *Cold Mountain,* Miramax, 2003.

August Nicholson, *The Village* (also known as *M. Night Shyamalan's "The Village"*), Buena Vista, 2004.

Donnelly, *Six Shooter* (short film), The Works, 2004.

Menelaus, *Troy,* Warner Bros., 2004.

Alastor "Mad–Eye" Moody, *Harry Potter and the Goblet of Fire,* Warner Bros., 2005.

De Jager, *Country of My Skull* (also known as *In My Country*), Sony Pictures Classics, 2005.

Keegan and Walter, *Studs,* Brother Films, 2005.

Reynald, *Kingdom of Heaven* (also known as *El reino de los cielos* and *Koenigreich der Himmel*), Twentieth Century–Fox, 2005.

Breakfast on Pluto, Pathe, 2005.

Desmond, *Black Irish,* Creanspeak Productions, 2006.

Television Appearances; Series:
Leslie Parry, *The Lifeboat,* BBC, 1994.

Television Appearances; Miniseries:
Red Fox, *Kidnapped,* ABC Family Channel, 1995.

Television Appearances; Movies:
Brendan Dowd, *Dear Sarah,* [Ireland], 1989.

Michael Collins, *The Treaty,* [Ireland], 1991, PBS, 1998.

Lester, *The Snapper,* BBC–2, 1993.

Thomas Macken, *Love Lies Bleeding,* BBC–2, 1993.

Flanagan, *Making the Cut,* [Ireland], 1998.

Television Appearances; Specials:
Lorry driver, *Hard Shoulder,* Channel 4 (England), 1990.

Saint Oscar, [Great Britain], 1991.

Pure Rage: The Making of "28 Days Later," 2002.

A Journey to "Cold Mountain," 2003.

The Words and Music of "Cold Mountain," 2003.

Himself, *Kingdom of Hope: The Making of "Kingdom of Heaven"* (documentary), 2005.

Television Appearances; Awards Presentations:
Presenter, *The Second Irish Film and Television Awards,* Irish Film and Television Network, 2004.

Stage Appearances:
Appeared in productions of *King Lear* and *King Richard II,* both Royal Shakespeare Company, Stratford–upon–Avon, England.

OTHER SOURCES

Periodicals:
Entertainment Weekly, July 23, 1999, p. 75.
NME, June 6, 1998, p. 10.
Radio Times, April 23, 1994, p. 6.

GOLDMAN, Danny

PERSONAL

Born in New York, NY.

Addresses: *Office*—Danny Goldman and Associates, 1006 N. Cole Ave., Los Angeles, CA 90038. *Agent*—Nancy Chaidez Agency & Associates, 1555 North Vine, Suite 223, Hollywood, CA 90028; TalentWorks, 3500 W. Olive Ave., Suite 1400, Burbank, CA 91505. *Contact*—c/o 11733 Goshen Ave., Brentwood, CA 90049.

Career: Actor and casting director. Also worked as a casting director for commercials and voice–overs, beginning in 1982, and as a theatre director.

Awards, Honors: L.A. Drama Critics Circle Award; *LA Weekly* Award, best ensemble director.

CREDITS

Film Appearances:
Captain Murrhardt, *M*A*S*H,* Twentieth Century–Fox, 1970.

Charlie, *The Strawberry Statement,* Metro–Goldwyn–Mayer, 1970.

Beware! The Blob (also known as *Son of Blob, Beware of the Blob,* and *Son of the Blob*), Jack H. Harris Enterprises, 1972.

Leopold Maxwell, *The World's Greatest Athlete,* Buena Vista, 1973.

(Uncredited) Bartender, *The Long Goodbye,* United Artists, 1973.

Mr. Crosby, *Busting,* United Artists, 1974.

Medical student, *Young Frankenstein,* Twentieth Century–Fox, 1974.

Barry Flanken, *Tunnel Vision* (also known as *Tunnelvision*), WorldWide Pictures, 1976.

Baggage clerk, *The Missouri Breaks,* United Artists, 1976.

Beyond Death's Door, Sunn Classic Pictures, 1979.

Ziggy, *Swap Meet,* Dimension Pictures, 1979.

Porter, *Where the Buffalo Roam,* Universal, 1980.

Voice, *Strong Kids, Safe Kids* (documentary short film), Paramount Home Video, 1984.

Dr. Blaustein, *My Man Adam,* TriStar, 1985.

Dr. Franklin Gibbles, *Free,* 2001.

Film Casting Director:

A Visit from the Sergeant Major with Unintended Consequences, 2000.

Small Emergencies (short film), 2002.

Staring at the Sun (short film), 2002.

Consent (short film), 2004.

Hearts as One (short film), 2004.

Straight Eye: The Movie (short film), 2004.

Television Appearances; Series:

Nick Dutton, *The Good Life,* NBC, 1971.

Lester Bellman, *Busting Loose,* CBS, 1977.

Voice of Brainy Smurf, *The Smurfs* (animated; also known as *Smurfs' Adventures*), NBC, 1981.

Voice, *The Kwicky Koala Show* (animated), CBS, 1981.

Ozzie the Answer, *Mike Hammer* (also known as *Mickey Spillane's "Mike Hammer"* and *The New Mike Hammer*), CBS, 1984–85.

Clarence Darrow, *General Hospital,* ABC, 1991.

Television Appearances; Movies:

Sidney, *Tribes* (also known as *The Soldier Who Declared Peace*), ABC, 1970.

Press photographer, *Columbo: Double Exposure,* 1973.

Judgement: The Trial of Julius and Ethel Rosenberg, 1974.

Kasey, *Terror on the 40th Floor* (also known as *The Blazing Tower*), NBC, 1974.

Billy, *The Secret Night Caller,* NBC, 1975.

Ozzie the Answer, *Return of Mickey Spillane's "Mike Hammer,"* 1986.

Dr. Abrahamson, *Street of Dreams,* CBS, 1988.

Dr. Denton, *Get Smart, Again!,* Fox, 1989.

Carlton, *Fugitive Nights: Danger in the Desert* (also known as *Fugitive Nights*), NBC, 1993.

Television Appearances; Pilots:

Nicholas Dutton, *The Good Life,* NBC, 1971.

Commercial director, *Savage* (also known as *The Savage File* and *Watch Dog*), NBC, 1973.

Corporal Harvey Green, *At Ease,* CBS, 1976.

Bert, *Dribble,* NBC, 1980.

Ozzie the Answer, *More than Murder* (also known as *Mickey Spillane's "Mike Hammer: More than Murder"*), CBS, 1983.

Gerald Klotz, *The World According Straw,* Fox, 1990.

Television Appearances; Specials:

Newsroom copy boy, *It's a Bird, It's a Plane, It's Superman* (also known as *Superman the Musical*), ABC, 1975.

Voices of Brainy Smurf, sergeant, and Ogre, *My Smurfy Valentine* (animated), NBC, 1983.

Voice of Brainy Smurf, *Smurfily Ever After* (animated), NBC, 1985.

Voice of Brainy Smurf, *The Smurfs Christmas Special* (animated), NBC, 1986.

Voice, *'Tis the Season to Be Smurfy* (animated), NBC, 1987.

Voice, *Cartoon All–Stars to the Rescue* (animated), Black Entertainment Television, Nickelodeon, Fox, USA, ABC, CBS, NBC, The Disney Channel, and syndicated, 1990.

Television Appearances; Episodic:

Waiter, "Mission Improbable: Parts 1," *That Girl,* 1969.

Counterman, "The Snow Must Go On: Part 1," *That Girl,* 1969.

Murray, "The Valedictorian," *Room 222,* ABC, 1970.

Director, "Bedknobs and Drumsticks," *The Partridge Family,* ABC, 1973.

"Love and the Mind Reader," *Love, American Style,* ABC, 1973.

"Do Your Own Thing," *Needles and Pins,* NBC, 1973.

Lawrence, "Great Expectations," *Happy Days,* ABC, 1974.

Eddie Josephs, "I'll Kill 'Em Again," *Hawaii Five–0,* CBS, 1974.

Dr. Crowley, "The Doctor Story," *Chico and the Man,* NBC, 1975.

Frankie, "The Noise of a Quiet Weekend," *Lucas Tanner,* NBC, 1975.

"Scruffy" Sutherland, "A Grave Too Soon," *Kojak,* CBS, 1976.

Doctor Bosca, "Crack–Up," *CHiPs,* NBC, 1978.

Professor Pober, "Slaughter," *Lou Grant,* CBS, 1978.

Dr. Bosca, "Quarantine," *CHiPs,* NBC, 1979.

Tony, "If the Shoe Fits," *Alice,* CBS, 1979.

Stenographer, *Soap,* ABC, 1980.

Otterholm, "Brain Child," *Trapper John, M.D.,* CBS, 1981.

Dr. Lindsey, "Fugitives," *The Powers of Matthew Star,* NBC, 1982.

Customer, "The Robot Wore Pink," *Alice,* CBS, 1983.

"The Georgia Street Motors," *Hardcastle and McCormick,* ABC, 1984.

Mailman, "One on One," *Alice,* CBS, 1985.

Public defender Shimmel, "Act of Conscience," *Cagney & Lacey,* CBS, 1986.

"The Boy Who Could Be King," *Scarecrow and Mrs. King,* CBS, 1986.

Man in theater, "Dorothy's Prized Pupil," *The Golden Girls,* NBC, 1987.

Voice of Sam Giddell, "See No Evil," *Batman* (animated), Fox, 1993.

"The Cyberskull Virus," *Mighty Max,* syndicated, 1994.

"Cyberskull: The Next Level," *Mighty Max,* syndicated, 1994.

Director, "My Best Shot," *Sabrina, the Teenage Witch,* The WB, 2001.

Jeweler, "Larva," *That's Life,* CBS, 2001.

Voice of Brainy Smurf, "Atta Toy," *Robot Chicken* (animated), Cartoon Network, 2005.

Also appeared in "Al Tells the Truth," *The Famous Teddy Z,* CBS; Mr. Schirmer, *Life Goes On,* ABC; in *Crazy Like a Fox,* CBS.

Television Work; Series:

Additional voices, *Capitol Critters* (animated), ABC, 1992.

Television Casting Director; Series:

Back to the Future, CBS, 1991.

Television Casting Director; Specials:

Neil Diamond ... Hello Again, CBS, 1986.

Television Casting Director; Pilots:

Hollywood Endings, AMC, 2004.

GREEN, Jenna Leigh 1977–
   (Jenna Leigh)

PERSONAL

Original name, Jennifer Leigh Greenberg; born August 22, 1977, in West Hills, CA; father, a musician; mother, an actress. *Education:* Graduate of Sid Haig's Stage and Video Education Theatre. *Avocational Interests:* Theater, Audrey Hepburn movies, musicals.

Career: Actress.

CREDITS

Television Appearances; Series:

Libby Chessler, *Sabrina, the Teenage Witch* (also known as *Sabrina* and *Sabrina Goes to College*), ABC, 1996–99.

Panelist for the series *Figure It Out* (also known as *Billy the Answer Head* and *What Do You Do?*), Nickelodeon.

Television Appearances; Movies:

Meredith, *A Friend to Die For* (also known as *Death of a Cheerleader*), NBC, 1994.

Risa, *Friends 'til the End,* NBC, 1997.

Jess Hayes, *First Shot,* TBS, 2002.

Television Appearances; Episodic:

Voice of Persefineathious, "Mole People," *Extreme Ghostbusters,* syndicated, 1997.

Voice of Wanda, "Witchy Woman," *Extreme Ghostbusters,* syndicated, 1997.

Kelly Kincaid, "She's with the Band," *Dharma & Greg,* ABC, 2002.

Tammy Gribbs, "Dead Again," *ER,* NBC, 2002.

Libby Chessler (in archive footage), "Cirque de Sabrina," *Sabrina, the Teenage Witch,* The WB, 2003.

Appeared in episodes of *America's Funniest Videos,* ABC; and *Saved by the Bell,* NBC.

Television Appearances; Other:

Tara Mather, "Borderline Normal," *Cover Me* (miniseries; also known as *Cover Me: Based on the True Life of an FBI Family*), CBC (Canada), 2001.

Appeared in *The Mystery Files of Shelby Wink* (pilot).

Film Appearances:

(As Jenna Leigh) Girl, *Captain Nuke and the Bomber Boys* (also known as *Demolition Day*), Concorde–New Horizons, 1995.

Wanda, *Sandman,* Black Lion Records, 1998.

Regret (short film), Point of View Films/Southern Cross Pictures, 1999.

Heather, *The Bogus Witch Project,* 2000.

Betty Lipschitz, *Open House,* Bugeater Films/NeoFight Film, 2004.

Some sources cite appearances in *Come See About Me, Mike the Detective,* and *Skin Deep.*

Stage Appearances:

Ivy, *Bare: A Pop Opera* (also known as *Bare the Musical*), American Theatre of Actors, Chernuchin Theatre, New York City, 2004.

Cabaret for the Cure (benefit), St. Clement's Theatre, New York City, 2004.

Nessarose and understudy for Elphaba, *Wicked* (musical), Pantages Theatre, Hollywood, CA, 2005.

Song Bird (benefit), Prohibition Theatre, New York City, 2005.

Also appeared in productions of *Antony and Cleopatra, The Crucible, The Diary of Anne Frank, The Fantasticks, Follies, Into the Woods, Macbeth,* and *Romeo and Juliet.*

Major Tours:

Nessarose and understudy for Elphaba, *Wicked* (musical), U.S. cities, 2005.

RECORDINGS

Video Games:
Voice of Libby, *Sabrina, the Teenage Witch: Spellbound,* Simon & Schuster Interactive, 1998.

GREY, Fettes
    See STRACZYNSKI, J. Michael

GUNN, James 1970–

PERSONAL

Born August 5, 1970, in St. Louis, MO; brother of Sean Gunn (an actor), Brian Gunn (a writer), Matthew Gunn (a filmmaker), and Patrick Gunn (a movie executive); married Jenna Fischer (an actress, director, writer), October 7, 2000. *Education:* St. Louis University, B.A., psychology; Columbia University, M.F.A., creative writing.

Addresses: *Agent*—United Talent Agency, 9560 Wilshire Blvd., Suite 500, Beverly Hills, CA 90212. *Manager*—Brillstein–Grey Entertainment, 9150 Wilshire Blvd., Suite 350, Beverly Hills, CA 90212.

Career: Director, writer, producer, composer, and actor. Previously a member of the Icons (a rock band); worked as a hospital orderly; wrote and drew comic strips.

CREDITS

Film Director:
(Uncredited) *Tromeo and Juliet,* Troma, 1996.
Hamster PSA, Troma, 1997.
Slither, Universal, 2005.

Film Executive Producer:
Tromeo and Juliet, Troma, 1996.
(With others) *Man Who Invented the Moon,* Normandie, 2003.
LolliLove, Ivywood, 2004.

Film Coproducer:
The Specials, Regent, 2000.
Scooby Doo 2: Monsters Unleashed, Warner Bros., 2004.

Film Appearances:
Found a peanut father, *Tromeo and Juliet,* Troma, 1996.

Minute Man/Tim Tilderbrook, *The Specials,* Regent, 2000.
Doctor Flem Hocking, *Citizen Toxie: the Toxic Avenger IV,* Troma, 2000.
Apocalypse Soon: The Making of "Citizen Toxie" (also known as *The Making of "Citizen Toxie": The Toxic Avenger 4*), Troma, 2002.
Scott, *Melvin Goes to Dinner,* Arrival, 2003.
Riley, *Doggie Tails, Vol. 1: Lucky's First Sleep–Over,* Troma, 2003.
The Ghouls, IFM, 2003.
James, *LolliLove,* Ivywood, 2004.
Tales from the Crapper, Troma, 2004.
Make Your Own Damn Movie!, Troma, 2005.

Television Director; Series:
The Tromaville Cafe, 1997.

Television Director; Specials:
Sgt. Kabukiman Public Service Announcement, 1997.

Television Appearances; Specials:
Insane masturbator, *Sgt. Kabukiman Public Service Announcement,* 1997.

Television Appearances; Series:
Mike the crazy boom guy, *The Tromaville Cafe,* 1997.

RECORDINGS

Albums; With The Icons:
Mom, We Like It Here on Earth, 1994.

WRITINGS

Screenplays:
Tromeo and Juliet, Troma, 1996.
Hamster PSA, Troma, 1997.
Terror Firmer, Troma, 1999.
The Specials, 2000.
Scooby–Doo, Warner Bros., 2002.
Tube, Instant, 2004.
Dawn of the Dead, Universal, 2004.
The Swidge, Instant, 2004.
Scooby Doo 2: Monsters Unleashed, Warner Bros., 2004.
LolliLove, Ivywood, 2004.
Slither, Universal, 2005.

Plays:
The Colorform Variety Show, produced in St. Louis, MO, 1992.
The James Gunn Show (performance monologues), performed in New York City, 1994.

Film Songs:

The Low Life, Cabin Fever, 1995.

"Demon Chant," *Scooby–Doo,* Warner Bros., 2002.

"Scooby's Terrific Rap," *Scooby Doo 2: Monsters Unleashed,* Warner Bros., 2004.

Television Specials:

Sgt. Kabukiman Public Service Announcement, 1997.

Television Series:

(And creator) *The Tromaville Cafe,* 1997.

Novels:

The Toy Collector, Bloomsbury Publishing, 2000.

Nonfiction:

(With Lloyd Kaufman) *Everything I Know about Filmmaking I Learned from "The Toxic Avenger,"* 1998.

OTHER SOURCES

Periodicals:

Hollywood Reporter, August 19, 1999; April 16, 2000.
Hollywood Scriptwriter, April, 2004, pp. 5–9.
Village Voice, August, 2000, pp. 16–22.
Wall Street Journal, March 26, 2004.

Electronic:

James Gunn Official Site, http://www.jamesgunn.com/, April 19, 2005.

H

HAGERTY, Michael G. 1954–
(Michael Hagerty, Mike Hagerty)

PERSONAL

Full name, Michael Gerard Hagerty; born May 10, 1954, in Chicago, IL; son of Michael and Margaret (maiden name, McFadden) Hagerty. *Education:* University of Illinois, B.A., 1978.

Addresses: *Agent*—Gold Coast Management, 1023 1/2 Abbott Kinney Blvd., Venice, CA 90291; Greater Vision Agency, 9229 Sunset Blvd., Suite 320, Hollywood, CA 90069. *Manager*—Roar LLC, 2400 Broadway, Suite 320, Santa Monica, CA 90404.

Career: Actor and director. Appeared in television commercials for Budweiser Beer, 1996, CoinStar, 2000, and Goodwrench, 2003.

CREDITS

Film Appearances:
Second cop, *Doctor Detroit,* Universal, 1983.
(As Mike Hagerty) Mayor's bodyguard, *Turk 182!,* Twentieth Century–Fox, 1985.
(As Mike Hagerty) Furniture warehouseman, *Brewster's Millions,* Universal, 1985.
(As Mike Hagerty) Eric, *Nothing in Common,* TriStar, 1986.
(As Michael Hagerty) Billy Pratt, *Overboard,* Metro–Goldwyn–Mayer, 1987.
(As Michael Hagerty) Pat Nunn, *Red Heat,* TriStar, 1988.
Doorman, *Dick Tracy,* Buena Vista, 1990.
Truck driver, *After Dark, My Sweet,* International Video, 1990.

Walsh, *One Good Cop,* Buena Vista, 1991.
Babe, *V. I. Warshawski* (also known as *V. I. Warshawski, Detective in High Heels*), Buena Vista, 1991.
Davy, *Wayne's World,* Paramount, 1992.
Frozen Assets, RKO Radio, 1992.
Obituary writer, *So I Married an Axe Murderer,* TriStar, 1993.
Cop, *Stuart Saves His Family,* Paramount, 1995.
Tommy, *Space Truckers* (also known as *Star Truckers*), Lions Gate Films, 1996.
Harvey, *Speed 2: Cruise Control,* Twentieth Century–Fox, 1997.
George, *Break Up,* Ascot Video, 1998.
Flop house manager, *I Woke Up Early the Day I Died* (also known as *Ed Wood's "I Woke Up Early the Day I Died"* and *I Awoke Early the Day I Died*), 1998.
Charlie, *Best Laid Plans,* Twentieth Century–Fox, 1999.
Peanut vendor, *Austin Powers: The Spy Who Shagged Me* (also known as *Austin Powers 2: The Spy Who Shagged Me*), New Line Cinema, 1999.
Sikes, *Inspector Gadget,* Buena Vista, 1999.
Gregg Beeson, *The Last Big Attraction,* 1999.
Steve, *North Beach,* 2000.
(As Mike Hagerty) Red, *Backflash,* Dimension Films, 2001.
(As Mike Hagerty) Earl, *Frank McKlusky, C.I.,* Buena Vista, 2002.

Television Appearances; Movies:
The Imposter, ABC, 1984.
Dyke Holland, *Rio Diablo,* CBS, 1993.

Television Appearances; Series:
Finley, *The Building,* CBS, 1993.
Frank MacNamara, *The George Carlin Show,* Fox, 1994.
Leo Blount, a recurring role, *The Home Court,* NBC, 1995–96.
The killer, *The Near Future,* 2000.

Television Appearances; Episodic:

Decker, "Strange Bedfellows: Part 1," *Cheers,* NBC, 1986.

(As Mike Hagerty) Furniture salesman, "Shadow Dancer," *Crime Story,* NBC, 1986.

(As Michael Hagerty) Schaffel, "The St. Louis Book of Blues," *Crime Story,* NBC, 1986.

(As Mike Hagerty) Coroner, "You Better Watch Out," *Married ... with Children,* Fox, 1987.

Vinnie, "The Boys Next Door," *Family Ties,* NBC, 1988.

Second deputy, "Stranger in a Strange Land," *Hard Time on Planet Earth,* 1989.

Howard Sutthoff, "The Bickners," *Murphy Brown,* CBS, 1989.

Al, "John's Night Out," *Dear John,* NBC, 1990.

Engineer, "Terror on the Hell Loop 2000," *Get a Life,* Fox, 1990.

Captain Larg, "Redemption: Part 2," *Star Trek: The Next Generation,* syndicated, 1991.

Davey, "Heartbreak Diner," *American Dreamer,* 1991.

Clerk, "The Lost Weekend," *The Wonder Years,* ABC, 1992.

Meter man, "Mann's Fate," *Mann & Machine,* NBC, 1992.

Plumber, "Dead Men Don't Flush," *Martin,* Fox, 1992.

"Grin and Bare It," *Civil Wars,* ABC, 1992.

"I Saw Gina Kissing Santa Claus," *Martin,* Fox, 1992.

Skoran, "Thine Own Self," *Star Trek: The Next Generation,* syndicated, 1994.

Rudy, "The Raincoats: Parts 1 & 2," *Seinfeld,* NBC, 1994.

Brazilla, "Brazilla vs. Rodney," *The Wayans Bros.,* The WB, 1995.

Head usher at movie theater, "Night at the Movies," *Kirk,* The WB, 1995.

Mr. Treeger, "The One Where Heckles Dies," *Friends,* NBC, 1995.

Mr. Treeger, "The One with Phoebe's Dad," *Friends,* NBC, 1995.

Eric, "The Fall," *Malibu Shores,* NBC, 1996.

Stuart, "Housecleaning," *Sisters,* NBC, 1996.

The Beer Guy, "Buzz Beer," *The Drew Carey Show,* ABC, 1996.

"Clark's Crisis," *The Faculty,* ABC, 1996.

Mr. Treeger, "The One with the Ballroom Dancing," *Friends,* NBC, 1997.

Ron, "The First Christmas Show," *Union Square,* NBC, 1997.

Mr. Ricky, "Riverboat Queen," *Grace under Fire,* ABC, 1997.

Ben Thompson, *The Practice,* ABC, 1997.

Robert, "Stuck in the Middle with You," *7th Heaven,* The WB, 1998.

Mr. Treeger, "The One with the Free Porn," *Friends,* NBC, 1998.

Michael Huttle, "Alone Again," *Ally McBeal,* Fox, 1998.

Mark Bales, "O Captain, My Captain," *L.A. Doctors,* CBS, 1999.

Zeke, "Our Past, Our Present, Our Future," *Arli$$,* HBO, 1999.

Golgi, "Mr. Irresistible," *The Michael Richards Show,* NBC, 2000.

Mike Duffy, "AAMCO," *Curb Your Enthusiasm,* HBO, 2000.

(As Mike Hagerty), Bartender, "Happy Anniversary," *Angel,* The WB, 2001.

Bartender, "The Problem with Corruption," *Dead Last,* The WB, 2001.

Mr. Treeger, "The One Where Rachel Tells ... ," *Friends,* NBC, 2001.

Store manager, "Take This Job and Love It," *Nikki,* The WB, 2001.

Stan, "She Was a Job–Jumper," *Nikki,* The WB, 2002.

(As Mike Hagerty) Mr. James, "It's All in Your Head," *ER,* NBC, 2002.

"Love and Let Die," *Strong Medicine,* Lifetime, 2003.

Fireman, "Assaulted Nuts," *Life with Bonnie,* ABC, 2003.

(As Mike Hagerty) Car wash manager, *Unscripted,* HBO, 2004.

Loud Wagoneer, "Deadwood," *Deadwood,* HBO, 2004.

Bill, "Don't Stress, Express," *Life with Bonnie,* ABC, 2004.

Uncle Bob, "Thanksgiving with the Savages," *Complete Savages,* ABC, 2004.

Steven, "82'—Schadenfreude," *Cold Case,* CBS, 2005.

Car wash manager, *Unscripted,* 2005.

Also appeared as Tim, *Beverly Hills, 90210,* Fox; Roger, *Drexell's Class,* Fox; Glen Cooper, *Walker, Texas Ranger,* CBS; Dave, *Good Advice,* CBS; Walter Pulaski, *Chicago Hope,* CBS; Private Officer Canton, *JAG,* CBS; Tom Sinclair, *Second Noah,* ABC; Billy Larsen, *The Pretender,* NBC; Christopher Weatherly, *Dark Skies,* NBC; Troy, *Nash Bridges,* CBS; Matt Caulfield, *Dawson's Creek,* The WB; Sean, *Jack & Jill,* The WB; Eli Goldberg, *Grosse Pointe,* The WB; Tom Jaffe, *Six Feet Under,* HBO; Will, *Scrubs,* NBC; Justin Spidell, *The Division,* Lifetime; (as Mike Hagerty) Steve, *Happy Family,* NBC; Tim Goodman, *CSI: New York,* CBS.

Television Appearances; Specials:

The Show Formerly Known as the Martin Short Show, NBC, 1995.

Television Appearances; Pilots:

Jack Duffy, *Glory Days,* NBC, 1987.

Moving man, *Lola,* CBS, 1990.

Stage Appearances:

James Joyce's "Dubliners," Roundabout Theatre Company, 1975.

Orwell That Ends Well, Village of New York, 1984.

Miguel the king, *Vincent Laresca,* Joseph Papp Public Theater, New York City, 1995.

Paul, *Questa,* Court Theatre, West Hollywood, CA, 2005.

Also appeared with Yale Repertory, New Haven, CT, 1985–86, and with Second City, Chicago, IL, 1978–85.

Stage Director:
Orwell That Ends Well, Village of New York, 1984.

RECORDINGS

Video Games:
Voice of bartender, *Star Trek: Klingon,* 1996.
(As Michael Hagerty) Voices of Dash, Elway, Orc leader, Markus, *Lands of Lore 3,* 1999.

HALE, Ron 1946–
　　(Ronald Hale)

PERSONAL

Born January 2, 1946, in Grand Rapids, MI; father, worked in carpet industry; married Dood, 1972 (divorced, 1989). *Education:* Graduated from the American Academy of Dramatic Art.

Career: Actor.

Awards, Honors: Daytime Emmy Award nominations, outstanding supporting actor in a daytime drama series, 1979, outstanding performance by an actor in a supporting role for a daytime drama series, 1980, *Soap Opera Digest* Award nomination, outstanding villain on a daytime serial, 1986, all for *Ryan's Hope.*

CREDITS

Film Appearances:
A Lovely Way to Die (also known as *A Lovely Way to Go*), Universal, 1968.
(As Ronald Hale) Stanley Dexter, *Me, Natalie,* National General Pictures, 1969.
Frank A. Sturgis, *All the President's Men,* Warner Bros., 1976.
Dr. Johnson, *Original Intent,* Skouras Pictures, 1992.
Bailiff, *Trial by Jury,* Warner Bros., 1994.
Pentakis, *The Dark Mist,* Smooth Pictures, 1996.
The Lord Protector, 1997.
Jack, *Sunstorm,* First Look Home Entertainment, 2001.

Television Appearances; Series:
Walt Driscoll, *Search for Tomorrow,* CBS, 1969.
Second Dr. Jim Abbot, *Love Is a Many Splendored Thing,* CBS, 1973.

Dr. Roger Coleridge, *Ryan's Hope,* ABC, 1975–89.
Mike Corbin, *General Hospital,* ABC, 1995—.
Michael "Mike" Corbin, Sr., *Port Charles,* ABC, 1997–98, 2000.

Television Appearances; Specials:
Mike, *General Hospital: Twist of Fate,* ABC, 1996.
Himself, *Intimate Portrait: Vanessa Marcil* (documentary), Lifetime, 2003.

Television Appearances; Episodic:
Eldon Williams, "The Scrooge," *Matlock,* NBC, 1989.
Mike Travers, "Hearts of Steel," *MacGyver,* ABC, 1990.
Lonnie, "Rodney's Mom," *Rodney,* 2004.

Also appeared in *N.Y.P.D.*

Stage Appearances:
Sailor, *The Time of Your Life,* Vivian Beaumont Theatre, New York City, 1969.
Gerard and understudy for the roles of Alberic of Rheims, Fulbert, and Hugh, *Abelard and Heloise,* Brooks Atkinson Theatre, New York City, 1971.
Dick, *Four Friends,* Lucille Lortel Theatre, New York City, 1975.

Also appeared in *Cat on a Hot Tin Roof; Prometheus Bound; Death of a Salesman.*

OTHER SOURCES

Periodicals:
Palm Springs Life Magazine, November, 2001.
.

HAMILTON, George 1939–

PERSONAL

Full name, George Stevens Hamilton IV; born August 12, 1939, in Memphis, TN; son of George Stevens Hamilton (a bandleader; known as Spike Hamilton) and Ann Potter Hamilton Hunt Spaulding; married Alana Collins (an actress and television personality; known as Alana Stewart), c. 1970 (divorced, c. 1976); children: Ashley Steven (an actor); (with Kimberly Blackford, a model) George Thomas.

Addresses: *Agent*—Agency for the Performing Arts, 9200 Sunset Blvd., Suite 900, Los Angeles, CA 90069.

Publicist—Jeffrey Lane, Jeffrey Lane and Associates, 9056 Santa Monica Blvd., Suite 304, Los Angeles, CA 90069.

Career: Actor and producer. Appeared in commercials and print advertisements. Creator of a line of skin care products, 1989; founder of a chain of tanning salons, 1990; former owner of restaurants, lounges, and nightclubs, including Hamilton's Miami.

Awards, Honors: Golden Globe Award (with others), most promising male newcomer, 1960; Golden Laurel Award nomination, top male new personality, Producers Guild of America, 1960; Film Award nominations, best foreign actor, British Academy of Film and Television Arts, 1961, for *Crime & Punishment, USA,* and 1963, for *Light in the Piazza;* Saturn Award, best actor, Academy of Science Fiction and Fantasy Films, and Golden Globe Award nomination, best motion picture actor—musical or comedy, both 1980, for *Love at First Bite;* Special Award, star of the year, ShoWest Convention, National Association of Theatre Owners, 1981; Golden Globe Award nomination, best motion picture actor—musical or comedy, 1982, for *Zorro, the Gay Blade.*

CREDITS

Film Appearances:
(Uncredited) Noah, *Lone Star,* 1952.
Robert Cole, *Crime & Punishment, USA* (also known as *Crime & Punishment*), Allied Artists, 1959.
Ryder Smith, *Where the Boys Are,* Metro–Goldwyn–Mayer, 1960.
Theron Hunnicutt, *Home from the Hill,* Metro–Goldwyn–Mayer, 1960.
Tony McDowall, *All the Fine Young Cannibals,* Metro–Goldwyn–Mayer, 1960.
Lieutenant Curtis McQuade, *A Thunder of Drums,* Metro–Goldwyn–Mayer, 1961.
Paul Strand, *Angel Baby,* Allied Artists, 1961.
Warren Winner, *By Love Possessed,* United Artists, 1961.
Davie Drew, *Two Weeks in Another Town,* Metro–Goldwyn–Mayer, 1962.
Fabrizio Naccarelli, *Light in the Piazza,* Metro–Goldwyn–Mayer, 1962.
Corporal Trower, *The Victors,* Columbia, 1963.
Moss Hart, *Act One,* Warner Bros., 1963.
Himself, *Looking for Love,* Metro–Goldwyn–Mayer, 1965.
Hank Williams, *Your Cheatin' Heart,* Metro–Goldwyn–Mayer, 1965.
Flores, *Viva Maria!,* United Artists, 1966.
Captain Dorrit Bentley, *A Time for Killing* (also known as *The Long Ride Home*), Columbia, 1967.

George, *That Man George* (also known as *Our Man in Marrakesh, El hombre de Marrakech, L'homme de Marrakech, Los saqueadores del Domingo,* and *L'uomo di Casablanca*), Allied Artists, 1967.
Harlan Wycliff, *Doctor, You've Got to Be Kidding!* (also known as *You've Got to Be Kidding*), Metro–Goldwyn–Mayer, 1967.
Jeff Hill, *Jack of Diamonds* (also known as *Der Diamantenprinz*), Metro–Goldwyn–Mayer, 1967.
(Uncredited; in archive footage) *Lionpower from MGM* (short film), Metro–Goldwyn–Mayer, 1967.
Professor Jim Tanner, *The Power,* Metro–Goldwyn–Mayer, 1968.
Togetherness, General Film Corporation, 1970.
(Uncredited) Himself, *Elvis: That's the Way It Is* (documentary), Warner Bros., 1970, also released as *Elvis: That's the Way It Is—Special Edition,* 2001.
Title role, *Evel Knievel,* Fanfare, 1972.
Crocker, *The Man Who Loved Cat Dancing,* Metro–Goldwyn–Mayer, 1973.
Jeffrey, *Medusa* (also known as *The Rhodes Incident, Twisted,* and *To Kynighi tis Medhoussas*), 1973.
David Milford, *Once Is Not Enough* (also known as *Jacqueline Susann's "Once Is Not Enough"*), Paramount, 1975.
Ward Thompson, *The Happy Hooker Goes to Washington,* Cannon, 1977.
Vance Norton, *Sextette,* Crown International Pictures, 1978.
Count Vladimir Dracula, *Love at First Bite,* American International Pictures, 1979.
David, *Express to Terror,* 1979.
Maurice Bernard, *From Hell to Victory* (also known as *Contro 4 bandiere, Da Dunkerque alla vittoria, De Dunkerque a la victoria, De Dunquerque a la victoire,* and *De l'enfer a la victoire*), New Film, 1979.
Don Diego Vega, Ramon Vega, Bunny Wigglesworth, and Margarita Wigglesworth, *Zorro, the Gay Blade,* Twentieth Century–Fox, 1981.
The Last of the Gladiators, Twin Tower Enterprises, 1988.
B. J. Harrison, *The Godfather, Part III* (also known as *Mario Puzo's "The Godfather, Part III"*), Paramount, 1990.
Dr. Halberstrom, *Doc Hollywood,* Warner Bros., 1991.
Alfonso de la Pena, *Once upon a Crime ... ,* Metro–Goldwyn–Mayer, 1992.
Rudolfo Carbonera, *Amore!,* PM Entertainment/Sunland Entertainment, 1993.
Channel 102 newscaster, *Double Dragon* (also known as *Double Dragon: The Movie*), Gramercy Pictures, 1994.
Gil Braman, *Playback,* Paramount Home Video, 1995.
Dick Bennett, *8 Heads in a Duffel Bag,* Orion, 1997.
Himself, *Meet Wally Sparks,* Trimark Pictures, 1997.
Alonso Palermo, *She's Too Tall,* 1998.
Desmond Spellman, *Casper Meets Wendy* (live action and animated), Twentieth Century–Fox Home Entertainment, 1998.

(Uncredited) Himself, *Bulworth,* Twentieth Century–Fox, 1998.

The great Allonso, *The Little Unicorn,* Peakviewing Transatlantic, 1998.

Von Steiger (the Hand), *Pets* (also known as *Pets to the Rescue*), 1999.

Armand Dupres, *Off Key* (also known as *Desafinado*), Lolafilms, 2001.

Special guest, *Crocodile Dundee in Los Angeles,* Paramount, 2001.

(In archive footage) Duncan Carlyle, *Reflections of Evil,* BijouFlix Releasing/Pookie Films, 2002.

Ed, *Hollywood Ending,* DreamWorks, 2002.

The king of Beverly Hills, *The L.A. Riot Spectacular,* Rockhard Pictures/Visionbox Pictures/Entitled Entertainment/El Camino Pictures/Cherry Road Films/RichKatz Entertainment, 2004.

Film Producer:

Evel Knievel, Fanfare, 1972.

Medusa (also known as *The Rhodes Incident, Twisted,* and *To Kynighi tis Medhoussas*), 1973.

(With others) Executive producer, *Love at First Bite,* American International Pictures, 1979.

(With C. O. Erickson) *Zorro, the Gay Blade,* Twentieth Century–Fox, 1981.

Some sources cite Hamilton as the executive producer of *The Trip,* 2003.

Television Appearances; Series:

Duncan Carlyle, *The Survivors* (also known as *Harold Robbins's "The Survivors"*), ABC, 1969–70.

Jack Brennan, *Paris 7000,* ABC, 1970.

Joel Abrigore, *Dynasty,* ABC, 1985–86.

Ian Stone, *Spies,* CBS, 1987.

Sonny Stone, *The Bold and the Beautiful* (also known as *Glamour, Top Models,* and *Belleza y poder*), CBS, 1987.

Host (with Alana Stewart), *The George & Alana Show* (also known as *George & Alana*), syndicated, 1995–96.

Alan Van Buren, *The Guilt,* c. 1996–97.

Guy Hathaway, *Jenny,* NBC, 1997–98.

Panelist, *Match Game,* syndicated, c. 1998–99.

Host, *The Family,* ABC, 2003.

Television Appearances; Miniseries:

Lieutenant Frederic Henry, *A Farewell to Arms,* BBC, 1966.

Stephen Bennett, *Roots,* ABC, 1977.

Lieutenant Hamilton Stovall, *The Seekers,* Operation Prime Time, 1979.

Jay Pomerantz, *Malibu,* ABC, 1983.

Harry Price, *Monte Carlo,* CBS, 1986.

William Randolph Hearst, *Rough Riders* (also known as *Teddy Roosevelt and the Rough Riders*), TNT, 1997.

Francis Olmsted, *P. T. Barnum,* Arts and Entertainment, 1999.

Television Appearances; Movies:

Dr. Mark Collier, *Columbo: A Deadly State of Mind,* NBC, 1975.

Don Drake, *The Dead Don't Die,* 1975.

Glenn Lyle, *Killer on Board,* 1977.

Greg Oliver, *The Strange Possession of Mrs. Oliver,* 1977.

Adam Baker, *The Users,* 1978.

Alan Roberto, *Institute for Revenge,* 1979.

Ray Jeffries, *Death Car on the Freeway* (also known as *Wheels of Death*), CBS, 1979.

Hightower, *The Great Cash Giveaway Getaway* (also known as *The Magnificent Hustle*), 1980.

Trent Bradley, *Two Fathers' Justice,* NBC, 1985.

Cousin John, *Poker Alice,* CBS, 1987.

Wade Anders, *Columbo: Caution! Murder Can Be Hazardous to Your Health* (also known as *The ABC Monday Mystery Movie, The ABC Saturday Mystery Movie,* and *Columbo*), ABC, 1991.

J. D. Gantry, *The House on Sycamore Street* (also known as *Murder on Sycamore Street* and *Remedy For Murder*), CBS, 1992.

Earl Henry von Hohenlodern, *Das Paradies am Ende der Berge,* 1993.

Trent Bradley, *Two Fathers: Justice For the Innocent* (also known as *Two Fathers Return*), NBC, 1994.

Malcolm Patterson, *Vanished* (also known as *Danielle Steel's "Vanished"*), NBC, 1995.

Karl Von Ostenberg, *Hart to Hart: Till Death Do Us Hart* (also known as *Hart to Hart: Double Trouble*), Family Channel, 1996.

Mall Santa Claus, *Too Cool for Christmas,* Lifetime, 2004.

Woody Prentice, *The Hollywood Mom's Mystery,* The Hallmark Channel, 2004.

Television Appearances; Specials:

Himself, *Celebrity Party* (also known as *Dick Clark's "Celebrity Party"*), ABC, 1963.

Ringmaster, *Circus of the Stars,* CBS, 1977.

Host, *An Evening at the Moulin Rouge,* HBO, 1981.

The Fantastic Miss Piggy Show, ABC, 1982.

Cohost, *Super Model Search: Look of the Year,* ABC, 1988.

Host, *Dracula: Live from Transylvania,* syndicated, 1989.

The 75th Anniversary of Beverly Hills, ABC, 1989.

Host, *The Lords of Hollywood,* syndicated, 1990.

Host (with Dr. Ruth Westheimer), *Comedy Battle of the Sexes,* Lifetime, 1992.

Host, *Heartstoppers ... Horror at the Movies,* syndicated, 1992.

Dame Edna's Hollywood, NBC, 1992.

Cohost, *The 1997 Miss Universe Pageant,* CBS, 1997.

Cohost, *The 1997 Miss USA Pageant,* CBS, 1997.

Host, *Canned Ham: 8 Heads in a Duffel Bag,* Comedy Central, 1997.

(In archive footage) *101 Biggest Celebrity Oops,* E! Entertainment Television, 2004.

Television Appearances; Awards Presentations:

Presenter, *The 34th Annual Academy Awards,* ABC, 1962.

Presenter, *The 38th Annual Academy Awards,* ABC, 1966.

Presenter, *The 52nd Annual Academy Awards,* ABC, 1980.

Cohost, *The 38th Annual Golden Globe Awards,* CBS, 1981.

The 46th Annual Golden Globe Awards (also known as *The Golden Globe Awards*), TBS, 1989.

Host, *The Soap Opera Digest Awards* (also known as *The Eighth Annual Soap Opera Digest Awards*), NBC, 1992.

Television Appearances; Episodic:

Herbie Shields, "Have Fun," *The Donna Reed Show,* ABC, 1959.

Marshal Elwood Masterson, "The Misfit Marshal," *The Adventures of Rin Tin Tin,* ABC, 1959.

Tom, "The Beauty and the Sorrow," *Cimarron City,* NBC, 1959.

"The Opposite Virtues," *Bus Stop,* ABC, 1962.

Clint Perry, "Who Killed the Richest Man in the World?," *Burke's Law,* ABC, 1964.

Jamie, "Two of a Kind," *The Rogues,* NBC, 1964.

Victor (some sources cite Peter) Thornton, "The Turncoat," *Bob Hope Presents the Chrysler Theater,* NBC, 1964.

Himself, *The Celebrity Game,* CBS, 1964.

Dr. Geoffrey Collicott, "Where Does the Boomerang Go?," *Ben Casey,* ABC, 1965.

Himself, "Olivia de Havilland vs. George Hamilton," *Password,* CBS, 1965.

Little John Lester, "Who Killed Mother Goose?," *Burke's Law,* ABC, 1965.

Guest panelist, *What's My Line?,* CBS, 1965.

Guest host, *Hullabaloo,* NBC, 1965, 1966.

Mystery guest, *What's My Line?,* CBS, 1965, 1966.

"Hell Cats," *Off to See the Wizard* (live action and animated), ABC, 1967.

Guest, *The Ed Sullivan Show* (also known as *Toast of the Town*), CBS, 1967, 1968, 1969, 1970, 1971.

Himself, *V.I.P.—Schaukel,* 1973.

Guest, *$10,000 Pyramid,* CBS, 1973, ABC and syndicated, 1975.

DeLucia, "The Other Side of the Fence," *Police Story,* NBC, 1976.

Keith Hampton, "The Great Taxicab Stampede," *McCloud,* NBC, 1977.

"Blackjack," *Sword of Justice,* NBC, c. 1978.

David, "Express to Terror," *Supertrain,* NBC, 1979.

Cohost, *Fridays,* ABC, 1981.

Himself, "The Big Date," *Hearts Afire,* CBS, 1992.

Himself, *Dame Edna's Hollywood,* NBC, 1992.

Dan McCadden, "And Bimbo Was His Name–O," *Dream On,* HBO, 1992, also broadcast on Fox.

Himself, "It Happened in Hollywood," *Birds of a Feather,* BBC, 1993.

She TV, ABC, 1994.

Himself, "How Can I Call You My Ex–Husbands If You Won't Go Away?," *Cybill,* CBS, 1995.

Craig Wohlman, "Mind over Murder," *Diagnosis Murder,* CBS, 1996.

Dirk Lawson, "Up All Night," *The Bonnie Hunt Show* (also known as *Bonnie*), CBS, 1996.

Don Green, "Zoso," *NewsRadio* (also known *News Radio* and *The Station*), NBC, 1996.

Himself, "Cosmetic Perjury," *The John Larroquette Show,* NBC, 1996.

Himself, "L.A. Times," *Dave's World,* CBS, 1996.

Himself, "Women Who Rises in World, Falls on Face," *The Naked Truth* (also known as *Pix* and *Wilde Again*), ABC, 1996.

Himself, "Joan Collins," *Biography,* Arts and Entertainment, 1997.

Himself, "The Curse of the Faro," *Buddy Faro,* CBS, 1998.

Himself, *Intimate Portrait: Vanna White,* Lifetime, 1998.

Guest, *Clive Anderson All Talk,* BBC, 1998.

Guest, *Late Lunch,* 1998.

Guest, *Late Night with Conan O'Brien,* NBC, 1998.

Guest, *The Late Show with David Letterman,* CBS, 1998, 1999.

Don Rio Sepulveda, "Getting Lucky," *Ladies Man,* CBS, 1999.

Himself, "Galaxy Girls," *Baywatch,* syndicated, 1999.

Don Rio Sepulveda, "Romance," *Ladies Man,* CBS, 2000.

Himself, "George Hamilton: Playing the Movie Star," *Biography,* Arts and Entertainment, 2000.

Raymond Peck, "Missing Key," *Nash Bridges* (also known as *Bridges*), CBS, 2000.

Guest, *Open House with Gloria Hunniford* (also known as *Open House*), Channel 5 (England), 2000.

Himself, *Love, Hate, and Joy,* 2002.

Guest, *The View,* ABC, 2002.

Himself, "Strap On," *Fastlane,* Fox, 2003.

Himself, *I'm a Celebrity, Get Me Out of Here!,* Independent Television, 2003.

Himself, *Intimate Portrait: Joan Collins,* Lifetime, 2003.

Himself, *V Graham Norton,* Channel 4 (England), 2003.

Bernard Taylor, "Good Run of Bad Luck," *Las Vegas,* NBC, 2004.

Himself, *Hollywood Squares,* syndicated, 2004.

Guest, *The Late Late Show with Craig Kilborn,* CBS, 2004.

Himself, *The Kumars at No. 42,* BBC, 2005.

Appeared as a guest host and guest in various episodes of *Live with Regis and Kathie Lee* (also known as *Live with Regis* and *Live with Regis & Kelly*), syndicated; appeared as a guest host, *Talk Soup,* E! Entertainment Television. Appeared as Krishna Vernoy in "Destination Nightmare" and "The Return of Madame Vernoy," both episodes of *The Veil.*

Television Appearances; Pilots:
Richard Manning III, *Poor Richard,* CBS, 1984.
Himself, *Life of Luxury,* ABC, 2003.

Television Appearances; Other:
The Last of the Powerseekers, 1971.

Television Producer:
Roots (miniseries), ABC, 1977.
(With others) *The George & Alana Show* (series; also known as *George & Alana*), syndicated, 1995–96.

Stage Appearances:
Andrew Makepeace Ladd III, *Love Letters,* Marines Memorial Theatre, San Francisco, CA, 2000.
Billy Flynn, *Chicago* (musical), Richard Rodgers Theatre, New York City, 2001–2002, then Shubert Theatre, New York City, 2002.

Appeared other productions, including *Barefoot in the Park, Gigi* (musical), *The Philadelphia Story,* and *The Star–Spangled Girl;* appeared in benefit performances.

Major Tours:
Nick Arnstein, *Funny Girl* (musical), U.S. cities, 1967.

RECORDINGS

Singles:
"Don't Envy Me," Metro–Goldwyn–Mayer, c. 1963.

WRITINGS

Nonfiction:
(With Alysse Minkoff) *Life's Little Pleasures,* Stoddart, 1998.

OTHER SOURCES

Periodicals:
People Weekly, August 8, 1994, p. 88; November 6, 1995, pp. 77–80; October 13, 1997, pp. 15–16; November 29, 1999, p. 13.
Restaurant Business, August 1, 1998, p. 120.

TV Guide, September 30, 1995, pp. 26–31; July 26, 2003, p. 9.
Vanity Fair, January, 1991, pp. 98–104, 118–20; August, 1994, pp. 106–114.

HARDY, Jonathan 1940–

PERSONAL

Born September 20, 1940, in Wellington, New Zealand.

Addresses: *Agent*—RGM Associates, 64–76 Kippax St., Level 2, Suite 202, Surry Hills, New South Wales 2010, Australia.

Career: Actor, writer, and director. Appeared in stage productions.

Awards, Honors: Australian Film Institute Award, best screenplay, original or adapted, 1980, and Academy Award nomination, best writing, screenplay based on material from another medium, 1981, both with others, both for *Breaker Morant;* Mystfest Award (with others), best artistic contribution, 1982, for *The Scarecrow;* Film Award, best short film performance, New Zealand Film and Television awards, 2001, for *Camping with Camus.*

CREDITS

Television Appearances; Series:
Harmar, *Mandog,* BBC, beginning c. 1972.
Shenlyn, *Andra,* Australian Broadcasting Corporation, beginning c. 1976.
Himself, *Butterfly Island,* [Australia], beginning c. 1988.
Brother Ignatius, *Family and Friends,* 9 Network (Australia), beginning c. 1990.
Voice of Dominar Rygel XVI, *Farscape* (also known as *Far Horizon*), Sci–Fi Channel, 1999–2004.

Television Appearances; Miniseries:
Paddy Kelleher, *Power without Glory,* Australian Broadcasting Corporation, 1976.
Father Emilio, *The Thorn Birds: The Missing Years,* ABC, 1996.
Voice of Rygel XVI, *Farscape: The Peacekeeper Wars* (also known as *The Farscape Miniseries*), Sci–Fi Channel, 2004.

Television Appearances; Movies:
The Trial of Ned Kelly, Australian Broadcasting Corporation, 1977.

Vlad, *The John Sullivan Story,* 9 Network (Australia), 1979.

Mr. Bretherton (a caretaker), *More Winners: His Master's Ghost,* [Australia], 1990.

Giles Ballard, *Terrain,* [Australia], 1997.

Television Appearances; Specials:

Voice of Dominar Rygel XVI, *Farscape Undressed,* Sci–Fi Channel, 2001.

Television Appearances; Episodic:

Benny Allman, "The Hydra," *Bluey,* 7 Network (Australia), 1977.

Colonel Flynn, "Story of a Shaggy Dog," *Young Ramsay,* 7 Network, 1977.

Mr. Potter, *Prisoner,* syndicated, 1980.

Waller, *Prisoner,* syndicated, 1981.

Etienne Reynard, "Submarine," *Mission: Impossible,* ABC, 1989.

Tyler Wells, "Milk Run," *The Flying Doctors,* 9 Network (Australia), 1989.

Patrick Gardiner, "When a Girl Marries," *A Country Practice,* 7 Network, c. 1990.

John Archer, Sr., "The Cutting Edge," *Snowy River: The McGregor Saga,* The Family Channel, 1994.

Mr. Rosenthal, *Medivac,* 10 Network (Australia), 1996.

"Borrowing Bazza," *Twisted Tales* (also known as *Twisted*), 9 Network, 1996.

Cliff Unwin, "Christmas Spice," *All Saints,* 7 Network, 1998.

Steve Capelli (some sources cite Jack Bailey), "Officers & Gentlemen," *State Coroner,* 10 Network, 1998.

Kahaynu, "Look at the Princess: I Do, I Think," *Farscape* (also known as *Far Horizon*), Sci–Fi Channel, 2000.

Kahaynu, "Look at the Princess: The Maltese Crichton," *Farscape* (also known as *Far Horizon*), Sci–Fi Channel, 2000.

Stan the fingers, "Special Services," *Above the Law,* 10 Network, 2000.

Justice Tulloch, "A Bird in the Hand," *MDA,* Australian Broadcasting Corporation, 2003.

Justice Tulloch, "A Closer Walk," *MDA,* Australian Broadcasting Corporation, 2003.

Stephen Betjeman, "Conversations with the Dead," *Stingers,* 9 Network, 2003.

Tribunal man, "Let the Burning Begin," *The Secret Life of Us,* 10 Network, 2003.

Television Appearances; Pilots:

Voice of Dominar Rygel XVI, *Farscape,* USA Network, 1999.

Television Puppeteer:

Farscape (pilot), USA Network, 1999.

Farscape (series; also known as *Far Horizon*), Sci–Fi Channel, 1999–2004.

Film Appearances:

Groove Courtenay, *The Adventures of Barry McKenzie,* Longford Productions, 1972.

Brother Arnold, *The Devil's Playground,* 1976.

Joe Speight, *The Mango Tree,* 1977.

Police commissioner Labatouche, *Mad Max,* Orion, 1979.

Bruce, *Lonely Hearts,* Samuel Goldwyn, 1982.

Charlie Dabney, *The Scarecrow* (also known as *Klynham Summer*), Oasis, 1982.

Randolf Grieve, *Constance,* 1984.

Doctor Max, *The Lie of the Land,* 1985.

John Macadam, *Wills and Burke—The Untold Story* (also known as *Wills & Burke*), Greater Union, 1985.

Ranji Gandhi, *Death Warmed Up,* 1985.

Burley, *Mesmerized* (also known as *Shocked*), 1986.

Magistrate, *The Delinquents,* Warner Bros., 1989.

Mayor, *Bloodmoon,* Carolco Pictures, 1990.

Henry Adams, *Tunnel Vision,* 1995.

Otis, *Down Rusty Down,* 1996.

Reverend McIntyre, *Mr. Reliable* (also known as *Mr. Reliable: A True Story* and *My Entire Life*), 1996.

Camping with Camus (short film), 2000.

Man in the moon, *Moulin Rouge!* (musical), Twentieth Century–Fox, 2001.

The great Orlando, *Ned Kelly* (also known as *Ned Kelly: Public Enemy No. 1*), Focus Features, 2004.

Film Work:

Associate to the director, *Return to Snowy River Part II, The Legend Continues,* Buena Vista, 1988.

Director, *Backstage,* Skouras Pictures, 1988.

RECORDINGS

Video Games:

Voice of Rygel XVI, *Farscape: The Game* (also known as *Farscape: War & Peacekeepers*), Simon & Schuster Interactive, 2002.

WRITINGS

Screenplays:

(With Bruce Beresford and David Stevens) *Breaker Morant,* New World, 1980.

Constance, 1984.

Backstage, Skouras Pictures, 1988.

Teleplays; Series:

The Adventures of Skippy, Australian Broadcasting Corporation, c. 1991–92.

HARPER, Tess 1950(?)–

PERSONAL

Original name, Tessie Jean Washam; born August 15, 1950 (some sources cite 1952), in Mammoth Spring, AR; married Ken Harper, 1971 (divorced, 1976). *Education:* Southwest Missouri State University, B.S.; also attended Arkansas State University.

Addresses: *Agent*—Don Buchwald and Associates, 6500 Wilshire Blvd., Suite 2200, Los Angeles, CA 90048; Bauman, Redanty and Shaul, 5757 Wilshire Blvd., Suite 473, Los Angeles, CA 90036.

Career: Actress. Performed in dinner theatre, children's theatre, and television commercials in Houston, TX, and Dallas, TX; performed at the theme parks Dogpatch USA in Jasper, AR, and Silver Dollar City in Branson, MO, both 1960s.

Member: Screen Actors Guild (vice president, beginning 2001), American Federation of Television and Radio Artists.

Awards, Honors: Golden Globe Award nomination, best performance by an actress in a supporting role in a motion picture, 1984, for *Tender Mercies;* Academy Award nomination, best actress in a supporting role, 1987, for *Crimes of the Heart.*

CREDITS

Film Appearances:
Linda Dawson, *Silkwood,* Twentieth Century–Fox, 1983.
Nancy Baxter, *Amityville 3–D* (also known as *Amityville: The Demon* and *Amityville III: The Demon*), Orion, 1983.
Rosa Lee Wadsworth, *Tender Mercies,* Universal, 1983.
Ellen, *Flashpoint,* TriStar, 1984.
Chick Boyle, *Crimes of the Heart,* De Laurentiis Entertainment Group, 1986.
Willa, *Ishtar,* Columbia, 1987.
Rita, *Far North,* Alive Films, 1988.
Detective Stillwell, *Criminal Law,* TriStar, 1989.
Sally Blackwood, *Her Alibi,* Warner Bros., 1989.
Sara Lee, *Daddy's Dyin' ... Who's Got the Will?,* Metro–Goldwyn–Mayer/United Artists, 1990.
Abigail Trant, *The Man in the Moon,* Metro–Goldwyn–Mayer/Pathe, 1991.
Cheryl Hornby, *My Heroes Have Always Been Cowboys,* Samuel Goldwyn, 1991.

Pretty Hattie's Baby (also known as *The Colors of Love*), 1991.
Kimmy Hayes, *My New Gun,* IRS Releasing, 1992.
Martha Harnish, *The Turning* (also known as *Home Fires Burning* and *Pocahontas, Virginia*), Phaedra Cinema, 1992.
Beth Greene, *Dirty Laundry,* Hollywood Productions/ Rogue Features/Artistic License Films, 1996.
The first lady, *The Jackal* (also known as *The Day of the Jackal, Der Schakal,* and *Le chacal*), Universal, 1997.
Dr. Amanda Giles, *The In Crowd,* Warner Bros., 2000.
Margaret, *Morning,* Down Home Entertainment/ Incognito Entertainment, 2000.
Rebecca Hodge, *The Rising Place,* Warner Bros./ Flatland Pictures, 2001.
Cindy's mom, *No Prom for Cindy* (short film), 2002.
Linda Little, *Studio City* (short film), Blind Mule Productions, 2003.
Liz O'Callahan, *Jesus, Mary and Joey,* Federal Hill Pictures, 2003.
Lonely Place, c. 2003.
Elizabeth, *Loggerheads,* Independent Dream Machine/ Lasalle Holland, 2005.
Molly Czehowicz (some sources cite Dorothy Homolka), *Karla* (also known as *Deadly*), Quantum Entertainment, 2005.

Television Appearances; Series:
Fairlight Spencer, *Christy* (also known as *Catherine Marshall's "Christy"*), CBS, 1994–95.
Lois Hobson, *Early Edition,* CBS, 1998–2000.

Television Appearances; Miniseries:
Carrie Lee, *Chiefs,* CBS, 1983.
Susan French, *Celebrity* (also known as *Tommy Thompson's "Celebrity"*), NBC, 1984.

Television Appearances; Movies:
Janet Briggs, *Starflight: The Plane That Couldn't Land* (also known as *Starflight One*), ABC, 1983.
Lorna Whateley, *Kentucky Woman,* CBS, 1983.
Gwen Palmer, *Promises to Keep,* CBS, 1985.
Jeannie Wyler, *A Summer to Remember,* CBS, 1985.
Meredith Craig, *Reckless Disregard,* Showtime, 1985.
Ann Burnette, *Daddy,* ABC, 1987.
Clara Brady, *Little Girl Lost,* ABC, 1988.
Betty McFall, *Incident at Dark River* (also known as *Dark River—A Father's Revenge* and *The Smell of Money*), TNT, 1989.
Mary Flowers, *Unconquered* (also known as *Invictus*), CBS, 1989.
Verna Heath, *Willing to Kill: The Texas Cheerleader Story* (also known as *Pom Pom Mom* and *Willing to Kill*), ABC, 1992.
Vicky Singer, *In the Line of Duty: Siege at Marion* (also known as *Children of Fury, In the Line of Duty: The*

Hostage Murders, In the Line of Duty: Standoff at Marion, and *Siege at Marion*), NBC, 1992.

Assistant district attorney Jerri Sims, *Death in Small Doses,* ABC, 1995.

Julia Archer, *The Road to Galveston,* USA Network, 1996.

Linda Grant, *A Stranger to Love* (also known as *Journey Home*), CBS, 1996.

Joanna Chandler, *A Child's Wish* (also known as *A Fight for Justice*), CBS, 1997.

Tina DeCapprio, *The Secret* (also known as *The Killing Secret* and *Whatever Happened to Angel?*), NBC, 1997.

Narrator and older Laura Ingalls Wilder, *Beyond the Prairie: The True Story of Laura Ingalls Wilder,* CBS, 2000.

Voice of Laura Ingalls Wilder, *Beyond the Prairie, Part 2: The True Story of Laura Ingalls Wilder,* CBS, 2002.

Mrs. Tompkins, *Angel in the Family,* The Hallmark Channel, 2004.

Television Appearances; Specials:

NBC 60th Anniversary Celebration, NBC, 1986.

Television Appearances; Awards Presentations:

The 59th Annual Academy Awards, ABC, 1987.

Television Appearances; Episodic:

Sarah, "Welcome to Winfield," *The Twilight Zone,* CBS, 1985.

"The Smiths," *George Burns Comedy Week,* CBS, 1985.

Sarah, "Quarantine," *The Twilight Zone,* CBS, 1986.

Irene Rutledge, "Simon Says Color Me Dead," *Murder, She Wrote,* CBS, 1987.

Patricia Pittman, "Sparky Brackman, R.I.P.?–1987," *L.A. Law,* NBC, 1987.

Debra "Deb" Krieger, "Post–Op," *thirtysomething,* ABC, 1990.

Dede, "After the Crash," *The Hidden Room,* Lifetime, 1993.

Joan, "Matthew's Old Lady," *Grace under Fire* (also known as *Grace under Pressure*), ABC, 1997.

Katie Malloy, "Sons of Thunder," *Walker, Texas Ranger,* CBS, 1997.

Virginia, "Ricochet," *Gun* (also known as *Robert Altman's "Gun"*), ABC, 1997.

Betsy Baxter, "The Empty Chair," *Touched by an Angel,* CBS, 2000.

Julia Barrett, "Bully for You," *CSI: Crime Scene Investigation* (also known as *CSI*), CBS, 2001.

Polly Danko, "Oh Mother, Who Art Thou?," *The Division* (also known as *Heart of the City*), Lifetime, 2003.

Karen Carmichael, "An Innocent Man" (also known as "You're No Jack McCallister"), *Jack & Bobby,* The WB, 2004.

May Scott, "Crash Course in Polite Conversations," *One Tree Hill,* The WB, 2004.

Barbara Nissman, "Sorry I Missed You," *Judging Amy,* CBS, 2005.

Appeared as Leanne in an episode of *Cracker* (also known as *Fitz*), ABC and Arts and Entertainment.

Television Appearances; Pilots:

Fairlight Spencer, *Christy* (also known as *Catherine Marshall's "Christy"*), CBS, 1994.

Karen Carmichael, *Jack & Bobby,* The WB, 2004.

Stage Appearances:

Macon Hill, *Abundance,* Manhattan Theatre Club, New York City, 1990.

RECORDINGS

Videos:

Herself, *Miracles & Mercies* (short documentary), Anchor Bay Entertainment, 2002.

OTHER SOURCES

Periodicals:

OzarksWatch, Volume IV, number 2, 1990.

Playboy, December, 1988, p. 202.

HARROLD, Jamie

PERSONAL

Born in Taylorville, IL; father, a truck driver. *Education:* Attended high school at the Academy for the Performing Arts, Chicago, IL; DePaul University, B.F.A.

Addresses: *Agent*—Rhonda Price, The Gersh Agency, 232 North Canon Dr., Beverly Hills, CA 90210.

Career: Actor.

CREDITS

Film Appearances:

The Violent Garden (short student film), Chalk Circle, 1990.

Stevie, *Up against the Wall,* African American Images, 1991.

Keith, *Chain of Desire,* October Films, 1992.

Waiter, *A Dog Race in Alaska,* 1993.

Pizza person, *Amateur,* Sony Pictures Classics, 1994.

Second child, *Natural Born Killers,* Warner Bros., 1994.

Billy Budd, *To Wong Foo, Thanks for Everything! Julie Newmar,* Universal, 1995.

Donnie, *Kalamazoo,* 1995.

Jackie Curtis, *I Shot Andy Warhol,* Samuel Goldwyn, 1996.

Jack's stepson, *Getting Away with Murder,* Savoy Pictures, 1996.

(Uncredited) Marc, *Bed of Roses* (also known as *Amelia and the King of Plants*), New Line Cinema, 1996.

Matthew "Matt" Edward Lynch, *I Think I Do,* Strand Releasing, 1997.

Air France airport clerk, *Too Tired to Die,* 1998.

Title role, *Henry Hill* (also known as *Play for Me*), The Asylum, 1999.

Ian, *101 Ways (The Things a Girl Will Do to Keep Her Volvo),* The Asylum, 2000.

Scott, *Erin Brockovich,* Universal, 2000.

(Uncredited) *Autumn in New York,* Metro–Goldwyn–Mayer, 2000.

Heath, *Swimming,* 2000, Oceanside Pictures, 2002.

(Uncredited) Baltimore State Forensic Hospital caretaker, *Hannibal,* Metro–Goldwyn–Mayer, 2001.

Steven, *The Score,* Paramount, 2001.

Dillon, *The Sum of All Fears* (also known as *Der Anschlag*), Paramount, 2002.

Frank, *Corn,* Revere Pictures, 2002.

Terry, *X, Y,* 2004.

Elliot Jenkins, *The Last Winter,* Antidote Films, 2005.

Whit Harrington, *Keep Your Distance,* Blue & Grey Film Ventures, 2005.

Flannel Pajamas, Carmichael Films/Gigantic Pictures, 2005.

Television Appearances; Series:

Dr. Elmer Traff, *Kingdom Hospital* (also known as *Stephen King's "Kingdom Hospital"*), ABC, 2004.

Television Appearances; Miniseries:

Randall Eberlin from the ages of fifteen to twenty–seven, *Family Pictures,* ABC, 1993.

Television Appearances; Movies:

Kendall Truitt, *A Glimpse of Hell,* FX Channel, 2001.

Television Appearances; Specials:

Nathan Leopold, *Darrow,* PBS, 1991.

Television Appearances; Episodic:

Sean, "'Tis Pity She's a Whore," *Cracker* (also known as *Fitz*), ABC, 1997.

Niall, "In a Yellow Wood," *Trinity,* NBC, 1998.

Niall, "In Loco Parentis," *Trinity,* NBC, 1998.

Niall, "... To Forgive, Divine," *Trinity,* NBC, 1998.

Niall, "Breaking In, Breaking Out, Breaking Up, Breaking Down," *Trinity,* NBC, 1999.

Bipolar patient, "20/20 Hindsight," *Wonderland,* ABC, 2000.

Dorian, "Collective," *Law & Order: Criminal Intent* (also known as *Law & Order: CI*), NBC, 2005.

OTHER SOURCES

Periodicals:

Interview, July, 2001, pp. 10, 21.

HART, Melissa Joan 1976–
(Melissa Hart)

PERSONAL

Full name, Melissa Joan Catherine Hart; born April 18, 1976, in Smithtown, NY (some sources cite Sayville, NY); daughter of William (an entrepreneur, shellfish purveyor, and clam hatchery worker) and Paula (a producer and talent manager) Hart; sister of Trisha, Elizabeth, and Emily Hart (actresses) and Brian Hart (an actor); half–sister of Alexandra Hart–Gilliams (an actress); married Mark Wilkerson (a singer and guitarist), July 19, 2003. *Education:* Attended New York University. *Avocational Interests:* Snowboarding, skiing, automobile racing, collecting Shirley Temple memorabilia, fine art, and estate jewelry.

Addresses: *Office*—Hartbreak Films, 5555 Melrose Ave., Los Angeles, CA 90038. *Agent*—Creative Artists Agency, 9830 Wilshire Blvd., Beverly Hills, CA 90212; (commercials) Brian Dubin, William Morris Agency, 1325 Avenue of the Americas, New York, NY 10019. *Publicist*—Brad Cafarelli, Bragman/Nyman/Cafarelli, Pacific Design Center, 8687 Melrose Ave., Eighth Floor, Los Angeles, CA 90069.

Career: Actress, voice performer, director, and producer. Hartbreak Films, Los Angeles, CA, cofounder, co–owner (with Paula Hart), and vice president. Appeared in commercials and print advertisements; appeared in campaigns of public service announcements, including "The More You Know" and "Express Yourself." Affiliated with charities, including the Starlight Foundation, the Hollywood for Children's Foundation, and Pediatric AIDS/Kids for Kids; Children's Museum of Manhattan, cochair. Appeared on merchandise related to *Clarissa Explains It All* and *Sabrina, the Teenage Witch.*

Awards, Honors: Youth in Film awards, best actress in a cable television show, 1992 and 1993, Young Artist awards, best young actress starring in an off–prime–

time or cable series, Young Artist Foundation, 1992, best young actress starring in a cable series, 1993, and best youth comedienne in a television show, 1995, Young Artist Award nomination, best youth actress in a leading role in a television series, 1994, and Annual CableAce Award nomination, best actress in a comedy series, National Cable Television Association, all for *Clarissa Explains It All;* Saturn Award nomination, best genre television actress, Academy of Science Fiction, Fantasy, and Horror Films, 1997, YoungStar Award nomination, best performance by a young actress in a comedy television series, *Hollywood Reporter,* 1997, Young Artist Award, best leading young performer in a television comedy series, 1998, Blimp Award, favorite television actress, Kids' Choice awards, 1998, and Blimp Award nominations, favorite television actress, 1999, 2000, 2001, 2002, and 2003, all for *Sabrina, the Teenage Witch;* Young Artist Award (with others), best performance by a young ensemble in a television movie or feature film, 1998, for *The Right Connections;* Blimp Award, favorite movie actress, 2000, for *Drive Me Crazy.*

CREDITS

Television Appearances; Series:

Clarissa Darling, *Clarissa Explains It All* (also known as *Clarissa*), Nickelodeon, 1991–94.

Title role, *Sabrina, the Teenage Witch* (also known as *Sabrina* and *Sabrina Goes to College*), ABC, 1996–2000, The WB, 2000–2003.

Host, *Mission: Makeover,* MTV, beginning 1998.

Voices of Aunt Hilda Spellman and Aunt Zelda Spellman, *Sabrina the Animated Series* (animated; also known as *Sabrina*), ABC, 1999–2000.

Television Appearances; Miniseries:

(As Melissa Hart) Florentyna Rosnovski at the age of seven, *Kane & Abel,* CBS, 1985.

(As Melissa Hart) Amy, *Christmas Snow,* NBC, 1986.

Herself, *Tying the Knot: The Wedding of Melissa Joan Hart,* ABC Family Channel, 2003.

I Love the '90s, VH1, 2004.

Television Appearances; Movies:

Samantha, *Family Reunion: A Relative Nightmare,* ABC, 1995.

Jennifer Stanton, *Twisted Desire,* NBC, 1996.

Sabrina Sawyer, "Sabrina, the Teenage Witch," *The Wonderful World of Disney,* Showtime, 1996.

Melanie Cambridge, *The Right Connections,* Showtime, 1997.

Susan Clarkson, *Two Came Back,* ABC, 1997.

Mary Stuartson, *Silencing Mary* (also known as *Campus Justice*), NBC, 1998.

Sabrina Spellman and Aunt Sophia, "Sabrina Goes to Rome," *The Wonderful World of Disney,* ABC, 1998.

Sabrina Spellman, "Sabrina Down Under," *The Wonderful World of Disney,* ABC, 1999.

Television Appearances; Specials:

Con Sawyer's little sister, "The Adventures of Con Sawyer and Hucklemary Finn," *ABC Afterschool Specials,* ABC, 1985.

NBA All–Star Stay in School Jam, multiple networks, 1992.

Cohost, *Nickelodeon's Big Helpathon,* Nickelodeon, 1994, 1995, 1996, 1997.

Host, *ABC Saturday Morning Preview Party,* ABC, 1996.

Host, *Halloween Jam V,* ABC, 1996.

Host, *Walt Disney World's Christmas Parade* (also known as *A Magical Walt Disney World Christmas*), ABC, 1997.

Host, *Walt Disney World's 25th Anniversary Party,* ABC, 1997.

Herself, *The Making of a Child Star,* E! Entertainment Television, 1997.

Christmas Miracles, ABC, 1997.

Totally California, 1997.

Host, *America's Teenagers: Growing Up on Television—A Museum of Television & Radio Special,* ABC, 1998.

Host, *Take a Moment,* The Disney Channel, 1998.

L'Oreal's Summer Music Mania '99, UPN, 1999.

Voice of Molly, *Santa Mouse and the Ratdeer* (animated), Fox Family Channel, 2000.

All–Star Bloopers, ABC, 2000.

Martha Stewart's Christmas Dream, CBS, 2000.

Host, *Holiday with the Stars,* E! Entertainment Television, 2001.

Host, *2001 Special Olympics World Winter Games,* PAX TV, 2001.

Host, *The Voyage to Atlantis: The Lost Empire,* ABC, 2001.

InStyle Celebrities at Home, NBC, 2001.

Herself, *Screen Tests of the Stars,* Independent Television, 2002.

ShirleyMania, Fox Movie Channel, 2002.

Television Appearances; Awards Presentations:

The Seventh Annual Nickelodeon Kids' Choice Awards, Nickelodeon, 1994.

Presenter, *The Eighth Annual Kids' Choice Awards,* Nickelodeon, 1995.

Presenter, *The 18th Annual CableAce Awards,* TNT, 1996.

The Ninth Annual Kids' Choice Awards, Nickelodeon, 1996.

Presenter, *The 24th Annual American Music Awards,* ABC, 1997.

The 10th Annual Kids' Choice Awards, Nickelodeon, 1997.

Presenter, *The 11th Annual Kids' Choice Awards,* Nickelodeon, 1998.

Presenter, *The 24th Annual People's Choice Awards,* CBS, 1998.

The Fourth Annual Screen Actors Guild Awards (also known as *Screen Actors Guild Fourth Annual Awards*), TNT, 1998.

Host, *The 26th Annual American Music Awards,* ABC, 1999.

Presenter, *The 25th Annual People's Choice Awards,* CBS, 1999.

The 1999 Teen Choice Awards, Fox, 1999.

Nickelodeon's 13th Annual Kids' Choice Awards, Nickelodeon, 2000.

The 2000 Teen Choice Awards, Fox, 2000.

Presenter, *Nickelodeon's 14th Annual Kids' Choice Awards,* Nickelodeon, 2001.

Presenter, *The 28th Annual American Music Awards,* ABC, 2001.

Prism Awards 2001, syndicated, 2001.

Presenter, *Nickelodeon Kids' Choice Awards '02,* Nickelodeon, 2002.

Presenter, *The 28th Annual People's Choice Awards,* CBS, 2002.

Presenter, *The 29th Annual American Music Awards,* ABC, 2002.

Presenter, *The Fifth Annual Family Television Awards,* The WB, 2003.

Presenter, *Nickelodeon's 16th Annual Kids' Choice Awards,* Nickelodeon, 2003.

Television Appearances; Episodic:

The Lucie Arnaz Show, CBS, 1985.

(As Melissa Hart) Laura Moore, "Torn," *The Equalizer,* CBS, 1986.

Roller skater, *Another World,* NBC, 1986.

Daphne, "The Tale of the Frozen Ghost," *Are You Afraid of the Dark?,* Nickelodeon, 1993.

America's Funniest People (also known as *AFV*), ABC, 1993.

Claire Latham, "Angels on the Air," *Touched by an Angel,* CBS, 1995.

Sabrina Spellman, "Genie without a Cause," *You Wish,* ABC, 1997.

Sabrina Spellman, "Mr. Wright," *Clueless,* ABC, 1997.

Sabrina Spellman, "One Dog Night," *Teen Angel,* ABC, 1997.

Sabrina Spellman, "The Witches of Pennbrook," *Boy Meets World,* ABC, 1997.

Guest, *Late Night with Conan O'Brien,* NBC, 1997.

Guest, *The Rosie O'Donnell Show,* syndicated, 1997.

Guest, *The Tonight Show with Jay Leno,* NBC, 1997, 2001.

Voice of Irma Adreen (Saturn Girl), "New Kids in Town," *The New Batman/Superman Adventures* (animated; also known as *Superman*), The WB and YTV, 1998.

Katrina, "The Good, the Bad, and the Luau," *Sabrina, the Teenage Witch* (also known as *Sabrina* and *Sabrina Goes to College*), ABC, 1999.

Mary, "Eric Gets Suspended," *That '70s Show,* Fox, 1999.

Herself, "Britney Spears: (You Drive Me) Crazy," *Making the Video,* MTV, 1999.

Guest, *The Martin Short Show,* syndicated, 1999.

Herself, *All That,* Nickelodeon, 1999.

Herself, *Total Request Live* (also known as *TRL*), MTV, 1999.

Katrina, "You Can't Twin," *Sabrina, the Teenage Witch* (also known as *Sabrina* and *Sabrina Goes to College*), The WB, 2000.

Krissy, "Fast Times at Finchmont High," *Just Shoot Me!,* NBC, 2000.

Petulant kid, "The Wild, Wild Witch," *Sabrina, the Teenage Witch* (also known as *Sabrina* and *Sabrina Goes to College*), The WB, 2000.

Herself, "Pirates," *2gether: The Series* (also known as *2gether*), MTV, 2001.

Guest, *The Late Late Show with Craig Kilborn,* CBS, 2001.

Herself, "Body by Shatzie/Sabrina/Canine Companions for Independence," *Amazing Tails,* Animal Planet, 2002.

Herself, "No Doubt," *Player$,* TechTV, 2002.

Sabrina's evil twin, "Deliver Us from E–mail," *Sabrina, the Teenage Witch* (also known as *Sabrina* and *Sabrina Goes to College*), The WB, 2002.

Guest, *The Caroline Rhea Show,* syndicated, 2002.

Guest, *Mad TV,* Fox, 2002.

Herself, *Intimate Portrait: Barbara Eden,* Lifetime, 2002.

Herself, *Intimate Portrait: Melissa Joan Hart,* Lifetime, 2002.

Herself, *Intimate Portrait: Young Hollywood,* Lifetime, 2002.

Cyrano Sabrina, "Getting to Nose You," *Sabrina, the Teenage Witch* (also known as *Sabrina* and *Sabrina Goes to College*), The WB, 2003.

Guest, *The Wayne Brady Show,* syndicated, 2003.

Herself, *Intimate Portrait: Eve Ensler,* Lifetime, 2003.

Herself, *JKX: The Jamie Kennedy Experiment* (also known as *The Jamie Kennedy Experiment* and *JKX*), The WB, 2003.

Contestant, "Tournament 1, Game 3," *Celebrity Blackjack,* GSN, 2004.

Herself, "Celebrity Weddings," *VH1: All Access* (also known as *All Access*), VH1, 2004.

Herself, "Secret Service," *North Shore,* Fox, 2004.

Guest, *On–Air with Ryan Seacrest,* syndicated, 2004.

Guest, *Tavis Smiley,* PBS, 2004.

Herself, "Small Screen, Big Stars," *TV Land's Top Ten,* TV Land, 2005.

Voice of DeeDee, "The Once and Future Thing: Time, Warped, Part 2," *Justice League: Unlimited* (animated), Cartoon Network, 2005.

Voice, "Operation Rich in Spirit," *Robot Chicken* (animated), Cartoon Network, 2005.

Appeared as Celena, *Hercules* (animated; also known as *Disney's "Hercules"*), ABC and syndicated; and as a contestant, *Get the Picture,* Nickelodeon. Appeared in episodes of *MTV Cribs* (also known as *Cribs*), MTV; *Saturday Night Live* (also known as *NBC's "Saturday Night,"* *Saturday Night,* and *SNL*), NBC; *Shelle's World; Storytime,* PBS; *Super Special Double Dare,* Nickelodeon; and *Where in the World Is Carmen Sandiego?,* PBS.

Television Appearances; Pilots:

Clarissa Darling, *Clarissa* (also known as *Clarissa, Now*), CBS, 1995.

Annabelle, "Love in the Old South," *Love American Style,* ABC, 1999.

Sabrina, *Witchright Hall,* broadcast as an episode of *Sabrina, the Teenage Witch* (also known as *Sabrina* and *Sabrina Goes to College*), The WB, 2001.

Sabrina, *Ralphie,* broadcast as an episode of *Sabrina, the Teenage Witch* (also known as *Sabrina* and *Sabrina Goes to College*), The WB, 2002.

Television Producer; Series:

Sabrina, the Teenage Witch (also known as *Sabrina* and *Sabrina, Goes to College*), ABC, 1996–2000, The WB, 2000–2003.

Sabrina, the Animated Series (animated; also known as *Sabrina*), ABC, 1999–2000.

Television Work; Miniseries:

Co–executive producer, *Tying the Knot: The Wedding of Melissa Joan Hart,* ABC Family Channel, 2003.

Television Work; Movies:

Producer, "Sabrina Goes to Rome," *The Wonderful World of Disney,* ABC, 1998.

Producer, "Sabrina Down Under," *The Wonderful World of Disney,* ABC, 1999.

Executive producer, *Child Star: The Shirley Temple Story,* ABC, 2001.

Television Director; Episodic:

"Snapshot," *So Weird,* The Disney Channel, 2000.

Sabrina, the Teenage Witch (also known as *Sabrina* and *Sabrina Goes to College*), The WB, multiple episodes, between 2000 and 2003.

"Bad Review," *Taina,* Nickelodeon, 2002.

Film Appearances:

(Uncredited) Vicki, *Can't Hardly Wait* (also known as *The Party*), Columbia, 1998.

Nicole Maris, *Drive Me Crazy* (also known as *Next to You*), Twentieth Century–Fox, 1999.

Sunlight Grrrll, *The Specials,* Regent Entertainment, 2000.

Voices of Delia Dennis and Deidre "Dee Dee" Dennis, *Batman Beyond: Return of the Joker* (animated; also known as *Batman of the Future: Return of the Joker* and *Return of the Joker*), Warner Bros., 2000.

C. J., *Backflash,* Paragon Film Group, 2001.

(Uncredited) Girl at party, *Not Another Teen Movie* (also known as *Sex Academy*), Columbia/TriStar, 2001.

Voice of Rebecca "Becky" Detweiller, *Recess: School's Out* (animated; also known as *Disney's "Recess: School's Out," Recess: The Ultimate Summer Vaca-*

tion, and *Summer Vacation: The Ultimate Recess*), Buena Vista/Walt Disney, 2001.

Holly Washburn, *Rent Control,* Hartbreak Films/ Hippofilms, 2002.

Hold On, 2002.

Jackie, *Jesus, Mary and Joey,* Federal Hill Pictures, 2003.

Lauren Wells, *Jack Satin,* 2005.

Kate, *Dirtbags,* Music Video Distributors, c. 2005.

Film Work:

Executive producer, *Rent Control,* Hartbreak Films/ Hippofilms, 2002.

Stage Appearances:

Alexandra, *Beside Herself,* Circle Repertory Theatre, New York City, 1989.

Valerie, *Imagining Brad,* Circle Repertory Theatre, Players Theatre, New York City, 1990.

Understudy, *The Crucible,* National Actors Theatre, Belasco Theatre, New York City, 1991–92.

The Vagina Monologues, off–Broadway production, 2000.

Naked TV, Los Angeles production, 2004.

RECORDINGS

Albums:

Narrator, *Britten: Young Person's Guide to the Orchestra—Prokofiev: Peter and the Wolf,* 1994.

(With Clarissa and the Straightjackets) *This Is What "NA NA" Means,* 1994.

Sabrina, the Teenage Witch: The Album, 1998.

Music Videos:

Britney Spears, "(You Drive Me) Crazy," 1999.

Videos:

(Uncredited) *Time Out with Britney Spears,* Jive/Zomba Video, 1999.

Video Games:

Nickelodeon Director's Lab, Viacom, 1994.

Voice of Sabrina Spellman, *Sabrina, the Teenage Witch: Spellbound* (also known as *Sabrina, the Teenage Witch: The Album*), 1998.

Voice of Sabrina Spellman, *Sabrina, the Teenage Witch: Brat Attack,* 1999.

WRITINGS

Teleplays; Stories for Movies:

Silencing Mary (also known as *Campus Justice*), NBC, 1998.

Juvenile:
(With others) *Hans Christian Andersen's "The Emperor's New Clothes": An All–Star Retelling of the Classic Fairy Tale,* Harcourt, Brace, 1998.

Advice columnist for *Teen Beat.*

OTHER SOURCES

Books:
Newsmakers, Issue 1, Gale, 2002.
Reisfeld, Randi, *Young Stars,* Aladdin, 1992.

Periodicals:
Cosmopolitan, July, 1999, p. 146.
Details, Volume 16, issue 5, 1997, pp. 148–55.
Entertainment Weekly, October 8, 1999, p. 47; October 15, 1999, p. 56.
Good Housekeeping, September, 1998, p. 27.
InStyle, March, 1999, pp. 308–313; February, 2000, p. 209.
Kid City, October, 1998, p. 6.
Maxim, October, 1999.
Movieline, August, 1999, pp. 48–53, 93.
Parade, June 8, 2003, p. 12.
People Weekly, December 6, 1996, p. 95; October 18, 1999, p. 170; April 24, 2000, p. 17; August 4, 2003, p. 52.
Seventeen, October, 1999, pp. 138–40.
Teen, June, 1998, pp. 44–45; March, 2001, p. 52; May, 2001, p. 58.
Time, October 4, 1999, p. 120.
TV Guide, April 6, 1996, p. 52; October 19, 1996, p. 26; April 19, 1997, p. 30; October 18, 1997, p. 18; October 2, 1999, pp. 16–19; July 26, 2003, p. 4.
Xpose, June, 2002, pp. 40–43.

HARTNETT, Josh 1978–
(Joshua Hartnett)

PERSONAL

Full name, Joshua Daniel Hartnett; born July 21, 1978, in San Francisco, CA; raised near St. Paul, MN; son of Daniel Hartnett (a building manager); stepson of Molly Hartnett (an artist). *Education:* Attended Purchase College State University of New York.

Addresses: *Office*—Roulette Productions, 6735 Yucca St., Hollywood, CA 90028. *Agent*—Creative Artists Agency, 9830 Wilshire Blvd., Beverly Hills, CA 90212.

Manager—Nancy Kremer, Kremer Management, 4545 Morse Ave., Studio City, CA 91604. *Publicist*—Susan Patricola, Patricola/Lust Public Relations, 8383 Wilshire Blvd., Suite 530, Beverly Hills, CA 90211.

Career: Actor and producer. Roulette Productions, Hollywood, CA, cofounder and partner. Appeared in commercials. Worked as a video store clerk.

Awards, Honors: Saturn Award nomination, best performance by a younger actor or actress, Academy of Science Fiction, Fantasy, and Horror Films, 1999, for *The Faculty;* MTV Movie Award nomination, best breakthrough male performance, and Blockbuster Entertainment Award nomination, favorite male newcomer, both 1999, for *Halloween H20: 20 Years Later;* named one of *Teen People* magazine's "twenty–one hottest stars under twenty–one," 1999, and "twenty-five hottest stars under twenty–five," 2002; Teen Choice Award nomination, choice breakout performance—film, 2000, for *Here on Earth;* ShoWest Award, male star of tomorrow, National Association of Theatre Owners, 2002; Teen Choice Award nomination, choice actor, drama/action adventure—film, and Phoenix Film Critics Society Award nomination (with others), best acting ensemble, both 2002, for *Black Hawk Down;* MTV Movie Award nomination, best male performance, 2002, for *Pearl Harbor;* Teen Choice Award nomination (with Shannyn Sossamon), choice chemistry—film, 2002, for *40 Days and 40 Nights.*

CREDITS

Film Appearances:
Bill, *Debutante* (also known as *Modern Girl*), 1998.
John Tate, *Halloween H20: 20 Years Later* (also known as *Halloween H20*), Miramax, 1998.
Zeke Tyler, *The Faculty,* Dimension Films/Miramax, 1998.
Trip Fontaine, *The Virgin Suicides* (also known as *Sofia Coppola's "The Virgin Suicides"*), Eternity Pictures, 1999, Paramount Classics, 2000.
Hugo Goulding, *O* (also known as *The One*), filmed 1999, Lions Gate Films, 2001.
Jasper Arnold, *Here on Earth,* Twentieth Century–Fox, 2000.
Brian Allen, *Blow Dry* (also known as *Ueber kurz oder lang*), Miramax, 2001.
Captain Danny Walker, *Pearl Harbor* (also known as *Pearl Harbour*), Buena Vista, 2001.
Gianni, *Member* (short film), 2001.
The neighbor, *The Same* (short film), Question Films, 2001.
Staff sergeant Matt Eversmann, *Black Hawk Down,* Columbia, 2001.
(As Joshua Hartnett) Tom Stoddard, *Town & Country,* New Line Cinema, 2001.

(In archive footage) John Strode/John Tate, *Halloween: Resurrection,* Dimension Films, 2002.

Matt Sullivan, *40 Days and 40 Nights* (also known as *40 jours et 40 nuits*), Miramax, 2002.

K. C. Calden, *Hollywood Homicide,* Columbia, 2003.

Matthew, *Wicker Park,* Metro–Goldwyn–Mayer, 2004.

Donald Morton, *Mozart and the Whale,* Millennium Films/Modern Digital/North by Northwest Entertainment/Swingin' Productions, 2005.

The salesman, *Sin City* (also known as *Frank Miller's "Sin City"*), Dimension Films, 2005.

Slevin, *Lucky Number Slevin,* FilmEngine/Ascendant Pictures/Capitol Films, 2005.

Stories of Lost Souls, America Video, 2005.

Bucky Bleichart, *The Black Dahlia,* Universal, 2006.

Film Producer:

Mozart and the Whale, Millenium Films/Modern Digital/North by Northwest Entertainment/Swingin' Productions, 2005.

Television Appearances; Series:

Michael Fitzgerald, *Cracker* (also known as *Fitz*), ABC and Arts and Entertainment, 1997–98.

Television Appearances; Specials:

Teen People's 21 Hottest Stars under 21, ABC, 1999.

Himself, *AFI's 100 Years, 100 Thrills: America's Most Heart–Pounding Movies,* CBS, 2001.

Himself, *Journey to the Screen: The Making of "Pearl Harbor,"* 2001.

(Uncredited; in archive footage) Himself, *Shirtless: Hollywood's Sexiest Men,* American Movie Classics, 2002.

MTV Presents Teen People Magazine's 25 Hottest Stars under 25, MTV, 2003.

Television Appearances; Awards Presentations:

Presenter, *The VH1/Vogue Fashion Awards,* VH1, 2001.

Presenter, *The 59th Annual Golden Globe Awards,* NBC, 2002.

Presenter, *The 74th Annual Academy Awards,* ABC, 2002.

The 2003 MTV Movie Awards, MTV, 2003.

Young Hollywood Awards, American Movie Classics, 2003.

Television Appearances; Episodic:

Guest, *The Late Show with David Letterman* (also known as *The Late Show*), CBS, 1998, 2002, 2004.

Guest, *The Tonight Show with Jay Leno,* NBC, multiple episodes in 2001, 2003.

Guest host, *Saturday Night Live* (also known as *NBC's "Saturday Night," Saturday Night,* and *SNL*), NBC, 2002.

Guest, *V Graham Norton,* Channel 4 (England), 2002.

Guest, *Late Night with Conan O'Brien,* NBC, 2003.

Guest, *Friday Night with Jonathan Ross,* BBC, 2004.

Guest, *The Graham Norton Effect,* Comedy Central, 2004.

Guest, *Jimmy Kimmel Live,* ABC, 2004.

Stage Appearances:

Appeared in various productions, including *Tom Sawyer.*

RECORDINGS

Videos:

Himself, *Unmasking the Horror* (documentary), 1998.

Himself, *The Essence of Combat: Making "Black Hawk Down"* (documentary), Columbia/TriStar Home Entertainment, 2003.

(Uncredited) Himself, *Sex at 24 Frames per Second* (documentary; also known as *Playboy Presents "Sex at 24 Frames per Second: The Ultimate Journey through Sex in Cinema"*), Playboy Entertainment Group, 2003.

Music Videos:

Air, "Playground Love," 1999.

Faith Hill, "There You'll Be," 2001.

OTHER SOURCES

Periodicals:

InStyle, April, 2000, p. 240.

Interview, January, 1999, pp. 68–71; February, 2000, p. 146; May 14, 2001, p. 49.

Movieline, March, 2000, pp. 78–79; July, 2001, pp. 42–46.

People Weekly, June 11, 2001, p. 69; July 2, 2001, p. 66; May 13, 2002, p. 168.

Rolling Stone, March 4, 1999, p. 75.

Teen People, May, 2000, p. 130.

HARVEY, Don

PERSONAL

Born in St. Clair Shores, MI. *Education:* Attended University of Michigan; Yale University, M.F.A.

Career: Actor.

CREDITS

Film Appearances:

Andy Cavanaugh, "Old Chief Wood'nhead," *Creepshow 2,* New World Pictures, 1987.

Officer Preseuski, *The Untouchables,* Paramount, 1987.

Kaminski, *The Beast* (also known as *The Beast of War*), Columbia, 1988.

Swede Risberg, *Eight Men Out,* Orion, 1988.

Corporal Thomas E. Clark, *Casualties of War,* Columbia, 1989.

Nathan, *After School* (also known as *Before God, Private Tutor,* and *Return to Eden*), Academy Entertainment/Moviestore Entertainment, 1989.

Garber, *Die Hard 2* (also known as *Die Hard 2: Die Harder*), Twentieth Century–Fox, 1990.

Snickers, *Hudson Hawk,* TriStar, 1991.

Rainey, *American Heart,* Triton Pictures, 1992.

Deputy Bono, *The Glass Shield* (also known as *The Johnny Johnson Trial*), Miramax, 1994.

Nolan, *Men of War* (also known as *Hombres de acero*), Miramax, 1994.

Sergeant Small, *Tank Girl,* United Artists, 1995.

Doug, *Last Dance,* Buena Vista, 1996.

The Continued Adventures of Reptile Man (And His Faithful Sidekick Tadpole), Northern Arts Entertainment, 1996.

Spota, *The Relic* (also known as *Das Relikt*), Paramount, 1997.

Flint, *Sparkler,* Strand Releasing, 1998.

Sergeant Becker, *The Thin Red Line* (also known as *La mince ligne rouge*), Twentieth Century–Fox, 1998.

Billy Bob, *Life,* MCA/Universal, 1999.

Murphy, *In Too Deep,* Miramax/Dimension Films, 1999.

Voice of Charles Buntz/Chucko, *Batman Beyond: Return of the Joker* (animated; also known as *Batman of the Future: Return of the Joker* and *Return of the Joker*), Warner Bros., 2000.

Ned Rogers, *Riders,* TheatreFire Films, 2001.

(Uncredited) Horace Rasmussen, *Corn,* Revere Pictures, 2002.

Ronnie, *Highway,* New Line Cinema, 2002.

G. Gordon Liddy, *She Hate Me,* Sony Pictures Classics, 2004.

Russell, *Swimmers,* Damage Control Productions, 2005.

Television Appearances; Miniseries:

Flight director, *From the Earth to the Moon,* HBO, 1998.

Television Appearances; Movies:

Kinderman, *Mission of the Shark: The Saga of the U.S.S. Indianapolis* (also known as *Mission of the Shark*), 1991.

Peter Resnick, *Prey of the Chameleon,* Showtime, 1992.

Del Collins, *Better Off Dead,* 1993.

Freddie Wakeman, *Jericho Fever,* USA Network, 1993.

T. M., *Saved by the Light,* Fox, 1995.

Willy Knapp, *Sawbones* (also known as *Prescription for Murder* and *Roger Corman Presents "Sawbones"*), Showtime, 1995.

Lieutenant Gus Kramer, *Crime of the Century,* HBO, 1996.

Quinn Harris, *Face of Evil,* CBS, 1996.

T. J., *The Con,* USA Network, 1998.

Kurt Lewis, *Never Say Die* (also known as *Outside the Law*), 2001.

Television Appearances; Specials:

Kevin, "High School Narc," *ABC Afterschool Special,* ABC, 1985.

Television Appearances; Episodic:

Don Beaks, "Hell Hath No Fury," *Miami Vice,* NBC, 1988.

Detective Hubie Flaherty, "Bad Girls," *New York Undercover* (also known as *Uptown Undercover*), Fox, 1995.

Voice of Gnaww, "The Main Man: Parts 1 & 2," *Superman* (animated; also known as *Superman: The Animated Series*), The WB, 1996.

Benny Flynn, "Days Past," *Walker, Texas Ranger,* CBS, 1997.

Voice of Milos Duncek, "The Haunted Sonata," *The Real Adventures of Jonny Quest* (animated; also known as *Jonny Quest*), TBS, Cartoon Network, and syndicated, 1997.

Joey Melino, "A Stand–Up Guy," *Pretender,* NBC, 1998.

Dirk, "Queasy Rider," *The King of Queens,* CBS, 1999.

Mr. Job, "Meltdown," *The Pretender,* NBC, 2000.

Voices of guard and Vincent D'Anacable, "The Last Resort," *Batman Beyond* (animated), The WB, 2000.

Mr. Schudy, "Never Say Never," *ER* (also known as *Emergency Room*), NBC, 2001.

"Most Likely," *Crossing Jordan,* NBC, 2004.

Darrell Yellen, "Coded," *Medium,* NBC, 2005.

Voice of Chucko, "The Once and Future Thing: Time Warped, Part 2," *Justice League: Unlimited* (animated), Cartoon Network, 2005.

Stage Appearances:

Frankie, *A Lie of the Mind,* Promenade Theatre, New York City, 1985–86.

Lenny, *Progress,* Long Wharf Theatre, New Haven, CT, 1986–87.

Demetrius, *Titus Andronicus,* New York Shakespeare Festival, Public Theatre, Delacorte Theatre, New York City, 1989.

RECORDINGS

Video Games:

Voices of pilot, SWAT team member, and techcom technician, *Terminator 3: Redemption,* Atari, 2004.

HASKINS, Dennis 1950–

PERSONAL

Born November 18, 1950, in Chattanooga, TN. *Education:* Attended the University of Tennessee at Chattanooga.

Career: Actor. Worked as a music manager, agent, and concert promoter in the music industry.

Member: Kappa Sigma.

CREDITS

Television Appearances; Series:
Mr. Richard Belding, *Good Morning, Miss Bliss* (also known as *Saved by the Bell: The Junior High Years*), The Disney Channel, c. 1987–89.
Mr. Richard Belding, *Saved By the Bell,* NBC, 1989–93.
Principal Richard Belding, *Saved By the Bell: The New Class,* NBC, c. 1993–2000.

Television Appearances; Miniseries:
Airline attendant, *Deadly Intentions,* ABC, 1985.
Himself, *I Love the '80s,* VH1, 2002.

Television Appearances; Movies:
Steven Fish, *The Image,* HBO, 1990.
Mr. Richard Belding, *Saved By the Bell—Hawaiian Style,* NBC, 1992.
Mr. Richard Belding, *Saved By the Bell—Wedding in Las Vegas,* NBC, 1994.
Captain Dale Landry, *Red Water,* TBS, 2003.

Television Appearances; Awards Presentations:
Prism Awards 2000, syndicated, 2000.

Television Appearances; Episodic:
Moss, "One Armed Bandits," *The Dukes of Hazzard,* CBS, 1979.
Charlie Watkins, "The Late J. D. Hogg," *The Dukes of Hazzard,* CBS, 1980.
Worker, "Growing Up Is Hard to Do: Part 1," *Archie Bunker's Place,* CBS, 1981.
Deputy, "Guess Who's Coming to Town?," *The Fall Guy,* ABC, 1982.
Plant worker, "Fallout," *CHiPs,* NBC, 1982.
Trigg, "Now You See It," *The Greatest American Hero,* ABC, 1982.
Officer, "Loss of Innocence," *Knots Landing,* CBS, 1983.

Elmo, "Cale Yarborough Comes to Hazzard," *The Dukes of Hazzard,* CBS, 1984.
Gate guard, "Undercover Dukes," *The Dukes of Hazzard,* CBS, 1984.
Del Haynes, "Autumn Warrior," *Magnum, P.I.,* CBS, 1986.
Man in station wagon, "What If ... ," *Amazing Stories,* NBC, 1986.
Bledsoe, "Voices in the Earth," *The Twilight Zone,* CBS, 1987.
Hal Latimer, "Hiroshima Maiden," *WonderWorks,* PBS, 1988.
Dr. Stan, "No Free Lunch," *Doctor Doctor,* CBS, 1990.
Coach MacIntyre, "The Ringer," *Hangin' with Mr. Cooper,* ABC, 1995.
Himself, "Murray for Mayor," *Malibu, CA,* syndicated, 1999.
Dr. Peters, "An Early Frost," *The Practice,* ABC, 2001.
Second CEO donor, "Bartlet for America," *The West Wing,* NBC, 2001.
Mr. Belding, "One Day a Time: Pressure/Saved by the Bell: Miss Bayside," *The Rerun Show,* NBC, 2002.
Himself, *Saved by the Bell: The E! True Hollywood Story,* E! Entertainment Television, 2002.
Traffic officer, "Stand Up," *7th Heaven* (also known as *7th Heaven: Beginnings*), The WB, 2003.
Airport security S–1, "Hard Time," *JAG,* CBS, 2004.

Appeared in episodes of *Frank's Place,* CBS; *Ohara,* ABC; *Scrabble,* NBC; and *Storytime,* PBS.

Television Appearances; Pilots:
Biker, *One Night Band,* CBS, 1983.
Mr. Richard Belding, *Saved By the Bell Graduation Special,* NBC, 1993.

Film Appearances:
Dr. Baldwin, *Eyewitness to Murder,* New Horizons Home Video, 1991.
Boyd Russell, *The Boy with the X–Ray Eyes* (also known as *X–Ray Boy* and *X–treme Teens*), Full Moon Entertainment/Kushner–Locke, 1999.
Ginger's Rise, c. 1999.
Laura's dad, *18,* Eighteen Productions/Misconstrued Productions, 2000.
Mr. Kohls (band teacher), *Max Keeble's Big Move,* Buena Vista/Walt Disney Pictures, 2001.
Dean Hendricks, *The Stoneman,* 2002.
Ronald Smith, *An Ordinary Killer,* Collective Development, 2002.
Toss Honeycut, *Tangy Guacamole,* York Entertainment, 2003.
Uncle Frank, *Going Down,* PAIA Pictures, 2003.
Mr. Makepiece, *Dead End Road,* 2004.
Joe, *Reverie,* Transdermal Entertainment, 2005.
Sheriff Folgar, *Wild Michigan,* American World Pictures, 2005.
Sheriff Thomas, *The Painted Forest,* Painted Pictures, 2005.

Appeared in a short film relating to *Wild Michigan.*

Stage Appearances:
The Taming of the Shrew, Alliance Theatre Company, Atlanta, GA, 1978.
Look Homeward, Angel, Pasadena Playhouse, Pasadena, CA, 1986.
Angry Housewives, Odyssey Theatre, Los Angeles, 1988.

RECORDINGS

Videos:
Behind the Scenes of "Going Down" (short documentary; also known as *The Making of "Going Down"*), PAIA Pictures, 2004.

WRITINGS

Nonfiction:
Rating the Agents, two volumes, 1988.

OTHER SOURCES

Periodicals:
People Weekly, October 22, 2001, p. 110.

HATOSY, Shawn 1975–
   (Shawn Wayne Hatosy)

PERSONAL

Surname is pronounced Hot–a–see; born December 29, 1975, in Ijamsville, Frederick County, MD; son of Wayne (a graphic designer) and Carol (some sources cite Cindy; a loan officer) Hatosy. *Avocational Interests:* Playing the guitar, playing tennis.

Addresses: *Agent*—Paradigm, 360 North Crescent Dr., North Building, Beverly Hills, CA 90210. *Manager*—Mary Erickson, Mary Erickson Entertainment, 8955 Norma Place, West Hollywood, CA 90069. *Publicist*—Kelly Bush, ID Public Relations, 8409 Santa Monica Blvd., West Hollywood, CA 90069.

Career: Actor. Appeared in local stage productions in Maryland, beginning c. 1985, in local public television programs, and in commercials; performed as musician, singer, and songwriter with the bands Lock Haven and Element.

Awards, Honors: Golden Satellite Award nomination, best performance by an actor in a supporting role in a series, miniseries, or motion picture made for television, International Press Academy, 2004, for *Soldier's Girl.*

CREDITS

Film Appearances:
(As Shawn Wayne Hatosy) Counter boy, *Home for the Holidays,* Paramount, 1995.
Gus, *All over Me,* Fine Line Features, 1996.
(As Shawn Wayne Hatosy) Sean, *No Way Home,* Live Film and Mediaworks, 1996.
Billy, *The Postman,* Warner Bros., 1997.
Jack, *In & Out,* Paramount, 1997.
Lead high school punk, *Niagara, Niagara* (also known as *Niagra Niagra*), 1997.
Victor, *Inventing the Abbotts,* Twentieth Century–Fox, 1997.
Stan Rosado, *The Faculty,* Miramax, 1998.
Benny, *Anywhere but Here,* Twentieth Century–Fox, 1999.
Cam, *The Joyriders,* DreamWorks/PorchLight Entertainment/Trident Releasing, 1999.
Timothy "Tim" Dunphy, *Outside Providence,* Miramax, 1999.
Young Vinnie Webb, *Simpatico,* Fine Line Features/Phaedra Cinema, 1999.
Eddie Hicks, *Down to You,* Miramax, 2000.
Brendan Behan (title role), *Borstal Boy,* 2000, Strand Releasing, 2002.
David Klein, *Tangled,* Dimension Films/Buena Vista Home Video, 2001.
Luther, *Deadrockstar,* Brink Films/Mosaic Films, 2002.
Mitch Quigley, *John Q,* New Line Cinema, 2002.
Duffy, *11:14,* Media 8 Entertainment, 2003.
Jim, *A Guy Thing,* Metro–Goldwyn–Mayer, 2003.
Mikey, *The Cooler,* Lions Gate Films, 2003.
Rusty, *Dallas 362* (also known as *Dallas and Rusty*), 2003, ThinkFilm, 2005.
Carter, *Little Athens,* Legaci Pictures, 2005.
Clyde Tyler, *Swimmers,* Damage Control Productions, 2005.
Elvis Schmidt, *Alpha Dog,* New Line Cinema, 2005.
Running Scared, New Line Cinema, c. 2005.

Television Appearances; Movies:
Quentin Vale, *Inflammable,* CBS, 1995.
Derek Kaminiski, *Double Jeopardy* (also known as *Victim of the Night*), Showtime, 1996.
Sean Batton, *Witness Protection,* HBO, 1999.
Justin Fisher, *Soldier's Girl,* Showtime, 2003.
Older Joe Stoshack, *The Winning Season,* TNT, 2004.
John McCain, *Faith of My Fathers,* Arts and Entertainment, 2005.

Television Appearances; Awards Presentations:
The 1999 MTV Movie Awards, MTV, 1999.

Television Appearances; Episodic:
(As Shawn Wayne Hatosy) Lyle Warner, "The Old and
the Dead," *Homicide: Life on the Street* (also
known as *Homicide* and *Homicide: LOTS*), NBC,
1995.
Chester Manning, "Savior," *Law & Order,* NBC, 1996.
Owen, "Moving On," *Felicity,* The WB, 2001.
Brody Farrell, "In the Game," *Six Feet Under,* HBO,
2002.
Owen, "Future Shock," *Felicity,* The WB, 2002.
Mario Devlin, "Pharaoh's Curse," *The Twilight Zone,*
UPN, 2003.
Himself, "Kevin Costner," *Biography* (also known as
A&E Biography: Kevin Costner), Arts and Entertain-
ment, 2003.
Jeff Simon, "Weeping Willows," *CSI: Crime Scene Inves-
tigation* (also known as *CSI*), CBS, 2005.

Stage Appearances:
Lost in Yonkers, Fredericktowne Players, MD, c. 1994.
Jock, *Roulette,* Ensemble Studio Theatre, John House-
man Theatre, New York City, 2004.

RECORDINGS

Music Videos:
Wheatus, "A Little Respect," 2001.

OTHER SOURCES

Periodicals:
Baltimore, July, 1999.
Detour, November, 1999.
Jump, August, 1999.
Los Angeles Times, August 29, 1999.
Mt. Airy Messenger, September 1, 1999.
Parade, July 25, 1999; October 31, 1999.
Ray Gun, July, 1999.
Seventeen, September, 1999.
Teen Movieline, summer, 2000.
TV Guide Ultimate Cable, December, 1999.

Electronic:
Shawn Hatosy Official Site, http://www.shawnhatosy.
com, March 14, 2005.
Washingtonian Online, January, 2000.

HAUSER, Cole 1975–

PERSONAL

Full name, Cole K. Hauser; born March 22, 1975, in
Laurel Springs (near Santa Barbara), CA; son of Wings

Hauser (an actor, director, and writer) and Cass Warner
Sperling (founder of the film production company
Warner Sisters); great–grandson of Harry M. Warner (a
film executive and founder of Warner Bros.). *Education:* Studied acting and improvisation.

Addresses: *Agent*—Jim Osborne, International Creative
Management, 8942 Wilshire Blvd., Beverly Hills, CA
90211. *Manager*—Nine Yards Entertainment, 8530
Wilshire Blvd., Beverly Hills, CA 90211. *Publicist*—
Platform Public Relations, 2666 North Beachwood Dr.,
Los Angeles, CA 90068.

Career: Actor. Appeared in summer theatrical
productions. Former semiprofessional soccer player.

Awards, Honors: Independent Spirit Award nomination,
best supporting male actor, Independent Features
Project/West, 2001, for *Tigerland;* Young Hollywood
Award, breakthrough male performance, *Movieline,*
2003.

CREDITS

Film Appearances:
Jack Connors, *School Ties,* Paramount, 1992.
Benny O'Donnell, *Dazed and Confused,* Gramercy
Pictures, 1993.
Cal, *Frame–Up II: The Cover–Up* (also known as *Deadly
Conspiracy*), 1993.
Bentz, *Skins* (also known as *Gang Boys*), Sunset Films
International, 1995.
Scott Moss, *Higher Learning,* Columbia, 1995.
Mark, *All over Me,* Fine Line Features, 1996.
Billy McBride, *Good Will Hunting,* Miramax, 1997.
Johnny, *Scotch and Milk,* Sundance Channel, 1998.
Little Boy Matson, *The Hi–Lo Country* (also known as
Hi–Lo Country—Im Land der letzten Cowboys),
Gramercy Pictures, 1998.
Staff Sergeant Cota, *Tigerland,* Twentieth Century–Fox,
2000.
William J. Johns, *Pitch Black* (also known as *The
Chronicles of Riddick: Pitch Black*), USA Films,
2000.
Kelsey O'Brian, *A Shot at Glory,* 2000, Mac Releasing,
2002.
Ray, *White Oleander* (also known as *Weisser Olean-
der*), Warner Bros., 2002.
Staff sergeant Vic W. Bedford, *Hart's War,* Metro–
Goldwyn–Mayer, 2002.
Carter Verone, *2 Fast 2 Furious,* Universal, 2003.
James "Red" Atkins, *Tears of the Sun,* Columbia/Sony
Pictures Entertainment, 2003.
Bo Laramie, *Paparazzi,* Twentieth Century–Fox, 2004.
Jack, *The Cave* (also known as *Prime Evil*), Screen
Gems, 2005.

Lieutenant, *Dirty,* Deviant Films/Silver Nitrate Pictures, 2005.

Lupus, *The Break Up,* Universal, 2006.

Television Appearances; Series:

Officer Randy Willitz, *High Incident,* ABC, 1996–97.

Television Appearances; Miniseries:

Rocky Jackson, *A Matter of Justice* (also known as *Final Justice*), NBC, 1993.

Television Appearances; Awards Presentations:

Presenter, *The 2001 IFP/West Independent Spirit Awards,* Independent Film Channel, 2001.

Presenter, *The Third Annual Taurus World Stunt Awards,* USA Network, 2003.

Young Hollywood Awards, American Movie Classics, 2003.

Television Appearances; Episodic:

Guest, *Dinner for Five,* Independent Film Channel, 2003.

Steve Curtis, "Drive," *ER* (also known as *Emergency Room*), NBC, 2004.

Steve Curtis, "Just a Touch," *ER* (also known as *Emergency Room*), NBC, 2004.

Steve Curtis, "Midnight," *ER* (also known as *Emergency Room*), NBC, 2004.

Steve Curtis, "Where There's Smoke," *ER* (also known as *Emergency Room*), NBC, 2004.

Guest, *The Late Late Show with Craig Kilborn,* CBS, 2004.

RECORDINGS

Videos:

Himself, *Journey to Safety: Making "Tears of the Sun"* (short documentary), Columbia/TriStar Home Video, 2003.

Video Games:

Voice of William J. Johns, *The Chronicles of Riddick: Escape from Butcher Bay,* Tigon Studios, 2004.

OTHER SOURCES

Periodicals:

Entertainment Weekly, October 25, 2002, p. 18.

Movieline, March, 2003, p. 14.

People Weekly, June 23, 2003, p. 121.

HAYDEN, Michael 1963–

PERSONAL

Born July 28, 1963, in St. Paul, MN; married Elizabeth Sastre (an actress); children: one daughter. *Education:* Graduated from St. John's University, Jamaica, NY; Juilliard School, M.F.A. *Avocational Interests:* Travel, animals, sports, family activities.

Career: Actor. Shakespeare Theatre, Washington, DC, member of company, 1999–2000.

Awards, Honors: *Theatre World* Award, Drama Desk Award nomination, and Laurence Olivier Award nomination, Society of West End Theatre, all c. 1994, for *Carousel;* Best Actor Award, AFI Fest, 1999, for *Charming Billy;* Antoinette Perry Award nomination, best featured actor in a play, 2001, for *Judgment at Nuremberg.*

CREDITS

Stage Appearances:

Ambrose/August, *The Matchmaker,* Roundabout Theatre Company, Union Square Theatre, New York City, 1991.

Dean Swift, *Nebraska,* Theatre Row Theatre, New York City, 1992.

Billy Bigelow, *Carousel* (musical), Royal National Theatre, London, 1993, then Vivian Beaumont Theatre, Lincoln Center, New York City, 1994–95.

Easter Bonnet Competition: A Salute to 100 Years of Broadway, Minskoff Theatre, New York City, 1994.

Chris Keller, *All My Sons,* Roundabout Theatre Company, Laura Pels Theatre (now Criterion Theatre), New York City, 1997.

Chance Wayne, *Sweet Bird of Youth,* Shakespeare Theatre, Lansburgh Theatre, Washington, DC, 1998.

Christy Mahon, *Playboy of the Western World,* Guthrie Theatre, Minneapolis, MN, 1998.

Lieutenant Sparky Watts, *Far East,* Mitzi E. Newhouse Theatre, New York City, 1999.

Burning Blue (reading), Westside Theatre, New York City, 1999.

Clifford Bradshaw, *Cabaret* (musical), Roundabout Theatre Company, Studio 54, between 1999 and 2001.

Title role, *Coriolanus,* Shakespeare Theatre, 2000.

Kilroy, *Camino Real,* Shakespeare Theatre, 2000.

Oscar Rolfe, *Judgment at Nuremberg,* National Actors Theatre, Longacre Theatre, New York City, 2001.

Camila, Philadelphia, PA, 2001.

Franklin Shephard, *Merrily We Roll Along* (musical), Eisenhower Theatre, John F. Kennedy Center for the Performing Arts, Washington, DC, 2002.

The Enchanted Cottage (musical), National Alliance for Musical Theatre, New York City, 2002.

Sondheim Concert Spectacular, Avery Fisher Hall, Lincoln Center, New York City, 2002.

Antony Wilding, *Enchanted April*, Belasco Theatre, New York City, 2003.

Henry (Prince Hal), *Henry IV*, Vivian Beaumont Theatre, Lincoln Center, 2003–2004.

110 Stories (staged reading), Public Theatre, New York City, 2004.

Paris Bound (staged reading), Bleecker Street Theatre, New York City, 2004.

Adam Nehemiah, *Dessa Rose* (musical), Mitzi E. Newhouse Theatre, 2005.

Also appeared in *End of the Day, Hello Again,* and *Off–Key.*

Television Appearances; Series:

Chris Docknovich, *Murder One*, ABC, 1995–97.

Also appeared in *Another World*, NBC, and *As the World Turns.*

Television Appearances; Miniseries:

Chris Docknovich, *Murder One: Diary of a Serial Killer*, ABC, 1997.

Michael Luciano, *Bella Mafia*, 1997.

Television Appearances; Episodic:

Henri Girard, "Soldier of Fortune," *Law & Order*, NBC, 2001.

Dr. Walt Massey, "Angels," *Law & Order: Special Victims Unit*, NBC, 2002.

Nick Bennett, "Husbands and Wives," *Hack*, CBS, 2002.

Kenneth Rayfield, "Suite Sorrow," *Law & Order: Criminal Intent*, NBC, 2003.

Television Appearances; Specials:

Some Enchanted Evening: Celebrating Oscar Hammerstein II (also known as *Celebrating Oscar Hammerstein II*), PBS, 1995.

Sparky Watts, *Far East*, PBS, 2001.

Television Appearances; Other:

Luke Constable, *In the Name of Love: A Texas Tragedy* (movie; also known as *After Laurette* and *Texas Heat: Love and Murder*), Fox, 1995.

Witt Porter, *Glory, Glory* (pilot), CBS, 1998.

Film Appearances:

Jeremiah William "Billy" Starkman, *Charming Billy*, WinStar Cinema, 1998.

HAYNIE, Jim

PERSONAL

Addresses: *Agent*—GVA Talent Agency, 9229 Sunset Blvd., Suite 320, Hollywood, CA 90069.

Career: Actor.

CREDITS

Film Appearances:

Guard, *Escape from Alcatraz*, Paramount, 1979.

First cop, *Time After Time*, Avco Embassy/Warner Bros., 1979.

Hank Jones, *The Fog* (also known as *John Carpenter's "The Fog"*), Avco Embassy, 1980.

First hot dog man, *Chu Chu and the Philly Flash*, 1981.

Old cop, *48 Hrs.,* Paramount, 1982.

Tommy, optometrist, and Carl, *Out* (also known as *Deadly Drifter*), Cinegate, 1982.

Air Force major, *The Right Stuff*, Warner Bros., 1983.

Arlon Brewer, *Country*, Buena Vista, 1984.

Owen Riley, *On the Edge*, Skouras Pictures, 1985.

Bradley, *Silverado*, 1985.

Lieutenant Fisher, *Hard Traveling*, New World, 1986.

Donnelly, *Pretty in Pink*, Paramount, 1986.

Morty Morton, *Action Jackson*, Warner Bros. Home Video, 1988.

Jack Haines, *From Hollywood to Deadwood*, Island Pictures, 1988.

Sergeant Gabriel, *Jack's Back*, Paramount, 1988.

Jake McDermott, *Staying Together*, Hemdale, 1989.

Captain Malone, *I Come in Peace* (also known as *Dark Angel*), Media Home Entertainment, 1990.

Mr. Buckley, *Men Don't Leave*, Warner Bros., 1990.

Father Seamus Kelly, *Too Much Sun*, RCA–Columbia, 1991.

Sheriff, *Big Girls Don't Cry ... They Get Even* (also known as *Stepkids*), New Line Cinema, 1992.

Sheriff Ira, *Sleepwalkers* (also known as *Sleepstalkers* and *Stephen King's "Sleepwalkers"*), Columbia, 1992.

Richard Johnson, *The Bridges of Madison County*, Warner Bros., 1995.

General Garnett, *The Peacemaker*, DreamWorks, 1997.

Jerry, *The Last Time I Committed Suicide*, 1997.

Bill Stone, *Bulworth*, Twentieth Century–Fox, 1998.

Jack, *The Gold Cup*, Full Circle Films, 2000.

Andy, *Andy Across the Water* (short film), Jean–Michel Dissard, 2002.

Ed Tobias, *Bringing Down the House*, Buena Vista, 2003.

Meyer, *Hide* (short film), Amado Pictures, 2003.

Ben, *The United States of Leland*, Paramount Classics, 2004.

Television Appearances; Movies:

First officer, *Undercover with the KKK* (also known as *The Freedom Riders* and *My Undercover Years with the KKK*), NBC, 1979.

Vernon Richards, *Homeward Bound*, CBS, 1980.

Doc Vandecamp, *Bitter Harvest*, NBC, 1981.

Swathmore, *Midnight Lace*, NBC, 1981.

Executive, *The Princess and the Cabbie*, CBS, 1981.

Lloyd, *Toughlove*, ABC, 1985.

Sheriff, *Brotherhood of Justice*, ABC, 1986.

Federal marshal, *Kung Fu: The Movie*, CBS, 1986.

Judge Winthrop, *Three on a Match*, NBC, 1987.

David Hartzfield, *The Image*, HBO, 1990.

Cantrell, *Hell Hath No Fury*, NBC, 1991.

Oscar, *Grand Tour: Disaster in Time* (also known as *Disaster in Time*, *The Grand Tour*, and *Timescape*), Showtime, 1992.

Star (also known as *Danielle Steel's "Star"*), NBC, 1993.

Tom Tyson, *Kiss of a Killer*, ABC, 1993.

Mr. Gil Sutton, *The Odd Couple: Together Again*, CBS, 1993.

Brad St. Clair, *Armed and Innocent*, CBS, 1994.

Byron Estes, *Betrayed by Love*, ABC, 1994.

Television Appearances; Miniseries:

Salkin, *Alcatraz: The Whole Shocking Story* (also known as *Alcatraz* and *Clarence Carnes*), NBC, 1980.

Power, NBC, 1980.

Ned Tuckmill, *Blood Feud*, syndicated, 1983.

Dob Fowler, *A Death in California* (also known as *Psychopath*), ABC, 1985.

Chief Kulbeth (some sources cite Officer Scott), *I Know My First Name Is Steven* (also known as *The Missing Years*), NBC, 1989.

Deputy Kingsolving, *The Stand* (also known as *Stephen King's "The Stand"*), ABC, 1994.

Television Appearances; Episodic:

Frank Reston, "No Big Thing," *Knight Rider*, 1982.

Deke Larson, Sr., "One Fresh Batch of Lemonade: Parts 1 & 2," *Highway to Heaven*, 1984.

Detective Flynn, "You're in Alice's," *Hill Street Blues*, 1985.

Detective Flynn, "Grin and Bear It," *Hill Street Blues*, 1985.

Kyle, "North by North Dipesto," *Moonlighting*, 1986.

Jake, "Body & Soul," *Falcon Crest*, 1987.

"The Execution of John Saringo," *Midnight Caller*, 1988.

"Some of That Jazz," *Hooperman*, 1989.

Judge Nelson Dunley, "The Mouse that Soared," *L.A. Law*, NBC, 1989.

Father Pete Riley, "The Talisman," *The Young Riders*, 1991.

Judge Stuart Thompson, "Alice Oakley Doesn't Live Here Anymore," *I'll Fly Away*, NBC, 1992.

Captain Lewis, "The Abduction," *Matlock*, 1992.

Gillis Toomey, "Midnight Sun," *Northern Exposure*, 1992.

Sheriff John Hoyt, "Killin' Time—June 18, 1958," *Quantum Leap*, 1992.

Jefferson K. Wallace, "The President's Coming," *Bakersfield P.D.*, Fox, 1993.

Grit, "Life Goes On: Parts 1 & 2," *Empty Nest*, NBC, 1995.

Jake Hilfiger, "These Successful Friends of Mine," *Ellen*, ABC, 1995.

"The Cattle Drive," *The Lazarus Man*, 1996.

Ben Miller, "Exposed," *The Pretender*, NBC, 1997.

Ben Miller, "Mirage," *The Pretender*, NBC, 1997.

Don Borman, "Devotion," *Michael Hayes*, CBS, 1998.

Nelson Hickes, "Gun with the Wind," *Chicago Hope*, CBS, 1998.

Albert Hall, "Liar's Club: Part 1," *Family Law*, CBS, 2001.

Floyd, "Bachelor Party," *Titus*, Fox, 2002.

"The Glass Ceiling," *American Family*, 2002.

Tom, "She's Positive," *The Parkers*, UPN, 2004.

Appeared as Sheriff Ford in *Crossroads*, ABC.

Television Appearances; Series:

Garrett Gordon, a recurring role, *Dallas*, 1986–87.

Lenny Goodman, *Take Five*, CBS, 1987.

Television Appearances; Specials:

Alfred Newton, *God, the Universe, and Hot Fudge Sundaes*, CBS, 1986.

Narrator, *Private Debts*, Showtime, 1993.

Preacher, *On Hope*, Showtime, 1994.

Distinguished man at table, *The Gift*, Showtime, 1994.

Desert's Edge, The Movie Channel, 1997.

Television Appearances; Pilots:

Potts, *Rowdies*, ABC, 1986.

Stage Appearances:

Walt Bates, *Book of Days*, St. Louis, MO, and Hartford, CT, both 1999, then Signature Theatre Company, Peter Norton Space, New York City, 2002.

Also appeared in *Looking for Normal*, Geffen Playhouse, Los Angeles; and as Lee, *True West*, Magic Theatre, San Francisco, CA.

HEINRICHS, Rick
(Richard Heinrichs)

PERSONAL

Born in San Rafael, CA; married, wife's name Dawn. *Education:* California Institute of the Arts, graduated; Boston University, B.F.A.; attended School of Visual Arts, New York City; studied with cartoonists Will Eisner and Harvey Kurtzman.

Addresses: *Manager*—Sandra Marsh Management, 9150 Wilshire Blvd., Suite 220, Beverly Hills, CA 90212.

Career: Production designer, art director, and set designer. WED Enterprises, sculptor for audio–animatronic figures for theme parks, 1979; Walt Disney Studios, assistant animator and model creator, beginning 1979; Greenlite, worked as stop–motion animator; also worked as animation effects and models supervisor and as visual consultant; frequent collaborator with filmmaker Tim Burton.

Awards, Honors: Los Angeles Film Critics Association Award, best production design, 1999, Academy Award, best art direction or set decoration (with Peter Young), Film Award, British Academy of Film and Television Arts, best production design, Golden Satellite Award, best art direction or production design (with others), Sierra Award, Las Vegas Film Critics Society, best production design, and Art Directors Guild Award, excellence in production design for a feature film (with others), all 2000, all for *Sleepy Hollow*; Art Directors Guild Award, excellence in production design for a period or fantasy feature film (with others), and Academy Award nomination, best achievement in art direction (with Cheryl Carasik), both 2005, for *Lemony Snicket's A Series of Unfortunate Events.*

CREDITS

Film Work; Production Designer:
Fargo, Gramercy, 1996.
The Big Lebowski, Gramercy, 1998.
Sleepy Hollow, Paramount, 1999.
Bedazzled (also known as *Teuflisch*), Twentieth Century–Fox, 2000.
Planet of the Apes, Twentieth Century–Fox, 2001.
Hulk, Universal, 2003.
Lemony Snicket's A Series of Unfortunate Events, Paramount, 2004.

Film Work; Art Director:
Batman Returns, Warner Bros., 1992.
Last Action Hero, Columbia, 1993.

Film Work; Set Designer:
Ghostbusters II, Columbia, 1989.
Edward Scissorhands, Twentieth Century–Fox, 1990.
Joe Versus the Volcano, Warner Bros., 1990.
The Fisher King, TriStar, 1991.

Film Work; Other:
Producer and sculpture designer, *Vincent* (animated short film), 1982.
Stop–motion animator, *The Adventures of Buckaroo Banzai: Across the 8th Dimension,* Twentieth Century–Fox, 1984.
Associate producer, *Frankenweenie,* 1984.
Animation effects supervisor, *Pee–Wee's Big Adventure,* Warner Bros., 1985.
Models and miniatures supervisor, *Nutcracker: The Motion Picture,* Atlantic, 1986.
Supervising art director, *Tall Tale* (also known as *Tall Tale: The Unbelievable Adventures of Pecos Bill*), 1995.

Television Work:
Stop–motion animator, *Hansel and Gretel,* 1982.
Art director, *To the Moon, Alice* (special), Showtime, 1990.
Production designer, *Fallen Angels* (series), Showtime, 1995.

Television Appearances; Specials:
The Making of "Planet of the Apes," 2001.

Television Appearances; Episodic:
"Planet of the Apes," *HBO First Look,* HBO, 2001.

RECORDINGS

Videos:
Sleepy Hollow: Behind the Legend, Mandalay/ Paramount, 2000.

OTHER SOURCES

Periodicals:
Washington Post, December 18, 2004, pp. C1, C2.

HENNESSY, Jill 1968–
(Jillian Hennessy)

PERSONAL

Born November 25, 1968, in Edmonton, Alberta, Canada; daughter of John (a sales and marketing executive) and Maxine (a secretary) Hennessy; twin sister of

Jacqueline Hennessy (an actress; also known as Jac Hennessy); married Paolo Mastropietro (an actor and bartender), October 1, 2000; children: Marco. *Avocational Interests:* Playing the guitar, riding motorcycles, cooking.

Addresses: *Agent*—International Creative Management, 8942 Wilshire Blvd., Beverly Hills, CA 90211.

Career: Actress. The New Originals (an alternative and folk band), guitarist; also worked as a model. Hennessy's Tavern (restaurant), Northvale, NJ, 1999; also worked as a bartender, waitress, and street performer.

Awards, Honors: Screen Actors Guild Award nomination (with others), outstanding performance by an ensemble in a drama series, 1997, for *Law and Order;* Golden Satellite Award, best performance by an actress in a miniseries or a motion picture made for television, 2001, for *Nuremberg;* Golden Satellite Award nomination, best performance by an actress in a supporting role in a miniseries or a motion picture made for television, 2002, for *Jackie, Ethel, Joan: The Women of Camelot.*

CREDITS

Film Appearances:

(As Jillian Hennessy) Mimsy, *Dead Ringers* (also known as *Gemini* and *Twins*), Twentieth Century–Fox, 1988.

Kathryn Darby, *Trip nach Tunis,* 1993.

Dr. Marie Lazarus, *Robocop 3* (also known as *RoboCop 3*), Orion, 1993.

Deanne White, *The Paper,* Universal, 1994.

Laura, *I Shot Andy Warhol,* Samuel Goldwyn Company, 1996.

Detective Angela Pierce, *Kiss & Tell,* 1996.

Lindsay Hamilton, *A Smile Like Yours,* Paramount, 1997.

Dr. Victoria Constantini, *Most Wanted,* New Line Cinema, 1997.

Lily, *Weekend Getaway,* 1998.

Kate, *Dead Broke,* 1998.

Mike the bartender, *Two Ninas,* King Brook Entertainment, 1999.

Lisa, *Chutney Popcorn,* Pryor, Cashman, Sherman & Flynn, 1999.

Susan Brookes, *Molly,* Metro–Goldwyn–Mayer, 1999.

Victoria the shrink, *Komodo,* Amuse Video, 1999.

Brenda, *The Florentine,* 1999.

Patti, *Row Your Boat,* Gullane Pictures, 2000.

Amanda Smythe, Jill, and anonymous, *The Acting Class,* 2000.

Lynne McCale, *Autumn in New York,* United Artists, 2000.

Annette Mulcahy, *Exit Wounds,* Warner Bros., 2001.

Ellen Walker, *Love in the Time of Money,* Blow Up Pictures, 2002.

Mariana Peck, *Pipe Dream,* Castle Hill Productions, 2002.

Herself, *Abby Singer,* 2003.

Film Work:

(With Elizabeth Holder) Director, camera operator, production designer, producer, and executive producer, *The Acting Class,* 2000.

Television Appearances; Series:

Assistant district attorney Claire Kincaid, *Law and Order,* NBC, 1993–96.

Voice of Commander Claire O'Brien, *Mobile Suit Gundam Wing* (animated), Cartoon Network, 1999—.

Dr. Jordan Cavanaugh, *Crossing Jordan,* NBC, 2001—.

Host, *Medical Intelligence,* MSNBC, Tech TV, and Rogers Television, 2003.

Television Appearances; Miniseries:

Elsie Douglas, *Nuremberg,* TNT, 2000.

Jackie Kennedy, *Jackie, Ethel, Joan: The Women of Camelot* (also known as *Jackie, Ethel, Joan: The Kennedy Women*), NBC, 2001.

Television Appearances; Specials:

The 75th Anniversary Macy's Thanksgiving Day Parade, NBC, 2001.

VH1 Big in 2002 Awards, VH1, 2002.

The 54th Annual Primetime Emmy Awards, NBC, 2002.

Presenter, *The 60th Annual Golden Globe Awards,* NBC, 2003.

Television Appearances; Episodic:

Patty, "Goliath Is My Name," *War of the Worlds* (also known as *War of the Worlds: The Second Invasion*), syndicated, 1988.

Marla, "Striptease," *The Hitchhiker,* USA Network, 1989.

Elisabeth, "Pawns," *The Hitchhiker,* USA Network, 1989.

Men, ABC, 1989.

Spanish hooker, "Wedding in Black," *Friday the 13th,* 1989.

Vampire woman, "Night Prey," *Friday the 13th,* 1989.

Hooker, "The Prom," *C.B.C.'s Magic Hour,* CBC (Canada), 1990.

Secretary, "Year of the Monkey," *Friday the 13th: The Series,* syndicated, 1990.

Scott, "Max," *War of the Worlds* (also known as *War of the Worlds: The Second Invasion*), syndicated, 1990.

Lex, "The Dealbreaker," *Counterstrike,* USA Network, 1990.

Lauren Benjamin, "Crazy for You ... And You," *Flying Blind,* Fox, 1992.

Assistant district attorney Claire Kincaid, "For God and
Country," *Homicide: Life on the Street* (also known
as *Homicide* and *H: LOTS*), NBC, 1996.
Herself, *Late Night with Conan O'Brien,* NBC, 1997,
2005.
Herself, *The Tonight Show with Jay Leno,* NBC, 2001.
Herself, *Mad TV,* Fox, 2001, 2002.
Herself, *Seitenblicke,* 2002.
Herself, *Last Call with Carson Daly,* NBC, 2004.
Herself, *The Tony Danza Show,* syndicated, 2004.
Dr. Jordan Cavanaugh, "Two of a Kind," *Las Vegas,*
NBC, 2004.
Herself, "Decision Time," *The Apprentice 2,* NBC,
2004.
Herself, *Live with Regis and Kelly,* syndicated, 2004.
Herself, *Inside Dish with Rachael Ray,* 2004.
Herself, *Ellen: The Ellen DeGeneres Show,* syndicated,
2005.
Herself, *The View,* ABC, 2005.

Also appeared in *Ed's Night Party,* City–TV; and *Street
Legal,* CBC.

Stage Appearances:
Maria Elena, *Buddy: The Buddy Holly Story,* Shubert
Theatre, New York City, 1990–91.

Also appeared in *Those Summer Nights When the Dark
Comes Late,* Off–Broadway production.

RECORDINGS

Videos:
Herself, *The Best of Ed's Night Party,* Morningstar
Entertainment, 1996.

Taped Readings:
Iris Johansen's *The Face of Deception,* BDD Audio,
1999.

WRITINGS

Screenplays:
The Acting Class, 2000.

OTHER SOURCES

Books:
Newsmakers, Issue 2, Gale Group, 2003.

Periodicals:
Parade, February 4, 2001, p. 8.

People Weekly, November 27, 1995, p. 113; May 13,
2002, p. 111; April 26, 2004, p. 33.
TV Guide, May 4, 1996, pp. 36–37.

HENRY, Tim

PERSONAL

Mother's name Anne Henry (a playwright); brother of
Donnelly Rhodes (an actor).

Addresses: *Manager*—Lisa King, King Talent, Inc., 228
East Fourth Ave., Suite 303, Vancouver, British Columbia, Canada V5T 1G5.

Career: Actor.

CREDITS

Television Appearances; Miniseries:
Richard, *Living with the Dead* (also known as *Talking
to Heaven*), CBS, 2002.
Used car salesperson, *Taken* (also known as *Steven
Spielberg Presents "Taken"*), Sci–Fi Channel, 2002.
Dr. Westin, *Battlestar Galactica,* Sci–Fi Channel, 2003.

Television Appearances; Movies:
Second detective, *A Deadly Business,* CBS, 1986.
Jim Sawyer, *Drop–out Mother,* CBS, 1988.
Deadly Vows, Fox, 1994.
Captain Beckman, *Mask of Death,* HBO, 1996.
Older cop, *The Invader,* HBO, 1997.
Bill Redman, *As Time Runs Out,* CBS, 1999.
Bell Baines, *By Dawn's Early Light,* Showtime, 2000.
Sergeant Campbell, *Deadlocked* (also known as *Dead-
locked—Die fuenft gewalt*), TNT, 2000.
James Biggs, *Video Voyeur: The Susan Wilson Story,*
Lifetime, 2002.
Aza Coffey, *12 Mile Road,* CBS, 2003.
Officer Rod Kresge, *I Accuse* (also known as *J'accuse*),
Lifetime, 2003.
Johnny, *Lies My Mother Told Me,* Lifetime, 2005.

Television Appearances; Episodic:
Nicosia, "Desperate Alibi," *Street Legal,* CBC (Canada),
1987.
First plain–clothes officer, "Not for Nothing," *Wiseguy,*
CBS, 1988.
Lloyd, "Fire Jumper," *Danger Bay,* 1988.
"Daddy Dearest," *Unsub,* 1989.
Red Ridley, "Keenan's Raiders," *Bordertown,* Family
Channel, 1989.

"Sight Unseen," *Bordertown,* Family Channel, 1990.

Frank Walters, "Film at Eleven," *21 Jump Street,* Fox, 1991.

Marshall, "Colony," *The X–Files,* Fox, 1995.

Agent Jones, "Luck of the Draw," *Sliders,* Fox, 1995.

Jim Rainey, "Double Eagle," *Highlander* (also known as *Highlander: The Series*), syndicated, 1995.

Leon Lorie, "Hat Trick," *Strange Luck,* Fox, 1995.

Colonel Winters, "The Switchman," *The Sentinel,* UPN, 1996.

Plain–clothed man, "Wetwired," *The X–Files,* Fox, 1996.

Bartender, "Man in the Mist," *Poltergeist: The Legacy,* Showtime, 1996.

Sam Grinkhov, "Money No Object," *Highlander* (also known as *Highlander: The Series*), syndicated, 1996.

Sheriff Powers, "No Man's Land," *Two,* syndicated, 1996.

Marshal Tom Randall, "Buryin' Sam," *Dead Man's Gun,* Showtime, 1997.

Paxton Oaks, "The Getaway," *Viper,* syndicated, 1998.

Jimmy Lee (some sources cite Joe Egerton), "Bob and May Lee," *Cold Squad,* CTV (Canada), 1998.

Sheriff Taylor, "Closure," *Millennium,* Fox, 1998.

Officer Nash, "Joshua," *First Wave,* Sci–Fi Channel, 1998.

George Harris, "The Really Real Reenactment," *Viper,* syndicated, 1998.

The mayor, "Gomez, the People's Choice," *The New Addams Family,* Fox Family Channel, 1999.

Second sheriff, "Bad Boys," *Dead Man's Gun,* Showtime, 1999.

"Spirit Falls," *Strange World,* ABC, 1999.

Burly sergeant, "Kein Ausgang," *Harsh Realm,* FX Channel, 2000.

FBI agent, "Underworld," *First Wave,* Sci–Fi Channel, 2000.

Henry Mars, "Bring Back the Dead," *Da Vinci's Inquest,* CBC, 2000.

Jack Laird, "Through the Looking Glass," *Level 9,* UPN, 2000.

Detective, "Intentions," *Mysterious Ways,* PAX, 2000.

Judge Arpano, "The Love," *Special Unit 2,* UPN, 2002.

Father, "John Deux," *John Doe,* Fox, 2002.

Skipper of fishing boat, "Dogs Don't Bite People," *Da Vinci's Inquest,* CBC, 2003.

Amory Sutton, "Deep Midnight's Voice," *Andromeda* (also known as *Gene Roddenberry's "Andromeda"*), syndicated, 2003.

Private Investigator Mason, "Relic," *Smallville,* The WB, 2003.

Private Investigator Mason, "Magnetic," *Smallville,* The WB, 2003.

Jim Ellis, "On the Beach," *The Mountain,* The WB, 2004.

Preston Stokes, "Cock of the Walk," *Cold Squad,* CTV, 2004.

Appeared as John Patton in "Dunne's Choice," an episode of *Breaking News.*

Television Appearances; Other:

The Dawson Patrol, 1978.

Appeared in the series *Famous Jury Trials,* CTV (Canada).

Film Appearances:

Luke, *Eye of the Cat* (also known as *Wylie*), Universal, 1969.

Eddie Cochran, *Homer,* National General Pictures, 1970.

Billie Joyce, *125 Rooms of Comfort,* 1974.

Eddie, *Vengeance Is Mine* (also known as *Blood for Blood*), American International Pictures, 1975.

Rick, *Find the Lady* (also known as *Call the Cops!* and *Kopek and Broom*), Danton Films, 1976.

Ralph McKinnon, *Age of Innocence* (also known as *Ragtime Summer*), Danton Films, 1977.

Captain Marriott, *Les liens du sang* (also known as *Blood Relatives*), 1978, Filmcorp Productions, 1981.

Tony, *Improper Channels,* Crown International, 1981.

West Virginia trooper, *Murder One,* Miramax, 1988.

FBI Lieutenant Dickson, *Fear of Flying* (also known as *Turbulence II: Fear of Flying*), Trimark Pictures, 2000.

Arlen Morris, *The Stickup,* Blockbuster Video, 2001.

Weeks, *D–Tox* (also known as *Eye See You* and *Im auge der angst*), DEJ Productions/Universal, 2002.

Jones, *My Boss's Daughter,* Dimension Films, 2003.

Sheriff Williams, *Neverwas,* Senator Film, 2005.

ADAPTATIONS

"A Question of Attitude," an episode of the television series *Danger Bay,* broadcast in 1989, was based on a story by Henry.

HEWITT, Jennifer Love 1979–
(Love Hewitt)

PERSONAL

Original name, Jennifer Hewitt; born February 21, 1979, in Waco, TX; daughter of Danny (a medical technician; some sources cite father's name, Tom) and Pat (a speech pathologist) Hewitt.

Addresses: *Office*—Love Spell Entertainment, 500 South Buena Vista Dr., Bldg. 1E, Rooms 24–25, Burbank, CA 91521. *Agent*—Endeavor, 9601 Wilshire Blvd., 3rd Floor, Beverly Hills, CA 90210. *Manager*—Danielle Thomas, Untitled Entertainment, 331 North Maple Dr., 2nd Floor, Beverly Hills, CA 90210. *Publicist*—PYR Public Relations, 6725 Sunset Blvd., Suite 570, Los Angeles, CA 90028.

Career: Actress, singer, songwriter, and producer. Love Spell Entertainment, Burbank, CA, principal. Appeared with the Texas Show Team (international tour group), c. 1988; L.A. Gear, trade show dancer on world tour, 1989; appeared in commercials, 1989—, including appearances for Neutrogena hair products, 1998–2003. Spokesperson for the Sears and *Seventeen* magazine Peak Performance Scholarship Program, 1996; U.S. Department of Veterans Affairs, national spokesperson, 2003; also affiliated with Disabled American Veterans, Veterans of Foreign Wars, and Tuesday's Child (pediatric AIDS foundation).

Awards, Honors: Young Artist Award nominations, outstanding young ensemble cast (with others), 1990, and outstanding young ensemble cast in a youth series or variety show (with others), 1993, and Young Artist Award, outstanding youth ensemble in a cable or off–primetime series (with others), 1994, all for *Kids Incorporated;* Young Artist Award nomination, best professional actress/singer, 1996; YoungStar Award nomination, *Hollywood Reporter,* best young actress in a television drama series, 1997, Teen Choice Award nomination, choice television actress, 1999, and Blimp Award nomination, Kids' Choice Awards, favorite television actress, 2000, all for *Party of Five;* Blockbuster Entertainment Award, favorite female newcomer in a film, Blockbuster Entertainment Award nomination, favorite horror actress, and Young Artist Award nomination, best leading young actress in a feature film, all 1998, for *I Know What You Did Last Summer;* Teen Choice Award, choice actress in a film, and Blockbuster Entertainment Award, favorite horror actress, both 1999, for *I Still Know What You Did Last Summer;* Young Artist Award nomination, best leading young actress in a feature film, and MTV Movie Award nomination, best female performance, both 1999, for *Can't Hardly Wait;* People's Choice Award, Proctor & Gamble Productions, favorite female performer in a new television series, 2000, for *Time of Your Life;* Teen Choice Award nomination, choice actress in a film, 2001; Teen Choice Award nomination, choice crossover artist (music/acting), 2003; DVD Premiere Award, best original song (with Chris Canute), 2003, for "I'm Gonna Love You," *The Hunchback of Notre Dame II;* Blimp Award, "favorite female butt kicker," 2003, for *The Tuxedo.*

CREDITS

Television Appearances; Series:
Robin, *Kids, Incorporated* (also known as *Kids, Inc.*), The Disney Channel, 1989–91.
Bernadette Moody, *Shaky Ground,* Fox, 1992–93.
Franny Byrd, *The Byrds of Paradise,* ABC, 1994.
Cassidy McKenna, *McKenna,* ABC, 1994–95.
Sarah Reeves, *Party of Five,* Fox, 1995–2000.
Sarah Reeves Merrin, *Time of Your Life,* Fox, 1999–2000.
Voice, *The Weekenders* (animated; also known as *Disney's "The Weekenders"*), ABC, 2000–2001.
Riley Reed, *In the Game,* ABC, 2005.

Television Appearances; Movies:
Title role, *The Audrey Hepburn Story,* ABC, 2000.
Samantha Andrews, *If Only,* ABC Family Channel, 2004.
Emily, *A Christmas Carol* (also known as *A Christmas Carol: The Musical*), NBC, 2004.
Katya Livingston, *Confessions of a Sociopathic Social Climber,* Oxygen, 2005.

Television Appearances; Specials:
Interviewee, *Intimate Portrait: Audrey Hepburn,* Lifetime, 1996.
Christmas Miracles, ABC, 1997.
Host, *The Senior Prom,* ABC, 1997.
Host, *MTV's New Year's Eve Live,* MTV, 1998.
Host, *Director's Cut: World AIDS Day '99,* MTV, 1999.
Teen People's 21 Hottest Stars Under 21, ABC, 1999.
The AFI's 100 Years ... 100 Stars, CBS, 1999.
Comedy Central Presents the New York Friars Club Roast of Jerry Stiller, Comedy Central, 1999.
Interviewee, *Celebrity Profile: Jennifer Love Hewitt,* E! Entertainment Television, 2000.
The 25 Hottest Stars Under 25 (also known as *Teen People's 25 Hottest Stars Under 25*), MTV, 2001.
AFI's 100 Years ... 100 Passions, CBS, 2002.
Host, *100 Greatest Love Songs,* 2002.
Summer Music Mania 2002, Fox, 2002.
The 3rd Annual Women Rock! Girls and Guitars, Lifetime, 2002.
MTV Bash: Carson Daly, MTV, 2003.
Scream Queens: The E! True Hollywood Story, E! Entertainment Television, 2004.
Host, *The Story of Veterans Day,* History Channel, 2004.
The Greatest: The 40 Hottest Rock Star Girlfriends ... and Wives, 2005.

Also appeared as host of *True Tales of Teen Romance* and *True Tales of Teen Trauma,* both MTV.

Television Appearances; Episodic:

Mad TV, Fox, 1997, 2000.

Herself, *Later with Greg Kinnear,* 1997.

Herself, *Arthel & Fred,* 1997.

Guest, *Late Night with Conan O'Brien,* NBC, 1998, 1999, 2004.

Guest host, *Saturday Night Live,* NBC, 1998.

Herself, *The View,* ABC, 1998, 2002.

Jennifer Love Fefferman, "And Then There Was Shawn," *Boy Meets World,* ABC, 1998.

Herself, *The Howie Mandel Show,* 1998.

Co–host, *Total Request Live* (also known as *TRL*), MTV, 1998.

Voice of Medusa, "Hercules and the Gorgon," *Hercules* (animated; also known as *Disney's Hercules*), ABC and syndicated, 1999.

Herself, *The Martin Short Show,* syndicated, 1999.

Guest, *The Tonight Show with Jay Leno,* NBC, 2001, 2002, 2004.

Guest, *Late Show with David Letterman,* 2001, 2002.

Guest, *The Big Breakfast,* Channel 4 (England), 2001.

Voice, "Stuck Together, Torn Apart," *Family Guy,* Fox, 2002.

Guest, *The Panel,* 10 Network (Australia), 2002.

Guest, *Revealed with Jules Asner,* E! Entertainment Television, 2002.

Guest, *The Late Late Show with Craig Kilborn,* CBS, 2002.

Guest, *The O'Reilly Factor,* Fox News Channel, 2002.

Herself, "Barenaked," *Making the Video,* 2002.

Herself, "TV & Movie Week," *Supermarket Sweep,* 2002.

(In archive footage) *Love Chain,* E! Entertainment Television, 2003.

Herself, *Banzai,* Fox, 2003.

Guest, *Ellen: The Ellen DeGeneres Show,* syndicated, 2003, 2004, 2005.

Guest, *Tinseltown TV,* International Channel, 2003.

Guest, *The Wayne Brady Show,* syndicated, 2003.

(In archive footage) *Celebrities Uncensored,* E! Entertainment Television, 2003.

Guest, *V Graham Norton,* 2003.

Chameleon, "Chameleon Chaos/Weedkiller," *The Cramp Twins,* 2003.

Nancy Sinatra, "The 7–10 Split," *American Dreams,* NBC, 2004.

Guest, *On–Air with Ryan Seacrest,* syndicated, 2004.

Nancy Sinatra, "Old Enough to Fight," *American Dreams,* NBC, 2004.

Herself, *Punk'd,* MTV, 2004.

Guest host, "And the Winner Is ... ," *American Idol: The Search for a Superstar,* Fox, 2004.

Guest, *The Daily Show,* Comedy Central, 2004.

Guest, *The Late Late Show with Craig Ferguson,* CBS, 2005.

Also appeared as herself, *Home Team with Terry Bradshaw.*

Television Appearances; Awards Presentations:

Presenter, *The 1998 MTV Movie Awards,* MTV, 1998.

Presenter, *The 1998 MTV Video Music Awards,* MTV, 1998.

Blockbuster Entertainment Awards, UPN, 1998.

Presenter, *The 25th Annual American Music Awards,* ABC, 1998.

The 1999 Billboard Music Awards, Fox, 1999.

Presenter, *The 1999 Teen Choice Awards,* Fox, 1999.

The 5th Annual Blockbuster Entertainment Awards, Fox, 1999.

Presenter, *The 57th Annual Golden Globe Awards,* NBC, 2000.

2000 MTV Movie Awards, MTV, 2000.

Presenter, *VH1/Vogue Fashion Awards,* VH1, 2000.

The 2000 Teen Choice Awards, Fox, 2000.

The Teen Choice Awards 2001, Fox, 2001.

Nickelodeon Kids' Choice Awards, Nickelodeon, 2002.

Presenter, *The Teen Choice Awards 2002,* Fox, 2002.

Presenter, *The 29th Annual American Music Awards,* ABC, 2002.

Host, *The 2002 World Music Awards,* ABC, 2002.

MTV Video Music Awards 2002 (also known as *VMAs 2002*), MTV, 2002.

Nickelodeon Kids' Choice Awards '03 (also known as *Nickelodeon's 16th Annual Kids' Choice Awards*), Nickelodeon, 2003.

(In archive footage) *Saturday Night Live: The Best of Cheri Oteri,* NBC, 2004.

Presenter, *Nickelodeon's 17th Annual Kids' Choice Awards,* Nickelodeon, 2004.

Television Appearances; Other:

Host, *The Greatest,* 1997.

Melinda Gordon, *The Ghost Whisperer* (pilot), CBS, 2005.

Television Work; Series:

Producer, *Time of Your Life,* Fox, 1999–2000.

Executive producer, *In the Game,* ABC, 2005.

Television Work; Other:

Co–executive producer, *The Audrey Hepburn Story,* ABC, 2000.

Singer of theme song, *Scooby Doo and the Alien Invaders* (animated movie), Cartoon Channel, 2000.

Film Appearances:

(As Love Hewitt) Andrea Kurtz, *Munchie,* New Horizons Home Video, 1992.

(As Love Hewitt) Heather Lofton, *Little Miss Millions* (also known as *Home for Christmas* and *Little Miss Zillions*), New Horizons Home Video, 1993.

Margaret, *Sister Act 2: Back in the Habit,* Buena Vista, 1993.

Brooke Figler, *House Arrest*, Rysher Entertainment, 1996.

Julie James, *I Know What You Did Last Summer*, Columbia, 1997.

Leah Jones, *Trojan War* (also known as *Rescue Me*), Warner Bros., 1997.

Deb Friedman, *Telling You* (also known as *Love Sucks*), Division I Entertainment, 1998.

Amanda Beckett, *Can't Hardly Wait*, Columbia, 1998.

Julie James, *I Still Know What You Did Last Summer*, Sony Pictures Entertainment, 1998.

Cate, *The Suburbans*, Columbia TriStar, 1998.

Voice of Helen, *Zoomates*, 1998.

The devil, *The Devil and Daniel Webster*, Family Room Entertainment, 2001.

Page Connors, Wendy, Jane Helstrom, and Allison Brechenhall, *Heartbreakers*, Metro–Goldwyn–Mayer, 2001.

Voice of Madelaine, *The Hunchback of Notre Dame II* (animated), Buena Vista Home Video/Walt Disney Home Video, 2002.

Voice of Thumbelina, *The Adventures of Tom Thumb & Thumbelina* (animated), Miramax, 2002.

Del Blaine, *The Tuxedo*, DreamWorks, 2002.

Voice of Chrissy, *Groove Squad* (animated; also known as *Groove Squad Cheerleaders*), Metro–Goldwyn–Mayer, 2002.

Alice Holbrook, *The Truth about Love*, FF Film and Music, 2004.

Voice of Dr. Liz Wilson, *Garfield* (animated; also known as *Garfield: The Movie*), Twentieth Century–Fox, 2004.

Voice of Princess Kyla, *Delgo* (animated), Key Creatives, 2005.

Film Work:

Producer, *One Night*, Eagle Cove Entertainment/Love Spell Entertainment/Winchester Films, 2002.

RECORDINGS

Albums:

(As Love Hewitt) *Love Songs*, released in Japan, 1992.

Let's Go Bang, Atlantic Records, 1995.

Jennifer Love Hewitt (includes "I Believe In ... ," "It's Good to Know I'm Alive" and "No Ordinary Love"), Atlantic Records, 1996.

Barenaked, Jive, 2002.

Recorded the singles "No Ordinary Love," Atlantic, 1996; "How Do I Deal," 143 Records, 1999; "Can I Go Now," Jive International, 2003; and "Barenaked," Jive.

Videos:

(As Love Hewitt) *Dance! Workout with Barbie* (exercise video), 1991.

Recorded the music videos "How Do I Deal," 1998, and "Can I Go Now," Jive, 2003; also appeared in the music videos "High" by Feeder, 1997; "Can't Get Enough of You Baby" by Smash Mouth, 1998; "Girl on TV" by LFO, 1999; and "Hero" by Enrique Iglesias, 2001.

WRITINGS

Film Music:

(With Chris Canute) Composer and lyricist, "I'm Gonna Love You," *The Hunchback of Notre Dame II* (animated), Buena Vista Home Video/Walt Disney Home Video, 2002.

Other:

Contributor to the book *Chicken Soup for the Teenage Soul*, Health Communications, 1996.

ADAPTATIONS

The 2005 television series *In the Game*, broadcast by ABC, is based on a story by Hewitt.

OTHER SOURCES

Books:

Contemporary Musicians, Volume 41, Gale, 2003.
Newsmakers 1999, Issue 2, Gale, 1999.

Periodicals:

Biography, September, 1999, pp. 52–56, 102.
Cosmopolitan, November, 1998, p. 228; February, 2000, pp. 24, 86.
Detour, June, 1998, pp. 70–71, 74.
Entertainment Weekly, April 17, 1998, p. 41; June 26, 1998, p. 24; October 30, 1998, p. 24; November 13, 1998, pp. 28–34; April 30, 1999, p. 95; September 10, 1999, p. 40; October 15, 1999, p. 48; December 3, 1999, p. 80.
Girlfriend, July, 1998, pp. 16–19.
In Style, November, 1998, p. 308.
Jane, September, 2002, pp. 178–181.
Lifetime, June, 2004, pp. 104–109.
Movieline, June, 1998, pp. 70–71, 74; November, 1998, pp. 40–44, 49, 80–81; September, 2002, pp. 48–53, 90.
Parade, March 26, 2000, p. 22.
People Weekly, September 23, 1996, p. 121; April 21, 1997, p. 100; September 29, 1997, p. 41; March 23, 1998, p. 43; November 30, 1998, p. 214; February 15, 1999, p. 45; March 27, 2000, p. 20.
Playboy, December, 1998, p. 20; December, 1999, p. 104.

Rolling Stone, May 27, 1999, p. 38; October 3, 2002, pp. 46–50.

Teen, May, 1998, pp. 52–53; January, 2000, p. 56.

Teen People, June, 2000, p. 92.

Texas Monthly, September, 1998, p. 108.

Time, March 27, 2000, p. 98.

Total Film, January, 1998, p. 36.

TV Guide, August 3, 1996, p. 48.

Urban Cinefile, July 5, 2001.

US, February, 1999, pp. 54–58, 95.

USA Weekend, March 24, 2000, p. 12.

Women's Wear Daily, March 13, 1998, p. 7.

Other:

Celebrity Profile: Jennifer Love Hewitt (television special), E! Entertainment Television, 2000.

HOGAN, Jonathan 1951–

PERSONAL

Born June 13, 1951, in Chicago, IL. *Education:* Goodman Theatre and School of Drama, graduated.

Career: Actor and composer. Circle Repertory Company, New York City, member of company, 1973—.

Awards, Honors: Antoinette Perry Award nomination, best actor in a play, 1985, and Drama Desk Award nomination, both for *As Is.*

CREDITS

Stage Appearances:

Paul Granger III, *The Hot L Baltimore,* Circle Theatre Company, Circle in the Square Downtown, New York City, 1973.

Understudy for Ged Murray and Mick Connor, *Comedians,* Music Box Theatre, New York City, 1976–77.

Bob McCullough, *Two from the Late Show,* Circle Repertory Company, New York City, 1978.

Robbie, *Glorious Morning,* Circle Repertory Company, 1978–79.

Carl, *Getting Out,* Lucille Lortel Theatre, New York City, 1979–80.

Ernie Blagg, *Innocents, Thoughts, Harmless Intentions,* Circle Repertory Company, 1980.

John Landis, *Fifth of July,* Circle Repertory Company, New Apollo Theatre, New York City, 1980–82.

Clyde Owens, *Threads,* Circle Repertory Company, 1981.

Lieutenant William Seward Keith, *The Caine Mutiny Court–Martial,* Circle in the Square, 1983.

Martin, *Balm in Gilead,* Circle Repertory Company, 1984.

Rich, *As Is,* Circle Repertory Company, Lyceum Theatre, New York City, 1985–86.

Burton, *Burn This,* Theatre 890, New York City, 1987–88.

Teddy, *The Homecoming,* Roundabout Theatre Company, Criterion Theatre, New York City, 1991.

Alvin, *The Balcony Scene,* Circle Repertory Company, 1991.

Mark, *Taking Steps,* Circle in the Square, 1991.

Kroger, *The Rhythm Club,* Oriental Theatre, Ford Center for the Performing Arts, Chicago, IL, 1998, then Signature Theatre, Arlington, VA, 2000, and Virginia Theatre, New York City, 2000.

Boyd Middleton, *Book of Days,* Signature Theatre Company, Peter Norton Space, New York City, 2002.

Gus Belmont, *Ctrl+Alt+Delete,* George Street Playhouse, New Brunswick, NJ, 2002.

Also appeared in *Otherwise Engaged,* Broadway production, and *The Red Address,* off–Broadway production.

Film Appearances:

Bernie, *Tattoo,* Twentieth Century–Fox, 1981.

Alan, *The House on Carroll Street,* Orion, 1988.

Larry, *In Country,* Warner Bros., 1989.

Eldon Krantz, *A Fish in the Bathtub,* Curb Entertainment, 1999.

Bob, *Hit and Runway,* Lot 47 Films, 2001.

Dr. Phil Karlson, *Revolution #9,* Exile Pictures, 2002.

Gary Dean, *December Ends,* Autumn Entertainment, 2005.

Television Appearances; Series:

Dr. Jerry Dancy, *The Doctors,* 1976–77.

Miles Miller (some sources cite Mitchell Miles), *Ryan's Hope,* 1980.

Walter Douglas, *One Life to Live,* 1992–93.

Jason Benedict, *As the World Turns,* 1992–93.

Television Appearances; Movies:

Dennis, *Living Proof: The Hank Williams Jr. Story,* NBC, 1983.

David Horan, *Dreams of Gold: The Mel Fisher Story,* CBS, 1986.

Trix's friend, *Getting to Know You* (also known as *Getting to Know All about You*), Sundance Channel, 2000.

Television Appearances; Specials:

Doctor Dan Loggins, *The Mound Builders,* PBS, 1976.

John Landis, *Fifth of July,* Showtime, 1982.

Television Appearances; Miniseries:
General Timothy Pickering, *Liberty! The American Revolution,* PBS, 1997.

Television Appearances; Episodic:
Cocoran, "Life Choice," *Law & Order,* NBC, 1991.
Ronald Price, "Silence of the Lambskins," *L.A. Law,* NBC, 1991.
Gus Vernon, "Promised Land—December 22, 1971," *Quantum Leap,* CBS, 1992.
John Curren, "Scoundrels," *Law & Order,* NBC, 1994.
James Clarkson, "Allen Strikes Back," *Central Park West,* CBS, 1995.
Mr. Latimer, "Hate," *Law & Order,* NBC, 1999.
Reverend Norman Mills, "Malignant," *Law & Order: Criminal Intent,* NBC, 2002.
Headmaster, "Privilege," *Law & Order: Special Victims Unit,* NBC, 2003.
Dr. Ellis Heinz, "House Calls," *Law & Order,* NBC, 2003.
Everett Phelps, "Skeleton," *Law & Order: Trial by Jury,* NBC, 2005.

WRITINGS

Television Music; Specials:
Score, *Fifth of July,* Showtime, 1982.

Stage Music:
Song "Taxi," *Taxi Tales,* Century Theatre, New York City, 1978.
Original music, *Fifth of July,* Circle Repertory Company, New Apollo Theatre, New York City, 1980–82.
Original music, *The Mound Builders,* Circle Repertory Company, Triplex Theatre II, New York City, 1986.

HOGAN, Susan

PERSONAL

Married Michael Hogan (an actor); children: Jennie Rebecca (an actress), Gabriel (an actor), Charlie. *Education:* Graduated from Canada's National Theatre School.

Addresses: *Manager*—Northern Exposure Talent Management Group, Ltd., G3–1099 Marinaside Crescent, Vancouver, British Columbia V6Z 2Z3, Canada.

Career: Actress. Appeared in Canada's Shaw Festival for five seasons and Stratford Festival for one season; Studio 58, acting teacher.

Awards, Honors: Jessie Richardson Theatre Award nomination, outstanding performance by an actress in a leading role, 1998, for *Grace;* Jessie Richardson Theatre Award, outstanding performance by an actress in a leading role, 2000, for *Communicating Door.*

CREDITS

Film Appearances:
Sylvia, *Title Shot,* Ambassador Film Distributors, 1970.
Linda, *A Sweeter Song* (also known as *Snapshot*), Ambassador Film Distributors, 1976.
Secretary, *I Miss You, Hugs and Kisses* (also known as *Drop Dead, Dearest* and *Left for Dead*), Astral Films, 1978.
Ruth Mayer, *The Brood* (also known as *La clinique de la terreur* and *David Cronenberg's "The Brood"*), New World Pictures, 1979.
Jenny St. Clair, *Phobia,* Paramount, 1980.
Kathy Rosso, *Rolling Vengeance,* Apollo Pictures, 1987.
Narrator, *The Midday Sun,* 1989.
Kathryn Weller, *Narrow Margin,* TriStar, 1990.
Belinda Casey, *White Fang,* Buena Vista, 1991.
Gloria Sardone, *Impolite,* The Asylum, 1992.
Marlene, *Bordertown Cafe,* 1993.
Braston's wife, *Boozecan,* Annex Entertainment, 1994.
Cynthia Clark, *Disturbing Behavior* (also known as *Disturbing Behaviour*), Metro–Goldwyn–Mayer, 1998.
Jeannie, *Legs Apart* (short film), Toronto International Film Festival, 2000.

Television Appearances; Series:
Kate Ashcroft, *Ritter's Cove,* CBC, 1980.
Elizabeth Vanderberg, *Vanderberg,* CBC, 1983.
Comedy Factory, ABC, 1985.
Nicole "Nickie" Rimbaud, *Night Heat,* CBS, 1985–89.
Helga Bohnsack, *The Little Vampire* (also known as *Der Kleine Vampir*), 1986.
Libby McDeere, *Family Passions* (also known as *Macht der Leidenschaft*), CTV, 1993.

Television Appearances; Miniseries:
Marie Dewey, *In Cold Blood,* CBS, 1996.

Television Appearances; Movies:
Sharon, *One Night Stand,* CBC, 1978.
Helen Brewster, *An American Christmas Carol,* 1979.
Carol Risicio, *Easy Prey,* ABC, 1986.
Helen Browne, *Liar, Liar* (also known as *Liar, Liar: Between Father and Daughter*), CBC and CBS, 1992.
Race to Freedom: The Underground Railroad, CTV, Black Entertainment Television, and The Family Channel, 1994.

Dr. Sandra Baldwin, *Thicker than Blood: The Larry McLinden Story* (also known as *The Larry McLinden Story*), CBS, 1994.
Dr. Dillard, *Visitors of the Night,* NBC, 1995.
Mrs. Dobson, *Ebbie,* TNT, 1995.
Kate Winfield, *No Greater Love* (also known as *Danielle Steel's "No Greater Love"*), NBC, 1996.
Closer and Closer, Lifetime, 1996.
Marilyn Copeland, *Golden Will: The Silken Laumann Story,* The Disney Channel, 1996.
Alicia, *When Danger Follows You Home,* USA Network, 1997.
Helen Stuartson, *Silencing Mary* (also known as *Campus Justice*), NBC, 1998.
Madeline Kempers. *Quarantine,* ABC, 1999.
Gayle Miller, *A Father's Choice,* CBS, 2000.
Irma, *Take Me Home: The John Denver Story,* CBS, 2000.
Dr. Ann Shirley Constable, *The New Beachcombers,* CBC, 2002 Ann Shirley Constable, *A Beachcombers Christmas,* CBC, 2004.
Florence, *Hush,* Lifetime, 2005.
Senator Bates, *Saving Milly,* CBS, 2005.
Marguerite, *Marker,* 2005.
Amber Frey: Witness for the Prosecution, CBS, 2005.

Television Appearances; Episodic:
"1832," *The Newcomers,* CBC, 1978.
Reporter, "The Secret of Red Hill," *The Littlest Hobo,* CTV and syndicated, 1981.
Meg Ferrell, "Voyageurs: Parts 1 & 2," *The Littlest Hobo,* CTV and syndicated, 1985.
Ruby Prynne, "Even Lawyers Sing the Blues," *Street Legal,* CBC, 1987.
Joyce Martin, "Don't Sell Yourself Short," *Alfred Hitchcock Presents,* USA Network, 1989.
Allison Walker, "Live Wires," *Danger Bay,* 1990.
Bridgette, "A Little Purity," *Counterstrike,* USA Network, 1990.
Trudy, "Writer Wrong," *Sweating Bullets,* CBS, 1991.
Maggie Becker, "Range of Motion," *Beyond Reality,* USA Network, 1991.
Brigitte Arnell, "Bosnian Connection," *Counterstrike,* USA Network, 1992.
Miriam Blair, "Moths to a Flame," *Matrix,* USA Network, 1993.
Phoebe Collins, "I Hear You Calling," *The Outer Limits,* Showtime and syndicated, 1996.
Clare Spencer, "A Traitor among Us," *Poltergeist: The Legacy,* Showtime and syndicated, 1996.
Dr. Marissa Golding, "Dark Rain," *The Outer Limits,* Showtime and syndicated, 1997.
Michelle Hoth, "Mind's Eye," *Poltergeist: The Legacy,* Showtime and syndicated, 1997.
Angela, "The Imposter," *Dead Man's Gun,* Showtime, 1997.
Vivian Logozzo, "Jane Klosky," *Cold Squad,* CTV, 1998.
Dlavan's wife, "Promised Land," *The Outer Limits,* Showtime and syndicated, 1998.

Sister Katherine, "Sisters of Mercy," *Dead Man's Gun,* Showtime, 1998.
Vivian Logozzo, "Jane Doe: Part 2," *Cold Squad,* CTV, 1998.
Megan Loomis, "Breeding Ground," *First Wave,* Sci–Fi Channel, 1998.
Vivian Logozzo, "Edmund Kritch," *Cold Squad,* CTV, 1998.
Una Saxum, "Antipas," *Millennium,* Fox, 1999.
Mary McGarrity, "Boo," *So Weird,* The Disney Channel, 1999.
"Top Dog," *Seven Days,* UPN, 2001.
Aunt Margo, "Art Attack," *Dark Angel,* Fox, 2001.
Carol Singleterry, "Condemned," *Mysterious Ways,* PAX, 2001.
"Dying to Be Thin," *Just Cause,* PAX, 2003.
Sharon Fairbanks, "Listen Up," *The L Word,* Showtime, 2004.
Sharon, "Lap Dance," *The L Word,* Showtime, 2005.

Also appeared as Ria, "Gentleman Caller," *The Fearing Mind.*

Stage Appearances:
One Last Kiss, The Playhouse, Vancouver, British Columbia, Canada, 2004, 2005.
Copenhagen, The Playhouse, 2005.

Appeared in *Dinner with Friends* and *Communicating Doors,* both Stanley Theatre, Vancouver; *Adult Entertainment,* Vancouver East Cultural Centre, Vancouver; *King Lear,* Necessary Angel; *Pal Joey,* National Arts Centre; *Grace,* Touchstone.

HOWARD, Shawn Michael 1969–
(Shawn M. Howard)

PERSONAL

Born July 31, 1969, in Newark, NJ; son of Frank, Jr. and Olivia C. Howard; children: Elijah Kovacevich Howard. *Education:* Attended New York University.

Addresses: *Agent*—Andrew Ruf, Paradigm, 360 North Crescent Dr., North Building, Beverly Hills, CA 90210. *Manager*—Shelly Browning, Magnolia Entertainment, 1620 26th St., Suite 480 South, Santa Monica, CA 90404. *Contact*—c/o Dig a Pony, Inc., 8391 Beverly Blvd., Suite 235, Los Angeles, CA 90048.

Career: Actor, voice performer, singer, guitarist, and songwriter. Appeared in commercials, including an AT&T commercial directed by and starring Spike Lee;

Invisible Culture (band), lead vocalist and songwriter; hopejunkies (alternative rock band), rhythm guitarist, lead singer, and songwriter.

CREDITS

Film Appearances:
Bobby, *Above the Rim,* New Line Cinema, 1994.
Basketball player, *The Cable Guy,* Columbia, 1996.
Kurt, *Sunset Park* (also known as *Coach*), TriStar, 1996.
Roger, *Flirting with Disaster,* Miramax, 1996.
Lee, *Plump Fiction,* 1997, Legacy Releasing, 1998.
Coco, *The Velocity of Gary,* Next Millennium Films, 1998.
Jimmy, *Thursday,* Gramercy Pictures/Volcanic Films, 1998.
Junie, *Men of Honor* (also known as *Men of Honour*), Twentieth Century–Fox, 2000.
Mason Becker, *Ritual,* Gotham Entertainment Group/Raslan Company of America, 2000.
Roller Elvis, *3000 Miles to Graceland,* Warner Bros., 2001.
Nestor, *Masked and Anonymous,* Sony Pictures Classics, 2003.
Rawlings, *Extreme Dating,* Franchise Pictures, 2004.

Television Appearances; Series:
Russell, *The Single Guy,* NBC, 1996–97.
Voice of Smokey, *The PJs* (animated), Fox, 1999–2001.

Television Appearances; Movies:
Fred D. Gray, *Boycott,* HBO, 2001.
Ty, *The Rats,* Fox, 2002.

Television Appearances; Episodic:
(As Shawn M. Howard) Franco, "Profile," *Law & Order,* NBC, 1993.
Antoine Jackson–Jones, "Skirt Chasers," *Nash Bridges* (also known as *Bridges*), CBS, 1996.
Barney, "Spring Break: Parts 1 & 2," *Married ... with Children,* Fox, 1996.
"Trackdown," *Nash Bridges* (also known as *Bridges*), CBS, 1996.
Lionel Polynice, "A Better Place," *413 Hope St.,* Fox, 1997.
Todd, "Oh, You Men," *Mr. Show* (also known as *Mr. Show with Bob and David*), HBO, 1997.
Guest host, *Soul Train,* syndicated, 1997.
Ben, "It's My Party," *Ally McBeal,* Fox, 1998.
Ben, "You Never Can Tell," *Ally McBeal,* Fox, 1998.
Dino, "Top Gum," *NYPD Blue,* ABC, 1998.
Mitchell Markson, "My Two Dads," *Smart Guy,* The WB, 1998.
(Uncredited) Rickey Dukes, "Shanghai Express," *Martial Law,* CBS, 1998.
Warren Cruickshank, "Another Day," *The Practice,* ABC, 1998.

Warren Cruickshank, "In Deep," *The Practice,* ABC, 1998.
"Hung Jury," *Cupid,* ABC, 1998.
Clay, "Nocturnal Omissions," *Becker,* CBS, 2001.
Flossy Carver, "It's to Die For," *NYPD Blue,* ABC, 2003.
Voice of Volkswagen Beetle, "A Bug's Wife," *The Pitts,* Fox, 2003.

Appeared in *Jack & Jill,* The WB; appeared as Patrick in "Hoop Dreams," an unaired episode of *It's Like, You Know ... ,* ABC.

Television Appearances; Pilots:
Warren Cruickshank, *The Practice,* ABC, 1997.

Stage Appearances:
Crowbar, Victory Theater, New York City, beginning c. 1990.

HUGHES, Finola 1960–

PERSONAL

Born October 29, 1960, in London, England; married Russell Young, July 4, 1992; children: Dylan Joseph, Cash Justice. *Avocational Interests:* Swimming, doing aerobics, reading, watching MTV, and viewing films.

Addresses: *Manager*—Iannucci Management, 300 S. Rexford Dr., Apt. 106, Beverly Hills, CA 90212. *Office*—c/o E! Networks, 5750 Wilshire Blvd., Los Angeles, CA 90036.

Career: Actress.

Awards, Honors: *Soap Opera Digest* Award nomination, outstanding actress in a leading role on a daytime serial, 1986, *Soap Opera Digest* Award nominations (with Ian Buchanan), favorite super couple: daytime, 1988, 1989, *Soap Opera Digest* Award nomination, outstanding heroine: daytime, 1989, *Soap Opera Digest* Awards, outstanding heroine: daytime, 1990, 1991, Daytime Emmy Award nomination, outstanding lead actress in a drama series, 1990, Daytime Emmy Award, outstanding lead actress in a drama series, 1991, *Soap Opera Digest* Award nomination, outstanding lead actress: daytime, 1992, all for *General Hospital; Soap Opera Digest* Award, favorite return, 2000, Daytime Emmy Award nominations, outstanding lead actress in a drama series, 2000, 2002, all for *All My Children.*

CREDITS

Film Appearances:
Dancer, *The Apple* (also known as *Star Rock*), Cannon, 1980.

Nadia Gargarin, *Nutcracker* (also known as *Nutcracker Sweet*), Rank, 1982.
Laura, *Staying Alive,* Paramount, 1983.
(Uncredited) "All My Trials" actress, *Soapdish,* Paramount, 1991.
Bryce Kellogg, *Aspen Extreme,* Buena Vista, 1993.
Jennifer Cole, *Dark Side of Genius,* 1994.
Voice of Dr. Woodward, *The Corporate Ladder,* 1997.
Amy Lowe, *Tycus,* New City Releasing, 1998.
Ronnie Fredericks, *Jekyll Island,* 1998.
Additional voices, *Pocahontas II: Journey to a New World* (also known as *Disney's "Pocahontas II: Journey to a New World"* and *Pocahontas: Journey to a New World;* animated), 1998.
Ginger, *Rockin' Good Times,* 1999.
Katherine Jessel, *Intrepid* (also known as *Deep Water*), Starlight, 2000.

Television Appearances; Series:
Dancer, *The Hot Shoe Show,* 1983.
Anna Devane Scorpio Lavery Scorpio Hayward, *General Hospital,* ABC, 1985–91, 1995.
Chelsea Duffy, *Jack's Place,* ABC, 1992–93.
Carol Russo, *Blossom,* 1993–95.
Kate Russo, *Pacific Palisades,* Fox, 1997.
Patty Halliwell, *Charmed,* The WB, 1999–2004.
Dr. Alexandra Devane Marick, *All My Children,* ABC, 1999–2001.
Police Chief Anna Devane Scorpio Lavery Scorpio Hayward, *All My Children,* ABC, 2001–2003.
Host, *How Do I Look?,* Style Network, 2004—.

Television Appearances; Miniseries:
Herself, *I Love the '80s* (documentary), VH1, 2002.
Herself, *I Love the '80s Strikes Back* (documentary), VH1, 2003.

Television Appearances; Movies:
Alison Graeme, *The Master of Ballantrae,* CBS, 1984.
Megan McGuire, *Haunted by Her Past* (also known as *Secret Passions*), NBC, 1987.
Cybil Cobb, *The Bride in Black,* ABC, 1990.
Iris, *Above Suspicion* (also known as *The Rhinehart Theory*), HBO, 1995.
Jo Parker, *The Crying Child,* 1996.
Emma Frost/White Queen, *Generation X,* Fox, 1996.
Voice of Lara, *Superman: The Last Son of Krypton* (animated), 1996.
Angie, *Prison of Secrets,* Lifetime, 1997.

Also appeared in *The Prime of Miss Jean Brodie,* BBC; *Grace Kennedy; The Monte Carlo Show.*

Television Appearances; Specials:
The Hollywood Christmas Parade, 1988.
Gwen, *Best Sellers: Men Who Hate Women and the Women Who Love Them: The Relationship,* 1994.

The General Hospital 35th Anniversary Show, ABC, 1998.
Herself, *Intimate Portrait: Kelly Ripa,* Lifetime, 2001.
Herself, *Intimate Portrait: Finola Hughes,* Lifetime, 2002.
Herself, *E! 101 Most Starlicious Makeovers,* E! Entertainment Television, 2004.

Television Appearances; Awards Presentations:
The 14th Annual Daytime Emmy Awards, ABC, 1987.
Soap Opera Digest Awards, NBC, 1988.
The 17th Annual Daytime Emmy Awards, 1990.
The 18th Annual Daytime Emmy Awards, 1991.
The 29th Annual Academy of Country Music Awards, 1994.
The 26th Annual Daytime Emmy Awards, CBS, 1999.
Presenter, *The 27th Annual Daytime Emmy Awards,* NBC, 2000.
The 29th Annual Daytime Emmy Awards, CBS, 2002.

Television Appearances; Pilots:
Betty, *Philby,* ABC, 1989.
Host, *Who's My Daddy?,* Fox, 2005.

Television Appearances; Episodic:
Lauren Sevilla, "Rohner vs. Gradinger," *L.A. Law,* 1987.
Lauren Sevilla, "Goldilocks and the Three Barristers," *L.A. Law,* 1987.
Lauren Sevilla, "Divorce with Extreme Prejudice," *L.A. Law,* 1987.
Laura North, prostitute, "'Tis a Pity She's a Neighbor," *Dream On,* HBO, 1990.
Rhonda, "Who Killed Romeo?," *Burke's Law,* CBS, 1994.
Voice of Lara–El, "Last Son of Krypton: Parts 1 & 2," *Superman* (animated), The WB, 1996.
Tracey Takes On..., HBO, 1996.
Helena Greer, *Sunset Beach,* 1997.
Alison Townsend, "Affairs to Remember," *The Love Boat: The Next Wave,* 1998.
Josie, "Obsession," *Tracey Takes On...,* HBO, 1999.
Herself, *The View,* ABC, 2000, 2002.
Tea with Fi, Romance Classics, 2000.
Herself, "AMC Stars on the Montel Show!," *The Montel Williams Show,* ABC, 2003.
Herself, "All My Children," *Biography,* Arts and Entertainment, 2003.
Herself, *The Wayne Brady Show,* syndicated, 2003, 2004.
Herself, "The Most Dramatic Changes Revealed!," *The Montel Williams Show,* ABC, 2004.
Herself, *The Oprah Winfrey Show,* syndicated, 2004.
Herself, *Soap Talk,* Soap Net, 2004.
Herself, "Daytime Emmys: Parts 1 & 2," *Hope & Faith,* ABC, 2004.
Herself, "Finola Hughes," *Soapography,* Soap Net, 2004.
Herself, *Live with Regis and Kelly,* syndicated, 2005.

Stage Appearances:
Victoria, the white cat, *Cats,* London, 1981.

Also a featured dancer, *Song and Dance,* 1982.

RECORDINGS

Videos:
Anna Devane Scorpio Lavery Scorpio Hayward and Dr. Alexandra "Alex" Devane Marick, *Daytime's Greatest Weddings,* Buena Vista Home Video, 2004.

WRITINGS

Novels:
(With Digby Diehl) *Soapsuds: A Novel,* Ballantine Books, 2005.

HUSTON, Danny 1962–

PERSONAL

Born May 14, 1962, in Rome, Italy; son of John Huston (an actor) and Zoe Sallis (an actress); half–brother of Anjelica Huston (an actress) and Tony Huston (a screenwriter); married Virginia Madsen (an actress), October, 1989 (divorced, 1992); married Katie Jane Evans, 2001; children: (second marriage) Stella. *Education:* Attended Overseas School, Rome, Italy, international branch of Milford School in Exeter, and London Film School.

Addresses: *Agent*—Victoria Belfrage, 46 Albermarle St., London W1X 4PP England; International Creative Management, 8942 Wilshire Blvd., Beverly Hills, CA 90211. *Manager*—Relativity Management, 8899 Beverly Blvd., Suite 510, Los Angeles, CA 90048.

Career: Director and actor.

Awards, Honors: Independent Spirit Award nomination, best male lead, 2003, for *Ivansxtc;* Phoenix Film Critics Society Award (with others), best ensemble acting, 2004, for *21 Grams;* Screen Actors Guild Award nomination (with others), outstanding performance by a cast in a motion picture, 2005, for *The Aviator.*

CREDITS

Film Director:
(Main title sequences only), *Under the Volcano,* Universal, 1984.
Mr. North, Samuel Goldwyn Co., 1988.

Becoming Colette (also known as *Colette*), Scotti Bros., 1992.
The Maddening, 1995.

Film Appearances:
Second barman, *Leaving Las Vegas,* Metro–Goldwyn–Mayer/United Artists, 1995.
Stiva, *Anna Karenina* (also known as *Anna Karenine*), British Lion, 1997.
John, *Spanish Fly,* EMI, 1998.
Jimmy's manager, *Rockin' Good Times,* 1999.
Ivan Beckman, *Ivansxtc* (also known as *Ivans xtc. (To Live and Die in Hollywood)*), Artistic License, 2000.
Randy, *Timecode,* Screen Gems, 2000.
Kalman, *Eden,* 2001.
Hotel manager, *Hotel,* Moonstone Entertainment, 2001.
Gary Silverman, *Torture TV,* 2002.
Herdsman, *The Bacchae,* 2002.
Michael, *21 Grams,* Focus Features, 2003.
The Golden Man, 2003.
Danny O'Brien, *Silver City,* Newmarket Films, 2004.
Joseph, *Birth,* Fine Line Features, 2004.
Jack Frye, *The Aviator,* Miramax, 2004.
Jim Ferris, *Alpha Male,* 2005.
Sandy, *The Constant Gardener,* Focus Features, 2005.
Arthur Burns, *The Proposition,* 2005.

Television Movies; Director:
Bigfoot, ABC, 1987.
Mr. Corbett's Ghost, 1987.
Die Eisprinzessin (also known as *Ice Princess*), HBO, 1995.

Television Specials; Director:
Santa Claus: The Making of the Movie (documentary), ABC, 1987.

Television Appearances; Movies:
Second gambler, *Susan's Plan* (also known as *Dying to Get Rich*), Cinemax, 1998.

Television Appearances; Specials:
Intimate Portrait: Anjelica Huston (documentary), Lifetime, 1998.
Himself, *John Huston: The Man, The Movies, The Maverick* (also known as *John Huston*), 1998.
The Hustons: Hollywood's Maverick Dynasty (documentary), Arts and Entertainment, 1998.
Himself, *Hollywood Legends* (documentary), 2004.

Television Appearances; Episodic:
Ty Caulfield, casino manager, "Suckers," *CSI: Crime Scene Investigation,* CBS, 2004.

Jack Frye, "The Aviator," *History vs. Hollywood,* History Channel, 2004.

Himself, "Lauren Bacall," *The Hollywood Greats,* BBC1, 2005.

OTHER SOURCES

Periodicals:
Parade Magazine, November 9, 2003, p. 20.

HYDE, Jonathan 1947–

PERSONAL

Born May 21, 1947, in Brisbane, Australia (some sources cite England). *Education:* Royal Academy of Dramatic Art, graduated.

Addresses: *Agent*—Artists Rights Group, 4 Great Portland St., London W1W 8PA, England.

Career: Actor. Royal Shakespeare Company, member of the company; Royal Academy of Dramatic Art, associate member; performer with the Glasgow Citizens' Company (later Glasgow Citizens' Theatre), Glasgow, Scotland, and Royal National Theatre.

Awards, Honors: Screen Actors Guild Award nomination (with others), outstanding performance by a cast, 1998, for *Titanic.*

CREDITS

Television Appearances; Series:
Charles, *Thomas and Sarah,* London Weekend Television, 1979.

Twenty Good Years, Australian Broadcasting Corporation, beginning 1979.

Mayor Waldo, *Dinotopia* (also known as *Dinotopia: The Series*), ABC, Hallmark Channel, CanWest Global Television, and Sky TV, 2002.

Television Appearances; Miniseries:
"Gambling Lady," *The Racing Game* (also known as *The Racing Game, Series I*), Yorkshire Television, 1979–80, broadcast on *Mystery!,* PBS, c. 1980.

Paul, *Lace,* NBC, 1984.

Philippe, *Mistral's Daughter,* CBS, 1985.

Tigellinus, *A.D.* (also known as *A.D.—Anno Domini*), NBC, 1985.

Edward Marshall Hall, *Shadow of the Noose,* BBC, 1989.

Jim Mollison, *The Great Air Race* (also known as *Half a World Away*), Australian Broadcasting Corporation, 1990.

Tony Dalton, *The Paper Man,* Australian Broadcasting Corporation, 1990.

Shrapnell, *Children of the North,* BBC–2, 1991.

Solderini, *A Season of Giants,* TNT, 1991.

Dr. Oliver Pleasance, *Bliss,* Carlton Television, 1995.

Duke of Bedford, *Joan of Arc* (also known as *Jeanne d'Arc*), CBS, 1999.

Dussan, *Jack and the Beanstalk: The Real Story* (also known as *Jim Henson's "Jack and the Beanstalk: The Real Story"*), CBS, 2001.

Felix, *Attila* (also known as *Attila the Hun*), USA Network, 2001.

Television Appearances; Movies:
Honour, Profit & Pleasure, Channel 4 (England), 1985.

St. Quentin Miller, *The Death of a Heart,* Granada Television, broadcast as *The Death of the Heart* on *Masterpiece Theatre,* PBS, c. 1986–87.

Professor Joseph Goebbels, *The Plot to Kill Hitler,* CBS, 1990.

Sheriff of Nottingham in Robin Hood performances, *Fellow Traveller,* HBO, 1990.

Cesar Baroodi, *I Spy Returns,* CBS, 1994.

Lord Hertford, *The Prince and the Pauper,* pay–per–view, 2000.

Prince John, *Princess of Thieves,* ABC, 2001.

George Pentney, *Sherlock Holmes and the Case of the Silk Stocking,* BBC, 2004.

Television Appearances; Specials:
Rosencrantz, "Hamlet, Prince of Denmark," *BBC Television Shakespeare* (also known as *The Complete Dramatic Works of William Shakespeare: Hamlet, Prince of Denmark*), BBC–2, 1980.

Corinthian representative, *The War That Never Ends,* BBC, 1991.

Slyme, *Woodcock,* BBC, 1994.

Television Appearances; Episodic:
Tommy, "Killer with a Long Arm," *The Professionals,* London Weekend Television, 1978.

Rudy, "Conjugal Wrongs," *Agony,* London Weekend Television, 1979.

Paisley, "Remembrance," *Chancer,* Central Television and PBS, 1991.

Jonathan Wilsher, "Three Men and a Brittle Lady," *Lovejoy,* BBC and Arts and Entertainment, 1993.

Dr. Stuart Mosely, "Brave Face," *Peak Practice,* Central Independent Television, 1994.

Culverton Smith, "The Dying Detective," *The Memoirs of Sherlock Holmes,* Granada Television, 1994, broadcast on *Mystery!,* PBS, c. 1994.

Godfrid Piccard, "The Leper of St. Giles," *Cadfael,* Central Independent Television, 1994, broadcast on *Mystery!,* PBS, c. 1995.

Dr. Keith Michaelson, "Deep Waters," *A Touch of Frost,* Yorkshire Television, 1996.

Frank Webster, "A Tale of Two Hamlets," *Midsomer Murders,* BBC and Arts and Entertainment, 2003.

Film Appearances:

Napier, *Phoelix,* 1979.

Neil Parkinson, *An Indecent Obsession,* PBL Productions, 1985.

Baglione, *Caravaggio,* Cinevista/Zeitgeist Films, 1986.

Francisco, *Being Human,* Warner Bros., 1994.

George Joseph Smith, *Deadly Advice,* Castle Hill Productions, 1994.

Herbert A. R. Cadbury, *Richie Rich,* Warner Bros., 1994.

Hunter Van Pelt/Samuel Alan Parrish, *Jumanji,* Columbia/TriStar, 1995.

J. Bruce Ismay, *Titanic,* Paramount, 1997.

Warren Westridge, *Anaconda,* Sony Pictures Entertainment, 1997.

Dr. Allen Chamberlain, *The Mummy,* MCA/Universal, 1999.

Meyerhold, *Eisenstein* (also known as *The Furnace*), Amerique Film, 2000.

Cavendish, *The Tailor of Panama,* Columbia/Sony Pictures Entertainment, 2001.

Morgan Sinclaire, *The Curse of King Tut's Tomb,* 2006.

Smith, *Land of the Blind,* Lucky 7 Productions, 2006.

Stage Appearances:

Nightwork, *Swansdown Gloves,* Royal Shakespeare Company, Stratford–upon–Avon, England, 1982.

Laxton, *The Roaring Girl,* Royal Shakespeare Company, 1984.

Octavius Caesar, *Antony and Cleopatra,* Royal Shakespeare Company, 1984.

Duke Ferdinand of Calabria, *The Duchess of Malfi,* Royal National Theatre, London, 1985.

Major Magnus Muldoon, *The Real Inspector Hound,* Royal National Theatre, 1985.

Mr. Sneer, *The Critic,* Royal National Theatre, 1985.

Yasha, *The Cherry Orchard,* Royal National Theatre, 1985.

Vasquez, *'Tis Pity She's a Whore,* Royal Shakespeare Company, 1991.

Christopher Columbus, *Columbus and the Discovery of Japan,* Royal Shakespeare Company, Barbican Theatre, London, 1992.

Charles, *Sleep with Me,* Royal National Theatre, 1999.

Creon, *Antigone,* Old Vic Theatre, London, 1999.

Additional appearances with Royal Shakespeare Company include appearances as Oliver, *As You Like It;* as Edgar, *King Lear;* as the porter, *Macbeth;* as Bassanio, *The Merchant of Venice;* as Aumerle, *Richard II;* as Mercutio, *Romeo and Juliet;* and in *The Alchemist* and *Julius Caesar.* Appeared in operas, including *The Case of Charles Dexter Ward, A Midsummer Night's Dream,* and *A Night in Old Peking.*

RECORDINGS

Video Games:

J. Bruce Ismay, *Titanic Explorer* (also known as *James Cameron's "Titanic Explorer"*), Twentieth Century–Fox Home Entertainment, 1997.

I-J

ITZIN, Gregory
(Gregory Itzen, Greg Itzin)

PERSONAL

Addresses: *Agent*—Donna Massetti, SMS Talent, Inc., 8730 West Sunset Blvd., Suite 440, West Hollywood, CA 90069.

Career: Actor. Appeared in commercials.

Awards, Honors: Antoinette Perry Award nomination, best featured actor in a play, 1994, for *The Kentucky Cycle.*

CREDITS

Television Appearances; Series:
Dennis, *The Nutt House,* NBC, 1989.
Jack Travis, *Something Wilder,* NBC, 1994–95.
District attorney Roger Garfield, *Murder One,* ABC, 1995–96.
Joel Marks, a recurring role, *Profiler,* NBC, 2000.
Sergei, *Strip Mall,* Comedy Central, 2000–2001.
Charles Logan, *24* (also known as *24 Hours*), Fox, beginning 2005.

Television Appearances; Miniseries:
Newsman, *Murder in Texas,* NBC, 1981.
Innocent Victims, ABC, 1996.
Arlen Specter, *The Hunt For the Unicorn Killer,* NBC, 1999.

Television Appearances; Movies:
Polygraph tester, *Thornwell,* CBS, 1981.
Mario, *The Other Woman,* CBS, 1983.
Harold Taplinger, *Carly's Web,* NBC, 1987.

Phil, *Hi Honey, I'm Dead,* Fox, 1991.
Gavin Hill, *Drive Like Lightning,* USA Network, 1992.
Cornell, *Donato and Daughter* (also known as *Dead to Rights* and *Under Threat*), CBS, 1993.
Rick Boyer, *Moment of Truth: Stalking Back,* NBC, 1993.
The Ultimate Lie, HBO, 1996.
Mr. Romley, *Friends 'til the End,* NBC, 1997.
Crook, *The Day Lincoln Was Shot,* TNT, 1998.
Headmaster Pritchard, *Johnny Tsunami,* The Disney Channel, 1999.
Joe, *One Last Flight* (also known as *Fly Boy*), HBO, 1999.
Attorney general John Ashcroft, *DC 9/11: Time of Crisis,* Showtime, 2003.

Television Appearances; Specials:
(As Greg Itzin) Goldsmith, "Miss Lonelyhearts," *American Playhouse,* PBS, 1983.

Television Appearances; Episodic:
Second man, "Dr. Morkenstein," *Mork & Mindy,* ABC, 1979.
Waiter, "Fallen Angel," *Charlie's Angels,* ABC, 1979.
Davis, "Bully and Billy," *Voyagers!,* NBC, 1982.
Dr. Reston, "To Soar and Never Falter," *Fame,* NBC, 1982.
(As Gregory Itzen) Young reporter, "Unthinkable," *Lou Grant,* CBS, 1982.
"Pursuit," *Voyagers!,* NBC, 1983.
Dr. Bitters, "The Trial," *Falcon Crest,* CBS, 1985.
Dr. Kaplan, "Seoul on Ice," *Hill Street Blues,* NBC, 1985.
Ed Banner, "Echoes," *Hotel,* ABC, 1985.
Harvey, "Vegas Run," *Street Hawk,* ABC, 1985.
(As Greg Itzin) Newton, "Grandma's Last Wish," *Tales from the Darkside,* syndicated, 1985.
Paul Cavanaugh, "You Only Die Twice," *Scarecrow and Mrs. King,* CBS, 1985.
"The Biggest Man in Town," *Hunter,* NBC, 1985.
"Deeds and Misdeeds," *Dallas,* CBS, 1985.

Lawyer, *Santa Barbara,* NBC, 1985.

Tom Cavanaugh, "Final Approach," *MacGyver,* ABC, 1986.

"Lost Weekend," *St. Elsewhere,* NBC, 1986.

"Wheel of Fortune," *The A Team,* NBC, 1986.

Carl Richardson, "The Rat Pack," *Matlock,* NBC, 1987.

Gregory, "Deities," *Max Headroom,* ABC and Cinemax, 1987.

Jack Angeletti, "Divorce with Extreme Prejudice," *L.A. Law,* NBC, 1987.

Michael Fitzmorris, "The Power Brokers," *Matlock,* NBC, 1987.

Dr. Wilcher, "Gladiator," *Something Is Out There,* NBC, 1988.

Jack Angeletti, "Belle of the Bald," *L.A. Law,* NBC, 1988.

"Brother Hanson & the Miracle of Renner's Pond," *21 Jump Street,* Fox, 1988.

Frank, "The More Things Change ... ," *Empty Nest,* NBC, 1989.

Val's lawyer, "A Grave Misunderstanding," *Knots Landing,* CBS, 1989.

Warren Karr, "From Snoop to Nuts: Parts 1 & 2," *Night Court,* NBC, 1989.

Cosby, "No Ifs, Ands, or Butlers," *Over My Dead Body,* CBS, 1990.

Cosby, "Obits and Pieces," *Over My Dead Body,* CBS, 1990.

Gil Porter, "On the Road Again," *Murphy Brown,* CBS, 1990.

Meriner, "Cement Hi–Tops," *Head of the Class,* ABC, 1990.

Tom, "Hayden's in the Kitchen with Dinah," *Coach,* ABC, 1990.

"Thirty ... Something," *Anything but Love,* ABC, 1990.

Mancuso F.B.I., NBC, 1990.

Allan Carmichael, "Man, This Joint Is Jumping," *Homefront,* ABC, 1991.

Assistant district attorney, "The Parents," *Matlock,* NBC, 1991.

Bill Wallace, "Lonely Are the Brave," *Empty Nest,* NBC, 1991.

Evan Stahl, "A Prayer for the Goldsteins," *Gabriel's Fire,* ABC, 1991.

The mayor, "The ATM with the Heart of Gold" (also known as "The ATM Machine"), *Eerie, Indiana,* NBC, 1991.

Mugger, "Where There's a Will, There's a Tony: Parts 1 & 2," *Night Court,* NBC, 1991.

Sam Blankenship, "The Fat Lady Sings Alone," *DEA* (also known as *DEA: Special Task Force*), Fox, 1991.

(As Gregory Itzen) Sterling Pope, "What Comes Around," *Dark Justice,* CBS, 1991.

Host, *Davis Rules,* ABC, 1991.

"It Never Entered My Mind," *Jake and the Fatman,* CBS, 1991.

Father Chris, "Destiny Rides Again," *Beverly Hills 90210,* Fox, 1992.

Judge Russell, "... Or Forever Hold Your Peace," *Empty Nest,* NBC, 1992.

The mayor, "The Loyal Order of Corn" (also known as "The Lodge"), *Eerie, Indiana,* NBC, 1992.

The mayor, "Marshall's Theory of Believability" (also known as "Professor Hill"), *Eerie, Indiana,* NBC, 1992.

The mayor, "Mr. Chaney" (also known as "Mr. Talbot"), *Eerie, Indiana,* NBC, 1992.

Phillip Montgomery, "Time Served," *Bodies of Evidence,* CBS, 1992.

"Devil's Advocate," *Civil Wars,* ABC, 1992.

"Honi soit qui mal y pense," *Civil Wars,* ABC, 1992.

Charlie Tuggle (some sources cite Jonathan), "The Vacation," *Matlock,* ABC, 1993.

Ilon Tandro, "Dax," *Star Trek: Deep Space Nine* (also known as *Deep Space Nine, DS9,* and *Star Trek: DS9*), syndicated, 1993.

Mr. Phillips, "Memphis Melody—July 3, 1954," *Quantum Leap,* CBS, 1993.

Mitch Hewitt, "Come Rain or Come Shine," *Major Dad,* CBS, 1993.

Repairman, "Asbestos and Costello," *Shaky Ground,* Fox, 1993.

Alvin, "The Funeral" (also known as "Funeral Episodes"), *Dave's World,* CBS, 1994.

Jack Angeletti, "The Age of Insolence," *L.A. Law,* NBC, 1994.

Michael Kramer, "The Bus Stops Here," *Picket Fences,* CBS, 1994.

Michael Kramer, "System Down," *Picket Fences,* CBS, 1994.

George Sherman, "The Burning of Atlanta," *The Client* (also known as *John Grisham's "The Client"*), CBS, 1995.

Ralph Brewer, "Frozen Stiff," *Murder, She Wrote,* CBS, 1995.

Ted Glenn, "Hat Trick," *Strange Luck,* Fox, 1995.

Andrew King, "X Marks the Murder: Part 1," *Diagnosis Murder,* CBS, 1996.

Burn doctor, "The Healers," *ER* (also known as *Emergency Room*), NBC, 1996.

Dr. Kyle Mitchell, "Sexual Perversity in Chicago Hope," *Chicago Hope,* CBS, 1996.

Mr. Lepner, "Caroline and the Kid," *Caroline in the City* (also known as *Caroline*), NBC, 1996.

(As Gregory Itzen) Tom Gale, "The Client's Best Interest," *Arli$$,* HBO, 1996.

Albert Daley, "Save the Mule," *The Practice,* ABC, 1997.

Hans Ingram, "Walkabout," *Millennium,* Fox, 1997.

Phil Campbell, "Jaroldo!," *The Pretender,* NBC, 1997.

Quentin Belkey, "Three of a Con," *Players,* NBC, 1997.

Undersecretary of state Lawrence Culbertson, "Above and Beyond," *JAG,* CBS, 1997.

Bob, "Car Trouble," *Suddenly Susan,* NBC, 1998.

Council member Emmett Kearn, "No Comment," *Any Day Now,* Lifetime, 1998.

Hain, "Who Mourns for Morn?," *Star Trek: Deep Space Nine* (also known as *Deep Space Nine, DS9,* and *Star Trek: DS9*), syndicated, 1998.

Hank, "Caroline and the Diva," *Caroline in the City* (also known as *Caroline*), NBC, 1998.

Larry Colburn, "My Best Friend's Funeral," *The Closer,* CBS, 1998.

Lawrence Culbertson, "Tiger, Tiger," *JAG,* CBS, 1998.

Mr. Weaver, "Who's Your Daddy?," *Brother's Keeper,* ABC, 1998.

Royce Bender, "Green Card," *C–16* (also known as *C–16: FBI*), ABC, 1998.

Bruce Bryce, "Camera Shy," *Early Edition,* CBS, 1999.

Chuck Van Straw, "The Apartment," *It's Like, You Know ... ,* ABC, 1999.

Chuck Van Straw, "Two Days in the Valley," *It's Like, You Know ... ,* ABC, 1999.

Max Brody, "Double Date," *Wasteland,* ABC, 1999.

Ronnie Beeman, "Midnight in the Garden of Ronnie Beeman," *V.I.P.* (also known as *V.I.P.—Die Bodyguards*), syndicated, 1999.

School psychologist, "Judgment Day," *Party of Five,* Fox, 1999.

School psychologist, "Party of Freud," *Party of Five,* Fox, 1999.

District attorney Michael Stanfield, "Liberty Bells," *The Practice,* ABC, 2000.

Dr. Dysek, "Critical Care," *Star Trek: Voyager* (also known as *Voyager*), UPN, 2000.

Matty Stillman, "It's Only Personal," *The Michael Richards Show,* NBC, 2000.

Richard Allegro, "Media Relations," *Family Law,* CBS, 2000.

"Russian Roulette," *Beggars and Choosers,* Showtime, 2000.

Ethan Donahue, "The Beginning, the End, and the Murky Middle," *Judging Amy,* CBS, 2001.

Lloyd Styner, "What the Past Will Bring," *Bull,* TNT, 2001.

Norman Stirling, "Boom," *CSI: Crime Scene Investigation* (also known as *CSI*), CBS, 2001.

"Leader of the Pack," *Wolf Lake,* CBS and UPN, 2001.

Attorney, "Judge Knot," *The Practice,* ABC, 2002.

Captain Sopek, "Shadows of P'Jem," *Enterprise* (also known as *Star Trek: Enterprise*), UPN, 2002.

Ethan Donahue, "Nobody Expects the Spanish Inquisition," *Judging Amy,* CBS, 2002.

Judge Donald Kingman, "The Double Standard," *For the People* (also known as *Para la gente*), Lifetime, 2002.

Magistrate Higgins, "Jaynestown," *Firefly,* Fox, 2002.

Martin Walsh, "Healthy McDowell Movement," *NYPD Blue,* ABC, 2002.

Paul Cabretti, "Thanks for the Mammaries," *Philly,* ABC, 2002.

State department representative, "Enemies Foreign and Domestic," *The West Wing,* NBC, 2002.

Theodore Hanigan, "The One with Ross's Inappropriate Song," *Friends,* NBC, 2002.

Aaron Thomas, "The Other Side of Caution," *The Lyon's Den,* NBC, 2003.

Attorney Mark Grundel, "Down the Hatch," *The Practice,* ABC, 2003.

Attorney Mark Grundel, "Final Judgment," *The Practice,* ABC, 2003.

Attorney Wayne Pyne, "Blessed Are They," *The Practice,* ABC, 2003.

FBI director, "Sea Dog," *Navy NCIS: Naval Criminal Investigative Service* (also known as *Naval CIS, Navy CIS, Navy NCIS, NCIS,* and *NCIS: Naval Criminal Investigative Service*), CBS, 2003.

FBI director, "Yankee White," *Navy NCIS: Naval Criminal Investigative Service* (also known as *Naval CIS, Navy CIS, Navy NCIS, NCIS,* and *NCIS: Naval Criminal Investigative Service*), CBS, 2003.

"Fallout: Part 1," *Without a Trace* (also known as *Vanished*), CBS, 2003.

Howard Lewson, "Progeny," *Medical Investigation,* NBC, 2004.

Stephen Herbert, "The New Era," *The O.C.,* Fox, 2004.

Theodore Hanigan, "The One with Phoebe's Wedding," *Friends,* NBC, 2004.

Admiral Black, "In a Mirror, Darkly: Part 2," *Enterprise* (also known as *Star Trek: Enterprise*), UPN, 2005.

Ethan Donahue, "Too Little, Too Late," *Judging Amy,* CBS, 2005.

"Gray Murders," *Crossing Jordan,* NBC, 2005.

Appeared as Kiritsis in an episode of *FBI: The Untold Stories,* ABC.

Television Appearances; Pilots:

V. Ogelthorpe, *Bulba,* ABC, 1981.

Cosby, *Over My Dead Body,* CBS, 1990.

Things That Go Bump, NBC, 1997.

Fearless, The WB, 2004.

Film Appearances:

First religious zealot, *Airplane!* (also known as *Flying High*), Paramount, 1980.

Member of Melvin's crew, *The Best Little Whorehouse in Texas* (musical; also known as *The Best Little Cathouse in Texas*), Universal, 1982.

Young man, *Airplane II: The Sequel,* Paramount, 1982.

Owen, *Hard to Hold,* Universal, 1983.

English teacher, *Teen Wolf,* Atlantic Releasing, 1985.

Ralph Kramer, *Dad,* Universal, 1989.

Vince Nancy, *The Fabulous Baker Boys,* Twentieth Century–Fox, 1989.

Walter Mallinson, *Born to Be Wild* (also known as *Katie*), Warner Bros., 1995.

George Burroughs, *Young Goodman Brown* (also known as *Nathaniel Hawthorne's "Young Goodman Brown"*), 50th Street Films, 1997.

Clerk at Mint Hotel, *Fear and Loathing in Las Vegas,* MCA/Universal, 1998.

Mr. Florens, *Small Soldiers* (live action and animated), DreamWorks, 1998.

James Moore, *What's Cooking?,* Trimark Pictures, 2000.

Scott's father, "$30," *Boys Life 3,* Strand Releasing, 2000.

Barry Cartwright, *Evolution,* DreamWorks, 2001.

Colonel Worth, *Original Sin* (also known as *Peche originel*), Metro–Goldwyn–Mayer, 2001.

(As Greg Itzin) Dennis, *Life or Something Like It,* Twentieth Century–Fox, 2002.

Prosecutor, *Adaptation* (also known as *The Orchid Thief*), Columbia/Sony Pictures Entertainment, 2002.

Gone, 2006.

Stage Appearances:

Andrew Talbert Winston, Jeremiah, J. T. Wells, Richard Talbert in 1861, and Sheriff Ray Blanko, *The Kentucky Cycle,* John F. Kennedy Center for the Performing Arts, Eisenhower Theater, Washington, DC, 1993, then Royale Theatre, New York City, 1993.

Lee Atwater, *Twilight's Last Gleaming and Atwater: Fixin' to Die,* Skirball Cultural Center, Los Angeles, 2000.

Waiting for Godot, Matrix Theatre, Hollywood, CA, 2000.

Lincolnesque (staged reading), South Coast Repertory Theatre, Costa Mesa, CA, 2003.

Mother Courage and Her Children, Antaeus Company, NewPlace Theatre Center, North Hollywood, CA, 2005.

Radio Appearances:

Appeared as Lee Atwater, *Twilight's Last Gleaming and Atwater: Fixin' to Die.*

IVEY, Dana 1942(?)–

PERSONAL

Full name, Dana Robins Ivey; born August 12, 1942 (some sources cite August 14 or 1941), in Atlanta, GA; daughter of Hugh Daugherty Ivey (a physicist and professor) and Mary Nell Ivey Santacroce (an actress, teacher, and speech therapist); maiden name, McKoin). *Education:* Rollins College, B.A., 1963; trained for the stage at London Academy of Music and Dramatic Art. *Avocational Interests:* Classical music, reading (historical fiction and mysteries), traveling, supporting animal rights groups.

Addresses: *Agent*—Richard Schmenner, Paradigm, 500 Fifth Ave., 37th Floor, New York, NY 10010.

Career: Actress and teacher. WGKA–AM Radio, Atlanta, GA, music announcer, interviewer, and classical music programmer, 1974–76; Georgia Institute of Technology, director of technical drama, 1974–77; South Coast Repertory, Costa Mesa, CA, guest artist, 1989–90; instructor at Circle in the Square Theatre School, National Theatre School of Canada, and Academy Theatre School; presenter at awards presentations.

Member: Actors' Equity Association, American Federation of Television and Radio Artists, Screen Actors Guild, Canadian Actors' Equity Association, Alliance of Canadian Cinema, Television, and Radio Artists.

Awards, Honors: Fulbright grant, 1964; Atlanta Circle of Drama Critics Award, best actress, 1977, for *Come Back to the Five and Dime, Jimmy Dean, Jimmy Dean;* DramaLogue Award, 1979, for *Romeo and Juliet;* Drama League Award, California Shakespeare Festival, 1979; Clarence Derwent Award, outstanding performance, Obie Award (with others), outstanding ensemble performance, *Village Voice,* and Drama Desk Award nomination, all 1983, for *Quartermaine's Terms;* Drama Desk Award nomination, 1983, for *Present Laughter;* Antoinette Perry Award nomination, best featured actress in a play, 1984, for *Heartbreak House;* Antoinette Perry Award nomination, best featured actress in a musical, 1984, for *Sunday in the Park with George;* Obie Award, outstanding performance, 1987, Outer Critics Circle Award, 1988, and Drama Desk Award nomination, best featured actress in a play, 1988, all for *Driving Miss Daisy;* Outer Critics Circle Award, 1988, for *Wenceslas Square;* Drama Desk Award, best featured actress in a play, 1997, for *The Last Night of Ballyhoo* and *Sex and Longing;* Antoinette Perry Award nomination, best featured actress in a play, 1997, for *The Last Night of Ballyhoo;* Helen Hayes Award nomination, outstanding supporting actress in a resident play, Washington Theatre awards Society, 2005, for "Cat on a Hot Tin Roof," *Tennessee Williams Explored;* Bayfield Award, for *Hamlet.*

CREDITS

Stage Appearances:

Hermia, *A Midsummer Night's Dream,* Front Street Theatre, Memphis, TN, 1964–65.

Madame Rosepettle, *Oh Dad, Poor Dad, Mama's Hung You in the Closet and I'm Feeling So Sad,* Front Street Theatre, 1964–65.

Marian's mother, *The Music Man* (musical), Front Street Theatre, 1964–65.

Mrs. Higgins, *My Fair Lady* (musical), Front Street Theatre, 1964–65.

Mrs. Teale, *Roberta,* Front Street Theatre, 1964–65.

Sara, *Major Barbara,* Front Street Theatre, 1964–65.

Wife, *The Seven Year Itch,* Front Street Theatre, 1964–65.

Wife and mother, *Ah! Wilderness,* Front Street Theatre, 1964–65.

Mrs. Mullins, *Carousel* (musical), Theatre of the Stars, Atlanta, GA, 1965.

Anna, *The Firebugs,* Canadian Players, Toronto, Ontario, Canada, 1965–66.

Member of chorus, *Murder in the Cathedral,* Canadian Players, 1965–66.

Sara Tansey, *The Playboy of the Western World,* Canadian Players, 1965–66.

Kitty, *Charley's Aunt,* Manitoba Theatre Centre, Winnipeg, Manitoba, Canada, 1966.

Margaret, *Galileo,* Manitoba Theatre Centre, 1966.

Mrs. Sowerberry, *Oliver!* (musical), Theatre of the Stars, 1966.

Solange, *The Maids,* Manitoba Theatre Centre, 1966.

Title role, *Antigone,* Hartford Stage Company, Hartford, CT, 1968.

Lucy Brown, *The Threepenny Opera* (musical), Hartford Stage Company, 1968.

Amanda, *Private Lives,* Theatre Calgary, Calgary, Alberta, Canada, 1969–70.

Baroness and Clea, *White Liars/Black Comedy,* Theatre Calgary, 1969–70.

Fay, *Loot,* Theatre Calgary, 1969–70.

Gillian, *Bell, Book, and Candle,* Theatre Calgary, 1969–70.

Gwendolyn, *The Importance of Being Earnest,* Theatre Calgary, 1969–70.

Mia, *The Three Desks,* Theatre Calgary, 1969–70.

Mrs. Gargary, *Great Expectations,* Theatre Calgary, 1969–70.

Pioneer woman and singer, *You Two Stay Here, the Rest Come with Me,* Theatre Calgary, 1969–70.

Emilia, *Othello,* Centaur Theatre, Montreal, Quebec, Canada, 1970–71.

Lill, *Revenge,* Centaur Theatre, 1970–71.

Miss Moscowitz, *The Electronic Nigger,* Centaur Theatre, 1970–71.

Mrs. Harford, *A Touch of the Poet,* Centaur Theatre, 1970–71.

Nurse, *The Death of Bessie Smith,* Centaur Theatre, 1970–71.

Ruth, *The Homecoming,* Centaur Theatre, 1970–71.

Sonya, *Uncle Vanya,* Centaur Theatre, 1970–71.

Claire, *The Maids,* Centaur Theatre, 1971–72.

Title role, *Electra,* Centaur Theatre, 1971–72.

Isabelle, *Total Eclipse,* Centaur Theatre, 1971–72.

Jean, *The Entertainer,* Centaur Theatre, 1971–72.

Narrator, *At the Hawk's Well,* Centaur Theatre, 1971–72.

Queen, *Full Moon in March,* Centaur Theatre, 1971–72.

Woman, *The Exception and the Rule,* Centaur Theatre, 1971–72.

Gwendolyn Pidgeon, *The Odd Couple,* Theatre of the Stars, 1972.

Helene, *En pieces detachees,* Manitoba Theatre Centre, 1973.

Sara, *Sunrise on Sara,* Festival Lennoxville, Lennoxville, Quebec, Canada, 1973.

Sara, *A Touch of the Poet,* National Arts Centre, Theatre at St. Lawrence Centre, Ottawa, Ontario, Canada, 1973.

Shen–Te, *The Good Woman of Setzuan,* Theatre London, London, Ontario, Canada, 1973.

Stella, *A Streetcar Named Desire,* Manitoba Theatre Centre, 1973.

Woman, *Thurber Carnival,* Manitoba Theatre Centre, 1973.

Jenny, *Everything in the Garden,* Druid Cellar Dinner Theatre, 1974.

Nurse, *Romeo and Juliet,* Alliance Theatre, Atlanta, GA, 1974.

Sister woman, *Cat on a Hot Tin Roof,* Alliance Theatre, 1974.

Elizabeth Proctor, *The Crucible,* Alliance Theatre, 1975.

Annie Sullivan, *The Miracle Worker,* Alliance Theatre, 1976.

Catherine, *Great Catherine,* Shaw Festival, Niagara–on–the–Lake, Ontario, Canada, 1977.

Title role, *Hedda Gabler,* Alliance Theatre, 1977.

Lina, *Misalliance,* Alliance Theatre, 1977.

Mary, *All the Way Home,* Alliance Theatre, 1977.

Mistress Quickly, *Henry IV, Part I,* Alliance Theatre, 1977.

Mona, *Come Back to the Five and Dime, Jimmy Dean, Jimmy Dean,* Alliance Theatre, 1977.

Alma, *Eccentricities of a Nightingale,* Alaska Repertory Theatre, Anchorage, AK, 1978.

Elaine, *The Last of the Red Hot Lovers,* Newport Actors Company, Newport, RI, 1978.

Miss Casewell, *The Mousetrap,* Newport Actors Company, 1978.

Mrs. Linde, *A Doll's House,* Manitoba Theatre Centre, 1978.

Pearl and Dot, *Patio/Porch,* Dallas, TX, 1978.

Claire, *The Taking Away of Little Willie,* Mark Taper Forum, Los Angeles, 1979.

Elvira, *Blithe Spirit,* Vancouver Playhouse, Vancouver, British Columbia, Canada, 1979.

Katherine, *The Taming of the Shrew,* California Shakespeare Festival, Visalia, CA, 1979.

Lady Capulet, *Romeo and Juliet,* California Shakespeare Festival, 1979.

Miss Giddens, *The Innocents,* Vancouver Playhouse, 1979.

Regina, *The Little Foxes,* Alliance Theatre, 1979.

Julia, *The Philanderer,* Shaw Festival, 1980.

Lucienne, *A Flea in Her Ear,* Shaw Festival, 1980.

Andrea, *Twinkle, Twinkle,* Hartford Stage Company, 1981.

Ellie, *Bing and Walker,* Peterborough Players, Peterborough, NH, 1981.

Gentlewoman, lady, and witch, *Macbeth,* Lincoln Center, Vivian Beaumont Theater, New York City, 1981.

Hilda, *Am I Blue?,* Hartford Stage Company, 1981.

Isabel, *A Call from the East,* Manhattan Theatre Club, New York City, 1981.

Lizzie Borden and actress, *Blood Relations,* Centaur Theatre, 1981.

Madwoman, *The Hunchback of Notre Dame,* New York Shakespeare Festival, Public Theatre, New York City, 1981.

Miss Prism, *The Importance of Being Earnest,* Peterborough Players, 1981.

Renata, *Forbidden Copy,* Hartford Stage Company, 1981.

Miss Tendesco, *Vivien,* Arc Theatre, New York City, 1982.

Monica Reed, *Present Laughter,* Circle in the Square, New York City, 1982–83.

Melanie Garth, *Quartermaine's Terms,* Long Wharf Theatre, New Haven, CT, and Playhouse 91, New York City, both 1983.

Nanny, Kate, and principal, *Baby with the Bathwater,* Playwrights Horizons Theatre, New York City, 1983.

Lady Ariadne Utterword, *Heartbreak House,* Circle in the Square, 1983–84.

Helen Kroger, *Pack of Lies,* Royale Theatre, New York City, 1984.

Naomi Eisen and Yvonne, *Sunday in the Park with George* (musical), Booth Theatre, New York City, 1984–85.

Countess, *The Marriage of Figaro,* Circle in the Square, 1985.

Daisy Werthan, *Driving Miss Daisy,* Playwrights Horizons Theatre, 1987, then John Houseman Theatre, 1987–89.

One of the women, *Wenceslas Square,* New York Shakespeare Festival, Public Theatre, Martinson Hall, New York City, 1988.

Melissa Gardner, *Love Letters,* Promenade Theatre, New York City, 1989.

Gertrude, *Hamlet,* New York Shakespeare Festival, Public Theatre, Anspacher Theatre, New York City, 1990.

Ma–Noreen, *Beggars in the House of Plenty,* Manhattan Theatre Club, City Center Theatre Stage II, New York City, 1991.

Nettie Cleary, *The Subject Was Roses,* Roundabout Theatre Company, New York City, 1991.

Julia Budder, *It's Only a Play,* Center Theatre Group, James A. Doolittle Theatre, Los Angeles, 1992.

Evelyn, *Kindertransport,* Manhattan Theatre Club, City Center Theatre Stage I, New York City, 1994.

Naomi Eisen and Yvonne, *Sunday in the Park With George* (concert performance), St. James Theatre, New York City, 1994.

Sonia, *It Changes Every Year* [and] *Sons and Fathers* (two one–acts), Malaparte Theatre Company, New York City, 1994.

Leonie (Leo), *Indiscretions (Les Parents Terribles),* Royal National Theatre, Ethel Barrymore Theatre, New York City, 1995.

Bridget McCrea, *Sex and Longing,* Cort Theatre, New York City, 1996.

Boo Levy, *The Last Night of Ballyhoo,* Helen Hayes Theatre, New York City, 1997–98.

Mrs. Malaprop, *The Rivals,* Williamstown Theatre Festival, 1998.

Ms. Amelia Pickles, *The Uneasy Chair,* Manhattan Theatre Club, Playwrights Horizons Theatre, 1998.

The Glass Menagerie, Williamstown Theatre Festival, Williamstown, MA, 1998.

Madame Pernelle, *Tartuffe,* New York Shakespeare Festival, Public Theatre, Delacorte Theatre, New York City, 1999.

The Death of Papa, Hartford Stage Company, 1999.

Sylvia Archibald, *Waiting in the Wings,* Skylight Productions, Colonial Theatre, Boston, MA, 1999, then Walter Kerr Theatre, New York City, 1999–2000, later Eugene O'Neill Theatre, New York City, 2000.

Mademoiselle Colombe (staged reading), Theatre Ten Ten, New York City, 2000.

Lady Britomark Undershaft, *Major Barbara,* Roundabout Theatre Company, American Airlines Theatre, New York City, 2001.

Big Mama, "Cat on a Hot Tin Roof," *Tennessee Williams Explored,* John F. Kennedy Center for the Performing Arts, Washington, DC, 2003.

Grace, *A Day in the Death of Joe Egg,* Roundabout Theatre Company, American Airlines Theatre, 2003.

Under Milk Wood, Williamstown Theatre Festival, Main Stage, 2003.

Lady Northumberland and Mistress Quickly, *Henry IV,* Lincoln Center, Vivian Beaumont Theater, 2003–2004.

Jubilee: Williamstown Theatre Festival's 50th Anniversary Bash, Williamstown Theatre Festival, Main Stage, 2004.

Lettice and Lovage (benefit performance), Coronet Theatre, West Hollywood, CA, 2004.

Mrs. Malaprop, *The Rivals,* Lincoln Center, Vivian Beaumont Theater, 2004–2005.

Appeared as the seventh fairy and a palace guard, *Sleeping Beauty,* Children's Civic Theatre, Atlanta, GA. Appeared in *In the Summerhouse,* London production; in *Richard III,* regional production; and in various concerts, including *Candida in Concert.*

Major Tours:

Anna, *The Firebugs,* Canadian Players, Canadian cities, 1966.

Member of chorus, *Murder in the Cathedral,* Canadian Players, Canadian cities, 1966.

Sara Tansey, *Playboy of the Western World,* Canadian Players, Canadian cities, 1966.

Avdotya, *The Government Inspector,* Stratford Shakespearean Festival Centennial tour, Canadian cities, 1967.

Lady-in-waiting, *Twelfth Night,* Stratford Shakespearean Festival Centennial tour, Canadian cities, 1967.

Androgyne, *Volpone,* National Shakespeare Company, U.S. cities, 1967.

Juliet, *Romeo and Juliet,* National Shakespeare Company, U.S. cities, 1967.

Viola, *Twelfth Night,* National Shakespeare Company, U.S. cities, 1967.

Miss McCormack and Mimsey, *Plaza Suite,* U.S. cities, 1969.

The Taming of the Shrew, Canadian schools, 1970.

Television Appearances; Series:

Dr. Maria Thompson, *Search for Tomorrow,* CBS, 1977–78.

Eleanor Stander, *Easy Street,* NBC, 1986–87.

All My Children, ABC, beginning 1989.

Television Appearances; Miniseries:

Little Gloria ... Happy at Last, NBC, 1982.

Television Appearances; Movies:

Gabrielle Harwood, "Die Laughing," *B. L. Stryker,* broadcast as part of *The ABC Saturday Mystery,* ABC, 1989.

Lois Jurgens, *A Child Lost Forever* (also known as *A Child Lost Forever: The Jerry Sherwood Story*), NBC, 1992.

Mrs. Julia Peyton, *Class of '61,* ABC, 1993.

Anna Guidry, *A Lesson before Dying,* HBO, 1999.

Beatrice Vernon, *Walking across Egypt,* Hallmark Channel, 1999.

Television Appearances; Specials:

Witch, *Macbeth,* 1982.

Lady Ariadne Utterword, "Heartbreak House," *American Playhouse,* PBS and Showtime, 1984.

Naomi Eisen and Yvonne, "Sunday in the Park with George," *American Playhouse* (musical), PBS and Showtime, 1985.

Newscaster, *Steven Wright in "The Appointments of Dennis Jennings"* (also known as *The Appointments of Dennis Jennings*), HBO, 1989.

Gertrude, *Hamlet,* PBS, 1990.

Television Appearances; Awards Presentations:

The 59th Annual Tony Awards, 2005.

Television Appearances; Episodic:

Kahlana, "Tribal Law," *The Beachcomber,* syndicated, c. 1961.

Margie Bolander, "Dead End," *Homicide: Life on the Street* (also known as *Homicide* and *Homicide: LOTS*), NBC, 1995.

Margie Bolander, "End Game," *Homicide: Life on the Street* (also known as *Homicide* and *Homicide: LOTS*), NBC, 1995.

Margie Bolander, "Law and Disorder," *Homicide: Life on the Street* (also known as *Homicide* and *Homicide: LOTS*), NBC, 1995.

Shore, "Girlfriends," *Law & Order,* NBC, 1996.

Ms. Langer, "Three Days of the Condo," *Frasier* (also known as *Dr. Frasier Crane*), NBC, 1997.

Patricia Nathan, "The Bill of Wrongs," *Oz,* HBO, 2000.

Patricia Nathan, "Obituaries," *Oz,* HBO, 2000.

Dr. Camille Willoughby, "Bottlecaps," *100 Centre Street,* Arts and Entertainment, 2001.

Judge Natalie Brown, "Cause of Action," *The Practice,* ABC, 2003.

Trudy Stork, "Out of the Frying Pan," *Sex and the City,* HBO, 2004.

Mrs. Eels, "Mr. Monk and the Other Detective," *Monk,* USA Network, 2005.

Also appeared in *Under Fire.*

Film Appearances:

Mrs. Freda Mueller, *The Explorers* (also known as *Explorers*), Paramount, 1984.

Miss Millie, *The Color Purple,* Warner Bros., 1985.

Wedding speaker, *Heartburn,* Paramount, 1986.

Engagement party guest, *Another Woman,* Orion, 1988.

Mrs. Reed, *Dirty Rotten Scoundrels,* Orion, 1988.

Wardrobe mistress, *Postcards from the Edge,* Columbia, 1990.

Margaret Alford/Margaret Addams, *The Addams Family,* Paramount, 1991.

Mrs. Stone, *Home Alone 2: Lost in New York* (also known as *Home Alone II*), Twentieth Century–Fox, 1992.

Claire, *Sleepless in Seattle,* TriStar, 1993.

Judge Tompkins, *Guilty as Sin,* Buena Vista, 1993.

Margaret Addams, *Addams Family Values,* Paramount, 1993.

The widow Douglas, *The Adventures of Huck Finn* (also known as *The Adventures of Huckleberry Finn*), Buena Vista, 1993.

Mack, *Sabrina,* Paramount, 1995.

Meredith Stonehall, *The Scarlet Letter,* Buena Vista, 1995.

Grandmother Wenteworth, *Simon Birch* (also known as *Angels and Armadillos*), Buena Vista, 1998.

Mrs. Essendine, *The Imposters,* Twentieth Century–Fox, 1998.

Mrs. Crisp, *Mumford,* Buena Vista, 1999.

Dr. Suzanne Alexander, *The Kid* (also known as *Disney's "The Kid"*), Buena Vista, 2000.

Ruth Kelson, *Two Weeks Notice,* Warner Bros., 2002.

Vera Gantner, *Orange County,* Paramount, 2002.

Congressperson Libby Hauser, *Legally Blonde 2: Red, White & Blonde* (also known as *Legally Blonde 2* and *Legally Blonde 2: Bigger, Bolder & Blonder*), Metro-Goldwyn–Mayer, 2003.

RECORDINGS

Audiobooks:

Larry McMurtry, *The Evening Star,* Simon & Schuster, 1992.

Mary Catherine Bateson, *Composing a Life,* Penguin HighBridge, 1992.

Barbara Delinsky, *For My Daughters,* Harper, 1994.

Frank B. Gilbreth, Jr. and Ernestine Gilbreth Carey, *Cheaper by the Dozen,* Bantam Doubleday Dell Audio, 1995.

Belva Plain, *Legacy of Silence,* Bantam, Doubleday Dell Audio, 1998.

Jan Karon, *A Common Life: The Wedding Story,* Penguin Audiobooks, 2001.

OTHER SOURCES

Periodicals:

American Theatre, April, 1997, pp. 24–29.

Playbill, January 18, 2005.

JEANNIN, Marcel

(Marcel Jeanin)

PERSONAL

Addresses: *Agent*—Jean–Jacques Desjardins, 3575 Boul., St. Laurent, Suite 503, Montreal, Quebec H2X 2T7, Canada.

Career: Actor. ASM Performing Arts, Montreal, Quebec, Canada, instructor.

CREDITS

Film Appearances:

Eddie lookalike, *Eddie and the Cruisers II: Eddie Lives!,* Alliance, 1989.

State trooper, *Affliction,* Lions Gate Films, 1997.

Editor, *Hemingway: A Portrait,* Direct Cinema, 1999.

Teller, *The Collectors,* New City Releasing, 1999.

Hiker, *Grey Owl,* New City Releasing, 1999.

Neighborhood guy, *One Eyed King,* Lions Gate Films, 2001.

(As Marcel Jeanin) Baltimore cop, *The Sum of All Fears* (also known as *Der Anschlag*), Paramount, 2002.

Train man, *Taking Lives,* Warner Bros., 2004.

Theater director, *Wicker Park,* Metro–Goldwyn–Mayer, 2004.

Television Appearances; Series:

Princess Sissi, Fox, 1997.

Voice of police man, *X–Chromosome* (animated), Oxygen, 1999.

Voice of Mr. Parker, Mona's dad, *Mona the Vampire* (animated), YTV, 1999.

Ti Jean Joual, *Blackfly,* CanWest Global, 2000.

Christopher Price, *Les poupees russes,* 2002–2003.

Staff executive assistant Patrick Arthur Lewis, *Snakes & Ladders,* CBC, 2004.

Voice of Bo Baxter, *Postcards from Buster* (animated), PBS, 2004.

Television Appearances; Movies:

Corporal, *Time at the Top* (also known as *L'ascenseur du temps*), Showtime, 1999.

Givenchy, *The Audrey Hepburn Story,* ABC, 2000.

Thaddeus, *The Sign of Four* (also known as *Le signe des quatre*), Odyssey and Hallmark Channel, 2001.

Teddy Leary, *Life in the Balance,* Lifetime, 2001.

Stewart Dan, *The Killing Yard,* Showtime, 2001.

Kirby Grantham, *Deadly Isolation,* Lifetime, 2005.

Television Appearances; Miniseries:

Junior lawyer, *The Sleep Room* (also known as *Le pavillon de l'oubli*), Lifetime, 1998.

Ernie Soldier, *Too Rich: The Secret Life of Doris Duke,* CBS, 1999.

Nils, *Revenge of the Land,* CBC, 1999.

Carl, *Further Tales of the City* (also known as *Armistead Maupin's "Further Tales of the City"*), Showtime, 2001.

Police RCMP civil, *Il duce canadese,* 2004.

Television Appearances; Episodic:

Crane, "The First Time," *Sirens,* syndicated, 1994.

The corpse, "The Tale of the Dead Man's Float," *Are You Afraid of the Dark?,* Nickelodeon, 1995.

Amirge, "The Sporting Kind," *Space Cases,* Nickelodeon, 1996.

The lumanian, "On the Road to Find Out," *Space Cases,* Nickelodeon, 1996.

Peter Givens, "The Horse Healer," *Lassie,* YTV, 1997.

Adrian, "Tale of the Walking Shadow," *Are You Afraid of the Dark?,* Nickelodeon, 1999.

Eddie, "Approaching Desdemona," *The Hunger,* Showtime, 2000.

Jeffrey Haberman, "Blind Eye," *Largo Winch,* Mystery Channel, 2001.

Voice of Orville, "Snow Job," *Arthur* (animated), PBS, 2003.

Voice of Mustapha, "Dear Adil/Bitzi's Break–Up," *Arthur* (animated), PBS, 2003.

Also appeared as Jesse, "Breath of a Salesman," *Space Cases,* Nickelodeon; Daniel Rexford, "Lights, Camera, Fatman," *Misguided Angels;* Hynreck, *Tales from the*

Neverending Story, Hallmark Channel; and voice of record executive, *Live through This,* MTV and YTV.

Television Appearances; Pilots:
Richard Grace, *All Souls,* UPN, 2001.

Stage Appearances:
Gynty, Factory Studio Theatre, 2002.
Girl in the Goldfish Bowl, 2005.

Also appeared as Mitch Albom, *Tuesdays with Morrie,* Leanor and Alvin Segal Theatre; in *Vinci,* Centaur Theatre; in productions with the National Arts Centre, Stratford Festival, and Globe Theatre, Regina, Saskatchewan, Canada.

RECORDINGS

Video Games:
Splinter Cell (also known as *Tom Clancy's "Splinter Cell"*), Ubisoft, 2002.
Prince of Persia: Warrior Within, Ubisoft, 2004.
Voice of Douglas Shetland, *Splinter Cell: Chaos Theory,* Ubisoft, 2005.

JOHNSON, Brad 1959–

PERSONAL

Born October 24, 1959, in Tucson, AZ; son of Grove (a cowboy) and Virginia Johnson; married Laurie (a model), October 11, 1986; children: six daughters and one son. *Education:* Attended Southern Oregon State College and College of Southern Idaho.

Addresses: *Agent*—Metropolitan Talent Agency, 4526 Wilshire Blvd., Los Angeles, CA 90010. *Manager*—The Pitt Group, 9465 Wilshire Blvd., Suite 480, Beverly Hills, CA 90212.

Career: Actor. Previously a professional rodeo cowboy; appeared in television commercials, including as a Marlboro Man and as a model for Calvin Klein.

CREDITS

Film Appearances:
Calhoun, *Nam Angels,* New Horizon, 1989.
Ted Baker, *Always,* United Artists, 1989.

Lieutenant Jake 'Cool Hand' Grafton, *Flight of the Intruder,* Paramount, 1991.
David Herdeg, *Philadelphia Experiment II,* Trimark Pictures, 1993.
Ned Blessing, *Lone Justice 2,* Triboro, 1995.
Harris, *Dominion,* Prism, 1995.
Ned Blessing, *Lone Justice 3* (also known as *Lone Justice: Showdown at Plum Creek*), Triboro, 1996.
Rayford Steele, *Left Behind* (also known as *Left Behind: The Movie*), Columbia TriStar Home Video, 2000.
Grant Johnson, *Across the Line,* High Water, 2000.
The Making of "Left Behind: The Movie," 2000.
The Making of "Left Behind II: Tribulation Force," 2002.
Rayford Steele, *Left Behind II: Tribulation Force* (also known as *Tribulation Force*), Cloud Ten, 2002.
Duane Edwards, *Truce,* Top Knot, 2004.
The actor playing Phil, *No Regrets,* Lifetime, 2004.
Rayford Steele, *Left Behind: World War III,* Columbia, 2005.

Television Appearances; Movies:
George Meade, *An American Story* (also known as *After the Glory*), CBS, 1992.
Charlie Siringo, *Siringo,* 1994.
Dennis, *Cries Unheard: The Donna Yaklich Story* (also known as *Victim of Rage*), CBS, 1994.
Ted, *The Birds II: Land's End,* Showtime, 1994.
Kyle Townes, *XXX's & OOO's,* CBS, 1994.
Ruben Mason, *Silk Hope,* CBS, 1999.
Beau Dorn, *Crossfire Trail* (also known as *Louis L'Amour's "Crossfire Trail"*), TNT, 2001.
Jack Fletcher, *Blind Obsession,* Lifetime, 2001.
Jeff Hale, *Riverworld,* Sci–Fi Channel, 2003.
Jay Clifford, *Wild Things: Diamonds in the Rough,* 2005.
Stephen Chase, *Alien Blood* (also known as *Alien Siege*), Sci–Fi Channel, 2005.

Television Appearances; Series:
Title role, *Ned Blessing: The Story of My Life and Times,* 1993.
Judge Wyatt E. Jackson, *Courthouse,* CBS, 1995.
Dr. Dominick O'Malley, a recurring role, *Melrose Place,* Fox, 1996.
Major Matthew Quentin Shepherd, *Soldier of Fortune, Inc.* (also known as *S.O.F. Special Ops Force, S.O.F., Inc.,* and *SOF, Inc.*), syndicated, 1997–99.

Television Appearances; Miniseries:
Henry Nash, *Rough Riders,* TNT, 1997.

Television Appearances; Episodic:
Mr. Wess, "Rule Number One," *A Different World,* 1991.
Jeff, "Veronica's Sliding Doors," *Veronica's Closet,* NBC, 1999.

Captain, UFS Mercury, "Manifest Destiny," *The Outer Limits,* Showtime and syndicated, 2000.

Paul Newsome, district engineer, "$35K O.B.O.," *CSI: Crime Scene Investigation* (also known as *C.S.I.*), CBS, 2001.

Paul Newsome, district engineer, "Justice Is Served," *CSI: Crime Scene Investigation* (also known as *C.S.I.*), CBS, 2001.

Roger Ballard/Mike Negley, "Phoenix," *Mysterious Ways,* PAX, 2001.

Paul Newsome, district engineer, "Scuba Doobie–Doo," *CSI: Crime Scene Investigation* (also known as *C.S.I.*), CBS, 2001.

Television Appearances; Pilots:

Al Bonitelli, *Sisters,* CBS, 1990.

Major Matthew Quentin Shepherd, *Soldier of Fortune,* syndicated, 1997.

James Bishop, *Day One,* The WB, 2000.

Destiny, CBS, 2001.

Lieutenant Ray Mathers, *Alaska,* ABC, 2003.

John Robinson, *The Robinsons: Lost in Space,* The WB, 2004.

JOHNSON, David

PERSONAL

Addresses: *Agent*—Sara Pritchard, Casarotto Marsh, Ltd., National House, 60–66 Wardour St., London W1V 4ND, England.

Career: Cinematographer. Camera operator and photographer for commercials.

Member: British Society of Cinematographers.

CREDITS

Film Cinematographer:

The Universe of Dermot Finn (short film), 1988.

Othello, Sony Pictures Releasing, 1995.

Saint–Ex, Bonneville Worldwide Entertainment, 1996.

Hilary and Jackie, October Films, 1998.

An Ideal Husband, Miramax, 1999.

Toy Boys (short film), Stray Dog Films, 1999.

The Very Thought of You (also known as *Martha, Meet Frank, Daniel and Laurence*), Miramax, 1999.

Honest, Winchester Films, 2000.

Football (short film), 2001.

The Martins (also known as *Tosspot*), Icon Film Distribution, 2001.

Joy–Rider, Mediterranean Films, 2002.

Resident Evil, Sony Pictures Entertainment/Screen Gems, 2002.

Bienvenue au gite (also known as *Bed and Breakfast*), Mars Distribution/A–Film Distribution, 2003.

AVP: Alien vs. Predator (also known as *Alien vs. Predator* and *AvP*), Twentieth Century–Fox, 2004.

On a Clear Day, Icon Film Distribution, 2005.

Film Camera Operator:

Second assistant camera operator, *The Darkening* (also known as *Black Gate* and *Dark Encounters*), Mainline Releasing, 1995.

Saint–Ex, Bonneville Worldwide Entertainment, 1996.

Honest, Winchester Films, 2000.

Football (short film), 2001.

The Martins (also known as *Tosspot*), Icon Film Distribution, 2001.

Resident Evil, Sony Pictures Entertainment/Screen Gems, 2002.

Television Cinematographer; Series:

Free Spirit, ABC, 1989–90.

Television Cinematographer; Movies:

(And camera operator) *Basil,* Romance Classics, 1998.

Tube Tales, Sky TV (England), 1999.

The Sight, FX Channel, 2000.

Television Cinematographer; Specials:

Chasing Shadows (documentary), 1996.

"The Mill on the Floss," *Masterpiece Theatre,* PBS, 1997.

Television Cinematographer; Episodic:

"The Yob," *The Comic Strip Presents,* Channel 4 (England), 1988.

JONES, Christine

PERSONAL

Born October 13.

Career: Actress.

CREDITS

Film Appearances:

Sandra, *Cooley High,* American International, 1975.

Dorrie, *Annie Hall,* United Artists, 1977.

Laurie, *Wild Thing,* Paramount Home Video, 1987.

Grace Chandler, *Stealing Home,* Warner Bros., 1988.

Thea's mother, *Minotaur* (also known as *Mossad*), Columbia TriStar Home Video, 1997.

(Uncredited) Miriam, *Meet Joe Black,* MCA/Universal, 1998.

(Uncredited) *The Devil and Daniel Webster,* Cutting Edge, 2001.

Christine Young Jenkins, *Triangles and Tribulations,* E.I. Independent Cinema, 2001.

Brenda, *Gang of Roses,* DEJ Productions, 2003.

Mother Superior, *The Drum Beats Twice,* Justice for All, 2004.

Television Appearances; Series:

Sheila Refferty, *One Life to Live,* ABC, 1977.

Anne Gifford Cushing, *Lovers and Friends* (also known as *For Richer, for Poorer*), 1977–78.

Amy Gifford, *Another World,* NBC, 1977.

Second Janice Frame Cory, *Another World,* NBC, 1978–80, 1989.

Lisa Brendon, *Number 96,* NBC, 1980.

Victoria 'Viki' Lord Riley, a temporary role, *One Life to Live,* ABC, 1981–82.

Catsy Kirkland, *Ryan's Hope,* ABC, 1982–83.

Christina Robertson, *Rituals,* syndicated, 1984–85.

Pamela Buchanan O'Neill, *One Life to Live,* ABC, 1986–88, 2001.

Tracy Quartermaine Williams, a temporary role, *General Hospital,* ABC, 1989.

Television Appearances; Miniseries:

Sarah Jackson, *Queen* (also known as *Alex Haley's "Queen"*), 1993.

Television Appearances; Pilots:

Kim, *Serpico: The Deadly Game* (also known as *The Deadly Game*), NBC, 1976.

Ilene Charlesworth, *Dakota's Way,* ABC, 1988.

Television Appearances; Episodic:

"Palm Springs Answer," *City of Angels,* NBC, 1976.

Helen, "Hear No Evil," *A Man Called Hawk,* ABC, 1989.

"The Secret Life of Mary Margaret: Portrait of a Bulimic," *Lifestories: Families In Crisis,* NBC, 1992.

Stapleton, "Burden," *Law & Order,* NBC, 1998.

Melanie, "Fire and Ice," *Now and Again,* CBS, 2000.

Deborah, "Just Another Night at the Opera," *Third Watch,* NBC, 2000.

Upper East Side woman, "Attack of the Five Foot Ten Woman," *Sex and the City,* HBO, 2000.

Mrs. Griscom, "The Third Horseman," *Law & Order: Criminal Intent,* NBC, 2002.

Laura Dietrich, "Monster," *Law & Order: Criminal Intent,* NBC, 2003.

K

KALFUS, Renee Ehrlich
(Renee Kalfus)

PERSONAL

Addresses: *Agent*—International Creative Management, 8942 Wilshire Blvd., Beverly Hills, CA 90211.

Career: Costume Designer.

Awards, Honors: Costume Designers Guild Award nomination, excellence for costume design in a period or fantasy film, and Film Award nomination, British Academy of Film and Television Arts, best costume design, both 2001, for *Chocolat.*

CREDITS

Film Costume Designer:
(As Renee Kalfus) *Once Around,* Universal, 1991.
What's Eating Gilbert Grape, Paramount, 1993.
Safe Passage, New Line Cinema, 1994.
With Honors, Warner Bros., 1994.
Dead Man Walking, Gramercy, 1995.
The Evening Star, Paramount, 1996.
Addicted to Love (also known as *Forlorn*), Warner Bros., 1997.
The Cider House Rules, Miramax, 1999.
Snow Falling on Cedars, MCA/Universal, 1999.
Pay It Forward, Warner Bros., 2000.
Chocolat, Miramax, 2000.
The Shipping News (also known as *Noeuds et denouements*), Miramax, 2001.
The Life of David Gale (also known as *Das leben des David Gale*), Universal, 2003.
Ladder 49, Buena Vista, 2004.
Game 6, Serenade Films/ShadowCatcher Entertainment, 2005.

Television Costume Designer; Movies:
Crazy in Love, TNT, 1992.
Let It Be Me (also known as *Love Dance*), Starz!, 1998.

KARASZEWSKI, Larry
(L. A. Karaszewski)

PERSONAL

Raised in South Bend, IN; married, wife's name Emily; children: Carver, Jack. *Education:* Attended University of Southern California.

Addresses: *Agent*—Endeavor, 9701 Wilshire Blvd., 10th Floor, Beverly Hills, CA 90212.

Career: Writer, producer, director, and script consultant. Worked as a television film critic in South Bend, IN.

Awards, Honors: Chicago International Film Festival Award for *Beyond Our Control;* awards with Scott Alexander include Screen Award nomination, Writers Guild of America, best original screenplay, and Saturn Award nomination, Academy of Science Fiction, Fantasy, and Horror Films, best writing, both 1995, for *Ed Wood;* Paul Selvin Honorary Award, Writers Guild of America, Golden Satellite Award, International Press Academy, best original screenplay, and Golden Globe Award, best motion picture screenplay, all 1997, for *The People vs. Larry Flynt.*

CREDITS

Film Work:
Director, *Screwed* (also known as *Fool Proof*), Universal Home Entertainment, 2000.
Producer, *Auto Focus,* Sony Pictures, 2002.

Television Work; Series:
Director, *Beyond Our Control,* between 1978 and 1980.
Executive producer, *Problem Child,* 1993.

Television Work; Movies:
Executive producer, *Problem Child 3: Junior in Love* (also known as *Problem Child 3*), NBC, 1995.

Television Appearances; Series:
Member of ensemble, *Beyond Our Control,* 1977–80.

WRITINGS

Screenplays:
(With Scott Alexander) *Problem Child,* Universal, 1990.
(With Alexander) *Problem Child 2* (also based on a story by Karaszewski), Universal, 1991.
(With Alexander) *Ed Wood,* Buena Vista, 1994, published by Farrar, Straus & Giroux, 1995.
(With Alexander) *The People vs. Larry Flynt* (also known as *Larry Flynt*), Columbia, 1996, published as *The People vs. Larry Flynt: The Shooting Script,* W. W. Norton and Co., 1996.
(As L. A. Karaszewski; with Alexander) *That Darn Cat,* Buena Vista, 1997.
(Uncredited; with Alexander) *Cats Don't Dance* (animated), 1997.
(With Alexander) *Man on the Moon* (also known as *Der mondmann*), Universal, 1999, published as *Man on the Moon: The Shooting Script,* W. W. Norton and Co., 2000.
(With Alexander) *Screwed* (also known as *Fool Proof*), Universal Home Entertainment, 2000.
(With Alexander) *Agent Cody Banks* (also known as *L'agent Cody Banks*), Metro–Goldwyn–Mayer, 2003.
(Uncredited) *The Pacifier,* Buena Vista, 2004.

Also contributes rewrites and dialogue changes to other screenplays.

Television Series:
Beyond Our Control, 1977–80.

ADAPTATIONS

The television movie *Problem Child 3: Junior in Love* was based on a story by Karaszewski.

OTHER SOURCES

Periodicals:
Time, December 31, 1999, p. 223.

KATIMS, Robert 1927–

PERSONAL

Born April 22, 1927, in Brooklyn, NY; married, wife's name Ruth; children: three, including Jason (a television producer and playwright). *Education:* Attended Brooklyn College of the City University of New York.

Career: Actor. Worked for thirty years as a seller of law books.

CREDITS

Television Appearances; Series:
Hal Roth, *Relativity,* ABC, 1996–97.

Television Appearances; Movies:
Moscowitz, *Double Exposure: The Story of Margaret Bourke–White* (also known as *Double Exposure* and *Margaret Bourke–White*), TNT, 1989.
Detective Goldman, *The Bride in Black* (also known as *The Bride Wore Black*), ABC, 1990.

Television Appearances; Pilots:
Sergeant Polsky, *Ladies on Sweet Street,* ABC, 1990.

Television Appearances; Episodic:
Husband, "The Ventriloquist's Dummy," *Tales from the Crypt,* 1990.
Jacob Bloom, "Misconceptions," *Law & Order,* NBC, 1991.
Jacob Bloom, "Consultation," *Law & Order,* NBC, 1992.
"F.O.B.," *L.A. Law,* 1993.
Officer Bobby Schneider, "So–Called Angels," *My So–Called Life,* 1994.
Arnold Deensfrei, "The Jimmy," *Seinfeld,* NBC, 1995.
Stanley Angrist, "Unembracable You," *NYPD Blue,* 1996.
Andy Havens, "A Penny Saved," *Mike Hammer, Private Eye,* 1997.
Arnold Deensfrei, "The Finale: Parts 1 & 2," *Seinfeld,* NBC, 1998.
Elliott, "The Rock," *The King of Queens,* CBS, 1998.
Judge Lewis, "Independence Day," *Roswell,* The WB, 2000.

Mike Campbell, "Dog Days," *Judging Amy,* CBS, 2000.
Judge Lewis, "To Serve and Protect," *Roswell,* The WB, 2001.
Judge Lewis, "We Are Family," *Roswell,* The WB, 2001.
Rabbi Solomon, "The Wedding," *For Your Love,* The WB, 2001.
"Chapter Sixty–one," *Boston Public,* Fox, 2003.

Appeared as Dr. Arnold Hunziger in an episode of *Civil Wars,* and as Benjamin Tuttlebaum, *Vengeance Unlimited,* ABC; also appeared in an episode of *Divorce Court.*

Television Work; Specials:
Additional voices, *Lincoln,* ABC, 1992.

Film Appearances:
Bob Fertilizer, *Eat or Be Eaten,* 1985.
Martin Klein, *Broadcast News,* Twentieth Century–Fox, 1987.
Histoires d'Amerique, 1988.
Cody, *Presumed Innocent,* Warner Bros., 1990.
Minister, *The Pallbearer,* Miramax, 1996.
Waiting for Woody, 1998.
Gerald Auerbach, *Zero Effect,* 1998.
Mr. Carmichael, *Early Bird Special,* 2001.
Ray Hott, *Mulholland Dr.* (also known as *Mulholland Drive*), Universal Focus, 2001.
Dry cleaner, *Down with Love* (also known as *Down with Love—Zum teufel mit der liebe!*), Twentieth Century–Fox, 2003.

Stage Appearances:
Troilus and Cressida, Globe Playhouse, Los Angeles, 1985.
Colonel, *The Invasion of Aratooga,* Classic Stage Company, New York City, 1987.
Uncle Umbi, *Bricklayers,* Winterfest 11, Yale Repertory Company, New Haven, CT, 1990.
Father, *Shmulnik's Waltz,* Jewish Repertory Theatre, then Houseman Theatre, both New York City, 1991.
Understudy for Mike Fransisco and Lou Graziano, *Breaking Legs,* Promenade Theatre, New York City, 1991–92.
No Conductor, Threshold Theatre, New York City, 1992.
In Shadow, Threshold Theatre, 1992.
Rabbi, *Teible and Her Demon,* Jewish Repertory Theatre, 1994.

Also appeared as Ben, *Broadway Bound,* South Jersey Regional Theatre; in *A Dybbuk,* Denver Center Theatre Conservatory, Denver, CO; and in *Men in Pits, On the Wing,* and *The Penguin.*

KATZ, Clark
See PROVAL, David

KAVA, Caroline

PERSONAL

Education: State University of New York Empire State College, B.A.

Addresses: *Agent*—Michael Slessinger & Associates, 8730 Sunset, Suite 270, West Hollywood, CA 90069.

Career: Actress, producer, director, film editor, and writer.

Awards, Honors: Grand Prize, Independent Film Channel, 1995, for *Polio Water.*

CREDITS

Film Appearances:
Stefka, *Heaven's Gate* (also known as *Johnson County Wars*), United Artists, 1980.
Connie White, *Year of the Dragon,* Metro–Goldwyn–Mayer, 1985.
Elizabeth Grant, *Little Nikita* (also known as *The Sleepers*), Columbia, 1988.
Mrs. Kovic, *Born on the Fourth of July,* Universal, 1989.
Elvira Elbrick, *O que e isso, companheiro?* (also known as *Four Days in September* and *Four Days in September (O que e isso companheiro?)*), Miramax, 1997.
Helen Chambers, *Snow Falling on Cedars,* MCA/Universal, 1999.
Bill's mother, *Final,* Lions Gate Films, 2001.
Up–tight customer, *The Favor* (short film), Heartcore Productions, 2001.

Film Producer and Director:
(And film editor) *Polio Water* (short film), 1995.
Number One (short film), 1998.

Television Appearances; Movies:
Charlotte Yoblonski, *Act of Vengeance,* HBO, 1986.
Dr. Blackwell, *Nobody's Child,* CBS, 1986.
Jean, *Body of Evidence,* CBS, 1988.
Jean, *Murder Times Seven* (also known as *Murder x 7*), CBS, 1990.
Jean, *Murder in Black and White,* CBS, 1990.

Mary Hohne, *Guilty until Proven Innocent* (also known as *Presumed Guilty*), NBC, 1991.
Martha Tremayne, *Shattered Mind* (also known as *The Terror Inside*), NBC, 1996.
Anne Clark, *Amy & Isabelle* (also known as *Oprah Winfrey Presents: Amy and Isabelle*), ABC, 2001.

Television Appearances; Miniseries:
Young woman, *The Scarlet Letter*, 1979.
Detective Jean Harp, *Internal Affairs*, 1988.
Barbara, *Cross of Fire*, NBC, 1989.
Janice Miller, *In a Child's Name*, CBS, 1991.

Television Appearances; Episodic:
"Shades of Darkness," *The Equalizer*, 1986.
Harriet Garth, "Grossberg's Return," *Max Headroom*, 1987.
"Race Traitors," *The Equalizer*, 1989.
Thelma Beckett, "The Leap Home—November 25, 1969," *Quantum Leap*, NBC, 1990.
Rose Schwimmer, "Life Choice," *Law & Order*, NBC, 1991.
Dr. Toby Russell, "Ethics," *Star Trek: The Next Generation*, 1992.
Prosecutor, "Cold Shower," *L.A. Law*, NBC, 1993.
Doris Kearns, "Our Town," *The X–Files*, Fox, 1995.
Betty Abrams, "Corruption," *Law & Order*, NBC, 1996.
Mrs. McPhee, "Full Moon Rising," *Dawson's Creek*, The WB, 1998.
Mrs. McPhee, "The Reluctant Hero," *Dawson's Creek*, The WB, 1998.
Mary Donovan, "Death Penalties," *The Practice*, ABC, 2000.
Mary Donovan, "'Till Death Do Us Part: Part 1," *The Practice*, ABC, 2000.
Mary Donovan, "Liberty Bells: Part 2," *The Practice*, ABC, 2000.
Mrs. Truskie, "Love Stories," *100 Centre Street*, Arts and Entertainment, 2001.
Grace Owens, "The Relay," *Third Watch*, NBC, 2001.
Wanda Skulnick, "Blind Faith," *Hack*, CBS, 2003.
Vivian Gleason, "Day," *Law & Order: Trial by Jury*, NBC, 2005.

Appeared as Dr. Scott in *Matt Waters*, CBS.

Television Appearances; Other:
Sonia Petrovsky, *Ivan the Terrible* (series), CBS, 1976.
Hallie's mother, *It's Only Rock 'n' Roll* (special), ABC, 1991.
Irene Dugan, *Jumpin' Joe* (pilot), ABC, 1992.

Stage Appearances:
Salaria and understudy for Nerissa, *The Merchant of Venice*, Vivian Beaumont Theatre, Lincoln Center, New York City, 1973.
Understudy for Nora Clitheroe and Mollser, *The Plough and the Stars*, Vivian Beaumont Theatre, Lincoln Center, 1973.
Becky, *Gorky*, American Place Theatre, New York City, 1975.
Polly Peachum and Glenn Kezer Smith, *The Threepenny Opera*, Vivian Beaumont Theatre, Lincoln Center, 1976–77, then New York Shakespeare Festival, Delacorte Theatre, New York City, 1977.
Jill Kahn in "Stage I—Denial," and Linda in "Stage IV—Depression," *Stages*, Belasco Theatre, New York City, 1978.
Maud and Lin, *Cloud 9*, Lucille Lortel Theatre, New York City, 1981.
Constance and the Musician, Women's Project and Productions, American Place Theatre, New York City, 1981.
Little Victories, Women's Project and Productions, American Place Theatre, 1983.
Ellen Porter, *Domestic Issues*, Circle Repertory Company, New York City, 1983.
Widow Quin, *The Playboy of the Western World*, Roundabout Theatre Company, Stage I, New York City, 1985.

Stage Director:
A Body of Water, Circle Repertory Company, New York City, 1994.
As It Is in Heaven, University of Illinois, Urbana–Champaign, IL, 2004.

WRITINGS

Screenplays:
Polio Water (short film), 1995.
Number One (short film), 1998.

Stage Plays:
(And song lyrics) *Constance and the Musician*, Women's Project and Productions, American Place Theatre, New York City, 1981.
The Early Girl, produced in staged reading by Women's Project and Productions, New York City, 1983–84, then Circle Repertory Company, New York City, 1986.

KELLMAN, Barnet 1947–

PERSONAL

Full name, Barnet Kramer Kellman; born November 9, 1947, in New York, NY; son of Joseph A. G. (an attorney) and Verona D. (maiden name, Kramer) Kellman; married Nancy Mette (an actress), June 26, 1982;

children: Katherine Mette, Eliza Mette, Michael Mette. *Education:* Colgate University, B.A., 1969; attended Yale University, 1970; Union Graduate School, Ph.D., 1972. *Religion:* Jewish.

Addresses: *Agent*—Richard Weitz, Endeavor, 9601 Wilshire Blvd., 3rd Floor, Beverly Hills, CA 90210.

Career: Director, producer, and educator. North Carolina School of the Arts, instructor and guest director, 1973–80; City College of the City University of New York, instructor and guest director, 1975–76; Columbia University, instructor and guest director, 1984–87; also instructor at Leonard Davis Center for the Arts, Circle in the Square Acting School, and Corner Loft Studio.

Member: Society of Stage Directors and Choreographers (member of board of directors, 1984–86; member of executive board, 1985), Directors Guild of America, Actors' Equity Association, Screen Actors Guild, New Dramatists (member of board of directors).

Awards, Honors: Thomas J. Watson fellow, 1969–71; Danforth fellow, 1969–72; Emmy Award nomination, outstanding direction in a comedy series, 1989, for "Respect" (premiere episode), *Murphy Brown;* Emmy Award, 1990, and Emmy Award nomination, 1991, both outstanding comedy series (with others), for *Murphy Brown;* Directors Guild of America Award (with others) and Emmy Award nomination, both outstanding direction in a comedy series, 1990, for "Brown Like Me," *Murphy Brown;* Emmy Award nomination, outstanding direction in a comedy series, 1991, for "On Another Plane," *Murphy Brown;* Directors Guild of America Award nomination, outstanding direction in a comedy series, 1991, for "Bob & Murphy & Ted & Avery," *Murphy Brown;* Emmy Award nomination, outstanding direction in a comedy series, 1992, for "Birth 101," *Murphy Brown;* also received Emmy Award nomination for *Another World.*

CREDITS

Film Director:
Key Exchange, Twentieth Century–Fox, 1985.
Straight Talk, Buena Vista, 1992.
Stinkers (also known as *Slappy and the Stinkers*), TriStar, 1997.

Film Appearances:
The director, *Key Exchange,* Twentieth Century–Fox, 1985.
The television director, *Straight Talk,* Buena Vista, 1992.

Television Producer; Series:
Murphy Brown, CBS, 1989–92.

Co–executive producer, *Mad About You,* NBC, 1992–93.
Executive producer, *The Second Half,* NBC, 1993.
Co–executive producer, *Good Advice,* CBS, 1993–94.
Executive producer (and creator), *Something Wilder,* NBC, 1994.
For Your Love, The WB, 1998.
Co–executive producer, *Family Affair,* The WB, 2002.
Executive producer (and developer), *My Life Is a Sitcom,* ABC, 2003.

Television Director; Series:
Murphy Brown, CBS, between 1988 and 1991.
Mad About You, NBC, between 1992 and 1993.
Good Advice, CBS, 1993.
Something Wilder, NBC, between 1994 and 1995.
Bless This House, CBS, 1995.
For Your Love, The WB, between 1998 and 2000.
Madigan Men, ABC, 2000.
Family Affair, The WB, between 2002 and 2003.
George Lopez, ABC, between 2002 and 2003.
It's All Relative, between 2003 and 2004.
Under One Roof, The WB, between 2003 and 2004.

Television Director; Episodic:
"Past Perfect," *All Is Forgiven,* 1986.
"Mother's Day," *All Is Forgiven,* 1986.
"And Justice for Oliver" (also known as "And Justice for Ollie"), *All Is Forgiven,* 1986.
"Old Spouses Never Die: Parts 1 & 2," *Designing Women,* CBS, 1987.
"Monette," *Designing Women,* CBS, 1987.
"Grand Slam, Thank You Ma'am," *Designing Women,* CBS, 1987.
Take Five, CBS, two episodes, 1987.
"Goodbye Steve," *My Sister Sam,* CBS, 1987.
"And They Said It Would Never Last," *My Sister Sam,* CBS, 1987.
The Robert Guillaume Show, ABC, 1988.
"Mixed Doubles," *Just in Time,* ABC, 1988.
"2 rms, no vu," *Just in Time,* ABC, 1988.
"Birth," *Murphy Brown,* CBS, 1992.
"The Thrill of the Hunt," *Murphy Brown,* CBS, 1994.
"The Prototype" (premiere episode), *Thunder Alley,* ABC, 1994.
"Are We Having Fun Yet?" (premiere episode), *Hope and Gloria,* NBC, 1995.
(With Thomas Schlamme) "Detour Ahead" (premiere episode), *If Not for You* (also known as *One of Those Things*), CBS, 1995.
"Baby Shower," *ER,* NBC, 1996.
"The Walk–Out," *Suddenly Susan,* NBC, 1996.
"The Fighting Irish," *Ink,* CBS, 1997.
"Never Can Say Goodbye: Parts 1 & 2," *Murphy Brown,* CBS, 1998.
"The List," *Felicity,* The WB, 1999.
"Revolutions," *Felicity,* The WB, 1999.
"Blackout," *Felicity,* The WB, 1999.

"Daddy's Girl," *Once and Again,* ABC, 2000.
"... And Then He Had to Give a Thumbs Up," *The Weber Show* (also known as *Cursed*), NBC, 2000.
"... And Then Wendell Wore Candy Stripes," *The Weber Show* (also known as *Cursed*), NBC, 2001.
"... And Then Jack Found Out," *The Weber Show* (also known as *Cursed*), NBC, 2001.
"... And Then Jack Had Two Dates," *The Weber Show* (also known as *Cursed*), NBC, 2001.
"Best of Enemies," *Once and Again,* ABC, 2001.
"Honest Bob," *Bob Patterson,* ABC, 2001.
"Naked Bob," *Bob Patterson,* ABC, 2001.
"Awards Bob," *Bob Patterson,* ABC, 2001.
"I'm Okay, You're Okay," *The Fighting Fitzgeralds,* NBC, 2001.
"The Loud Man," *The Fighting Fitzgeralds,* NBC, 2001.
"Snowman," *Alias,* ABC, 2001.
"The Great Escape," *For Your Love,* The WB, 2002.
"Mickey Swallows a Bee," *Listen Up,* 2004.
"Volleybrawl," *8 Simple Rules* (also known as *8 Simple Rules for Dating My Teenage Daughter*), ABC, 2005.
"The Snow Episode," *Committed,* NBC, 2005.
"The Mother Episode," *Committed,* NBC, 2005.
The Bad Girl's Guide, UPN, 2005.

Also directed episodes of *Ally McBeal,* Fox; *Another World* (also known as *Another World: Bay City*), NBC, 1980s; *As the World Turns,* CBS; *Beverly Hills Buntz,* NBC; *The Big House,* ABC; *Brothers and Sisters,* NBC; *For Richer, for Poorer,* NBC; *Gemini,* Showtime; *Hometown,* CBS; and *Imagine That,* NBC.

Television Director; Pilots:
Sons of Gunz, CBS, 1987.
Cowboy Joe, NBC, 1988.
Good Advice, CBS, 1993.
The Second Half, NBC, 1993.
Daddy's Girls, CBS, 1994.
Bless This House, CBS, 1995.
Suddenly Susan, NBC, 1996.
Life with Roger, The WB, 1996.
For Your Love, The WB, 1998.
Bob Patterson, ABC, 2001.
Family Affair, The WB, 2002.
Rock Me Baby, The WB, 2003.
Like Family, The WB, 2003.
Me, Me, Me, UPN, 2004.
Hidden Howie: The Private Life of a Public Nuisance, Bravo, 2005.
Deal, NBC, 2005.

Television Director; Other:
Orphans, Waifs, and Wards, CBS, 1981.
The Designing Women Special: Their Finest Hour (special), CBS, 1990.
Mary and Rhoda (movie), ABC, 2000.

Stage Director:
Comanche Cafe/Domino Courts, American Place Theatre, New York City, 1976.
Key Exchange, Workshop of the Players Art Theatre, then Orpheum Theatre, both New York City, 1981.
Breakfast with Les and Bess, Hudson Guild, Lamb's Theatre, New York City, 1982.
The Good Parts, Astor Place Theatre, New York City, 1982.
Friends, Manhattan Theatre Club, Stage 73, New York City, 1983–84.
Danny and the Deep Blue Sea, Actors' Theatre of Louisville, Louisville, KY, then Circle in the Square Downtown, New York City, 1984.
Eden Court, Promenade Theatre, New York City, 1985.
The Loman Family Picnic, Manhattan Theatre Club Stage II, New York City, 1989.
Defiled, Geffen Playhouse, University of California, Los Angeles, 2000.

Also directed productions at Public Theatre, New York City; Eugene O'Neill Theatre Center, New York City; Yale Repertory Theatre, New Haven, CT; Folger Theatre, Washington, DC; and Williamstown Theatre Festival, Williamstown, MA.

WRITINGS

Television Episodes:
(With Lee Kalchein) "Hell No, They Won't Go," *Something Wilder,* NBC, 1994.

KENZLE, Leila 1960(?)–

PERSONAL

Born July 16, 1960 (some sources cite 1961), in Patchogue, Long Island, NY; daughter of Kurt (in electrical supply sales) and Lee (an antiques dealer) Kenzle; married Neil Monaco (an acting coach, writer, and director), April 26, 1994. *Education:* Rutgers University, B.F.A., 1984. *Avocational Interests:* Yoga, hiking, antique shopping.

Addresses: *Agent*—Metropolitan Talent Agency, 4526 Wilshire Blvd., Los Angeles, CA 90010; Karen Forman, Agency for the Performing Arts, 9200 Sunset Blvd., Suite 900, Los Angeles, CA 90069; (voice work) William Morris Agency, One William Morris Place, Beverly Hills, CA 90212. *Manager*—Ted Schachter, Schachter Entertainment, 1157 South Beverly Dr., Second Floor, Los Angeles, CA 90035.

Career: Actress and producer. Appeared in "The More You Know," a series of public service announcements broadcast on NBC. Hotel telephone operator. Volunteer for multiple sclerosis charities.

Awards, Honors: Screen Actors Guild Award nominations (with others), outstanding performance by an ensemble in a comedy series, 1997 and 1998, both for *Mad about You*; several awards, including South Carolina Worldfest Charleston Award and Houston Annual Worldfest Award, both best short film, for *Bigger Fish*.

CREDITS

Television Appearances; Series:
Fran Devanow, *Mad about You* (also known as *Loved by You*), NBC, 1992–98.
Kate DiResta, *DiResta*, UPN, 1998–99.

Television Appearances; Miniseries:
The Charmer, Independent Television, c. 1987, broadcast on *Masterpiece Theatre*, PBS, 1988.

Television Appearances; Movies:
Jessie Frank, *All She Ever Wanted* (also known as *Mother's Day* and *The Ties That Bind*), ABC, 1996.
Arlene, *Breast Men*, HBO, 1997.
Amy, "Dogomatic" (also known as "Dogmatic"), *The Wonderful World of Disney*, ABC, 1999.

Television Appearances; Specials:
The 17th Annual All New Circus of the Stars and Side Show, CBS, 1992.

Television Appearances; Episodic:
Second girl, "Theo's Women," *The Cosby Show*, NBC, 1989.
First student, "The Guilty Party," *thirtysomething*, ABC, 1990.
Prostitute, "A Passing Inspection," *Over My Dead Body*, CBS, 1990.
Tamara, "Blanche Delivers," *The Golden Girls*, NBC, 1990.
Debra Kirshner–Kleckner, "Someday My Prince Will Gum," *Princesses*, CBS, 1991.
Guest, *Late Night with Conan O'Brien*, NBC, 1994.
Fran Devanow, "The One with the Two Parts: Parts 1 & 2," *Friends*, NBC, 1995.
Lena, "For the Boys," *Something Wilder*, NBC, 1995.
Guest, *The Jon Stewart Show*, MTV, 1995.
Marsha McArthur, "The Murder Trade," *Diagnosis Murder*, CBS, 1996.
Voice of Janeane, "Ebony Baby," *Duckman* (animated), USA Network, 1997.

Guest, *The Rosie O'Donnell Show*, syndicated, 1997.
Herself, *Pictionary*, syndicated, 1997.
Guest, *The Late Show with David Letterman* (also known as *The Late Show*), CBS, c. 1997.
Naomi Demble, "The Reunion Show," *The Nanny*, CBS, 1998.
Fran, "The Final Frontier," *Mad about You* (also known as *Loved by You*), NBC, 1999.
Voice of Arctic hare, "Show Me the Bunny," *The Wild Thornberrys* (animated), Nickelodeon, 1999.
Voice of Bobri, "You Otter Know," *The Wild Thornberrys* (animated), Nickelodeon, 1999.
Tammy Bomgarden, "All Dressed Up and Nowhere to Die," *Diagnosis Murder*, CBS, 2000.
Leigh, "Angels Anonymous," *Touched by an Angel*, CBS, 2001.
Attorney, "The Paper Chase," *Felicity*, The WB, 2002.
Mrs. McKinney, "Looking for Quarters," *Judging Amy*, CBS, 2003.
Herself, *Kitty Bartholomew: You're Home*, Home & Garden Television, 2004.

Appeared in episodes of other series, including *Happy Hour*, USA Network; *Instant Comedy with the Groundlings* (multiple episodes), FX Channel; and *Politically Incorrect with Bill Maher* (also known as *Politically Incorrect*), Comedy Central and ABC.

Television Appearances; Pilots:
Gina DeSalvo, *The World according to Straw*, Fox, 1990.
Debra Kirshner–Kleckner, *Princesses*, CBS, 1991.
Julia, "Love and the Internet," *Love American Style*, ABC, 1999.

Film Appearances:
Marcia, *Other People's Money* (also known as *Riqueza ajena*), Warner Bros., 1991.
Bigger Fish (short film), Second Hand Smoke, 1996.
First woman, *Enemies of Laughter*, Outrider Pictures, 2000.
Ann Greenway, *White Oleander* (also known as *Weisser Oleander*), Warner Bros., 2002.
Julie Thomas, *The Hot Chick*, Buena Vista, 2002.
Alice York, *Identity*, Columbia/Sony Pictures Entertainment, 2003.

Film Producer:
Bigger Fish (short film), Second Hand Smoke, 1996.

Stage Appearances:
Madeline Monroe, *Tony 'n' Tina's Wedding*, Washington Square Church and Carmelita's, then Theatre at St. John's Church, later Vinnie Black's Coliseum, all New York City, 1988–89, then in Los Angeles, 1989.

OTHER SOURCES

Periodicals:
People Weekly, December 11, 1995, pp. 107–108.

KERNS, Joanna 1953–
(Joanna DeVarona, Joanne DeVarona)

PERSONAL

Original name, Joanna Crussie DeVarona; born February 12, 1953, in San Francisco, CA; daughter of David Thomas (an insurance agent) and Martha Louise (a clothing store manager; maiden name, Smith) DeVarona; sister of Donna DeVarona (an Olympic athlete and sportscaster); married Richard Martin Kerns (a director and producer), December 11, 1976 (divorced, December, 1986); married Marc Francis Appleton (an architect), 1995; children: (first marriage) Ashley Cooper. *Education:* Attended University of California, Los Angeles, 1970–71; studied acting with Lee Strasberg, Peggy Feury, Jeff Corey, and David Craig. *Politics:* Democrat.

Addresses: *Agent*—Sean Freidin, Broder, Webb, Chervin, Silbermann Agency, 9242 Beverly Blvd., Suite 200, Beverly Hills, CA 90210. *Manager*—Susan B. Landau, Thompson Street Entertainment, 754 North Kilkea Dr., Los Angeles, CA 90046. *Publicist*—Jim Broutman, Broutman Public Relations, 8225 Santa Monica Blvd., Los Angeles, CA 90046.

Career: Actress, producer, director, and writer. Appeared in "The More You Know," a series of public service announcements broadcast on NBC. Worked as a dancer at Disneyland; also a competitive gymnast.

CREDITS

Television Appearances; Series:
Pat Devon, *The Four Seasons,* CBS, 1984.
Margaret Katherine "Maggie" Malone Seaver, *Growing Pains,* ABC, 1985–92.

Television Appearances; Miniseries:
Marjorie Donovan, *V* (also known as *V: The Original Mini Series*), NBC, 1983.
Dr. Clare Winslow, *The Big One: The Great Los Angeles Earthquake* (also known as *The Great Los Angeles Earthquake*), NBC, 1990.
Maria Marshall, *Blind Faith* (also known as *The Toms River Case*), NBC, 1990.

Television Appearances; Movies:
(As Joanna DeVarona) Jessie, *The Million Dollar Rip–Off,* 1976.
Meg, *Marriage Is Alive and Well,* NBC, 1980.
Doris Marshall, *A Day of Thanks on Walton's Mountain,* NBC, 1982.
Doris Marshall, *Mother's Day on Walton's Mountain,* NBC, 1982.
Doris Marshall, *A Wedding on Walton's Mountain,* NBC, 1982.
Pamela Saletta, *The Return of Marcus Welby, M.D.,* ABC, 1984.
Andrea, *A Bunny's Tale,* ABC, 1985.
Anita Parrish, *The Rape of Richard Beck* (also known as *The Broken Badge* and *Violated*), ABC, 1985.
Lana Singer, *Stormin' Home,* CBS, 1985.
Stephanie Blume, *Mistress,* CBS, 1987.
Diane Pappas, *Those She Left Behind,* NBC, 1989.
Linda Fairstein, *The Preppie Murder,* ABC, 1989.
Kathy Plunk, *Captive* (also known *Season of Fear*), ABC, 1991.
Sally Raynor, *Deadly Intentions ... Again?,* ABC, 1991.
Eve Rhodes, *The Nightman* (also known as *The Watchman*), NBC, 1992.
Mary Ellen "Mel" Robbins, *Desperate Choices: To Save My Child* (also known as *The Final Choice* and *Solomon's Choice*), NBC, 1992.
Katy, *The Man with Three Wives,* CBS, 1993.
Maryanne Walker–Tate, *Shameful Secrets* (also known as *Going Underground*), ABC, 1993.
Veronica Ricci, *Not in My Family* (also known as *Breaking the Silence* and *Shattering the Silence*), ABC, 1993.
Dr. Jennifer Kessler, *Robin Cook's "Mortal Fear"* (also known as *Mortal Fear*), NBC, 1994.
Jane Ravenson, *See Jane Run,* ABC, 1995.
Laura Eagerton, *Whose Daughter Is She?* (also known as *For the Love of My Daughter, Moms,* and *Semi–Precious*), CBS, 1995.
Cynthia Martin, *Terror in the Family,* Fox, 1996.
Jessica Rayner, *No One Could Protect Her,* ABC, 1996.
Celeste Cooper, *Mother Knows Best,* ABC, 1997.
Gail Connelly Metzger, *Sisters and Other Strangers* (also known as *Suspicion of Innocence*), CBS, 1997.
Emma Bridges, *Emma's Wish,* CBS, 1998.
Elizabeth Cooper, *At the Mercy of a Stranger,* CBS, 1999.
Margaret "Maggie" Katherine Malone Seaver, "The Growing Pains Movie," *The Wonderful World of Disney,* ABC, 2000.
Matt's mother, *Someone to Love,* 2001.
Margaret "Maggie" Seaver, "Growing Pains: Return of the Seavers" (also known as "Growing Pains II: Home Equity"), *The Wonderful World of Disney,* ABC, 2004.

Television Appearances; Specials:
Are You a Missing Heir?, ABC, 1978.
Lifetime Salutes Mom, Lifetime, 1987.

Host, *The National Love and Sex Test,* ABC, 1988.

Host, *Second Annual Star–Spangled Celebration,* ABC, 1988.

Like Mother, Like Daughter, Lifetime, 1988.

Host, *Sea World's Miracle Babies and Friends* (also known as *The Miracle Babies of Sea World*), ABC, 1989.

The Hollywood Christmas Parade, syndicated, 1989.

Walt Disney World's Very Merry Christmas Parade 1989, 1989.

Starathon '90, syndicated, 1990.

The Tube Test, ABC, 1990.

Host, *Fantasies,* ABC, 1991.

Host, *Starathon '91,* syndicated, 1991.

Herself, *Welcome Home, America!—A USO Salute to America's Sons and Daughters,* ABC, 1991.

Voices That Care, Fox, 1991.

Television Appearances; Awards Presentations:

The 15th Annual People's Choice Awards, CBS, 1989.

The 16th Annual People's Choice Awards, CBS, 1990.

The Television Academy Hall of Fame (also known as *The Sixth Annual Television Academy Hall of Fame*), Fox, 1990.

Presenter, *The 53rd Annual Golden Globe Awards,* NBC, 1996.

Television Appearances; Episodic:

(As Joanna DeVarona) Joy, "Gillian," *Starsky and Hutch,* ABC, 1976.

"Officer Luca, You're Dead," *S.W.A.T.,* ABC, 1976.

Beth, "Romance Roulette," *The Love Boat,* ABC, 1977.

Customer, "Love for Sale," *Rhoda,* CBS, 1977.

Lily, "Touch of Death," *Quincy* (also known as *Quincy, M.E.*), NBC, 1977.

Natalie Sands, "The Blue Angels," *Charlie's Angels,* ABC, 1977.

(As Joanne DeVarona) "Firehouse Quintet," *Emergency!,* NBC, 1977.

"Playoff," *Switch,* CBS, 1978.

Bobby Trilling, "The Love Lesson," *Three's Company,* ABC, 1980.

Colleen, "Dead Man's Riddle," *CHiPs,* NBC, 1981.

"Difficult Lesson," *Fitz and Bones,* NBC, 1981.

Mary Kanfer, "The Last Page," *Magnum, P.I.,* CBS, 1982.

Woman, "The Fashion Show," *Laverne & Shirley,* ABC, 1982.

"Spring Is in the Air," *Star of the Family,* ABC, 1982.

Cassie, "Fatal Error," *Whiz Kids,* CBS, 1983.

Cheryl, "Jack Be Quick," *Three's Company,* ABC, 1983.

Jenny "Jen" Hunter, "Two Birds of a Feather," *Magnum, P.I.,* CBS, 1983.

Trish Brenner, "A Nice Place to Visit," *The A Team,* NBC, 1983.

Ryan's 4, ABC, 1983.

State liquor agent, "Hair Apparent," *Hill Street Blues,* NBC, 1984.

Mona Williams, "Hot Target," *Street Hawk,* ABC, 1985.

Regis Philbin's "Lifestyles" (also known as *The Regis Philbin Show*), Lifetime, 1987.

Cheryl Blaste, "Blaste from the Past," *Hooperman,* ABC, 1988.

"Love Struck," *Short Stories,* Arts and Entertainment, 1988.

Animal Crack–Ups, ABC, 1988.

Guest, *The Tonight Show Starring Johnny Carson,* NBC, 1990.

Christine, "Enter Christine," *The Mommies,* NBC, 1995.

Herself, "The Face with Two Men," *Hope and Gloria,* NBC, 1995.

Voice, "Bobut Conquers All," *Aliens in the Family,* ABC, 1996.

Claire McLaren, "The Closure," *The Closer,* CBS, 1998.

Stephanie Serone, "Broken Hearts," *Chicago Hope,* CBS, 1998.

Stephanie Serone, "Physician, Heal Thyself," *Chicago Hope,* CBS, 1998.

Herself, *Intimate Portrait: Victoria Principal,* Lifetime, 1998.

"Touched by an Angel," *Beggars and Choosers,* Showtime, 1999.

Herself, *Intimate Portrait: Joanna Kerns,* Lifetime, 2000.

Herself, *Intimate Portrait: Katey Sagal,* Lifetime, 2000.

Herself, *Larry King Live,* Cable News Network, 2000.

Herself, "Tracey Gold," *Biography* (also known as *A&E Biography: Tracey Gold*), Arts and Entertainment, 2001.

Herself, *Growing Pains: The E! True Hollywood Story,* E! Entertainment Television, 2001.

Herself, *I Am My Mother's Daughter,* Lifetime, 2001.

Kathryn Cahill, "Money Changes Everything," *The Education of Max Bickford,* CBS, 2002.

Judy, "Claude's Alternative Thanksgiving," *Less Than Perfect,* ABC, 2003.

Guest, *The Wayne Brady Show,* syndicated, 2003.

Herself, *Intimate Portrait: Tracey Gold,* Lifetime, 2003.

Judy, "Mom's the Word," *Less Than Perfect,* ABC, 2004.

Guest, *The Tony Danza Show,* syndicated, 2004.

Appeared in episodes of *Dr. Vegas,* CBS; and *One Tree Hill,* The WB.

Television Appearances; Pilots:

Dr. Kettering, *Hunter,* NBC, 1984.

Carrie, *Morning Glory, S.C.,* CBS, 1996.

Claire McLaren, *The Closer,* CBS, 1998.

I Love You—The Three Worst Words You'll Ever Hear, 1999.

Television Work; Movies:

Co–executive producer, *The Nightman* (also known as *The Watchman*), NBC, 1992.

Director, *Defending Our Kids: The Julie Posey Story,* Lifetime, 2003.

Director, "Growing Pains: Return of the Seavers" (also known as "Growing Pains II: Home Equity"), *The Wonderful World of Disney,* ABC, 2004.

Television Director; Episodic:
"The Truck Stops Here," *Growing Pains,* ABC, 1992.
"The Dupree Family Christmas," *Hope and Gloria,* NBC, 1995.
"The New Actor," *Remember WENN,* American Movie Classics, 1997.
"Trick or Treat," *Clueless,* UPN, 1997.
"Affairs to Remember," *The Love Boat: The Next Wave,* UPN, 1998.
"Life Is a Beach," *Clueless,* UPN, 1998.
"Poetry in Notion," *Suddenly Susan,* NBC, 1998.
"Pratfall," *Remember WENN,* American Movie Classics, 1998.
"Such Sweet Dreams," *The Love Boat: The Next Wave,* UPN, 1999.
"Troubled Water," *Ally McBeal,* Fox, 1999.
"Disinformed Sources," *Beggars and Choosers,* Showtime, 2000.
"Payback's a Bitch," *Titans,* NBC, 2000.
"Three Lucky Ladies on the Line," *Any Day Now,* Lifetime, 2000.
"Where's the Justice in That?," *Any Day Now,* Lifetime, 2000.
"You Think I Am Lying to You?," *Any Day Now,* Lifetime, 2000.
"Chapter Fourteen," *Boston Public,* Fox, 2001.
"Fire," *Felicity,* The WB, 2001.
"The Obstacle Course," *Ally McBeal,* Fox, 2001.
"The Right Thing to Do," *Judging Amy,* CBS, 2001.
"Something Battered, Something Blue," *That's Life,* CBS, 2001.
"Call Him Macaroni," *Any Day Now,* Lifetime, 2002.
"Carmic Behavior," *Leap of Faith,* NBC, 2002.
"Come Blow Your Whistle," *For the People* (also known as *Para la gente*), Lifetime, 2002.
"Felicity Interrupted," *Felicity,* The WB, 2002.
"The Importance of Not Being Too Earnest," *Dawson's Creek,* The WB, 2002.
"Stages," *Strong Medicine,* Lifetime, 2002.
"Addicted to Love," *Strong Medicine,* Lifetime, 2003.
"Power Play," *For the People* (also known as *Para la gente*), Lifetime, 2003.
"Skin," *Strong Medicine,* Lifetime, 2003.
"Substitute Teacher," *The O'Keefes,* The WB, 2003.
"My Common Enemy," *Scrubs,* NBC, 2004.
"Rush for the Door," *The Division* (also known as *Heart of the City*), Lifetime, 2004.
"Tanner," *Phil of the Future,* The Disney Channel, 2004.
"Trade Talks," *Clubhouse,* CBS, 2004.
"Romancing the Joan," *Joan of Arcadia,* CBS, 2005.

Directed episodes of *The Mommies,* NBC.

Film Appearances:
(As Joanna DeVarona) Marilyn Baker, *A*P*E* (also known as *Ape, Attack of the Giant Horny Gorilla, Hideous Mutant, The New King Kong, Super Kong,* and *King Kongui daeyeokseub*), New World, 1976.
Diana, *Coma,* United Artists, 1978.
Nancy, *Cross My Heart,* Universal, 1987.
(Uncredited) Herself, *She's Having a Baby,* Paramount, 1988.
Katharine Watson, *Street Justice,* Lorimar, 1989.
Aunt Sunny, *An American Summer,* Castle Hill Productions, 1991.
Carol Cochran, *No Dessert Dad, Till You Mow the Lawn,* New Horizons Picture Corporation, 1994.
Annette Kaysen, *Girl, Interrupted* (also known as *Durchgeknallt* and *Durchgeknallt—Girl, Interrupted*), Columbia, 1999.
Lydia, *All over the Guy,* Lions Gate Films, 2001.

Stage Appearances:
(As Joanna DeVarona) Zoe, blushing bride, nymph, pygmy, and Yew, *Ulysses in Nighttown,* Winter Garden Theatre, New York City, 1974.

As Joanna DeVarona, appeared as a dancer in *Clown Around.*

Stage Work:
Director, *What Every Woman Knows,* West Coast Ensemble Theatre, Los Angeles, 1989.

Major Tours:
(As Joanna DeVarona) *Two Gentlemen of Verona* (musical), New York Shakespeare Festival, U.S. and Canadian cities, 1973.

Also toured in a production of *My Fair Lady* (musical).

RECORDINGS

Music Videos:
"Voices That Care," 1991.

WRITINGS

Teleplays; Episodic:
(With Becky Ayers) "Family Ties," *Growing Pains,* ABC, 1988.
"Guess Who's Coming to Dinner," *Growing Pains,* ABC, 1989.

Screenplays:
Author of the unproduced screenplay *Freestyle.*

OTHER SOURCES

Periodicals:

InStyle, May, 1998, p. 258.
People Weekly, June 26, 2000, p. 137.

KOPACHE, Thomas 1945–
(Tom Kopache)

PERSONAL

Born October 17, 1945, in Manchester, NH; son of Dorothy E. (maiden name, Sterling) Kopache. *Education:* San Diego State University, B.A., 1971; California Institute of the Arts, M.F.A., 1973; studied acting with Sam Schact.

Addresses: *Agent*—Geddes Agency, 8430 Santa Monica Blvd., Suite 200, West Hollywood, CA 90069.

Career: Actor. Camera Obscura (touring company), Amsterdam, the Netherlands, founding member, 1973, and performer throughout Europe, 1973–76; Cleveland Playhouse, Cleveland, OH, guest artist, 1986–87. Teacher of acting classes at University of California, La Jolla, and San Diego City College. *Military service:* U.S. Navy, 1963–66; served in Vietnam; received Armed Forces Expedition Army Medal.

Member: Actors' Equity Association, Screen Actors Guild, American Federation of Television and Radio Artists.

CREDITS

Film Appearances:

Warden, *Hot Money* (also known as *Getting Centered, Going for Broke, The Great Madison County Robbery, Never Trust an Honest Thief,* and *Zen Business*), Westfront Productions, 1979, 1983.
Police officer, *Without a Trace,* Twentieth Century–Fox, 1982.
Highway patrol officer, *Strange Invaders,* Orion, 1983.
(As Tom Kopache) Truck driver, *Home Free All,* Almi Classics, 1983.
Cory, *Agent on Ice,* 1985, Shapiro Entertainment, 1986.
Television station man, *Loose Cannons,* TriStar, 1990.
Dr. Parker, *Liebestraum,* Metro–Goldwyn–Mayer/Pathe, 1991.
Geiger counter vendor, *This Boy's Life,* Warner Bros., 1993.
Mr. Wilson, *Mr. Jones,* TriStar, 1993.

Communications officer, *Star Trek: Generations* (also known as *Star Trek 7*), Paramount, 1994.
Mr. Simpson, *Leaving Las Vegas,* United Artists, 1995.
Thorn McIntyre, *Ghosts of Mississippi* (also known as *Ghosts from the Past*), Columbia, 1996.
Calhoun, *Breakdown* (also known as *The Breakdown Mile*), Paramount, 1997.
(As Tom Kopache) Captain Trent, *Recoil,* PM Entertainment Group, 1997.
Merv, *One Night Stand,* New Line Cinema, 1997.
Father Durning, *Stigmata,* Metro–Goldwyn–Mayer, 1999.
Principal Evans, *Catch Me If You Can,* DreamWorks, 2002.
Student, *Reality School* (short film), Hypnotic Films, 2002.
Chief Neal, *A Man Apart* (also known as *Extreme Rage*), New Line Cinema, 2003.
Killian, *Hard Scrambled,* New Visions Fellowship, 2004.
Mr. Duke, *Ten 'til Noon,* 2005.
Frank Patton, *110%: When Blood, Sweat and Tears Are Not Enough,* 2006.

Television Appearances; Series:

Bob Slattery, *The West Wing,* NBC, 2001–2004.

Television Appearances; Miniseries:

Mike O'Rourke, *People Like Us,* NBC, 1990.

Television Appearances; Movies:

Squad leader, *The Red Spider,* 1988.
Carl Fitzpatrick, *A Woman Scorned: The Betty Broderick Story* (also known as *Till Murder Do Us Part*), CBS, 1992.
Blood bank executive, *And the Band Played On,* HBO, 1993.
Dr. Mason, *For Their Own Good,* 1993.
Mason, *Hart to Hart Returns,* NBC, 1993.
Steve Dahlberg, *A Case for Murder,* USA Network, 1993.
(As Tom Kopache) Arlo Trask, *Children of the Dark,* 1994.
Ray Keyes, *Breaking Through* (also known as *After the Silence* and *Breaking Free*), ABC, 1996.
Arlo, *All Lies End in Murder* (also known as *Behind Every Good Man*), 1997.

Television Appearances; Specials:

Mr. Carter, Professor Willard, Constable Warren, and Farmer McCarty, "Our Town," *Great Performances,* PBS, 1989.
Janos, "Miss Rose White," *Hallmark Hall of Fame,* NBC, 1992.
Dr. Darrold Treffert, *On Trial,* NBC, 1994.
Jed, "Journey," *Hallmark Hall of Fame,* CBS, 1995.

Television Appearances; Episodic:
Cab driver, *Another World,* NBC, 1983.
Carl, *Guiding Light,* CBS, 1985.
Grady, "On the Night He Was Betrayed," *Spenser: For Hire,* ABC, 1987.
Dr. Miles, "Spleen It to Me, Lucy," *L.A. Law,* NBC, 1991.
(As Tom Kopache) Sam Drucker, "Mushrooms," *Law & Order,* NBC, 1991.
Donald Bobeck, "Looking for Loans in All the Wrong Places," *Roseanne,* ABC, 1992.
Mirok, "The Next Phase," *Star Trek: The Next Generation* (also known as *The Next Generation* and *Star Trek: TNG*), syndicated, 1992.
Second reporter, "No Man Loyal and Neutral," *Homefront,* ABC, 1992.
Chief, "Dead–End for Delia," *Fallen Angels* (also known as *Perfect Crimes*), Showtime, 1993.
(As Tom Kopache) Hughes, "Friday the 13th," *Sirens,* ABC, 1993.
Sawyer, "Endangered Species," *Bodies of Evidence,* CBS, 1993.
Engineer, "Emergence," *Star Trek: The Next Generation* (also known as *The Next Generation* and *Star Trek: TNG*), syndicated, 1994.
Sal DalBazzo, "Dirty Deeds," *The John Larroquette Show,* NBC, 1994.
Tu'Pari, "The Parliament of Dreams," *Babylon 5,* syndicated, 1994.
"Family Values," *Law & Order,* NBC, 1994.
Dr. Leland O'Conner, "Chapter Three," *Murder One,* ABC, 1995.
Dr. Stevens, "And the Winner Is ... ," *Melrose Place,* Fox, 1995.
Dr. Stevens, "Melrose Impossible," *Melrose Place,* Fox, 1995.
General Thomas Callahan, "The Walk," *The X–Files,* Fox, 1995.
Leonard, "Nan's Ghost: Parts 1 & 2," *Murder, She Wrote,* CBS, 1995.
Viorsa, "The Thaw," *Star Trek: Voyager* (also known as *Voyager*), UPN, 1996.
Kaplinger, "The Last Five Pounds Are the Hardest," *The Burning Zone,* UPN, 1997.
Kira Taban, "Ties of Blood and Water," *Star Trek: Deep Space Nine* (also known as *Deep Space Nine, DS9,* and *Star Trek: DS9*), syndicated, 1997.
Terry Albright, "Citizen Canine," *Total Security,* ABC, 1997.
"Power Corrupts," *Profiler,* NBC, 1997.
Dr. Stanford Forsythe, "The Gettysburg Virus," *7 Days,* UPN, 1998.
Kira Taban, "Wrongs Darker Than Death or Night," *Star Trek: Deep Space Nine* (also known as *Deep Space Nine, DS9,* and *Star Trek: DS9*), syndicated, 1998.
Mr. Schramm, "Body Count," *The Practice,* ABC, 1998.
Mr. Abbott, "See Dharma Run," *Dharma & Greg,* ABC, 1999.
Attorney, "The Getaway," *Ally McBeal,* Fox, 2001.
Denver, "Reprise," *Angel,* The WB, 2001.
Dr. Harold Manning, "Honor Code," *The Practice,* ABC, 2001.
Dr. Thompson, "Separation," *Family Law,* CBS, 2001.
Irwin Slater, "To Walk on Wings," *JAG,* CBS, 2001.
Mr. Purcell, "Hero," *The Division,* Lifetime, 2001.
Mr. Willoughby (some sources cite James Jasper), "You've Got Male," *CSI: Crime Scene Investigation* (also known as *CSI*), CBS, 2001.
Ellori, "Prophecy," *Stargate SG–1,* Sci–Fi Channel and syndicated, 2003.
Ike Gukor, "Babylon," *Carnivale,* HBO, 2003.
Judge Seymour, "Final Judgment," *The Practice,* ABC, 2003.
The alien, "Harbinger," *Enterprise* (also known as *Star Trek: Enterprise*), UPN, 2004.
Judge Dale Wallace, "Change of Course," *Boston Legal,* ABC, 2004.
Judge Dale Wallace, "A Greater Good," *Boston Legal,* ABC, 2004.
Creepy guy/God, "Jump," *Joan of Arcadia,* CBS, 2004.
Michael Wilkins, "Omissions," *Strong Medicine,* Lifetime, 2004.
Paul Danner, "American Dreamers," *CSI: NY* (also known as *CSI: New York*), CBS, 2004.
Vic Feldspar, "Living Will," *Malcolm in the Middle,* Fox, 2005.

Appeared as Judge Boyle, *Ally McBeal,* Fox; as Ralph Pistone, *Michael Hayes,* CBS; as Judge Letts, *The Practice,* ABC; as Lawrence Mason, *Six Feet Under,* HBO; and in *Civil Wars,* ABC.

Television Appearances; Pilots:
Tos, *Enterprise: Broken Bow* (also known as *Star Trek Enterprise: Broken Bow*), UPN, 2001.

Stage Appearances:
Conrade, *Much Ado about Nothing,* San Diego Shakespeare Festival, San Diego, CA, 1970.
The emperor, *The Architect and Emperor of Assyria,* La MaMa Experimental Theatre Club, New York City, 1976.
Macbeth, *Macbeth,* La MaMa Experimental Theatre Club, 1977.
Butcher, *The Resistible Rise of Arturo Ui* (also known as *Arturo Ui*), La MaMa Experimental Theatre Club, 1978.
Prospero, *The Tempest,* La MaMa Experimental Theatre Club, 1978.
Scipio, *Caligula,* La MaMa Experimental Theatre Club, 1978.
Wagner, *Faust,* La MaMa Experimental Theatre Club, 1978.
Morris, *The Bloodknot,* Syracuse Stage, Syracuse, NY, then Walnut Street Theatre, Philadelphia, PA, both 1979.
Recruiting officer, *Mother Courage,* Center Stage, Baltimore, MD, 1980.

George, *Hunting Scenes from Lower Bavaria,* Manhattan Theatre Club, Stage 73, New York City, 1981.

Harry Roat, *Wait Until Dark,* Wye Mills Theatre, 1981.

Rover, *Hurrah for the Bridge,* La MaMa Experimental Theatre Club, 1981.

First presser, *The Workroom,* Center Stage, 1982.

Ioga, *The Extravagant Triumph ... ,* INTAR Hispanic American Theatre, New York City, 1982.

Kevin Morrow, *Friends Too Numerous to Mention,* Jewish Repertory Theatre, New York City, 1982.

Macduff, *Macbeth,* Shakespeare and Company, 1982.

Pedro, *The Senorita from Tacna,* INTAR Hispanic American Theatre, 1982.

Bob Cratchit, *A Christmas Carol,* Indiana Repertory Company, 1983.

The dark man, *The Woman,* Center Stage, 1983.

Deeley, *Old Times,* Indiana Repertory Company, 1983.

Morris, *The Bloodknot,* New Stage, 1983.

Westmoreland, *Henry IV, Parts I and II,* Indiana Repertory Company, 1983.

Coach, *Baseball Play,* Ensemble Studio Theatre, New York City, 1984.

Jack, *Plainsong,* Ensemble Studio Theatre, 1984.

Waiter, doctor, Kovacs, and barber, *The Danube,* American Place Theatre, New York City, 1984.

Jimmy, *Cayuses,* Ensemble Studio Theatre, 1985.

Polixenes, *The Winter's Tale,* Lincoln Center, Symphony Space, New York City, 1985.

Dr. Bailey, Buford Bullough, and Griswold Plankman, *Laughing Stock,* Long Wharf Theatre, New Haven, CT, 1987.

Smith, *The Last Temptation of Joe Hill,* INTAR Hispanic American Theatre, Stage 2, New York City, 1988.

Titus Lartius, *Coriolanus,* New York Shakespeare Festival, Public Theatre, Anspacher Theatre, New York City, 1988.

Mr. Carter, Professor Willard, Constable Warren, and Farmer McCarty, *Our Town,* Lyceum Theatre, New York City, 1988–89.

Mr. Dubinsky, first man and understudy for Jabe Torrance, *Orpheus Descending,* Neil Simon Theatre, New York City, 1989.

Julian, "The Encanto File," *The Encanto File and Other Short Plays,* Women's Project and Productions, Judith Anderson Theatre, New York City, 1991.

Karl Streber, *Temporary Help,* Long Wharf Theatre, 1991.

Karl Streber, *Temporary Help,* A Contemporary Theatre, Seattle, WA, 1999.

(As Tom Kopache) Creon, *Antigone,* Circus Theatricals Studio Ensemble, Odyssey Theatre, Los Angeles, 2003.

(As Tom Kopache) Duke Senior, *As You Like It,* Circus Theatricals Studio Ensemble, Lex Theatre, Hollywood, CA, 2003.

Major Tours:

The emperor, *The Architect and Emperor of Assyria,* European cities, 1976.

OTHER SOURCES

Periodicals:

Cult Times, February, 1998; February, 1999; January, 2002.

TV Zone, February, 1997, pp. 40–43; January, 2002, p. 11.

KOROMZAY, Alix 1971–
  (Alix Koromazay)

PERSONAL

Full name, Alexandra Elizabeth Koronzay; born April 22, 1971, in Washington, DC; children: Sasha. *Education:* Studied acting at Circle in the Square. *Avocational Interests:* Yoga.

Career: Actress.

CREDITS

Film Appearances:

Cindy, *Kindergarten Cop,* Universal, 1990.

Girl, *A Smile in the Dark* (also known as *A Day in L.A., California 405, Destination Unknown,* and *Jungle of Love*), 1991.

Saloon girl, *Mad at the Moon,* Republic, 1992.

Punk girl, *Ghost in the Machine* (also known as *Deadly Terror*), Twentieth Century–Fox, 1993.

Angel, *The Pornographer* (also known as *Family Values*), World Movies, 1994.

Tea lady, *Hard Drive* (also known as *Enter Deliah*), Triboro, 1994.

Elphin girl, *The Girl with the Hungry Eyes,* Columbia TriStar, 1995.

Angie, *Somebody Is Waiting,* Live Entertainment, 1996.

Nicky, *Dogstar,* Golden Shadow, 1997.

Joyce, *Nightwatch,* Miramax, 1997.

Remy, *Mimic,* Dimension Films, 1997.

Natalie, *Lucinda's Spell,* Golden Shadow, 1998.

Mary Lambetta, *The Haunting* (also known as *La maldicion*), DreamWorks, 1999.

Sheriff Cora, *Children of the Corn 666: Isaac's Return* (also known as *Children of the Corn 666*), Buena Vista Home Video, 1999.

Liddy Adams, *Net Worth,* Curb Entertainment, 2000.

Lisa, *Dear Emily,* Wolfe, 2001.

Remi, *Mimic 2* (also known as *Mimic 2: Hardshell*), Miramax, 2001.

Alex, *The Complex,* Complex, 2002.

Mrs. Cordell, *Blood Work,* Warner Bros., 2002.

Denise, *Family Tree,* 2003.

Ms. Mann, *7 Songs,* Soft Serve, 2003.
Nina, *Tre,* Cinema Libre Studio, 2005.

Television Appearances; Movies:
Woman in quarantine, *Daybreak,* HBO, 1993.
Josie, *Reform School Girl,* Showtime, 1994.
(As Alix Koromazay) Alicia, *A Friend to Die For* (also known as *Death of a Cheerleader*), NBC, 1994.

Television Appearances; Miniseries:
Cheryl, *Mr. Murder* (also known as *Dean Koontz's "Mr. Murder"*), ABC, 1998.

Television Appearances; Series:
Dawn, *Tribes,* 1990.

Television Appearances; Episodic:
Leah, "Mr. Right," *The Trials of Rosie O'Neill,* CBS, 1990.
Lisa, "Heal Thyself," *Northern Exposure,* CBS, 1993.
Valerie, "The Bounty Hunter," *The Marshal,* The Family Channel, 1995.
Pretty girl, "Madwoman," *Cracker,* ABC, 1997.
Karin Shaw, "Celano v. Foster," *Family Law,* CBS, 2002.

Also appeared as Suzanne, *Crime & Punishment,* NBC; Colleen Fernandez, "Good Question," *Presidio Med,* CBS.

Television Appearances; Specials:
The Hollywood Christmas Parade, syndicated, 1990.

KOVE, Martin 1946–
(Martin Cove, Marty Kove)

PERSONAL

Born March 6, 1946, in Brooklyn, NY; married Vivienne. *Avocational Interests:* Tennis, horse training, racquetball, skiing, gourmet cooking.

Addresses: *Agent*—Cunningham/Escott/Slevin & Doherty Talent Agency, 10635 Santa Monica Blvd., Suite 140, Los Angeles, CA 90025.

Career: Actor and producer. Appeared in television commercials for King Cobra Beer; previously worked as a substitute math teacher, Ward Melville High School, New York, NY. Tarzana, CA, honorary marshal.

CREDITS

Film Appearances:
(Film debut; uncredited) *Little Murders,* Twentieth Century–Fox, 1971.

(As Marty Kove) Marty, *Women in Revolt* (also known as *Andy Warhol's "Women in Revolt"*), 1971.
Deputy, *Last House on the Left* (also known as *Krug and Company, Grim Company, Night of Vengeance,* and *The Sex Crime of the Century*), Hallmark/Atlas International, 1972.
(As Martin Cove) Ambulance attendant, *Cops and Robbers,* United Artists, 1973.
Archie, *Savages,* Angelika, 1974.
Weigh station cop, *Road Movie,* 1974.
Editor, *The Wild Party,* American International Pictures, 1975.
Nero the Hero, *Deathrace 2000,* New World, 1975.
The Four Deuces, Avco Embassy, 1975.
Pete Gusenberg, *Capone,* Twentieth Century–Fox, 1975.
Clem, *White Line Fever,* Columbia, 1975.
Smokey Ross, the "Deuce of Diamonds," *The Four Deuces,* 1976.
Jack McCall, *The White Buffalo* (also known as *Hunt to Kill*), United Artists, 1977.
Texas gambler, *Mr. Billion* (also known as *The Windfall*), Twentieth Century–Fox, 1977.
Skip, *Seven* (also known as *Sevano's Seven*), American International Pictures, 1979.
Laboratory, 1980.
Partners, Paramount, 1982.
Neil, *Blood Tide* (also known as *The Red Tide, Bloodtide,* and *Demon Island*), 21st Century, 1982.
John Kreese, *Karate Kid,* Columbia, 1984.
Jackson, the helicopter pilot, *Rambo: First Blood Part II,* TriStar, 1985.
John Kreese, *Karate Kid, Part II,* Columbia, 1986.
John Steele, *Steele Justice,* Atlantic, 1987.
John Kreese, *Karate Kid, Part III,* Columbia, 1989.
Sean Craig, *White Light,* Academy, 1991.
Michael DeSilva, *Project: Shadowchaser* (also known as *Shadowchaser*), Prism Entertainment, 1992.
Sam Nicholson, *The President's Target* (also known as *The Man from Nowhere*), Hemdale Home Video, 1993.
Agent Baker, *The Outfit,* MCA/Universal Home Video, 1993.
Stewart, *Firehawk,* Concorde, 1993.
Rick Kulhane, *To Be the Best,* PM Home Video, 1993.
Mr. Lee, *Shootfighter: Fight to the Death* (also known as *Shootfighter*), Columbia TriStar Home Video, 1993.
Stewart, *Future Shock,* 1993.
Wolf Larsen, *Without Mercy* (also known as *Outraged Fugitive*), Live Entertainment, 1994.
Jabal, *Savage Land,* Motion Picture Village/Savage Land Productions, 1994.
Dr. Langdon, *Future Shock,* Hemdale Home Video, 1994.
DeVoe, *Endangered* (also known as *Uncivilized, The Most Dangerous Predator Is Man,* and *The Hunted*), Academy Entertainment, 1994.
Paul Landis, *Death Match,* Monarch Home Video, 1994.

Ed Ross, *Wyatt Earp* (also known as *Wyatt Earp: Return to Tombstone*), Warner Bros., 1994.

John Dillinger, *Baby Face Nelson,* Concorde/New Horizons, 1995.

Michael Silvano, *Judge and Jury,* A–Pix Entertainment, 1996.

Torman, *The Final Equinox* (also known as *Alien Weapon I*), Triad Studios, 1996.

Admiral Teegs, *Timelock,* 1996.

Marshal Jackson, *Grizzly Mountain,* Legacy Releasing, 1997.

Carl, *Top of the World* (also known as *Cold Cash* and *Showdown*), 1997.

Samuel J. Weber, *The Marksmen* (also known as *Sliding Home*), 1997.

James Ricks, *The Waterfront* (also known as *Maximum Justice*), 1998.

Face, *The Thief & the Stripper* (also known as *Strip 'n Run*), 1998.

Hank, *Nowhere Land,* 1998.

Thompson, *Joseph's Gift,* 1998.

Hyacinth, 1998.

Frank, *Savage Season,* 2001.

Captain Peter James, *Final Payback,* Amsell Entertainment, 2001.

Black Scorpion Returns, New Concorde, 2001.

Father Brazinksi, *Going Back* (also known as *Under Heavy Fire*), M.I.B., 2001.

Packard, *Extreme Honor* (also known as *Last Line of Defence 2*), MTI Home Video, 2001.

Redick, *Con Games,* Westar Entertainment, 2001.

Tom Reynolds, *Shattered Lies,* Hart Sharp Video, 2002.

Theodore Huntley, *American Gun,* 2002.

Robert Leoni, *Trance,* Trimark, 2002.

Roland, *Crocodile 2: Death Swamp* (also known as *Crocodile 2: Death Roll*), Nu Image, 2002.

It's Only a Movie: The Making of "Last House on the Left" (documentary short), Metro–Goldwyn–Mayer/United Artists Home Entertainment, 2002.

Himself, *Celluloid Crime of the Century* (documentary short), 2003.

Taxi driver, *Paradise,* 2003.

Zeff, *Devil's Knight,* MTI Home Video, 2003.

Munkar, *Barbarian,* New Concorde, 2003.

Captain Ron Williams, *Rice Girl,* 2003.

Caleb, *Curse of the Forty–Niner* (also known as *Curse of the 49er* and *Miner's Massacre*), DEJ Productions, 2003.

Corrigan, *Glass Trap,* 2004.

The clown, *Big Chuck, Little Chuck,* Maricopa Films, 2004.

Jake Lawlor, *Soft Target,* Gorilla Pictures, 2005.

The bartender, *Seven Mummies,* American World Pictures, 2005.

Jess, *Miracle at Sage Creek,* Talmarc Pictures, 2005.

Also appeared in *Janis; The Lion of Ireland.*

Film Work:

Associate producer, *Curse of the Forty–Niner* (also known as *Curse of the 49er* and *Miner's Massacre*), 2003.

Associate producer, *Miracle at Sage Creek,* 2005.

Television Appearances; Series:

George Baker, *Code R,* CBS, 1977.

Ken Redford, *We've Got Each Other,* CBS, 1977–78.

Romeo Slade, *The Edge of Night,* ABC, 1982.

Detective Victor Isbecki, *Cagney and Lacey,* CBS, 1982–88.

Jesse, *Hard Time on Planet Earth,* CBS, 1989.

Television Appearances; Miniseries:

Captains and Kings, NBC, 1976.

Black Jack Ketchum, *The Gambler V: Playing for Keeps,* CBS, 1994.

Also appeared in *City of Angels.*

Television Appearances; Movies:

The Spy Who Returned from the Dead, ABC, 1974.

Dealey, *Kingston: The Power Play* (also known as *The Newspaper Game*), NBC, 1976.

The Sky Trap, 1978.

Willie Yeager, *Trouble in High Timber Country* (also known as *The Yeagers*), ABC, 1980.

Jeff, *Cry for the Strangers,* CBS, 1982.

Rick Loden, *Higher Ground,* CBS, 1988.

Cecil Harding, *Without a Kiss Goodbye* (also known as *The Laurie Samuels Story, The Patricia Stallings Story,* and *Falsely Accused*), CBS, 1993.

Duane Furber, *Lightning in a Bottle,* Lifetime, 1994.

Victor Isbecki, *Cagney and Lacey: The Return,* CBS, 1994.

Andy Powers, *Assault on Devil's Island* (also known as *Shadow Warriors: Assault on Devil's Island*), TNT, 1997.

Phoenix, *Mercenary,* 1997.

Admiral Teegs, *Timelock,* Sci–Fi Channel, 1998.

Carl, *Top of the World,* HBO, 1998.

Andy Powers, *Shadow Warriors II: Hunt for the Death Merchant* (also known as *Assault on Death Mountain*), 1999.

Cully, *Gentle Ben* (also known as *Terror on the Mountain*), Animal Planet, 2002.

Cully, *Gentle Ben 2: Danger on the Mountain* (also known as *Black Gold*), Animal Planet, 2003.

Floyd, *Hard Ground,* Hallmark Channel, 2003.

Sandy Palumbo, *The Hollywood Mom's Mystery,* Hallmark Channel, 2004.

Anslow, *Alien Lockdown,* Sci–Fi Channel, 2004.

Also appeared in *Donovan's Kid; The Optimist.*

Television Appearances; Specials:
Detroit parade host, *The CBS All–American Thanksgiving Day Parade,* 1985.
Voices That Care, Fox, 1991.
Himself, *Super Secret Movie Rules: Sports Underdogs,* VH1, 2004.

Television Appearances; Episodic:
Rollo, "The Spy Who Returned from the Dead," *Wide World of Mystery,* 1974.
(Uncredited) Punk, "This Must Be the Alamo," *McCloud,* 1974.
"Downshift to Danger," *McMillan and Wife,* 1974.
Guthrie, "In Performance of Duty," *Gunsmoke,* CBS, 1974.
Gary, "Anything Wrong?," *Rhoda,* 1974.
"The Deadly Missiles Caper," *Switch,* CBS, 1975.
Three for the Road, CBS, 1975.
Jimmy Jay, "Measure of Mercy," *The Rookies,* ABC, 1975.
Frank Harris, "Six Strings of Guilt," *Petrocelli,* NBC, 1976.
Burl Slote, "Law Dance," *Kojak,* CBS, 1976.
Willis Hines, "The Drop," *Streets of San Francisco,* ABC, 1976.
Harry Smick, "Dirty Money, Black Light," *The Rockford Files,* NBC, 1977.
Pete Miller, "The Mystery of the Solid Gold Kicker," *Nancy Drew Mysteries,* ABC, 1977.
"The Shortest Yard," *San Pedro Beach Bums,* ABC, 1977.
Georgie, "The Sammy Davis Jr. Kidnap Caper," *Charlie's Angels,* ABC, 1977.
Henry "Rocky" Welsh, "Final Round," *The Incredible Hulk,* CBS, 1978.
Greg Saunders, "Nest of Scorpions," *Barnaby Jones,* CBS, 1978.
Jimmy Lucas, "Birds of a Feather," *Starsky and Hutch,* ABC, 1979.
Joe Kirby, "Death's Challenge," *Quincy, M.E.,* NBC, 1979.
Stan Benson, "Girl on the Road," *Barnaby Jones,* CBS, 1979.
"Lady Bug," *A Man Called Sloane,* NBC, 1979.
Sherwood, "Hot Wheels," *CHiPs,* 1979.
"Savage Says: What Are Friends For?," *Tenspeed and Brownshoe,* ABC, 1980.
"Highway Robbery," *Freebie and the Bean,* CBS, 1981.
Code Red, ABC, 1981.
Father, "Opening Day," *The Twilight Zone,* CBS, 1985.
Lyle Rainwood, "Don't Keep the Home Fires Burning," *Wildside,* 1985.
Dr. Gary Ellison, "Armed Response," *Murder, She Wrote,* CBS, 1985.
America's Most Wanted, Fox, 1988.
Mitch Raines, "Fighting Cage," *Renegade,* syndicated, 1992.
Chi'ru master, "Shadow Assassin," *Kung Fu: The Legend Continues,* syndicated, 1993.

Detective, "Half–Way Horrible," *Tales from the Crypt,* 1993.
Joe Tanner, "Who Killed Nick Hazard?," *Burke's Law,* 1994.
Dealey, *Walker, Texas Ranger,* CBS, 1994.
Fred Kimble, "Flashback," *Walker, Texas Ranger,* CBS, 1995.
Demetrius, "The Mother of All Monsters," *Hercules: The Legendary Journeys,* syndicated, 1996.
Captain Walter Newman, "The Last Resort," *Diagnosis Murder,* CBS, 1998.
"Bloody Valentine," *V.I.P.,* syndicated, 1998.
Captain Walter Newman, "Trapped in Paradise," *Diagnosis Murder,* CBS, 1999.
Captain Walter Newman, "Voices Carry," *Diagnosis Murder,* CBS, 1999.
"Cell Phone," *Hollywood Off–Ramp,* E! Entertainment Television, 2000.
FireArm, "Armed and Dangerous," *Black Scorpion,* Sci–Fi Channel, 2001.

Stage Appearances:
"The Two Things in Life That I Really Love," *Great Writers Series* (staged readings), MET Theatre, Los Angeles, CA, 1993.

Made New York stage debut in *Woyceck,* La MaMa Experimental Theatre Club (ETC); appeared as Lenny, *Of Mice and Men,* MET Theatre; Stanley, *A Streetcar Named Desire;* in *Volpone,* Off–Broadway production; *Toyland,* Off–Broadway production; *Delicate Champions; Poor Bitos; Revengers Tragedy; Man and Superman; Moby Dick;* and *The Rainmaker.*

KRAUSE, Brian 1969–

PERSONAL

Born February 1, 1969, in El Toro, CA; married Beth Bruce (a model), 1996 (divorced, 2000); married; wife's name, Linda; children: (first marriage) Jamen (son). *Education:* Attended Orange Coast College. *Avocational Interests:* Golf, automobile racing.

Addresses: *Agent*—Leland LaBarre, Diverse Talent Group, 1875 Century Park East, Suite 2250, Los Angeles, CA 90067. *Publicist*—Andi Schecter, Jonas Public Relations, 240 26th St., Suite 3, Santa Monica, CA 90402.

Career: Actor. Appeared in commercials. Worked as a semiprofessional soccer player.

CREDITS

Television Appearances; Series:
Matthew Cory, *Another World* (also known as *Another World: Bay City*), NBC, 1997–98.
Leo Wyatt, *Charmed*, The WB, 1998—.

Television Appearances; Miniseries:
Bart, *Match Point*, broadcast on *MMC* (also known as *The All New Mickey Mouse Club, Club MMC,* and *The Mickey Mouse Club*), The Disney Channel, 1989.
Greg Thayer, *Family Album* (also known as *Danielle Steel's "Family Album"*), NBC, 1994.
Himself, *I Love the '80s,* VH1, 2002.
Himself, *I Love the '70s,* VH1, 2003.

Television Appearances; Movies:
Mike, *Earth Angel,* ABC, 1991.
Lynn, *Bandit: Bandit, Bandit* (also known as *Bandit, Bandit*), syndicated, 1994.
Lynn, *Bandit: Bandit Goes Country* (also known as *Bandit Goes Country*), syndicated, 1994.
Lynn, *Bandit: Bandit's Silver Angel* (also known as *Bandit: Bandit and the Silver Angel*), syndicated, 1994.
Lynn, *Bandit: Beauty and the Bandit,* syndicated, 1994.
Clay Nelson, *Breaking Free,* The Disney Channel, 1995.
Court Van Degen, *919 Fifth Avenue* (also known as *Dominick Dunne's "919 Fifth Avenue"*), 1995.
Edward, *Naked Souls,* HBO, 1996.
Luke Harrison, *Within the Rock,* Sci–Fi Channel, 1996.
Mike Helton, *Return to Cabin by the Lake,* USA Network, 2001.

Television Appearances; Specials:
Matt Henderson, *American Eyes,* CBS, 1990.
The Women of Charmed (documentary), 2000.
Charmed: Behind the Magic (documentary), LivingTV, 2003.

Television Appearances; Episodic:
Second boy, "Goodbye, Mr. Zelinka," *Highway to Heaven,* NBC, 1989.
Student, "Kangaroo Gate," *TV 101,* CBS, 1989.
Tex Crandell, "House of Horror," *Tales from the Crypt* (also known as *HBO's "Tales from the Crypt"*), HBO, 1993.
Billy Kramer, "Collision Course," *Walker, Texas Ranger,* CBS, 1995.
Scott Wilson, "Killshot," *High Tide,* syndicated, 1996.
Himself, *Celebrity Profile: Alyssa Milano* (also known as *Celebrity Profile* and *E! Celebrity Profile*), E! Entertainment Television, 1999.
(Uncredited) Leo, "Alyssa Milano," *Revealed with Jules Asner,* E! Entertainment Television, 2002.

Himself, "Sum 41, 3 Doors Down, Brian Krause," *Player$,* TechTV, 2003.
Himself, *Intimate Portrait: Alyssa Milano,* Lifetime, 2003.
Guest, *Good Day Live,* Fox, 2004.
Guest, *The Sharon Osbourne Show* (also known as *Sharon*), syndicated, 2004.

Appeared as a panelist in *The List,* VH1; appeared in *The Test,* FX Channel.

Television Appearances; Pilots:
Johnny Doyle, *Extreme Blue,* UPN, 1996.

Film Appearances:
Joey, *An American Summer,* Castle Hill Productions, 1991.
Richard, *Return to the Blue Lagoon,* Columbia, 1991.
Tim Mitchell, *December,* IRS Releasing, 1991.
Charles Brady, *Sleepwalkers* (also known as *Sleepstalkers* and *Stephen King's "Sleepwalkers"*), Columbia, 1992.
Pat, *The Liar's Club,* New Horizons Picture Corporation, 1993.
Matt Jarvis, *Mind Games,* Brimstone Productions/Shadow Film Partners, 1996.
Get a Job (also known as *The Red Lion*), Taurus Entertainment, 1998.
Pete Leiber, *Dreamers,* American Anvil Motion Picture Distribution, 1999.
Will Fowler (some sources cite Will Porter), *Trash* (also known as *Nobody's Children* and *No Fear*), Xscapade Pictures, 1999.
The husband, *The Party* (short film), Baltic International, 2000.
Danson, *To Kill a Mockumentary,* Pizza Guy Films, 2005.
Jay, *Pissed,* Artist View Entertainment, 2005.

RECORDINGS

Videos:
Himself, *Teen Vid II,* BMG Video, 1991.

WRITINGS

Teleplays; Episodic:
(Author of story with Ed Bokinskie) "Sense and Sense Ability," *Charmed,* The WB, 2003.

OTHER SOURCES

Periodicals:
Cult Times, January, 2004, pp. 38–41.
Cult Times Special, November, 2002, pp. 42–45.
Steppin' Out, June 14, 2000.

TV Zone, April, 2002, pp. 30–32.
Xpose, February, 2001, pp. 28–31; November, 2002, pp. 42–45; June, 2003, pp. 16–22; July, 2004, pp. 38–42; February, 2005, pp. 44–46, 48–49, 50.

Electronic:
Brian Krause Official Site, http://www.brian-krause. com, March 15, 2005.

KRIGE, Alice 1954–

PERSONAL

Born June 28, 1954, in Upington (some sources say Cape Town), South Africa; married Paul Schoolman (a filmmaker). *Education:* Rhodes University, B.A., 1975; also studied at the Central School of Speech and Drama, London, England, and Royal Shakespeare Company, London.

Addresses: *Manager*—McKeon–Valeo–Myones Management, 9150 Wilshire Blvd., Suite 102, Beverly Hills, CA 90212.

Career: Actress. Royal Shakespeare Company, Stratford–Upon–Avon, England, and London, member of company, 1984–85.

Awards, Honors: Society of West End Theatres Award, most promising newcomer, Plays and Players, London Theatre Critics Award, most promising newcomer, both 1981, Laurence Olivier Theatre Award, best promising newcomer, 1982, all for *Arms and the Man;* Fantafestival Award, best actress, 1992, for *Sleepwalkers;* Saturn Award, best supporting actress, Academy of Science Fiction, Fantasy & Horror Films, 1997, for *Star Trek: First Contact.*

CREDITS

Stage Appearances:
Arms and the Man, London, 1981.
The Tempest, Royal Shakespeare Company, Stratford–upon–Avon, England, Royalty Theatre, London, 1984–85.
King Lear, Royal Shakespeare Company, Stratford–upon–Avon and London, 1984–85.
The Taming of the Shrew, Royal Shakespeare Company, Stratford–upon–Avon and London, 1984–85.
Cyrano de Bergerac, Royal Shakespeare Company, Stratford–upon–Avon and London, 1984–85.

Bond's Lear, Royal Shakespeare Company, Stratford–upon–Avon and London, 1984–85.
Belvidera, *Venice Preserv'd,* Almedia Theatre, London, 1995.

Also appeared in *Forever Yours,* London; and *Maylou,* London.

Film Appearances:
Sybil Gordon, *Chariots of Fire,* Twentieth Century–Fox, 1981.
Alma Mobley and Eva Galli, *Ghost Story,* Universal, 1981.
Bathsheba, *King David,* Paramount, 1985.
Tully Sorenson, *Barfly,* Cannon, 1987.
Mary Godwin, *Haunted Summer,* Cannon, 1988.
Isabelle, *Spies, Inc.* (also known as *Code Name: Chaos, Spies, Lies, and Alibis,* and *S.P.O.O.K.S.*), Vestron Pictures/Electric Shadows Partners, 1988.
Beth Goodwin, *See You in the Morning,* Warner Bros., 1989.
Mary Brady, *Sleepwalkers* (also known as *Stephen King's "Sleepwalkers"*), Columbia, 1992.
Wife, *Sea Beggars,* 1994.
Lisa Benjamenta, *Institute Benjamenta* (also known as *Institute Benjamenta,* or *This Dream People Call Human Life*), Zeitgeist Films, 1995.
Borg Queen, *Star Trek: First Contact* (also known as *Star Trek: Borg, Star Trek: Destinies, Star Trek: Future Generations, Star Trek: Generations II, Star Trek 8,* and *Star Trek: Resurrection*), Paramount, 1996.
Amanda, Sony Pictures Entertainment, 1996.
Zephyr Eccles, *Twilight of the Ice Nymphs,* Zeitgeist Films, 1997.
Herself, *Guy Maddin: Waiting for Twilight,* 1997.
Clarissa Symes, *Habitat,* 1997.
Mother Marianne Cope, *Molokai: The Story of Father Damien* (also known as *Damiaan, Father Damien,* and *Molokai: The Forbidden Island*), 1999.
Freda, *The Little Vampire* (also known as *Der kleine vampir* and *De kleine vampier*), New Line Cinema, 2000.
Elizabeth Plummer, *The Calling,* 2000.
Mirella Cenci, *Superstition,* 2001.
Monique, *Vallen* (also known as *Falling*), 2001.
Karen Abercromby, *Reign of Fire,* Buena Vista, 2002.
Borg Queen, *Star Trek: The Experience—Borg Invasion 4D,* Paramount, 2004.
Margie Henderson, *Shadow of Fear,* Millennium Films, 2004.
Cristabella, *Silent Hill,* Sony Pictures Entertainment, 2006.
Janet, *Lonely Hearts,* 2006.

Television Appearances; Series:
Maddie, *Deadwood,* HBO, 2005—.

Television Appearances; Miniseries:

Bridget O'Donnell, *Ellis Island,* CBS, 1984.

Baroness Lisl Kemery, *Wallenberg: A Hero's Story,* NBC, 1985.

Jessie Benton Fremont, *Dream West,* CBS, 1986.

Olga, *The Strauss Dynasty,* 1991.

Parvaneh Limbert, *Iran: Days of Crisis* (also known as *444 Days* and *L'Amerique en Otage*), TNT, 1991.

Rachel, *Joseph* (also known as *The Bible: Joseph, Die Bibel: Josef,* and *Joseph in Egypt*), TNT, 1995.

Madame De Renal, *The Scarlet and Black* (also known as *Scarlet & Black*), BBC, 1993.

Louise, *Close Relations,* BBC (England), 1998.

Placidia, *Attila* (also known as *Attila the Hun*), USA Network, 2001.

Rosemary Waldo, *Dinotopia,* ABC, 2001.

Lady Jessica Atreides, *Children of Dune* (also known as *Duen–bedrohung des imperiums, Dune–der messias, Dune–die kinder des wustenplaneten, Dune-krieg um den wustenplaneten,* and *Frank Herbert's "Children of Dune"*), Sci–Fi Channel, 2003.

Television Appearances; Movies:

Lucy Manette, *A Tale of Two Cities,* CBS, 1980.

Gwen, *Second Serve* (also known as *I Changed My Life*), CBS, 1986.

Patsy Cline and performer of song "Faded Love," *Baja Oklahoma,* HBO, 1988.

Helen Weiss, *Max and Helen,* TNT, 1990.

May Packard, *Ladykiller* (also known as *Lady Killer*), USA Network, 1992.

Jean Syfert, *Judgment Day: The John List Story* (also known as *Deliver Them from Evil: The John List Story* and *To Save Their Souls*), CBS, 1993.

Pamela Sparrow, *Double Deception* (also known as *Crimes of Passion* and *Kane*), NBC, 1993.

Joan Anatole, *Jack Reed: Badge of Honor* (also known as *Jack Reed: An Honest Cop*), NBC, 1993.

Alice Stillman, *Donor Unknown* (also known as *Dangerous Heart*), USA Network, 1995.

Alessandra Locatelli, *Devil's Advocate,* BBC, 1995.

Dee, *Hidden in America,* Showtime, 1996.

Clarissa Symes, *Habitat* (also known as *Ecophoria, Ecotopia, The Fifth Season,* and *Hothouse*), Sci–Fi Channel, 1997.

Rebecca Daly, *Indefensible: The Truth about Edward Brannigan* (also known as *A Father's Betrayal*) CBS, 1997.

Isabelle Morton, *The Commissioner,* The Movie Channel, 1998.

Annalise Jurgenson, *Deep in My Heart,* CBS, 1999.

Sarah Gold, *In the Company of Spies,* Showtime, 1999.

Snubby Eaton, *The Death and Life of Nancy Eaton,* Oxygen, 2003.

Maria Gurdin, *The Mystery of Natalie Wood,* ABC, 2004.

Joan Collins, *Dynasty: The Making of a Guilty Pleasure,* ABC, 2005.

Also appeared in *Summer.*

Television Appearances; Specials:

Marquesa Dorada, "Sharpe's Honour" (also known as "Sharpe II"), *Masterpiece Theatre,* PBS, 1995.

Ultimate Trek: Star Trek's Greatest Moments, UPN, 1999.

Rosemary, *Discovering Dinotopia* (documentary), 2002.

Also appeared in *The Happy Autumn Fields,* British television.

Television Appearances; Episodic:

Diana Molner, "Operation Susie," *The Professionals,* 1982.

Nita Cochran, "Murder in the Afternoon," *Murder, She Wrote,* CBS, 1985.

Jennifer, "Dream Child," *The Hidden Room,* Lifetime, 1991.

Anne Beresford, "64 Wild Horses," *Beverly Hills, 90210,* Fox, 1992.

Nita Cochran, "Murder in the Afternoon," *Murder, She Wrote,* CBS, 1994.

Aura Mendoza, "Acute Triangle," *Welcome to Paradox,* Sci–Fi Channel, 1998.

Dr. Sondra Rush, "Activate Your Choices," *Becker,* CBS, 1999.

Borg Queen, "Endgame: Parts 1 & 2," *Star Trek: Voyager,* UPN, 2001.

Alma, "Out, Out Brief Candle," *Six Feet Under,* HBO, 2002.

Alma, "The Plan," *Six Feet Under,* HBO, 2002.

Senator Lily Randolph, "Flipping," *Threat Matrix,* ABC, 2003.

Senator Lily Randolph, "19 Seconds," *Threat Matrix,* ABC, 2004.

RECORDINGS

Video Games:

Voice of the Borg Queen, *Star Trek: Armada II,* Activision, 2001.

Taped Readings:

Ronald Harwood's Another Time, L.A. Theatre Works, 2001.

OTHER SOURCES

Periodicals:

Entertainment Weekly, December 20, 1996, p. 50.

Femme Fatales, June, 1997, pp. 40–43.

Maclean's, December 2, 1996, p. 82.

KRULL, Suzanne 1966–

PERSONAL

Born July 8, 1966, in New York, NY.

Addresses: *Agent*—Origin Talent Agency, 4705 Laurel Canyon, Suite 306, Studio City, CA 91607.

Career: Actress, writer, and producer.

CREDITS

Film Appearances:
The Fox, *The Tie That Binds,* 1995.
Mona, *Open Season,* 1996.
Julie, *Por vida,* 1996.
Woman at phone, *8 Heads in a Duffel Bag,* Metromedia Entertainment Group, 1997.
First waitress, *Mouse Hunt,* DreamWorks, 1997.
(Uncredited) Macrobiotic Customer, *Trial and Error,* 1997.
Polly, *Stripping for Jesus,* 1998.
Vanessa, *The Souler Opposite,* 1998.
Sam, *Sam and Mike,* 1999.
Stringy–haired woman, *Go,* Columbia, 1999.
Annabel, *The Next Best Thing,* Paramount, 2000.
Who, *How the Grinch Stole Christmas* (also known as *Dr. Seuss's "How the Grinch Stole Christmas,"* *The Grinch,* and *Der Grinch*), MCA/Universal, 2000.
Skinny woman, *Camouflage,* PM Entertainment Group, 2001.
Sneezy woman, *Jackpot,* Sony Pictures Classics, 2001.
Lima lips, *Meet Market,* 2004.
Reporter #3, *Kids in America,* 2005.

Film Work:
Executive producer, *Sam and Mike,* 1999.

Television Appearances; Series:
Betty Ann McCurry, *Nash Bridges,* CBS, 2001.

Television Appearances; Pilots:
The Simple Life, CBS, 1998.

Television Appearances; Episodic:
Melissa, "On the Edge," *The Facts of Life,* 1988.
Junie, *NYPD Blue,* ABC, 1993.
Gretchen, *General Hospital,* ABC, 1994.
Junie, "Serge the Concierge," *NYPD Blue,* ABC, 1994.
Wife, "Where There's Smoke...," *Sisters,* 1996.
Heidi, "Obsession," *Night Stand,* 1997.
Wife, "The Shot," *Gun,* 1997.
Lucy, "Blackout," *Nash Bridges,* CBS, 1997.
Gwen, "The Strike," *Seinfeld,* NBC, 1997.
"A Candidate for Murder," *Mike Hammer, Private Eye,* 1998.
Nurse, "What Would I Do Without Wu?," *Arli$$,* HBO, 1998.
Mrs. Pimner, "Shanghai Express," *Martial Law,* 1998.
Trish McFarland, "Numb & Number," *NYPD Blue,* ABC, 1998.
Clerk, "Lover's Walk," *Buffy the Vampire Slayer,* The WB, 1998.
Olga, "And the Sabrina Goes to...," *Sabrina, the Teenage Witch,* ABC, 1998.
Mrs. Pimner, "Red Storm," *Martial Law,* CBS, 1998.
Bates Balou, "A New Hope," *Two Guys, a Girl, and a Pizza Place,* ABC, 1999.
Terry, "Girl Trouble," *Will & Grace,* NBC, 2000.
Louise Farcher, "The Telltale Nation," *The Practice,* ABC, 2002.
Lucinda Roane, "Marry, Marry Quite Contrary," *Judging Amy,* CBS, 2003.
Miss Winston, "Tanner," *Phil of the Future,* Disney Channel, 2004.
Miss Winston, "Raging Bull," *Phil of the Future,* Disney Channel, 2004.
Aileen, "First Response," *Strong Medicine,* Lifetime, 2005.
Judge, "Dog Day After–Groom," *That's So Raven,* Disney Channel, 2005.
Miss Winston, "Milkin' It," *Phil of the Future,* Disney Channel, 2005.
Imara, "Freaky Phoebe," *Charmed,* The WB, 2005.

Also appeared as Miss Burvich, "Back to P.C.A.," *Zoey 101,* Nickelodeon.

RECORDINGS

Video Games:
Stand–up performances #1, *Don't Quit Your Day Job,* 1996.

WRITINGS

Screenplays:
Sam and Mike, 1999.

KUNIS, Mila 1983–

PERSONAL

Original name, Milena Markovna Kunis; born August 14, 1983, in Kiev, Ukraine; immigrated to the United States, 1991; daughter of Mark (a mechanical engineer and cab company executive) and Elvira (a physics teacher and drugstore manager) Kunis. *Education:* Studied acting at Beverly Hills Studios. *Avocational Interests:* Salsa dancing, bowling.

Addresses: *Agent*—Creative Artists Agency, 9830 Wilshire Blvd., Beverly Hills, CA 90212. *Publicist*—PMK/HBH Public Relations, 700 San Vicente Blvd., Suite G910, West Hollywood, CA 90069.

Career: Actress. Also worked as a model for Guess? girls clothing, 1997, and Lisa Frank products; appeared in television commercials for Mattel's Barbie and Payless Shoes.

Awards, Honors: Young Artist Award nomination (with others), best performance in a TV series—young ensemble, 1999, YoungStar Awards, best performance by a young actress in a comedy TV series, 1999, 2000, Young Artist Award nominations, best performance in a TV comedy series—leading young actress, 2000, 2001, Teen Choice Award nominations, TV–choice actress, 2000, 2001, Teen Choice Award nominations, TV–choice actress— comedy, 2002, 2003, 2004, 2005, all for *That '70s Show;* Young Hollywood Award, one to watch–female, 2002.

CREDITS

Film Appearances:
Melinda, *Make a Wish, Molly,* 1995.
Sarah, *Santa with Muscles,* 1996.
Jill, *Honey, We Shrunk Ourselves,* 1997.
Abbey Tournquist, *Krippendorf's Tribe,* Buena Vista, 1998.
(Uncredited) Martice, *Milo,* 1998.
Basin, *Get Over It* (also known as *Get Over It!*), Miramax, 2001.
Rachael Newman, *American Psycho II: All American Girl* (also known as *American Psycho 2*), Lions Gate Films, 2002.
Tina, *Tony 'n' Tina's Wedding,* 2004.
Voice of Meg Griffin and additional voices, *Stewie Griffin: The Untold Story!* (animated), Twentieth Century–Fox, 2005.
Tom 51, 2005.
Michelle, *Moving McAllister,* 2005.

Television Appearances; Series:
Anna Marie Del–Bono, *Nick Freno: Licensed Teacher,* The WB, 1996–97.
Jackie Beulah Burkhardt, *That '70s Show,* Fox, 1998—.
Voice of Megan Griffin, *Family Guy* (also known as *Padre de familia* and *Padre del familia;* animated), Fox, 1999–2000, 2005—.

Television Appearances; Movies:
Susie Grogan, *Piranha* (also known as *Roger Corman Presents "Piranha"*), UPN, 1995.
Gia at age 11, *Gia,* HBO, 1998.

Television Appearances; Specials:
The 1999 Teen Choice Awards, 1999.
Teen People's 25 Hottest Stars Under 25, ABC, 2000.
Holiday Music Spectacular from Miami Beach 2000, Fox, 2000.
The 2000 Teen Choice Awards, Fox, 2000.
The 2000 Billboard Music Awards, Fox, 2000.
Presenter, *Nickelodeon's 14th Annual Kids' Choice Awards,* Nickelodeon, 2001.
Making the Show: That '70s Show (documentary), MTV, 2001.
Stars team member, *Basebrawl: MTV Rock n' Jock,* MTV, 2001.
Herself, *Young Hollywood Awards,* 2001.
MTV Icon: Aerosmith (documentary), MTV, 2002.
Herself, *Nickelodeon Kids' Choice Awards '02,* Nickelodeon, 2002.
Host, *Seaside Survivor* (also known as *MTV's "Seaside Survivor"*), MTV, 2002.
That '70s Show Special, Fox, 2002.

Television Appearances; Episodic:
Anne, "Aftershock," *Baywatch,* 1994.
Lucy Sanchez, "The Defiant One," *The John Larroquette Show,* NBC, 1995.
Devon, "Here's Just Looking at You, Kid," *Hudson Street,* CBS, 1995.
Bonnie, "Hot Stuff," *Baywatch,* 1995.
Chloe, "In the Stars," *Unhappily Ever After,* The WB, 1996.
Ashley, "Saturday," *7th Heaven,* The WB, 1996.
Theresa, *Moloney,* CBS, 1996.
Pepper, "Last Hope," *Walker, Texas Ranger,* CBS, 1997.
Ashley, "With a Little Help From My Friends," *7th Heaven,* The WB, 1997.
Ashley, "See You in September," *7th Heaven,* The WB, 1997.
Ashley, "Truth or Dare," *7th Heaven,* The WB, 1997.
Jessie Kerwoord, "Company Town," *Penascola: Wings of Gold,* 1998.
Taylor Vaughn, "Tested," *Get Real,* Fox, 2000.
The Late Late Show with Craig Kilborn, CBS, 2001.
Daisy, *Mad TV,* Fox, 2002.
The Michael Essany Show, E! Entertainment Television, 2003.
The Sharon Osbourne Show, syndicated, 2003.
Late Night with Conan O'Brien, NBC, 2004.
Lana, "Space Camp Oddity," *Grounded for Life,* The WB, 2004.
Lana, "Policy of Truth," *Grounded for Life,* The WB, 2004.
The Oprah Winfrey Show, syndicated, 2005.
Voice of Susan, "Gold Dust Gasoline," *Robot Chicken* (animated), Cartoon Network, 2005.

Voice of Pyramid contestant, "Badunkadunk," *Robot Chicken* (animated), Cartoon Network, 2005.
Guest host, *The View,* ABC, 2005.
Last Call with Carson Daly, NBC, 2005.
Herself, *Punk'd,* MTV, 2005.

Also appeared as Taylor Vaughn, "The Last Weekend," *Get Real,* Fox; in *E! Hollywood Hold'em,* E! Entertainment Television; narrator, *TNN's Lifegame,* TNN.

Television Work; Series:
Singer (theme song), *Family Guy* (also known as *Padre de familia* and *Padre del familia*; animated), Fox, 1999.

RECORDINGS

Music Videos:

Appeared in Aerosmith's "Jaded," 2001; Vitamin C's "The Itch"; and The Stroke's "The End Has No End."

OTHER SOURCES

Periodicals:
People Weekly, April 2, 2001, p. 79.

L

LADD, Cheryl 1951–

(Cheryl Stoppelmoor Ladd, Cherie Moor, Cherie Moore, Cheryl Stoppelmoor, Cheryl Jean Stoppelmoor, Jean Stoppelmoor)

PERSONAL

Original name, Cheryl Jean Stoppelmoor; born July 12, 1951, in Huron, SD; daughter of Marion (a railroad engineer) and Dolores (a waitress; maiden name, Katz) Stoppelmoor; married first husband (divorced); married David Ladd (an actor and producer), May 1973 (divorced, September 1980); married Brian Russell (a musician and film producer), January 3, 1981; children: (second marriage) Jordan Elizabeth (an actress); stepchildren: (third marriage) Lindsay Russell (a musician). *Education:* Studied acting at the Milton Katselas Acting Workshop. *Politics:* Republican. *Avocational Interests:* Golf, collecting and creating art, writing.

Addresses: *Agent*—Don Buchwald & Associates, 6500 Wilshire Blvd., Suite 2200, Los Angeles, CA 90048. *Publicist*—JDS, 3151 Cahuenga Blvd. West, Suite 220, Los Angeles, CA 90068.

Career: Actress, singer, dancer, and writer. Member of the touring musical group the Music Shop Band, 1968–70; Buick Motor Division, golf ambassador, 1997–?; appeared in television commercials, including Prell, 1975, Ultra Brite, c. early 1970s, Freixenet, 1982, Dento–Med Hydron Plus Hand and Body Moisturizer, Max Factor, and ShapeMate. Retinitis Pigmentosa International, spokesperson; Childhelp USA, official ambassador, 1979—.

Member: Screen Actors Guild, American Federation of Television and Radio Artists, American Guild of Variety Artists.

Awards, Honors: Photoplay Award, 1978; Gold singles from the albums *Cheryl Ladd,* 1978, and *Dance Forever,* 1979; Woman of the World Award, Childhelp USA, 1987; Hubert H. Humphrey Humanitarian Award, Washington, D.C., Touchdown Club, 1987; Child Caring Award, Center for the Improvement of Child Care, for *When She Was Bad...*

CREDITS

Film Appearances:
The Marriage of a Young Stockbroker, Twentieth Century–Fox, 1971.
(As Cherie Moor) Kathy, *Chrome and Hot Leather,* American International Pictures, 1971.
(Jean Stoppelmoor) Teenage girl, *Harry O: Such Dust as Dreams Are Made On,* 1973.
Zabby, *The Treasure of Jamaica Reef* (also known as *Evil in the Deep* and *Treasure of the Jamaica Deep*), Golden–Selected (unreleased), 1976.
Jessie Clark, *Now and Forever,* InterPlanetary, 1983.
Deborah Solomon, *Purple Hearts,* Warner Bros., 1984.
Louise Baltimore, *Millennium,* Twentieth Century–Fox, 1989.
Katherine, *Lisa* (also known as *Candlelight Killer*), Metro–Goldwyn–Mayer/United Artists, 1990.
Georgie Cooper, *Poison Ivy,* New Line Cinema, 1992.
Pamela Verlaine, *Permanent Midnight,* Artisan Entertainment, 1998.
Anna Cogez, *A Dog of Flanders,* Warner Bros., 1999.

Television Appearances; Series:
The Andy Williams Show, 1969–71.
(As Cherie Moore) Singing voice of Melody Valentine, *Josie and the Pussycats* (animated), CBS, 1970–72, NBC, 1975–76.
The D.A., 1971–72.
(As Cheryl Jean Stoppelmoor) Regular performer, *The Ken Berry Wow Show* (also known as *Ken Berry's Wow*), ABC, 1972.

(As Cheryl Stoppelmoor) Amy (a Probe control agent), *Search* (also known as *Probe*), NBC, 1972–73.

(As Cherie Moore) Singing voice of Melody Valentine, *Josie and the Pussycats in Outer Space* (animated), CBS, 1972–74.

Kris Monroe, *Charlie's Angels,* ABC, 1977–81.

Dr. Dawn "Holli" Holliday, *One West Waikiki,* CBS, 1994, syndicated, 1995–96.

Jillian Deline, *Las Vegas,* NBC, 2003–2004.

Television Appearances; Miniseries:

(As Cheryl Jean Stoppelmoor) Nelly, *Alexander Zwo* (also known as *Alexandre Bis* and *Double Identity*), 1972.

Black Beauty, NBC, 1978.

Hope Masters, *A Death in California* (also known as *Psychopath*), ABC, 1985.

Liane De Villiers, *Crossings,* ABC, 1986.

Maude Sage Breen, *Bluegrass,* CBS, 1988.

Herself, *The Ultimate Hollywood Blonde,* E! Entertainment Television, 2004.

Herself, *TV Land Moguls* (documentary), TV Land, 2004.

Television Appearances; Movies:

The Devil's Daughter, 1972.

(As Cheryl Jean Stoppelmoor) Jody Keller, *Satan's School for Girls,* ABC, 1973.

Thaddeus Rose and Eddie, 1978.

Betina "Teeny" Morgan, *When She Was Bad...,* ABC, 1979.

Willa, 1979.

Guyana Tragedy: The Story of Jim Jones (also known as *The Mad Messiah*), CBS, 1980.

Joan Robinson Hill, *Murder in Texas,* 1981.

Title role, *Grace Kelly* (also known as *The Grace Kelly Story*), ABC, 1983.

Maggie Telford, *Kentucky Woman,* CBS, 1983.

Margaret, *The Hasty Heart,* 1983.

Lily Parker, *Romance on the Orient Express,* NBC, 1985.

Crime of Innocence, 1985.

Anne Halloran, *Deadly Care,* CBS, 1987.

Mary Gray, *The Fulfillment of Mary Gray* (also known as *Fulfillment*), CBS, 1989.

The Lookalike, 1990.

Diane Halstead, *Crash: The Mystery of Flight 1501* (also known as *Aftermath* and *Aftermath: The Fate of Flight 1501*), 1990.

Sara Crawford, *Jekyll and Hyde* (also known as *Dr. Jekyll and Mr. Hyde*), ABC, 1990.

Laura Huntoon, *The Girl Who Came between Them* (also known as *Face of Love* and *Victim of Innocence*), NBC, 1990.

Melanie Adams, *Changes* (also known as *Danielle Steel's "Changes"*), NBC, 1991.

Annie Gallagher, *Locked Up: A Mother's Rage* (also known as *The Delores Donovan Story, Other Side of Love,* and *They're Doing My Time*), CBS, 1991.

Pam Cheney, *Broken Promises: Taking Emily Back* (also known as *Broken Promises*), CBS, 1993.

Linda DeSilva Edelman, *Dead before Dawn,* ABC, 1994.

Mary Dannon, *Dancing with Danger* (also known as *The Last Dance*), USA Network, 1994.

The Lady, 1995.

Lucinda/Lucy Ann Michaels, *A Tangled Web* (also known as *Deadly Seduction* and *Vows of Deception*), CBS, 1996.

Jean McAvoy, *Kiss and Tell* (also known as *Please Forgive Me*), ABC, 1996.

Ellen Downey, *The Haunting of Lisa* (also known as *Les premonitions de Lisa*), Lifetime, 1996.

Elaine Freedman, *Perfect Little Angels,* Fox Family Channel, 1998.

Connie Hoagland, *Every Mother's Worst Fear,* USA Network, 1998.

Lynn Landon, *Michael Landon, the Father I Knew* (also known as *A Father's Son*), CBS, 1999.

Jane Thorton, *Her Best Friend's Husband,* Lifetime, 2002.

Diane Simon, *Eve's Christmas,* Lifetime, 2004.

Television Appearances; Specials:

ABC team member, *Battle of the Network Stars III,* ABC, 1977.

Ben Vereen: Showcase for a Man of Many Talents (also known as *Ben Vereen ... His Roots, Ben Vereen: His Roots,* and *The Sentry Collection Presents Ben Vereen: His Roots*), ABC, 1978.

Herself, *General Electric's All–Star Anniversary,* NBC, 1978.

John Denver and the Ladies, ABC, 1978.

National Collegiate Cheerleading Championships, 1978.

Holiday Star Telethon, 1978.

That Thing on ABC, 1978.

The Muppets Go Hollywood, 1979.

AFI Salute to Alfred Hitchcock, 1979.

Host, *The Cheryl Ladd Special* (also known as *Cheryl Ladd*), ABC, 1979.

Host, *Cheryl Ladd ... Looking Back—Souvenirs* (also known as *Cheryl Ladd—Souvenirs* and *Looking Back: Souvenirs*), ABC, 1980.

Herself, *The Barbara Walters Special,* 1980.

A Time for Love, 1980, 1981.

Coast to Coast U.S.A., 1981.

Get High On Yourself Special, 1981.

Is There a Family in the House, 1981.

Women Who Rate a 10, 1981.

Perry Como's "Spring in San Francisco" (also known as *Spring in San Francisco*), ABC, 1981.

Host, *Cheryl Ladd: Scenes from a Special* (also known as *Scenes from a Special*), ABC, 1982.

Cheryl Ladd: Fascinated, 1982.

The Paul Anka Show, 1982.

Fascinated, syndicated, 1983.

The Presidential Inaugural Gala, CBS, 1989.

Innocent Skin, 1991.

Cheryl Ladd's Body Slide Instruction, 1992.

Cheryl Ladd's Body Slide Sliding into Shape, 1992.

Cheryl Ladd's Shape Up with Shapemate, 1993.

Host, *Your Skin and How to Save It,* CNBC and WGN, 1995.

50 Years of Television: A Celebration of the Academy of Television Arts and Sciences Golden Anniversary, HBO, 1997.

Hollywood Glamour Girls, E! Entertainment Television, 1998.

King of Primetime: Aaron Spelling, 1998.

Intimate Portrait: Jaclyn Smith, Lifetime, 1998.

Intimate Portrait: Cheryl Ladd, Lifetime, 1999.

Entertainment Tonight Charlie Angels Uncovered II, 2000.

The 74th Annual Macy's Thanksgiving Day Parade, NBC, 2000.

A&E Biography: Cheryl Ladd, Arts and Entertainment, 2000.

Champions of Industry: "Children's Wish Foundation," 2000.

Charlie's Angels Night 2000, 2000.

Time & Again: Charlie's Angels, 2000.

TV Guide's Truth behind the Rumors: "Charlie's Angels," 2000.

Movieguide Awards Gala, 2001.

Herself, *Tvography: Charlie's Angels—Girls with Guns* (documentary), Arts and Entertainment, 2002.

Herself, *Charlie's Angels: TV Tales* (documentary), E! Entertainment Television, 2002.

Charlie's Angels: The Story, 2003.

TV Land Awards—Red Carpet Countdown, TV Land, 2003.

TV Movie Superstars: Women You Love (documentary), Lifetime, 2004.

Television Appearances; Awards Presentations:

The 35th Annual Golden Globe Awards, 1978.

The 57th Annual Photoplay Gold Medal Awards, 1978.

American Music Awards, 1979.

Cohost, *The 31st Annual Primetime Emmy Awards,* ABC, 1979.

The 32nd Annual Primetime Emmy Awards, 1980.

The 6th Annual People's Choice Awards, 1980.

The 12th Annual People's Choice Awards, CBS, 1986.

The 43rd Annual Golden Globe Awards, 1987.

Host, *The 44th Annual Golden Globe Awards,* 1987.

Presenter, *The 48th Annual Golden Globe Awards,* TBS, 1991.

Presenter, *The 18th Annual People's Choice Awards,* CBS, 1992.

Presenter, *The 18th Annual CableACE Awards,* TNT, 1996.

Host, *The 9th Annual Movieguide Awards,* PAX, 2001.

Herself, *TV Land Awards: A Celebration of Classic TV* (also known as *1st Annual TV Land Awards*), TV Land, 2003.

Television Appearances; Pilots:

Teenage girl, *Such Dust as Dreams Are Made On,* ABC, 1973.

That Thing on ABC, ABC, 1978.

Dr. Dawn "Holli" Holliday, *One West Waikiki,* CBS, 1994.

Television Appearances; Episodic:

(As Cheryl Jean Stoppelmoor) "The Good Die Young," *The Rookies,* ABC, 1972.

(As Cheryl Stoppelmoor) Amy, "Flight to Nowhere," *Search,* 1972.

(As Cheryl Stoppelmoor) Amy, "Let Us Prey," *Search,* 1973.

(As Cheryl Jean Stoppelmoor) Bank manager, "The Wheel of Fortune," *The Rookies,* ABC, 1973.

Gwen, "A Game of Showdown," *Ironside,* NBC, 1973.

(As Cheryl Stoppelmoor) Amy, "Suffer My Child," *Search,* 1973.

(As Cheryl Stoppelmoor) Joanna, "Double Trouble," *The Partridge Family,* ABC, 1973.

Cindy Shea, "Wish Upon a Star," *Happy Days,* ABC, 1974.

Teenage girl, "Such Dust As Dreams Are Made On," *Harry O,* ABC, 1974.

(As Cheryl Stoppelmoor) Susan Ellen Morley, "Blockade," *The Streets of San Francisco,* ABC, 1974.

Jill Lauimer, "Death by Resurrection," *Switch,* CBS, 1975.

Buffy, "Prime Rib," *Police Story,* NBC, 1976.

Natica, "The Innocent Prey," *The Fantastic Journey,* NBC, 1977.

Herself, *Donny and Marie,* ABC, 1977, 1978.

(As Cheryl Stoppelmoor Ladd) Kate, "Silky Chamberlain," *Police Woman,* NBC, 1977.

"Angels and the Bums," *The San Pedro Beach Bums,* ABC, 1977.

Code R, 1977.

Herself, *The Muppet Show,* syndicated, 1978.

The Tonight Show Starring Johnny Carson, NBC, 1978, 1979, 1982, 1991.

Herself, *The Midnight Special,* 1978.

Herself, "Mickey's 50," *Disneyland,* 1978.

Dick Clark's Live Wednesdays, 1978.

Don Kirshner's Rock Concert, 1978.

Omnibus: General Electric Theatre, 1978.

Carol Burnett & Company, 1979.

Herself, *Omnibus: General Electric Theatre,* 1980.

Herself, *The American Sportsman,* 1982.

Late Night with David Letterman, NBC, 1985.

The Rosie O'Donnell Show, syndicated, 1996.

Mercedes Haverset, "The Black Book," *Ink,* CBS, 1997.

Mary Anne, "Crazy White Female," *Jesse,* NBC, 1999.

Berg's mother, "Foul Play," *Two Guys and a Girl* (also known as *Two Guys, a Girl, and a Pizza Place*), ABC, 1999.

Berg's mother, "The Undercard," *Two Guys and a Girl* (also known as *Two Guys, a Girl, and a Pizza Place,* ABC, 2000.

"Charlie's Angels," *Inside TV Land,* TV Land, 2000.
The Wayne Brady Show, syndicated, 2002.
"Style and Fashion," *Inside TV Land,* TV Land, 2002.
Who Wants to be a Millionaire, 2002.
Doris Bennett, "The Day the Magic Died," *Charmed,* The WB, 2003.
Herself, "Pictures of Lily," *Just Shoot Me!,* NBC, 2003.
The Yesterday Show with Johnny Kerwin, Trio, 2004.
Mary Jo Fairfield, "9021–Uh–Oh," *Hope & Faith,* ABC, 2004.
"The '70s—Part II," *TV Land Moguls,* TV Land, 2004.
Live with Regis and Kelly, syndicated, 2005.
The Tony Danza Show, syndicated, 2005.
Herself, *The O'Reilly Factor,* Fox News, 2005.
The Late Late Show with Craig Ferguson, CBS, 2005.

Television Executive Producer; Specials:

Cheryl Ladd ... Looking Back—Souvenirs (also known as *Cheryl Ladd—Souvenirs* and *Looking Back: Souvenirs*), ABC, 1980.

Stage Appearances:

Reno Sweeney, *Anything Goes,* Santa Barbara Theatre Festival, Santa Barbara, CA, 1986.
Annie Get Your Gun, Marquis Theatre, New York City, 2000.

Also appeared in *The Hasty Heart.*

RECORDINGS

Albums:

Cheryl Ladd, Capitol, 1978.
Dance Forever, Capitol, 1979.
(Japan only) *Take a Chance,* 1981.
(Japan only) *The Best of Cheryl Ladd,* 1981.
(Japan only) *You Make It Beautiful,* 1982.

Also released *The Best of Cheryl Ladd,* Capitol; appeared on *Josie & the Pussycats,* Rhino.

Videos:

Herself, *Jim Henson's "Muppet Video: The Kermit and Piggy Story,"* Playhouse Home Video, 1985.

WRITINGS

Children's Books:

(With Brian Russell) *The Adventures of Little Nettie Windship,* illustrated by Ezra Tucker and Nancy Krause, Dove Kids/Penguin USA (West Hollywood, CA), 1996.

Memoir:

Token Chick: A Woman's Guide to Golfing with the Boys, 2005.

OTHER SOURCES

Periodicals:

Barron's, February 1, 1993, p. 62.
Drug Topics, April 10, 1995, p. 34.
Entertainment Weekly, August 5, 1994, pp. 42–43; August 19, 1994, p. 50.
Newsweek, June 13, 2005, p. 69.
People Weekly, June 9, 1997, pp. 67–68; January 11, 1999, p. 53; September 27, 1999, pp. 97–98.
Redbook, July, 1994, pp. 70–74.

LAGERFELT, Caroline 1947–
(Carolyn Lagerfelt)

PERSONAL

Full name, Caroline Eugenie Lagerfelt; born September 23, 1947, in Paris, France; daughter of Baron Karl–Gustav Israel (an ambassador) and Mary Charmian Sara Chapion (maiden name, de Crespigny; some sources cite name as Sara Champion de Crespigny) Lagerfelt; married; children: two sons. *Education:* Attended Sigtuna Stiftelsens Humanistiska Larouerket, Sigtuna, Sweden; studied acting at the American Academy of Dramatic Arts.

Career: Actress. Tyrone Guthrie Theatre, Minneapolis, MN, member of acting company, 1987–88. Stage manager for theatrical productions. Children's Village, Dobbs Ferry, NY, volunteer.

Member: Actors' Equity Association (member of council), American Academy of Dramatic Arts Alumni Association (president).

Awards, Honors: Villager Downtown Theatre Award, 1982, for *The Sea Anchor.*

CREDITS

Stage Appearances:

(As Carolyn Lagerfelt) Liz and understudy for Celia, *The Philanthropist,* Ethel Barrymore Theatre, New York City, 1971.
(As Carolyn Lagerfelt) Understudy for various roles, *Four on a Garden* (four one–acts), Broadhurst Theatre, New York City, 1971.

(As Carolyn Lagerfelt) Lady Ursula Itchin, *The Jockey Club Stakes,* Cort Theatre, New York City, 1973.

Marie–Louise Durham, *The Constant Wife,* Shubert Theatre, New York City, 1975.

Della, *Clarence,* Roundabout Theatre Company, Stage II, New York City, 1975–76.

(As Carolyn Lagerfelt) Beth, *Otherwise Engaged,* Plymouth Theatre, New York City, 1977.

Judith, *The Devil's Disciple,* Meadow Brook Theatre, Rochester, MI, c. 1978.

Standby for Emma, *Betrayal,* Trafalgar Theatre, New York City, 1980.

Jean, *The Sea Anchor,* Open Space, New York City, c. 1982.

Ruth Carson, *Night and Day,* Huntington Theatre Company, Boston, MA, 1982.

Anita Manchip, *Quartermaine's Terms,* Long Wharf Theatre, New Haven, CT, and Playhouse 91, New York City, both 1983.

Gila/Pauline, *Other Places,* Manhattan Theatre Club, Stage 73, New York City, 1984.

Annie, *The Real Thing,* Plymouth Theatre, New York City, c. 1984–85.

The Wall of Water, produced as a part of *Winterfest 8: Four New Plays in Repertory,* Yale Repertory Theatre, New Haven, CT, 1988.

Governor's wife, *Phaedra Britannica,* Classic Stage Company, New York City, 1988–89.

Diana, *Lend Me a Tenor,* Really Useful Theatre Company, Royale Theatre, New York City, 1989–90.

Izz, *Swim Visit,* Primary Stages, New York City, 1990.

Anita, *A Small Family Business,* Music Box Theatre, New York City, 1992.

Suzanne, *Don't Dress for Dinner,* Paper Mill Playhouse, Millburn, NJ, 1992.

Tekla, *Creditors,* Classic Stage Company, New York City, 1992.

Simone, *The Workroom,* American Jewish Theatre, New York City, 1993.

The Misanthrope, Long Wharf Theatre, 1993.

Death Takes a Holiday, Lobero Theater, Santa Barbara, CA, 1997.

Elizabeth I, *Mary Stuart,* San Francisco, CA, then Huntington Theatre Company, Boston University Theatre, Boston, MA, 2000.

Gareth Peirce, *Guantanamo: Honor Bound to Defend Freedom,* Culture Project, Forty–Five Bleecker Street Theatre, New York City, 2004.

Appeared as Margaret, *Close of Play,* as Edward/Victoria, *Cloud Nine,* and as Alison, *Look Back in Anger,* all Manhattan Theatre Club; as Gwendolyn, *The Importance of Being Earnest,* Pittsburgh Public Theatre, Pittsburgh, PA; as Monika Stettler, *The Physicists,* John F. Kennedy Center for the Performing Arts, Washington, DC; as Clarissa, *Spider's Web,* Nassau Repertory; as Mary, *Vanities,* George Street Playhouse, New Brunswick, NJ; as Stephanie Dickinson, *Cactus Flower;* and in other productions, including dinner theatre productions.

Major Tours:

Appeared as Sister Margaret, *The Hasty Heart;* Sally Boothroyd, *Lloyd George Knew My Father;* Nia, *The Right Honorable Gentleman;* and Beatrice, *To Grandmother's House We Go.*

Stage Work; As Carolyn Lagerfelt:

Assistant stage manager, *Four on a Garden* (four one–acts), Broadhurst Theatre, New York City, 1971.

Stage manager, *The Philanthropist,* Ethel Barrymore Theatre, New York City, 1971.

Film Appearances:

Elizabeth Masters, *Iron Eagle,* TriStar, 1986.

Sidewalk Motel, 1990.

Check–in nurse, *Father of the Bride Part II* (also known as *Father of the Bride 2*), Buena Vista, 1995.

First mother at McDonald's, *Bye Bye, Love,* Twentieth Century–Fox, 1995.

Joleen Lemon, *Glam,* Storm Entertainment, 2001.

Miss Greta Van Eyck, *Minority Report,* Twentieth Century–Fox, 2002.

Mrs. Carter, *Homecoming,* Myriad Arts Productions, 2005.

Television Appearances; Series:

Patricia Devereaux, *The Edge of Night,* ABC, 1983.

Elaine Hargrove, *As the World Turns,* CBS, 1986.

Carrie Gordon, *One Life to Live,* ABC, 1988–89.

Sheila Silver, *Beverly Hills 90210,* Fox, 1995–96.

Inger Dominguez, *Nash Bridges* (also known as *Bridges*), CBS, 1996–2001.

Appeared in *Guiding Light,* CBS.

Television Appearances; Movies:

Liz Shaw, *Do You Remember Love,* CBS, 1985.

Emily Fukes, *No Way Back,* 1996.

Lady of the house, *Journey of the Heart,* 1997.

Mayor Louise Terry, *The Lake,* NBC, 1998.

Television Appearances; Specials:

Serena, "Missing Pieces," *Hallmark Hall of Fame,* CBS, 2000.

Television Appearances; Episodic:

(As Carolyn Lagerfelt) Ruth Kendall, "The Shabbat Dinner," *Archie Bunker's Place,* CBS, 1979.

Julia, "The Throwaway," *T. J. Hooker,* ABC, 1985.

April Hamilton, "The Misfortune Cookie," *The Twilight Zone,* CBS, 1986.

Rita Quintero, "DWI," *Cagney & Lacey,* CBS, 1986.

"Keeper of the Flame," *Bridges to Cross,* CBS, 1986.

Christina, "Home at Last," *WonderWorks,* PBS, 1988.

Evelyn, "Eighteen with a Bullet," *The Equalizer,* CBS, 1988.

Governess, "Haunting," *Spenser: For Hire,* ABC, 1988.

Mary Ann Miller, "But Now a Word from Our Sponsor," *Murphy Brown,* CBS, 1990.

Danielle Keyes, "Black Tie," *Law & Order,* NBC, 1993.

Sally Lewis, "Over a Barrel: Parts 1–4," *Ghostwriter,* PBS, 1993.

Andrea, "ER Confidential," *ER* (also known as *Emergency Room*), NBC, 1994.

Kitty Lear, "Good Time Charlie," *NYPD Blue,* ABC, 1994.

Makbar, "Tribunal," *Star Trek: Deep Space Nine* (also known as *Deep Space Nine, DS9,* and *Star Trek: DS9*), syndicated, 1995.

Nurse Holder, "The Virus," *Chicago Hope,* CBS, 1995.

Rhinebeck Retreat receptionist, "Showgirls," *Central Park West* (also known as *CPW*), CBS, 1995.

Amazing Grace, NBC, 1995.

Marta Beiler, "To Forgive Is Divine," *Picket Fences,* CBS, 1996.

Mrs. Hoyt, "Atomic Cat Fight," *The Drew Carey Show,* ABC, 1996.

Rae, "Bogey Man," *Pensacola: Wings of Gold,* syndicated, 1997.

Marcia Zindler, "The Grinch," *Snoops,* ABC, 1999.

Mother, "Egg Lessons," *Chicken Soup for the Soul,* PAX TV, 1999.

Attorney, "Children Are the Most Important Thing," *Any Day Now,* Lifetime, 2001.

Rustic woman, "The Gift," *The X–Files,* Fox, 2001.

Barbara Evans, "Right to Die," *First Monday,* CBS, 2002.

Corinne, "The Fever Episode," *Maybe It's Me,* The WB, 2002.

Alternate wife, "Perfect Circles," *Six Feet Under,* HBO, 2003.

Anne, "Lies My Parents Told Me," *Buffy the Vampire Slayer* (also known as *Buffy* and *Buffy the Vampire Slayer: The Series*), UPN, 2003.

Glinka (some sources cite Ginka), "The Doctor Is Out," *Frasier* (also known as *Dr. Frasier Crane*), NBC, 2003.

Hannah Heltman, "The Posthumous Collection," *Law & Order: Criminal Intent* (also known as *Law & Order: CI*), NBC, 2004.

Television Appearances; Pilots:

Veronica Pierson, *Red Skies,* USA Network, 2002.

LANE, Stewart F. 1951–

PERSONAL

Born May 3, 1951, in New York, NY; son of Leonard Charles (a business executive) and Mildred C. (maiden name, Chesnow) Lane; married Robin Etta Lavin (an actress), May 16, 1981 (marriage ended); married Bonnie Comley (a producer); children: (first marriage) Eliana Constance. *Education:* Boston University, B.F.A., 1973.

Career: Producer. Brooks Atkinson Theater, assistant house manager, New York City; member of New York City Mayor Rudolph Guliani's transition committee, Department for Cultural Affairs and the Department of Film, Theatre, and Broadcasting; member of board of governors, City Center of Music and Drama at Lincoln Center; co–owner and operator of Palace Theatre, New York City; co–owner (with Robert DeNiro) of restaurant Tribeca Grill and film house Tribeca Film Centre, New York City.

Awards, Honors: Antoinette Perry Award nomination, best revival of a play or musical, 1980, for *West Side Story;* Antoinette Perry Award nomination, best musical, 1981, for *Woman of the Year;* Drama League Critics Award, best new play, 1983, for *Teaneck Tanzi: The Venus Flytrap;* Antoinette Perry Award, best musical, Outer Critics Circle Award, and Drama Desk Award nomination, 1984, all for *La Cage Aux Folles;* Antoinette Perry Award and New York Drama Critics Circle Award, both best musical, and Drama Desk Award, 1991, all for *The Will Rogers Follies: A Life in Revue;* Antoinette Perry Award nomination, best musical, 1993, for *The Goodbye Girl;* Antoinette Perry Award nomination, best revival—musical, and Outer Critics Circle Award nomination and Drama Desk Award nomination, both outstanding revival of a musical, 1998, all for *1776;* American Theater Critics Association Award nomination, best new play, *If It Was Easy...* (with Ward Morehouse III); Antoinette Perry Award, best musical, 2002, for *Thoroughly Modern Millie;* Antoinette Perry Award, best revival of a musical, 2003, for *Gypsy;* Antoinette Perry Award, best revival of a musical, 2004, for *Fiddler on the Roof.*

CREDITS

Stage Producer:

Can–Can (revival), Minskoff Theatre, New York City, 1981.

Frankenstein, Palace Theatre, New York City, 1981.

Woman of the Year, Palace Theatre, 1981–83.

La Cage Aux Folles, Palace Theatre, 1983–87.

The Apprenticeship of Duddy Kravitz, Off–Broadway production, 1987.

A Change in the Heir, Edison Theatre, New York City, 1989.

The Will Rogers Follies: A Life in Revue, Palace Theatre, 1991–93.

Sarah and Abraham, 1992.

Eating Raoul, Union Square Theatre, New York City, 1992.

(With James M. Nederlander), *Candles, Snow, and Mistletoe,* Palace Theatre, 1993.

The Goodbye Girl, Marquis Theatre, New York City, 1993.

Fortune's Fools, Cherry Lane Theatre, New York City, 1995.

1776, Gershwin Theatre, New York City, 1997–98.

JFK: A Musical Drama, Olympia Theatre, Dublin, Ireland, 1997.

Wait Until Dark, Brooks Atkinson Theatre, New York City, 1998.

Minnelli on Minnelli, Palace Theatre, 1999.

Thoroughly Modern Millie, Marquis Theatre, 2002–2004.

Fiddler on the Roof, Minskoff Theatre, New York City, 2004.

Stage Coproducer:

Teaneck Tanzi: The Venus Flytrap, Nederlander Theatre, New York City, 1983.

Stage Associate Producer:

Lone Star/Private Wars, Century Theatre, New York City, 1979.

West Side Story (revival), Minskoff Theatre, New York City, 1980.

Stage Assistant Producer:

Whose Life Is It Anyway?, 1979.

Stage Produced in Association With:

The Grand Tour, Palace Theatre, New York City, 1979.

The Two and Only, Atlantic Theater, New York City, 2004.

Stage Director:

Fortune's Fools, New Dramatists, 1994.

Accentuate the Positive, Weitzenhoffer Theatre, Norman, OK, 1996.

The Golden Age, Actors Theatre of Nantucket, Nantucket, MA, 1999.

If It Was Easy..., Berkshire Theatre Festival, Stockbridge, MA, 1999.

If It Was Easy..., 7 Stages, Atlanta, GA, 2000.

If It Was Easy..., Douglas Fairbanks Theatre, New York City, 2001.

The Gig, Lyric Theatre, Boston, MA, 2002.

Ain't Misbehavin', Vineyard Playhouse, Vineyard, MA, 2002.

Major Tours; Producer:

Woman of the Year, tour of U.S. cities, 1983.

Film Appearances:

George Lemay, *Puppet on a Chain,* 1970.

Film Work:

Executive producer, *Show Business,* 2005.

Television Appearances:

Host, *Curtain Time,* Crosswalks Television Network (New York City), 1994–95.

Television Work; Producer:

Curtain Time, Crosswalks Television Network (New York City), 1994–95.

WRITINGS

Stage Plays:

(With Ward Morehouse III) *If It Was Easy...,* Douglas Fairbanks Theatre, New York City, 2001.

In the Wings, Promenade Theatre, New York City, 2005.

OTHER SOURCES

Periodicals:

Back Stage, July 24, 1998, p.3; December 10, 1999, p.2.

LANGE, Ted 1947(?)–

PERSONAL

Full name, Theodore William Lange; born January 5, 1947 (some sources say 1948), in Oakland, CA; son of Ted and Geraldine L. (a television show host) Lange; married Sheryl Thompson, 1978; children: Ted IV, Turner Wallace. *Education:* Attended San Francisco City College and Merritt Junior College; graduated from the Royal Academy of Dramatic Arts.

Addresses: *Agent*—The Schiowitz/Clay/Ankrum & Ross FKA Talent Syndicate, 1680 N. Vine St., Suite 614, Los Angeles, CA 90028.

Career: Actor, director, producer, and writer. Performed with New Shakespearean Company; appeared in television commercial for Bud Light, 2003.

Member: Directors Guild of America.

Awards, Honors: Renaissance Man Theatre Award, National Association for the Advancement of Colored People; Paul Robeson Award, American Film Institute.

CREDITS

Film Appearances:

Melvin the Pimp, *Trick Baby* (also known as *The Double Con*), Universal, 1972.

Himself, *Wattstax* (documentary), Columbia, 1973.

Henry Watson, *Blade,* Joseph Green Pictures, 1973.

(Uncredited) Militant, *Black Belt Jones,* 1974.

Fancy Dexter, *Friday Foster,* American International Pictures, 1975.

The Wiz, *Record City,* 1978.

Fantastic, *Double Exposure* (also known as *Terminal Exposure*), United Film Distribution, 1987.

DuBois, *Glitch!,* Omega, 1988.

Title role, *Othello,* Uptown Films, 1989.

The deacon, *Penny Ante* (also known as *Penny Ante: The Motion Picture*), Motion Picture Corporation of America, 1990.

George, *Perfume,* 1991.

The flower peddler, *The Naked Truth,* 1992.

Gnome, *Sandman,* 1998.

Reverend, *The Redemption,* 2000.

Is This Your Mother? (short), 2002.

Professor Williams, *Banana Moon,* 2003.

Bartender #2, *Gang of Roses,* DEJ Productions, 2003.

Himself, *The N–Word,* 2004.

Film Work:

Executive producer and director, *Othello,* Uptown Films, 1989.

Coproducer, *Banana Moon,* 2003.

Also directed *Toe to Toe.*

Television Appearances; Series:

Junior, *That's My Mama,* ABC, 1974–75.

Harvard, *Mr. T and Tina,* ABC, 1976.

Bartender Isaac Washington, *The Love Boat,* ABC, 1977–87.

Television Appearances; Movies:

Banacek: Detour to Nowhere, NBC, 1972.

Larry, 1974.

The Love Boat, ABC, 1976.

Isaac Washington, *The Love Boat II,* 1977.

Isaac Washington, *The New Love Boat* (also known as *The Love Boat III*), ABC, 1977.

Isaac Washington, *The Love Boat: The Christmas Cruise,* ABC, 1986.

Isaac Washington, *The Love Boat: The Shipshape Cruise,* ABC, 1986.

Isaac Washington, *The Love Boat: Who Killed Maxwell Thorn?,* ABC, 1986.

Napoleon, *It Nearly Wasn't Christmas* (also known as *It Almost Wasn't Christmas*), syndicated, 1989.

Isaac Washington, *The Love Boat: A Valentine Voyage* (also known as *Valentine's Day Love Boat Reunion* and *The Love Boat: A Summer Cruise*), CBS, 1990.

The Naked Truth, Cinemax, 1993.

Television Appearances; Specials:

Love Boat team member, *All–Star Family Feud Special,* ABC, 1977.

The Celebrity Football Classic, NBC, 1979.

Circus of the Stars #5, CBS, 1980.

Kraft Salutes Disneyland's 25th Anniversary, 1980.

Good Evening, Captain, CBS, 1981.

ABC Team contestant, *Battle of the Network Stars XVI,* ABC, 1984.

The ABC All–Star Spectacular, ABC, 1985.

Ghost of Christmas Present, *Christmas* (also known as *John Grin's "Christmas"*), ABC, 1988.

Living the Dream: A Tribute to Dr. Martin Luther King, syndicated, 1988.

Super Bloopers and New Practical Jokes, NBC, 1989.

An All Star Party for Aaron Spelling, ABC, 1998.

Interviewee, *TV Guide's Truth behind the Sitcoms 3* (documentary), Fox, 2000.

The Love Boat (documentary), Arts and Entertainment, 2001.

The Love Boat: TV Tales (documentary), E! Entertainment Television, 2002.

ABC's 50th Anniversary Celebration, ABC, 2003.

The Second Annual TV Land Awards: A Celebration of Classic TV, TV Land and Nickelodeon, 2004.

TV Land Landmarks: Breaking the Mold (documentary), TV Land, 2004.

BET Comedy Awards, BET, 2004.

Also appeared in *The American Film Institute's Salute to James Cagney.*

Television Appearances; Pilots:

The Real Trivial Pursuit, ABC, 1985.

That's My Mama Now, 1986.

Television Appearances; Episodic:

The Great Scott, "Amusement Park/Rock Stars," *Fantasy Island,* ABC, 1979.

Isaac Washington, "Love Boat Angels: Part 1 and 2," *Charlie's Angels,* ABC, 1979.

Bartender, "The Last Drive," *The Fall Guy,* ABC, 1983.

"Malibu Man," *The New Gidget,* syndicated, 1987.

James Jeffson, "A Necessary Evil," *In the Heat of the Night,* NBC, 1988.

Lou, "Snow Bound," *227,* NBC, 1988.

"Warzone," *The Highwayman,* NBC, 1988.

Mr. Taxerman, "Teaching Is a Good Thing," *Evening Shade,* 1993.

Mr. Angel, "Out of the Mouths of Babes," *Platypus Man,* 1995.

Frank Winslow, "The Brother Who Came to Dinner," *Family Matters*, ABC, 1996.

Himself, "Tom and Them," *The Show*, Fox, 1996.

Himself, "The Commercial," *Malcolm and Eddie* (also known as *Top of the Stairs*), UPN, 1996.

Isaac, "Chet–A–Nator," *Weird Science*, 1996.

Himself, "Fraternity Row," *Boy Meets World*, ABC, 1997.

Isaac, "Goin' Overboard: Part 1 and 2," *Martin*, Fox, 1997.

Himself, *Ed's Night Party*, 1997.

Isaac Washington, "Reunion," *The Love Boat: The Next Wave*, The WB, 1998.

Frank Millan, "Rap Sheet," *L.A. Heat*, TNT, 1999.

Voice of Robot Bartender iZak, "A Flight to Remember," *Futurama* (animated), 1999.

Himself, *Who Wants to Be a Millionaire*, ABC, 2001.

Mr. Henderson, "How Hattie Got Her Groove Back," *The Hughleys*, UPN, 2002.

Mr. Blair, "My New Coat," *Scrubs*, NBC, 2002.

Repairman, "The Big Butting In Episode," *Half & Half*, UPN, 2003.

Teacher, "Guitar," *Drake & Josh*, Nickelodeon, 2004.

Himself, "Top 10 TV Dads," *TV Land's Top Ten*, TV Land, 2004.

Himself, "Top 10 TV Cars," *TV Land's Top Ten*, TV Land, 2004.

Mr. Calvert, "Mindy's Back," *Drake & Josh*, Nickelodeon, 2005.

Himself, "Wacky Neighbors," *TV Land's Top Ten*, TV Land, 2005.

Himself, "Perfect 10's the Women," *TV Land's Top Ten*, TV Land, 2005.

Also appeared in *The New Mike Hammer* (also known as *Mickey Spillane's "Mike Hammer"*), CBS; and *The Last Detail*.

Television Director; Episodic:

"Friend or Foe?," *Eve*, ABC, 1983.

"Trauma," *The Fall Guy*, ABC, 1983.

"The Last Drive," *The Fall Guy*, ABC, 1983.

"Spring Break," *The Fall Guy*, ABC, 1985.

"Fathers and Sons," *Starman*, ABC, 1987.

"Hakeem's Birthday," *Moesha*, UPN, 1997.

"Halloween Part 1: Kim's Revenge," *Moesha*, UPN, 1997.

"Reunion," *The Love Boat: The Next Wave*, UPN, 1998.

"My Pest Friend's Wedding," *In the House*, UPN, 1998.

"Independence Day," *The Wayans Bros.*, The WB, 1998.

"Good Child/Curtain Call," *Fantasy Island*, UPN, 1999.

"Divorce, Downbeat, and Distemper," *The Love Boat: The Next Wave*, UPN, 1999.

"Blind Love," *The Love Boat: The Next Wave*, UPN, 1999.

"Guest Dad," *In the House*, UPN, 1999.

"There's Something About Tiffany," *In the House*, UPN, 1999.

"Not as Good as It Gets," *In the House*, UPN, 1999.

"Out House," *In the House*, UPN, 1999.

"Arriving Right on Q," *Moesha*, UPN, 2000.

"The Candidate," *Moesha*, UPN, 2000.

"Home Is Where the Art Is," *Dharma & Greg*, ABC, 2001.

"The End of Innocence: Part 1," *Dharma & Greg*, ABC, 2001.

Also directed episodes of *The Love Boat*, ABC; *The New Mike Hammer* (also known as *Mike Hammer* and *Mickey Spillane's "Mike Hammer"*).

Stage Appearances:

(New York debut) *Hair*, 1969.

Hoke, *Driving Miss Daisy*, Jupiter Theatre, Jupiter, FL, 1991–92.

Hoke, *Driving Miss Daisy*, Bushnell Theatre, Hartford, CT, 1994.

Weird Willie and the B.L.C., Whitefire Theatre, Los Angeles, 1999.

Lemon Meringue Facade, New Perspectives Theatre, New York City, 2003, 2004.

Also appeared in *Dialogue Black and White; Golden Boy; Tell Pharaoh; Ain't Supposed to Die a Natural Death;* and *Big Time Buck White*.

Stage Director:

The Visit, 1996.

The Marriage, Stage 52, Los Angeles, 2000.

Also directed productions of *Richard III, Hamlet, The Odd Couple,* and *Little Footsteps*.

RECORDINGS

Music Videos:

Appeared in Van Gogh's Daughter's "Through the Eyes of Julie," 1996, which featured actors from *The Love Boat;* Barry White's "Come On."

WRITINGS

Plays:

Weird Willie and the B.L.C., Whitefire Theatre, Los Angeles, CA, 1999.

Lemon Meringue Facade, New Perspectives Theatre, New York City, 2003, 2004.

Screenplays:
Passing Through, 1977.
Othello (adaptation), Uptown Films, 1989.

Television Episodes:
Wrote episodes of *The Love Boat,* ABC.

LANGHAM, Wallace 1965–
    (Wally Ward)

PERSONAL

Full name, James Wallace Langham II; born March 11, 1965, in Fort Worth, TX; raised in Los Angeles, CA; son of James (an elevator repairman) and Sunni (a costume designer) Langham; married Laura, December 28, 1986 (divorced, 1998); married Karey Richard (a flamenco dancer), November 3, 2002; children: (first marriage) Alex, Chloe. *Education:* Los Angeles City College, A.A., business; also attended California State University at Northridge. *Avocational Interests:* Skiing.

Addresses: *Agent*—United Talent Agency, 9560 Wilshire Blvd., Suite 500, Beverly Hills, CA 90212. *Manager*—Schachter Entertainment, 1157 S. Beverly Dr., 2nd Floor, Los Angeles, CA 90035.

Career: Actor. Appeared in commercials; part of the pre–show ride, Dinosaur!, in Disney's Animal Kingdom, Orlando, FL.

CREDITS

Film Appearances:
(As Wally Ward) Paul, *Thunder Run,* Cannon, 1985.
(As Wally Ward) The Weeny, *Weird Science,* Universal, 1985.
(As Wally Ward) Barky Brewer, *Soul Man* (also known as *The Imposter*), New World, 1986.
(As Wally Ward) *The Invisible Kid,* Taurus Entertainment, 1988.
(As Wally Ward) Archie, *The Chocolate War,* Management Company Entertainment, 1988.
(As Wally Ward) Backwash, *Under the Boardwalk,* New World, 1989.
Gant, *Vital Signs,* Twentieth Century–Fox, 1990.
(As Wally Ward) Voyeur Martian, *Martians Go Home,* Taurus Entertainment, 1990.
Rick, *God's Lonely Man,* Cinequanon Pictures International, 1995.
Bruce Craddock, *Michael,* New Line Cinema, 1996.
Jimmy Hand, *On Edge,* KBK Entertainment, 2000.
Voice of narrator, *Uncle Saddam,* 2000.

Jim Fields, *Daddy Day Care,* Revolution Studios, 2003.
Jack, *Hot Night in the City,* 2004.
Claude Clochet, *I Want Someone to Eat Cheese With,* 2005.

Television Appearances; Series:
(As Wally Ward) Mark Ratner, *Fast Times* (also known as *Fast Times at Ridgemont High*), CBS, 1986.
(As Wally Ward) Willis Teitlebaum, *WIOU,* CBS, 1990–91.
Phil, *The Larry Sanders Show,* HBO, 1992–98.
Josh Blair, *Veronica's Closet,* NBC, 1997–2000.
Voice of Andy French, *Mission Hill,* The WB, 1999—.
Mark Ludlow, *What About Joan,* ABC, 2001.
David Hodges, *CSI: Crime Scene Investigation,* CBS, 2003—.

Television Appearances; Miniseries:
Himself, *I Love the '80s* (documentary), VH1, 2002.

Television Appearances; Movies:
(As Wally Ward) Kevin, *Children of the Night,* CBS, 1985.
(As Wally Ward) Percival "Perry" Barnett, *Combat High* (also known as *Combat Academy*), NBC, 1986.
(As Wally Ward) Jimmy Pierson, *A Deadly Silence,* ABC, 1989.
Don Kirshner, *The Monkees: Daydream Believers,* VH1, 2000.
Aloysius Benheim, *Sister Mary Explains It All,* Showtime, 2001.
Jay, *Behind the Camera: The Unauthorized Story of "Three's Company,"* NBC, 2003.
Jay Bernstein, *Behind the Camera: The Unauthorized Story of "Charlie's Angels,"* NBC, 2004.

Television Appearances; Specials:
(As Wally Ward) Babe, *Ace Hits the Big Time,* CBS, 1985.
(As Wally Ward) Paul Hendler, *Just a Regular Kid: An AIDS Story* (also known as *Just a Regular Kid*), ABC, 1987.
Voice, *Life with Louie: A Christmas Surprise for Mrs. Stillman* (animated), Fox, 1994.
Voice of Prince Bobby/Fish, *The Frog Princess: An Animated Special from the "Happily Ever After: Fairy Tales for Every Child"* Series, 2000.
Himself, *Rocky Horror 25: Anniversary Special,* PBS, 2000.
Special correspondent, *Grease 20th Anniversary Re–release Party,* VH1, 2002.

Television Appearances; Pilots:
(As Wally Ward) Mark Ratner, *Fast Times* (also known as *Fast Times at Ridgemont High*), CBS, 1986.
Jeff, *NewsRadio,* NBC, 1995.
Rubbing Charlie, CBS, 2003.

Also appeared in *Tinsel Tales.*

Television Appearances; Episodic:
(As Wally Ward) "Past Tense, Future Tense: Parts 1 & 2," *Our House,* 1987.
(As Wally Ward) "Time and Teresa Golowitz," *The Twilight Zone,* 1987.
(As Wally Ward) Dennis Austin, "The Cult," *Matlock,* 1989.
Michael, "The Murphy Brown School of Broadcasting," *Murphy Brown,* CBS, 1990.
Poole, "Research and Destroy," *21 Jump Street,* Fox and syndicated, 1990.
John Hemingway, "The Fairy Tale," *Life Goes On,* 1992.
Todd Merlin, "Dead to Rights," *Murder, She Wrote,* 1993.
"Family Membership," *Dave's World,* CBS, 1994.
Dr. Melvoin, "Doctor Carter, I Presume," *ER,* NBC, 1996.
Stewart, "Physical Graffiti," *NewsRadio,* NBC, 1996.
Eric, "Grace's New Job," *Grace Under Fire,* ABC, 1997.
Levi, "Shooting Mickey," *F/X: The Series,* syndicated, 1997.
Flotter T. Water, "Once Upon a Time," *Star Trek: Voyager,* UPN, 1998.
The Rosie O'Donnell Show, 1998.
Hollywood Squares, 1998.
Instant Comedy with the Groundlings, 1998.
Happy Hour, USA Network, 1999.
Ezekiel, "Final Appeal," *The Outer Limits,* Showtime and syndicated, 2000.
Voice of Smoltz, "Return to Karn," *Buzz Lightyear of the Star Command* (also known as *Disney/Pixar's "Buzz Lightyear of Star Command"*; animated), ABC, 2000.
Voice of Care–bots, "Speed Trap," *Buzz Lightyear of the Star Command* (also known as *Disney/Pixar's "Buzz Lightyear of Star Command"*; animated), ABC, 2000.
A. J., "Comic Relief Pitcher," *Inside Schwartz,* NBC, 2001.
Charlie Stickney, "Mr. Motivation," *The Twilight Zone,* UPN, 2002.
Willie, "To Market, To Market," *Sex and the City,* HBO, 2003.
Julian Kerbis, "Donny, We Hardly Knew Ye," *Las Vegas,* NBC, 2003.
Lucas, "Kate in Extasy," *Miss Match,* NBC, 2003.
Ken, "With Friends Like These, Who Needs Emmys?," *Good Morning, Miami,* NBC, 2003.
Terry Anders, "The Hubbert Peak," *The West Wing,* NBC, 2004.
Alan, "Suspicions and Certainties," *Medium,* NBC and CTV (Canada), 2005.
Alan, "The Other Side of the Tracks," *Medium,* NBC and CTV, 2005.
Himself, "How Do I Measure Up?," *Love Lounge,* 2005.

Also appeared in *Madman of the People,* NBC; *The Tracey Ullman Show,* Fox.

Television Director; Episodic:
Directed "Veronica's Clips," *Veronica's Closet,* NBC.

OTHER SOURCES

Periodicals:
Entertainment Weekly, October 10, 1997, p. 73.
People Weekly, February 10, 1997, pp. 208–10.

LARESCA, Vincent 1974–

PERSONAL

Born January 21, 1974, in New York, NY.

Addresses: *Agent*—Paradigm Talent Agency, 360 N. Crescent Dr., North Bldg., Beverly Hills, CA 90210. *Manager*—MJ Management, 130 W. 157th Street, Suite 11A, New York, NY 10019.

Career: Actor.

Awards, Honors: Screen Actors Guild Award nomination (with others), outstanding performance by an ensemble in a drama series, 2005, for *24.*

CREDITS

Film Appearances:
Radames, *Juice* (also known as *Angel Town 2*), Paramount, 1992.
J. C., *Bad Lieutenant,* Artisan, 1992.
Angel, *I Like It Like That,* Columbia, 1994.
Subway robber, *Money Train,* Columbia, 1995.
Rodriguez, *The Substitute,* Artisan, 1996.
The Money Shot, Bigel/Mailer, 1996.
Vincent, *Basquiat* (also known as *Build a Fort, Set It on Fire*), Miramax, 1996.
Jimmy, *Ripe,* Trimark Pictures, 1996.
Patches, *Extreme Measures,* Columbia, 1996.
Jose, *The Associate,* Buena Vista, 1996.
Thief, *Destination Unknown,* 1996.
Abra, *Romeo + Juliet* (also known as *Romeo and Juliet* and *William Shakespeare's "Romeo + Juliet"*), Twentieth Century–Fox, 1996.
Ranaldo, *I'm Not Rappaport,* Gramercy, 1996.
Bopo, *Arresting Gena,* Good Machine, 1997.
Second medic, *Cop Land,* Miramax, 1997.

Trey, *The Real Blonde,* Paramount, 1997.
First big guy, *The Devil's Advocate* (also known as *Im Auftrag des Teufels*), Warner Bros., 1997.
Jesus, *Music from Another Room,* Orion, 1998.
The Money Shot, 1999.
Javier Cesti, *Forever Mine,* J&M, 1999.
Nick, *Just One Time,* Cowboy Pictures, 1999.
Raymond Camacho, *Flawless,* United International, 1999.
Ernie, *Animal Factory,* New City, 2000.
Jose Abreu, *Before Night Falls* (also known as *Antes que anochezca*), Fine Line, 2000.
Navarro, *K–PAX,* Universal, 2001.
Jimmy, *Empire,* Universal, 2002.
Corrections Officer Rodriguez, *Hollywood Homicide,* Columbia, 2003.
Jorge, *The Aviator,* Miramax, 2004.
Renny, *Coach Carter,* Paramount, 2005.
Chino, *Lords of Dogtown,* Columbia, 2005.
Aurielo, *Kiss, Kiss, Bang, Bang,* Warner Bros., 2005.
Doug Davenport, *Alpha Dog,* New Line Cinema, 2005.

Television Appearances; Series:
Carlos Martinez, *413 Hope St.,* Fox, 1997–98.
Hector Salazar, a recurring role, *24,* Fox, 2003–2004.

Television Appearances; Movies:
Tyro Corter, *Thicker Than Blood,* TNT, 1998.
Nikita, *Run for the Money* (also known as *Hard Cash*), USA Network, 2002.

Television Appearances; Episodic:
Danny, "Sisters of Mercy," *Law & Order,* NBC, 1992.
Fuenta Partaga, "The Lottery Winner Murders," *The Cosby Mysteries,* NBC, 1994.
Hector Belaflores, "Without Mercy," *New York Undercover,* Fox, 1996.
Tomas Paredes, "God and Country," *Touched by an Angel,* CBS, 1998.
Dr. Alvarez, "Letting Go," *Chicago Hope,* CBS, 2000.
Reggie Garland, "Foreign Affair," *The District,* CBS, 2001.
Tito Perez, "Humpty Dumped," *NYPD Blue,* ABC, 2002.
Buddy, "The Lineman," *The Twilight Zone,* UPN, 2002.
Feo Ruiz, "The Brotherhood," *Law & Order,* NBC, 2004.

Also appeared as Jesse Torres, *Family Law,* CBS.

Television Appearances; Pilots:
Marco, *Tru Calling,* Fox, 2003.

LARKIN, Linda 1970–

PERSONAL

Born March 20, 1970, in Hollywood, CA; married Yul Vazquez (an actor and voice performer), May 18, 2002.

Addresses: *Agent*—Cunningham, Escott and Dipene, 257 Park Ave. South, Ninth Floor, New York, NY 10010.

Career: Actress, voice performer, and producer.

CREDITS

Film Appearances:
Joanne, *Zapped Again!,* Pathfinder Pictures, 1990.
Voice of Princess Jasmine, *Aladdin* (animated), Buena Vista, 1992.
Voice of Princess Jasmine, *The Return of Jafar* (animated; also known as *Aladdin 2*), Buena Vista Home Video, 1994.
Caroline Ballard, *Childhood's End,* Open City Films/ Planview Pictures, 1996.
Fan, *Basquiat* (also known as *Build a Fort, Set It on Fire*), Miramax, 1996.
Voice of Princess Jasmine, *Aladdin and the King of Thieves* (animated), Buena Vista, 1996.
Voice of Princess Jasmine, *Aladdin's Arabian Adventures: Creatures of Invention* (animated), 1998.
Voice of Princess Jasmine, *Aladdin's Arabian Adventures: Fearless Friends* (animated), 1998.
Voice of Princess Jasmine, *Aladdin's Arabian Adventures: Magic Makers* (animated), 1998.
Voice of Princess Jasmine, *Aladdin's Arabian Adventures: Team Genie* (animated), 1998.
Voice of Princess Jasmine, *The Greatest Treasure* (animated; also known as *Disney's Princess Collection: The Greatest Treasure*), 1998.
Voice of Princess Jasmine, *Magic and Mystery* (animated; also known as *Disney's Princess Collection: Magic and Mystery*), 1998.
Carrie Boxer, *Two Ninas,* Trident Releasing, 1999.
Cory Lindross, *My Girlfriend's Boyfriend,* Enlightenment Productions, 1999.
Gill's girlfriend, *Runaway Bride,* Paramount, 1999.
Melanie, *Personals* (also known as *Hook'd Up*), Unapix Entertainment, 1999.
Trudy Tackle, *Final Rinse,* Bruder Releasing, 1999.
Voice of Princess Jasmine, *Jasmine's Wish* (animated; also known as *Disney's Princess Collection: Jasmine's Wish*), 1999.
Voice of Princess Jasmine, *True Hearts* (animated; also known as *Disney's Princess Collection: True Hearts*), 1999.
Kelly, *The Next Best Thing,* Paramount, 2000.
Liz, *Fear of Fiction,* Pow Wow, 2000.
Polly, *Custody* (short film), Life of Riley Productions, 2000.
Annette, *Knots,* Cross River Pictures/Davis Entertainment Filmworks/GDN/Parts Unknown Productions, 2004.
Voice of Princess Jasmine, *Disney Princess Party: Volume Two* (animated), 2005.

Film Producer:
Running Time (short film), 2002.

Television Appearances; Series:
Voice of Princess Jasmine, *Aladdin* (animated; also known as *Disney's "Aladdin"*), CBS and syndicated, 1994–95.
Voice of Jasmine, *House of Mouse* (animated; also known as *Disney's "House of Mouse"*), ABC, c. 2001–2004.

Television Appearances; Movies:
Melanie Miller, *Our Son, the Matchmaker,* CBS, 1996.
Annette, *Sex, Love and Lies,* Lifetime, 2005.

Television Appearances; Specials:
Voice of Princess Jasmine, *Aladdin on Ice* (also known as *Disney's "Aladdin on Ice"*), 1995.

Television Appearances; Episodic:
Karen Ann, "Family Doctor," *Murder, She Wrote,* CBS, 1991.
Kelly, "Dances with Wanda," *Doogie Howser, M.D.,* ABC, 1991.
Kim, "You Ought to Be in Pictures," *Almost Home* (also known as *The Torkelsons*), ABC, 1993.
Lisa, "Bye–Bye, Bunny," *Wings,* NBC, 1993.
Gwen, *The Boys,* CBS, 1993.
"You Thought the Pope Was Something," *New York News,* CBS, 1995.
Alycia, "In a Yellow Wood," *Trinity,* NBC, 1998.
Alycia, "In Loco Parentis," *Trinity,* NBC, 1998.
Voice of Princess Jasmine, "Hercules and the Arabian Night," *Hercules* (animated; also known as *Disney's "Hercules"*), ABC and syndicated, 1999.

Appeared as Denise, *Evening Shade,* CBS.

RECORDINGS

Video Games:
Voice of Princess Jasmine, *Disney's "Math Quest with Aladdin"* (also known as *Aladdin's Math Quest* and *Math Quest with Aladdin*), Buena Vista Home Video, 1998.
Voice of Princess Jasmine, *Aladdin in Nasira's Revenge* (also known as *Disney's "Aladdin in Nasira's Revenge"*), Sony Computer Entertainment America, 2001.
Voice of Princess Jasmine, *Kingdom Hearts* (also known as *Kingudamu hatsu*), Square Electronic Arts, 2002.
Voice of Skye of Lynlorra, *Darkened Skye,* TDK Interactive, 2002.
Voice of Princess Jasmine, *Kingdom Hearts II,* Square Electronic Arts, 2005.

LAURIE, Piper 1932–
(Laurie Piper)

PERSONAL

Original name, Rosetta Jacobs; born January 22, 1932, in Detroit, MI; daughter of Alfred (a furniture dealer) and Charlotte Sadie Jacobs; married Joseph Morgenstern (a journalist, critic, and writer), 1962 (divorced, 1981); children: Anne Grace. *Education:* Attended high school in Los Angeles; studied acting at Neighborhood Playhouse. *Avocational Interests:* Baking, making pottery, painting.

Addresses: *Agent*—William Morris Agency, One William Morris Place, Beverly Hills, CA 90212; Judy Schoen, Judy Schoen and Associates, 606 North Larchmont Blvd., Suite 309, Los Angeles, CA 90004.

Career: Actress. Also a sculptor.

Member: Screen Actors Guild, American Federation of Television and Radio Artists, Academy of Motion Picture Arts and Sciences.

Awards, Honors: Emmy Award nomination, outstanding single performance by an actress, 1958, for "The Deaf Heart," *Studio One;* Emmy Award nomination, outstanding single performance by an actress, 1959, for "The Days of Wine and Roses," *Playhouse 90;* Academy Award nomination, best actress, Film Award nomination, best foreign actress, British Academy of Film and Television Arts, and nomination for Golden Laurel, top female dramatic performance, Laurel awards, Producers Guild of America, all 1962, for *The Hustler;* named Hasty Pudding Woman of the Year, Hasty Pudding Theatricals, Harvard University, 1962; Academy Award nomination, best supporting actress, and Golden Globe Award nomination, best motion picture actress in a supporting role, both 1977, for *Carrie;* Saturn Award nomination, best actress in a horror film, Academy of Science Fiction, Fantasy, and Horror Films, 1978, for *Ruby;* Emmy Award nomination, outstanding supporting actress in a limited series or special, 1981, for *The Bunker;* Emmy Award nomination, outstanding supporting actress in a limited series or special, 1983, and Golden Globe Award, best performance by an actress in a supporting role in a series, miniseries, or movie made for television, 1984, both for *The Thorn Birds;* Emmy Award nomination, outstanding supporting actress in a drama series, 1984, for "Lust et Veritas," *St. Elsewhere;* Academy Award nomination, best supporting actress, 1987, for *Children of a Lesser God;* Emmy Award, outstanding supporting actress in a miniseries or special, and Golden Globe Award nomination, best performance by an actress in a supporting role in a television series, miniseries, or movie made for television, both 1987, for "Promise," *Hallmark Hall of Fame;* Emmy Award nominations, outstanding lead actress in a drama series, 1990, and outstanding supporting actress in a drama series, 1991, Golden Globe Award, best performance by an actress in a supporting role in a series, miniseries, or movie made for television, 1991, and *Soap Opera Digest* Award nominations, outstanding villainess in prime time, 1991, and outstanding actress in prime time, 1992, all for *Twin Peaks;* Southeastern Film Critics Association Award, best supporting actress, 1997, for *The Grass Harp;* American Independent Award, special jury prize, and Golden Space Needle Award, best actress, both Seattle International Film Festival, 1999, for *The Mao Game;* Emmy Award nomination, outstanding guest actress in a comedy series, 1999, for "Dr. Nora," *Frasier.*

CREDITS

Film Appearances:
Cathy Norton, *Louisa,* Universal, 1950.
Chris Abbott, *The Milkman,* Universal, 1950.
Frances Travers, *Francis Goes to the Races,* Universal, 1951.
Herself, *Cancer Fund Film Notables Attend Glittering Benefits* (short documentary), Warner Bros., 1951.
Tina, *The Prince Who Was a Thief,* Universal, 1951.
Kiki, *Son of Ali Baba,* Universal, 1952.
Lee Kingshead, *No Room for the Groom,* Universal, 1952.
Millicent Blaisdell, *Has Anybody Seen My Gal?,* Universal, 1952.
Angelique "Leia" Duroux, *The Mississippi Gambler,* Universal, 1953.
Princess Khairuzan, *The Golden Blade,* Universal, 1953.
Liz Fielding, *Johnny Dark,* Universal, 1954.
Louise Graham, *Dangerous Mission* (also known as *Rangers of the North*), RKO Radio Pictures, 1954.
Rannah Hayes, *Dawn at Socorro,* Universal, 1954.
Laura Evans, *Smoke Signal,* Universal, 1955.
Sarah Hatfield, *Ain't Misbehavin',* Universal, 1955.
Delia Leslie, *Until They Sail,* Metro–Goldwyn–Mayer, 1957.
Mina Van Runkel, *Kelly and Me,* Universal, 1957.
Sarah Packard, *The Hustler* (also known as *Robert Rossen's "The Hustler"*), Twentieth Century–Fox, 1961.
Margaret White, *Carrie,* United Artists, 1976.
Ruby Claire, *Ruby* (also known as *Blood Ruby*), Dimension Films, 1977.
Mary Horton, *Tim* (also known as *Colleen McCullough's "Tim"*), Australian Film Commission/Pisces Production, 1979, Satori, 1981.
Lady Macbeth, *Macbeth,* 1981.
(In archive footage) Margaret White, *Terror in the Aisles* (documentary), Universal, 1984.

Aunt Em Blue, *Return to Oz* (also known as *The Adventures of the Devil from the Sky* and *Oz*), Buena Vista, 1985.
Mrs. Norman, *Children of a Lesser God,* Paramount, 1986.
Emily Boynton, *Appointment with Death,* Cannon, 1988.
Frances Warsaw, *Tiger Warsaw* (also known as *The Tiger*), Columbia, 1988.
Margot Caldwell, *Distortions,* Cori, 1988.
The Boss' Son, New American Cinema, 1988.
Gena Ettinger, *Dream a Little Dream,* Vestron Pictures, 1989.
Martha Cousins, *Mother, Mother,* 1989.
Bea Sullivan, *Other People's Money* (also known as *Riqueza ajena*), Warner Bros., 1991.
Constance Fowler, *Storyville,* Twentieth Century–Fox, 1992.
Adriana Petrescu, *Trauma* (also known as *Aura's Enigma* and *Dario Argento's "Trauma"*), Overseas Film-Group, 1993.
Georgia, *Wrestling Ernest Hemingway,* Warner Bros., 1993.
Vera Delmage, *Rich in Love,* Metro–Goldwyn–Mayer, 1993.
Dolly Talbo, *The Grass Harp,* Fine Line Features, 1995.
Helen Booth, *The Crossing Guard* (also known as *Three Days for the Truth*), Miramax, 1995.
The Passion of Darkly Noon (also known as *Darkly Noon*), Entertainment Film Distributors/New Capital Group, 1995.
Karen Olson, *The Faculty,* Dimension Films/Miramax, 1998.
Evangelist, *Palmer's Pick Up,* Framework Entertainment Group/Winchester Films, 1999.
Ida Highland, *The Mao Game,* Untitled Entertainment, 1999.
Mary Pat Donnelly–McDonough, *St. Patrick's Day,* The Asylum, 1999.
(In archive footage) Voice of Margaret White, *The Rage: Carrie 2* (also known as *Carrie 2* and *Carrie 2, Say You're Sorry*), United Artists, 1999.
(In archive footage) Herself, *A Decade under the Influence* (documentary), IFC Films, 2003.
Charlotte Collins, *Eulogy,* Lions Gate Films/Artisan Entertainment, 2004.

Television Appearances; Series:
Jo Skagska, *Skag,* NBC, 1980.
Catherine Packard Martell, *Twin Peaks* (also known as *Northern Passage*), ABC, 1990–91.
Cora Trapchek, *Traps,* CBS, 1994.
Roberta Stahler, *Partners,* CBS, 1999.

Television Appearances; Miniseries:
Anne Mueller, *The Thorn Birds,* ABC, 1983.
(As Laurie Piper) Elsie Speers, *Tender Is the Night,* Showtime, 1985.
Miriam Braynard, *Intensity* (also known as *Dean Koontz's "Intensity"*), Fox, 1997.

Television Appearances; Movies:

Julie Quinlan, *In the Matter of Karen Ann Quinlan*, NBC, 1977.

Ethel Gumm, *Rainbow*, NBC, 1978.

Magda Goebbels, *The Bunker* (also known as *Le bunker*), CBS, 1981.

Matilda West, *Mae West*, ABC, 1982.

Christine Groda, *Love, Mary*, CBS, 1985.

Darlene Marsh, *Toughlove*, ABC, 1985.

Margo, *Toward the Light* (also known as *Go to the Light* and *Go toward the Light*), CBS, 1988.

Martha Robinson, *Rising Son*, TNT, 1990.

Margaret Kinsey, *Love, Lies & Lullabies* (also known as *For the Good of the Child* and *Sad Inheritance*), ABC, 1993.

Ellis Snow, *Shadows of Desire* (also known as *The Devil's Bed*), CBS, 1994.

Judge Edna Burton, *Fighting for My Daughter* (also known as *Fighting for My Daughter: The Anne Dion Story*), ABC, 1995.

Kay Trafero, *In the Blink of an Eye*, ABC, 1996.

Wanda Kirkman, *The Road to Galveston*, USA Network, 1996.

Jennie, *A Christmas Memory* (also known as *Truman Capote's "A Christmas Memory"*), CBS, 1997.

Lillie Dawson, *Alone* (also known as *Horton Foote's "Alone"*), Showtime, 1997.

Sarah Brady, *Inherit the Wind*, Showtime, 1999.

Aunt Hanna, *Possessed*, Showtime, 2000.

Cheryl Visco, *Midwives*, Lifetime, 2001.

Ruth Anne Potter, *The Last Brickmaker in America*, CBS, 2001.

Television Appearances; Specials:

Viola, "Twelfth Night," *Hallmark Hall of Fame*, NBC, 1957.

Miriamne, "Winterset," *Hallmark Hall of Fame*, NBC, 1959.

Caesar and Cleopatra, 1976.

Anne Gilbert, "Promise," *Hallmark Hall of Fame*, CBS, 1986.

Herself, *Dario Argento: An Eye for Horror*, Independent Film Channel, 2000.

Television Appearances; Awards Presentations:

The 25th Annual Academy Awards, NBC, 1953.

Presenter, *The 19th Annual Tony Awards*, WWOR (New York City), 1965.

The 59th Annual Academy Awards, ABC, 1987.

The 49th Annual Golden Globe Awards, TBS, 1992.

Television Appearances; Episodic:

Herself, "Rock Hudson," *This Is Your Life*, NBC, 1952.

Guest, *The Ed Sullivan Show* (also known as *Toast of the Town*), CBS, 1953.

Billie Moore, "Broadway," *The Best of Broadway*, CBS, 1955.

Stacey Spender, "Quality Town," *Robert Montgomery Presents*, CBS, 1955.

Judy Jones, "Winter Dreams," *Front Row Center*, CBS, 1956.

Phoebe Durkin, "The Road That Led Afar," *General Electric Theater*, CBS, 1956.

Ruth Cornelius, "The Deaf Heart," *Studio One*, CBS, 1957.

Ruth McAdam, "The Ninth Day," *Playhouse 90*, CBS, 1957.

"The Changing Ways of Love," *The Seven Lively Arts*, CBS, 1957.

Kirsten Arnesen Clay, "The Days of Wine and Roses," *Playhouse 90*, CBS, 1958.

Cleopatra, "Caesar and Cleopatra," *General Electric Theater*, CBS, 1959.

Eileen Gorman, "The Innocent Assassin," *Desilu Playhouse* (also known as *Westinghouse Desilu Playhouse*), CBS, 1959.

Edna Cartey, "You Can't Have Everything," *The U.S. Steel Hour* (also known as *The United States Steel Hour*), CBS, 1960.

Eurydice, "Legend of Lovers," *The Play of the Week*, syndicated, 1960.

Jessica Galloway, "A Musket for Jessica," *General Electric Theater*, CBS, 1961.

Mystery guest, *What's My Line?*, CBS, 1961.

Kathleen Dooley, "Light Up the Dark Corners," *Ben Casey*, ABC, 1963.

Lee Wiley, "Something about Lee Wiley," *Bob Hope Presents the Chrysler Theater*, NBC, 1963.

Mary Highman, "Howard Running Bear Is a Turtle," *Naked City*, ABC, 1963.

"Mission of Fear," *The U.S. Steel Hour* (also known as *The United States Steel Hour*), CBS, 1963.

Alice Marin, "The Summer House," *Breaking Point*, ABC, 1964.

Alicia Carter, "My Door Is Locked and Bolted," *The Eleventh Hour*, NBC, 1964.

Margaret Sanger, "The Woman Rebel" (also known as "The Life of Margaret Sanger" and "A Woman's Rebel"), *Nova*, PBS, 1976.

Fran Singleton, "Lust et Veritas," *St. Elsewhere*, NBC, 1983.

Fran Singleton, "Newheart," *St. Elsewhere*, NBC, 1983.

Fran Singleton, "Ties That Bind," *St. Elsewhere*, NBC, 1983.

Aunt Neva, "The Burning Man," *The Twilight Zone*, CBS, 1985.

Jessica, "Illusions," *Hotel*, ABC, 1985.

Peggy Shannon, "Murder at the Oasis," *Murder, She Wrote*, CBS, 1985.

Claire Leigh, "The Judge," *Matlock*, NBC, 1986.

Mrs. Davis, "A Gentle Rain," *Beauty and the Beast*, CBS, 1989.

(In archive footage) Claire Leigh, "The Kidnapper," *Matlock*, NBC, 1990.

Marianne, "Guess Who's Coming to Breakfast," *Frasier* (also known as *Dr. Frasier Crane*), NBC, 1994.

Sarah Ross, "Home," *ER* (also known as *Emergency Room*), NBC, 1995.

Assistant district attorney Susan Turner, "The ABCs of Murder," *Diagnosis Murder,* CBS, 1996.

Herself, "Tyrone Power: The Last Idol," *Biography* (also known as *A&E Biography: Tyrone Power*), Arts and Entertainment, 1996.

Sarah Ross, "Take These Broken Wings," *ER* (also known as *Emergency Room*), NBC, 1996.

Annie Doyle, "Venice," *Touched by an Angel,* CBS, 1997.

Jane Waide, "Everybody Says I Love You," *Brother's Keeper,* ABC, 1999.

Mrs. Mulhern, "Dr. Nora," *Frasier* (also known as *Dr. Frasier Crane*), NBC, 1999.

Sharon Timmers, "There but for the Grace of Grace," *Will & Grace,* NBC, 2000.

Dorothy Russ, "Care," *Law & Order: Special Victims Unit* (also known as *Law & Order: SVU* and *Special Victims Unit*), NBC, 2001.

Herself, "Paul Newman," *Bravo Profiles,* Bravo, 2001.

Aunt Sophie, "Where the Boys Are," *State of Grace,* ABC Family Channel, 2002.

Nina Romney, "Forget Me Not," *Dead Like Me,* Showtime, 2004.

Herself, *Scream Queens: The E! True Hollywood Story,* E! Entertainment Television, 2004.

Rose 2005, "Best Friends," *Cold Case,* CBS, 2005.

Television Appearances; Pilots:

Jo Skagska, *Skag,* NBC, 1980.

Catherine Martell, *Twin Peaks* (also known as *Northern Passage*), ABC, 1990.

Wolf Pack, CBS, 1996.

Roberta Stahler, *Partners,* CBS, 1999.

Stage Appearances:

Laura Wingfield, *The Glass Menagerie,* Brooks Atkinson Theatre, New York City, 1965.

Flo Varney, *Rosemary* [and] Candy Simpson, *The Alligators* (double–bill), York Playhouse, New York City, c. 1969.

The Innocents, Ivanhoe Theatre, Chicago, IL, 1970–71.

Marco Polo Sings a Solo, regional production, 1973.

Marion Froude, *Biography,* Manhattan Theatre Club Downstage, New York City, 1980.

Zelda Fitzgerald, *The Last Flapper* (solo show), 1986.

Rena Weeks, *The Destiny of Me,* Circle Repertory Company, Lucille Lortel Theatre, New York City, 1992–93.

Madame Ranyevskaya, *The Cherry Orchard,* Great Lakes Theatre Festival, Cleveland, OH, 1993–94.

Esther Crampton, *Morning's at Seven,* Lyceum Theatre, New York City, 2002, then Ahmanson Theatre, Los Angeles, 2002–2003.

Appeared in other productions, including regional productions of *Macbeth* and *Twelfth Night* (also known as *Twelfth Night, or What You Will*).

Major Tours:

Zelda Fitzgerald, *The Last Flapper* (solo show), c. 1986.

RECORDINGS

Videos:

Herself, *Acting "Carrie"* (short documentary), Metro–Goldwyn–Mayer/United Artists Home Entertainment, 2001.

Herself, *Mel Gibson: The High Octane Birth of a Superstar* (short documentary), Metro–Goldwyn–Mayer Home Entertainment, 2001.

(In archive footage) Herself, *The Hustler: The Inside Story* (short documentary), Twentieth Century–Fox Home Entertainment, 2002.

OTHER SOURCES

Periodicals:

People Weekly, April 30, 1990, p. 27.

LEGGIO, Jerry 1935–

PERSONAL

Born September 23, 1935, in Baton Rouge, LA; married Gloria, November 7, 1959. *Education:* Louisiana State University, B.A., speech/psychology.

Career: Actor. Appeared in television commercials, including ads for Holiday Inn, Lee Jeans, and Cracker Barrel. Previously worked as a personnel administrator and as a research analyst for Gulf South Research Institute.

CREDITS

Stage Appearances:

Boolie, *Driving Miss Daisy,* Cabaret Theatre, Baton Rouge, LA, 1990.

Ben Chambers, *Norman, Is That You?,* Cabaret Theatre, 1993.

Appeared as Erwin Leeds, *Subject to Change,* Sol Weisenheimer, *Drop Dead,* Officer Welch, *Rumors,* all at Cabaret Theatre; Senex and Miles Gloriosus, *Funny Thing Happened on the Way to the Forum,* Col Jessep, *A Few Good Men,* Sen Malbeaux, *Home Spin,* Judge Bastardson, *Sly Fox,* Doc, *Westside Story,* Henry Drummond, *Inherit the Wind,* Herb Tucker, *I Oughta be in Pictures,* Lieutenant Shrank, *Westside Story,* Virgil Blessing, *Bus Stop,* Sheriff Dodd, *Best Little Whorehouse in Texas,* Cap'm Andy, *Show Boat,* Captain Von Trapp, *Sound of Music,* Watson Frye, *Close Ties,* Lancelot, *Camelot,* Desmonde, *Happy Time,* Dr. Carrasco, *Man of LaMancha,* Lou Tanner, *Gingerbread Lady,* Peter Marriott, *Sound of Murder,* Bert Jefferson, *The Man Who Came to Dinner,* Phil Romano, *That Championship Season,* Hajj, *Kismet,* King Arthur, *Camelot,* Stanley Kowalsky, *Streetcar Named Desire,* Bertram Cates, *Inherit the Wind,* Allen Baker, *Come Blow Your Horn,* Paul Sevine, *Shot in the Dark,* Bernie Dodd, *Country Girl,* Sky Masterson, *Guys and Dolls,* Nerone, *Devil's Advocate,* Thomas Cromwell, *Man for All Seasons,* Bill Sykes, *Oliver,* Billy Bigelow, *Carousel,* all Baton Rouge Little Theatre; G. Patton, *All the King's Men,* Swine Palace Productions; Sir Charles Clarke, *Gross Indecency, the Three Trials of Oscar Wilde;* Reader D, *The Hollow Crown,* Sudden Theatre Group; President Jefferson, *PASSAGES: A Story of Lewis and Clark;* Miles Gloriosus, *Funny Thing Happened On the Way to the Forum,* Dr. Chumley, *Harvey,* Julian Winston, *Cactus Flower,* King of Siam, *The King and I,* Sheriff Oglesby, *The Death and Life of Sneaky Fitch,* Captain Von Trapp, *Sound of Music,* all Aubin Lane Dinner Theatre; King, *Sleeping Beauty;* Paul Verral, *Born Yesterday,* The Dinner Theatre; Jack/George, *You Know I Can't Hear You When the Water's Running,* Skyline Theatre; Adam, *Creation of the World and Other Business;* Moony, *Moony's Kid Don't Cry,* Opelousas Little Theatre; Bonario, *Volpone,* and Linzman, *Lilliom,* both Louisiana State University Theatre.

Film Appearances:

(Uncredited) Doctor, *Hush ... Hush, Sweet Charlotte* (also known as *Cross of Iron* and *What Ever Happened to Cousin Charlotte?*), 1964.

(Uncredited) Doctor, *Hurry Sundown,* Paramount, 1967.

Guard, *Sounder,* Twentieth Century–Fox, 1972.

Mr. Bonnard, *Sister, Sister,* New World, 1987.

(Uncredited) Photographer, *Blaze,* Buena Vista, 1989.

(Uncredited) Doctor, *Heaven's Prisoners,* New Line Cinema, 1996.

Television Appearances; Movies:

Carpetbagger, *The Autobiography of Miss Jane Pittman,* 1974.

Mr. Valchex, *The Deadly Tower* (also known as *Sniper*), NBC, 1975.

Jack Williamson, *The Life and Assassination of the Kingfish* (also known as *Every Man a King*), NBC, 1977.

Coach, *Superdome,* 1978.

First policeman, *Murder at the Mardi Gras,* CBS, 1978.

(Uncredited) Businessman, *Big Bob Johnson and His Fantastic Speed Circus,* NBC, 1978.

Farmer, *Rascals and Robbers: The Secret Adventures of Tom Sawyer and Huck Finn,* CBS, 1982.

Charlie, *Hot Pursuit,* NBC, 1984.

Sixth reporter, *Margaret Bourke–White* (also known as *Double Exposure*), TNT, 1989.

Dr. Melvin, *False Witness* (also known as *Double Exposure*), NBC, 1989.

Judge Altzo, *Doublecrossed,* HBO, 1991.

Mayor Mann, *The Ernest Green Story,* The Disney Channel, 1993.

Deputy coroner, *House of Secrets* (also known as *Conspiracy of Terror*), NBC, 1993.

Morris McGonigal, *Jake Lassiter: Justice on the Bayou,* NBC, 1995.

Farley's aide, *Kingfish: A Story of Huey P. Long,* TNT, 1995.

Warden, *Old Man* (also known as *William Faulkner's "Old Man"*), CBS, 1997.

Henry, *The Badge,* Starz!, 2001.

Ackerman, *Malpractice,* Lifetime, 2002.

Dr. Harns, *Torn Apart,* Lifetime, 2004.

Doctor, *Infidelity,* Lifetime, 2004.

Television Appearances; Series:

Harry, *In the Heat of the Night,* NBC, 1988.

Judge Hopewell, *Sweet Justice,* NBC, 1994.

Television Appearances; Pilots:

Preacher, *The Night Rider,* ABC, 1979.

Television Appearances; Miniseries:

Coleman's third man, *A Woman Called Moses,* NBC, 1978.

Varnedoe, *Beulah Land,* NBC, 1980.

District attorney, *The Mississippi,* CBS, 1983.

Banker, *Louisiana* (also known as *Louisiane*), Cinemax, 1984.

(Uncredited) Policeman, *If Tomorrow Comes,* CBS, 1986.

Television Appearances; Episodic:

"An Eye for an Eye," *Dangerous Curves,* CBS, 1992.

David Larkin, "Deathwatch," *Dangerous Curves,* CBS, 1992.

Governor, "Luther's Temptation," *Orleans,* CBS, 1997.

Television Appearances; Specials:

Banker, *Hollywood Gets MADD* (documentary), TBS, 1993.

OTHER SOURCES

Electronic:

Jerry Leggio Official Site, http://www.sremploy.org/, April 21, 2005.

LEIGH, Jenna
   See GREEN, Jenna Leigh

LEITCH, Ione Skye
   See SKYE, Ione

LEMCHE, Kris 1978–
   (Kristopher Lemche)

PERSONAL

Full name, Kristopher Lemche; born 1978, in Brampton, Ontario, Canada; mother, a schoolteacher; father, a proprietor of a heating business; brother of Matthew Lemche (an actor).

Addresses: *Agent*—The Gersh Agency, 232 N. Canon Dr., Beverly Hills, CA 90210; Great North Artists Management Inc., 350 Duponte, Toronto M5R 1V9, Canada. *Manager*—Evolution Entertainment, 901 N. Highland Ave., Los Angeles, CA 90038.

Career: Actor.

Awards, Honors: Gemini Award, best performance by an actor in a featured supporting role in a dramatic series, Academy of Canadian Cinema and Television, 1998, for *Emily of New Moon.*

CREDITS

Television Appearances; Series:
Zed Goldhawk, *Flash Forward,* ABC, 1996.
Perry Miller, *Emily of New Moon,* CBC, 1998.
Lucas Zank, *My Guide to Becoming a Rock Star,* The WB, 2002.
Cute boy/God, a recurring role, *Joan of Arcadia,* CBS, 2003–2004.

Television Appearances; Movies:
Shane Roberson, *Children of Fortune,* CBS, 2000.
Malachy, *Bailey's Mistake,* ABC, 2001.
Scott, *The Last Casino,* 2004.

Television Appearances; Miniseries:
Emile, *Joan of Arc* (also known as *Jeanne d'Arc*), CBS, 1999.

Television Appearances; Episodic:
Sticks, "The Scarecrow Walks at Midnight," *Goosebumps,* Fox, 1996.
Rodney Covington, "The Goody Two–Shoes People," *Eerie, Indiana: The Other Dimension,* NBC, 1998.
Greg Hillinger, "Fuzzy Logic," *La Femme Nikita,* USA Network, 1998.
Greg Hillinger, "Outside the Box," *La Femme Nikita,* USA Network, 1999.
Greg Hillinger, "Any Means Necessary," *La Femme Nikita,* USA Network, 1999.
Greg Hillinger, "Three Eyed Turtle," *La Femme Nikita,* USA Network, 1999.
Clinton, "People Who Don't Care about Anything," *Twitch City,* CBC and Bravo, 2000.
Clinton, "The Life of Reilly," *Twitch City,* CBC and Bravo, 2000.
Greg Hillinger, "Line in the Sand," *La Femme Nikita,* USA Network, 2000.
RI:SE, 2002.
"Murder.com," *The Division,* Lifetime, 2003.
Randy Southbrook, "Sticks and Stones," *Dragnet* (also known as *L.A. Dragnet*), ABC, 2003.

Television Appearances; Specials:
Humphrey Newton, *Newton: A Tale of Two Isaacs,* HBO, 1998.

Television Appearances; Pilots:
Cute boy/God, *Joan of Arcadia,* CBS, 2003.

Film Appearances:
(As Kristopher Lemche) Peter, *Teen Knight,* Full Moon, 1998.
Sean, *Johnny,* The Asylum, 1999.
Noel Dichter, *eXistenZ,* Dimension Films, 1999.
Sam, *Ginger Snaps,* Lions Gate Films, 2000.
Saint Jude, Behavior, 2000.
Decker, *Knockaround Guys,* New Line Cinema, 2001.
Rex, *My Little Eye,* United International, 2001.
Patrick, *State's Evidence,* Cush, 2004.
Caleb, *A Simple Curve,* Domino, 2005.
Keith, *Vinyl,* Romano, 2005.

LEVITAN, Steven

PERSONAL

Born in Chicago, IL; married Krista; children: Hannah, Alexa, Griffin. *Education:* University of Wisconsin, B.A., journalism, 1984.

Career: Producer, writer, and director. Previously worked as a television news reporter, Madison, WI, and at Leo Burnett Advertising, Chicago, IL, 1987–90.

Awards, Honors: Humanitas Prize, 30 minute category, Television Producer of the Year Award in Episodic (with others), PGA Golden Laurel Awards, 1996, for *Frasier;* Emmy Award nomination, outstanding writing for a comedy series, 1999, and Golden Globe Award nominations, for *Just Shoot Me;* Ursa Major Award, 2002, for *Greg the Bunny;* Emmy Award nomination, for *The Larry Sanders Show;* People's Choice Award, best new comedy, for *Stark Raving Mad;* also won a CableACE Award and Writer's Guild nomination.

CREDITS

Television Executive Producer; Series:
Men Behaving Badly, NBC, 1996.
Just Shoot Me!, NBC, 1997.
Stark Raving Mad, NBC, 1999.
Greg the Bunny, Fox, 2002.
Oliver Beene, Fox, 2003.
Stacked, Fox, 2005.

Television Director; Episodic:
"Rescue Me," *Just Shoot Me!,* NBC, 1998.
"Slow Donnie," *Just Shoot Me!,* NBC, 1999.
"The Odd Couple: Parts 1 & 2," *Just Shoot Me!,* NBC, 1999.
"Fast Times at Finchmont High," *Just Shoot Me!,* NBC, 2000.
"My Bodyguard" (also known as "Guarding Tess"), *Stark Raving Mad,* NBC, 2000.
"The Grade," *Stark Raving Mad,* NBC, 2000.
"You Wanna?," *Yes, Dear,* CBS, 2000.
"All I Want for Christmas Is My Dead Uncle's Cash," *Yes, Dear,* CBS, 2000.

Television Director; Pilots:
Stacked, Fox, 2005.

Television Co–Executive Producer; Series:
Wings, NBC, 1990.
The Larry Sanders Show, HBO, 1992.

Television Co–Executive Producer; Movies:
With You In Spirit, ABC, 2003.

Television Co–Executive Producer; Pilots:
Say Uncle, CBS, 2001.

WRITINGS

Television Episodes:
Wings, NBC, 1991–95.
"Seat of Power," *Frasier,* NBC, 1994.
"Miserable," *The Critic,* ABC, 1994.

"L.A. Jay," *The Critic,* ABC, 1994.
(With Mary Forbes) "Roseanne's Return," *The Larry Sanders Show,* HBO, 1995.
(With Garry Shandling) "Nothing Personal," *The Larry Sanders Show,* HBO, 1995.
"Breaking the Ice," *Frasier,* NBC, 1995.
"It's Hard to Say Goodbye If You Won't Leave," *Frasier,* NBC, 1996.
"Come Lie with Me," *Frasier,* NBC, 1996.
"After Midnight," *Men Behaving Badly,* NBC, 1997.
"Back Issues," *Just Shoot Me!,* NBC, 1997.
"Your Dreams," *Just Shoot Me!,* NBC, 1997.
"Old Boyfriends," *Just Shoot Me!,* NBC, 1997.
"My Dinner with Woody," *Just Shoot Me!,* NBC, 1997.
"Rescue Me," *Just Shoot Me!,* NBC, 1998.
"Slow Donnie," *Just Shoot Me!,* NBC, 1999.
"The Stalker," *Stark Raving Mad,* NBC, 1999.
"The Dance," *Stark Raving Mad,* NBC, 1999.
(With Spencer Chinoy and Dan Milano) "Welcome to Sweetknuckle Junction," *Greg the Bunny,* Fox, 2002.
"The Singing Mailman," *Greg the Bunny,* Fox, 2002.
"Father and Son Reunion," *Greg the Bunny,* Fox, 2002.
"Future Issues," *Just Shoot Me!,* NBC, 2003.
"Space Race," *Oliver Beene,* Fox, 2003.
(With Howard Gewirtz) "Dibs," *Oliver Beene,* Fox, 2004.

Television Pilots:
Stark Raving Mad, NBC, 1999.
Stacked, Fox, 2005.

Also (with Dan Milano and Spencer Chinoy) wrote the unaired pilot for *Greg the Bunny,* Fox.

Television Stories; Episodic:
"Hello Goodbye," *Just Shoot Me,* NBC, 1999.
(With Robert Leddy, Jr.) "The Singing Mailman," *Greg the Bunny,* Fox, 2002.

Television Movies:
With You In Spirit, ABC, 2003.

Television Music; Series:
Theme lyrics, *Stark Raving Mad,* NBC, 1999.

LEWIS, Geoffrey 1935–
(Geoffery Lewis, Jeoffery Lewis)

PERSONAL

Born January 1 (some sources cite July 31), 1935; married Glenis Batley (a graphic artist; divorced, 1975); married Paula Hochhalter; children: ten, including Juliette (first marriage; an actress), Deirdre (an actress), Lightfield (an actor and writer), Peter (an actor), Matthew (an actor), and Brandy (a producer). *Religion:* Scientologist.

Addresses: *Agent*—Tom Harrison, Diverse Talent Group, 1875 Century Park E., Suite 2250, Los Angeles, CA 90067.

Career: Actor. Celestial Navigations (storytellers and performance artists), member.

Awards, Honors: Golden Globe Award nomination, best supporting actor in a series, miniseries, or television movie, 1981, for *Flo;* Annual CableACE Award nomination, National Cable Television Association, best actor in a dramatic series, 1985, for *Maximum Security.*

CREDITS

Film Appearances:
Man in park, *The Fat Black Pussycat,* 1963.
Francis Rapture, *Welcome Home, Soldier Boys* (also known as *Five Days Home*), 1971.
Hobbs, *Bad Company,* Paramount, 1972.
Russ Sterve (some sources cite Caldwell), *The Culpepper Cattle Company* (also known as *Dust, Sweat, and Gunpowder*), Twentieth Century–Fox, 1972.
Harry Pierpoint, *Dillinger,* American International Pictures, 1973.
Stacey Bridges, *High Plains Drifter,* Universal, 1973.
(Uncredited) leader of Wild Bunch, *My Name is Nobody* (also known as *Lonesome Gun, Mein Name ist Nobody, Il mio nome e Nessuno,* and *Mon nom est personne*), 1973.
Eddie Goody, *Thunderbolt and Lightfoot,* United Artists, 1974.
Hamp, *Macon County Line,* 1974.
Damion Gummere, *The Wind and the Lion,* United Artists, 1975.
Captain Aaron Mosely, *Lucky Lady,* Twentieth Century–Fox, 1975.
Wilson Shears, *Smile,* United Artists, 1975.
Newt, *The Great Waldo Pepper,* Universal, 1975.
Zenas Morro, *The Return of a Man Called Horse,* United Artists, 1976.
Orville Boggs, *Every Which Way But Loose,* Warner Bros., 1978.
Doubletten–Snake (also cited as 2 Strike Snake), *Sella d'argento* (also known as *The Man in the Silver Saddle, Silver Saddle,* and *They Died with Their Boots On*), 1978.
Truck driver, *Tilt,* Warner Bros., 1979.
Walter Stoll, *Tom Horn,* 1980.
Dr. Kline, *Human Experiments* (also known as *Beyond the Gate*), Crown, 1980.

Trapper, *Heaven's Gate* (also known as *Johnson County Wars*), United Artists, 1980.
John Arlington, *Bronco Billy,* Warner Bros., 1980.
Orville Boggs, *Any Which Way You Can,* Warner Bros., 1980.
Scalp hunter, *Shoot the Sun Down,* 1981.
Joe Butler, *I, the Jury,* Twentieth Century–Fox, 1982.
Dave Dante, *10 to Midnight,* Cannon, 1983.
Dr. Carter, *Night of the Comet,* Atlantic Releasing, 1984.
Hard Case Williams, *Lust in the Dust,* New World, 1985.
Ralph Rizzo, *Stitches,* 1985.
Steve Smith, *Time Out,* 1987.
Mr. Johnson, *Catch Me if You Can,* Management Company Entertainment Group, 1989.
Ku Klux Klan leader, *Fletch Lives,* Universal, 1989.
Dennis, *Out of the Dark,* New Line Cinema, 1989.
Ricky Z, *Pink Cadillac,* Warner Bros., 1989.
(Uncredited) Captain Schroeder, *Tango & Cash,* Warner Bros., 1989.
Paint It Black, Live Entertainment, 1990.
Michael Kahn, *Disturbed,* International Video Entertainment, 1991.
Frank Avery, *Double Impact,* Columbia, 1991.
Terry McKeen, *The Lawnmower Man* (also known as *Stephen King's "The Lawnmower Man"* and *Virtual Wars*), New Line Cinema, 1992.
Hitchcock, *Wishman,* 1992.
Drugstore owner, *Point of No Return* (also known as *The Assassin, La Femme Nikita, Nikita,* and *The Specialist*), Warner Bros., 1993.
Chief Wayne Stark, *The Man without a Face,* Warner Bros., 1993.
Kerrigan, *Only the Strong* (also known as *Street Fighters*), Twentieth Century–Fox, 1993.
God's janitor (voice), *The Janitor,* 1993.
Sheriff Cepeda, *Army of One* (also known as *Joshua Tree*), 1993.
Matthew Wicker/Eugene, *Maverick,* Warner Bros., 1994.
(As Geoffery Lewis) Uncle Rex Carver, *Last Resort* (also known as *National Lampoon's "Last Resort"* and *National Lampoon's "Scuba School"*), Rose & Ruby Productions, 1994.
Shin–ichi, *The Dragon Gate,* Century Group, 1994.
Heath, *White Fang 2: Myth of the White Wolf* (also known as *White Fang 2*), Buena Vista, 1994.
Cyclops Baby (short film), 1996.
Willy, *American Perfekt,* American Perfekt Productions, Inc., 1997.
Luther Driggers, *Midnight in the Garden of Good and Evil,* Warner Bros., 1997.
First guest, *The Prophet's Game,* Moonstone Entertainment, 1999.
Abner Mercer, *The Way of the Gun,* Artisan Entertainment, 2000.
Highway 395, Creative Light Worldwide, 2000.
Browner, *Sunstorm,* First Look Home Entertainment, 2001.

Geoff, *Song of the Vampire* (also known as *Vampire Resurrection*), 2001, Shadow Entertainment, 2003.

Stanley Melnick, *A Light in the Darkness,* Bearsmouth Entertainment, 2002.

Principal Zaylor, *The New Guy,* Columbia, 2002.

(As Jeoffery Lewis) Bolton, *Brazilian Brawl,* York Entertainment, 2003.

Melvin Reeves, *Mind Games* (also known as *Something Borrowed*), 2003, Ventura Distribution, 2005.

Walters, *May Day,* 2003.

Old man, *Old Man Music* (short film), Ez Company Productions/Jaded Craze, 2004.

Sullivan, *Renegade* (also known as *Blueberry* and *Blueberry: L'experience secrete*), Columbia TriStar, 2004.

Lucky Marshall, *Formosa,* High Road Productions, 2005.

Crazy Old Martin, *Moving McAllister,* Camera 40 Productions/Revel Entertainment, 2005.

Roy Sullivan, *The Devil's Rejects,* Lions Gate Films, 2005.

Television Appearances; Series:
Earl Tucker, *Flo,* CBS, 1979–80.
Amos Tucker, *Gun Shy,* CBS, 1983.
Lucas Crosby, *Falcon Crest,* 1984.
Frank Murphy, *Maximum Security,* 1984–85.
Willis P. Dunleevy, *Land's End,* syndicated, 1995–96.

Television Appearances; Miniseries:
Bishop Fisher, *The Six Wives of Henry VIII,* 1971.
Ed Duncan, *Attack on Terror: The FBI versus the Ku Klux Klan* (also known as *Attack on Terror: The FBI vs. the Ku Klux Klan*), 1975.
Sheriff Bogardus, *Centennial,* 1978.
Mike Ryerson, *Salem's Lot* (also known as *Blood Thirst, Salem's Lot: The Miniseries,* and *Salem's Lot: The Movie*), 1979.
Lynch, *The Gambler V: Playing For Keeps,* CBS, 1994.
Eli, *Rough Riders* (also known as *Teddy Roosevelt and the Rough Riders*), TNT, 1997.

Television Appearances; Movies:
Lawrence Burrifors, *Moon of the Wolf,* 1972.
Roper, *Honky Tonk,* 1974.
Archie, *The Great Ice Rip–Off,* 1974.
Jason McCoy, *The Gun and the Pulpit,* 1974.
Dr. Crandon, *The Great Houdini* (also known as *The Great Houdinis*), 1976.
Dutton, *The New Daughters of Joshua Cabe,* 1976.
Red Bayliss, *The Deadly Triangle,* 1977.
Mr. Eckert, *The Hunted Lady,* 1977.
Albert Cavanaugh (The Snowman), *When Every Day Was the Fourth of July,* 1978.
Harold Tigner, *Samurai,* 1979.
Dr. Bill Janowski, *The Jericho Mile,* 1979.
Reverend Meeks, *Belle Starr,* 1980.

Captain Charley Rawlins, *Life of the Party: The Story of Beatrice,* 1982.

Major Cooper Ashbury, *The Shadow Riders* (also known as *Louis L'Amour's "The Shadow Riders"*), 1982.

Sheriff Gilbert Johnson, *September Gun,* 1983.

Janus, *The Return of the Man from U.N.C.L.E.* (also known as *The Fifteen Years Later Affair*), 1983.

John Tuckerman, *Travis McGee* (also known as *Travis McGee: The Empty Copper Sea*), 1983.

Scooter Lee, *Stormin' Home,* CBS, 1985.

Ed Porter, *Dallas: The Early Years* (also known as *The Early Years*), CBS, 1986.

Professor Alan Jeffries, *The Annihilator,* NBC, 1986.

Dirty Jerry, *Spot Marks the X,* 1986.

Del Rains, *Desert Rats,* NBC, 1988.

Ben Catlin, *Pancho Barnes* (also known as *The Happy Bottom Riding Club* and *The Pancho Barnes Story*), CBS, 1988.

Oliver Ostrow, *Desperado: The Outlaw Wars,* NBC, 1989.

Bodine, *Gunsmoke: The Last Apache* (also known as *Gunsmoke II: The Last Apache*), CBS, 1990.

Frank Harper, *Matters of the Heart,* USA Network, 1990.

Matt Corman, *Day of Reckoning* (also known as *The Wisdom Keeper*), NBC, 1994.

J. D., *Kansas,* ABC, 1995.

Parmenter, *When the Dark Man Calls,* USA Network, 1995.

Draper Jewett, *An Occasional Hell,* HBO, 1996.

Stubbs, "The Graveyard Rats," *Trilogy of Terror II,* USA Network, 1996.

Sloan, *Five Aces,* Cinemax, 1999.

Mr. Spruill, "A Painted House" (also known as "John Grisham's 'A Painted House'"), *Hallmark Hall of Fame,* CBS, 2003.

Raymond McPheron, "Plainsong," *Hallmark Hall of Fame,* CBS, 2004.

Gus Ferguson, *The Fallen Ones,* Sci–Fi Channel, 2005.

Television Appearances; Pilots:
Officer Tilwick, *Mork & Mindy,* 1978.
Koup, *Skyward Christmas,* NBC, 1981.
Rudy Hopper, *Poor Richard,* CBS, 1984.
Andy Johnson, *The Johnsons Are Home,* CBS, 1988.
Joe Haaksman, *The Underworld,* NBC, 1997.
Paul, *My Life with Men,* ABC, 2003.

Television Appearances; Specials:
Bill, "Blue Suits," *NBC Presents the AFI Comedy Special,* NBC, 1987.
The Smothers Brothers Comedy Special, CBS, 1988.
The Smothers Brothers Thanksgiving Special, CBS, 1988.
The Smothers Brothers Comedy Hour ... Lonesome Doves and Lonely Guys, CBS, 1989.
The Smothers Brothers Comedy Hour ... Fun 'n' Games, CBS, 1989.

The Smothers Brothers Comedy Hour ... Dangerous Comedy Liaisons, CBS, 1989.

Pirate story teller, *Disney's Greatest Hits on Ice,* CBS, 1994.

Interviewee, "Clint Eastwood: Out of the Shadows," *American Masters,* PBS, 2000.

Television Appearances; Episodic:

"Don't Interrupt," *Alfred Hitchcock Presents,* 1958.

Voice, "The Radio Ham," *Hancock's Half Hour,* 1961.

Dr. Geers, *A for Andromeda,* 1961.

Dr. Geers, *The Andromeda Breakthrough,* 1962.

Rogers, "A Matter of Faith," *Bonanza,* NBC, 1970.

Scott Russell, "The Russell Incident," *The Young Lawyers,* ABC, 1970.

Gus, "The Ninety–nine Mile Circle," *Then Came Bronson,* 1970.

Second bum, "Spokes," *The High Chaparral,* 1970.

Bates, "Los Angeles 2017," *The Name of the Game,* 1971.

Patch, "Stagecoach Seven," *Alias Smith and Jones,* ABC, 1971.

Al, "The Bounty Hunter," *Alias Smith and Jones,* ABC, 1971.

Roederer, "Safe Deposit," *Cade's County,* 1971.

Ernest, "Days Beyond Recall," *Mannix,* 1971.

George, "To Kill a Guinea Pig," *Cannon,* CBS, 1972.

James Bancroft, "Nobody Beats the House," *Cannon,* CBS, 1972.

Harris, "School of Fear," *The Streets of San Francisco,* ABC, 1972.

Deputy Burk Stover, "What Happened at the XST?," *Alias Smith and Jones,* ABC, 1972.

Kaye Lusk, "Committed," *Mission: Impossible,* CBS, 1972.

Proctor, "Kidnap," *Mission: Impossible,* CBS, 1972.

Killer, "Cry Silence," *Mannix,* 1972.

Lafitte, "Hostage!," *Gunsmoke,* 1972.

Johnson, "Chains," *Kung Fu,* ABC, 1973.

Sheriff Otis Dale, "Murder–Go–Round," *Barnaby Jones,* 1973.

"Cry Uncle," *Mod Squad,* 1973.

Elwood Dobbs, "The Runaway," *The Waltons,* 1974.

Gates, "Sidewinder," *Police Woman,* 1975.

Senator John Elton, "Mayday," *Harry O,* ABC, 1975.

Jack Bonelli, "The Killing Ground," *S.W.A.T.,* ABC, 1975.

Alan "Monk" Philos, "The Fix," *Starsky and Hutch,* 1975.

Harris, "School of Fear," *The Streets of San Francisco,* 1975.

Vern Spear, "Farewell, Mary Jane," *Police Woman,* 1975.

Richie, "Journey to Oblivion," *The Rookies,* 1976.

Deputy Barnes, "A Call to Arms," *Alice,* 1976.

Andy Kline, "Bonnie and McCloud," *McCloud,* 1976.

Sam Galender, "The Bully Boys," *Little House on the Prairie,* 1976.

"The Death of a Dream," *Police Woman,* 1976.

Title role, "Orkus," *Ark II,* 1976.

Danzig, "Mirror Image," *Hunter,* CBS, 1977.

Mr. Gunther, "Honeymoon Hotel," *Laverne & Shirley,* 1977.

Charlie Wynn, "Bigfoot V," *The Six Million Dollar Man,* 1977.

Sheriff, "Henhouse," *Lou Grant,* 1977.

Earl, "The Captives," *Barnaby Jones,* 1977.

Commander Chris Nolan, "Deep Cover," *Hawaii Five–0,* 1977.

Admiral Flint, "The Good, the Bad, and the Ficus," *Quark,* 1978.

Weldon Gray, "Photo Finish," *The Amazing Spider–Man,* 1979.

"Wild Bill" McEnvoy, "Tuned for Destruction," *A Man Called Sloane,* 1979.

Waldon "Wally" Gannus, "The Killing Point," *Barnaby Jones,* 1980.

John Kirk, "Siege," *B. J. and the Bear,* 1980.

Jim Lawrence, "Dogs," *Lou Grant,* 1980.

Barney Broomick, "Hallie," *Bret Maverick,* NBC, 1982.

Cole Younger, "The Older Brothers," *Little House on the Prairie,* 1983.

Claude Cainmaker, "Mama's Silver," *Mama's Family,* 1983.

Claude Cainmaker, "Alien Marriage," *Mama's Family,* 1983.

Sheriff Kyle C. Tenney, "A Clear and Present Danger," *Blue Thunder,* ABC, 1984.

Lloyd DeWitt, "The Return of Luther Gillis," *Magnum, P.I.,* CBS, 1984.

Kale Sykes, "Semi–Friendly Persuasion," *The A–Team,* NBC, 1984.

Colonel Mack Stoddard, "The Doctor Is Out," *The A–Team,* NBC, 1984.

Louis, "Villa's Gold," *The Yellow Rose,* 1984.

Honest Eddy, "Another Song for Christmas," *Highway to Heaven,* 1984.

Harry Patterson, "Promised Land," *Spenser: For Hire,* 1985.

Matt Barris (some sources cite Garrett), "King of the Stuntmen," *The Fall Guy,* 1985.

Cooper, "The Middle of Somewhere," *Shadow Chasers,* ABC, 1985.

Peter Sacker, "Sour Grapes," *Scarecrow and Mrs. King,* CBS, 1985.

Peter Sacker, "Utopia Now," *Scarecrow and Mrs. King,* CBS, 1985.

Rileback, "Until The Fat Lady Sings," *Wildside,* ABC, 1985.

Gus "Gus the geek" Zimmer/Donald Gilbert, "I Never Wanted to Go to France, Anyway," *Magnum, P.I.,* CBS, 1986.

David Crane, "Silent World," *MacGyver,* ABC, 1986.

Dan, "One for the Road," *Amazing Stories,* 1986.

Lester Grinshaw, "No Accounting for Murder," *Murder, She Wrote,* CBS, 1987.

Dr. Davis Jackson, "Mary Jo's Dad Dates Charlene," *Designing Women,* 1987.

Chuck, "Empty Nests," *The Golden Girls,* 1987.

Chuck/Mr. Fix–It, "Empty Nests," *Empty Nest,* 1987.

Slydel Toomes, "Graveyard Shift," *J. J. Starbuck,* 1987.

Kenny Oats, "Who Threw the Barbitals in Mrs. Fletcher's Chowder?," *Murder, She Wrote,* CBS, 1988.

Norman Tedge, "The Case of the Willing Parrot," *Mathnet,* 1988.

Mickey Morrison, "The Investigation: Parts 1 & 2," *Matlock,* 1988.

Norman Tedge, *Square One TV,* 1988.

"The Burial Ground," *Paradise,* 1989.

Captain Jenkins, "Brotherly Love: Parts 1 & 2," *In the Heat of the Night,* 1990.

Hank Crenshaw, "Deadly Misunderstanding," *Murder, She Wrote,* 1990.

Rooney Wilson, "Dead Dogs Tell No Tales," *Shades of L.A.,* 1991.

Beau Langley, "Badge of Honor," *Walker, Texas Ranger,* CBS, 1994.

Roger Yates, "What You Don't Know Can Kill You," *Murder, She Wrote,* 1996.

Alfred Fellig, "Tithonus," *The X–Files,* Fox, 1999.

Himself, "The Films of Clint Eastwood," *The Directors,* c. 2000.

Wylie Johnson, "Brothers," *Pensacola: Wings of Gold,* syndicated, 2000.

Martin Hurkle, "Generations," *The Huntress,* USA Network, 2001.

Calvin and homeless man, "Private Dave," *Titus,* Fox, 2001.

Freddy the Fish, "Dey Got de Degas," *Thieves,* ABC, 2001.

Leyton Scott, "Rapture," *Odyssey 5,* Showtime, 2002.

Mr. Copeland, "You Belong to Me," *The Guardian,* CBS, 2003.

Uncle Bill, "Rock Bottom," *Dawson's Creek,* The WB, 2003.

Bill Braxton, "Goodbye, Yellow Brick Road," *Dawson's Creek,* The WB, 2003.

Dr. Marcus Grayson, "Sofia Lopez," *Nip/Tuck,* FX Channel, 2003.

Nathan "Jonesy" Jones in 2004, "The Letter," *Cold Case,* CBS, 2004.

Pops Castille, "New Orleans," *Las Vegas,* NBC, 2004.

Mr. Harmon, "Unbroken," *The Mountain,* The WB, 2004.

Leyton Scott, "Fossil," *Odyssey 5,* Showtime, 2004.

Butch Perkins, "In the Dark," *Law & Order: Criminal Intent,* NBC, 2004.

Kirstie's dad, "Crack for Good," *Fat Actress,* Showtime, 2005.

Appeared as Harry, *The Oldest Rookie,* CBS.

Stage Appearances:

Celestial Navigations, Matrix Theatre, Los Angeles, 1984.

Once appeared in summer stock productions at Plymouth Theatre in Massachusetts.

Television Director; Series:

Land's End, syndicated, 1995–96.

RECORDINGS

Videos:

A Woman's Guide to Firearms, Lyon House Productions, 1987.

Macon County Line: 25 Years down the Road, Anchor Bay Entertainment, 2000.

Albums:

(With Celestial Navigations) *Chapter II,* K–tel International, 1989.

WRITINGS

Screenplays:

(As Jeoffery Lewis) *Brazilian Brawl,* York Entertainment, 2003.

Television Series:

Land's End, syndicated, 1995–96.

ADAPTATIONS

The 1993 film *The Janitor* was based on a story by Lewis.

LIMA, Kevin 1962(?)–

PERSONAL

Born c. 1962; married Brenda Chapman (a director and writer).

Addresses: *Agent*—Endeavor, 9601 Wilshire Blvd., 3rd Floor, Beverly Hills, CA 90210.

Career: Director and producer.

Awards, Honors: Annie Award nomination, International Animated Film Society, outstanding direction in an animated feature production (with Chris Buck), 1999, for *Tarzan;* Directors Guild of America Award, outstanding direction in children's programs (with others), 2004, for "Eloise at Christmastime," *The Wonderful World of Disney.*

CREDITS

Film Director:
A Goofy Movie (animated), Buena Vista, 1995.
Tarzan (animated), Buena Vista/Walt Disney, 1999.
102 Dalmatians, Buena Vista, 2000.

Film Work; Other:
Animation director and character designer, *The Brave Little Toaster* (animated), 1987.
Character animator, *Oliver & Company* (animated), Buena Vista, 1988.
Character designer, *The Little Mermaid* (animated), Buena Vista, 1989.

Film Appearances:
Voice of Lester, *A Goofy Movie* (animated), Buena Vista, 1995.

Television Coproducer and Director; Movies:
Eloise at the Plaza, ABC, 2003.
"Eloise at Christmastime," *The Wonderful World of Disney,* ABC, 2003.

Television Director; Episodic:
Director for the animated series *Goof Troop* (also known as *Disney's "Goof Troop"*), ABC; and *The Legend of Tarzan* (also known as *Disney's "The Legend of Tarzan"*), UPN and syndicated.

ADAPTATIONS

The animated films *Aladdin* and *Oliver & Company* were based on stories by Lima.

OTHER SOURCES

Periodicals:
Cinefantastique, August, 1999, p. 20.

LIPNICKI, Jonathan 1990–

PERSONAL

Full name, Jonathan William Lipnicki; born October 22, 1990, in Westlake Village, CA; son of Joseph and Rhonda (maiden name, Rosen) Lipnicki; brother of Al-

exis Gabrielle Lipnicki (an actress). Religion: Jewish. *Religion:* Jewish. *Avocational Interests:* Basketball, skate–boarding.

Addresses: *Agent*—Mitchell Gossett, Cunningham/ Escott/Slevin & Doherty, 10635 Santa Monica Blvd., Suite 140, Los Angeles, CA 90025.

Career: Actor. Began career acting in commercials, including advertisements for Nestle's Quik drink mix, 1997, Radio Shack electronics stores, 2000, Sav–On drug stores, Shell Oil Co., Hormel foods, and Hellman's mayonnaise. Supporter of charitable organizations.

Awards, Honors: Young Artist Award, best actor age ten or under in a feature film, YoungStar Award nomination, *Hollywood Reporter,* best young actor in a drama film, and Broadcast Film Critics Association Award, best child performance, all 1997, for *Jerry Maguire;* YoungStar Award nomination, best young actor in a comedy television series, 1998, for *Meego;* Young Artist Award nomination, best young actor age ten or under in a feature film, and YoungStar Award, best young actor in a motion picture comedy, both 2000, for *Stuart Little;* Saturn Award nomination, Academy of Science Fiction, Fantasy, and Horror Films, best younger actor, and Young Artist Award nomination, best young actor age ten or under in a feature film, both 2001, for *The Little Vampire.*

CREDITS

Film Appearances:
Ray Boyd, *Jerry Maguire,* TriStar, 1996.
Voice of baby tiger, *Doctor Dolittle,* Twentieth Century–Fox, 1998.
George Little, *Stuart Little,* Columbia, 1999.
Tony Thompson, *The Little Vampire* (also known as *De kleine vampier* and *Der kleine vampir*), New Line Cinema, 2000.
Murph, *Like Mike,* Twentieth Century–Fox, 2002.
George Little, *Stuart Little 2,* Columbia TriStar, 2002.
Toby Wilson, *When Zachary Beaver Came to Town,* Echo Bridge Entertainment, 2003.
Tom Saltine, Jr., *The L.A. Riot Spectacular,* Rockhard Pictures/Visionbox Pictures/Entitled Entertainment/ El Camino Pictures/ Cherry Road Films/RichKatz Entertainment, 2005.

Television Appearances; Series:
Justin Foxworthy, *The Jeff Foxworthy Show* (also known as *Somewhere in America*), NBC, 1996–97.
Alex Parker, *Meego,* CBS, 1997.

Television Appearances; Episodic:
Rudy, "Big Baby," *The Single Guy,* NBC, 1997.
Guest, *The Rosie O'Donnell Show,* syndicated, 1997.

Guest, *Late Show with David Letterman,* 1997.
Buzz Thompson, "Cinderella Story," *Dawson's Creek,* The WB, 2000.
Buzz Thompson, "Neverland," *Dawson's Creek,* The WB, 2000.
Buzz Thompson, "The Longest Day," *Dawson's Creek,* The WB, 2000.
Guest, *The Late Late Show with Craig Kilborn,* CBS, 2002.
Stan, "The Good Earth," *Touched by an Angel,* CBS, 2003.
Himself, "Pirates," *The Brendan Leonard Show,* ABC Family Channel, 2003.
Guest, *The Sharon Osbourne Show,* syndicated, 2003.

Also appeared in *The Screen Savers.*

Television Appearances; Specials:
All–Star TGIF Magic, ABC, 1997.
Hollywood Unites: An E! News Special, E! Entertainment Television, 2001.
AFI's 100 Years ... 100 Passions, CBS, 2002.
The Osbourne Family Christmas Special, MTV, 2003.
Frankie Muniz HoopLA Celebrity Basketball Event, Fox Sports Network, 2004.
Interviewee, *100 Greatest Kid Stars,* VH1, 2005.

Television Appearances; Awards Presentations:
The 11th Annual American Comedy Awards, ABC, 1997.
Host, *American Comedy Honors,* Fox, 1997.
Presenter, *The 4th Annual VH1 Honors,* VH1, 1997.
The 2000 MTV Movie Awards, MTV, 2000.
The 16th Annual Genesis Awards, Animal Planet, 2002.
The 1st 13th Annual Fancy Anvil Award Show Program Special ... Live! ... in Stereo, Cartoon Network, 2002.

OTHER SOURCES

Electronic:
Jonathan Lipnicki Official Site, http://www.jonathanlipnicki.com, August 10, 2005.

LIPTON, Dina

PERSONAL

Career: Production designer, art director, and set designer.

Awards, Honors: Art Directors Guild Award nomination, excellence in production design for a single–camera television series, 2005, for "An Innocent Man," *Jack & Bobby.*

CREDITS

Film Production Designer:
Mallrats, Gramercy, 1995.
Mad Dog Time (also known as *Trigger Happy*), Metro–Goldwyn–Mayer/United Artists, 1996.
The Players Club, New Line Cinema, 1998.
Very Bad Things, Polygram, 1998.
The Muse, October Films/USA Films, 1999.
Next Friday, New Line Cinema, 2000.
Here on Earth, Twentieth Century–Fox, 2000.
(With others) *Down to You,* Miramax, 2000.
The New Guy, Sony Pictures Releasing, 2002.
Dickie Roberts: Former Child Star (also known as *Dickie Roberts: (Former) Child Star*), Paramount, 2003.
Eulogy, Lions Gate Films, 2004.
Life of the Party (also known as *Glory Days*), Warner Bros., 2005.

Film Art Director:
The Public Eye, Universal, 1992.
The Last Seduction, October Films, 1993.
Corrina, Corrina, New Line Cinema, 1994.
Mr. Holland's Opus, Buena Vista, 1995.
Celtic Pride, Buena Vista, 1996.

Television Work; Movies:
Set designer, *For Richer, for Poorer* (also known as *Father, Son, and the Mistress*), 1992.
Production Designer, *The Assassination File,* Starz!, 1996.

Television Work; Series:
Art director, *Generations,* NBC, between 1989 and 1991.
Production designer, *Jack & Bobby,* The WB, 2004.

Also art director for *The Fresh Prince of Bel–Air,* NBC.

LITTLEFORD, Beth 1968–

PERSONAL

Full name, Elizabeth Ann Halcyon Littleford; born July 17, 1968, in Nashville, TN; daughter of Philip O. (a cardiologist and inventor) and Jackie (a professor) Littleford; married Rob Fox (a writer, producer, and director), July 1998.

Addresses: *Agent*—Agency for the Performing Arts, 9200 Sunset Blvd., Suite 900, Los Angeles, CA 90069.

Manager—Relevant Entertainment Group, 144 S. Beverly Dr., Suite 400, Beverly Hills, CA 90212. *Publicist*—PYR Public Relations, 6725 Sunset Blvd., Suite 570, Los Angeles, CA 90028.

Career: Actress. Appeared in television commercials for Citrona, 2002, IBM, 2002, Diet Pepsi, 2003, and Cheez–It snack crackers, 2003.

Member: Screen Actors Guild.

CREDITS

Television Appearances; Series:
Correspondent, *The Daily Show* (also known as *The Daily Show with Jon Stewart* and *The Daily Show with Jon Stewart Global Edition*), Comedy Central, 1996–2000.
Deirdre, *Spin City*, ABC, 1998–2000.
Nancy Bladford, *Method & Red*, Fox, 2004.

Television Appearances; Miniseries:
Herself, *I Love the '80s Strikes Back* (documentary), VH1, 2003.
Herself, *I Love the '90s* (documentary), VH1, 2004.
Herself, *I Love the '90s: Part Deux* (documentary), VH1, 2005.

Television Appearances; Specials:
Correspondent, *The Daily Show Holiday Spectacular*, Comedy Central, 1996.
Host, *The Beth Littleford Interview Special*, Comedy Central, 1998.
Correspondent, *The Daily Show Year–End Spectacular '98*, Comedy Central, 1998.
Colin Cowie's Millennium Party, Romance Classics, 1999.
Host, *The Beth Littleford Interview Special*, Comedy Central, 1999.
Herself, *The Daily Show with Jon Stewart: The Greatest Millennium*, Comedy Central, 1999.
Host, *Reel Comedy: Bringing Down the House*, Comedy Central, 2003.
Commentator, *Mouthing Off: 51 Greatest Smartasses*, Comedy Central, 2004.

Television Appearances; Pilots:
Dr. "Mrs." Casey, *Life with Bonnie*, ABC, 2002.
Laurie Laemke, *The Big Wide World of Carl Laemke*, Fox, 2003.

Also appeared in *Why Blitt?*, Fox.

Television Appearances; Episodic:
Host, *Three Blind Dates*, Lifetime, 1997.

Herself, "Comedians Special #2," *Weakest Link*, NBC, 2001.
Marcia Fennel, "Chapter Twenty–Four," *Boston Public*, Fox, 2001.
Television anchor Leslie, "The U.S. Poet Laureate," *The West Wing*, NBC, 2002.
Kristy Duncan, "Still in School," *Still Standing*, CBS, 2002.
Marna, "Popularity," *Greetings from Tucson*, The WB, 2002.
Susan, "Copy That," *What I Like About You*, The WB, 2002.
Reggie Meadows, "The Show Might Go On," *Andy Richter Controls the Universe*, Fox, 2002.
Marna, "Student Council," *Greetings from Tucson*, The WB, 2003.
Dr. "Mrs." Casey, "No Matter Where You Go, There You Are," *Life with Bonnie*, ABC, 2003.
Geraldine Murphy, "Tears of a Clown," *One on One*, UPN, 2003.
Geraldine Murphy, "Dream Seller," *One on One*, UPN, 2004.
Creationism date, "Match Game," *Frasier*, NBC, 2004.
Geraldine Murphy, "The Play's the Thing," *One on One*, UPN, 2004.
Geraldine Murphy, "Bright Lights, Big City," *One on One*, UPN, 2004.
Jimmy Kimmel Live, ABC, 2004.
Late Night with Conan O'Brien, NBC, 2004.
Carla, "Joey and the Premiere," *Joey*, NBC, 2005.

Also appeared in *Hollywood Squares*; *Politically Incorrect*; *The Family Guy* (animated), Fox; *O2Be*, Oxygen; and as guest host, *Talk Soup*, E! Entertainment Television.

Film Appearances:
Lynn Shapiro, *The 24–Hour Woman*, Artisan Entertainment, 1998.
Suzanne, *A Cool, Dry Place*, 1998.
Patt, *Picture This*, 1999.
Janice Pettiboe, *Mystery, Alaska*, Buena Vista, 1999.
Television host, *Unconditional Love*, New Line Cinema, 2002.

Also appeared in *Saddam 17*.

Stage Appearances:
This Is Where I Get Off (one–woman show), Circle Repertory Theatre, New York City, 1996.

Also appeared in *CHOP*, Arcade Theater; *Shaving Heads and Tales*, Playwright's Horizons, New York City; *Brutality of Fact*, Circle Rep Lab; *The Artifacts*, Ohio Theater; *In the Jungle of Cities*, Playwright's Horizon's, New York City.

WRITINGS

Stage Plays:
This Is Where I Get Off (one–woman show), Circle Repertory Theatre, New York City, 1996.

LIVINGSTON, Ron 1968–

PERSONAL

Born June 5, 1968, in Cedar Rapids, IA; son of Kurt (an aerospace engineer) and Linda (a Lutheran minister) Livingston; brother of John Livingston (an actor). *Education:* Yale University, B.A.

Addresses: *Agent*—Kevin Volchok, Endeavor, 9601 Wilshire Blvd., 3rd Floor, Beverly Hills, CA 90210. *Manager*—J. B. Roberts, Thruline Entertainment, 9250 Wilshire Blvd., Ground Floor, Beverly Hills, CA 90212.

Career: Actor. Narrator of commercials, including one for Hewlett Packard computer products, 2004.

Awards, Honors: Golden Globe Award nomination, best supporting actor in a television series, miniseries, or movie made for television, 2002, for *Band of Brothers.*

CREDITS

Film Appearances:
Soldier, *Straight Talk,* Buena Vista, 1992.
Some Folks Call It a Sling Blade, 1994.
Chad, *The Low Life,* 1995.
Rob, *Swingers,* 1996.
Steve, *The Small Hours,* 1997.
Rick, "The Honeymoon," and recreational vehicle driver, "The Campfire," *Campfire Tales,* New Line Cinema, 1998.
Trent, *Body Shots,* New Line Cinema, 1999.
Peter Gibbons, *Office Space* (also known as *Cubiculos de la oficina*), Twentieth Century–Fox, 1999.
Ron Statlin, *Dill Scallion,* Asylum, 1999.
Marty Sachs, *Two Ninas,* Trident Releasing, 1999.
Allen Ginsberg, *Beat,* Background Productions/Beat LLC/Martien Holdings/Millenium Pictures/Pendragon Film/Pfilmco/Walking Pictures, 2000.
Uncle Charlie, *A Rumor of Angels,* Metro–Goldwyn–Mayer/United Artists, 2000.
Marty Bowen, *Adaptation,* Columbia, 2002.
Pirates (short film), Ma & Pa Pictures, 2003.
Larry Sokolov, *The Cooler,* Lions Gate Films, 2003.

Eric Gatley, *King of the Ants,* Anthill Productions/Asylum, 2003.
Derek, *Little Black Book,* Columbia, 2004.
Mr. Bricker, *Winter Solstice,* Paramount Classics, 2005.
Ron, *Life Coach: The Movie,* Broad Appeal Productions, 2005.
Percy Anderson, *Pretty Persuasion,* Samuel Foldwyn Films/Roadside Attractions/Renaissance Films, 2005.
Richard Clayton, *Relative Strangers,* Nu Image, 2005.
(Uncredited) Rudolf, *McCartney's Genes,* Project Mayhem Pictures/Purple Mountain Productions, 2005.
Patric, *Holly,* Max Entertainment/Priority Films, 2005.
Johnny, *American Crude,* Sheffer/Kramer Productions, 2005.

Television Appearances; Series:
Kurt, *Townies,* ABC, 1996.
Mitch, *That's Life,* ABC, 1998.
Assistant District Attorney Alan Lowe, *The Practice,* ABC, 2001–2002.
Jack Berger, a recurring role, *Sex and the City,* HBO, 2002–2003.

Television Appearances; Miniseries:
Captain Lewis Nixon, *Band of Brothers,* HBO, 2001.

Television Appearances; Movies:
Sheldon Buckle, *The Big Brass Ring,* Showtime, 1999.
Tyler Carter Bellows, *Buying the Cow,* Starz!, 2002.
Donnie Anderson, *44 Minutes: The North Hollywood Shoot–Out,* FX Channel, 2003.

Television Appearances; Episodic:
Corporal David Anderson, "Scimitar," *JAG,* NBC, 1995.
Jordan, "Con Law," *Players,* NBC, 1997.
Eliot Ness, "Public Enemy," *Timecop,* Universal, 1997.
Max, "Then Came Cousin Aidan," *Then Came You,* ABC, 2000.
Guest, *The Late Late Show with Craig Kilborn,* CBS, 2001.
Guest, *Dinner for Five,* Independent Film Channel, 2002, 2004.
Guest, *Late Night with Conan O'Brien,* 2003.
Guest, *The View,* ABC, 2003.
Contestant, "Tournament 1, Game 4," *Celebrity Poker Showdown,* Bravo, 2003.
Contestant, "Tournament 3, Game 2," *Celebrity Poker Showdown,* Bravo, 2004.
Guest, *Coming Attractions,* 2004.
Guest, *The Late Late Show with Craig Ferguson,* CBS, 2005.
Voice of Bob, "Homeland Insecurity," *American Dad!,* Fox, 2005.

Television Appearances; Specials:

The Making of "Band of Brothers," HBO, 2001.
Host, *VH1 50 Greatest Album Covers,* VH1, 2003.
TV Guide: Greatest Moments of 2003, 2003.
Sex and the City: A Farewell, HBO, 2004.
Still Swingin', Independent Film Channel, 2005.

Television Appearances; Pilots:

Co–owner of struggling "dot.com," *Silicon Stories,* ABC, 2001.

Television Appearances; Awards Presentations:

Presenter, *The 9th Annual Screen Actors Guild Awards,* TNT, 2003.
Presenter, *The 9th Annual Critics' Choice Awards,* E! Entertainment Television, 2004.

Stage Appearances:

Appeared in productions at Goodman Theatre, Chicago, IL, with Manhattan Class Company, New York City, and at Williamstown Theatre Festival, Williamstown, MA.

RECORDINGS

Audio Books:

Narrator of *Mission Flats,* by William Landay and *A Week in the Woods,* by Andrew Clements.

OTHER SOURCES

Periodicals:

Entertainment Weekly, August 9, 2002, p. 57.
Movieline, March, 1999, p. 22.
People Weekly, July 14, 2003, p. 96.
TV Guide, October, 2001, pp. 50–53, 65.

LODER, Kurt 1945–

PERSONAL

Born May 5, 1945, in Ocean City, NJ.

Career: Writer, journalist, and actor. Appeared in a television commercial for Amnesty International, 2001. Previously worked as a writer with *Circus* magazine and as the senior editor of *Rolling Stone. Military Service:* United States Army.

CREDITS

Film Appearances:

MTV VJ, *The Adventures of Ford Fairlane,* Twentieth Century–Fox, 1990.
Hitman, *Who's the Man?,* New Line Cinema, 1993.
Himself, *The Paper,* Universal, 1994.
Himself, *Fear of a Black Hat,* Samuel Goldwyn, 1994.
Himself, *Airheads,* Twentieth Century–Fox, 1994.
Himself, *Dead Man on Campus,* Paramount, 1998.
Himself, *Belly,* Artisan, 1998.
Himself, *The Suburbans,* TriStar, 1999.
Himself, *Entropy,* Magic Light, 1999.
Himself, *Pups,* Monarch, 1999.
Himself, *My Generation,* PolyGram, 2000.
Himself as MTV newscaster, *Book of Shadows: Blair Witch 2* (also known as *BW2, BWP2* and *Book of Shadows: Blair Witch Project 2*), Artisan, 2000.
Himself, *Sugar & Spice,* New Line Cinema, 2001.
Angryman, Blue Mutt, 2001.
Himself, *Pauly Shore Is Dead,* Regent, 2003.
(In archive footage) *Tupac: Resurrection,* Paramount, 2003.
Himself, *Ramones Raw,* 2004.

Television Appearances; Series:

News reporter, *MTV News:The Week in Rock,* MTV, 1987.
Correspondent, *MTV News,* MTV, 1988—.
Famous Last Words, 1990.
Host, *MTV Live,* 1997.
Total Request Live (also known as *TRL* and *Total Request with Carson Daly*), MTV, 1998.
Host, *MTV News 1515,* MTV, 1998.

Also appeared in *Doggy Fizzle Televizzle,* MTV.

Television Appearances; Specials:

Host, *Moscow Music Peace Festival Rockumentary* (documentary), MTV, 1989.
Narrator, *Sex in the '90s,* (documentary), CBS, 1990.
MTV, Give Me Back My Life: A Harvard Lampoon Parody, Comedy Central, 1991.
Narrator, *MTV Generation* (documentary), MTV, 1991.
Host, *The Year in Rock: '92* (documentary), MTV, 1992.
Host, *Rolling Stone 25: The MTV Special* (documentary), 1992.
Host, *Fox/MTV Guide to Summer '92,* Fox, 1992.
Host, *The Year in Rock: '93,* MTV, 1993.
Narrator, *Seven Deadly Sins: An MTV News Special Report* (documentary), MTV, 1993.
Host, *Hate Rock* (documentary), MTV, 1993.
Host, *Straight Dope* (documentary), MTV, 1994.
Narrator, *Sex in the 90s V: Love Sucks* (documentary), MTV, 1994.
Host, *Conversations with the Rolling Stones* (documentary), MTV, 1994.

Host, *Madonna: No Bull! The Making of "Take a Bow"* (documentary), 1994.

Host, *A New Madonna: The Making of "Evita"* (documentary), 1994.

Host, *24 Hours in Rock and Roll* (documentary), MTV, 1995.

Host, *MTV News Raw* (documentary), MTV, 1995.

Host, *New Religions: The Cult Question*, MTV, 1995.

Host, *Smashed: An MTV News Special Report* (documentary), MTV, 1996.

Narrator, *The Year in Rock 1997*, MTV, 1997.

Host, *Fight for the Right* (documentary), MTV, 1997.

Host, *Tibetan Freedom Concert*, 1997.

Host, *MTV New Year's Eve 1998*, MTV, 1998.

Host, *Sex in the 90s XIII: Generation Sex* (documentary), MTV, 1999.

Host, *Sex in the 90s XII: Fact or Fiction* (documentary), MTV, 1999.

Host, *MTV 2 Large New Year's Eve Party*, MTV, 1999.

9 Days That Rocked the 90's (documentary), MTV, 1999.

MTV Uncensored, MTV, 1999.

Host, *MTV Video Music Awards Opening Act*, MTV, 1999.

Host, *MTV Backstage at the Grammy's*, MTV, 2000.

Host, *When Lyrics Attack*, MTV, 2000.

2000 MTV Video Music Awards Post Show, MTV, 2000.

2000 MTV Video Music Awards Opening Act, MTV, 2000.

Host, *Testimony: 20 Years of Rock on MTV*, MTV, 2001.

MTV's New Year's Eve 2002, MTV, 2001.

Correspondent, *MTV Newsnow Special Report*, MTV, 2001.

Narrator, *Hips, Lips & Gender Benders: MTV History of Sex* (documentary), MTV, 2001.

2001 MTV Video Music Awards Post Show, MTV, 2001.

MTV Video Music Awards Opening Act, MTV, 2001 and 2003.

MTV Video Music Awards 2002 (also known as *VMA's 2002*), MTV, 2002.

Host, *Tupac: Resurrection MTV Movie Special* (documentary), MTV, 2003.

2003 MTV Movie Awards, MTV, 2003.

MTV Video Music Awards 2003, MTV, 2003.

Host, *2004 MTV Video Music Awards Pre–Show by the Shore*, MTV, 2004.

Television Appearances; Episodic:

Saturday Night Live, NBC, 1996.

"A Star Is Abhorred," *Duckman*, USA Network, 1997.

"Foul Bull," *Kenan & Kel*, Nickelodeon, 1997.

Late Night with Conan O'Brien, NBC, 1998.

"Leap of Faith," *Movie Stars*, The WB, 1999.

"May a Takes a Stan," *Girlfriends*, UPN, 2001.

RECORDINGS

Videos:

(In archive footage) *Welcome to Death Row*, 2001.

Himself, *Purple Rain: Backstage Pass*, Warner Home Video, 2004.

WRITINGS

Screenplays:

(With others) *What's Love Got to Do with It* (adapted from his book *I, Tina*, cowritten with Tina Turner; also known as *Tina: What's Love Got to Do with It*), Buena Vista, 1993.

Television Specials:

Sex in the '90s, (documentary), CBS, 1990.

MTV Generation (documentary), MTV, 1991.

Rolling Stone 25: The MTV Special (documentary), 1992.

Fox/MTV Guide to Summer '92, Fox, 1992.

Seven Deadly Sins: An MTV News Special Report (documentary), MTV, 1993.

Hate Rock (documentary), MTV, 1993.

Straight Dope (documentary), MTV, 1994.

Smashed: An MTV News Special Report (documentary), MTV, 1996.

When Lyrics Attack, MTV, 2000.

Testimony: 20 Years of Rock on MTV, MTV, 2001.

Hips, Lips & Gender Benders: MTV History of Sex (documentary), MTV, 2001.

Spider–Man: An MTV Movie Special, MTV, 2002.

Tupac: Resurrection MTV Movie Special (documentary), MTV, 2003.

Television Series:

House of Style, MTV, 1989.

Ultra Sound, MTV, 1998.

Nonfiction:

(With Tina Turner) *I, Tina*, William Morrow, 1986.

Bat Chain Puller: Rock and Roll in the Age of Celebrity, Cooper Square Press, 1990.

Contributor to periodicals, including *Esquire*, *Details*, *New York*, and *Time*.

M

MALINA, Rolondo
   See MOLINA, Rolando

MANCINA, Mark

PERSONAL

Born in Santa Monica, CA; married Jill Ann Meyer, May 9, 1999; children: Molly Rose. *Education:* Attended California State University, Fullerton. *Avocational Interests:* Collecting guitars and rare instruments.

Addresses: *Agent*—Gorfaine/Schwartz Agency, 13245 Riverside Dr., Suite 450, Sherman Oaks, CA 91423.

Career: Composer, music producer, and orchestrator. Performs as a singer, guitarist, pianist, and percussionist, including appearances on tour with Trevor Rabin; also music producer and composer for Yes and collaborator with recording artist such as Phil Collins and Kenny Loggins. Composer (with Collins) of the Brother Bear live show for Disneyland theme park; also composer for numerous television commercials, including music for Mountain Dew soft drinks, Jaguar automobiles, McDonald's restaurants, U.S. Army, and American Express.

Awards, Honors: Two BMI Film Music Awards, Broadcast Music Inc., 1995, for *Bad Boys* and *Speed;* Grammy Award, National Academy of Recording Arts and Sciences, best musical album for children, and American Music Award, best popular album, both 1994, for producing *The Lion King;* BMI Film Music Awards, 1997, for *Twister,* and 1998, for *Con Air;* Grammy Award, best musical show album, 1998, for producing stage version of *The Lion King;* Antoinette Perry Award nomination, best original musical score (with others), 1998, and Ivor Novello Award, international achievement in musical theatre, 2000, both for *The Lion King;* Grammy Award, best soundtrack album, 1999, and BMI Film Music Award, 2000, both for *Tarzan;* BMI Film Music Award, 2002, for *Training Day;* Annie Award nomination, International Animated Film Society, outstanding music in an animated feature production (with Phil Collins), and BMI Film Music Award, both 2004, for *Brother Bear;* platinum record certification, Recording Industry Association of America, for film soundtrack recording *The Lion King.*

CREDITS

Film Work:
Music orchestrator and song arranger, "I Just Can't Wait to be King," "Hakuna Matata," and "Can You Feel the Love Tonight," *The Lion King* (animated), Buena Vista, 1994.
Music producer, *Monkey Trouble,* New Line Cinema, 1994.
(Uncredited) Orchestrator, *Twister,* Warner Bros., 1996.
Music arranger, *Speed 2: Cruise Control,* Twentieth Century–Fox, 1997.
Orchestrator, *Return to Paradise,* Twentieth Century–Fox, 1998.
Score producer, song arranger, and orchestra conductor, *Tarzan* (animated), Buena Vista/Walt Disney, 1999.
Music producer, *Training Day,* Warner Bros., 2001.

Also arranger and producer of songs for other films.

Television Work; Series:
Music arranger and performer, *Millennium: Tribal Wisdom and the Modern World,* PBS, 1992.
Executive music producer (and arranger and producer of song "Two Worlds"), *Disney's "The Legend of Tarzan,"* 2001.

Television Appearances; Specials:
The Making of "Speed 2: Cruise Control," 1997.

Stage Work:

Music arranger, *The Lion King* (musical; also known as *The Lion King on Broadway*), New Amsterdam Theatre, New York City, beginning, 1997, then London, c. 2000.

RECORDINGS

Albums:

Soundtrack recordings include *The Lion King* (film soundtrack), *The Lion King* (stage version), and *Tarzan.* Composer (with others) and producer of *Black Moon* by Emerson, Lake, and Palmer, Polygram; composer and producer of *Miracle of Life,* Arista; composer (with others), arranger, and producer, *Rhythm of the Pride Lands by Lebo M,* Walt Disney Records. Also arranger of music for other recordings.

WRITINGS

Film Music:

Mankillers, Sony Pictures Entertainment, 1987.
Death Chase (also known as *Chase*), New Star Entertainment, 1988.
Night Wars, Action International Pictures, 1988.
Space Mutiny, Action International Pictures, 1988.
Code Name Vengeance, Action International Pictures, 1989.
Hell on the Battleground (also known as *Battleground*), Action International Pictures, 1989.
Rage to Kill, Action International Pictures, 1989.
Born Killer, 1990.
Where Sleeping Dogs Lie, Columbia TriStar Home Video, 1991.
Additional music, *True Romance* (also known as *Breakaway*), Warner Bros., 1993.
Monkey Trouble (also known as *Pet*), New Line Cinema, 1994.
Speed, Twentieth Century–Fox, 1994.
Assassins (also known as *Day of Reckoning*), Warner Bros., 1995.
Bad Boys, Columbia, 1995.
Fair Game, Warner Bros., 1995.
Money Train, Columbia, 1995.
Running Wild (also known as *Born Wild*), 1995.
Man of the House (also known as *Man 2 Man* and *Pals Forever*), Buena Vista, 1995.
Moll Flanders, Twentieth Century–Fox, 1996.
Twister, Warner Bros., 1996.
Con Air, Buena Vista, 1997.
(Including song "Speed TK Re–mix") *Speed 2: Cruise Control,* Twentieth Century–Fox, 1997.
Return to Paradise (also known as *All for One*), Twentieth Century–Fox, 1998.
(Including songs "Two Worlds" and "You'll Be In My Heart") *Tarzan* (animated), Buena Vista/Walt Disney, 1999.

Auggie Rose (also known as *Beyond Suspicion*), Roxie Releasing, 2000.
Bait (also known as *Piege*), Warner Bros., 2000.
Training Day, Warner Bros., 2001.
Domestic Disturbance, Paramount, 2001.
Early Bloomer (animated short film), Columbia, 2003.
(With Phil Collins) *Brother Bear* (animated; also known as *Tierra de osos*), Buena Vista, 2003.
The Haunted Mansion (also known as *Disney's "Haunted Mansion"*), Buena Vista, 2003.
The Reckoning (also known as *Morality Play* and *El misterio de Wells*), Paramount Classics, 2004.
Asylum, Paramount Classics, 2005.
Tarzan II (animated), Buena Vista Home Video, 2005.

Songs Featured in Films:

"You and Me" and "Home," *Jetsons: The Movie,* Universal, 1990.

Television Music; Movies:

Future Force, syndicated, 1992.
(Including theme music), *Lifepod,* Fox, 1993.
Taking Liberty, ABC, 1996.
Theme, *Houdini,* TNT, 1998.

Television Music; Series:

Millennium: Tribal Wisdom and the Modern World, PBS, 1992.
Space Rangers, CBS, 1993.
(Including theme music), *The Outer Limits* (also known as *The New Outer Limits*), Showtime, 1995.
Theme music, *Poltergeist: The Legacy,* Showtime, 1996.
Soldier of Fortune, Inc. (also known as *S.O.F., Inc.* and *S.O.F. Special Ops Force*), 1997.
Theme music, *The Strip,* UPN, 1999.

Television Music; Miniseries:

"Apollo 1" segment, *From the Earth to the Moon,* HBO, 1998.

Stage Music:

Lyricist and composer of additional music, *The Lion King* (musical; also known as *The Lion King on Broadway*), New Amsterdam Theatre, New York City, beginning, 1997, then London, 2000.

ADAPTATIONS

The music from the 1994 film *Speed* has been featured in subsequent films, including *Don't Say a Word,* released by Twentieth Century–Fox in 2001, and *Road,* released by Varma Corporation in 2002.

OTHER SOURCES

Periodicals:

Playbill, June 20, 2003.

Electronic:
Mark Mancina Official Site, http://www.markmancina. com, July 21, 2005.

MANGOLD, James 1964–
(Jim Mangold)

PERSONAL

Full name, James Allen Mangold; born 1964, in New York, NY; son of Robert (an artist) and Sylvia (an artist) Mangold; married Cathy Konrad (a producer), August 7, 1998. *Education:* California Institute of the Arts, graduated, 1985; attended Columbia University, 1989.

Addresses: *Office*—Tree Line Films, 1708 Berkeley St., Santa Monica, CA 90040. *Agent*—Joanne Wiles, William Morris Agency, 1 William Morris Pl., Beverly Hills, CA 90212. *Manager*—Daniel Rappaport, Management 360, 9111 Wilshire Blvd., Beverly Hills, CA 90210. *Publicist*—Bumble, Ward and Associates, 8383 Wilshire Blvd., Suite 340, Beverly Hills, CA 90211.

Career: Director, producer, writer, and actor. Walt Disney Productions, director and writer, c. 1985–89; Tree Line Films, Santa Monica, CA, partner and producer.

Awards, Honors: Special Jury Prize, best direction, and nomination for Grand Jury Prize, dramatic category, both Sundance Film Festival, and Grand Prix Asturias and Best Screenplay Award, both Gijon International Film Festival, all 1995, for *Henry.*

CREDITS

Film Director:
Future View, 1982.
Victor, 1991.
Heavy, Columbia TriStar Home Video, 1995.
Cop Land, Buena Vista, 1997.
Girl, Interrupted (also known as *Durchgeknallt* and *Durchgeknallt—Girl, interrupted*), Columbia, 1999.
Kate & Leopold, Miramax, 2001.
Identity, Columbia, 2003.
Walk the Line, Twentieth Century–Fox, 2005.

Film Appearances:
Himself, *At Sundance,* 1995.
Dr. Greg, *The Sweetest Thing,* Columbia, 2002.
Himself, *Mackendrick on Film* (documentary), Sticking Place Films, 2004.

Television Executive Producer:
Lift (movie), Showtime, 2001.
Cop Land (pilot), HBO, 2001.

Television Appearances; Specials:
The Making of "Girl, Interrupted," HBO, 1999.

Television Appearances; Episodic:
Guest, "Girl, Interrupted," *HBO First Look,* HBO, 2000.

WRITINGS

Screenplays:
Future View, 1982.
Coauthor, *Oliver & Company* (animated), Buena Vista, 1988.
Victor, 1991.
Heavy (based on the novel *Nickel Mountain* by John Gardner), Columbia TriStar Home Video, 1995, published with novelization *Cop Land,* Farrar, Straus & Giroux, 2000.
Cop Land, Buena Vista, 1997.
Girl, Interrupted (also known as *Durchgeknallt* and *Durchgeknallt—Girl, interrupted*), Columbia, 1999, published as *Girl, Interrupted: The Screenplay,* Faber & Faber, 2000.
Kate & Leopold, Miramax, 2001.
Walk the Line, Twentieth Century–Fox, 2005.

Television Specials:
(As Jim Mangold) *The Deacon Street Deer,* ABC, 1986.

ADAPTATIONS

The film *Cop Land* was adapted as a novel by Mike McAlary and published by Hyperion Books in 1997. It was published with *Heavy* by Farrar, Straus & Giroux in 2000.

OTHER SOURCES

Periodicals:
Premiere, December, 1997, pp. 84–85.

MANTOOTH, Randolph 1945–
(Randy Mantooth)

PERSONAL

Born September 19, 1945, in Sacramento, CA; son of Donald and Sadie Mantooth; married Rose Para (divorced); married Kristen Connors, August 10, 2002.

Education: Attended college in Santa Barbara, CA; studied at the American Academy of Dramatic Arts.

Addresses: *Agent*—Stone Manners Agency, 6500 Wilshire Blvd., Suite 550, Los Angeles, CA 90048.

Career: Actor and director. Project 51 (a nonprofit organization), committee member, 2000. Sometimes credited as Randy Mantooth.

Awards, Honors: Soap Opera Digest Award nomination, outstanding hero and supporting actor, 1990, 1995, and 1996, for *Loving;* Soap Opera Digest Award nomination, outstanding supporting actor, 1997, for *The City.*

CREDITS

Television Appearances; Series:
Paramedic John Gage, *Emergency!* (also known as *Emergencia* and *Emergency One*), NBC, 1972–77.
Voice of John Gage, *Emergency +4* (animated), syndicated, 1973–76.
Lieutenant Mike Bender, *Operation Petticoat,* ABC, 1978–79.
Eddie Dawkins, *Detective School,* ABC, 1979.
First Alex Masters (also known as Clay Alden), *Loving,* ABC, 1987–90, 1993–95.
Richard Halifax, *General Hospital,* ABC, 1992–93.
Alex Masters, *The City,* ABC, 1995–97.
Hal Munson, *As the World Turns,* CBS, 2003—.

Television Appearances; Movies:
Vanished, ABC, 1971.
Dan, *Marriage: Year One,* NBC, 1971.
Lieutenant Lewis, *The Bravos,* ABC, 1972.
Gage, *Greatest Rescues of Emergency!,* 1978.
John Gage, *Emergency: Survival on Charter #220,* 1978.
Most Deadly Passage, 1979.
Joe Nez, *Bridge across Time* (also known as *Arizona Ripper* and *Terror at London Bridge*), NBC, 1985.
Bing Tupper, *Spy Games,* ABC, 1991.
Bing Tupper, *Before the Storm,* ABC, 1991.
Michael's father, *Please, God, I'm Only Seventeen,* CBS, 1992.

Television Appearances; Miniseries:
Father Frank McNulty, *Testimony of Two Men,* syndicated, 1977.
Abraham Kent, *The Seekers,* syndicated, 1979.

Television Appearances; Pilots:
Sarge (also known as *Sarge: The Badge or the Cross* and *The Badge or the Cross*), NBC, 1971.
Paramedic John Gage, *Emergency!,* NBC, 1972.

Television Appearances; Specials:
The 14th Annual Daytime Emmy Awards, ABC, 1987.
Presenter, *The 21st Annual Daytime Emmy Awards,* ABC, 1994.
Presenter, *The 11th Annual Soap Opera Awards,* NBC, 1995.
Interviewee, *Television: The First 50 Years* (documentary), PBS, 2001.
Himself, *VH–1 Where Are They Now: TV Hunks,* VH1, 2003.

Television Appearances; Episodic:
Intern, "Man from Taos: Part 1: Who Says You Can't Make Friends in New York City?," *McCloud,* NBC, 1970.
Paul, "Angie," *Matt Lincoln,* ABC, 1970.
"A Continual Roar of Musketry: Parts 1 & 2," *The Bold Ones: The Senator,* 1970.
Lieutenant Dorn, "The Regimental Line," *The Virginian,* NBC, 1971.
Dan Loomis, "Stagecoach Seven," *Alias Smith and Jones,* ABC, 1971.
Neil Williams, "Log 88—Reason to Run," *Adam–12,* NBC, 1971.
Elkins, "Class of '99," *Night Gallery,* NBC, 1971.
Terence "Terry" Kimble, "The Strange Secret of Yermo Hill," *The Bold Ones: The Lawyers,* NBC, 1971.
Fince, "The Combatants," *Sarge,* NBC, 1971.
Lonnie, "Until Proven Innocent," *Owen Marshall: Counselor at Law,* ABC, 1971.
Philip Yerby, "The Disposal Man," *McCloud,* NBC, 1971.
"Solomon's Choice," *Marcus Welby, M.D.,* ABC, 1972.
Paramedic John Gage, "Lost and Found," *Adam–12,* NBC, 1972.
Keith Ryder, "The Desertion of Keith Ryder," *Owen Marshall: Counselor at Law,* ABC, 1974.
Mailman, "New Family/Traffic Rules," *Cos,* ABC, 1976.
Tim Jenkins, "Sighting 4016: The Pipeline Incident," *Project U.F.O.,* NBC, 1978.
Bobby Howard, "Serve, Volley and Kill," *Vega$,* ABC, 1978.
Alan Billingsly, "Like Father Like Son/Don't Push Me/Second Choice," *The Love Boat,* ABC, 1979.
Michael, "Greetings from Earth: Parts 1 & 2," *Battlestar Galactica,* ABC, 1979.
Mark Williams, "Island Angels," *Charlie's Angels,* 1980.
Todd Peterson, "French Twist," *Vega$,* ABC, 1981.
Todd Peterson, "No Way to Treat a Victim," *Vega$,* ABC, 1981.
Dr. Paul Todd, "Devil and Mr. Roarke/Ziegfeld Girls/Kid Corey Rides Again," *Fantasy Island,* ABC, 1981.
Dr. Paul Todd, "Delphine/The Unkillable," *Fantasy Island,* ABC, 1981.
"The Star/The Trouble with Chester/Fran's Worst Friend," *Aloha Paradise,* ABC, 1981.
Larry, "To the Finish," *The Fall Guy,* ABC, 1983.
Joe Don Ford, "Jamie," *Dallas,* CBS, 1984.
Veckler, "The Winner," *The Fall Guy,* ABC, 1984.

Raymond Two Crows/DeMarco, "Murder Digs Deep," *Murder, She Wrote,* CBS, 1985.

Jerry Andrews, "The Lucky Stiff," *The Fall Guy,* ABC, 1986.

Gil Tecowsky, "The Princess and the Pee," *L.A. Law,* NBC, 1988.

Joaquin, "100 Klicks Out," *China Beach,* ABC, 1991.

Earl Stringer, "The Prometheus Syndrome," *MacGyver,* ABC, 1991.

Sam Dietz, "Dead of Summer," *Baywatch,* syndicated, 1992.

Mayor Bill Tremont, "Malibu Fire," *Diagnosis Murder,* CBS, 1997.

Colonel Ron Barret, "Impact," *JAG,* CBS, 1997.

James Lee Crown, "Rainbow's End," *Walker, Texas Ranger,* CBS, 1997.

Ben Camden, "When Darkness Falls," *Promised Land,* CBS, 1998.

"Trash TV: Parts 1 & 2," *Diagnosis Murder,* CBS, 1999.

Policeman, "May Day," *ER,* NBC, 2000.

Hollywood Squares, syndicated, 2004.

Also appeared in *This Is the Life; Scene of the Crime,* NBC; *The West,* PBS; as firefighter–paramedic John Gage, "The Urban Rangers," *Sierra;* Lieutenant Michael Bender, *The New Operation Petticoat,* NBC.

Television Director; Episodic:

"The Nuisance," *Emergency!* (also known as *Emergencia* and *Emergency One*), NBC, 1976.

Film Appearances:

Solonsky, *Enemy Action,* New Horizons, 1999.

Ken Crandall, *Time Share* (also known as *Bitter Suite* and *Time Share—Doppelpack im Ferienhaus*), Fox, 2000.

Admiral Edwards, *Captured* (also known as *Agent Red*), Columbia TriStar, 2000.

Stage Appearances:

Tony, *Rain Dance,* Signature Theatre Company, Peter Norton Space, New York City, 2003.

OTHER SOURCES

Electronic:

Randolph Mantooth Official Site, http://www. randymantooth.com, April 21, 2005.

MARIANO, John

PERSONAL

Addresses: *Agent*—Robert Haas, Osbrink Talent Agency, 4343 Lankershim Blvd., Suite 100, Universal City, CA 91602.

Career: Actor and voice artist.

CREDITS

Television Appearances; Series:

Johnny the waiter, a recurring role, *Caroline in the City* (also known as *Caroline*), NBC, 1995–97.

Chris, a recurring role, *Veronica's Closet,* NBC, 1999–2000.

Felix, *The Young and the Restless* (also known as *Y&R*), CBS, 2002.

Voice of Bobby Pigeon, *Animaniacs* (animated; also known as *Steven Spielberg Presents "Animaniacs"*); voice of Bobby for *Pinky and the Brain* (animated; also known as *Steven Spielberg Presents "Pinky and the Brain"*).

Television Appearances; Pilots:

John, *Life with Roger,* The WB, 1996.

Man, *Dharma & Greg,* ABC, 1997.

Television Appearances; Episodic:

"The Cop," *Matlock,* 1986.

Wakefield, "Chao Ong," *China Beach,* 1988.

Tommy Miranda, "Molly and Eddie," *Booker,* 1990.

Stickman, "Busted," *Family Matters,* ABC, 1991.

Repair person, "An Affair to Forget," *Who's the Boss?,* 1991.

Zippy, *Good & Evil,* 1991.

"TV or Not TV," *L.A. Law,* NBC, 1991.

Travis Gerkin, "The System Works," *Night Court,* 1991.

Travis Gerkin, "Shave and a Haircut," *Night Court,* 1992.

Travis Gerkin, "To Sir with ... Ah, What the Heck ... Love," *Night Court,* 1992.

Voices, "Heart of Ice," *Batman* (animated; also known as *Batman: The Animated Series*), 1992.

Dave, "Big Doings: Part 2," *Blossom,* NBC, 1993.

Pete, "No Ma'am," *Married ... with Children,* Fox, 1993.

Voice of Danny D., "Taming of the Screwy," *Animaniacs* (animated; also known as *Steven Spielberg Presents "Animaniacs"*), 1993.

Voice of Gagnort, "Potty Emergency," *Animaniacs* (animated; also known as *Steven Spielberg Presents "Animaniacs"*), 1993.

Voice of Guenther, "The Warners 65th Anniversary Special," *Animaniacs* (animated; also known as *Steven Spielberg Presents "Animaniacs"*), 1994.

Bobby Vinera, "Ghosts of the Past," *Silk Stalkings,* 1994.

Voice of head gendarme, "Napoleon Brainaparte," *Pinky and the Brain* (animated; also known as *Steven Spielberg Presents "Pinky and the Brain"*), 1995.

Leonard Apfenbach, "Men Plan, God Laughs," *ER,* NBC, 1995.

Phillip, "The Mating Season," *The Crew,* Fox, 1995.

Voice of C. W., "Manhattan Maneater," *The Real Adventures of Jonny Quest* (animated), 1996.

Voice of sewer czar, "The Tick vs. Filth," *The Tick* (animated), 1996.

Tom, "The Milk Carton Kid," *Renegade,* 1996.

Rhett, "Chett World," *Weird Science,* 1996.

Voices of Vic, Morrie, and Zamboni Jones, "Downtown as Fruits/Eugene's Bike," *Hey Arnold!* (animated), 1996.

Voices of Vic and Morrie, "Door #16/Arnold as Cupid," *Hey Arnold!* (animated), 1996.

Voices of Vic and Morrie, "Das Subway/Wheezin' Ed," *Hey Arnold!* (animated), 1996.

Armand Miller, "Lost and Found," *Pacific Blue,* 1997.

Voice, "The Alpha Syndrome," *Men in Black: The Series,* The WB, 1997.

Voice, "A Temporary Insanity," *Extreme Ghostbusters,* syndicated, 1997.

Voice, "Casting the Runes," *Extreme Ghostbusters,* syndicated, 1997.

Voice, "The Psychic Link Syndrome," *Men in Black: The Series,* The WB, 1997.

Ring announcer, "The Brother Who Came to Dinner," *Family Matters,* ABC, 1997.

Morgan Driscoll, "Sheedy Dealings," *NYPD Blue,* ABC, 1997.

Voice of Robert, "Pinky & the Brain and ... Larry/Where the Deer and the Mousealopes Play," *Pinky and the Brain* (animated; also known as *Steven Spielberg Presents "Pinky and the Brain"*), 1997.

Voice of third agent, "Where There's Smoke," *The New Batman/Superman Adventures* (animated), The WB, 1998.

Vincenzo, "Torch Song," *Batman Gotham Knights,* 1998.

Enrico Amati, "Soul Searching," *JAG,* CBS, 1999.

Voice of short–order cook, "Superman's Pal," *Superman* (animated), The WB, 1999.

Voice of Vic, "Back to School/Egg Story," *Hey Arnold!* (animated), 1999.

Voice of Vic and Morrie, "Weird Cousin/Baby Oskar," *Hey Arnold!* (animated), 1999.

Voice of driver, "Eyewitness," *Batman Beyond* (animated), The WB, 2000.

Ralph Giorgio, "Do Not Resuscitate," *The Sopranos,* HBO, 2000.

Nick Giovanni, "Con Truck," *18 Wheels of Justice,* The Nashville Network, 2000.

Bertram, "Shibboleth," *The West Wing,* NBC, 2000.

Sonny Martone, "Saturday Night," *Walker, Texas Ranger,* CBS, 2001.

Ray Bolzano, "Philly Folly," *Philly,* ABC, 2001.

Joey Marx, "Tarzan and One Punch Mullargan," *The Legend of Tarzan,* 2001.

Voice of Ray, "Gerald's Game/Fishing Trip," *Hey Arnold!* (animated), 2002.

Davey Penrod, "MIA/NYC Nonstop," *CSI: Miami,* CBS, 2004.

Officer Gary Moretti, "I Like Ike," *NYPD Blue,* ABC, 2004.

Also appeared as first cemetery worker, *Judging Amy,* CBS; in *Lucky,* FX Network; as Lieutenant Light, *The Monroes,* ABC; as Ronnie Traylor, *NYPD Blue,* ABC; in *On the Television,* Nickelodeon; as pizza guy, *Room for Two,* ABC; as witch detective, *Sabrina, The Teenage Witch,* ABC; as voice of commandant, *The Sylvester & Tweety Mysteries* (animated), The WB; in *The Unnaturals,* Comedy Central; as Eddie Coburn, *Walker, Texas Ranger,* CBS; and as Blake, *The Watcher,* UPN.

Television Work; Series:

Additional voices for the series *The Toxic Crusaders* and *Where's Waldo?* (animated; also known as *Where's Wally?*), CBS.

Film Appearances:

When Nature Calls, Troma, 1982.

Second teller, *Tough Guys,* Buena Vista, 1986.

Jack, *Life Could Be Worse,* 1989.

Nick Sorvino, *The Finishing Touch,* Columbia TriStar Home Video, 1992.

Arthur, *With Friends like These ... ,* 1998.

Brunie, *A Wake in Providence,* 1999, Indican Pictures, 2005.

Roberto, *Cool Crime,* Phaedra Cinema, 1999.

Voice of Bobby, *Wakko's Wish* (animated; also known as *Steven Spielberg Presents "Animaniacs: Wakko's Wish"*), Amblin Entertainment/Warner Bros. Animation, 1999.

Carlo, *Jesus, Mary, and Joey,* Federal Hill Pictures, 2003.

RECORDINGS

Videos:

Additional voices, *Batman: Mystery of the Batwoman* (animated), Warner Bros., 2003.

Video Games:

Voices of Brage, Kagain, Slythe, Tiax, and Tuth, *Forgotten Realms: Baldur's Gate,* 1998.

Voice, *Y2K: The Game,* 1999.

Voices of Tiax, Talon Yarryl, and Naljier, *Forgotten Realms: Baldur's Gate II—Shadows of Amn,* Bioware/Black Isle Studios/Interplay Productions, 2000.

Voices of Jojo Jr. and Salty the bait shop owner, *Escape from Monkey Island,* LucasArts Entertainment, 2000.

Voice, *Fallout Tactics: Brotherhood of Steel,* Interplay Productions, 2001.

Voice, *Lionheart* (also known as *Lionheart: Legacy of the Crusader*), Black Isle Studios, 2003.

Voice of Rexus, *Armed & Dangerous,* LucasArts Entertainment, 2003.

Voices of wasteland bartender, "psycho" ghoul user, "rader" torch, and soldier, *Fallout: Brotherhood of Steel,* Interplay Productions, 2004.

Voices of generic male dark elf merchant, generic male dwarf merchant, generic male halfling merchant, and generic male Iksar merchant, *EverQuest II,* Sony Online Entertainment, 2004.

MARTIN, Dan
(Jake Daniels, Jake Martin)

PERSONAL

Married Ella Joyce (an actress).

Addresses: *Agent*—Michael Linden Greene, Michael Greene and Associates, 7080 Hollywood Blvd., Suite 1017, Hollywood, CA 90028. *Manager*—Jeff Ross, Jeff Ross Management, 14560 Benefit St., Suite 206, Sherman Oaks, CA 91403.

Career: Actor, voice performer, and director. Towne Street Theatre Conservatory, teacher of acting classes. Appeared in commercials for McDonald's restaurants, 2003, and Gateway computer systems, 2004.

CREDITS

Television Appearances; Series:
Lou Adams, *Katts and Dog* (also known as *Rin Tin Tin: K–9 Cop*), The Family Channel, 1988–91.
(As Jake Martin) Voice of Captain Zanbarusu in English version, *Saibogu* (anime; also known as *Cyborg 009* and *Cyborg 009: The Cyborg Soldier*), Cartoon Network, 2003.
Voice, *Trigun* (anime; also known as *Trigun #1: The $60,000,000,000 Man*), Cartoon Network, 2003.
(As Jake Martin) Voice of Inspector Kouichi Zenigata for English version, *Rupan sansei: Part II* (anime; also known as *The New Lupin III*), Cartoon Network, 2003.
Lieutenant Baker, a recurring role, *The Bold and the Beautiful,* CBS, 2003–2004.
Raphael Suzuki, a recurring role, *The Legend of Black Heaven,* 2004.

Television Appearances; Miniseries:
Woodrow "Woody" Arnett, *Laurel Avenue,* HBO, 1993.
Rich Moffat, *The Stand* (also known as *Stephen King's "The Stand"*), ABC, 1994.

Television Appearances; Movies:
Frank Donnelly, *Donor Unknown* (also known as *Dangerous Heart*), USA Network, 1995.

Lieutenant Barnes, *Alien Avengers* (also known as *Roger Corman Presents "Alien Avengers"* and *Welcome to Planet Earth*), Showtime, 1996.
Carter, *Executive Target,* HBO, 1997.
Ed Lang, *Host* (also known as *Virtual Obsession*), ABC, 1998.
Weems, *Always Outnumbered* (also known as *Always Outnumbered, Always Outgunned*), HBO, 1998.
Officer, *Horse Sense,* The Disney Channel, 1999.
Sam Kinsett, *Three Secrets,* CBS, 1999.
Agent Neely, *Murder, She Wrote: A Story to Die For,* CBS, 2000.
Tommy's father, *Dancing in September,* HBO, 2001.
Huge cop, *Earth vs. the Spider,* Cinemax, 2001.

Television Appearances; Pilots:
Lieutenant Douglas, *Pacific Blue,* USA Network, 1996.
First security guard, *Clubhouse,* CBS, 2004.

Television Appearances; Episodic:
Jackie Stubbs, "Poison," *A Man Called Hawk,* ABC, 1989.
Dr. Martin Tomkins, "Providence," *Doctor Doctor,* CBS, 1990.
Snar (some sources cite Snaz), "Split Second," *Tales from the Crypt,* HBO, 1991.
George, "Requiem for a Garbage Man," *Roc,* Fox, 1991.
"Stormy Weather: Part 1," *Jake and the Fatman,* CBS, 1992.
Barry, "The Guilty Party," *Dream On,* HBO, 1992.
Officer Walters, "The Green, Green Grass of Home," *L.A. Law,* NBC, 1993.
Vince Meyers, "Pros and Convicts," *Hangin' with Mr. Cooper,* ABC, 1994.
Detective Richard Duarte, "The Bitch is Back," *Melrose Place,* Fox, 1994.
First cop, "The Shawn–Shank Redemption," *The Wayans Bros.,* The WB, 1995.
Lieutenant, "The Healers," *ER,* NBC, 1996.
Father Ray, "The Dark Side of the Moon," *Nowhere Man,* UPN, 1996.
Lieutenant Douglas, "Captive Audience," *Pacific Blue,* USA Network, 1996.
(Uncredited) "The One with the Race Car Bed," *Friends,* NBC, 1996.
Bouncer, "Where's 'Swaldo," *NYPD Blue,* ABC, 1996.
Reverend Thomas, "Do the Wrong Thing," *The Wayans Bros.,* The WB, 1996.
"A Rock and a Hard Place," *High Tide,* syndicated, 1997.
Lloyd, "The Goode, the Bad, and the Willie," *Goode Behavior,* UPN, 1997.
Dr. Fletcher, "Under the Reds," *The Pretender,* NBC, 1997.
"Primal Scream," *Profiler,* NBC, 1997.
Officer Tedesco, "The Means," *The Practice,* ABC, 1997.

Lieutenant Hecker, "There's an Old Flame: Part 2," *The Good News,* UPN, 1997.

Prosecutor, "Existence," *Prey,* ABC, 1998.

Bentley Langford, "My Pest Friend's Wedding," *In the House,* UPN, 1998.

Simon, "Amazing Grace," *Night Man,* syndicated, 1998.

Daniel, "Telling the Office," *Oh Baby,* Lifetime, 1998.

Ron Jarek, "Lucky Burger," *NewsRadio,* NBC, 1998.

Referee, "Popularity," *Clueless,* UPN, 1999.

Bernard Harding, "True Stories," *Pensacola: Wings of Gold,* syndicated, 1999.

Ed Adams, "Games," *Family Law,* CBS, 1999.

Megan Whoopie, "Secrets and Lies," *Dawson's Creek,* The WB, 1999.

Principal, "Heat Wave," *Roswell,* The WB, 1999.

Remick, "Santa on Ice," *Becker,* CBS, 1999.

Principal, "Sexual Healing," *Roswell,* The WB, 2000.

Reverend Maurice Haybrook, "The Fire Next Time," *18 Wheels of Justice,* The Nashville Network, 2000.

Coach Wilson, "History Lessons," *Get Real,* Fox, 2000.

"Separation Anxiety," *The Invisible Man,* Sci–Fi Channel, 2000.

School Principal Bradford Jolie, "The Man with the Bag," *Ally McBeal,* Fox, 2000.

Mr. Pennix, "I Wanna Be Suspended," *Grounded for Life,* Fox, 2001.

Demolition expert, "Mr. Wrong," *That's Life,* CBS, 2001.

Curley, "The Iron Coffin," *JAG,* CBS, 2001.

Mr. Pennix, "Eddie's Dead," *Grounded for Life,* Fox, 2001.

Sergeant Matthew Richter, "Loyalties," *The Guardian,* CBS, 2001.

Bradley Baker, *The Bold and the Beautiful,* CBS, 2001.

Malik, "Poker: Parts 1 & 2," *Malcolm in the Middle,* Fox, 2002.

Mr. Pennix, "We Didn't Start the Fire" (some sources cite "I Didn't Start the Fire"), *Grounded for Life,* Fox, 2002.

"When Approaching a Let–Go," *Presidio Med,* CBS, 2002.

Dr. Mumford, "The Deflower Half–Hour," *Off Centre,* The WB, 2002.

Police officer, "Just a Formality," *Everybody Loves Raymond,* CBS, 2003.

Malik, "Long Drive," *Malcolm in the Middle,* Fox, 2003.

Joseph Vigna, "Absolute Perfection," *Robbery Homicide Division,* CBS, 2003.

Malik, "Baby: Parts 1 & 2," *Malcolm in the Middle,* Fox, 2003.

Police officer, "Robert's Wedding," *Everybody Loves Raymond,* CBS, 2003.

(Uncredited) Detective Avery, "Going Down," *Judging Amy,* CBS, 2003.

Mechanic, "Under Color of Law," *The Handler,* CBS, 2003.

"Crash," *JAG,* CBS, 2004.

Detective Avery, "Order and Chaos," *Judging Amy,* CBS, 2004.

Maurice "Mad Mo" Banks, "Yo, Adrian," *Cold Case,* CBS, 2005.

Pretzel man, "Still Bonding," *Still Standing,* 2005.

Also appeared as an officer, *Life with Roger,* The WB; Richard Haas, *Moloney,* CBS; a paramedic, *Nothing Sacred,* ABC; and security guard, *7 Days,* UPN.

Television Work; Additional Voices; Anime Series:

Serial Experiments: Lain (also known as *Wirtualna Lain*), Tech TV Channel, 1998.

Kido senshi Gundam: Dai 08 MS shotai (also known as *Gundam 08th MS Team, Gundam MS08, Mobile Suit Gundam: The 08th MS Team,* and *08th MS Team*), Cartoon Network, 2001–2002.

Also provided additional voices for *Cowboy Bebop.*

Film Appearances:

Hawthorne, *Casualties of War,* Columbia, 1989.

Joe, *Bloodfist IV: Die Trying* (also known as *Die Trying*), California, 1992.

Andy Simpson, *Sleepwalkers* (also known as *Sleepstalkers* and *Stephen King's "Sleepwalkers"*), Columbia, 1992.

Cooper, *Beverly Hills Cop III,* Paramount, 1994.

Harry Dieter, *Heat,* Warner Bros., 1995.

Croupier, *Fox Hunt,* Capcom Entertainment, 1996.

Los Angeles police sergeant, *Nothing to Lose,* Buena Vista/Touchstone Pictures, 1997.

Second FBI gate guard, *Rush Hour,* New Line Cinema, 1998.

Leprechaun in the Hood, 2000.

Bailiff, *The Man Who Wasn't There,* USA Films, 2001.

Sacred Is the Flesh (also known as *Sacred*), Strange Fruit Films, 2001.

Lieutenant Paul Jackson, *Angel Blade,* Vegas Knights Film Productions, 2002.

FBI agent, *Enough,* Columbia, 2002.

Pilot, *Crocodile 2: Death Swamp* (also known as *Crocodile 2: Death Roll*), Nu Image, 2002.

(As Jake Martin) Voice of police captain in English version, *WXIII: Patlabor the Movie 3* (anime), Pioneer Entertainment, 2003.

Captain Morgan, *Groom Lake* (also known as *The Visitor*), Shadow Entertainment, 2003.

(As Jake Martin) Jack, *The Reception* (short film), 2004.

Patrol officer, *3–Way,* Columbia TriStar Home Video, 2004.

Stage Appearances:

Hank, *The Phonograph,* Towne Street Theatre Conservatory, Raven Playhouse, North Hollywood, CA, 2002.

Summers in Suffolk, Theatre–Theatre, Hollywood, CA, 2003.

Appeared in *Cobb,* Yale Repertory Theatre, New Haven, CT; and *Five on the Black Hand Side.*

Major Tours:

Toured as Theo, *Ceremonies in Dark Old Men,* Negro Ensemble Company; in *One Flew over the Cuckoo's Nest,* Classic Theatre International; and as Captain Davenport, *A Soldier's Story,* Negro Ensemble Company.

Stage Director:

Directed productions of *Ambiguity,* Towne Street Theatre Conservatory; and *Fences,* National Black Theatre Festival.

RECORDINGS

Anime Videos:

Voice of Onuma for English version, *Kyoshoku soko Guyver Act II* (also known as *Guyver: Bio–Booster Armor, Act Two*), 1991.

Voice, *Hand Maid May,* Pioneer Entertainment, 2001.

(As Jake Martin) Voice of Inspector Daisuke Hashimoto for English version, *Gate Keepers* (also known as *Gate Keepers 21*), Pioneer Entertainment, 2001.

(As Jake Daniels) Voices of Neil Olsen and others in English version, *Heat Guy J,* Pioneer Entertainment, 2002.

(As Jake Martin) Voice of Master Chief Ginpun in English version, *Maho tsukai ni taisetsu na koto,* TV Asahi, 2003.

(As Jake Martin) Voice, *Galerians: Ash* (video game), Sammy Studios, 2003.

Voice for English version, *Orguss 02* (also known as *Super Dimension Century Orguss Two: Orguss 02* and *Cho Jiku Seiki Orguss 02*), Manga Entertainment, 2003.

(As Jake Martin) Voice of Inspector Koichi Zenigata, *Rupan sansei: Majutsu–ou no isan* (video game; also known as *Lupin the 3rd: Treasure of the Sorcerer King*), Bandai America, 2004.

Voice, *Akira,* Geneon, 2004.

Voice of Professor Shizuma for English version, *Jaianto robo: The Animation* (also known as *Giant Robo: The Animation—The Day the Earth Stood Still*), AnimeWorks, 2004.

Voice for *Panda! Go, Panda!* (also known as *Panda Kopanda*) and *Panda! Go, Panda! Rainy Day* (also known as *Panda–Kopanda: Amefuri Circus no Makai*); and *The Wings of Honneamise* (also known as *Royal Space Force, Star Quest, Wing of Royal Space Troop Honneamise,* and *Oritsu Ucuugun—Honneamise no Tsubasa*). Several of these anime videos were broadcast originally in Japanese as television series.

Anime Videos; Additional Voices:

Kyoshoku soko Guyver (also known as *Guyver: Bio–Booster Armor*), 1989.

Battle Athletes, AIC/Domu/Genco, 1997.

Battle Athletes daiundokai (also known as *Battle Athletes Victory*), Pioneer Entertainment, 1998.

Morudaiba (also known as *Moldiver*), AIC/Pioneer, 1993.

Yugen kaisha (also known as *Phantom Quest Corp.* and *You gen kai sya*), Pioneer Entertainment, 1994.

Street Fighter II: V (also known as *Street Fighter II: Victory*), 1995.

Shinpi no sekai Eru Hazado (also known as *El Hazard: The Magnificent World*), AIC/Pioneer, 1995.

Rakusho! Hyper Doll (also known as *Hyperdoll* and *Hyperdoll: Mew & Mica the Easy Fighter*), Bandai Entertainment, 1995.

(As Jake Daniels) *Vandread* (also known as *Vandread: The Second Stage*), Pioneer Entertainment, 2000.

Chojiku yosai Macross II Lovers, Again (also known as *Macross II: Lovers Again* and *Superdimensional Fortress Macross II: Lovers Again*), PolyGram Home Video, 2000.

Sol Bianca: The Legacy (also known as *Ship of the Sun: The Legacy*), Pioneer Entertainment, 2003.

Several of these anime videos were broadcast originally in Japanese as television series.

MARTIN, Jake
    See MARTIN, Dan

MARTINEZ, Cliff 1954–

PERSONAL

Full name, Clifford Martinez; born February 5, 1954, in New York, NY.

Addresses: *Agent*—Soundtrack Music Associates, 15760 Ventura Blvd., #2021, Encino, CA 91436.

Career: Composer and actor. Drummer with rock bands, including Captain Beefheart, Red Hot Chili Peppers, Dickies, and Weirdos.

Awards, Honors: Golden Satellite Award nomination, best original score, BMI Film Music Award, 2001, Grammy Award nomination, best score soundtrack, National Academy of Recording Arts and Sciences, 2002, for *Traffic.*

CREDITS

Film Appearances:
Member of Red Hot Chili Peppers, *Tough Guys,* 1986.
Dickies band member, *18 Again,* New World Pictures, 1988.
Red Hot Chili Peppers: What Hits?, 1992.

WRITINGS

Film Scores:
Sex, Lies, and Videotape (also known as *Sex, Lies...*), Miramax, 1989.
Pump Up the Volume (also known as *Plein volume* and *Y a–t–il une vie apres le lycee?*), New Line Cinema, 1990.
Kafka, Miramax, 1991.
Night and the City, Twentieth Century–Fox, 1992.
King of the Hill, United International, 1993.
Underneath (also known as *The Underneath*), Gramercy, 1995.
Gray's Anatomy, Northern Arts, 1996.
Schizopolis (also known as *Steven Soderbergh's "Schizopolis"*), Wellspring Media, 1996.
Wicked, 1998.
Out of Sight, Universal, 1998.
The Limey, Artisan, 1999.
Traffic (also known as *Traffic—Die Macht des Kartells*), Alliance Atlantis, 2000.
Narc (also known as *Narco*), Paramount, 2002.
Solaris, Twentieth Century–Fox, 2002.
Narc: Shooting Up, Paramount Home Video, 2003.
Wonderland, Lions Gate Films, 2003.
Wicker Park, Metro–Goldwyn–Mayer, 2004.
Havoc, Media & Entertainment, 2005.

Film Songs:
(Uncredited) "Black Eyed Blonde," *Thrashin',* AIP, 1986.

Television Music; Specials:
The Pee–Wee Herman Show, HBO, 1981.

Television Songs; Series:
"I'm Gonna Drawl," *G String Divas,* 2000.

Television Music; Movies:
Black Magic, Showtime, 1992.

MAZUR, Monet 1976–

PERSONAL

Full name, Monet Happy Mazur; born April 17, 1976, in Los Angeles, CA; daughter of Ruby (an illustrator).

Addresses: *Agent*—United Talent Agency, 9560 Wilshire Blvd., Suite 500, Beverly Hills, CA 90212. *Manager*—Principal Entertainment, 1964 Westwood Blvd., Suite 400, Los Angeles, CA 90025. *Publicist*—Baker/Winokur/Ryder, 9100 Wilshire Blvd., 6th Floor, West Tower, Beverly Hills, CA 90212.

Career: Actress. Nancy Raygun (a rock band), member. Appeared in television commercials, including Nice 'n' Easy hair color and Gap.

Awards, Honors: Young Hollywood Award, new stylemaker–female, 2002.

CREDITS

Film Appearances:
Flirting woman, *Addams Family Values,* Paramount, 1993.
Lila Ridgeway, *Raging Angels,* Borde, 1995.
Mod girl, *Austin Powers: International Man of Mystery,* New Line Cinema, 1997.
Dolly, *The Mod Squad,* United International, 1999.
Becky Beaner, *Mystery Men,* United International, 1999.
Girlfriend, *Welcome to Hollywood,* 2000.
Maria, *Blow,* New Line Cinema, 2001.
Kathy Pogue, *Angel Eyes,* Warner Bros., 2001.
Georgia, *The Learning Curve* (also known as *Dangerous Seduction*), Metro–Goldwyn–Mayer, 2001.
Lead model, *Sadie's Daydream,* Rica Jones, 2002.
Kiki, *Comic Book Villains,* Lions Gate Films, 2002.
Candy, *40 Days and 40 Nights* (also known as *40 jours et 40 nuits*), Universal, 2002.
Vanessa, *Stark Raving Mad,* Columbia TriStar, 2002.
Antonia "Toni" Sposato, *Kiss the Bride,* Imageworks, 2002.
Lauren, *Just Married* (also known as *Voll verheiratet*), Twentieth Century–Fox, 2003.
Title role, *Whirlygirl,* All the Way Round, 2004.
Shane, *Torque,* Warner Bros., 2004.
Fiona, *Monster–in–Law,* Warner Bros., 2005.
Anita Pallenberg, *The Wild and Wycked World of Brian Jones,* 2005.
Monet, *In Memory of My Father,* Persona, 2005.

Television Appearances; Series:
First Brandee Fields, *Days of Our Lives* (also known as *DOOL* and *Days*), NBC, 1993.

Television Appearances; Pilots:
Kansas, ABC, 1995.

Television Appearances; Episodic:
Erica, "Ready or Not," *Party of Five,* Fox, 1995.
Erica, "Falsies," *Party of Five,* Fox, 1995.

Cassandra Tyson, "Lullaby," *Strange World,* ABC, 1999.
Laurie Tindell, "Not Just a River in Egypt," *Jack & Jill,* The WB, 1999.
Last Call with Carson Daly, 2002.
The Howard Stern Show, 2002.

RECORDINGS

Music Videos:
Appeared in "Revolving Door" by Crazy Town.

OTHER SOURCES

Periodicals:
Movieline, June, 2001, p. 16.
Premiere, May, 2003, pp. 73–74.

McCORKLE, Kevin

PERSONAL

Career: Actor and producer. Also worked as assistant director and scenic artist.

CREDITS

Film Appearances:
Autograph seeker, *Six Pack,* Twentieth Century–Fox, 1982.
Customer, *Stroker Ace,* Universal/Warner Bros., 1983.
Tommy Cage, *Out of Bounds,* Columbia, 1986.
Zeke, *Oasis Cafe,* 1994.
Jack, *Shooter on the Side,* New City Releasing, 1996.
George, *Hero, Lover, Fool,* Golden Shadow Pictures, 1996.
Psycho soup bum, *Blood Type,* KHW Entertainment and Skonto Films Partnership/Tuppence Productions, 1999.
Jeff, *Swallows,* Arrival Entertainment, 1999.
The lost dog, *The Remote,* Warner Home Video, 2000.
James, *Mic and the Claw,* Golden Shadow Pictures/ Asylum, 2000.
Peter Fromm, *March,* Kanan/Hammerschlag, 2001.
Fredo, *Natural Selection,* 2003.
Gary, *Reckless Abandon* (short film), Stupid Genius Productions, 2003.
The Pearl, Bullet Productions, 2004.
Laurent's shadow, *The Island,* DreamWorks, 2005.

Film Work:
Producer, *Hero, Lover, Fool,* Golden Shadow Pictures, 1996.

Producer, *Mic and the Claw,* Golden Shadow Pictures/ Asylum, 2000.
Coproducer, *Solomon Bernstein's Bathroom* (short film), Montauk Films, 2000.

Television Appearances; Series:
Detective Gil Sherman, a recurring role, *Cold Case,* CBS, 2003–2004.

Television Appearances; Movies:
News photographer, *For Us the Living: The Medgar Evers Story* (also known as *For Us the Living*), PBS, 1983.
Tagget (also known as *Dragonfire*), USA Network, 1991.
Bellhop, *The Great Pretender* (also known as *Dead End Brattigan*), NBC, 1991.
(Uncredited) *Death Dreams,* Lifetime, 1991.

Television Appearances; Episodic:
Alien captain, "The Omega Directive," *Star Trek: Voyager,* UPN, 1998.
Bartender, "Monday: Time in a Bottle," *Port Charles* (also known as *Port Charles: Desire, Port Charles: Fate, Port Charles: Miracles Happen, Port Charles: Naked Eyes, Port Charles: Secrets, Port Charles: Superstitions, Port Charles: Surrender, Port Charles: Tainted Love, Port Charles: Tempted, Port Charles: The Gift, Port Charles: Time in a Bottle,* and *Port Charles: Torn*), ABC, 2001.
Tony, "The Warsaw Closes," *The Drew Carey Show,* ABC, 2001.
SD–6 agent, "Spirit," *Alias,* ABC, 2001.
Second cult man, "Providence," *The X–Files,* Fox, 2002.
Captain Franklin, "Born to Run," *Line of Fire,* ABC, 2003.
Commander Edwards, "Free Byrd," *The District,* CBS, 2003.
Dan McClafferty, "Minimum Security," *Navy NCIS: Naval Criminal Investigative Service,* CBS, 2003.
Los Angeles police officer, "Day 2: 12:00 p.m.–1:00 p.m.," *24,* Fox, 2004.
Captain Jack Pine, "Pro Per," *CSI: Miami,* CBS, 2004.
Astronaut Gus Grissom, "It's My Life," *American Dreams,* NBC, 2005.

McCULLOUGH, Kim 1978–

PERSONAL

Full name, Kimberly Anne McCullough; born March 5, 1978, in Bellflower, CA. *Education:* Attended New York University.

Addresses: *Agent*—Metropolitan Talent Agency, 4526 Wilshire Blvd., Los Angeles, CA 90010.

Career: Actress and producer.

Awards, Honors: Soap Opera Digest Award, outstanding child star, 1986 and 1993, Soap Opera Digest Award nomination, outstanding younger leading actress, 1992, Young Artist Award, outstanding young actress, 1986 and 1987, Young Artist Award nominations, best young actress, 1988, 1989, 1990, and 1997, Daytime Emmy Awards, outstanding juvenile female, 1989, and outstanding younger leading actress, 1996, Daytime Emmy Award nominations, outstanding young actress, 1990 and 1997, YoungStar Award nomination, best performance by a young actress, 1997, all for *General Hospital.*

CREDITS

Television Appearances; Series:
Robin Scorpio, *General Hospital,* ABC, 1985–2000, 2004.
Jennifer, a recurring role, *Once and Again,* ABC, 1999–2000.
Robin Scorpio, *All My Children,* ABC, 2001.
Beth Reinhart, a recurring role, *Joan of Arcadia,* CBS, 2004–2005.

Television Appearances; Movies:
Alyssa Lennox, *Dying to Dance,* NBC, 2001.

Television Appearances; Specials:
The 17th Annual Daytime Emmy Awards, ABC, 1990.
Positive: A Journey into AIDS (documentary; also known as *The ABC Afterschool Special*), ABC, 1995.
In a New Light: Sex Unplugged, ABC, 1995.
Hot Summer Soaps, ABC, 1995.
Robin Scorpio, *General Hospital: Twist of Fate,* ABC, 1996.
April, *Crosstown* (also known as *Schoolbreak Special: Crosstown*), CBS, 1996.
Sex with Cindy Crawford, ABC, 1998.
The General Hospital 35th Anniversary Show, ABC, 1998.
ABC Soaps' Most Unforgettable Love Stories, ABC, 1998.
Maternity Ward: Fragile Balance (documentary), The Learning Channel, 2002.
Intimate Portrait: Finola Hughes, Lifetime, 2002.

Appeared as a dancer, *People's Choice Awards.*

Television Appearances; Episodic:
Rachel's classmate, "Speaking in Tongues," *Nothing Sacred,* ABC, 1997.

Robin Scorpio, *Port Charles,* ABC, 1998.
Jennifer Hobson, "Underground," *Sons of Thunder,* CBS, 1999.
Phoebe, "Taboo or Not Taboo," *Party of Five,* Fox, 2000.
Becky Jo Jensen, "America's Sweetheart," *DAG,* NBC, 2001.
Nori, "Fear of Commitment," *ER,* NBC, 2001.
Melissa Johnston, "Who Shot Dick?," *Judging Amy,* CBS, 2002.
Isabelle, "Four Fathers," *Crossing Jordan,* NBC, 2002.
Carly Sifton, "Big Brother," *Family Law,* CBS, 2002.
Deena, "Blowback," *The Shield,* F/X, 2002.
Deena, "Pay in Pain," *The Shield,* F/X, 2002.
Chari, "Heart of Gold," *Firefly,* Fox, 2003.
Audra, "She Ain't Heavy, She's My Sister," *The Stones,* CBS, 2004.
Second vampire, "Suckers," *CSI: Crime Scene Investigation* (also known as *C.S.I.*), CBS, 2004.
Audra, "Seamus on You," *The Stones,* CBS, 2004.
Deena, "Streaks and Tips," *The Shield,* F/X, 2004.
Audra, "The Lawyer Trap," *The Stones,* CBS, 2004.

Also appeared as a dancer, *Fame* and *Solid Gold.*

Television Appearances; Pilots:
Audra, *The Stones,* 2004.

Also appeared as Gina in the unaired pilot for *Undressed.*

Television Producer; Specials:
A Passion for Faith (documentary), ABC, 1990.

Film Appearances:
Kimberly, *Breakin' 2: Electric Boogaloo* (also known as *Breakdance 2: Electric Boogaloo*), TriStar, 1984.
Dorra Orfus, *Purple People Eater,* Concorde, 1988.
Barbara Siegel, *Bugsy,* TriStar, 1991.
Lori Parker, *Consenting Adults,* Buena Vista, 1992.
Amy, *Legally Blonde,* Metro–Goldwyn–Mayer, 2001.
Mindy, *Cigarette,* Film Makers, 2003.
Alice, *Greener Mountains,* Waterfall, 2004.
Inn Trouble, 2004.

Stage Appearances:
Little Cosette, *Les miserables,* Los Angeles, 1988.

WRITINGS

Television Specials:
A Passion for Earth (documentary), ABC, 1990.

McNEICE, Ian 1950–

PERSONAL

Born October 2, 1950, in Bashingstoke, Hampshire, England; married (divorced); children: Travers, Angus, Maisie. *Education:* Studied acting at the Salisbury Playhouse and the London Academy of Music and Dramatic Art.

Addresses: *Agent*—Markham and Froggatt Ltd., 4 Windmill Street, London W1P 1HF, England.

Career: Actor. Royal Shakespeare Company, member for four years.

CREDITS

Film Appearances:
"Fats" Bannerman, *Voice Over,* Welsh Arts, 1983.
Blindman, *Top Secret!,* Paramount, 1984.
Thrush, *Whoops Apocalypse,* Metro–Goldwyn–Mayer, 1986.
Harry, *Personal Services,* Vestron, 1987.
Bill Humphries, *84 Charing Cross Road,* Columbia, 1987.
(Uncredited) *Cry Freedom,* Universal, 1987.
Bernard Rice, *The Lonely Passion of Judith Hearne,* Island, 1987.
The farmer, *The Raggedy Rawney,* L. W. Blair, 1988.
Azolan, *Valmont,* Orion, 1989.
Prince of Wales, *1871,* ICA, 1990.
Merrydew, embassy representative, *The Russia House,* United International, 1990.
First Businessman, *Secret Friends,* Briarpatch, 1991.
Ian, *Year of the Comet,* Columbia, 1992.
King, *No Escape* (also known as *Escape from Absolom*), Savoy, 1994.
Stanley Sharkey, *Funny Bones,* Buena Vista, 1995.
George Garrad, *The Englishman Who Went Up a Hill But Came Down a Mountain,* Miramax, 1995.
Fulton Greewall, *Ace Ventura: When Nature Calls* (also known as *Ace Ventura Goes to Africa*), Warner Bros., 1995.
Ira Grushinsky, *The Beautician and the Beast,* Paramount, 1997.
Mayhew, *A Life Less Ordinary,* United International, 1997.
Sir Maximilian Fair Brown, *The Auteur Theory,* Pathfinder, 1999.
Pishchik, *The Cherry Orchard* (also known as *O Byssinokipos* and *La cerisaie*), Kino, 1999.
The inspector, *The Nine Lives of Tomas Katz* (also known as *Die Neun Leben des Tomas Katz*), E.D., 2000.

Bishop, *Anazapta,* Imagine, 2001.
Dr. Sproul, *The Body,* TriStar, 2001.
Peter Principal, *Town & Country,* New Line Cinema, 2001.
Lewiston, MI5 officer, *The Fourth Angel* (also known as *Vengeance secrete*), Artisan, 2001.
Robert Drudge, *From Hell,* Twentieth Century–Fox, 2001.
Doug Chandler, *Amnesia,* Medusa, 2002.
Priest, *The Final Curtain,* Universal, 2002.
Harry Kane, *Chaos and Cadavers,* High Point, 2003.
Hugh the Sideburns, *Blackball,* First Look, 2003.
Graham, *I'll Be There,* Warner Bros., 2003.
Forensic profiler Saul Seger, *Freeze Frame,* Universal, 2004.
Colonel Kitchener, *Around the World in 80 Days,* Buena Vista, 2004.
Quizmaster, *Bridget Jones: The Edge of Reason* (also known as *Bridget Jones 2* and *Bridget Jones: L'age de raison*), United International, 2004.
Raymond Price, *White Noise,* United International, 2005.
Vogon Kwaltz, *The Hitchhiker's Guide to the Galaxy,* Buena Vista, 2005.

Television Appearances; Miniseries:
Wackford Squeers/Scaley/Croupier, *The Life and Adventures of Nicholas Nickleby,* The Disney Channel and syndicated, 1983.
Alexander, *The Cleopatras,* 1983.
Henry Harcourt, *Edge of Darkness,* syndicated, 1985.
Sefton Boyd, *A Perfect Spy* (also known as *John Le Carre's "A Perfect Spy"*), BBC and PBS, 1987.
Philip Benton, *Wipe Out,* 1988.
Batcular, *Around the World in 80 Days* (also known as *Il giro del mondo in 80 giorni* and *In 80 Tagen um die Welt*), NBC, 1989.
Tate lecturer, *Look At It This Way,* 1992.
George Collard, *The Blackheath Poisonings,* PBS, 1992.
Prosecutor, *The Scarlet and the Black,* 1993.
Dent, *The Wimbledon Poisoner,* BBC, 1994.
Zief, *Have Your Cake and Eat It,* 1997.
Canon Eloard, "The Devil's Novice," *Cadfael 2,* PBS, 1997.
Desmond Ulrick, *A Certain Justice,* PBS, 1999.
Mr. Dick, *David Copperfield,* BBC and PBS, 2000.
Dr. Bliss, *Longitude,* Arts and Entertainment, 2000.
Baron Vladimir Harkonnen, *Dune* (also known as *Duna, Frank Herbert's "Dune," Frank Herbert's Dune—Der Wuestenplanet,* and *Der Wuestenplanet*), Sci–Fi Channel, 2000.
Baron Vladimir Harkonnen, *Children of Dun* (also known as *Dune—Bedrohung des Imperiums, Dune—Der Messias, Dune—Die Kinder de Wuestenplaneten* and *Frank Herbert's "Children of Dune"*), Sci–Fi Channel, 2003.
Lentulus Batiatus, *Spartacus,* USA Network, 2004.
Professor Krempe, *Frankenstein,* Hallmark Channel, 2004.

Television Appearances; Series:
Leather Hardbones, *Time Riders,* 1991.
Franklyn Bysouth, *Stay Lucky,* YTV, 1993.
First Gustave LaRoche, *Chef!,* BBC, 1994.
Chuck Purvis, *Ain't Misbehavin,* 1994.
Testament: The Bible in Animation (animated), HBO, 1996.
Pelham Denning, *Paradise Heights* (also known as *The Eustace Brothers*), 2002.
Bert Large, *Doc Martin,* 2004.

Television Appearances; Movies:
Shrike, *Dark River,* 1990.
Dick Baker, *An Ungentlemanly Act,* 1992.
Norman, *Running Late,* 1992.
Dr. Holly, *The Cloning of Janna May,* 1992.
Oscar Bhilardi, *Don't Leave Me This Way,* BBC, 1993.
Runciman, *Sharpe's Battle,* 1995.
Professor Davenport, *The Canterville Ghost,* ABC, 1997.
Tapling, *Hornblower: The Examination for Lieutenant* (also known as *Horatio Hornblower: The Fire Ship*), Arts and Entertainment, 1998.
Mr. Albert Fezziwig, *A Christmas Carol,* TNT, 1999.
Mr. Tarbuck, *The Sleeper,* BBC, 2000.
Dr. Gerhard Klopfer, *Conspiracy,* HBO, 2001.
Ivan, *Armadillo,* Arts and Entertainment and BBC, 2001.
Haywood Donovan, *Murder Rooms: The Kingdom of Bones,* BBC, 2001.
Nigel Batty, *Man and Boy,* 2002.
Lentulus Batiatus, *Spartacus,* USA Network, 2004.
Bill Bache, *Cherished,* BBC, 2005.

Television Appearances; Pilots:
Louie, *Three of a Kind,* ABC, 1989.
Casca, *Age of Treason,* 1993.
Gideon, *7:08,* 1997.

Television Appearances; Specials:
Potiphar, *Joseph and the Amazing Technicolor Dreamcoat* (also known as *Great Performances: Joseph and the Amazing Technicolor Dreamcoat*), PBS, 2000.
Contributor, *Happy Birthday BBC Two,* 2004.

Television Appearances; Episodic:
Eric Morgan, "Rocky Eight and a Half," *Minder,* ITV, 1984.
Fowler, "Avenge, O Lord," *Bergerac,* BBC1, 1985.
Kerber, "Passage Hawk," *C.A.T.S. Eyes,* ITV, 1986.
Graham Barker, "In It for the Monet," *Boon,* ITV, 1989.
Gervase Rackham, "The Italian Venus," *Lovejoy,* Arts and Entertainment, 1991.
Ivan Teal, "Murder Being Once Done," *The Ruth Rendell Mysteries,* 1991.

Pathologist, "Deadly Slumber," *Inspector Morse,* ITV and PBS, 1993.
Sir Nigel Hussey, "Seven Deadly Sinners," *Cluedo,* ITV, 1993.
Leon, "La solitude," *Paris,* CBS, 1994.
Barry Wilkes, "Who Only Stand and Wait," *Pie in the Sky,* 1994.
Coroner, "Inquest," *The Bill,* ITV1, 1994.
Barry Wilkes, "The Mystery of Pikey," *Pie in the Sky,* 1995.
Peter Hunter, "A Sporting Chance," *Bugs,* BBC, 1995.
Dr. Oliver Burgess, "Who Killed Cock Robin?," *Midsomer Murders,* ITV, 2001.
Lord Andrew, "Fountain of Youth," *Relic Hunter,* syndicated, 2002.
Harrison, "Incubus," *Strange,* BBC, 2003.
Judge, "Persephone," *Spooks,* BBC, 2004.

Also appeared as Wilkie, "The Place of Cold Fires," *Moon and Son.*

Stage Appearances:
His man, *Henry VI Part One,* Royal Shakespeare Company, Stratford–upon–Avon, England, 1977.
Apprentice/first gentleman, *Henry VI Part Two,* Royal Shakespeare Company, 1977.
Young Wackford Squeers, Scaley, and Croupier, *The Life and Adventures of Nicholas Nickleby,* Plymouth Theatre, New York City, 1981–82.
Kean, Old Vic Theatre, London, 1990.

MEDRANO, Frank 1954–

PERSONAL

Born April 9, 1954, in Brooklyn, NY.

Addresses: *Agent*—Charles Silver, SMS Talent, Inc., 8730 West Sunset Blvd., Suite 440, West Hollywood, CA 90069. *Manager*—Kathy Carter, Axiom Management, 10701 Wilshire Blvd., Suite 1202, Los Angeles, CA 90024.

Career: Actor.

CREDITS

Film Appearances:
Student waiter, *The Waiter,* 1993.
Steve, *High Kicks,* 1993.

Teamster, *... And God Spoke* (also known as *The Making of "... And God Spoke"*), Live Entertainment, 1993.

Vic, *Amongst Friends,* Fine Line, 1993.

Fat Ass, *The Shawshank Redemption,* Columbia, 1994.

Graybera (some sources cite Guaybera), *Fair Game,* Warner Bros., 1995.

Yevgeny, *The Destiny of Marty Fine,* 1995.

Rizzi, *The Usual Suspects* (also known as *Die ueblichen verdaechtigen*), Gramercy, 1995.

Eddie Agajan, *Cover Me,* 1995.

Larry Giancarlo, *Chameleon,* 1995.

Man in plane, *Bogus,* Warner Bros., 1996.

Fat Mancho, *Sleepers,* Warner Bros., 1996.

Leon, *The Fan,* TriStar, 1996.

Mechanic, *Father's Day,* Warner Bros., 1997.

Heckle, *Suicide Kings,* Live Entertainment, 1997.

Bartender, *Enemy of the State,* Buena Vista, 1998.

Charles' killer, *Fallen,* Warner Bros., 1998.

Cliff Randal, *Kissing a Fool,* Universal, 1998.

Fat Eddie, *Southie,* Lions Gate Films, 1998.

Rawlins, *The Replacement Killers,* Columbia, 1998.

Frank, *Shock Television* (also known as *Shock TV*), 1998.

Sal Lombardo, *Telling You* (also known as *Love Sucks*), 1999.

The Boss, 1999.

Frank, *Blue Streak* (also known as *Der diamanten–cop*), Columbia, 1999.

Walt, *Coyote Ugly,* Buena Vista, 2000.

Orestes, *The Specials,* Regent Entertainment, 2000.

Manny, *Gabriela,* Power Point Films, 2001.

Sal, *Shade,* RKO International, 2003.

Stanley, *P.S. Your Cat Is Dead,* TLA Releasing, 2003.

El Cojo, *El pasaporte rojo* (also known as *Red Passport*), Dimension Films, 2004.

Television Appearances; Movies:

Jorge de la Paz, *Above Suspicion* (also known as *The Rhinehart Theory*), HBO, 1995.

On Seventh Avenue, NBC, 1996.

Melvin Diamond, *Winchell,* HBO, 1998.

Father Neil, *Michael Angel* (also known as *The Apostate*), Cinemax, 1998.

Television Appearances; Pilots:

Heckler, *Hardball,* Fox, 1994.

First rowdy fan, *Clubhouse,* CBS, 2004.

Television Appearances; Episodic:

Bobby Del Giotto, "Rhyme and Punishment," *L.A. Law,* NBC, 1993.

Heckler, "Whose Strike Is It Anyway?," *Hardball,* Fox, 1994.

Heckler, "Frank Buys an Island, Mike Pays the Price," *Hardball,* Fox, 1994.

Theo Costas, "Good Time Charlie," *NYPD Blue,* ABC, 1994.

(Uncredited) Theo Costas, "A.D.A. Sipowicz," *NYPD Blue,* ABC, 1995.

Cabbie, "Lower East Side Story," *Platypus Man,* UPN, 1995.

"3 Card Monte" Santa, "25 Hours of Christmas," *Nash Bridges,* CBS, 1996.

Sal, "Dead Man Sleeping," *Brooklyn South,* CBS, 1998.

Pete Kokiko, "Yesterday," *Law & Order: Criminal Intent,* NBC, 2002.

Jake, "Dolls," *Law & Order: Special Victims Unit,* NBC, 2002.

Liquor store cashier, "The Review," *Entourage,* HBO, 2004.

Shop employee, "New York," *Entourage,* HBO, 2004.

Bruno, "American Dreamers," *C.S.I.: NY* (also known as *CSI: New York*), CBS, 2004.

Appeared as Al Tashjian in an episode of *High Incident,* ABC; and as Mel Krupp, *Michael Hayes,* CBS.

Television Appearances; Other:

Ephraim's friend, *The Investigator* (special), Showtime, 1994.

Peacock Blues, 1996.

RECORDINGS

Video Games:

Voice of Eddie Pantucci, *Blue Heat: The Case of the Cover Girl Murders,* 1997.

MICHOS, Anastas N.
(Anastas Michos, Tass Mikos)

PERSONAL

Addresses: *Agent*—Gersh Agency, 232 North Canon Dr., Beverly Hills, CA 90210.

Career: Cinematographer and lighting director. Also worked as camera operator, sometimes credited as Anastas Michos or Tass Mikos. Photographer of music videos for Phil Collins, Whitney Houston, and other recording artists.

Member: Society of Cinematographers.

CREDITS

Film Cinematographer:

The Hooters: Nervous Night, 1986.

The Education of Little Tree (also known as *L'education de Little Tree*), Paramount, 1997.

(As Anastas Michos) *Man on the Moon* (also known as *Der mondmann*), Universal, 1999.

The Big Kahuna (also known as *Hospitality Suite*), Lions Gate Films, 1999.

Keeping the Faith, Touchstone, 2000.

What's the Worst that Could Happen?, Metro–Goldwyn–Mayer, 2001.

Death to Smoochy (also known as *Toetet Smoochy*), Warner Bros., 2002.

Duplex (also known as *Our House* and *Der appartement–schreck*), Miramax, 2003.

Mona Lisa Smile, Columbia, 2003.

The Forgotten, Columbia, 2004.

Lady Luck, 2005.

Television Work; Movies:

Lighting director, *Seriously ... Phil Collins,* CBS, 1990.

RECORDINGS

Videos:

Himself, *Scene Stealers* (documentary), Metro–Goldwyn–Mayer Home Entertainment, 2002.

MOLINA, Rolando 1971–
(Rolondo Malina)

PERSONAL

Full name, Rolando Alberto Argueta–Molina; born August 13, 1971, in San Salvador, El Salvador; mother's name, Ana. *Education:* Attended high school in Hollywood, CA.

Addresses: *Agent*—Ellis Talent Group, 4705 Laurel Canyon Blvd., Suite 300, Valley Village, CA 91607. *Manager*—Manny Jimmenez, Suspect Entertainment, 5482 Wilshire Blvd., Suite 293, Los Angeles, CA 90036.

Career: Actor. Universal Studios, worked as a security guard.

CREDITS

Film Appearances:

Gary, *Jamie's Secret,* 1992.

Lenny, *To Protect and Serve,* Apsicon Productions, 1992.

Police officer, *American Me,* Universal, 1992.

Vato, *Menace II Society,* New Line Cinema, 1993.

Police officer, *Im Sog des Boesen* (also known as *Deadly Measures, Desperate Measures, In the Flesh, Nanny's Nightmare, Undercurrent,* and *Desperate—Verzweifelt*), Neverland Films, 1995.

Video store salesperson, *Virtuosity,* Paramount, 1995.

Gang member, *The Rich Man's Wife,* Buena Vista, 1996.

Parent of murdered child, *Eye for an Eye,* Paramount, 1996.

Ruben, *Street Corner Justice,* 1996.

Second man, *Mojave Moon,* Trimark Pictures, 1996.

Hector, *Do Me a Favor* (also known as *Trading Favors*), Imperial Entertainment, 1997.

Anthony Ramirez, *Primary Colors* (also known as *Perfect Couple* and *Mit aller Macht*), Universal, 1998.

Ernie, *Brown's Requiem,* Avalanche Releasing, 1998.

Mr. Big (Jefe), *The Pandora Project,* 1998.

Support van driver, *The Unknown Cyclist,* 1998.

Warehouse worker, *Edtv* (also known as *Ed TV*), MCA/Universal, 1999.

Baby joker, *Next Friday,* New Line Cinema, 2000.

Hector, *Crazy/Beautiful,* Buena Vista, 2001.

Javier, *King Rikki* (also known as *The Street King*), Dream Rock/Moonstone Entertainment, 2002.

Hood, *Bruce Almighty,* Universal, 2003.

Show security person, *Grind,* Warner Bros., 2003.

Benzito, *Cake,* Xenon Pictures, 2004.

Chewi, *Party Animalz,* Artisan Entertainment, 2004.

Oso, *Platinum Illusions,* Urban Dynasty/Fantasy World Entertainment, 2006.

Television Appearances; Series:

Rolando, a recurring role, *ER* (also known as *Emergency Room*), NBC, 1995–96.

Bartender, *Kingpin,* NBC, 2003.

Television Appearances; Miniseries:

Raymond, *The Invaders,* Fox, 1995.

Television Appearances; Movies:

Ramon, *Rockford Files: If the Frame Fits,* CBS, 1996.

Chach, *A Better Way to Die,* HBO, 2000.

Television Appearances; Episodic:

Simmy, "Bitter Fruit," *Street Justice,* syndicated, 1993.

First punk, "The Opposite," *Seinfeld,* NBC, 1994.

Waiter, "There's Got to Be a Morning After," *Living Single,* Fox, 1994.

Grip, "Since I Lost My Baby," *Cybill,* CBS, 1995.

Orson, "I'm Too Sexy for My Brother," *The Wayans Bros.,* WB, 1995.

Joker, "Jumped," *Dangerous Minds,* ABC, 1996.

Munchkin, "Bangers," *Pacific Blue,* USA Network, 1996.

District attorney, "The Green Cover," *Public Morals,* CBS, c. 1996.

First guard, "Columbus Day," *Gun* (also known as *Robert Altman's "Gun"*), ABC, 1997.

Joker, "The Feminine Mystique," *Dangerous Minds*, ABC, 1997.

Hector, "Are You Ready for Some Football?," *Dharma & Greg*, ABC, 1998.

Second bar patron, "Numb & Number," *NYPD Blue*, ABC, 1998.

Camera operator, "Two Guys, a Girl, and the Storm of the Century," *Two Guys, a Girl and a Pizza Place* (also known as *Two Guys and a Girl*), ABC, 1999.

Christian Rudecki, "My Man Sammo," *Martial Law*, CBS, 1999.

(As Rolondo Malina) Dragon Fly bouncer, "Lady Evil," *GvsE* (also known as *Good versus Evil, Good vs. Evil,* and *G vs. E*), USA Network, 1999.

Louis, "Baby, It's Cold Outside," *L.A. Doctors*, CBS, 1999.

Bennie, "Renunciation," *Good versus Evil* (also known as *Good vs. Evil, GvsE,* and *G vs. E*), Sci–Fi Channel, 2000.

Hernandez, "Reckless Abandon," *Charmed*, The WB, 2000.

Juror, "Twelve Angry People," *7th Heaven* (also known as *7th Heaven: Beginnings*), The WB, 2000.

Manolo, "A Thousand Words," *Pacific Blue*, USA Network, 2000.

Mark Vasquez, "Spoil the Child," *Judging Amy*, CBS, 2000.

Iladio, "The 31–Inch–High Club," *Ladies Man*, CBS, 2001.

Randy Drago, "Without a Sound," *Walker, Texas Ranger*, CBS, 2001.

Bolles, "War Stories," *Firefly*, Fox, 2002.

Hector Estanza, "Throwaway," *The Shield*, FX Channel, 2002.

Second father, "Let's Talk about Sex," *Becker*, CBS, 2002.

Valet, "Table for Too Many: Parts 1 & 2," *My Wife and Kids*, ABC, 2002.

Hector Chirullo, "Sunset Division," *Crossing Jordan*, NBC, 2003.

Idalo Tavarez, "Laughlin All the Way to the Clink," *NYPD Blue*, ABC, 2003.

Jesus Linares, "Bleak House," *The Handler*, CBS, 2004.

Security person, "You Can Leave the Lights On," *Less Than Perfect*, ABC, 2005.

Trash collector/God, "Secret Service," *Joan of Arcadia*, CBS, 2005.

Appeared as a criminal, *Bakersfield P.D.*, Fox; as a neighbor, *Cracker* (also known as *Fitz*), ABC; as Erno Pender, *Diagnosis Murder*, CBS; as a technician, *Late-Line*, NBC; as a voice, *Sammy* (animated), NBC; and in *Tracey Takes On ...* , HBO.

MOOR, Cherie
    See LADD, Cheryl

MOORE, Cherie
    See LADD, Cheryl

MOORE, Demi 1962–

PERSONAL

Original name, Demetria Gene Guynes; born November 11, 1962, in Roswell, NM; daughter of Charles Harmon and Virginia King Guynes (some sources cite first name as Victoria); married Freddy Moore (a musician), 1980 (divorced, c. 1984); married Bruce Willis (an actor and producer), November 21, 1987 (divorced, October 18, 2000); children: (second marriage) Rumer Glenn, Scout LaRue, Tallulah Belle. *Education:* Studied acting with Zina Provendie. *Avocational Interests:* Collecting dolls, shopping, soccer.

Addresses: *Agent*—Creative Artists Agency, 9830 Wilshire Blvd., Beverly Hills, CA 90212. *Manager*—Jason Weinberg, Untitled Entertainment, 8436 West Third St., Suite 650, Los Angeles, CA 90048. *Publicist*—PMK/HBH Public Relations, 700 San Vicente Blvd., Suite G910, West Hollywood, CA 90069 (some sources cite 8500 Wilshire Blvd., Suite 700, Beverly Hills, CA 90211).

Career: Actress and producer. Rufglen Films, founder and producer, 1991; Moving Pictures (production company), owner; voice–over artist for commercials; model; costume designer for the theatre. Planet Hollywood (restaurants), co–owner. Worked for a collection agency in Los Angeles. CityKids Foundation, national spokesperson. Some sources cite Moore as a songwriter.

Awards, Honors: Named one of the most "promising new actors of 1986," by *John Willis's "Screen World,"* 1986; *Theatre World* Award, 1987, for *The Early Girl*; Saturn Award, best actress, Academy of Science Fiction, Fantasy, and Horror Films, and Golden Globe Award nomination, best performance by an actress in a musical or comedy, both 1991, for *Ghost*; People's Choice Award, favorite actress in a dramatic motion picture, Proctor & Gamble Productions, 1993; MTV Movie Award nomination, best female performance, 1993, for *A Few Good Men*; MTV Movie Award, best kiss (with Woody Harrelson), and MTV Movie Award nominations, best female performance and most desirable female, all 1994, for *Indecent Proposal*; named ShoWest female star of the year, National Association of Theatre Owners, 1995; MTV Movie Award nominations, best villain and most desirable female, both 1995, for *Disclosure*; MTV Movie Award nomination, most desirable female, 1996, for *The Scarlet Letter;* Emmy Award nominations, President's Award and outstanding made for television movie, and Golden Globe Award nomination, best performance by an actress in a television miniseries or movie made for television, all 1997, for *If These Walls Could Talk;* MTV Movie Award nomination (with Viggo Mortensen), best fight, 1998, for *G.I. Jane;* DVD Premiere Award nomination (with Ritsuko Notani), best animated character performance, DVD Exclusive awards, 2003, for *The Hunchback of Notre Dame II;* Mexican MTV Movie Award, sexiest female villain, and MTV Movie Award nomination, best villain, both 2004, for *Charlie's Angels: Full Throttle.*

CREDITS

Film Appearances:
Corri, *Choices,* 1981.

Patricia Welles, *Parasite,* Embassy Pictures, 1981.

(Uncredited) New intern, *Young Doctors in Love,* Twentieth Century–Fox, 1982.

Laura Victor, *No Small Affair,* Columbia, 1984.

Nicole "Nikki" Hollis, *Blame It on Rio,* Twentieth Century–Fox, 1984.

Jules Jacoby, *St. Elmo's Fire,* Columbia, 1985.

Cassandra Eldrich, *One Crazy Summer* (also known as *Greetings from Nantucket*), Warner Bros., 1986.

Debbie Sullivan, *About Last Night* (also known as *Sexual Perversity in Chicago*), TriStar, 1986.

Karen Simmons, *Wisdom,* Twentieth Century–Fox, 1986.

Abby Quinn, *The Seventh Sign,* TriStar, 1988.

Molly, *We're No Angels,* Paramount, 1989.

Molly Jensen, *Ghost,* Paramount, 1990.

Cynthia Kellogg, *Mortal Thoughts,* Columbia, 1991.

Diane Lightston, *Nothing but Trouble,* Warner Bros., 1991.

Marina Lemke, *The Butcher's Wife,* Paramount, 1991.

Lieutenant commander JoAnne Galloway, *A Few Good Men,* Columbia, 1992.

Diana Murphy, *Indecent Proposal,* Paramount, 1993.

Meredith Johnson, *Disclosure,* Warner Bros., 1994.

A Century of Cinema (documentary), 1994.

Hester Prynne, *The Scarlet Letter,* Buena Vista, 1995.

Samantha Albertson, *Now and Then* (also known as *The Gaslight Addition*), New Line Cinema, 1995.

Your Studio and You (short film), Universal, 1995.

Annie Laird, *The Juror,* Columbia, 1996.

Erin Grant, *Striptease,* Columbia, 1996.

(Uncredited) Voice of Dallas Grimes, *Beavis and Butt–Head Do America* (animated), Paramount, 1996.

Voice of Esmeralda, *The Hunchback of Notre Dame* (animated; also known as *The Hunchback*), Buena Vista, 1996.

Helen, *Deconstructing Harry,* Fine Line Features, 1997.

(Uncredited) Herself, *I Think I Cannes* (also known as *All Access*), BuyIndies.com, 1997.

Helen, *Deconstructing Harry,* Fine Line Features, 1997.

Lieutenant Jordan O'Neil, *G.I. Jane* (also known as *In Pursuit of Honor, A Matter of Honor, Navy Cross,* and *Undisclosed*), Buena Vista, 1997.

Maria/Martha "Marty" Talmadge, *Passion of Mind,* Paramount, 2000.

Code of Conduct (short documentary film), 2001.

Voice of Esmeralda, *The Hunchback of Notre Dame II* (animated), Buena Vista Home Video/Walt Disney Home Video, 2002.

Madison Lee, *Charlie's Angels: Full Throttle,* Columbia, 2003.

Rachel Carson, *Half Light,* Lakeshore International, 2005.

Film Producer:
(With others) *Mortal Thoughts,* Columbia, 1991.

Now and Then (also known as *The Gaslight Addition*), New Line Cinema, 1995.

(With others) *Austin Powers: International Man of Mystery,* New Line Cinema, 1997.

G.I. Jane (also known as *In Pursuit of Honor, A Matter of Honor, Navy Cross,* and *Undisclosed*), Buena Vista, 1997.

Austin Powers: The Spy Who Shagged Me (also known as *Austin Powers 2: The Spy Who Shagged Me*), New Line Cinema, 1999.

Austin Powers in Goldmember (also known as *Austin Powers: Goldmember*), New Line Cinema, 2002.

Slugger, Miramax, 2002.

Television Appearances; Series:
Jackie Templeton, *General Hospital,* ABC, 1982–83.

Television Appearances; Miniseries:
I Love the '70s, VH1, 2003.

Television Appearances; Movies:
Claire Donnelly, "1952," *If These Walls Could Talk,* HBO, 1996.

Janie, *Destination Anywhere,* VH1, 1997.

U–Z–Onesa, *The Magic 7* (animated), 2005.

Television Appearances; Specials:
Nancy, *Bedrooms,* HBO, 1984.

Sandy Darden, *Judge Reinhold and Demi Moore in The New Homeowners' Guide to Happiness,* Cinemax, 1987.

Ron Reagan Is the President's Son, 1988.

Entertainers 91: The Top 20 of the Year, ABC, 1991.

First Person with Maria Shriver, NBC, 1991.

Herself, *Hollywood's Most Powerful Women,* E! Entertainment Television, 1995.

Planet Hollywood Comes Home, ABC, 1995.

Herself, *The Barbara Walters Special,* ABC, 1996.

Host, *CityKids All Star Celebration* (also known as *All Star CityKids Celebration*), ABC, 1996.

Herself, *The Making of Disney's "The Hunchback of Notre Dame,"* ABC, 1996.

Disney's Most Unlikely Heroes, ABC, 1996.

Hollywood & Vinyl: Disney's 101 Greatest Musical Moments, VH1, 1998.

Herself, *Charlie's Angels Uncensored,* MTV, 2003.

Herself, *The Making of "Charlie's Angels: Full Throttle,"* HBO, 2003.

(In archive footage) *Celebrity Naked Ambition,* Channel 5 (England), 2003.

(In archive footage) *MTV Bash: Carson Daly,* MTV, 2003.

(In archive footage) Herself, *E! 101 Most Starlicious Makeovers,* E! Entertainment Television, 2004.

(In archive footage) *Die geschichte des erotischen Films,* 2004.

Television Appearances; Awards Presentations:

Presenter, *The 61st Annual Academy Awards Presentation,* ABC, 1989.

Presenter, *The 1992 MTV Movie Awards,* MTV, 1992.

Presenter, *The 64th Annual Academy Awards Presentation,* ABC, 1992.

Presenter, *The 49th Annual Primetime Emmy Awards,* CBS, 1997.

The 69th Annual Academy Awards, ABC, 1997.

VH1 97 Fashion Awards, VH1, 1997.

The 2003 MTV Movie Awards, MTV, 2003.

Television Appearances; Episodic:

Holly Trumbull, "Max," *The Master* (also known as *Master Ninja I*), NBC, 1984.

Guest host, *Saturday Night Live* (also known as *NBC's "Saturday Night," Saturday Night,* and *SNL*), NBC, 1988.

Woman in elevator, "When Girls Collide," *Moonlighting,* ABC, 1989.

Cathy Marno, "Dead Right," *Tales from the Crypt* (also known as *HBO's "Tales from the Crypt"*), HBO, 1990.

Guest, *Late Night with David Letterman,* NBC, 1990, 1991.

Guest, *The Late Show with David Letterman* (also known as *The Late Show*), CBS, multiple appearances, 1993–2003.

Guest, *The Rosie O'Donnell Show,* syndicated, 1996, 1997.

(Uncredited) Sample lady, "The Puppy Episode: Parts 1 & 2," *Ellen* (also known as *These Friends of Mine*), ABC, 1997.

Guest, *Clive Anderson All Talk,* 1997.

Guest, *Lo mas plus* (also known as *Lo + plus*), 1997.

Herself, "Charlie's Angels: Full Throttle," *HBO First Look,* HBO, 2003.

Sissy Palmer–Ginsburg, "Women and Children First," *Will & Grace,* NBC, 2003.

Guest, *Extra* (also known as *Extra: The Entertainment Magazine*), syndicated, 2003.

(In archive footage) "Ashton Kutcher," *Love Chain,* E! Entertainment Television, 2003.

(In archive footage) *Celebrities Uncensored,* E! Entertainment Television, 2003, 2004.

Herself, *Demi Moore: The E! True Hollywood Story,* E! Entertainment Television, 2004.

(Uncredited) Herself, *Saturday Night Live* (also known as *NBC's "Saturday Night," Saturday Night,* and *SNL*), NBC, 2005.

Appeared in episodes of *Kaz,* CBS; and *Vega$,* ABC.

Television Executive Producer:

If These Walls Could Talk (movie), HBO, 1996.

CityKids All Star Celebration (special; also known as *All Star CityKids Celebration*), ABC, 1996.

Stage Appearances:

Lily, *The Early Girl,* Circle Repertory Company, New York City, 1987.

RECORDINGS

Videos:

Hollywood's Hottest (documentary), Foglight Entertainment/Insomnia Media Group, 2003.

Music Videos:

John Parr, "St. Elmo's Fire (Man in Motion)," 1985.

Jon Bon Jovi, "Ugly," 1998.

OTHER SOURCES

Books:

International Dictionary of Films and Filmmakers, Volume 3: *Actors and Actresses,* fourth edition, St. James Press, 2000.

Newsmakers 91, Issue 4, Gale, 1991.

St. James Encyclopedia of Popular Culture, St. James Press, 2000.

Periodicals:

Cosmopolitan, December, 1990, p. 204; March, 1997.

Daily News, March 31, 1988, pp. 51, 61.

Empire, Issue 48, 1993, pp. 64–71; Issue 88, 1996, pp. 94–100.

Entertainment Weekly, July 12, 1996; June 20, 2003, pp. 32–33.

InStyle, March, 1996, pp. 88–93.

Interview, July, 1996.

Movieline, January/February, 1993.

Newsweek, June 23, 2003, p. 62.

New Woman, October, 1996.

New York Newsday, April 18, 1991, p. 72.

People Weekly, May 6, 1996; April 19, 1999, pp. 116–
17; September 6, 1999, p. 108; November 6, 2000,
p. 70; April 23, 2001, p. 88; September 2, 2002,
p. 54; November 4, 2002, p. 102; June 16, 2003,
p. 108.
Premiere, April, 1991, pp. 56–60, 62.
Prevue, May, 1991, pp. 18–19, 57; October, 1991,
p. 46.
US, May, 1993, p. 31.
Vanity Fair, August, 1991.
Washington Post, June 27, 2003, pp. C1–C2.

MULGREW, Kate 1955–

PERSONAL

Full name, Katherine Kiernan Mulgrew; born April 29,
1955, in Dubuque, IA; daughter of Thomas James (a
contractor) and Joan Virginia (a painter; maiden name,
Kiernan) Mulgrew; married Robert Harry Egan (a direc-
tor), July 31, 1982 (divorced, 1995); married Timothy
"Tim" Hagan (a politician and consultant), April 19,
1999; children: (first marriage) Ian Thomas, Alexander
James (Alec); stepchildren: Eleanor, Marie. *Education:*
Attended Northwestern University and University of
Iowa; New York University, A.A., 1976; studied with
Stella Adler; trained at Tyrone Guthrie Theatre, Min-
neapolis, MN. *Religion:* Roman Catholicism.

Addresses: *Agent*—Innovative Artists, 1505 10th St.,
Santa Monica, CA 90401.

Career: Actress and voice performer. American Shakespeare Company, Stratford, CT, member of company,
1975; appeared in commercials; model; participant at
awards presentations. Cornish Institute, Seattle, WA,
instructor of audition technique, 1982. Appeared as
Admiral Kathryn Janeway in *Star Trek: The Experience—Borg Invasion 4D,* a short film included as part
of a *Star Trek* exhibit. Worked as a waitress. Committee
for the Right to Life, member of board of directors;
Alzheimer's Association, spokesperson and fund–raiser.

Member: Actors' Equity Association, Screen Actors
Guild, American Federation of Television and Radio
Artists.

Awards, Honors: Golden Globe Award nomination,
best television actress—drama, 1980, for *Mrs.
Columbo;* Tracey Humanitarian Award, c. 1992, for
"On the Rocks," *Murphy Brown;* Saturn Award, best
genre television actress, Academy of Science Fiction,
Fantasy, and Horror Films, and Golden Satellite Award,
best actress in a series—drama, International Press

Academy, both 1998, and Saturn Award nominations,
best genre television actress, 1999 and 2000, and best
actress on television, 2001, all for *Star Trek: Voyager;*
Audience Award, favorite solo performance, Broadway.
com, Outer Critics Circle Award nomination, outstanding solo performance, and Lucille Lortel Award
nomination, outstanding lead actress, League of Off–
Broadway Theatres and Producers, all 2003, and Car-
bonell Award, best actress, 2004, all for *Tea at Five;*
honorary doctorate of letters, Seton Hill University.

CREDITS

Television Appearances; Series:
Mary Ryan Fenelli, *Ryan's Hope,* ABC, c. 1975–78 and
c. 1983.
Kate Columbo/Kate Callahan, *Mrs. Columbo* (also
known as *Kate Columbo, Kate Loves a Mystery,* and
Kate the Detective), NBC, 1979.
Dr. Joanne Springsteen (later known as Dr. Joanne Hal-
loran), *Heartbeat,* ABC, 1988–89.
Mayor Lisbeth Chardin, *Man of the People,* NBC, 1991.
Captain Kathryn Janeway, *Star Trek: Voyager* (also
known as *Star Trek: Voyager*), UPN, 1995–2001.

Television Appearances; Miniseries:
Tony Nicholson, *The Word,* CBS, 1978.
Rachel Clement, *The Manions of America,* ABC, 1981.

Television Appearances; Movies:
Mother Elizabeth Bayley Seton, *A Time for Miracles,*
ABC, 1980.
Kendall Murphy, *Roses Are for the Rich,* CBS, 1987.
Hattie Carraway, *Roots: The Gift,* ABC, 1988.
Sarah Watson, *Daddy* (also known as *Danielle Steel's
"Daddy"*), NBC, 1991.
Sue Bradley, *Fatal Friendship* (also known as *Friends
and Enemies*), NBC, 1991.
Antonia Doyle, *For Love and Glory* (also known as *Ely-
sian Fields* and *Shenandoah*), CBS, 1993.
Victoria Riddler, *Nightworld: Riddler's Moon* (also
known as *Riddler's Moon*), UPN, 1998.

Television Appearances; Specials:
Deborah Sampson, *The American Woman: Portraits of
Courage,* 1976.
Host, *The Parent Survival Guide,* Lifetime, 1989.
Narrator, *Expecting Miracles,* PBS, 1989.
Inside the New Adventure—Star Trek: Voyager, syndi-
cated, 1995.
It's Hot in Here: UPN Fall Preview, UPN, 1996.
Star Trek: 30 Years and Beyond, UPN, 1996.
Narrator, *Rocketships,* The Disney Channel, 1998.
(In archive footage) *Ultimate Trek: Star Trek's Greatest
Moments,* UPN, 1999.
Herself, *America Loves ... Star Trek,* The National
Network, 2001.

Television Appearances; Awards Presentations:

Segment host, *The 11th Annual Soap Opera Awards,* NBC, 1995.

Presenter, *The Blockbuster Entertainment Awards,* UPN, 1996.

Presenter, *The 1996 Emmy Awards,* ABC, 1996.

Television Appearances; Episodic:

Susan, "Alien Lover," *Wide World of Mystery,* ABC, 1975.

Garnett McGee, "Act of Love," *Dallas,* CBS, 1978.

Garnett McGee, "Triangle," *Dallas,* CBS, 1978.

Maureen McLaughlin, "McLaughlin's Flame," *Jessie,* ABC, 1984.

Trapper John, M.D., CBS, 1985.

Helen O'Casey, "Time Heals: Parts 1 & 2," *St. Elsewhere,* NBC, 1986.

Janet Eldridge, "Strange Bedfellows: Parts 1–3," *Cheers,* NBC, 1986.

Maura, "Ryan's Doubts," *Ryan's Hope,* ABC, 1986.

Maura, "Ryan's Wedding," *Ryan's Hope,* ABC, 1986.

Leslie Chase, "Reservations," *Hotel,* ABC, 1987.

Sonny Greer, "The Corpse Flew First Class," *Murder, She Wrote,* CBS, 1987.

Mary Ryan Fenelli, "The Final Show," *Ryan's Hope,* ABC, 1989.

Hillary Wheaton, "On the Rocks," *Murphy Brown,* CBS, 1992.

Joanna Rollins, "Ever After," *Murder, She Wrote,* CBS, 1992.

Voice of Red Claw, "The Cat and the Claw: Parts 1 & 2," *The Adventures of Batman and Robin* (animated; also known as *Batman* and *Batman: The Animated Series*), syndicated, 1992.

Maude Gillis, "The Dying Game," *Murder, She Wrote,* CBS, 1994.

Voice of Isis, "The Mommy's Hand," *Mighty Max,* 1994.

Voice of Queen Hippsodeth, "From Hippsodeth, with Love," *Aladdin* (animated; also known as *Disney's "Aladdin"*), CBS and syndicated, 1994.

Voice of Queen Hippsodeth, "A Sultan Worth His Salt," *Aladdin* (animated; also known as *Disney's "Aladdin"*), CBS and syndicated, 1994.

Voice of Red Claw, "The Lion and the Unicorn," *The Adventures of Batman and Robin* (animated; also known as *Batman* and *Batman: The Animated Series*), syndicated, 1995.

Herself, *Live with Regis and Kathie Lee,* syndicated, 1995.

Voice of Anastasia Renard, "Walkabout," *Gargoyles* (animated), ABC and syndicated, 1996.

Voices of Anastasia Renard and Titania, "The Gathering: Part 1," *Gargoyles* (animated), ABC and syndicated, 1996.

Voice of Titania, "The Gathering: Part 2," *Gargoyles* (animated), ABC and syndicated, 1996.

Voice of Titania, "Ill Met by Moonlight," *Gargoyles* (animated), ABC and syndicated, 1996.

Voice of Titania, "For It May Come True," *Gargoyles: The Goliath Chronicles* (animated), ABC and syndicated, 1996.

Guest, *The Rosie O'Donnell Show,* syndicated, 1996, 1998.

Guest, *Politically Incorrect with Bill Maher* (also known as *Politically Incorrect*), ABC, 1997.

Herself, "William Shatner: At Home in the Universe," *Life and Times,* CBC, 1999.

Shannon O'Donnell, "11:59," *Star Trek: Voyager* (also known as *Voyager*), UPN, 1999.

Guest, *The Late Late Show with Craig Kilborn,* CBS, 2000, 2001.

"America's Big Cat Crisis," *National Geographic Explorer,* MSNBC, c. 2002.

Appeared as Admiral Janeway, *Star Trek: The Next Generation* (also known as *The Next Generation* and *Star Trek: TNG*), syndicated.

Television Appearances; Pilots:

Joan Russell, *Jennifer: A Woman's Story,* NBC, 1979.

Kate Columbo, *Kate Loves a Mystery* (also known as *Mrs. Columbo: Word Games*), NBC, 1979.

Title role, *Carly Mills,* 1986.

Laura Adams, *My Town,* ABC, 1986.

Dr. Joanne Springsteen, *Heartbeat,* ABC, 1988.

Diana Summerfield, *Life in Desire,* 1990.

Captain Kathryn Janeway, *Star Trek Voyager: Caretaker* (also known as *Caretaker*), UPN, 1995.

Queen Tyris, *Battle Force: Andromeda* (also known as *Galaxy Force* and *Nemesis Enforcers*), Sci-Fi Channel, 2003.

Television Additional Voices; Animated Series:

Pirates of Darkwater (also known as *Dark Water*), ABC, 1991–92.

The Wild West C.O.W. Boys of Moo Mesa, ABC, 1992–94.

Film Appearances:

Iseult (Isolde), *Lovespell* (also known as *Summer of the Falcon, Tristan and Iseult,* and *Tristan and Isolde*), 1979, Clar Films, 1981.

Sharon Martin, *A Stranger Is Watching,* Metro–Goldwyn–Mayer/United Artists, 1982.

Major Rayner Fleming, *Remo Williams: The Adventure Begins...* (also known as *Remo: Unarmed and Dangerous*), Orion, 1985.

Margaret Donner, *Throw Momma from the Train,* Orion, 1987.

Judith Schweitzer, *Round Numbers,* 1992.

Rachel Prescott, *Camp Nowhere,* Buena Vista, 1994.

Mrs. Pescoe, *Captain Nuke and the Bomber Boys* (also known as *Demolition Day*), New Horizons Home Video, 1995.

Trekkies (documentary), Paramount Classics, 1999.

Narrator, *Sisters in Resistance* (documentary), Women Make Movies, 2000.

(Uncredited) *Judgment* (also known as *Apocalypse IV: Judgment*), Cloud Ten Pictures, 2001.

Admiral Kathryn Janeway, *Star Trek: Nemesis* (also known as *Star Trek: Insurrection*), Paramount, 2002.

Narrator, *Of Ashes and Atoms* (documentary), National Aeronautics and Space Administration, 2004.

Mary, *Perception,* Liquid Films, 2004.

Stage Appearances:

Blanche, *Widower's House,* Cyrano Repertory, New York City, 1974.

Emily, *Our Town,* American Shakespeare Theatre, Stratford, CT, 1975.

Desdemona, *Othello,* Hartman Theatre Company, Stamford, CT, 1977.

Jennie Malone, *Chapter Two,* Coachlight Dinner Theatre, Nanuet, NY, 1980.

Regina, *Another Part of the Forest,* Seattle Repertory Theatre, Seattle, WA, 1981.

Title role, *Major Barbara,* Seattle Repertory Theatre, 1982.

Margaret (Maggie the cat), *Cat on a Hot Tin Roof,* Syracuse Stage, Syracuse, NY, 1982.

Kitty Strong, *The Ballad of Soapy Smith,* Seattle Repertory Theatre, 1983.

Tracy Lord, *The Philadelphia Story,* Alaska Repertory Theatre, Anchorage and Fairbanks, AK, 1983.

Celemine, *The Misanthrope,* Seattle Repertory Theatre, 1984.

Isabella, *Measure for Measure,* Center Theatre Group, Mark Taper Forum, Los Angeles, 1984.

Charlotte, *The Real Thing,* Center Theatre Group, James A. Doolittle Theatre, Mark Taper Forum, 1986.

Title role, *Hedda Gabler,* Center Theatre Group, James A. Doolittle Theatre, Mark Taper Forum, 1986.

Nan Sinclair, *The Film Society,* Los Angeles Theatre Center, Los Angeles, 1987.

Tamora, *Titus Andronicus,* New York Shakespeare Festival, Public Theatre, Delacorte Theatre, New York City, 1989.

Alice, *Aristocrats,* Center Theatre Group, Mark Taper Forum, 1990.

Mrs. Prentice, *What the Butler Saw,* Mandell Weiss Theatre, La Jolla Playhouse, La Jolla, CA, 1992.

Clea, *Black Comedy* (produced with *White Lies* in a double-bill production titled *White Liars*), Roundabout Theatre Company, Criterion Center Stage Right Theatre, New York City, 1993.

Mrs. Patrick Campbell, *Dear Liar* (staged reading), Youngstown State University Theatre, Youngstown, OH, 2002.

Katharine Hepburn, *Tea at Five* (solo show), Hartford Stage Company, Hartford, CT, 2002, then Promenade Theatre, New York City, 2003.

Kate Hammond, *Stay,* Zipper Theatre, New York City, 2003.

Julie Cavendish, *The Royal Family,* Center Theatre Group, Ahmanson Theatre, Los Angeles, 2004.

Title role, *Mary Stuart* (staged reading), Classic Stage Company Theatre, New York City, 2004.

Only We Who Guard the Mystery Shall Be Unhappy (staged reading), Hartford Stage Company, 2004.

Appeared in other productions, including *Orpheus Descending,* Circle in the Square, New York City; *The Plow and the Stars,* Irish Rebel Theatre; and *Three Sisters,* City Center Theatre, New York City. Appeared in productions at the O'Neill Festival.

Major Tours:

Emily Webb, *Absurd Person Singular,* Encore Productions, U.S. cities, 1976.

Katharine Hepburn, *Tea at Five* (solo show), U.S. cities, beginning 2003.

Radio Appearances:

Narrator of *Her–Story: Then—Women Pioneers in Science, Technology, Engineering and Mathematics,* a series of radio stories, WAMC (public radio).

RECORDINGS

Video Games:

Voice of Captain Kathryn Janeway, *Star Trek Voyager: Elite Force,* Activision, 2000.

Voice of Dr. Mek, *Run Like Hell* (also known as *RLH* and *Run Like Hell: Hunt or Be Hunted*), Interplay Entertainment, 2002.

Voice of Lady Kreya, *Lords of Everquest,* Sony Online Entertainment, 2003.

Audiobooks:

James Joyce, *The Dead and Other Stories from "Dubliners,"* Audio Editions, 1989.

Elizabeth Gage, *Taboo,* HarperAudio, 1993.

Barbara Taylor Bradford, *Everything to Gain,* HarperAudio, 1994.

Edna Buchanan, *Miami, It's Murder,* HarperAudio, 1994.

Jeri Taylor, *Star Trek Voyager—Mosaic* (also known as *Mosaic*), Simon & Schuster, 1996.

(With others) H. G. Wells, *The Invisible Man,* Simon & Schuster, 1998.

Matthew Lombardo, *Tea at Five,* HighBridge Audio, 2003.

OTHER SOURCES

Periodicals:

Catholic Digest, August, 2003, pp. 42–48.
Chicago Tribune, January 3, 2000.
Cinefantastique, November, 1997, pp. 84–86.

Cleveland, February, 2000.
Cult Times, June, 1997, pp. 10–13.
Entertainment Weekly, January 20, 1995, p. 14.
InStyle, December, 1997, p. 179.
McCall's, January, 2000.
Ms., May, 1995.
Parade, July 14, 1996, p. 10.
People Weekly, July 5, 1999, p. 114.
Sci-Fi TV, February, 1999.
Starburst Special, October, 1999, pp. 16–23.
Starlog, March, 1995; July, 1996.
Star Trek, October, 2000.
Star Trek Monthly, January, 2001.
TV Guide, October 8, 1994, pp. 16–17; January 14, 1995, pp. 14–15; July 15, 1995, pp. 6–8, 10, 11; August 24, 1996, p. 18; March 29, 2003, p. 13.
TV Zone, September, 1996, pp. 29–37; July, 2000.
TV Zone Special, May, 2001, pp. 10–13.
Working Mother, September, 1995.

Electronic:

Playbill Online, http://www.playbill.com, March 16, 2003.
Totally Kate, http://www.totallykate.com, March 14, 2005.

MULLIGAN, Terry David 1942–
(Terry D. Mulligan)

PERSONAL

Born June 30, 1942, in New Westminster, British Columbia, Canada; children: four. *Avocational Interests:* Fly–fishing, riding, golf, swimming, biking, and sailing.

Addresses: *Office*—c/o Citytv/CP24/Star!, 299 Queen St. W, Toronto, Ontario M5V 2Z5, Canada.

Career: Actor. Worked as a Royal Canadian Mounted Police officer in Olds and Red Deer, Alberta, Canada, 1960–64; worked as a radio disc jockey for CKRD, CFUN, and CHUM, and programmer for CKLG–FM (later CFOX), c. 1964–?; MuchMusic (a music video cable network), veejay and host; MusicWest, producer, c. 1984–98; CHUMTV, cohost of MT–Movie Television, senior segment producer, west coast correspondent, and live host for Star Network and Startv, 1998—; appeared in television commercials for Molson Golden beer.

Awards, Honors: Canadian Announcer of the Year.

CREDITS

Film Appearances:

Policeman, *Christina,* International Amusements Corp., 1974.

Midruff, *The Supreme Kid,* Canadian Filmmakers' Distribution Centre, 1976.
(As Terry D. Mulligan) Mr. Brandt, *The Boy Who Could Fly,* Twentieth Century–Fox, 1986.
Minister, *Betrayed,* United Artists, 1988.
Lieutenant Duncan, *The Accused* (also known as *Appel a la justice*), Paramount, 1988.
Mac Carthy, *Eye of the Widow,* 1989.
IRS inspector, *Look Who's Talking Too,* TriStar, 1990.
Mr. McHugh, *Mystery Date,* Orion, 1991.
Young Jo, *Hear My Song,* 1992.
Doc, *Deadly Sins,* WarnerVision Films, 1995.
Host, *Big Sky: High River Concert,* 1995.
Mulligan, *Hard Core Logo,* Miramax, 1996.
Nathan Clark, *Disturbing Behavior* (also known as *Disturbing Behaviour*), Metro–Goldwyn–Mayer, 1998.
Himself, *Barenaked in America* (documentary), The Shooting Gallery, 1999.
Dr. Henry Savage, *Mystery, Alaska,* Buena Vista, 1999.
Potential buyer, *Mr. Rice's Secret,* Panorama Entertainment, 2000.
TV host, *Suddenly Naked* (also known as *Mise a nu*), 2001.

Television Appearances; Series:

Host, *Hits a Poppin,* CBC, 1968.
Host, *A Second Look,* CBC, 1969.
Host, *Piffle & Co.,* CBC, 1971.
Hey, Taxi, CBC, 1972.
Host, *Star Chart,* syndicated, 1980.
Host, *Movie Television,* 1997.

Also appeared as *Good Rockin' Tonight,* CBC.

Television Appearances; Miniseries:

Terry, *Big Sky,* 1997.
CNI anchor, *Atomic Train,* NBC, 1999.
Captain Blaine, *Sole Survivor* (also known as *Dean Koontz's "Sole Survivor"*), Fox, 2000.
Interviewer, *Taken* (also known as *Steven Spielberg Presents "Taken"*), Sci–Fi Channel, 2002.

Television Appearances; Movies:

Second man, *Bitter Harvest,* NBC, 1981.
Reporter, *Jane Doe,* CBS, 1983.
Steve Roye, *The Haunting Passion,* NBC, 1983.
Announcer, *Going for the Gold: The Bill Johnson Story,* CBS, 1985.
Dr. Powers, *Love, Mary,* CBS, 1985.
Zack Coley, *The Girl Who Spelled Freedom,* ABC, 1986.
Captain Romano, *Firefighter,* CBS, 1986.
Stanley Jones, *Sworn to Silence,* ABC, 1987.
Wayne Tyler, *A Stranger Waits,* CBS, 1987.
Rafael Abramovitz, *The Amy Fisher Story* (also known as *Beyond Control*), ABC, 1993.

Don Delgado, *Miracle on Interstate 880* (also known as *Miracle on I–880*), NBC, 1993.

Radio show host, *Someone Else's Child* (also known as *Lost and Found*), Lifetime, 1994.

Sheriff Beck, *Have You Seen My Son,* ABC, 1996.

George Preston, *Justice for Annie: A Moment of Truth Movie,* NBC, 1996.

Alan Kelly, *Stand against Fear* (also known as *Moment of Truth: Stand against Fear* and *Unlikely Suspects*), NBC, 1996.

Martin Walsh, *Dirty Little Secret,* USA Network, 1998.

The president, *Nick Fury: Agent of Shield,* Fox, 1998.

Skeptical TV reporter, *Big and Hairy,* 1998.

Mr. Kearns, *Playing to Win: A Moment of Truth Movie,* NBC, 1998.

Wheeler, *Crash and Byrnes,* 1999.

Coach Trembly, *Can of Worms,* The Disney Channel, 1999.

Bob Richards, *Our Guys: Outrage at Glen Ridge* (also known as *Outrage in Glen Ridge*), ABC, 1999.

Fred Herrera as an older man, *Sweetwater* (also known as *Sweetwater: A True Rock Story*), VH1, 1999.

Farah attorney, *Behind the Camera: The Unauthorized Story of Charlie's Angels,* NBC, 2004.

Television Appearances; Episodic:

Danny Barrett, "Fire and Ice," *MacGyver,* ABC, 1987.

Coach Watson, "How Much Is That Body in the Window?," *21 Jump Street,* Fox, 1987.

Deputy Chief Bill Glanson, "School's Out," *21 Jump Street,* Fox, 1988.

"Partners and Other Strangers," *Street Legal,* CBC, 1989.

Giles Hope, "Outlaw," *The Beachcombers,* CBC, 1989.

Frank Rogan, "Two Times Trouble," *MacGyver,* ABC, 1989.

First mission controller, "Space," *The X–Files,* Fox, 1993.

Police chief, "Fast Forward," *M.A.N.T.I.S.,* Fox, 1995.

Barry Donnelly, "Off Broadway: Part 1," *The Commish,* 1995.

Dr. Barzman, "The Crystal Scarab," *Poltergeist: The Legacy,* Showtime, 1996.

J. P. Orland, "Games People Play," *Two,* CBC and syndicated, 1996.

"Second Thoughts," *The Outer Limits,* Showtime and syndicated, 1997.

Bob Birckenbuehl, "Weeds," *Millennium,* Fox, 1997.

Secretary of Defense David Swift, "The Nox," *Stargate SG–1,* Showtime and syndicated, 1997.

Max Lundy, "Next of Kin," *Dead Man's Gun,* Showtime, 1997.

Judge Lance Giffen, "Marcey Bennett," *Cold Squad,* CTV, 1998.

Dr. Harvey, "Collateral Damage," *Millennium,* Fox, 1999.

Donald Burton, victim #4, "Eye–see–you.com," *The Net,* USA Network, 1999.

Steve Fentress, "Lazarus Rising," *The Crow: Stairway to Heaven,* syndicated, 1999.

Chancellor Wilder, "Mind Reacher," *The Outer Limits,* Showtime and syndicated, 2001.

Himself, *This Hour Has 22 Minutes,* CBC, 2002.

Himself, "Teen Angel," *Cold Squad,* 2004.

Also appeared as Detective Cooke, *Birdland;* Detective Shannahan, *Traps,* CBS.

Radio Appearances:

Appeared as host, *Great Canadian Goldrush,* CBC Radio; host, *Discumentary,* syndicated; host, *Mulligan Stew,* CKUA Radio.

MUMY, Bill 1954–
(Art Barnes, Billy Mumy)

PERSONAL

Surname pronounced "Moo–my"; original name, Charles William Mumy, Jr.; born February 1, 1954, in San Gabriel, CA; son of Charles William (a cattle rancher) and Muriel Gertrude (maiden name, Gould) Mumy; married Eileen Joy Davis (a childbirth educator), October 9, 1986; children: Seth (an actor), Liliana (an actress). *Education:* Attended Santa Monica City College, CA, 1972–73. *Politics:* Democrat. *Avocational Interests:* Comic book collecting, racquetball, swimming, sketching.

Career: Actor, voice performer, musician (guitar, bass guitar, keyboards, banjo, mandolin, harmonica, percussion), singer, writer, and recording artist. Member of the rock band America, 1970s; Barnes & Barnes (performing duo), founder and performer (with Robert Haimer), group sometimes cited as the Bore Brothers; Be Five, member of ensemble (with others from the cast of *Babylon 5*); performer with various groups, including Energy, Gully, Redwood, the Mumy–Gordon Band, Bill Mumy and the Igloos, and the Jenerators. Appeared in commercials. Creator and writer of comic books and graphic novels. Participant at conventions.

Member: Academy of Motion Picture Arts and Sciences, Screen Actors Guild, American Federation of Musicians, American Federation of Television and Radio Artists, American Society of Composers, Authors, and Publishers.

Awards, Honors: Emmy Award nomination, outstanding music composition, 1992, for Disney's *"Adventures in Wonderland"*; Annual CableACE Award nomination, outstanding children's series, National Cable Television Association, 1996, for *Space Cases;* some sources cite an induction into the Comedy Music Hall of Fame, 2005.

CREDITS

Television Appearances; Series:

Voice of Matty Matel, *Matty's Funday Funnies* (animated), ABC, 1959–61.

Will Robinson, *Lost in Space* (also known as *Space Family Robinson*), CBS, 1965–68.

Weaver, *Sunshine*, NBC, c. 1974–75.

Host, *Inside Space*, beginning 1992.

Narrator, *Biography* (also known as *A&E Biography*), Arts and Entertainment, beginning 1993.

Lennier, *Babylon 5* (also known as *B5*), syndicated, 1994–99.

Host, *The Mars Series*, Sci–Fi Channel, beginning 1995.

Narrator, *What's So Funny?*, Arts and Entertainment, beginning 1995.

Host, *TVography*, Arts and Entertainment, beginning 2001.

Narrator, *Animal Icons*, Animal Planet, beginning 2005.

Television Appearances; Movies:

Petey Loomis, "Sammy, the Way–Out Seal," *Walt Disney's Wonderful World of Color*, NBC, 1962.

Freddy Gray, *For the Love of Willadean*, 1964.

Weaver, *Sunshine Christmas*, NBC, 1977.

Host, *Blast from the Past*, Sci–Fi Channel, 1996.

Television Appearances; Specials:

Host, *The Fantasy Worlds of Irwin Allen*, Sci–Fi Channel, 1995.

Himself, *Lost in Space Forever*, Fox, 1998.

Host and narrator, *Attack of the 50 Ft. Monster Mania*, American Movie Classics, 1999.

Himself, *Child Stars: Their Story*, Arts and Entertainment, 2000.

Host, *Boom! Hollywood's Greatest Disaster Movies*, American Movie Classics, 2000.

Narrator of *Leonardo DiCaprio: A Life in Progress*, American Movie Classics.

Television Appearances; Episodic:

(As Billy Mumy) Willy, "Donald's Friend," *National Velvet*, NBC, 1960.

The Law and Mr. Jones, ABC, 1960.

Anthony Fremont, "It's a Good Life," *The Twilight Zone*, CBS, 1961.

Billy Bayles, "Long Distance Call," *The Twilight Zone*, CBS, 1961.

Buzz, "A Friendly Tribe," *General Electric Theater*, CBS, 1961.

(As Billy Mumy) Jackie Chester, "Bang! You're Dead," *Alfred Hitchcock Presents*, NBC, 1961.

(As Billy Mumy) Jimmy Harrison, "The Lie," *The Loretta Young Show* (also known as *Letter to Loretta*), NBC, 1961.

(As Billy Mumy) Rennie, "My Own Master," *The Loretta Young Show* (also known as *Letter to Loretta*), NBC, 1961.

"Furnishing the Apartment" (also known as "The Apartment"), *Father of the Bride*, CBS, 1961.

The Bob Hope Show, NBC, 1961.

The Dick Powell Show, NBC, 1961.

The New Breed, ABC, 1961.

(As Billy Mumy) David Bennett, "The Royce Bennett Story," *The Wide Country*, NBC, 1962.

(As Billy Mumy) Jeffrey, "The Bronc–Buster," *Dr. Kildare*, NBC, 1962.

Little boy, "Jack and the Crying Cab Driver," *The Jack Benny Program*, CBS, 1962.

(As Billy Mumy) Mickey Hollins, "The Door without a Key," *Alfred Hitchcock Presents*, CBS, 1962.

(As Billy Mumy) Toddy, "The Sam Darland Story," *Wagon Train*, NBC, 1962.

(As Billy Mumy) Tony Mitchell, "House Guest," *The Alfred Hitchcock Hour*, CBS, 1962.

(As Billy Mumy) "The Boy Who Wasn't Wanted," *Alcoa Premiere*, ABC, 1962.

Going My Way, ABC, 1962.

(As Billy Mumy) Freddy, "End of an Image," *Empire* (also known as *Redigo*), NBC, 1963.

(As Billy Mumy) Jeff, "Lady in Limbo," *The Greatest Show on Earth*, ABC, 1963.

Miles, "The Case of the Shifty Shoebox," *Perry Mason*, CBS, 1963.

Young Pip, "In Praise of Pip," *The Twilight Zone*, CBS, 1963.

Barry, "Sunday Father," *The Eleventh Hour*, NBC, 1964.

(As Billy Mumy) Billy, "The Ballerina," *The Adventures of Ozzie & Harriet*, ABC, 1964.

(As Billy Mumy) Billy, "The Pennies," *The Adventures of Ozzie & Harriet*, ABC, 1964.

(As Billy Mumy) Billy, "Rick's Old Printing Press," *The Adventures of Ozzie & Harriet*, ABC, 1964.

(As Billy Mumy) David, "Home Is the Hunted," *The Fugitive*, ABC, 1964.

"A Taste of Melon," *Walt Disney's Wonderful World of Color*, NBC, 1964.

"Treasure in the Haunted House," *Walt Disney's Wonderful World of Color*, NBC, 1964.

Custer, "Whatever Became of Baby Custer?," *I Dream of Jeannie*, NBC, 1965.

Darrin as a boy, "Junior Executive," *Bewitched*, ABC, 1965.

Googie Miller, "Come Back, Little Googie," *The Munsters*, CBS, 1965.

(In archive footage) Michael, "A Vision of Sugar Plums," *Bewitched*, ABC, 1965.

(As Billy Mumy) Victor Chase, "Did Your Mother Come from Ireland, Ben Casey?," *Ben Casey*, ABC, 1965.

(As Billy Mumy) Willy, "Old Cowboy," *The Virginian*, NBC, 1965.

(As Billy Mumy) Andy, "The Kid," *Lancer*, CBS, 1969.

"Break the Bank of Tacoma," *Here Come the Brides*, ABC, 1970.

Trask, "Aura Lee, Farewell," *The Rockford Files*, NBC, 1975.

Roger, *Me and Mom*, ABC, c. 1985.

Dr. Irwin Bruckner, "The Genius," *Matlock*, NBC, 1988.

Guest, *The Howard Stern Show*, 1990.

Roger Braintree, "Goodnight, Central City," *The Flash*, CBS, 1991.

Tommy Puck, "A Change of Heart: Parts 1 & 2," *Superboy* (also known as *The Adventures of Superboy*), syndicated, 1991.

Tommy Puck, "Obituary for a Super Hero," *Superboy* (also known as *The Adventures of Superboy*), syndicated, 1992.

Voice of Farmer Bill, "Witch One," *Animaniacs* (animated; also known as *Steven Spielberg Presents "Animaniacs"*), Fox, 1993.

"Monstrous Meltdown (Gabora)," *Ultraman: The Ultimate Hero* (animated; also known as *Ultraman Powered*), [Japan], 1993.

"The Last Show," *The Steven Banks Show*, PBS, 1994.

Voice of Brainchild, "Blazing Entrails/Lumber Jerks," *The Ren & Stimpy Show* (animated), Nickelodeon, 1995.

Warren Lawford (the Fox), "The Terrible Trio," *Batman: The Animated Series* (animated; also known as *Batman*), Fox, 1995.

Guest, *Howard Stern*, 1995.

Ferna Herna, "A Day in the Life," *Space Cases*, Nickelodeon, 1996.

Himself, "Jimmy Stewart," *Biography* (also known as *A&E Biography*), Arts and Entertainment, 1997.

Himself, "Switcheroo," *Space Ghost Coast to Coast* (live action and animated), Cartoon Network, 1997.

Delivery person, "Back to School," *The Weird Al Show*, CBS, 1997.

Voice of Sam, "The Monkey Prince," *The Oz Kids* (animated; also known as *Little Wizard Stories*), 1997.

Voice of Sam, "Underground Adventure," *The Oz Kids* (animated; also known as *Little Wizard Stories*), 1997.

Engineer Kellin, "The Siege of AR–558," *Star Trek: Deep Space Nine* (also known as *Deep Space Nine, DS9*, and *Star Trek: DS9*), syndicated, 1998.

Nervous man, "Alienated," *Diagnosis Murder*, CBS, 1998.

Narrator, *Famous Families*, The Disney Channel, 1999.

Voice of Eon, "Tag Team," *Buzz Lightyear of Star Command* (animated; also known as *Disney/Pixar's "Buzz Lightyear of Star Command"*), UPN and syndicated, 2000.

Voice of Eon, "A Zoo Out There," *Buzz Lightyear of Star Command* (animated; also known as *Disney/Pixar's "Buzz Lightyear of Star Command"*), UPN and syndicated, 2000.

Narrator, *Cheech & Chong: The E! True Hollywood Story*, E! Entertainment Television, 2000.

Narrator, *The Mod Squad: The E! True Hollywood Story*, E! Entertainment Television, 2000.

Guest, *The List* (also known as *VH1 The List*), VH1, 2000.

Himself, "Goofy Greats," *One Hit Wonders*, VH1, 2002.

Anthony Fremont, "It's Still a Good Life," *The Twilight Zone*, UPN, 2003.

Voice of Harry Noze, "Toy Scary Boo," *What's New, Scooby–Doo?* (animated), The WB, 2003.

Appeared in "The Party," an episode of *Insight*, syndicated; appeared in episodes of other television series, including *The Chevy Show* (also known as *The Blair and Raitt Show*), NBC; *Have Gun, Will Travel*, CBS; *Playhouse 90*, CBS; *The Red Skelton Show*, NBC and CBS; *Riverboat*, NBC; *Romper Room*, syndicated; *The Tennessee Ernie Ford Show*, NBC and ABC; and *The Tom Ewell Show*, CBS.

Television Appearances; Pilots:

Will Robinson, *Lost in Space* (also known as *Space Family Robinson*), CBS, 1965.

(As Billy Mumy) Chris Williams, *The Two of Us*, broadcast on *Vacation Playhouse*, CBS, 1966.

Weaver, *Sunshine*, CBS, 1973.

Nick Butler, *The Rockford Files* (also known as *The Rockford Files: Backlash of the Hunter*), NBC, 1974.

Larry, *Archie*, ABC, 1976.

Television Appearances; Other:

My Uncle Elroy, 1961.

Scooter Deere Day, 1961.

From Dragonettes and Gargoyles (animated), c. 1995.

Appeared in *The Mangaboos* (animated).

Television Work; Series:

Creator (with Peter David) and producer, *Space Cases*, Nickelodeon, 1996–97.

Film Appearances:

Aladdin, *The Wizard of Baghdad*, Twentieth Century–Fox, 1960.

(As Billy Mumy) Neil Bateman, *Tammy, Tell Me True*, Universal, 1961.

(As Billy Mumy) "Boom–Boom" Yates, *Palm Springs Weekend*, Warner Bros., 1963.

(As Billy Mumy) Alex Martin, *A Ticklish Affair*, Metro–Goldwyn–Mayer, 1963.

(As Billy Mumy) Boy counting pearls, *A Child Is Waiting*, United Artists, 1963.

(As Billy Mumy) Erasmus Leaf, *Dear Brigitte*, Twentieth Century–Fox, 1965.

Boy, *Wild in the Streets*, 1968.

Sterling North, *Rascal*, Buena Vista, 1969.

Teft, *Bless the Beasts & Children*, Columbia, 1971.

Lariot, *Papillon*, Allied Artists, 1973.

Weaver, *Sunshine Part II* (also known as *My Sweet Lady*), 1976.
(As Art Barnes in the group Barnes & Barnes) *Fish Heads* (live action and animated short film), 1982.
Tim, "It's a Good Life," *Twilight Zone—The Movie*, Warner Bros., 1983.
Keyboard player with the James Roberts Band, *Hard to Hold*, Universal, 1983.
Young General Fleming, *Captain America*, Columbia/TriStar, 1992.
Bob, *Double Trouble*, Motion Picture Corporation of America, 1992.
Host, *Apollo 13: The Untold Story* (documentary), 1992.
Neighbor, *Three Wishes*, Savoy Pictures, 1995.
Austin, *Dirk and Betty*, AMCO Entertainment Group/Standard Film Trust/Surfer Girl Entertainment/Zephyr Entertainment, c. 1999.
Derailroaded (documentary), 2005.
Ringers: Lord of the Fans (documentary), Planet BB Entertainment, 2005.

RECORDINGS

Albums:
BB, 1980.
(As Member of choir) Jay Gruska, *Which One of Us Is Me*, Rhino, 1984.
(With Seduction of the Innocent) *Golden Age*, 1990.
(As Art Barnes in the group Barnes & Barnes) *Loozanteen*, Rhino, 1991.
(As Art Barnes in the group Barnes & Barnes) *The Dinosaur Album*, Kid Rhino, 1993.
(As Art Barnes in the group Barnes & Barnes) *The Yogi Bear Environmental Album: This Land Is Your Land*, Kid Rhino/Hanna Barbera, 1993.
(With the Jenerators) *The Jenerators*, Asil Records, 1994.
Dying to be Heard, Renaissance, 1997.
In the Current, Renaissance, 1997.
(With the Jenerators) *Hitting the Silk*, Wildcat Records, 1998.
(With Be Five) *Trying to Forget*, Renaissance, 1998.
Kiss My Boo Boo, Infinite Visions, c. 1998.
(As Art Barnes in the group Barnes & Barnes) *Yeah: The Essential Barnes & Barnes*, Varese Sarabande, 1999.
(With the Jenerators) *Little Drummer Boys*, KLOS–Radio, 2000.
Pandora's Box, Renaissance, 2000.
After Dreams Come True, Oglio Records, 2001.
(With Redwood) *Lost, but Not Really: The History of Tree Music*, 2003.
Ghosts: The Best of Bill Mumy, Renaissance, 2005.

Contributor to albums by other recording artists.

Albums with America:
View from the Ground, Capitol, 1982.
Your Move, Capitol, 1983.
Perspective, Capitol, 1984.

The Very Best of America, Gibson, 1990.
Encore: More Greatest Hits, Warner Bros., 1991.
Hourglass, American Gramophone, 1994.
America in Concert, King Biscuit Flower Hour, 1995.
Centenary Collection, EMI, 1996.
Premium Gold Collection, EMI, 1996.
You Can Do Magic, Disky, 1996.
Greatest Hits, Capitol/EMI, 1999.
Highway: 30 Years of America, Rhino, 2000.
Live, Capitol/EMI, 2000.
Hits You Remember Live, Madacy Records, 2001.

Singles:
(With Sarah Taylor) "I've Got Some Presents for Santa," Rhino, 1994.

Singles as Art Barnes in the group Barnes & Barnes:
"Fish Heads," 1982.
"Soak It Up," c. 1983.

Other singles with Barnes & Barnes include "Ah A," "Love Tap," "Party in My Pants," "Pizza Face," and "When You Die."

Videos:
(And producer) *Zabagabee: The Best of Barnes & Barnes*, 1987.
(As Art Barnes) *Dr. Demento 20th Anniversary Collection*, Rhino Home Video, 1991.
Comic Book: The Movie, Miramax Home Entertainment, 2004.

Music Videos as Art Barnes in the group Barnes & Barnes:
"Soak It Up," c. 1983.

Other music videos with Barnes & Barnes include "Ah A," "Love Tap," "Party in My Pants," "Pizza Face," and "When You Die."

WRITINGS

Television Music; Series:
Songwriter, *Disney's "Adventures in Wonderland"* (also known as *Adventures in Wonderland*), The Disney Channel, beginning 1992.
Composer, *Space Cases*, Nickelodeon, 1996–97.
Composer of theme music, *Backstory* (also known as *Hollywood Backstories*), American Movie Classics, beginning 2001.

Television Music; Specials:
The Fantasy Worlds of Irwin Allen, Sci–Fi Channel, 1995.
Lost in Space Forever, Fox, 1998.

Television Music; Episodic:
Main title theme music, *TV Guide Looks at Christmas*, USA Network, 1997.

Composer and songwriter for episodes of *Santa Barbara*, NBC; *The Simpsons* (animated), Fox; and *The Universe and I*, PBS.

Television Music; Pilots:
Composer and songwriter, *Archie*, ABC, 1976.

Teleplays; Episodic:
Sunshine, NBC, episodes between 1974 and 1975.
(With Peter David) "The Impossible Dram," *Space Cases*, Nickelodeon, 1996.
(Author of story) "Found and Lost," *The Twilight Zone*, UPN, 2002.

Author of episodes of *Swamp Thing*, USA Network.

Screenplays:
(As Art Barnes in the group Barnes & Barnes) *Fish Heads* (live action and animated short film), 1982.

Film Music:
(As Art Barnes in the group Barnes & Barnes) *Fish Heads* (live action and animated short film), 1982.

Songs Featured in Films:
Bless the Beasts & Children, Columbia, 1971.
Hard to Hold, Universal, 1983.
"You're Rich," *Plain Clothes*, Paramount, 1998.

Videos:
Zabagabee: The Best of Barnes & Barnes, 1987.

Albums:
BB, 1980.
(As Art Barnes in the group Barnes & Barnes) *Loozan-teen*, Rhino, 1991.
(As Art Barnes in the group Barnes & Barnes) *The Dinosaur Album*, Kid Rhino, 1993.
(As Art Barnes in the group Barnes & Barnes) *The Yogi Bear Environmental Album: This Land Is Your Land*, Kid Rhino/Hanna Barbera, 1993.
(With the Jenerators) *The Jenerators*, Asil Records, 1994.
Dying to be Heard, Renaissance, 1997.
In the Current, Renaissance, 1997.
(With the Jenerators) *Hitting the Silk*, Wildcat Records, 1998.
Kiss My Boo Boo, Infinite Visions, c. 1998.
(As Art Barnes in the group Barnes & Barnes) *Yeah: The Essential Barnes & Barnes*, Varese Sarabande, 1999.

(With the Jenerators) *Little Drummer Boys*, KLOS–Radio, 2000.
Pandora's Box, Renaissance, 2000.
After Dreams Come True, Oglio Records, 2001.
(With Redwood) *Lost, but Not Really: The History of Tree Music*, 2003.
Ghosts: The Best of Bill Mumy, Renaissance, 2005.

Albums with America:
View from the Ground, Capitol, 1982.
Your Move, Capitol, 1983.
Perspective, Capitol, 1984.
The Very Best of America, Gibson, 1990.
Encore: More Greatest Hits, Warner Bros., 1991.
Hourglass, American Gramophone, 1994.
America in Concert, King Biscuit Flower Hour, 1995.
Centenary Collection, EMI, 1996.
Premium Gold Collection, EMI, 1996.
You Can Do Magic, Disky, 1996.
Greatest Hits, Capitol/EMI, 1999.
Highway: 30 Years of America, Rhino, 2000.
Live, Capitol/EMI, 2000.
Hits You Remember Live, Madacy Records, 2001.

Singles:
(With Sarah Taylor) "I've Got Some Presents for Santa," Rhino, 1994.

Singles as Art Barnes in the group Barnes & Barnes:
"Fish Heads," 1982.
"Soak It Up," c. 1983.

Other singles with Barnes & Barnes include "Ah A," "Love Tap," "Party in My Pants," "Pizza Face," and "When You Die." Composer of songs featured in albums, films, television productions, and videos.

Graphic Novels:
(With Miguel Ferrer) *The Dreamwalker*, illustrated by Gray Morrow, Marvel Comics, 1989.

Issues of Comic Books:
(With Miguel Ferrer) *Comet Man*, illustrated by Kelley Jones, Marvel Comics, 1987.
The Hulk, illustrated by Marshall Rogers, Marvel Comics, 1989.
(With Ferrer) *Trypto the Acid Dog*, illustrated by Steve Leialoha, Renegade Press, 1989.
Spider Man, illustrated by Aaron Lopresti, Marvel Comics, 1990.
Star Trek, three issues subtitled "Return of the Worthy," DC Comics, 1990.
Wonder Man, illustrated by Brian Murray, Marvel Comics, 1990.
Iron Man, illustrated by Leialoha, Marvel Comics, 1991.

Lost in Space, four issues, illustrated by Michael Dutkiewicz, Innovation Comics, 1991–93.

Aquaman, 1998.

(With Peter David) *The Spectre,* illustrated by Steve Ditko, DC Comics, 1998.

Contributor to other comic book series, including *The Comet Man 2, She Hulk, Star Trek,* and *The Trainer.*

Short Fiction:

(With Peter David) "The Undeadliest Game," *Shock Rock,* Volume 1, edited by Jeff Gelb, foreword by Alice Cooper, Pocket Books, 1992.

Shock Rock, Volume 2, edited by Jeff Gelb, foreword by Lonn Friend, Pocket Books, c. 1994.

OTHER SOURCES

Periodicals:

Aspire!, July, 1998, pp. 3, 4.

Babylon 5, May, 1998, pp. 16–24.

Entertainment Weekly, March 17, 1995, p. 97.

People Weekly, July 17, 1995, pp. 46–47.

Sci–Fi TV, December, 1998.

Starlog, February, 1991; May, 1995; May, 1996.

Universe Today, May, 1996, pp. 6–7, 11.

Electronic:

Bill Mumy Official Site, http://www.billmumy.com, March 14, 2005.

O

O'DONOHUE, Ryan 1984–
(Ryan Sean O'Donohue)

PERSONAL

Full name, Ryan Sean O'Donohue; born April 26, 1984, in Pomona, CA; son of Sean Patrick O'Donohue and Anita Lynne Rultenberg.

Addresses: *Agent*—Cunningham, Escott & Dipene, 10635 Santa Monica Blvd., #130, Los Angeles, CA 90025.

Career: Actor.

Awards, Honors: Young Artist Award nomination, best performance in a voiceover—TV or film—young actor, 1998, for *Recess*.

CREDITS

Film Appearances:
(English version) Voice of Mimi–Siku, *Little Indian, Big City,* Buena Vista, 1994.
Voice of Young Kovu, *The Lion King II: Simba's Pride* (animated), Walt Disney Home Video, 1998.
Voice of Matthew "Matt" McGinnis, *Batman Beyond: Return of the Joker* (animated; also known as *Batman of the Future: Return of the Joker* and *Return of the Joker*), Warner Bros., 2000.
Voices of Randall Weems and Digger Dave, *Recess: School's Out* (animated), Buena Vista, 2001.

Film Work:
Additional voice, *Toy Story* (animated), Buena Vista, 1995.

Additional voices, *A Bug's Life* (animated), Buena Vista, 1998.
Additional voices, *The Iron Giant* (animated), Warner Bros., 1999.

Television Appearances; Series:
Zeke Byrd, *The Byrds of Paradise,* ABC, 1994.
Peter Hansen, *The Boys Are Back,* CBS, 1994.
What–A–Mess, *What a Mess,* ABC, 1995.
Voices of Randall Weems and Digger Dave, *Recess* (animated; also known as *Disney's "Recess": Created by Paul and Joe*), ABC, 1997.
Voice of Matthew "Matt" McGinnis, *Batman Beyond* (animated; also known as *Batman of the Future*), The WB, 1999–2000.

Television Appearances; Miniseries:
Young Alfie, *Mr. Murder* (also known as *Dean Koontz's "Mr. Murder"*), ABC, 1998.

Television Appearances; Movies:
Coop, *Safety Patrol* (also known as *Disney's "Safety Patrol"* and *Safety Patrol!*), ABC, 1998.
Roger Robinson, *Beverly Hills Family Robinson,* ABC, 1998.
Voice of Matt McGinnis, *Batman Beyond: The Movie* (animated), 1999.

Television Appearances; Episodic:
Danny, "Demon Knight," *Tales from the Crypt,* 1995.
Joey, "Acting Out," *Maybe This Time,* ABC, 1996.
Voice of boy #1, "Identity Crisis," *Superman* (animated), 1997.
Voice of Matt, "Legends of the Dark Knight," *Batman: Gotham Knights* (animated), The WB, 1998.

RECORDINGS

Video Games:
Voice of C.A., *Someone's in the Kitchen!,* 1996.

Voice of Young Kovu, *The Lion King II: Simbaa's Pride Activity Center* (also known as *Disney's "The Lion King II: Simbaa's Pride Activity Center"*), 1998.

Voice of Dr. Knobb, *Dark Chronicle* (also known as *Dark Cloud 2*), Sony Computer Entertainment America, 2002.

OSMENT, Haley Joel 1988–
(Haley Osment)

PERSONAL

Born April 10, 1988, in Los Angeles, CA; son of Eugene Michael (an actor; some sources cite name as Michael Eugene) and Theresa (a teacher) Osment; sister of Emily Osment (an actress). Avocational interests: Reading, playing the guitar, playing basketball, animals. *Avocational Interests:* Reading, playing the guitar, playing basketball, animals. Religion: Roman Catholicism.

Addresses: *Contact*—Meredith Fine, Coast to Coast Talent Group, 3350 Barham Blvd., Los Angeles, CA 90068.

Career: Actor and voice performer. Appeared in television commercials.

Awards, Honors: Young Artist Award, best performance by an actor under ten in a motion picture, Young Artist Foundation, 1995, for *Forrest Gump;* Young Artist Award nominations, best performance in a television comedy or drama by a supporting young actor age ten or under, 1996 and 1997, for *The Jeff Foxworthy Show;* Young Artist Award nomination, best performance in a feature film by an actor age ten or under, 1997, for *Bogus;* YoungStar Award nomination, best performance by a young actor in a made–for–television movie, *Hollywood Reporter,* 1997, for *Last Stand at Saber River;* Young Artist Award nomination, best performance in a television comedy series by a young actor age ten or under, 1998, for *Murphy Brown;* Young Artist Award nomination, best performance in a television drama series by a guest starring young actor, 1998, for "Lucas: Parts 1 & 2," *Walker, Texas Ranger;* YoungStar Award nomination, best performance by a young actor in a miniseries or made–for–television movie, 1999, for *Cab to Canada;* Saturn Award, best performance by a younger actor or actress, Academy of Science Fiction, Fantasy, and Horror Films, Golden Satellite Special Achievement Award, outstanding new talent, International Press Academy, Broadcast Film Critics Association Award, best child performance, Dallas–Fort Worth Film Critics Association Award, best supporting actor, Florida Film Critics Circle Award, best supporting actor, Kansas City Film Critics Circle Award, best supporting actor, Southeastern Film Critics Association Award, best supporting actor, Sierra awards, best supporting actor, most promising actor, and Youth in Film Award, all Las Vegas Film Critics Society, Young Artist Award, best leading young actor in a feature film, YoungStar Award, best young actor in a motion picture drama, Teen Choice Award, choice breakout performance in a film, Online Film Critics Society Award, best supporting actor, Blockbuster Entertainment Award, favorite male newcomer (Internet poll only), Academy Award nomination, best supporting actor, Golden Globe Award nomination, best performance by an actor in a supporting role in a motion picture, Screen Actors Guild Award nomination, outstanding performance by a male actor in a supporting role, Chicago Film Critics Association Award nominations, best supporting actor and most promising actor, MTV Movie Award nominations, breakthrough male performance and (with Bruce Willis) best on–screen duo, and Online Film Critics Society Award nomination, best debut, all 2000, for *The Sixth Sense;* Blockbuster Entertainment Award, favorite supporting actor in a drama or romance, and Young Artist Award nomination, best leading young actor in a feature film, both 2001, for *Pay It Forward;* ShoWest Award, supporting actor of the year, National Association of Theatre Owners, 2001; Saturn Award, best performance by a younger actor, Broadcast Film Critics Association Award nomination, best young actor or actress, Empire Award nomination, best actor, and Young Artist Award nomination, best leading young actor in a feature film, all 2002, for *Artificial Intelligence: AI;* Young Artist Award nomination, best performance by a young actor in a voice–over role, 2003, for *The Hunchback of Notre Dame II;* World Soundtrack Award nomination (with others), best original song written for a film, 2003, for "Jungle Rhythm," *The Jungle Book 2;* Young Artist Award nomination, best performance by a young actor in a voice–over role, 2004, for *The Jungle Book 2;* Young Artist Award nomination, best performance in a feature film by a leading young actor, 2004, for *Secondhand Lions.*

CREDITS

Film Appearances:

Forrest Junior, *Forrest Gump,* Paramount, 1994.

Little boy, *Mixed Nuts* (also known as *Lifesavers*), Columbia/TriStar, 1994.

Albert Franklin, *Bogus,* Warner Bros., 1996.

Danny, *For Better or Worse,* 1996.

Voice of Chip, *Beauty and the Beast: The Enchanted Christmas* (animated; also known as *Beauty and the Beast 2*), Walt Disney Home Video, 1997.

(Uncredited) *Pitch* (documentary), The Asylum, 1997.

Cole Sear, *The Sixth Sense,* Buena Vista, 1999.

Peewee Clayton, *I'll Remember April,* Regent Moonstone, 2000.

Trevor McKinney, *Pay It Forward,* Warner Bros., 2000.

Voice of Spot, *Discover Spot* (animated), Walt Disney Home Video, 2000.

Voice, *Edwurd Fudwupper Fibbed Big* (animated short film), Nickelodeon Movies, 2000.

David Swinton, *Artificial Intelligence: AI* (also known as *A.I.: Artificial Intelligence*), Warner Bros., 2001.

Romek, *Edges of the Lord* (also known as *Boze skrawki*), Miramax, 2001.

Voice of Beary Barrington, *The Country Bears* (also known as *The Bears*), Buena Vista, 2002.

Voice of Zephyr, *The Hunchback of Notre Dame II* (animated), Buena Vista Home Video/Walt Disney Home Video, 2002.

Voice of Mowgli, *The Jungle Book 2* (animated), Buena Vista, 2003.

Walter, *Secondhand Lions,* New Line Cinema, 2003.

Home of the Giants, 2006.

Television Appearances; Series:

Harry Turner, *Thunder Alley,* ABC, 1994–95.

Matt Foxworthy, *The Jeff Foxworthy Show* (also known as *Somewhere in America*), ABC, 1995–96, NBC, 1996–97.

Avery Brown, *Murphy Brown,* CBS, 1997–98.

Television Appearances; Movies:

(As Haley Osment) Kyle, *Lies of the Heart: The Story of Laurie Kellogg,* ABC, 1994.

Davis Cable, *Last Stand at Saber River,* TNT, 1997.

Andy Dorset, "The Ransom of Red Chief," *The Wonderful World of Disney,* ABC, 1998.

Bobby, *Cab to Canada,* CBS, 1998.

Dylan Hydecker, *The Lake,* NBC, 1998.

Television Appearances; Specials:

Voice of True, *The Puppies Present Incredible Animal Tales,* ABC, 1998.

Host, *Heroes for the Planet Featuring Special Guest Charlotte Church,* multiple channels, 2000.

(In archive footage) Himself, *The "Billy Elliot" Boy,* BBC, 2001.

Television Appearances; Awards Presentations:

The 72nd Annual Academy Awards, ABC, 2000.

Sixth Annual Screen Actors Guild Awards, TNT, 2000.

2000 Blockbuster Entertainment Awards, Fox, 2000.

AFI Life Achievement Award: A Tribute to Tom Hanks, USA Network, 2002.

Himself, *The Third Annual TV Land Awards: A Celebration of Classic TV,* TV Land, 2005.

Television Appearances; Episodic:

Little boy, "The Fourteenth Floor," *The Larry Sanders Show,* HBO, 1994.

Lucas Simms, "Lucas: Parts 1 & 2," *Walker, Texas Ranger,* CBS, 1997.

Davy Simpkins, "Bloodlines: Parts 1 & 2," *The Pretender,* NBC, 1998.

John Henry, "Flights of Angels," *Touched by an Angel,* CBS, 1998.

Nathan Cacaci, "Memento Mori," *Chicago Hope,* CBS, 1998.

Eric Stall, "Angels and Blimps," *Ally McBeal,* Fox, 1999.

Voice of Curly Gamelthorpe, "It Girl/Deconstructing Arnold," *Hey Arnold!* (animated), Nickelodeon, 1999.

Himself, "Pay It Forward," *HBO First Look,* HBO, 2000.

Voice of kid, "Dammit Janet," *Family Guy* (animated), Fox, 2000.

Voice of kid, "There's Something about Paulie," *Family Guy* (animated), Fox, 2000.

Voice of Myka, "Lone Wolf," *Buzz Lightyear of Star Command* (animated; also known as *Disney/Pixar's "Buzz Lightyear of Star Command"*), UPN and syndicated, 2000.

Guest, *Good Morning America* (also known as *GMA*), ABC, 2000.

Guest, *The Oprah Winfrey Show* (also known as *Oprah*), syndicated, 2000.

Guest, *Smap x Smap,* Fuji Television Network, 2000.

Voice of kid in bathroom, "The Thin White Line," *Family Guy* (animated), Fox, 2001.

Guest, *Rove Live,* 10 Network (Australia), 2001.

Guest, *The Tonight Show with Jay Leno,* NBC, 2001.

Guest, *The Early Show,* CBS, 2001, 2002.

Guest, *Today* (also known as *NBC News Today* and *The Today Show*), NBC, 2001, 2003.

Guest, *The Late Show with David Letterman* (also known as *The Late Show*), CBS, 2002.

Guest, *The Best Damn Sports Show Period,* Fox Sports Network, 2003.

Guest, *The Charlie Rose Show,* PBS, 2003.

Guest, *Coming Attractions,* E! Entertainment Television, 2003.

Guest anchor, *Channel One,* Channel One Network, 2003.

Himself, *Eigo de shabera–night,* NHK (Japan), 2004.

Appeared in episodes of other series, including *Larry King Live,* Cable News Network.

Television Appearances; Other:

Voice of Tom Terrific for *Curbside,* Nickelodeon.

Television Work; Series:

Provided additional voices (uncredited) for the series *Sesame Street* (also known as *Canadian Sesame Street, The New Sesame Street, Open Sesame, Sesame Park,* and *Les amis de Sesame*), PBS and other networks.

Stage Appearances:

Narrator, *Peter and the Wolf,* Toyota Symphonies for Youth, Performing Arts Center of Los Angeles

County, Los Angeles Music Center, Walt Disney Concert Hall, Los Angeles, 2003.

RECORDINGS

Videos; Documentaries:

AI: From Drawings to Sets, Warner Bros., 2002.

AI/FX, Warner Bros., 2002.

AI: A Portrait of David, 2002.

AI: A Portrait of Gigolo Joe, 2002.

Animating "AI," Warner Bros., 2002.

Dressing "AI," Warner Bros., 2002.

The Music of "AI," Warner Bros., 2002.

The Robots of "AI," 2002.

The Sixth Sense: Reflections from the Set, Buena Vista Home Video, 2002.

The Sound of "AI," Warner Bros., 2002.

Haley Joel Osment: An Actor Comes of Age, Mirage Productions, 2004.

Video Games:

Voice of Sora, *Kingdom Hearts* (also known as *Kingudamu hatsu*), Square Electronic Arts, 2002.

OTHER SOURCES

Periodicals:

Entertainment Weekly, August 13, 1999, p. 52; July 13, 2001, pp. 24–31.

Hollywood Reporter, August 2, 1999, p. 10.

People Weekly, August 30, 1999, p. 143; September 29, 2003, p. 74.

Premiere, September, 2004.

TV Guide, October 9, 1999, p. 3.

Electronic:

Haley Joel Osment Official Site, http://www.haleyjoel osment.net, April 14, 2005.

P

PARKER, Paula Jai 1971–

PERSONAL

Born 1971, in Cleveland, OH (some sources cite Farmington, MI); married Forrest D. Martin, 2005. *Education:* Graduated from Howard University. *Avocational Interests:* Writing, singing, dancing.

Addresses: *Agent*—Abrams Artists, 9200 Sunset Blvd., 11th Floor, Los Angeles, CA 90069. *Manager*—Leonard Torgan, Leverage Management, 3030 Pennsylvania Ave., Santa Monica, CA 90404. *Publicist*—Bragman/Nyman/Cafarelli, Pacific Design Center, 8687 Melrose Ave., Eighth Floor, Los Angeles, CA 90069; Marvet Britto, The Britto Agency, 234 West 56th St., Penthouse, New York, NY 10019.

Career: Actress. Appeared in "Express Yourself," a series of public service announcements.

Awards, Honors: Annual CableACE Award, best actress in a dramatic series, National Cable Television Association, 1994, for "Tang," *Cosmic Slop.*

CREDITS

Film Appearances:
Joi, *Friday,* New Line Cinema, 1995.
Sissy, *Tales from the Hood,* Savoy Pictures, 1995.
Drunk party girl, *Don't Be a Menace to South Central While Drinking Your Juice in the Hood* (also known as *Don't Be a Menace*), Miramax, 1996.
Jamilia, *Get on the Bus,* Columbia, 1996.
Adina, *Sprung,* Trimark Pictures, 1997.
Rumors, 1997.
Claudette, *Woo,* New Line Cinema, 1998.

Paula King, *Why Do Fools Fall in Love?,* Warner Bros., 1998.
Ann, *The Breaks,* Artisan Entertainment, 1999.
Felicia, *Phone Booth,* Twentieth Century–Fox, 2002.
Gracie, *High Crimes,* Twentieth Century–Fox, 2002.
Stephanie, *30 Years to Life,* Keystone Entertainment/ Exodus Entertainment, 2002.
Love Chronicles, Melee Entertainment, 2003.
Evelyn, *She Hate Me,* Sony Pictures Classics, 2004.
Rolonda, *My Baby's Daddy,* Miramax, 2004.
Lexus, *Hustle & Flow,* MTV Films, 2005.
Reecy, *Animal,* DEJ Productions, 2005.

Television Appearances; Series:
Member of ensemble, *The Apollo Comedy Hour,* syndicated, 1992–93.
Member of ensemble, *Townsend Television,* Fox, 1993.
Monique, *The Wayans Bros.,* The WB, 1995–96.
Val Brentwood (Gal Spy), *The Weird Al Show,* CBS, 1997–98.
Roberta Young, *Snoops,* ABC, 1999.

Television Appearances; Miniseries:
I Love the '80s Strikes Back, VH1, 2003.
I Love the '90s Part Deux, VH1, 2005.

Television Appearances; Movies:
Lisa, "Homecoming Day," *Riot* (also known as *Riot in the Streets*), Showtime, 1995.
Melodie, *Always Outnumbered* (also known as *Always Outnumbered, Always Outgunned*), HBO, 1998.
Voice of Trudy Parker–Proud, *The Proud Family Movie* (animated), The Disney Channel, 2005.

Television Appearances; Specials:
"Tang," *Cosmic Slop,* HBO, 1994.

Television Appearances; Episodic:
Guest host, *Soul Train,* syndicated, 1994.
Jill, "No Place Like Home," *Roc,* Fox, 1994.

Mia, "Pulp Marlon," *The Wayans Bros.*, The WB, 1995.

Udia, "Silent Auction," *Pointman*, syndicated, 1995.

Sabina, "Wendell and I Spy," *The Parent 'Hood*, The WB, 1997.

Tonya, "The Two Hilton Lucases," *Cosby*, NBC, 1997.

Cara Wilson, "Speak for Yourself, Bruce Clayton," *NYPD Blue*, ABC, 1998.

Billie Holiday, "God Bless the Child," *Touched by an Angel*, CBS, 2000.

Voice of Trudy Parker–Proud, "Romeo Must Wed," *The Proud Family* (animated), The Disney Channel, 2002.

Desirae, "Cracking Ice," *The Shield* (also known as *The Barn* and *Rampart*), FX Channel, 2004.

Voice of Trudy Parker–Proud, "Spats: Experiment #397," *Lilo & Stitch: The Series* (animated; also known as *The Adventures of Lilo & Stitch*), The Disney Channel, 2005.

Television Appearances; Pilots:

Hell, Fox, 1995.

Roberta Young, *Snoops*, ABC, 1999.

OTHER SOURCES

Periodicals:

Celebrity Sleuth, Volume 14, number 1, 2001, pp. 84–85.

PATRICK, Butch 1953–
(Butch Patrick–Lilly)

PERSONAL

Original name, Patrick Allen Lilly (some sources spell name Patrick Alan Lilley); born August 2, 1953, in Los Angeles, CA; stepson of Ken Hunt (a professional baseball player).

Career: Actor and musician. Performed with the musical group Eddie and the Monsters, beginning 1983; owner of a promotions company; appeared in commercials. Lecturer at various institutions, including Boston State University and at junior and senior high schools; participant at conventions.

Awards, Honors: Named one of the "100 greatest kid stars" by VH1.

CREDITS

Television Appearances; Series:

Greg Howard, *The Real McCoys* (also known as *The McCoys*), CBS, 1963.

Edward Wolfgang "Eddie" Munster, *The Munsters*, CBS, 1964–66.

Gordon Dearing, a recurring role, *My Three Sons*, CBS, 1968–69.

Mark, *Lidsville*, ABC, 1971–73.

Host, *Macabre Theatre*, syndicated, beginning 2002.

Television Appearances; Movies:

Bumper, *The Young Loner*, 1968.

Here Come the Munsters, Fox, 1995.

Television Appearances; Specials:

Edward Wolfgang "Eddie" Munster, *Marineland Carnival*, CBS, 1965.

Where Are They Now? Part 2, CBS, 1996.

Himself, *Inside TV Land: 40 Greatest Theme Songs* (documentary), TV Land, 2002.

Himself, *Child Stars: Then and Now* (documentary), NBC, 2003.

Himself, *Macabre Theatre Halloween Special*, syndicated, 2003.

Himself, *TV Land Convention Special* (documentary), TV Land, 2004.

Television Appearances; Awards Presentations:

The Second Annual TV Land Awards: A Celebration of Classic TV, Nickelodeon and TV Land, 2004.

Television Appearances; Episodic:

Bobby, "The Legend of Jim Riva," *The Detectives* (also known as *The Detectives Starring Robert Taylor* and *Robert Taylor's "Detectives"*), NBC, 1961.

(Uncredited) Charles, "The Night They Shot Santa Claus," *The Untouchables*, ABC, 1962.

Little boy, "Air Derby," *My Three Sons*, ABC, 1962.

Wesley, "The Time of the Tonsils," *Alcoa Premiere*, ABC, 1962.

"A Pleasant Thing for the Eyes," *Ben Casey*, ABC, 1962.

Jody Fletcher, "The Prime of Life," *Bonanza*, NBC, 1963.

Stevie, "How to Be a Hero without Really Trying," *My Favorite Martian*, CBS, 1963.

Tommy, "Kingdom for a Horse," *Death Valley Days*, syndicated, 1963.

Tommy Slater, "Don't Laugh at Horses," *Mister Ed*, CBS, 1963.

Runt, "Friend," *Gunsmoke*, CBS, 1964.

Stevie, "Ed the Desert Rat," *Mister Ed*, CBS, 1964.

"Incident of the Pied Piper," *Rawhide*, CBS, 1964.

Chad Turner, "A Crooked Line," *Pistols 'n' Petticoats*, CBS, 1966.

Richard, "My Master the Author," *I Dream of Jeannie*, NBC, 1966.

Melvin Vandersnoot, "The Christmas Show," *The Monkees*, NBC, 1967.

Tom John, "Mad Dog," *Gunsmoke*, CBS, 1967.

Frankie, "By a Whisker," *Family Affair*, CBS, 1968.

Frank Wilson, "Way Down Cellar: Parts 1 & 2," *Walt Disney's Wonderful World of Color,* NBC, 1968.

Black Cat Jack, "Copperhead Izzy," *Daniel Boone,* NBC, 1969.

Sailor Ballinger, "All Flags Flying," *Marcus Welby, M.D.,* ABC, 1969.

Tony Niccola, "Log 15: Exactly 100 Yards," *Adam–12,* NBC, 1969.

Paul Foster, "Log 75: Have a Nice Weekend," *Adam–12,* NBC, 1970.

Ritchie, *The Headmaster,* CBS, 1970.

Elmore Crocker, "Ernie Drives," *My Three Sons,* CBS, 1971.

"Ten O'Clock and All Is Well," *The Smith Family,* ABC, 1972.

Bill, "By the Numbers," *Lucas Tanner,* NBC, 1974.

Jack, "The Athlete," *Shazam!,* CBS, 1974.

Himself, "Fred Gwynne—More Than a Munster," *Biography* (also known as *A&E Biography: Fred Gwynne–More Than a Munster*), Arts and Entertainment, 1999.

Voice of himself, "Eight Misbehavin'," *The Simpsons* (animated), Fox, 1999.

(In archive footage) Voice, "Behind the Laughter," *The Simpsons* (animated), Fox, 2000.

Host, "A Munster Halloween," *Biography* (also known as *A&E Biography: A Munster Halloween*), Arts and Entertainment, 2001.

Himself, "Butch Patrick," *Star Dates,* E! Entertainment Television, 2002.

Himself, "The Munsters," *Biography* (also known as *A&E Biography: The Munsters*), Arts and Entertainment, 2003.

Himself, "*The Andy Griffith Show* episodes," *TV Land's Top Ten,* TV Land, 2004.

Himself, "Top 10 TV Cars," *TV Land's Top Ten,* TV Land, 2004.

Himself, "Top 10 TV Dads," *TV Land's Top Ten,* TV Land, 2004.

Appeared as Johnny in *General Hospital,* ABC. Appeared in episodes of other series, including *Divorce Court,* syndicated; *Good Morning America* (also known as *GMA*), ABC; *Solid Gold,* syndicated; and *Today* (also known as *NBC News Today* and *The Today Show*), NBC.

Television Work; Series:

Creator of *The Basement Tapes,* MTV.

Film Appearances:

Billy Davis, *The Two Little Bears,* Twentieth Century–Fox, 1961.

Davey, *Hand of Death* (also known as *Five Fingers of Death*), Twentieth Century–Fox, 1962.

(Uncredited) Imaginary playmate, *Pressure Point,* United Artists, 1962.

(Uncredited) Student, *A Child Is Waiting,* United Artists, 1963.

John Peale, *One Man's Way,* United Artists, 1964.

Eddie Munster, *Munster, Go Home,* Universal, 1966.

Johnny, *The One and Only, Genuine, Original Family Band* (musical), Buena Vista, 1968.

Brian, *80 Steps to Jonah,* Warner Bros., 1969.

Milo, *The Phantom Tollbooth* (animated; also known as *The Adventures of Milo in the Phantom Tollbooth*), Metro–Goldwyn–Mayer, 1969.

No Legs, *The Wild Pack* (also known as *The Defiant* and *The Sandpit Generals*), American International Pictures, 1972.

Scary Movie, Generic Video, 1989.

Sam the Sorcerer, *Magic Al and the Mind Factory,* Underdog Productions, 2000.

(As Butch Patrick–Lilly) Himself, *Dickie Roberts: Former Child Star* (also known as *Dickie Roberts: (Former) Child Star*), Paramount, 2003.

Surge of Power, Surge of Power Enterprises, 2004.

Roy Autry, *It Came from Trafalgar,* 2005.

Host of *San Diego Paranormal: City's Most Haunted* (short documentary film).

RECORDINGS

Videos:

Himself, *Al Lewis: Forever Grandpa* (short documentary), Foxstar Productions, 2000.

Music Videos:

(With Eddie and the Monsters) "What Ever Happened to Eddie?," 1983.

OTHER SOURCES

Electronic:

Butch Patrick Official Site, http://www.butch-patrick.com, March 15, 2005.

PIPER, Laurie
    See LAURIE, Piper

PISANA, Jennifer

PERSONAL

Born in Toronto, Ontario, Canada. *Education:* Studied singing at Royal Conservatory of Music. *Avocational Interests:* Competitive equestrian events.

Career: Actress and singer. Festival of the Sound (music festival), Parry Sound, Ontario, Canada, performed as soloist.

CREDITS

Television Appearances; Movies:

Marie, *When the Bullet Hits the Bone,* Terror Zone Productions, 1995.

Sally, *Giant Mine,* CBC (Canada), 1996.

Wilhelmina, *My Own Country,* Showtime, 1998.

Lindsey Witkowski, *Mail to the Chief,* ABC, 2000.

Little girl, *Dying to Dance,* NBC, 2001.

Young Pam, *Gilda Radner: It's Always Something,* ABC, 2002.

Taylor, *Get a Clue,* The Disney Channel, 2002.

Young Liz, *Homeless to Harvard: The Liz Murray Story,* Lifetime, 2003.

Joy, *More than Meets the Eye: The Joan Brock Story,* Lifetime, 2003.

Soccoro Greeley, *Finding John Christmas,* CBS, 2003.

Television Appearances; Series:

Lauren Zelmer, *The Power Strikers,* Nickelodeon, 2004.

Appeared as Becca Fisher at age five, *Flash Forward.*

Television Appearances; Specials:

Little girl, "The Haunted Mask," *Goosebumps,* Fox, 1995.

Television Appearances; Episodic:

Sally, "The Greenhouse Effect/The Buzz," *Psi Factor: Chronicles of the Paranormal,* 1997.

Lucy, "Mama Mia," *Twice in a Lifetime,* 2001.

Jessica, "Lesser Evils," *Street Time,* Showtime, 2002.

Sue Ellen, "Mr. Monk Meets Dale the Whale," *Monk,* USA Network, 2002.

Tracey Nolan, "Evaluate This," *Doc,* PAX, 2003.

Film Appearances:

Lorraine at age seven, *Bogus,* Warner Bros., 1996.

Second girl, *The Long Kiss Goodnight,* New Line Cinema, 1996.

Marie at age ten, *Perfect Pie* (also known as *La voie du destin*), Odeon Films, 2002.

Blizzard, Metro–Goldwyn–Mayer Home Entertainment, 2003.

Stage Appearances:

Alice, *Alice in the Orchestra,* Festival of the Sound, Parry Sound, Ontario, Canada, 2004.

PROVAL, David 1942–
(Clark Katz)

PERSONAL

Original name, Aron Proval; born May 20, 1942, in Brooklyn, New York, NY; son of Clara Katz (an actress); married Harriet Cohen; children: Marc, Brett.

Addresses: *Agent*—Gage Group, 9255 Sunset Blvd., Suite 515, Los Angeles, CA 90069; Mitchell K. Stubbs and Associates, 8675 West Washington Blvd., Suite 203, Culver City, CA 90232. *Manager*—Incognito Management, 345 North Maple Dr., Suite 348, Beverly Hills, CA 90210 (some sources cite 9440 Santa Monica Blvd., Suite 302, Beverly Hills, CA 90210).

Career: Actor. Worked as a teacher and in cosmetology. Also known as Clark Katz.

Awards, Honors: Screen Actors Guild Award nomination (with others), outstanding performance by an ensemble in a drama series, 2001, for *The Sopranos.*

CREDITS

Television Appearances; Series:

Richie Aprile, *The Sopranos,* HBO, 2000.

Signore Marco Fogagnolo, *Everybody Loves Raymond,* CBS, 2000–2001.

Television Appearances; Movies:

Ianucci, *Foster and Laurie,* CBS, 1975.

Rick, *Nowhere to Hide* (also known as *Fatal Chase*), CBS, 1977.

Angelo Cervi, *Courage,* 1986.

Lucca, *Perfect Witness,* HBO, 1989.

Dog man, *The Courtyard,* Showtime, 1995.

Hap Cartello, *The Rockford Files: Friends and Foul Play,* CBS, 1996.

Daniel Mann, *James Dean,* TNT, 2001.

James/Edward Talley, *Murder without Conviction,* The Hallmark Channel, 2004.

Uncle Fab, *Just Desserts,* The Hallmark Channel, 2004.

Television Appearances; Episodic:

Calvelli, "Siege of Terror," *Kojak,* CBS, 1973.

"Silent Knight," *Knight Rider,* NBC, 1983.

Felix Parinkchinko, "Taxicab Murders," *Cagney & Lacey,* CBS, 1984.

Doran, "Dreams," *Fame,* syndicated, 1985.

Hunk Pepitone, "White Light," *Fame,* syndicated, 1985.

Louie Gallo, "The Dutch Oven," *Miami Vice*, NBC, 1985.

Victor Haas, "Badge of Honor," *Friday the 13th* (also known as *Friday's Curse* and *Friday the 13th: The Series*), syndicated, 1988.

"13 O'Clock," *Friday the 13th* (also known as *Friday's Curse* and *Friday the 13th: The Series*), syndicated, 1989.

Mr. Gelormino, "My Cheatin' Heart," *The Marshall Chronicles*, ABC, 1990.

(Uncredited) William Mayer, "On Your Honor," *L.A. Law*, NBC, 1990.

Dr. Silverman, "Shock Theater—October 2, 1954," *Quantum Leap*, NBC, 1991.

"The Three–Minute Egg," *Palace Guard*, CBS, 1991.

Frank the potato man, "Frank the Potato Man," *Picket Fences*, CBS, 1992.

Frank the potato man, "Abominable Snowman," *Picket Fences*, CBS, 1994.

Frank the potato man, "Saint Zach," *Picket Fences*, CBS, 1995.

Norman Kendall, "The Heartbreak Kid," *The Marshal*, ABC, 1995.

Carl Will, "Prison Story," *Pretender*, NBC, 1997.

Harry, "Redemption," *Brimstone*, Fox, 1998.

Mr. Kinney, "Hot Objects," *Felicity*, The WB, 1998.

Rabbi Glassman, "Take This Sabbath Day," *The West Wing*, NBC, 2000.

Henry Pagnao, "The Last Word," *Judging Amy*, CBS, 2001.

Joe Sambarelli, "The Loud Man," *The Fighting Fitzgeralds*, NBC, 2001.

Edgar Lessing, "Long Day's Journey," *The Division* (also known as *Heart of the City*), Lifetime, 2002.

Paul Turcotte, "Reelin' in the Years," *Boomtown*, NBC, 2002.

Carmine Schiavelli, "Till Death Do Us Part," *A.U.S.A.*, NBC, 2003.

(Uncredited) Himself, "Dallas Cowboys at New York Giants," *NFL Monday Night Football*, ABC, 2003.

Paul Turcotte, "Lost Child," *Boomtown*, NBC, 2003.

"Stealing Home," *Life with Bonnie*, ABC, 2003.

Richie Aprile, "The Test Dream," *The Sopranos*, HBO, 2004.

Appeared in "So What Else Happened," an episode of *L.A. Firefighters*, Fox.

Television Appearances; Pilots:
Goldman, *The Equalizer*, CBS, 1985.

(Uncredited) Voice of Paul Turcotte, *Boomtown*, NBC, 2002.

Film Appearances:
First sailor, *Cinderella Liberty*, Twentieth Century–Fox, 1973.

Tony, *Mean Streets*, Warner Bros., 1973.

Title role, *Nunzio*, Universal, 1975.

Ben, *Harry and Walter Go to New York*, Columbia, 1976.

Voice of Peace, *Wizards* (animated), Twentieth Century–Fox, 1977.

Voice of Crazy Shapiro, *Hey, Good Lookin'* (animated), Warner Bros., 1982.

Officer Nelson, *The Star Chamber*, Twentieth Century–Fox, 1983.

Pilot, *The Monster Squad*, TriStar, 1987.

Larry, *Shakedown* (also known as *Blue Jean Cop*), Universal, 1988.

Turk, *Vice Versa*, Columbia, 1988.

Voice, *Mirai Ninja* (also known as *Cyber Ninja, Future Ninja, Robo Ninja*, and *Warlord*), Namco Productions, 1988.

Head thug, *UHF* (also known as *The Vidiot from UHF*), Orion, 1989.

Roy Wittle, *Martial Marshal*, 1990.

Phil Reardon, *The Walter Ego* (short film), Putch Productions, 1991.

Lenny, *Innocent Blood* (also known as *A French Vampire in America*), Warner Bros., 1992.

George, *Being Human*, Warner Bros., 1993.

McTeague, *Strike a Pose*, Moving Forward Films, 1993.

Scully, *Romeo Is Bleeding*, Gramercy Pictures, 1993.

Snooze, *The Shawshank Redemption*, Columbia, 1994.

Electrician, *The Brady Bunch Movie*, Paramount, 1995.

Joey Bambino, *To the Limit*, PM Entertainment Group, 1995.

Sigfried, "The Wrong Man," *Four Rooms*, Miramax, 1995.

Rolling Thunder, c. 1995.

Charlie Zephro, *The Phantom*, Paramount, 1996.

Billy White, Michael's lover, and narrator, *Flipping*, Dove International, 1997.

Frank, *Dumb Luck in Vegas*, 1997.

George Gianfranco, *Mob Queen*, First Run Features, 1997.

Johnson, *The Relic* (also known as *Das Relikt*), Paramount/PolyGram Filmed Entertainment, 1997.

(Uncredited) Security guard, *Skyscraper*, 1997.

Danny Sussman, *The Siege*, Twentieth Century–Fox, 1998.

Mike's father, *Zigs* (also known as *Double Down*), Lions Gate Films/Trimark Pictures, 1999.

Jim Lovero, *White Boy* (also known as *Menace*), Banned in America Films, c. 1999.

Charlie, *The Hollywood Sign* (also known as *Der Himmel von Hollywood*), Blue Rider Pictures/Pleswin Entertainment Group, 2000.

Jacob Johnson, *NewsBreak*, Rojak Films, 2000.

Moe Potter, *Thirteen Moons* (also known as *13 Moons*), Lot 47 Films, 2002.

Larry, *Bookies*, International Arts Entertainment, 2003.

The Circle, Bergman Lustig Productions, 2004.

Himself, *Nobody Wants Your Film* (documentary), 2005.

Angels with Angles, Sierra Mar Pictures, 2005.

Lucky Smith, *Frankie the Squirrel* (short film), Eagle Films/Unknown Productions, 2006.
Hollywood Dreams, The Rainbow Film Company, 2006.

Film Work:
Dialogue coach, *D.C. Cab* (also known as *Street Fleet*), Universal, 1983.

Stage Appearances:
The Basic Training of Pavlo Hummel, Inner City Cultural Company, Los Angeles, 1974.
Larry Mastice, *Momma's Little Angels,* Quaigh Theatre, New York City, 1978.
Army Hakes, *Requiem for a Heavyweight,* Long Wharf Theatre, New Haven, CT, 1985.
Mickey Marcus, *The Normal Heart,* Long Wharf Theatre, 1985–86.

Appeared in performances at the Arena Stage, Washington, DC, 1986–87.

RECORDINGS

Videos:
Himself, *Hope Springs Eternal: A Look Back at "The Shawshank Redemption"* (short documentary), Warner Home Video, 2004.

OTHER SOURCES

Periodicals:
New York Times, August 4, 1978.
Entertainment Weekly, February 18, 2000, p. 25.

PUTCH, John 1961–

PERSONAL

Born in July, 1961, in Fayetteville (some sources cite Chambersburg), PA; son of William H. Putch (a producer, director, and theatre operator) and Jean Stapleton (an actress); brother of Pamela Putch (a producer and actress).

Addresses: *Agent*—Janet Carol Norton, Broder/Webb/Chervin/Silbermann, 9242 Beverly Blvd., Suite 200, Beverly Hills, CA 90210.

Career: Actor, director, producer, and writer. Founder of Putch Films, Putch Productions, and (with Randal Patrick) Putch–Patrick Productions. Appeared in television commercials.

Awards, Honors: Bronze Award, WorldFest Flagstaff, best independent feature film, documentary category, 1998, and Bronze Award, WorldFest Houston, best documentary, 1999, both for *This Is My Father;* Jury Awards, Hertfordshire Film Festival, best direction and best feature, 2003, for *Valerie Flake;* Audience Award, Palm Beach International Film Festival, best feature, 10 Degrees Hotter Award, Valley Film Festival, best feature film, Audience Award, ARPA International Film Festival, Audience Award, Dahlonega International Film Festival, narrative comedy feature category, Audience Award, Dances with Films, feature film category, and Audience Award and Directors' Favorite Award, both Fort Myers Beach Film Festival, all 2003, for *BachelorMan.*

CREDITS

Film Appearances:
Sean Brody, *Jaws 3–D* (also known as *Jaws 3*), Universal, 1983.
Tom's director, *Waiting to Act* (short film), Putch–Patrick Productions, 1985.
Martin, *The Sure Thing,* Embassy, 1985.
Danny Stubbs, *Impure Thoughts,* RMC Films, 1985.
Corey, *Welcome to 18* (also known as *Summer Release*), American Distribution, 1986.
Spaceballs, Metro–Goldwyn–Mayer, 1987.
Bob Perkins, *Curfew,* New World, 1989.
Mike, *Men at Work,* Triumph Releasing, 1990.
Hamilton, *Skeeter,* New Line Home Video, 1994.
Neil Garbus, *Camp Nowhere,* Buena Vista, 1994.
Blackhawk copilot, *Clear and Present Danger,* Paramount, 1994.
Journalist with headset, *Star Trek: Generations* (also known as *Star Trek 7*), Paramount, 1994.
Skinner, *Same River Twice,* 1996.
Master of ceremonies at strip club, *The Confidence Man,* [Canada], 1996.
Doctor, *Spoiler,* Artist View Entertainment, 1998.
Lester, *The Souler Opposite,* Curb Entertainment/Movie Studio Apartment, 1998.
Stanley Shaw, *Freedom Strike,* A–Pix Entertainment, 1998.
Man in car, *City of Angels* (also known as *Stadt der Engel*), Warner Bros., 1998.
William Flake, *Valerie Flake,* Dream Entertainment, 1999.
Dave Bayne, *Fugitive Mind,* Flashstar/Royal Oaks Communications, 1999.
Amtorg driver, *Tycus,* New City Releasing, 2000.
George, *Crash Point Zero* (also known as *Extreme Limits*), New City Releasing, 2000.
Tim Mandell, *Mach 2,* Paramount Home Entertainment, 2001.

Film Director:
(And producer) *Waiting to Act* (short film), Putch–Patrick Productions, 1985.
Alone, 1985.

(And editor) *The Walter Ego* (short film), Putch Productions, 1991.

Alone in the Woods, New Horizons Home Video, 1996.

Curse of the ShadowBorg, 1997.

(And producer) *This Is My Father* (documentary; also known as *This Is My Father: A Documentary about William H. Putch*), Cinema Guild, 1998.

The Boy Who Saved Christmas, Hallmark Entertainment, 1998.

Valerie Flake, I.E. Films, 1999.

Storm Catcher, Columbia/TriStar Home Video, 1999.

Intrepid (also known as *Deep Water*), Starlight, 1999.

Tycus, New City Releasing, 2000.

Pursuit of Happiness, Showcase Entertainment, 2001.

(And coproducer) *BachelorMan,* Profile Entertainment, 2003.

Television Appearances; Movies:

Owen Eaton, *Angel Dusted* (also known as *Angel Dust*), 1981.

Randy, *Marian Rose White,* 1982.

A Matter of Sex, 1984.

Corporal, *The B.R.A.T. Patrol,* ABC, 1986.

Abercrombie, *Double Agent,* 1987.

Wilson (some sources say Winston), *You Ruined My Life,* ABC, 1987.

Sergeant Arnie, *Street of Dreams,* CBS, 1988.

Doctor, *After the Shock,* 1990.

Mitch, *Keeper of the City,* 1992.

Moderator, "The Water Engine," *TNT Screenworks,* TNT, 1992.

Art Lipsky, *Beyond Suspicion* (also known as *Appointment for a Killing*), 1993.

Host of "Pasta Talk," *Ghost Dog* (also known as *My Magic Dog*), 1997.

Thomas Cleardon, *The Patron Saint of Liars,* CBS, 1998.

Agent Lambert, *Chain of Command,* HBO, 2000.

Television Appearances; Miniseries:

Hanging deputy, *Kenny Rogers as the Gambler: The Adventure Continues,* CBS, 1983.

Detective Wendle, *Something Is Out There,* NBC, 1988.

Television Appearances; Pilots:

Johnny Muller, "The Adventures of Pollyanna," *The Wonderful World of Disney,* CBS, 1982.

Mike Swanson, *Acting Sheriff,* CBS, 1991.

Television Appearances; Episodic:

Boy Scout, "Archie Is Branded," *All in the Family,* CBS, 1973.

Pete, "Summer of '82," *Family Ties,* NBC, 1982.

Neil, "Birthday Boy," *Family Ties,* NBC, 1984.

Inn guest, "Dick Gets Larry's Goat," *Newhart,* 1985.

"Hail to the Chef," *It's a Living,* 1985.

"Spring Break," *The Fall Guy,* ABC, 1985.

Neil, "Starting Over," *Family Ties,* NBC, 1986.

"More Skinned Against than Skinning," *Hill Street Blues,* 1986.

Jeff Stave, "Love Kittens Go to High School," *Fame,* NBC, 1987.

"Reading, Writing, and Rating Points," *Newhart,* 1987.

Mordock, "Coming of Age," *Star Trek: The Next Generation* (also known as *Star Trek: TNG*), syndicated, 1988.

Ensign Mendon, "A Matter of Honor," *Star Trek: The Next Generation* (also known as *Star Trek: TNG*), syndicated, 1989.

"Out of Control," *21 Jump Street,* Fox, 1989.

Gary, "The Cocaine Mutiny," *Cop Rock,* 1990.

Second police officer, "Prisoner of Love," *Get a Life,* 1991.

Roy, "The Stranded," *Seinfeld,* NBC, 1991.

Detective Reese, "Variations on a Theme," *The Antagonists,* 1991.

Matt Draughon, "Winners and Other Losers," *Room for Two,* ABC, 1992.

Matt Draughon, "Help," *Room for Two,* ABC, 1992.

Matt Draughon, "Not Quite ... Room for Two," *Room for Two,* ABC, 1992.

Officer Barnes, "Dead–End for Delia," *Fallen Angels,* Showtime, 1993.

Attorney Kevin Flynn, *Jack's Place,* ABC, 1993.

Jeff, "Long Distance Lament," *Wings,* NBC, 1994.

Phil, *Muscle,* syndicated, 1995.

Todd Barber, "Angels on the Air," *Touched by an Angel,* CBS, 1995.

James, "The Mating Season" (also known as "The Dating Game"), *The Crew,* Fox, 1995.

Mort Kriendler, "Chapter Sixteen," *Murder One,* ABC, 1996.

Jake, "Pills," *Grace Under Fire* (also known as *Grace Under Pressure*), ABC, 1997.

Roger, *Over the Top,* ABC, 1997.

Dan, "The Long and Winding Road: Part 1," *Home Improvement,* ABC, 1999.

Birdie, "Strip Show," *L.A. Heat,* TNT, 1999.

Husband, "Therapy," *Stark Raving Mad,* NBC, 2000.

Television Appearances; Other:

Bob Morton, a recurring role, *One Day at a Time* (series), CBS, between 1977 and 1983.

David Collins, "The Wave," *ABC Afterschool Special,* ABC, 1981.

Television Director; Movies:

Ghost Dog (also known as *My Magic Dog*), 1997.

A Time to Remember, Hallmark Channel, 2003.

Love, Clyde, Hallmark Channel, 2004.

A Family of Strangers, Hallmark Channel, 2005.

Television Director; Episodic:

Chicken Soup for the Soul, PAX, 1999.

"Area 69," *Son of the Beach,* FX Channel, 2001.

"The Island of Dr. Merlot," *Son of the Beach,* FX Channel, 2001.

"A Tale of Two Johnsons," *Son of the Beach,* FX Channel, 2001.

"The Kids Are Alright," *Grounded for Life,* Fox, 2002.

"Eddie and This Guy with Diamonds," *Grounded for Life,* Fox, 2002.

"Welcome to the Working Week," *Grounded for Life,* Fox, 2003.

"Whatever Happened to Jane's Baby?," *Good Girls Don't,* Oxygen, 2004.

"Oh, Brother," *Good Girls Don't,* Oxygen, 2004.

"Can't Get Next to You," *Grounded for Life,* Fox, 2004.

"Beat on the Brat," *Grounded for Life,* Fox, 2004.

Also directed episodes of *Beetleborgs Metallix,* Fox; *Madison Heights,* PBS; and *The Tracy Morgan Show,* NBC.

Television Director; Other:
Beetleborgs (series; also known as *Big Bad Beetleborgs* and *Saban's Big Bad Beetleborgs*), Fox, 1996–97.
The Poseidon Adventure (miniseries), 2005.

WRITINGS

Screenplays:
(With Randal Patrick) *Waiting to Act* (short film), Putch–Patrick Productions, 1985.
This Is My Father (documentary; also known as *This Is My Father: A Documentary about William H. Putch*), Cinema Guild, 1998.

OTHER SOURCES

Electronic:
John Putch Official Site, http://putchfilms.com, July 21, 2005.

R

REBHORN, James 1948–
(James R. Rebhorn)

PERSONAL

Born September 1, 1948, in Philadelphia, PA. *Education:* Wittenberg University, graduated 1970; Columbia University, M.F.A., 1972.

Addresses: *Agent*—SMS Talent, Inc., 8730 West Sunset Blvd., Suite 440, West Hollywood, CA 90069.

Career: Actor. Whole Theatre Company, Montclair, NJ, guest artist, 1977–78; Mirror Repertory Company, New York City, member of company, 1983–86; Ensemble Studio Theatre, New York City, member of company.

Member: Actors' Equity Association.

Awards, Honors: *Soap Opera Digest* Award nomination, outstanding supporting actor in daytime, 1992, for *As the World Turns.*

CREDITS

Film Appearances:
Casting director, *The Yum–Yum Girls* (also known as *Bright Lights*), 1976.
Professor Carl Mason, *He Knows You're Alone* (also known as *Blood Wedding*), Metro–Goldwyn–Mayer/United Artists, 1980.
Lawyer, *Soup for One,* Warner Bros., 1982.
Los Alamos doctor, *Silkwood,* Twentieth Century–Fox, 1983.
Drunk businessperson, "Wuitters Inc.," *Cat's Eye* (also known as *Stephen King's "Cat's Eye"*), Metro–Goldwyn–Mayer/United Artists, 1985.

Michael Manion, *Whatever It Takes,* Aquarius Films, 1986.
The official, *The House on Carroll Street,* Orion, 1988.
Richard, *Heart of Midnight,* Samuel Goldwyn Company, 1988.
Prosecutor, *Desperate Hours,* Metro–Goldwyn–Mayer/United Artists, 1990.
Dr. Sultan, *Regarding Henry,* Paramount, 1991.
George, *Wind,* TriStar, 1992.
Mr. Trask, *Scent of a Woman,* Universal, 1992.
Ellard Muscatine, *Lorenzo's Oil,* Universal, 1992.
Vigilante, *Shadows and Fog,* Orion, 1992.
George Wilbur, *My Cousin Vinny,* Twentieth Century–Fox, 1992.
Dr. McElwaine, *Basic Instinct* (also known as *Ice Cold Desire*), TriStar, 1992.
Flynn, *White Sands,* Warner Bros., 1992.
District Attorney Norwalk, *Carlito's Way,* Universal, 1993.
Clyde Frost, *8 Seconds* (also known as *The Lane Frost Story*), New Line Cinema, 1994.
Fred Waters, *Blank Check* (also known as *Blank Cheque*), Buena Vista, 1994.
Howard Shaeffer, *Guarding Tess,* TriStar, 1994.
Mando, *I Love Trouble,* Buena Vista, 1994.
How to Make an American Quilt (also known as *An American Quilt*), Universal, 1995.
Tyler, *White Squall,* Buena Vista, 1996.
John Merino, *Up Close & Personal,* Buena Vista, 1996.
Simon Ackerman, *If Lucy Fell,* TriStar, 1996.
Albert Nimzikj, *Independence Day* (also known as *ID4*), Twentieth Century–Fox, 1996.
Charlie Reynolds, *My Fellow Americans,* Warner Bros., 1996.
Jim Feingold, *The Game,* PolyGram Filmed Entertainment, 1997.
Bill Holbeck, *All of It* (also known as *Marriage Material*), 1999.
Herbert Greenleaf, *The Talented Mr. Ripley* (also known as *The Mysterious Yearning Secretive Sad Lonely Troubled Confused Loving Musical Gifted Intel-*

ligent Beautiful Tender Sensitive Haunted Passionate Talented Mr. Ripley), Paramount, 1999.

Alvin Hooks, *Snow Falling on Cedars*, MCA/Universal, 1999.

Mr. Corcoran, *Last Ball*, Sugar Pond Films, 2000.

Larry Banks, *Meet the Parents*, Universal, 2000.

Voice of President Signoff, *The Adventures of Rocky and Bullwinkle* (animated; also known as *Die abenteuer von Rocky und Bullwinkle*), Universal, 2000.

Norm Duncan, *Scotland, Pa.*, Lot 47 Films, 2001.

Dirk Bentley, *Vacuums* (also known as *Stealing Bess*), BVI Bust the Dust/Cobalt Media Group/MediaPro Pictures/Middle Fork Productions/Quincy Jones Media Group, 2002.

Belcher, *The Adventures of Pluto Nash* (also known as *Pluto Nash*), Warner Bros., 2002.

Dr. Bowman, *Far from Heaven* (also known as *Loin du paradis*), Focus Features, 2002.

John Torman, *The Trade*, Lantern Lane Entertainment, 2003.

Senator Bill Arnot, *Head of State*, DreamWorks, 2003.

Doctor, *Cold Mountain*, Miramax, 2003.

Abe White, *The Last Shot*, Buena Vista, 2004.

Television Appearances; Series:

Tom Carroll, *The Doctors*, 1977.

John Brady, *Texas* (also known as *Another World: Texas*), NBC, 1981–82.

Bradley Raines, *The Guiding Light*, CBS, 1984–85, 1989.

Al Miller, *Search for Tomorrow*, 1985–86.

Henry Lange, *As the World Turns*, CBS, 1988–91.

Captain Elchisak, a recurring role, *Third Watch*, NBC, 1999–2000.

Television Appearances; Miniseries:

Federal prosecutor, *Kane and Abel*, CBS, 1985.

Major Anderson, *North and South*, ABC, 1985.

Lieutenant Lloyd Butler, *Deadly Matrimony* (also known as *Shattered Promises*), 1992.

St. John, *J.F.K.: Reckless Youth*, 1993.

Mr. Closson, "The Buccaneers," *Masterpiece Theatre*, PBS, 1995.

Harrison Storms, *From the Earth to the Moon*, HBO, 1998.

Erno Erdai, *Reversible Errors* (also known as *Scott Turow's "Reversible Errors"*), CBS, 2004.

Television Appearances; Movies:

Peter Maroulis, *Will: The Autobiography of G. Gordon Liddy*, NBC, 1982.

Harry, *Sessions*, ABC, 1983.

Man on phone, *He's Fired, She's Hired*, 1984.

Corbett, *A Deadly Business*, CBS, 1986.

Arthur Reardon, *Rockabye*, CBS, 1986.

Henry Quibro, *Kojak: The Price of Justice*, 1987.

Slusher, *Kojak: Ariana* (also known as *Ariana*), 1989.

Slusher, *Kojak: Fatal Flaw*, ABC, 1989.

William Wheaton, "Sarah, Plain and Tall," *Hallmark Hall of Fame*, CBS, 1991.

(As James R. Rebhorn) Ezra, *Plymouth*, ABC, 1991.

William Wheaton, *Skylark* (also known as *Sarah, Plain and Tall: Skylark*), CBS, 1993.

Timothy Lanigan, *Mob Justice* (also known as *Dead and Alive, Dead and Alive: The Race for Gus Farace*, and *In the Line of Duty: Mob Justice*), ABC, 1995.

Mayor Taylor, *Mistrial*, CBS, 1996.

American ambassador to Vietnam, *A Bright Shining Lie*, HBO, 1998.

Avery Clark, *Amy & Isabelle* (also known as *Oprah Winfrey Presents: Amy and Isabelle*), ABC, 2001.

Television Appearances; Specials:

Ira Smith, *Song of Myself*, CBS, 1976.

Charlie Riley, *The Adventures of Con Sawyer and Hucklemary Finn*, ABC, 1985.

Dan Jensen, *A Town's Revenge*, 1989.

Dr. Franklin Gibbs, *Our Town*, PBS, 1989.

Television Appearances; Episodic:

Paul Manning, "Blood Money," *Spenser: For Hire*, ABC, 1985.

Derek, "The Reunion," *Kate & Allie*, 1985.

Derek, "Privacy," *Kate & Allie*, 1986.

Father Hoyt, "On the Night He Was Betrayed," *Spenser: For Hire*, ABC, 1987.

Agent White, "Fruit of the Poisonous Tree: Parts 1 & 2," *Wiseguy*, CBS, 1990.

Agent White, "La Mina," *Wiseguy*, CBS, 1990.

I'll Fly Away, NBC, 1991.

Albert Lawrence Cheney, "Vengeance," *Law & Order*, NBC, 1992.

Charles Garnett, "Progeny," *Law & Order*, NBC, 1995.

Will Garrett, *The Wright Verdicts*, CBS, 1995.

Tucker (some source cite Tuckett), "The Promised Land," *New York Undercover*, Fox, 1997.

Charles Garnett, "Denial," *Law & Order*, NBC, 1997.

District Attorney Hoyt, "The Finale: Parts 1 & 2," *Seinfeld*, NBC, 1998.

Charles Garnett, "Patsy," *Law & Order*, NBC, 1999.

General Irving, "Deep in My Heart Is a Song," *Now and Again*, NBC, 2000.

General Irving, "Everybody Who's Anybody," *Now and Again*, NBC, 2000.

Hanson Garnett, "A Losing Season," *Law & Order*, NBC, 2001.

Attorney John Rapherson, "Home of the Brave," *The Practice*, ABC, 2001.

Attorney John Rapherson, "The Case of Harland Bassett," *The Practice*, ABC, 2001.

Deputy Warden Petrocelli, "The Siege" (also known as "Prison Riot"), *UC: Undercover*, NBC, 2001.

Captain Elchisak, "Thicker than Water," *Third Watch*, NBC, 2002.

Charles Garnett, "Dazzled," *Law & Order*, NBC, 2002.

"Head of State," *HBO First Look*, HBO, 2003.

Richard Farrell, "See No Evil," *Hack,* CBS, 2003.
Richard Farrell, "The Looking Glass," *Hack,* CBS, 2003.

Appeared as Jack McFlemp, "Goodbye My Little Viking: Parts 1 & 2," *The Adventures of Pete & Pete.*

Television Appearances; Pilots:
Captain Elchisak, *Third Watch,* NBC, 1999.
John Melville, *Hopewell,* CBS, 2000.

Television Appearances; Other:
Jim, *Everyday Heroes,* 1990.

Stage Appearances:
Understudy, *Blue Boys,* Martinique Theatre, New York City, 1972.
Frank, *Dearly Beloved,* Manhattan Theatre Club, New York City, 1976.
Father Gerry Powers, *Ballymurphy,* Manhattan Theatre Club, 1976.
Ed, "A Long Story," *Bosom Buddies,* Three Muses Theatre, New York City, 1978.
Sterling Hayden, Elliott Sullivan, and Arthur Miller, *Are You Now or Have You Ever Been,* Rutgers Theatre Company, 1978–79, then Century Theatre, New York City, 1979.
Roderigo, *Othello,* New York Shakespeare Festival, Delacorte Theatre, Public Theatre, New York City, 1979.
The Last Few Days of Willie Callendar, Philadelphia Drama Guild, Philadelphia, PA, 1979–80.
President Lehman, Ben Bragge, and first underworld figure, *The Trouble with Europe,* Marymount Manhattan Theatre, Phoenix Theatre, New York City, 1980.
George, *Period of Adjustment,* Perry Street Theatre, New York City, 1980–81.
The Front Page, Center Stage, Baltimore, MD, 1980–81.
Dr. Wesley Ketchum, *The Freak,* Workshop of the Players Art Theatre, New York City, 1981, then Douglas Fairbanks Theatre, New York City, 1982.
Tobias, "Half a Lifetime," *Triple Feature,* Stage 73, Manhattan Theatre Club, 1983.
David, *To Gillian on Her 37th Birthday,* Ensemble Studio Theatre, New York City, 1983, then Circle in the Square Downtown, New York City, 1984.
Harry, *Husbandry,* Stage 73, Manhattan Theatre Club, 1984.
Robert, "Blind Date," *Marathon '86: Series A,* Ensemble Studio Theatre, 1986.
Danforth, *I'm Not Rappaport,* Booth Theatre, New York City, c. 1986.
Leon, *Cold Sweat,* Playwrights Horizons Theatre, New York City, 1988.
Marathon '88, Ensemble Studio Theatre, 1988.
Dr. Gibbs, *Our Town,* Lyceum Theatre, New York City, 1988–89.

Charlie, Jerry, and Lance, *Ice Cream with Hot Fudge,* Estelle R. Newman Theatre, Public Theatre, New York City, 1990.
John Calvin, Fielding, Lieutenant Waters, and DeVries, *Life During Wartime,* Manhattan Theatre Club Stage II, 1991.
Karl, *The Innocent's Crusade,* Manhattan Theatre Club Stage II, 1992.
Tramp and Gil, *On the Bum,* Playwrights Horizons Theatre, 1992.
Atticus Finch, *To Kill a Mockingbird,* Peterborough Players, 1994.
Kyle, *Oblivion Postponed,* Second Stage Theatre Company, McGinn–Cazale Theatre, New York City, 1995–96.
Austin, *Later Life,* Peterborough Players, 1998.
Ancestral Voices (staged reading), Mitzi E. Newhouse Theatre, New York City, 1999.
Far East, Mitzi E. Newhouse Theatre, 1999.
Patterson "Pat" Beeves, *The Man Who Had All the Luck: A Fable,* Roundabout Theatre Company, American Airlines Theatre, New York City, 2002.
Oliver Jordan, *Dinner at Eight,* Vivian Beaumont Theatre, Lincoln Center, New York City, 2002–2003.
Fourth juror, *Twelve Angry Men,* Roundabout Theatre Company, 2004–2005.

Appeared in *Nebraska,* La Jolla Playhouse, La Jolla, CA; also appeared in productions of *The Hasty Heart, The Hunchback of Notre Dame, Isn't It Romantic?, Rain, Spoils of War,* and *Touch Black.*

RECORDINGS

Videos:
(Uncredited) Stranger, "Bad Girl," *Madonna: The Video Collection 93:99,* Warner Reprise, 1999.
Spotlight on Location: Meet the Parents, Universal, 2001.

Appeared in the music video "Bad Girl" by Madonna.

Audio Books:
Reader (with others), *From a Buick 8: A Novel,* by Stephen King, Simon & Schuster Audio, 2002.

REGOR, Yrava
   See AVARY, Roger

ROBERTS, Doris 1930(?)–

PERSONAL

Full name, Doris May Roberts; born November 4, 1930 (some sources cite or 1925 or 1929), in St. Louis, MO;

raised in New York City; daughter of Larry and Ann (maiden name, Meltzer) Roberts; married Michael E. Cannata (a lawyer; divorced, 1962); married William Goyen (a writer, editor, composer, and educator), November 10, 1963 (died, August 30, 1982 [some sources cite 1983]); children: (first marriage) Michael Robert (a personal manager). *Education:* Attended New York University, 1950–51; trained for the stage at Neighborhood Playhouse with Stanford Meisner and at Actors Studio with Lee Strasberg. *Avocational Interests:* Travel, painting, restoring old furniture, needlepoint.

Addresses: *Agent*—Innovative Artists, 1505 10th St., Santa Monica, CA 90401.

Career: Actress, voice performer, and director. Appeared in commercials.

Member: Actors' Equity Association, Screen Actors Guild, American Federation of Television and Radio Artists, Directors Guild of America.

Awards, Honors: Outer Critics Circle Award, 1974, for *Bad Habits;* Emmy Award, outstanding supporting actress in a drama series, 1983, for "Cora and Arnie," *St. Elsewhere;* Emmy Award nomination, outstanding supporting actress in a drama series, 1985, for *Remington Steele;* Emmy Award nomination, outstanding guest actress in a comedy series, 1989, for "Maid to Order," *Perfect Strangers;* Emmy Award nomination, outstanding supporting actress in a miniseries or special, 1991, for "The Sunset Gang," *American Playhouse;* Q awards, best supporting actress in a quality comedy series, Viewers for Quality Television, 1998, 1999, and 2000, American Comedy Award, funniest supporting female performer in a television series, 1999, Emmy Award nominations, 1999, 2000, 2004, and 2005, and Emmy awards, 2001, 2002, and 2003, all outstanding supporting actress in a comedy series, Screen Actors Guild Award nominations, 1999, 2000, 2002, 2004, and 2005, and Screen Actors Guild Award, 2003, all outstanding performance by an ensemble in a comedy series, all with others, American Comedy Award nomination, funniest supporting female performer in a television series, 2000, *TV Guide* Award, supporting actress of the year in a comedy series, 2001, Television Award nomination, actress of the year in a series, American Film Institute, 2002, Golden Satellite Award, best performance by an actress in a supporting role in a comedy or musical television series, International Press Academy, 2003, and Screen Actors Guild Award nominations, outstanding performance by a female actor in a comedy series, 2004 and 2005, all for *Everybody Loves Raymond;* received a star on the Hollywood Walk of Fame, 2003; Family Television Award, 2004; *Los Angeles Weekly* Award.

CREDITS

Television Appearances; Series:
Dorelda Doremus, *Mary Hartman, Mary Hartman,* syndicated, 1976–77.
Theresa Falco, *Angie,* ABC, 1979–80.
Loretta Davenport, *Maggie,* ABC, 1981–82.
Mildred Krebs, *Remington Steele,* NBC, 1983–87.
Doris Greenblatt, *The Boys,* CBS, 1993.
Marie Barone, *Everybody Loves Raymond,* CBS, 1996–2005.
Voice of Jaundice Mutton, *Zeroman* (animated), TeleToon, beginning 2004.

Television Appearances; Miniseries:
Tessie McBride, *Blind Faith* (also known as *The Toms River Case*), NBC, 1990.
(And in archive footage) Herself, *The Fifty* (documentary), 1998.

Television Appearances; Movies:
Ma Bailey, *It Happened One Christmas,* ABC, 1977.
Marion Davidson (some sources cite Marion Davidoff), *The Storyteller,* NBC, 1977.
Eva, *Ruby and Oswald* (also known as *Four Days in Dallas*), CBS, 1978.
Kay, *Jennifer: A Woman's Story,* NBC, 1979.
Mrs. Van Daan, *The Diary of Anne Frank,* NBC, 1980.
Myrna, *Another Woman's Child,* CBS, 1983.
Mrs. Bowzer, *California Girls,* ABC, 1985.
Sadie Finney, *A Letter to Three Wives,* NBC, 1985.
Edith Bernside, *Ordinary Heroes,* ABC, 1986.
Dottie Wilson, *If It's Tuesday It Still Must Be Belgium,* NBC, 1987.
Mildred Krebs, *Remington Steele: The Steele That Wouldn't Die,* NBC, 1987.
Philomena, *A Mom for Christmas,* NBC, 1990.
Maddy, *A Time to Heal* (also known as *Jenny's Story* and *Out of the Darkness*), NBC, 1994.
Sister Philomena, *A Thousand Men and a Baby* (also known as *Narrow Escape*), 1997.
Lillian, *One True Love,* CBS, 2000.
Marge, *Sons of Mistletoe* (also known as *Un noel pas comme les autres*), CBS, 2001.
Maggie Calhoun, *A Time to Remember,* Hallmark Channel, 2003.
Aunt Marie, *Raising Waylon,* CBS, 2004.
Our House, The Hallmark Channel, 2006.

Television Appearances; Specials:
Waitress, *The Trouble with People,* NBC, 1972.
The Lily Tomlin Special, ABC, 1975.
Doris, *Alvin Goes Back to School,* NBC, 1986.
NBC's 60th Anniversary Celebration, NBC, 1986.
Mimi Finkelstein, "Yiddish," a segment of "The Sunset Gang," *American Playhouse,* PBS, 1991.

Marie, *Sea World and Busch Gardens Adventures: Alien Vacation!,* CBS, 1997.

Funny Flubs and Screw–Ups III, CBS, 1999.

TV Moms at Home, Home and Garden Television, 1999.

Judge, *Miss USA 2001,* CBS, 2001.

Hollywood Unites: An E! News Special, E! Entertainment Television, 2001.

Herself, *Everybody Loves Raymond: The First Six Years,* CBS, 2002.

CBS at 75, CBS, 2003.

Herself, *TV Guide Close Up: From Comedy Club to Primetime* (documentary), TV Guide Channel, 2004.

Host, *Sitcom Super Moms,* Nickelodeon, 2004.

(Uncredited) *Sesame Street Presents: The Street We Live On,* PBS, 2004.

Appeared in other specials.

Television Appearances; Awards Presentations:

Presenter, *The 1999 Primetime Creative Arts Emmy Awards,* HBO Plus, 1999.

Presenter, *14th Annual Genesis Awards,* Animal Planet, 2000.

Presenter, *The 55th Annual Tony Awards,* CBS and PBS, 2001.

Presenter, *The Ninth Annual Movieguide Awards,* PAX TV, 2001.

Presenter, *The 2001 Genesis Awards,* Animal Planet, 2001.

The 2001 TV Guide Awards, Fox, 2001.

The 54th Annual Emmy Awards Show, 2002.

The 56th Annual Tony Awards, CBS, 2002.

16th Annual Genesis Awards, Animal Planet, 2002.

The 55th Annual Primetime Emmy Awards, Fox, 2003.

The Mark Twain Prize: Lily Tomlin, 2003.

TV Land Awards: A Celebration of Classic TV (also known as *First Annual TV Land Awards*), TV Land, 2003.

The Sixth Annual Family Television Awards, 2004.

Herself, *The 59th Annual Tony Awards,* 2005.

Television Appearances; Episodic:

"Jane Eyre," *Studio One,* CBS, 1952.

Edna Potter, "Side Show," *Way Out,* CBS, 1961.

Minnah, "Rider Number Six," *Look Up and Live,* CBS, 1961.

Marjorie Hill, "Madman: Parts 1 & 2," *The Defenders,* CBS, 1962.

"One of the Most Important Men in the Whole World," *Naked City,* ABC, 1962.

Claire Forrest, "Father Was an Intern," *Ben Casey,* ABC, 1963.

"Color Schemes Like Never Before," *Naked City,* ABC, 1963.

Helen Wyroski, "Next Stop, Valhalla," *The Doctors and the Nurses* (also known as *The Nurses*), CBS, 1964.

Minna Fraylock, "Claire Chevel Died in Boston," *The Defenders,* CBS, 1964.

Ann Hawley, "The Patient Nurse," *The Doctors and the Nurses* (also known as *The Nurses*), CBS, 1965.

Shimmy, "Shadow Game," *CBS Playhouse,* CBS, 1969.

Gladys Callahan, "Two against Death," *Medical Center,* CBS, 1975.

Helen Farrell, "Phyllis Whips Inflation," *The Mary Tyler Moore Show* (also known as *Mary Tyler Moore*), CBS, 1975.

Mrs. Asher, "Sharper Than a Serpent's Truth," *Baretta,* ABC, 1975.

Marge, "Edith's Night Out," *All in the Family,* CBS, 1976.

Mrs. Strauss, "The Thrill Killers: Parts 1 & 2," *The Streets of San Francisco,* ABC, 1976.

Sylvia Levy, "Meet the Levys," *Rhoda,* CBS, 1976.

"The Nurse's Pipes," *Viva Valdez,* ABC, 1976.

"Such Sweet Sorrow," *Family,* ABC, 1976.

Louise Kaufman, "Sex Surrogate," *Barney Miller,* ABC, 1977.

Harriet Brower, "The Sighting," *Barney Miller,* ABC, 1978.

Flo Flotski, *Soap,* ABC, multiple episodes in 1978.

Harriet Brower, "Wojo's Girl: Part 1," *Barney Miller,* ABC, 1979.

Marjorie Gibbs, "Goose for the Gander," *Fantasy Island,* ABC, 1979.

Crystal, *The Mary Tyler Moore Comedy Hour,* CBS, 1979.

Harriet Brower, "Agent Orange," *Barney Miller,* ABC, 1980.

Rose, "Sergeant Bull," *The Love Boat,* ABC, 1980.

Mona Spivak, "Alice's Big Four–Oh!," *Alice,* CBS, 1981.

Fantasy Island, ABC, 1981.

Cora, "Cora and Arnie," *St. Elsewhere,* NBC, 1982.

Mona Spivak, "Alice's Turkey of a Thanksgiving," *Alice,* CBS, 1982.

Helen Freitas, "Jane Doe #37," *Cagney & Lacey,* CBS, 1983.

"The Night Stalker," *The New Odd Couple,* ABC, 1983.

"Our Son, the Lawyer," *The Love Boat,* ABC, 1983.

"The Perils of Pauline," *The New Odd Couple,* ABC, 1983.

Mrs. Bush, "Call Me a Doctor," *The Love Boat,* ABC, 1984.

Mom, "The Three Little Pigs," *Faerie Tale Theater* (also known as *Shelley Duvall's "Faerie Tale Theater"*), Showtime, 1985.

Judge Westphall, "Deportation: Part 2," *Mr. Belvedere,* ABC, 1986.

Great Aunt Eliza, "The Fig Tree," *WonderWorks,* PBS, 1987.

Michele Loring, "The State of Oregon vs. Stanley Manning," *You Are the Jury,* NBC, 1987.

Ida Kankel, "School Daze," *Cagney & Lacey,* CBS, 1988.

Claire Tanner, "Granny Tanny," *Full House,* ABC, 1989.

Mrs. Bailey, "Maid to Order," *Perfect Strangers,* ABC, 1989.

Helen Owens, "Shear Madness," *Murder, She Wrote,* CBS, 1990.

Aunt Retha, "The Last Temptation of Laverne," *Empty Nest,* NBC, 1991.

Delores, "My Dinner with Jack and Delores," *Sunday Dinner,* CBS, 1991.

"Throw Momma from the House," *The Family Man,* CBS, 1991.

Angie Pedalbee, "The Book, the Thief, Her Boss, and His Lover," *Dream On,* HBO, 1993, also broadcast on Fox.

Angie Pedalbee, "Pop Secret," *Dream On,* HBO, 1993, also broadcast on Fox.

Angie Pedalbee, "Reach Out and Touch Yourself," *Dream On,* HBO, 1993, also broadcast on Fox.

Aunt Edna, "I'll Be Home for Christmas," *Step by Step,* ABC, 1994.

Mrs. Leah Colfax, "The Murder Channel," *Murder, She Wrote,* CBS, 1994.

Angie Pedalbee, "Flight of the Pedalbee," *Dream On,* HBO, 1995, also broadcast on Fox.

Angie Pedalbee, "Significant Author," *Dream On,* HBO, 1995, also broadcast on Fox.

Angie Pedalbee, "Toby's Choice," *Dream On,* HBO, 1995, also broadcast on Fox.

Betsy Meadows, "Who Killed Cock-a-Doodle Dooley?," *Burke's Law,* CBS, 1995.

Elaine Portugal, "The Big Bingo Bamboozle," *Walker, Texas Ranger,* CBS, 1995.

Hazel, "Touching Up Your Roots," *High Society,* CBS, 1996.

Guest, *The Late Show with David Letterman* (also known as *The Late Show*), CBS, 1998, 2003.

Marie Barone, "Rayny Day," *The King of Queens,* CBS, 1999.

Guest, *The Martin Short Show,* syndicated, 1999.

Guest, *Saturday Night Live* (also known as *NBC's "Saturday Night," Saturday Night,* and *SNL*), NBC, 1999.

Guest, *Mad TV,* Fox, 1999, 2001.

Herself, *Intimate Portrait: Patricia Heaton,* Lifetime, 2000.

Guest, *Larry King Live,* Cable News Network, 2000.

Guest, *The View,* ABC, 2001, 2002, 2003, 2004, 2005.

Rose, "The Bells of St. Peters," *Touched by an Angel,* CBS, 2002.

Herself, *Intimate Portrait: Doris Roberts,* Lifetime, 2002.

Guest, *The Late Late Show with Craig Kilborn,* CBS, 2002.

Guest, *Rove Live,* 10 Network (Australia), 2002.

Herself, "Blondes Have More Fun Week," *The Hollywood Squares,* 2003.

Herself, "Most Shocking Moments in Entertainment," *E!'s 101,* E! Entertainment Television, 2003.

Herself, "Peter Boyle," *Biography* (also known as *A&E Biography: Peter Boyle*), Arts and Entertainment, 2003.

Grandma Ruth, "Grand Ole' Grandma," *Lizzie McGuire* (live action and animated), The Disney Channel, 2003.

Guest, *Live with Regis and Kelly,* syndicated, 2003.

Guest, *The Wayne Brady Show,* syndicated, 2003.

Guest, *Good Day Live,* Fox, 2003, 2004.

Herself, "Doris Roberts," *ALF's Hit Talk Show,* TV Land, 2004.

Guest, *The Hollywood Squares,* 2004.

Guest, *On-Air with Ryan Seacrest,* syndicated, 2004.

Guest, *The Tony Danza Show,* syndicated, 2004, multiple episodes in 2005.

Herself, "Ray Romano," *Biography* (also known as *A&E Biography: Ray Romano*), Arts and Entertainment, 2005.

Herself, "Wacky Neighbors," *TV Land's Top Ten,* TV Land, 2005.

Guest, *Live with Regis and Kelly,* syndicated, 2005.

Guest, *The Oprah Winfrey Show* (also known as *Oprah*), syndicated, 2005.

Guest, *Sidewalks Entertainment* (also known as *Sidewalks* and *Sidewalks Entertainment Hour*), syndicated, 2005.

Guest, *Tavis Smiley,* PBS, 2005.

Appeared in episodes of other series, including *Blansky's Beauties,* ABC; and *Joe and Sons,* CBS.

Television Appearances; Pilots:

Aunt Enid, *Bell, Book and Candle,* NBC, 1976.

Paula Handy, *The Oath: Thirty-Three Hours in the Life of God,* ABC, 1976.

Irma DeGroot, *In Trouble,* ABC, 1981.

Ethel Connelly, *Me and Mrs. C.,* NBC, 1984.

Cecile Rickwald, *The Gregory Harrison Show,* CBS, 1989.

Bea, *The Ladies on Sweet Street,* ABC, 1990.

Mrs. Shenker, *The John Larroquette Show,* NBC, 1993.

Television Director; Episodic:

"Angie and Joyce Go to Jail," *Angie,* ABC, 1980.

Film Appearances:

Girl in 5 and 10, *Something Wild,* United Artists, 1961.

(Uncredited) Desk clerk, *Dear Heart* (also known as *Out of Towners*), Warner Bros., 1964.

Feeney, *A Lovely Way to Die* (also known as *A Lovely Way to Go*), Universal, 1968.

(Uncredited) Hotel maid, *Barefoot in the Park,* Paramount, 1968.

Sylvia Poppie, *No Way to Treat a Lady,* Paramount, 1968.

Bunny, *The Honeymoon Killers* (also known as *The Lonely Hearts Killers*), Cinerama, 1970.

Mrs. Chamberlain, *Little Murders,* Twentieth Century-Fox, 1971.

Mrs. Gold, *Such Good Friends,* Paramount, 1971.

Mrs. Traggert, *A New Leaf,* Paramount, 1971.

Mrs. Cantrow, *The Heartbreak Kid,* Twentieth Century-Fox, 1972.

The mayor's wife, *The Taking of Pelham 1–2–3* (also known as *Pelham 1–2–3* and *El tomar de Pelham uno dos tres*), United Artists, 1974.

Mrs. Kavarsky, *Hester Street,* First Run Features, 1975.

Mrs. Lambert, *Blood Bath,* 1976.

Lars Brady's ex–wife, *Once in Paris,* Leigh McLaughlin, 1978.

Mrs. Carpenter, *Rabbit Test,* Avco–Embassy, 1978.

Mrs. Foster, *The Rose,* Twentieth Century–Fox, 1979.

Rene (some sources cite Marie), *Good Luck Miss Wykoff* (also known as *Secret Yearnings, The Shaming,* and *The Sin*), 1979.

Mrs. Barzak, *Number One with a Bullet,* Cannon, 1986.

Anna DiLorenzo, *Simple Justice,* Panorama Entertainment, 1989.

Frances Smith, *National Lampoon's "Christmas Vacation"* (also known as *Christmas Vacation* and *National Lampoon's "Winter Holiday"*), Warner Bros., 1989.

Mrs. Nelson, *Honeymoon Academy* (also known as *For Better or for Worse*), Triumph Releasing, 1990.

Aunt Lonnie, *Used People,* Twentieth Century–Fox, 1992.

Neighbor, *The Night We Never Met,* Miramax, 1993.

Taffy, 1994.

Mrs. Richards, *The Grass Harp,* Fine Line Features, 1995.

Frieda, *A Fish in the Bathtub,* Curb Entertainment, 1998.

Rose Kaminski, *My Giant,* Columbia, 1998.

Voice of Auntie Shrew, *The Secret of NIMH 2: Timmy to the Rescue* (animated), 1998.

Esther, *All over the Guy,* Lions Gate Films, 2001.

Sylvia, *Full Circle,* Sinovoi Entertainment, 2001.

Peggy Roberts, *Dickie Roberts: Former Child Star* (also known as *Dickie Roberts: (Former) Child Star*), Paramount, 2003.

Rose Fiedler, *Lucky 13,* Road Picture/Winsome Productions, 2005.

Grandma Lilly, *Grandma's Boy* (also known as *Nana's Boy*), Twentieth Century–Fox, 2006.

Stage Appearances:

Prostitute, *The Time of Your Life,* City Center, New York City, 1955.

Miss Rumple, *The Desk Set,* Broadhurst Theatre, New York City, 1955–56.

Nurse, *The Death of Bessie Smith,* York Playhouse, New York City, 1961.

Mommy, *The American Dream,* York Playhouse, 1961, revived at Cherry Lane Theatre, New York City, 1971.

Color of Darkness, Writers Stage Theatre, New York City, 1963.

Cracks, Writers Stage Theatre, 1963.

Rae Wilson, *Marathon '33,* American National Theatre and Academy, New York City, 1963–64.

Miss Punk, *The Office,* Henry Miller's Theatre, New York City, 1966.

Standby for Flora Sharkey, Hilda, and Marcella Vankuchen, *Under the Weather,* Cort Theatre, New York City, 1966.

Understudy for Madame Girard and Eloisa, *Malcolm,* Shubert Theatre, New York City, 1966.

Edna, *The Natural Look,* Longacre Theatre, New York City, 1967.

Jeanette Fisher, *Last of the Red Hot Lovers,* Eugene O'Neill Theatre, New York City, 1969–71.

May, *Felix,* Actors Studio, New York City, 1972.

Miss Manley and standby for Mildred Wild, *The Secret Affairs of Mildred Wild,* Ambassador Theatre, New York City, 1972.

Dolly Scupp, "Ravenswood," and Becky Hedges, "Dunelawn," in *Bad Habits* (double–bill), Astor Place Theatre, then Booth Theatre, both New York City, 1974.

Dede, *Ladies at the Alamo,* Actors Studio, 1975.

Grace, *Cheaters,* Biltmore Theatre, New York City, 1978.

Emma, *It's Only a Play,* Center Theatre Group, James A. Doolittle Theatre, Los Angeles, 1992.

Appeared in other productions, including productions in Ann Arbor, MI, 1953; and Chatham, MA, 1955.

Major Tours:

Claudia, *The Opening,* U.S. cities, 1972.

Morning's at Seven, U.S. cities, 1976.

Stage Work:

Assistant stage manager, *The Desk Set,* Broadhurst Theatre, New York City, 1955–56.

Director of a play at the Skylight Theater, Los Angeles.

RECORDINGS

Audiobooks:

Doris Roberts and Danelle Morton, *Are You Hungry, Dear? Life, Laughs, Lasagna,* Audio Renaissance, 2003.

WRITINGS

Nonfiction:

(With Danelle Morton) *Are You Hungry, Dear? Life, Laughs, Lasagna,* St. Martin's Press, 2003.

Contributor to periodicals, including *Woman's World.*

OTHER SOURCES

Books:
Newsmakers, Issue 4, Gale, 2003.

Periodicals:
Parade, November 23, 2003, p. 24.
People Weekly, June 5, 2000, p. 69.
TV Guide, June 30, 2001, pp. 26–29; November 22, 2003, p. 22.

ROBINSON, Amy 1948–

PERSONAL

Born April 13, 1948, in Trenton, NJ; daughter of a doctor. *Education:* Attended Sarah Lawrence College. *Religion:* Judaism.

Addresses: *Office*—Amy Robinson Productions, 101 Fifth Ave., Eighth Floor, Suite R, New York, NY 10003; Serenade Films, 2901 Ocean Park Ave., Suite 217, Santa Monica, CA 90405.

Career: Producer, director, and actress. Triple Play Productions, founder (with Griffin Dunne and Mark Metcalfe), 1977; Double Play Productions, founder (with Dunne), 1982, partner, 1982–91; Jersey Tomato, Inc., New York City, producer; Amy Robinson Productions, New York City, founder and producer; Serenade Films, Santa Monica, CA, partner; Ruben/Robinson Productions, partner.

Awards, Honors: Independent Spirit Award (with Robert F. Colesberry and Griffin Dunne), best feature, Independent Features Project/West, 1986, for *After Hours;* Crystal Heart Award, Heartland Film Festival, 2004, for *When Zachary Beaver Came to Town.*

CREDITS

Film Producer:
(With Mark Metcalf and Griffin Dunne) *Head over Heels* (also known as *Chilly Scenes of Winter*), United Artists, 1979.
(With Dunne) *Baby, It's You,* Paramount, 1983.
(With Dunne and Robert F. Colesberry) *After Hours,* Warner Bros., 1985.
(With Dunne) *Running on Empty,* Warner Bros., 1988.
(With Dunne and Mark Rosenberg) *White Palace,* Universal, 1990.
(With Dunne) *Once Around,* Universal, 1991.

Isle of Joy, 1994.
(With Paula Weinstein) *With Honors,* Warner Bros., 1994.
Drive Me Crazy (also known as *Next to You*), Twentieth Century–Fox, 1999.
(With Armyan Bernstein) *For Love of the Game,* MCA/ Universal, 1999.
(With Gary Lucchesi and Tom Rosenberg) *Autumn in New York,* United Artists, 2000.
When Zachary Beaver Came to Town, Echo Bridge Entertainment, 2003.
Game 6, Serenade Films, 2005.
The Deep Blue Goodbye, Twentieth Century–Fox, 2006.

Film Executive Producer:
From Hell, Twentieth Century–Fox, 2001.
Marie and Bruce, New Films International, 2004.
The Great New Wonderful, Serenade Films/Sly Dog Films, 2005.
Twelve and Holding, Canary Films/Serenade Films, 2005.

Film Director:
Isle of Joy, 1994.

Film Appearances:
Teresa Ronchelli, *Mean Streets,* United Artists, 1973.

Television Producer; Specials:
Herself, *A View from Hell* (documentary), HBO, 2001.

Television Appearances; Movies:
Nancy, *A Brand New Life,* ABC, 1973.
The Neighborhood (also known as *Breslin's Neighborhood*), CBS, 1982.

Television Appearances; Specials:
Martin Scorsese Directs (documentary), PBS, 1990.

Television Appearances; Episodic:
Herself, "From Hell," *HBO First Look,* HBO, 2001.

Stage Appearances:
Appeared in productions of the La MaMa Experimental Theatre Club, New York City.

RECORDINGS

Videos:
Herself, *Filming for Your Life: Making "After Hours,"* Warner Home Video, 2004.

WRITINGS

Screenplays:
(And story) *Baby, It's You,* Paramount, 1983.

Nonfiction:
Contributor to periodicals, including *New York Times.*

OTHER SOURCES

Periodicals:
New York Times, March 24, 1974.
Variety, November 15, 1999, p. N5.

ROMANO, Larry
  (Lawrence John Romano)

PERSONAL

Raised in New York City; father, in garment business. *Education:* Trained at Lee Strasberg Institute and the Learning Annex.

Addresses: *Agent*—TalentWorks, 3500 West Olive Ave., Suite 1400, Burbank, CA 91505. *Manager*—Kim Matuka, Online Talent Group, 1522 North Formosa, Suite 211, West Hollywood, CA 90046.

Career: Actor, producer, musician, singer, and writer. Drummer, singer, and songwriter with the bands Deficit and Eljay Are. Appeared in commercials. Worked at a garment factory and as a pizza delivery person, bartender, bicycle messenger, and a telephone sales representative.

CREDITS

Television Appearances; Series:
Richie Catina, a recurring role, *NYPD Blue,* ABC, 1993–94.
Richie Biondi, *Public Morals,* CBS, 1996.
Richie Iannucci, *The King of Queens,* CBS, 1998–2001.
Aldo Bonnadonna, *Kristin,* ABC, 2001.

Television Appearances; Episodic:
Falcone, "F.O.B.," *L.A. Law,* NBC, 1993.
Vinnie, "My Boyfriend's Back!," *Mad about You* (also known as *Loved by You*), NBC, 1995.
Leo, "Thanksgiving," *What I Like about You,* The WB, 2002.

Appeared as a guest in *The Test,* FX Channel; also appeared in *Civil Wars,* ABC.

Television Appearances; Pilots:
Walt, *Guy Island,* NBC, 1997.

Film Appearances:
First Base, *Lock Up,* TriStar, 1989.
(As Lawrence John Romano) Howling punk, *She's Back* (also known as *Dead and Married*), Tycin Entertainment, 1989.
Black Rain, Paramount, 1989.
Salesclerk, *Out for Justice,* Warner Bros., 1991.
First tough man, *Vibrations* (also known as *Cyberstorm*), Dimension Films, 1995.
Emilio, *New York Cop* (also known as *Nyuyoku u koppu*), Overseas Film Group, 1996.
First waiter, *Love Is All There Is,* Samuel Goldwyn, 1996.
Frankie "Eyelashes," *Bullet,* New Line Cinema, 1996.
Second man, *Sleepers,* Warner Bros., 1996.
Tino Zapatti, *City Hall,* Columbia, 1996.
Tommy Ruggiero, *Donnie Brasco,* TriStar, 1997.
Carter, *No Way Home,* LIVE Entertainment/Live Film and Mediaworks, 1998.
Private Mazzi, *The Thin Red Line* (also known as *La mince ligne rouge*), Twentieth Century–Fox, 1998.
Jimmy the Pope, *18 Shades of Dust* (also known as *Hitman's Journal* and *The Sicilian Code*), New Films International, 1999.
Danny Russo, *Final Breakdown* (also known as *Truth Be Told* and *Turnaround*), Strange Fruit Films/Niko Filmworks, 2002.
John, *Spanish Fly,* Iron Heart Films, 2003.
Ryan, *Saved by the Rules,* 2003.
Fish without a Bicycle, Echelon Entertainment, 2003.
Herman, *Bald,* Endeavor Productions, 2005.
Detective Don Warner, *Roney's Point,* Bird's–Eye Media, 2006.

Film Producer:
Little Athens, Legaci Pictures, 2005.

RECORDINGS

Albums:
With Eljay Are, albums include *Deficit* and *Undefined.* Other recordings include "The House That Ruth Built" and *Johnny Bago.*

WRITINGS

Writings for the Stage:
Author of *We Ain't Kids No More,* produced by Lee Strasberg Institute, New York City; and *Suitcase of Memories,* off–Broadway production.

Albums:
With Eljay Are, albums include *Deficit* and *Undefined.* Other recordings include "The House That Ruth Built."

OTHER SOURCES

Electronic:
Larry Romano Official Site, http://www.larryromano. com, March 15, 2005.

ROWE, Nicholas 1966–
(Nick Rowe)

PERSONAL

Born November 22, 1966, in Edinburgh, Scotland (one source says London, England); son of Andrew (a politician and editor) and Alison (a singer) Rowe. *Education:* Attended University of Bristol.

Addresses: *Agent*—Lucy Brazier, Peters Fraser & Dunlop, 34–43 Russell St., London WC2B 5HA, England.

Career: Actor. Worked as a market researcher in London.

CREDITS

Film Appearances:
(As Nick Rowe) Spungin, *Another Country,* Orion, 1984.
Title role, *Young Sherlock Holmes* (also known as *Pyramid of Fear*), Paramount, 1985.
"J", *Lock, Stock and Two Smoking Barrels* (also known as *Two Smoking Barrels*), Gramercy, 1998.
Jeremy, *Hit List* (short film), 2000.
Maidanov, *All Forgotten* (also known as *Lover's Prayer*), Seven Hills Productions, 2000.
Villiers, *Enigma* (also known as *Enigma—Das geheimnis*), Manhattan Pictures International, 2002.
Lord Verisopht, *Nicholas Nickleby,* Metro–Goldwyn–Mayer, 2002.
Harry, *Girl on a Cycle,* 2003.
Lawyer, *Seed of Chucky,* Rogue Pictures, 2004.

Television Appearances; Series:
(As Nick Rowe) Boyer, *The Fugitives,* ITV (England), 2005.

Television Appearances; Miniseries:
David Pennistone, *A Dance to the Music of Time,* Channel 4 (England), 1997.

King George III, *Longitude,* Arts and Entertainment, 2000.
Professor Gibberne, *The Infinite Worlds of H. G. Wells,* Hallmark Channel, 2001.
Thomas Orde–Lees, *Shackleton,* Arts and Entertainment, 2002.
Duke of Buckingham, *La Femme Musketeer,* Hallmark Channel, 2004.

Television Appearances; Movies:
Captain Gilliand, "Sharpe's Enemy," *Sharpe II,* PBS, 1994.
Richard Hull (some sources cite David Ball), *True Blue* (also known as *Miracle at Oxford*), NBC, 1996.
Lord Edward Fitzmaurice, "Poldark," *Mystery!,* PBS, 1996.
Gervase Butt, *Dalziel and Pascoe: An Autumn Shroud,* Arts and Entertainment, 1996.
Dr. Gerry Saddler, *Outside the Rules,* BBC1 (England), 2002.
Ambassador, *Princes in the Tower,* Channel 4, 2005.

Television Appearances; Specials:
Tennessee Shad, *The Prodigious Mr. Hickey* (also known as *The Lawrenceville Stories: The Return of Hickey* and *The Prodigious Mr. William Hicks*), PBS, 1987.
Tennessee Shad, *The Beginning of the Firm,* PBS, 1989.
Gui De Chauliae, *World's Worst Century,* Channel 4 (England), 2004.

Television Appearances; Episodic:
Kevin Wright, "Lemon Twist," *Pie in the Sky,* 1995.
Charles Beaufort (some sources cite Beaulon), "Blood Money," *Kavanagh QC,* ITV (England), 1997.
Charles Beaufort (some sources cite Beaulon), "Diplomatic Baggage," *Kavanagh QC,* ITV, 1997.
Dan Spearill, "The Long Weekend," *Dangerfield,* BBC (England), 1998.
Julian Desire, "Murder," *Let Them Eat Cake,* BBC, 1999.
Peter Graham, "The Last Knight," *Relic Hunter,* syndicated, 2000.
Nathan Cairns, "Desperate Measures," *Holby City,* BBC, 2003.
David Heartley–Reade, "The Fisher King," *Midsomer Murders,* Arts and Entertainment, 2004.

Stage Appearances:
Guildenstern, *Hamlet,* Almeida Theatre Company, Belasco Theatre, New York City, 1995.

OTHER SOURCES

Periodicals:
People Weekly, February 3, 1986, pp. 89–90.

RUIVIVAR, Anthony Michael 1970–
(Anthony Ruivivar)

PERSONAL

Born November 4, 1970, in Honolulu, HI; father, a musician; married Yvonne Jung (an actress), January, 1998; children: Kainoa (son). *Education:* Boston University, B.F.A. *Avocational Interests:* Surfing, writing, and playing music.

Addresses: *Agent*—Gersh Agency, 232 North Canon Dr., Beverly Hills, CA 90210.

Career: Actor and writer. Member of the Imua! Theatre Company, Circle East Theatre Company, and the Lab, all New York City. Sometimes credited as Anthony Ruivivar.

CREDITS

Film Appearances:
Peter, *White Fang 2: Myth of the White Wolf* (also known as *White Fang 2*), Buena Vista, 1994.
Eduardo Braz, *Race the Sun,* TriStar, 1996.
(Uncredited) *In & Out,* Paramount, 1997.
Shujumi, *Starship Troopers,* Columbia/TriStar, 1997.
Xander, *High Art,* October Films, 1998.
Arturo (Satan), *Saturn* (also known as *Speed of Life*), Thousand Words, 1999.
Roberto Fuentes, *Harvest* (also known as *Cash Crop* and *A Desperate Season*), Artisan Entertainment, 1999.

Ramos, *Simply Irresistible* (also known as *Einfach unwiderstehlich*), Twentieth Century–Fox, 1999.
Kalani, *Swimming,* Oceanside Pictures, 2002.
John, *Express* (short film), Paradoxal, 2004.

Television Appearances; Series:
Enrique "Ricky," a recurring role, *All My Children* (also known as *All My Children: The Summer of Seduction*), ABC, 1997.
Carlos Nieto, *Third Watch,* NBC, 1999–2004.

Television Appearances; Episodic:
Raymond Cartena, "Mad Dog," *Law & Order,* NBC, 1997.
"Third Watch Edition," *Weakest Link,* NBC, 2001.
"Tit for Tat," *The Apprentice,* NBC, 2004.
Guest, *Good Day Live,* syndicated, 2004.
Paramedic Carlos Nieto, "Half Life," *Medical Investigation,* NBC, 2005.

Guest on *The Carolina Rhea Show.*

Television Appearances; Other:
Maverick Square (pilot), ABC, 1991.
NBC's Funniest Outtakes (special), NBC, 2002.

Stage Appearances:
Nestor, *Watcher,* Cap 21 Theatre, New York City, 2001.

WRITINGS

Published Plays:
Safe, Imua! Theatre Company, Jose Quintero Theatre, New York City, 2003.

S

SADLER, William 1950–
(Bill Sadler)

PERSONAL

Full name, William Thomas Sadler; born April 13, 1950, in Buffalo, NY; married Marni Joan Bakst (an actress); children: one. *Education:* State University of New York College at Geneseo, B.A. and B.S.; Cornell University, M.F.A.

Addresses: *Agent*—Don Buchwald and Associates, 6500 Wilshire Blvd., Suite 2200, Los Angeles, CA 90048. *Manager*—James Suskin, James Suskin Management, 253 West 72nd St., Suite 1014, New York, NY 10023.

Career: Actor. Trinity Square Repertory Company, Providence, RI, member of company, 1975–76. Once worked at a boatyard near Boston, MA.

Awards, Honors: Obie Award, *Village Voice,* and Villager Award, both 1981, for *Limbo Tales;* Clarence Derwent Award, Actors' Equity Association, and Drama–Logue Award, both 1985, for *Biloxi Blues;* Saturn Award, Academy of Science Fiction, Fantasy, and Horror Films, best supporting actor, 1992, for *Bill & Ted's Bogus Journey;* also received Drama Desk Award nomination.

CREDITS

Film Appearances:
(As Bill Sadler) Hotel clerk, *Hanky–Panky,* Columbia, 1982.
(As Bill Sadler) Dickson, *Off Beat,* Touchstone, 1986.

(As Bill Sadler) Dr. Lynnard Carroll, *Project X,* Twentieth Century–Fox, 1987.
(As Bill Sadler) Salesman Don, *K–9,* Universal, 1989.
Frank Sutton, *The Hot Spot,* Orion, 1990.
(As Bill Sadler) Vernon Trent, *Hard to Kill* (also known as *Seven Year Storm*), Warner Bros., 1990.
Colonel Stuart, *Die Hard 2* (also known as *Die Hard 2: Die Harder*), Twentieth Century–Fox, 1990.
Monroe, *Rush,* Metro–Goldwyn–Mayer, 1991.
Grim reaper/English family member, *Bill & Ted's Bogus Journey* (also known as *Bill and Ted Go to Hell*), Orion, 1991.
Don Perry, *Trespass* (also known as *Looters*), Universal, 1992.
Dick Brian, *Freaked* (also known as *Hideous Mutant Freekz*), 1994.
Heywood, *The Shawshank Redemption,* Columbia, 1994.
Brayker, *Tales from the Crypt Presents: Demon Knight* (also known as *Demon Keeper* and *Demon Knight*), Universal, 1995.
Colonel Frank Madden, *Solo,* Triumph, 1996.
The mummy, *Tales from the Crypt Presents: Bordello of Blood* (also known as *Bordello of Blood*), Universal, 1996.
Quinn, *Reach the Rock,* Gramercy, 1997.
Mission commander Captain "Wild Bill" Overbeck, *Rocket Man* (also known as *Space Cadets*), Buena Vista, 1997.
Ringo, *Skippy,* Taurus Entertainment, filmed, 1997, released 2001.
Dorian Newberry, *Disturbing Behavior* (also known as *Disturbing Behaviour*), Metro–Goldwyn–Mayer, 1998.
Klaus Detterick, *The Green Mile* (also known as *Stephen King's "The Green Mile"*), Warner Bros., 1999.
Man, *Another Life* (short film), Another Life Productions, 2002.
Abe Ernswiler, *The Battle of Shaker Heights,* Miramax, 2003.
Kenneth Braun, *Kinsey,* Fox Searchlight, 2004.

Dad, *Unspoken*, Pan Productions/Odyssey Entertainment, 2005.

Devour, Sony Pictures Home Entertainment, 2005.

Roger Lampert, *Confess*, Centrifugal Films, 2005.

Mr. Dewitt, *A New Wave*, Fitter Happier Films, 2005.

Also appeared in *By the Rivers of Babylon*, produced by Wolf Films/Crescendo Productions/Logo Productions.

Television Appearances; Series:

Assaulted Nuts, Cinemax, 1985.

(As Bill Sadler) Lieutenant Charlie Fontana, *Private Eye*, NBC, 1987–88.

Gideon Oliver, 1989.

Sheriff Jim Valenti, *Roswell* (also known as *Roswell High*), The WB, beginning 1999.

Dr. Darrin Tyler, *Wonderfalls*, Fox, 2004.

Television Appearances; Movies:

Dieter Schmidt, *The Great Wallendas*, NBC, 1978.

Joey, *Charlie and the Great Balloon Race* (also known as *Charlie's Balloon*), NBC, 1981.

Lieutenant Charles "Charlie" Fontana, *Private Eye*, NBC, 1987.

(As Bill Sadler) Coach Dickey, *Unconquered* (also known as *Invictus*), CBS, 1989.

Anthony Prine, *The Face of Fear*, CBS, 1990.

Uri (some sources cite Yuri) Chelenkoff, *Tagget* (also known as *Dragonfire*), USA Network, 1991.

Treat, *The Last to Go*, ABC, 1991.

Detective Sam Grace, *Bermuda Grace*, NBC, 1993.

David Anatole, *Jack Reed: Badge of Honor* (also known as *Jack Reed: An Honest Cop*), NBC, 1993.

Sarge, *Roadracers* (also known as *Rebel Highway*), Showtime, 1994.

Jim Natter, *Ambushed*, HBO, 1998.

Peterson, *Stealth Fighter*, HBO, 1999.

Sharp, *Witness Protection*, HBO, 1999.

Television Appearances; Pilots:

The Neighborhood (also known as *Breslin's Neighborhood*), NBC, 1982.

(As Bill Sadler) Colonel Tom Sturdivant, *Cadets* (also known as *Rotten to the Corps*), ABC, 1988.

Mr. Rush, *Two-Fisted Tales*, Fox, 1992.

Dr. Linus, *The Omen*, NBC, 1995.

Ray "Spider" Look, *Spider*, The WB, 1996.

Television Appearances; Specials:

"Henry Winkler Meets William Shakespeare," *The CBS Festival of Lively Arts for Young People*, CBS, 1977.

Die Harder: The Making of "Die Hard 2," 1990.

Eddy, "Night Driving," *Showtime 30-Minute Movie*, Showtime, 1993.

Shawshank: The Redeeming Feature, Channel 4 (England), 2001.

Voice of Ernest Hemingway, *F. Scott Fitzgerald: Winter Dreams*, PBS, 2001.

Also appeared in *The Other Side of Victory* and *The Rocking Chair Rebellion*.

Television Appearances; Episodic:

Guest, "Lady & the Tramps," *Newhart*, CBS, 1983.

(As Bill Sadler) Rick Dillon/Kevin Moore, "Shades of Darkness," *The Equalizer*, CBS, 1986.

Major Rigby, "Dislocations," *Tour of Duty*, 1987.

Richie Epson, "Blind Spot: Parts 1 & 2," *In the Heat of the Night*, NBC, 1988.

(As Bill Sadler) Ben, "The Younger Girl," *Dear John*, NBC, 1988.

(As Bill Sadler) "The Abby Singer Show," *St. Elsewhere*, NBC, 1988.

(As Bill Sadler) Colonel Fitzpatrick, "Off the Job Experience," *Murphy Brown*, CBS, 1989.

(As Bill Sadler) Dwight Hooper, "Dan's Birthday Bash," *Roseanne*, ABC, 1989.

(As Bill Sadler) Dwight Hooper, "Saturday," *Roseanne*, ABC, 1989.

(As Bill Sadler) Larry (some sources cite Lanny) Harbin, "Look Homeward, Dirtbag," *Hooperman*, ABC, 1989.

(As Bill Sadler) Niles Talbot, "The Man Who Was Death," *Tales from the Crypt*, HBO, 1989.

Officer Rollman, "The Way Home," *Hard Time on Planet Earth*, 1989.

The grim reaper, "The Assassin," *Tales from the Crypt*, HBO, 1994.

Frank Hellner, "Valerie 23," *The Outer Limits*, Showtime, 1995.

Shamus Bloom, "The Fifth Sepulcher" (premiere episode), *Poltergeist: The Legacy*, Showtime, 1996.

Luther Sloan, "Inquisition," *Star Trek: Deep Space Nine*, syndicated, 1998.

Luther Sloan, "Inter Arma Enim Silent Leges," *Star Trek: Deep Space Nine*, syndicated, 1998.

Luther Sloan, "Extreme Measures," *Star Trek: Deep Space Nine*, syndicated, 1999.

Lee Leetch, "The Case," *Ed*, NBC, 2003.

Kyle Devlin, "Graansha," *Law & Order: Criminal Intent*, NBC, 2003.

Saul Wainright, "Retrial," *JAG*, CBS, 2004.

Scotty Murray, "Forever Blue," *Third Watch*, NBC, 2005.

Travis Duffy, "Enough," *Tru Calling*, Fox, 2005.

Paul Rice, "Blue Wall," *Law & Order: Trial by Jury*, NBC, 2005.

Also appeared in an episode of *After M*A*S*H*, CBS; and *Project Greenlight*.

Television Director; Episodic:
"Four Aliens and a Baby," *Roswell* (also known as *Roswell High*), UPN, 2002.

Stage Appearances:
(Stage debut) Title role, *Hamlet,* Colorado Shakespeare Festival, 1973.

(Off–Broadway debut) Title role, *Ivanov,* City Play-works, 1975.

Ensemble, *Henry V,* New York Shakespeare Festival, Delacorte Theatre, Public Theatre, New York City, 1976.

Ensemble, *Measure for Measure,* New York Shakespeare Festival, Delacorte Theatre, Public Theatre, 1976.

Ramblings, Playwrights Horizons Theatre, New York City, 1977.

Cracks, Playwrights Horizons Theatre, 1977.

Dial M for Murder, Playwrights Horizons Theatre, 1978.

Journey's End, Long Wharf Theatre, New Haven, CT, 1978.

Editor, bellboy, janitor, body guard, Harry the Horse, priest, sound man, and pirate, *New Jerusalem,* New York Shakespeare Festival, Public Theatre, 1979.

Jimmy, *A History of the American Film,* Seattle Repertory Theatre, Seattle, WA, 1979.

Time Steps, Playwrights Horizons Theatre, 1980.

Ladies in Retirement, Royal Poinciana Playhouse, Palm Beach, FL, 1981.

Len Jenkins, *Limbo Tales,* off–Broadway production, 1981.

Jeweler, *Dark Ride,* Soho Repertory Theatre, New York City, 1981.

Betty and Gerry, *Cloud 9,* Theatre De Lys (now Lucille Lortel Theatre), New York City, 1981.

Hector, *The Chinese Viewing Pavilion,* Production Company, Actors and Directors Theatre, New York City, 1982.

Jasper, boyfriend of Ginger, and friend of Burt, *Necessary Ends,* New York Shakespeare Festival, Public Theatre, 1982.

Pete Shotton, Alan Williams, Victor Spinetti, Arthur Janov, and Andy Peebles, *Lennon,* Entermedia Theatre, New York City, 1982.

Night Must Fall, Hartman Theatre, Stamford, CT, 1982.

Much Ado about Nothing, Yale Repertory Theatre, New Haven, CT, 1982.

Sergeant Merwin J. Toomey, *Biloxi Blues,* Center Theatre Group, Ahmanson Theatre, Los Angeles, 1984, then (Broadway debut) Neil Simon Theatre, New York City, 1985–86.

U.S. Army investigator, *Burning Blue,* 1998.

Sheet, O'Casey, and judge, *The Resistible Rise of Arturo Ui,* National Actors Theatre, Michael Schimmel Center for the Arts, Pace University, New York City, 2002.

Samuel Clemens, *A Few Stout Individuals,* Signature Theatre Company, Peter Norton Space, New York City, 2002.

Title role, *Julius Caesar,* Belasco Theatre, New York City, 2005.

Appeared as Charley, *Charley's Aunt,* Academy Festival Theatre; in *Hannah,* off–Broadway production; as Bill Sprightly, *A Mad World, My Masters,* La Jolla Playhouse, La Jolla, CA; and in *The Relations of Paul Le June,* Street Theatre, Boston, MA.

Major Tours:
Toured as Hamm, *Endgame,* Florida Studio Theatre.

RECORDINGS

Videos:
Walking the Mile (also known as *Walking the Mile: The Making of "The Green Mile"*), Warner Home Video, 2000.

Hope Springs Eternal: A Look Back at "The Shawshank Redemption," Warner Home Video, 2004.

WRITINGS

Songs Featured in Films:
Additional lyrics, "The Reaper Rap," *Bill & Ted's Bogus Journey* (also known as *Bill and Ted Go to Hell*), Orion, 1991.

OTHER SOURCES

Periodicals:
TV Zone, June, 2000, pp. 32–36.

Electronic:
William Sadler Official Site, http://www.williamsadler. com, July 22, 2005.

SAGET, Bob 1956–

PERSONAL

Full name, Robert Lane Saget; born May 17, 1956, in Philadelphia, PA (some sources cite Norfolk, VA); son of Benjamin M. (a supermarket executive) and Rosalyn C. (a hospital administrator) Saget; married Sherri K. Kramer (an attorney), May 16, c. 1983 (divorced, c. 1997); children: Aubrey Michelle, Lara Melanie, Jennifer Belle. *Education:* Temple University, B.A., 1978; briefly attended University of Southern California; trained for the stage with Darryl Hickman, Harvey Lembeck, and Vincent Chase.

Addresses: *Agent*—William Morris Agency, 1 William Morris Pl., Beverly Hills, CA 90212. *Manager*—Brillstein–Grey Entertainment, 9150 Wilshire Blvd., Suite 350, Beverly Hills, CA 90212.

Career: Comedian, actor, producer, director, and writer. Groundlings (improvisational comedy troupe), former member; appeared as a comedian in nightclubs and concert halls throughout the United States and Canada, including Carnegie Hall, the Comedy Store, and the Improv in California, beginning 1979; host of Winter Olympics, 2002.

Member: Screen Actors Guild, American Federation of Television and Radio Artists, Directors Guild of America, Writers Guild of America, American Society of Composers, Authors, and Publishers.

Awards, Honors: Merit Award, Student Academy Awards, documentary category, 1978, for *Through Adam's Eyes;* Annual CableACE Award nomination, National Cable Television Association, best direction, 1991, for "Bob Saget—In the Dream State," *HBO Comedy Hour.*

CREDITS

Television Appearances; Series:
Cohost, *The Morning Program,* CBS, 1987.
Daniel Ernest "Danny" Tanner, *Full House,* ABC, 1987–95.
Danny, *ABC TGIF,* ABC, 1990.
Host, *America's Funniest Home Videos* (also known as *AFHV, America's Funniest,* and *America's Funniest Videos*), ABC, 1990–97.
Matt Stewart, *Raising Dad,* The WB, 2001.

Television Appearances; Specials:
The Fact, CBS, 1982.
Rodney Dangerfield Hosts the 9th Annual Young Comedians Special (also known as *Ninth Annual Young Comedians Special*), HBO, 1984.
HBO Young Comedians Special, HBO, 1986.
A Comedy Celebration: The Comedy & Magic Club's 10th Anniversary Special, Showtime, 1989.
Comic Relief III, HBO, 1989.
Host, *America's Funniest Home Videos: An Inside Look,* ABC, 1990.
"Bob Saget–In the Dream State," *HBO Comedy Hour,* HBO, 1990.
Comic Relief IV, HBO, 1990.
The MDA Jerry Lewis Telethon (also known as *The 25th Anniversary MDA Jerry Lewis Labor Day Telethon*), syndicated, 1990.
A User's Guide to Planet Earth: The American Environmental Test, ABC, 1991.
George Burns's 95th Birthday Party, CBS, 1991.
HBO's 20th Anniversary—We Hardly Believe It Ourselves (also known as *HBO's 20th Anniversary Special—We Don't Believe It Ourselves*), CBS and HBO, 1992.

Inside America's Totally Unsolved Lifestyles, ABC, 1992.
The Comedy Store's 20th Birthday, NBC, 1992.
What about Me? I'm Only 3!, CBS, 1992.
(Uncredited) Game show host, *To Grandmother's House We Go,* 1992.
Segment host, *ABC's 40th Anniversary Special,* ABC, 1994.
Comic Relief VI, HBO, 1994.
Host, *A Comedy Salute to Andy Kaufman,* NBC, 1995.
Host, *America's Funniest Home Videos Guide to Parenting,* ABC, 1995.
Comic Relief VII, HBO, 1995.
Host, *America's Funniest Home Videos Salute to Boneheads,* ABC, 1996.
Host, *America's Funniest Home Videos: Kids and Animals,* ABC, 1996.
Catch a Rising Star 50th Anniversary—Give or Take 26 Years, CBS, 1996.
"Rodney Dangerfield's 75th Birthday Toast," *HBO Comedy Hour,* HBO, 1997.
Canned Ham: Dirty Work, Comedy Central, 1998.
Behind the Walls of "Full House," 2000.
Interviewee, "Mary–Kate & Ashley Olsen," *Celebrity Profile,* E! Entertainment Television, 2001.
Interviewee, *VH1 Goes inside South Park,* VH1, 2003.
Interviewee, *Intimate Portrait: Dana Delany,* Lifetime, 2003.
Interviewee, "John Stamos," *Biography,* Arts and Entertainment, 2004.
Interviewee, "Mary–Kate and Ashley Olsen," *Biography,* Arts and Entertainment, 2004.
Interviewee, *Full House: The E! True Hollywood Story,* E! Entertainment Television, 2005.

Also appeared in *Comedy Break,* syndicated; *Comedy Tonight,* PBS; and *Comic of the Month,* Showtime.

Television Appearances; Episodic:
Contestant, *The Dating Game,* ABC, 1979.
Himself, *Make Me Laugh,* syndicated, 1980.
The comic, "The Show Must Go On," *Bosom Buddies,* ABC, 1981.
Student, "Wizards and Warlocks," *The Greatest American Hero,* ABC, 1983.
It's a Living, ABC, 1985.
Guest, *Late Night with David Letterman,* NBC, 1988.
Guest, *The Tonight Show Starring Johnny Carson,* NBC, multiple appearances, between 1989 and 1992.
Macklyn "Mack" MacKay, "Stand Up—April 30, 1959," *Quantum Leap,* NBC, 1992.
Himself, "Hey Now," *The Larry Sanders Show,* HBO, 1992.
Guest, *Late Show with David Letterman,* CBS, multiple appearances, beginning 1993.
Himself, "Office Romance," *The Larry Sanders Show,* HBO, 1994.
Himself, "Ellen's Improvement," *Ellen,* ABC, 1995.

Himself, "A Sore Winner," *The Jeff Foxworthy Show* (also known as *Somewhere in America*), ABC, 1995.

Himself, "Girl Buys Soup while Woman Weds Ape," *The Naked Truth* (also known as *Pix* and *Wilde Again*), ABC, 1995.

Guest host, *Saturday Night Live*, NBC, 1995.

(Uncredited) Himself, "One Man and a Baby," *The Parent 'Hood*, 1996.

Guest, *The Tonight Show with Jay Leno*, NBC, 1996.

Himself, "Alone Again ... Naturally," *Ellen*, ABC, 1997.

Guest, *Howard Stern*, E! Entertainment Television, 1997, 2000, 2002.

Guest, *The Howard Stern Radio Show*, syndicated, 1999.

Guest, *The Martin Short Show*, syndicated, 1999.

"What Is Funny?," *Turn Ben Stein On*, Comedy Central, 1999.

Mr. Atkitson, "Norm vs. Schoolin'," *The Norm Show* (also known as *Norm*), ABC, 2000.

Guest, *The View*, ABC, 2001, 2002.

Guest, *America's Funniest Home Videos* (also known as *AFHV*, *America's Funniest*, and *America's Funniest Videos*), ABC, 2003.

Himself, *The Late Late Show with Craig Kilborn*, CBS, 2003, 2004.

Jonathan Young, "Lipstick on Your Panties," *Huff*, Showtime, 2004.

Himself, "Joey and the Roadtrip," *Joey*, NBC, 2004.

Butch, "Flashpants," *Huff*, Showtime, 2004.

Entourage, HBO, 2004.

Guest, *The Daily Buzz*, 2005.

Mitch, "Coach Potato," *Listen Up*, CBS, 2005.

Appeared in episodes of *At Ease*, ABC; *Evening at the Improv*, syndicated; *Grace Under Fire*, ABC; and *The Merv Griffin Show*, syndicated.

Television Appearances; Awards Presentations:

The 4th Annual American Comedy Awards, ABC, 1990.

The 16th Annual People's Choice Awards, CBS, 1990.

The 43rd Annual Primetime Emmy Awards Presentation, Fox, 1991.

Master of ceremonies, *Jim Thorpe Pro Sports Awards*, ABC, 1992.

Host, *The World Magic Awards*, Fox Family Channel, 1999.

Television Appearances; Pilots:

Love, American Style '85, ABC, 1985.

Host, *America's Funniest Home Videos*, ABC, 1989.

Funny You Should Ask, CBS, 1990.

Cohost of the pilots *Knock–Knock*, syndicated, and *Surprise*, CBS; also appeared in *Good News/Bad News*.

Television Appearances; Movies:

Spencer Paley, "Father and Scout," *The ABC Family Movie*, ABC, 1994.

(Uncredited) Dean Tinker, *Sorority*, MTV, 1999.

(Uncredited) Bob, *Becoming Dick*, E! Entertainment Television, 2000.

Television Work; Movies:

Executive producer, "Father and Scout," *The ABC Family Movie*, ABC, 1994.

Executive producer and director, *For Hope*, ABC, 1996.

Director, *Jitters*, Lifetime, 1997.

Director, *Becoming Dick*, E! Entertainment Television, 2000.

Television Director; Episodic:

"Norm vs. Youth," *The Norm Show* (also known as *Norm*), ABC, 2000.

"Just Thinking of You," *The Mind of the Married Man*, HBO, 2001.

Television Work; Other:

Producer and director of video segments, *The Morning Program* (series), CBS, 1987.

Director, "Bob Saget–In the Dream State" (special), *HBO Comedy Hour*, HBO, 1990.

Film Appearances:

(Film debut) Student and sportscaster, *Full Moon High* (also known as *Moon High*), Orion, 1979.

Therapy patient, *Devices*, 1980.

Voice of jukebox, *Spaced Out* (also known as *Outer Reach* and *Outer Touch*), Miramax, 1981.

Himself, *Moving* (also known as *Apartment Hunting*), 1981.

Dr. Joffe, *Critical Condition*, Paramount, 1987.

For Goodness Sake, 1993.

Fourth reporter, *Meet Wally Sparks*, Trimark Pictures, 1997.

(Uncredited) Cocaine addict, *Half Baked*, 1998.

Walter Matthews (Charlie), *Dumb and Dumberer: When Harry Met Lloyd*, New Line Cinema, 2003.

Himself, *New York Minute*, Warner Bros., 2004.

Himself, *The Aristocrats*, ThinkFilm, 2005.

Film Work:

Producer, director, and editor, *Through Adam's Eyes* (documentary), 1978.

Director (with Alan Bloom), *Moving* (also known as *Apartment Hunting*), 1981.

Director, *Dirty Work* (also known as *Sale boulot*), Metro–Goldwyn–Mayer, 1998.

Stage Appearances:

(Stage debut) Douglas, *Audience*, Fig Tree Theatre, Hollywood, CA, 1986.

Ted, *Privilege*, Second Stage Theatre, New York City, 2005.

Stage Work:
Producer, *Audience,* Fig Tree Theatre, Hollywood, CA, 1986.

RECORDINGS

Videos:
Paramount Comedy Theatre, Vol. 1: Well Developed, 1986.
Host, *The Best of America's Funniest Home Videos,* 1991.
Host, *America's Funniest Pets,* CBS/Fox Home Video, 1992.

WRITINGS

Film Scripts:
Through Adam's Eyes (documentary), 1978.
Additional dialogue, *Spaced Out* (also known as *Outer Reach* and *Outer Touch*), Miramax, 1981.
Stepbrothers, 1985.
Two Orphans (short film), 1985.
Coffee Shop (short film), 1986.
Temporary Asylum, 1988.
The Shop Teacher, 1995.
The Merchants in Venice, 1998.

Television Specials:
America's Funniest Home Videos: An Inside Look, ABC, 1990.
"Bob Saget–In the Dream State," *HBO Comedy Hour,* HBO, 1990.
Jim Thorpe Pro Sports Awards, ABC, 1992.
America's Funniest Home Videos: Kids and Animals, ABC, 1996.

Television Series:
The Morning Program, CBS, 1987.

Television Episodes:
America's Funniest Home Videos (also known as *AFHV, America's Funniest,* and *America's Funniest Videos*), ABC, 1990, 1993.

Television Pilots:
America's Funniest Home Videos, ABC, 1989.
(With Marshall Herzkovitz) *Freeman,* ABC, 1999.

Television Music; Movies:
Songwriter, "He's Dick," *Becoming Dick,* E! Entertainment Television, 2000.

Other:
(With Tony Hendra) *Bob Saget's Tales from the Crib* (baby–picture book), Perigee, 1991.

SIDELIGHTS

Bob Saget's television movie *For Hope* is a semi–biographical account of his sister Gay Saget's fight with scleroderma, an autoimmune disease. Gay died from the disease at the age of forty–seven.

OTHER SOURCES

Periodicals:
Entertainment Weekly, May 19, 1995, pp. 38–39.
Los Angeles Magazine, November, 1990, p. 174.
People Weekly, March 26, 1990, p. 38; June 26, 2000, p. 74.
Redbook, September, 1990, p. 80.
TV Guide, March 31, 1990, p. 2.

ST. JOHN, Marco 1939–

PERSONAL

Original name, Marco John Figueroa, Jr.; born May 7, 1939, in New Orleans, LA; son of Marco John Figueroa and Iris (maiden name, Davidson) Springer; married Barbara Lincoln Bonnell (died, 1971); children: Marco II. *Education:* Fordham University, B.S., 1960. *Politics:* Democrat. *Religion:* Roman Catholic. *Avocational Interests:* Jogging and writing.

Addresses: *Agent*—People Store, 2004 Rockledge Rd. NE, Atlanta, GA 30324. *Contact*—P.O. Box 521, Ocean Springs, MS 35966–0521.

Career: Actor. *Military service:* U.S. Army, first lieutenant, 1960–61.

CREDITS

Film Appearances:
Bobo, *The Plastic Dome of Norma Jean,* 1965.
Cleopatra (also known as *Viva Viva*), 1970.
Lawrence Shannon, orderly, *The Happiness Cage* (also known as *The Demon Within* and *The Mind Snatchers*), Cinerama Releasing, 1972.
Justin, *The Next Man* (also known as *Double Hit* and *The Arab Conspiracy*), Allied Artists Pictures Corp., 1976.
Hampton Richmond Clayton III, *Night of the Juggler* (also known as *New York Killer*), Columbia, 1980.
Policeman, *Cat People,* MCA/Universal, 1982.
Leander Rolfe, *Tightrope,* Warner Home Video, 1984.

Sheriff Tucker, *Friday the 13th: A New Beginning* (also known as *Friday the 13th Part V: A New Beginning*), Paramount, 1985.

Marth, *The Package,* Orion, 1989.

Jimmy Cavello, *State of Grace,* Orion, 1990.

Truck driver, *Thelma & Louise,* Metro–Goldwyn–Mayer, 1991 Morton, *Hard Target,* Universal, 1993.

Polk, *The Dangerous,* 1994.

Deputy Wilkes, *The Waking* (also known as *Keeper of Souls*), 2001.

Defense attorney, *The Rising Place,* Warner Bros., 2001.

Big Six Rayburn, *The Badge,* Lions Gate Films, 2002.

Charlie, *Tough Luck,* Curb Entertainment, 2003.

Daley, *Runaway Jury,* Twentieth Century–Fox, 2003.

Evan/Undercover "John," *Monster,* Newmarket Films, 2003.

Vicious, MTI Home Video, 2003.

Dr. Fenton, *Beyond the Wall of Sleep,* 2004.

Police Chief Morris, *The Punisher,* Lions Gate Films, 2004.

Reporter, *Mr. 3000,* Buena Vista, 2004.

Cimanno, *In,* 2005.

Sheriff Hank Bullard, *Things That Hang from Trees,* 2005.

Frank Singleton, *At Last,* 2005.

Television Appearances; Series:

Sixth Dr. Paul Stewart, *As the World Turns,* CBS, 1969–70.

Erica's physician, *All My Children,* ABC, 1971.

Joey Kimball, *Search for Tomorrow,* CBS, 1975.

Rayford Plunkett, *Ball Four,* CBS, 1976.

Policeman, *Ryan's Hope,* ABC, 1977.

Television Appearances; Miniseries:

Blaylock, *Beulah Land,* NBC, 1980.

Television Appearances; Movies:

Eddie Manzaro, crime boss, *Contract on Cherry Street* (also known as *Stakeout on Cherry Street*), NBC, 1977.

Emcee, *Dixie: Changing Habits,* CBS, 1983.

Hot Pursuit, 1984.

Frederick Payton, *Fatal Flaw,* ABC, 1989.

Morley Rickerts, *Blue Bayou,* NBC, 1990.

Tom Scott, *This Gun for Hire,* USA Network, 1991.

Dr. Hector Salcodo, *Sacrifice,* HBO, 2000.

Literature professor, *The Brooke Ellison Story,* Arts and Entertainment, 2004.

Gaylord, *The Madam's Family: The Truth about the Canal Street Brothel,* CBS, 2004.

Chief, *Frankenfish,* Sci–Fi Channel, 2004.

Television Appearances; Pilots:

Rapist, *Hardcase,* NBC, 1981.

Kevin Tree, *The Six of Us,* NBC, 1982.

Television Appearances; Episodic:

Dom Capabo, "Daughter, Am I in My Father's House?," *Naked City,* ABC, 1962.

Johnnie, "Soda Pop and Paper Flags," *Route 66,* CBS, 1963.

Johnny Plank, "Riot," *Bonanza,* NBC, 1972.

Virgil Bonner, "Hostage!," *Gunsmoke,* CBS, 1972.

Darcy, "Disciple," *Gunsmoke,* CBS, 1974.

Tony Papas, "Birthday Party," *Kojak,* CBS, 1976.

"Old Hatreds Die Hard," *The Mississippi,* 1983.

Doc Gridley, "Second Base Steele," *Remington Steele,* NBC, 1984.

Joe Ed Thaxton, "Road Kill," *In the Heat of the Night,* NBC, 1988.

Payton, "Fatal Flaw," *Kojak,* 1989.

Jay Turkus, "Citizen Trundel: Parts 1 & 2," *In the Heat of the Night,* NBC, 1990.

Barney Flatt, "Major Moonlighting," *Major Dad,* 1991.

Officer Strangis, "The Committee," *Walker, Texas Ranger,* CBS, 1994.

Evan Calder, "The Avenger," *Walker, Texas Ranger,* CBS, 1996.

Bus driver, "Shades of Gray," *Homicide* (also known as *Homicide: Life on the Street* and *H: LOTS*), NBC, 1999.

Also appeared as Gebhardt, *Orleans,* CBS.

Stage Appearances:

Delanoue (Merda), *Poor Bitos,* Cort Theatre, New York City, 1964.

Clarence, *Things That Go Bump in the Night,* Royale Theatre, New York City, 1965.

Julien, *Colombe,* Garrick Theatre, New York City, 1965.

Young Walt, *We, Comrades Three,* Lyceum Theatre, New York City, 1966.

Charles Surface (alternate), *The School for Scandal,* Lyceum Theatre, 1966–67.

Tony Kirby, *You Can't Take It with You,* Lyceum Theatre, 1967.

Kuragin, *War and Peace,* Lyceum Theatre, 1967.

Rebel, *The Unknown Soldier and His Wife,* Vivian Beaumont Theatre, then George Abbott Theatre, New York City, 1967.

Beany Mac Gruder, *Weekend,* Broadhurst Theatre, New York City, 1968.

Peter Latham, *Forty Carats,* Morosco Theatre, New York City, 1968–70.

Standby Kurt, *Dance of Death,* Vivian Beaumont Theatre, 1974.

Richmond, *Richard III,* Mitzi E. Newhouse Theatre, New York City, 1974.

Understudy for the roles of the Gentleman Caller and the son, *The Glass Menagerie,* Circle in the Square Theatre, New York City, 1975–76.

Antonio, *Twelfth Night or What You Will,* Delacorte Theatre, New York City, 1986.

Lord Willoughby, *Richard II,* Delacorte Theatre, 1987.

Also appeared in *Hamlet,* San Diego Shakespeare Festival.

SAITO, James 1955–

PERSONAL

Born March 6, 1955, in Los Angeles, CA. *Education:* University of California, Los Angeles, graduated.

Career: Actor.

CREDITS

Film Appearances:

Eddie, *The Idolmaker,* United Artists, 1980.

Kendo Yamomoto, *Hot Dog ... The Movie,* Metro–Goldwyn–Mayer/United Artists, 1984.

Park Sung, *Mortal Sins* (also known as *Dangerous Obsession, Divine Obsession,* and *God's Payroll*), Panorama Entertainment, 1989.

Oroko Saki (The Shredder), *Teenage Mutant Ninja Turtles,* New Line Cinema, 1990.

Servant, *Wolf,* Columbia, 1994.

Nemura, *The Hunted,* Universal, 1995.

Korean proprietor, *Die Hard: With a Vengeance* (also known as *Die Hard 3* and *Simon Says*), Twentieth Century–Fox, 1995.

Mr. Deng, *Henry Fool,* Sony Pictures Classics, 1997.

Takaori Osumi, *The Devil's Advocate* (also known as *Diabolos* and *Im Auftrag des Teufels*), Warner Bros., 1997.

Chinese mob boss, *Home Alone 3,* Twentieth Century–Fox, 1997.

Paul Cheng, *The Thomas Crown Affair,* Metro–Goldwyn–Mayer, 1999.

First Japanese aide, *Pearl Harbor* (also known as *Pearl Harbour*), Buena Vista, 2001.

Akiri, *Love the Hard Way,* 2001, Kino International, 2003.

Bruce, *Another Bed* (short film), 2001.

Ray/Groper, "My Robot Baby," *Robot Stories,* Pak Film/Shotwell Media, 2003.

John Lu, *Ghost Dance,* ABL Communications, 2005.

Television Appearances; Miniseries:

The Golden Moment: An Olympic Love Story, NBC, 1980.

Tom Halehone, *Blood & Orchids,* CBS, 1986.

Operations Officer Yamato, *War and Remembrance,* ABC, 1988.

Tony Chiu, *To Be the Best,* CBS, 1992.

Television Appearances; Movies:

Richard Wakatsuki, *Farewell to Manzanar,* 1976.

Lieutenant Tatsuo Yamato, *Enola Gay: The Men, the Mission, and the Atomic Bomb* (also known as *Enola Gay*), NBC, 1980.

Professor, *The Two Lives of Carol Letner,* CBS, 1981.

Khan, *The Renegades,* ABC, 1982.

First officer, *Girls of the White Orchid* (also known as *Death Ride to Osaka*), NBC, 1983.

Cabbie, *Covenant,* NBC, 1985.

C.A.T. Squad: Python Wolf (also known as *Python Wolf*), 1988.

Johnny Chen, *Tongs,* ABC, 1989.

Japanese soldier, *Silent Cries* (also known as *Guests of the Emperor*), NBC, 1993.

Dr. Hiro Lorechi, *The Tomorrow Man,* 1996.

Police officer, *Rock the Boat* (also known as *Atlantis Conspiracy*), HBO, 2000.

Television Appearances; Episodic:

Third commando, "Up for Grabs," *Baa Baa Black Sheep* (also known as *Black Sheep Squadron*), 1976.

Ensign Kira, "Divine Wind," *Baa Baa Black Sheep* (also known as *Black Sheep Squadron*), 1977.

South Korean, "Comrades in Arms: Parts 1 & 2," *M*A*S*H,* CBS, 1977.

Korean soldier, "Dear Comrade," *M*A*S*H,* CBS, 1978.

Nakajima, "Hype," *Lou Grant,* 1979.

Sergeant, "The Last Ten Days," *The Waltons,* 1981.

Vietnamese interpreter, "Veteran," *The Incredible Hulk,* 1981.

Man, "All You Need Is Love," *Bosom Buddies,* 1981.

Park, "Communication Breakdown," *M*A*S*H,* CBS, 1981.

Kelly Kim, "The Hand–Painted Thai," *The Greatest American Hero,* ABC, 1982.

Police officer, "The Japanese Connection," *The Fall Guy,* ABC, 1982.

Japanese lieutenant, "Once a Tiger ... ," *Tales of the Gold Monkey,* 1982.

Third reporter, "The Fatal Blow," *Knots Landing,* 1983.

Sixth reporter, "Forsaking All Others," *Knots Landing,* 1984.

Yamahiro, "The Dog Who Knew Too Much," *Hart to Hart,* 1984.

Ronnie Quan, "The Mole," *Scarecrow and Mrs. King,* 1984.

Laboratory technician, "Hot Property," *T. J. Hooker,* ABC, 1984.

Ming, "The Golden Triangle," *MacGyver,* ABC, 1985.

Howie Wong, "Golden Triangle: Part 2," *Miami Vice,* NBC, 1985.

Joe Ching, "Chinatown Memories," *Street Hawk,* 1985.

First anesthesiologist, "Night Fever," *Alfred Hitchcock Presents,* 1985.

"Year of the Fox," *Crazy like a Fox,* 1985.

Kwai Li, "The Say U.N.C.L.E. Affair," *The A–Team,* NBC, 1986.

Mr. Ashida, "Days of Swine and Roses," *Hill Street Blues,* NBC, 1987.

Dr. Tim Shimizu, "X–Virus," *Airwolf,* 1987.

Ma Sek, "Heart of Night," *Miami Vice,* NBC, 1988.

General Loctuck, "Power Play," *Counterstrike,* 1990.

Mr. Tanaka, "Scoundrels," *Law & Order,* NBC, 1994.

Detective Chang, "Sins of the Father," *New York Undercover,* Fox, 1994.

Nogami, "The 37s," *Star Trek: Voyager,* UPN, 1995.

Voice of Taro, "Bushido," *Gargoyles* (animated), syndicated, 1996.

Korean man, "Ex and the City," *Sex and the City,* HBO, 1999.

Yoshi Yopshimura, "Dissonance," *Law & Order,* NBC, 2000.

"No Good Deed Goes Unpunished," *100 Centre Street,* Arts and Entertainment, 2001.

"Lost Causes," *100 Centre Street,* Arts and Entertainment, 2001.

Sergeant Yee, "The Long Guns," *Third Watch,* NBC, 2002.

Mr. Miyazaki, "Great Barrier," *Law & Order: Criminal Intent,* NBC, 2004.

Television Appearances; Pilots:

Food delivery person, *Charles in Charge,* CBS, 1984.

Stage Appearances:

You're on the Tee/Ripples in the Pond, East West Players, Los Angeles, 1983–84.

Bandit, *Rashomon,* Roundabout Theatre Company, Union Square Theatre, New York City, 1988.

Blackie Sakata, *The Wash,* Center Theatre Group, Mark Taper Forum, Los Angeles, 1990–91.

Wilderness, Pan Asian Repertory, Playhouse 46, New York City, 1994.

Yellow Fever, Pan Asian Repertory, St. Clement's Theatre, New York City, 1994.

Stage manager and Sam Craig, *Our Town,* Vineyard Theatre, New York City, 1994.

Servant and ghost, *Golden Child,* John F. Kennedy Center for the Performing Arts, Washington, DC, then Longacre Theatre, New York City, 1998.

The duke, *Othello, the Moor of Venice,* National Asian American Theatre Company, Connelly Theatre, New York City, 2000.

"Egads" and "Lilly Lee's Science Fair," in *Frozen Lemonade,* Asian American Writers' Workshop, New York City, 2003.

Appeared as understudy for Andrew Kwong and Eng Tieng–Bin, *Day Standing on Its Head,* American Conservatory Theatre, Manhattan Theatre Club, New York City; and in *The King and I,* Broadway production; also performed at Ensemble Studio Theatre, New York City, Williamstown Theatre Festival, Williamstown, MA, and Arena Stage, Baltimore, MD.

SAMS, Jeffrey D. 1967–
(Jeffrey Sams)

PERSONAL

Born June 18, 1967, in Cincinnati, OH; married Lisa Bourcier (an advertising executive), April 18, 1998; children: one. *Education:* Attended School of Creative and Performing Arts, St. Louis, MO; graduate of Webster University.

Addresses: *Agent*—Joseph Rice, Abrams Artists Agency, 9200 Sunset Blvd., 11th Floor, Los Angeles, CA 90069.

Career: Actor. Appeared in television commercials for Ford Motor Company, 1998, and others. Supporter of Book Pals and Equity Fighting AIDS.

Member: Actors' Equity Association, Screen Actors Guild, American Federation of Television and Radio Artists.

CREDITS

Television Appearances; Series:

Clate Baker, *Medicine Ball,* Fox, 1995.

Assistant District Attorney Edison "Ed" Moore, *Courthouse,* CBS, 1995.

Ben Costigan, *Sleepwalkers,* NBC, 1997.

Albert "Champ" Terrace, *Cupid,* ABC, 1998–99.

Vincent "Vince" Lewis, *Wasteland,* ABC, 1999.

Mel Thomas, *Breaking News,* Bravo, 2002.

Detective Cyrus Lockwood, a recurring role, *CSI: Crime Scene Investigation,* CBS, 2002–2003.

Todd Stevens, *Line of Fire,* ABC, 2003.

Television Appearances; Movies:

John King, *Green Dolphin Beat* (also known as *Green Dolphin Street*), Fox, 1994.

Harry, *Automatic,* 1994.

Adam Clayborne, "Rose Hill," *Hallmark Hall of Fame,* CBS, 1996.

R. J. Hampton, *Run for the Dream: The Gail Devers Story,* Showtime, 1996.

Peter Hall, *The Prosecutors,* 1996.

Jediah Walker, *Hope,* 1997.

John Pierce "JLP", *NTSB: The Crash of Flight 323,* ABC, 2001.

Television Appearances; Episodic:

Arthur, "Artie's Party," *Thea,* ABC, 1993.

Greg, "A Kiss before Lying," *Living Single,* Fox, 1993.

Percy Lewis, "Benny," *The Commish,* ABC, 1994.

Dr. Thomas, "A Triage Grows in Boston," *Boston Common,* NBC, 1996.

(As Jeffrey Sams) Jeffrey Craig, "Love Is Blind," *Early Edition,* CBS, 1997.

Evan Grant, "Judgment in L.A.: D–Girl," *Law & Order,* NBC, 1997.

Evan Grant, "Judgment in L.A.: Turnaround," *Law & Order,* NBC, 1997.

Jack, "Dependency," *Strong Medicine,* Lifetime, 2000.

Jack, "Second Opinion," *Strong Medicine,* Lifetime, 2000.

Jack, "Fix," *Strong Medicine,* Lifetime, 2001.

Dr. Trevor Collins, "Sex in the Suburbs," *That's Life,* CBS, 2001.

Terrence, "Space Race," *Oliver Beene,* Fox, 2003.

Fire Captain Scott McAllister, "Trip Box," *Without a Trace,* CBS, 2003.

Track coach, "A Man of Faith," *Jack & Bobby,* The WB, 2004.

(As Jeffrey Sams) Steve Nutting, "Sergeant Sipowicz' Lonely Hearts Club Band," *NYPD Blue,* ABC, 2005.

Mark Sutter, "Sabotage," *Numb3rs,* CBS, 2005.

Jason Hunter, "Trial," *Eyes,* ABC, 2005.

Appeared in an episode of *The Division,* Lifetime, and as Dr. Turner, *Loving,* ABC.

Television Appearances; Pilots:
Nick Tyler, *Five Up, Two Down,* CBS, 1991.

Junior Democratic congressman, *Capital City,* ABC, 2004.

Detective Marc Garcia, *Soccer Moms,* ABC, 2005.

Television Appearances; Awards Presentations:
The 14th Annual Stellar Awards, syndicated, 1999.

Film Appearances:
Rich, *Fly by Night,* Arrow Releasing, 1993.

Lionel, *Waiting to Exhale,* Twentieth Century–Fox, 1995.

(As Jeffrey Sams) Danny, *Just Write,* Curb Entertainment/ Heartland Film Releasing, 1997.

Kenneth "Kenny", *Soul Food,* Twentieth Century–Fox, 1997.

Sid Sampson, *Academy Boyz,* 1997.

Sheldon, *Checking Out,* Full Circle Productions, 2004.

Stage Appearances:
(As Jeffrey Sams) *Julius Caesar,* Repertory Theatre of St. Louis, St. Louis, MO, c. 1987–88.

Eat Moe, *Five Guys Named Moe* (musical revue), Eugene O'Neill Theatre, New York City, 1992–93.

Appeared in productions of *Little Shop of Horrors; A Midsummer Night's Dream,* Goodman Theatre, Chicago, IL; and *The Old Settler,* Broadway production.

OTHER SOURCES

Periodicals:
TV Zone, April, 1998, pp. 52–55; December, 1998, pp. 62–64.

SARSGAARD, Peter 1971–
(Peter Scarsgaard)

PERSONAL

Born March 7, 1971, at Scott Air Force Base, IL. *Education:* Washington University, St. Louis, MO, degree in history and literature; trained at Actors Studio, New York City.

Addresses: *Agent*—Creative Artists Agency, 9830 Wilshire Blvd., Beverly Hills, CA 90212. *Manager*—Jon Rubinstein, MJ Management, 130 West 57th St., Suite 11A, New York, NY 10019. *Publicist*—I/D Public Relations, 155 Spring St., Sixth Floor, New York, NY 10012 and 8409 Santa Monica Blvd., West Hollywood, CA 90069.

Career: Actor and writer. Drama Department, New York City, cofounder and member of company; Mama's Pot Roast (comedy improvisation group), Washington University, St. Louis, MO, cofounder.

Awards, Honors: Emerging Actor Award, St. Louis International Film Festival, 2000; Boston Society of Film Critics Award, San Francisco Film Critics Circle Award, and Toronto Film Critics Association Award, all 2003, National Society of Film Critics Award, Kansas City Film Critics Circle Award, Online Film Critics Society Award, Golden Globe Award nomination, Independent Spirit Award nomination, Independent Features Project/ West, and Chlotrudis Award nomination, all 2004, all best supporting actor, for *Shattered Glass;* Stockholm Film Festival Award, best actor, 2004, and Golden Satellite Award nomination, best actor in a supporting role in a comedy or musical, International Press Academy, 2005, both for *Garden State;* Chlotrudis Award, Glitter Award, International Gay and Lesbian Independent Film awards, Independent Spirit Award nomination, Broadcast Film Critics Association Award nomination, Golden Satellite Award nomination, and Online Film Critics Society Award nomination, all best supporting actor, all 2005, for *Kinsey.*

CREDITS

Film Appearances:
Walter Delacroix, *Dead Man Walking,* Paramount, 1995.

Billy Baxter, *Desert Blue,* Samuel Goldwyn, 1998.

Raoul, *The Man in the Iron Mask,* Metro–Goldwyn–Mayer/United Artists, 1998.

Ty, *Another Day in Paradise,* Trimark Pictures, 1998.

Minor Details, 1998.

John Lotter, *Boys Don't Cry* (also known as *Take It Like a Man*), Twentieth Century–Fox/Fox Searchlight Pictures, 1999.

Kitchen Privileges, Atmosphere Films, 1999.

Jimmy the Finn, *The Salton Sea,* Warner Bros., 2000.

(Uncredited) Julia Hickson's fiance, *The Cell,* New Line Cinema, 2000.

Richard Longman, *The Center of the World,* Artisan Entertainment, 2000.

Tom, *Housebound,* First Look Pictures Releasing, 2000.

Cowboy, *Bacon Wagon: The Movie* (short film), 2001.

Jack, *Empire,* Universal, 2002.

Vadim Ratchenko, *K–19: The Widowmaker* (also known as *K*19: The Widowmaker* and *K–19: Terreur sous la mer*), Paramount, 2002.

Brendon III, *Death of a Dynasty,* Intrinsic Value Films/R&B FM/Roc–a–fella Films, 2003.

Charles "Chuck" Lane, *Shattered Glass,* Lions Gate Films, 2003.

Clyde Martin, *Kinsey,* Fox Searchlight Pictures, 2004.

Mark, *Garden State,* Fox Searchlight Pictures, 2004.

Gene Carson, *Flightplan* (also known as *Flight Plan*), Buena Vista, 2005.

Luke, *The Skeleton Key,* Universal, 2005.

Robert, *The Dying Gaul,* Rebel Park Pictures/Holedigger Films, 2005.

Troy, *Jarhead,* Universal, 2005.

Appeared in the film *In God's Hands.*

Television Appearances; Movies:

(As Peter Scarsgaard) First boy, "Underground," *Subway Stories: Tales from the Underground,* HBO, 1997.

Cal Jackson, *Freak City,* Showtime, 1999.

Window washer, *Unconditional Love* (also known as *Who Shot Victor Fox?*), Starz!, 2002.

Television Appearances; Awards Presentations:

Himself, *The 61st Annual Golden Globe Awards,* NBC, 2004.

Himself, *The 2004 IFP/West Independent Spirit Awards,* Independent Film Channel, 2004.

Himself, *The 20th IFP Independent Spirit Awards,* Independent Film Channel and Bravo, 2005.

The 10th Annual Critics' Choice Awards, The WB, 2005.

Television Appearances; Episodic:

Josh Strand, "Paranoia," *Law & Order,* NBC, 1995.

Some sources cite an appearance as Spencer in *Cracker* (also known as *Fitz*), ABC.

Stage Appearances:

The Greatest and Most Exciting Gratuitous Exhibition Ever Exploited, Cunningham Space, New York City, beginning c. 1993.

Harvey Griswold, *Laura Dennis,* Signature Theatre Company, New York City, 1995.

Kingdom of Earth, Drama Department, Greenwich House Theatre, New York City, 1996.

Pale, *Burn This,* Union Square Theatre, New York City, 2002.

Reader, "I Woke Up Wicked," *Greater Writers Series* (reading series), MET Theatre, Hollywood, CA, 2004.

Also appeared in *American Archeology.*

RECORDINGS

Videos:

(In archive footage) John Lotter, *Sex at 24 Frames per Second* (documentary; also known as *Playboy Presents "Sex at 24 Frames per Second: The Ultimate Journey through Sex in Cinema"*), Playboy Entertainment Group, 2003.

Himself, *The Making of "Garden State"* (documentary), Twentieth Century–Fox Home Entertainment, 2004.

Himself, *The Kinsey Report: Sex on Film* (documentary), Twentieth Century–Fox Home Entertainment, 2005.

WRITINGS

Writings for the Stage:

The Greatest and Most Exciting Gratuitous Exhibition Ever Exploited, Cunningham Space, New York City, beginning c. 1993.

OTHER SOURCES

Periodicals:

Entertainment Weekly, November 7, 2003, p. 51.

Interview, March, 2001, pp. 160–63.

Movieline's Hollywood Life, February, 2004, pp. 68–69, 108.

SAWYER, Diane 1945(?)–
(Diane K. Sawyer)

PERSONAL

Full name, Lila Diane Sawyer (some sources cite Lila Diana Sawyer); born December 22, 1945 (some sources cite 1946), in Glasgow, KY; raised in Louisville,

KY; daughter of E. P. (a judge) and Jean W. (an elementary school teacher; maiden name, Dunagan) Sawyer; married Mike Nichols (a director and producer), April 29, 1988. *Education:* Wellesley College, B.A., 1967; attended the University of Louisville. *Avocational Interests:* Reading, watching films, singing.

Addresses: *Agent*—N. S. Bienstock, 1740 Broadway, 24th Floor, New York, NY 10019.

Career: Broadcast journalist. WLKY–TV, Louisville, KY, weather reporter and general reporter, 1967–70; assistant to White House deputy press secretary Jerry Warren, White House press secretary Ron Ziegler, and President Richard M. Nixon, Washington, DC, 1970–74; researcher for Nixon's memoirs, San Clemente, CA, 1974–78; CBS–News, New York City, general assignment reporter and State Department correspondent, 1978–81, coanchor for various programs, 1981–84, correspondent and coeditor, 1984–89; ABC News, New York City, coanchor and correspondent for news programs and occasional anchor for other programs, beginning 1989. Also known as Diane K. Sawyer.

Member: Council on Foreign Relations.

Awards, Honors: Kentucky's Junior Miss and America's Junior Miss (also known as America's Young Woman of the Year), both 1963; Emmy Award nominations, outstanding news and documentary program segment, 1979, for "Hostages—300 Days," and outstanding interview segment, 1981, for "Richard Nixon," both *CBS Morning News;* Emmy Award nomination, outstanding interview segment, 1983, for "Admiral Rickover," *60 Minutes;* Matrix Award, New York chapter of Women in Communications, 1984; Emmy Award nominations, outstanding interview segments, 1986, for "Dancing on Her Grave," and 1987, for "The City of Garbage—Sister Emanuelle," both *60 Minutes;* George Foster Peabody Broadcasting Award, Henry W. Grady School of Journalism and Mass Communications, University of Georgia, 1989; Emmy Award (with others), investigative journalism, 1989, for the story "Pan Am Flight 103"; Emmy Award nominations, outstanding investigative journalism segment, for "The Second Battlefield," outstanding interview segment, for "Katherine the Great," and outstanding coverage of a continuing news story, for "Murder in Beverly Hills," all 1991, *PrimeTime Live;* Robert F. Kennedy Journalism Award (Grand Prize), c. 1991–92, for investigative report about racism; National Headliner Award, Ohio State University Award, and Sigma Delta Chi Award, c. 1991–92, for investigative report about child care centers; Emmy Award (with others), interview segments, 1995, for "McNamara's War," *PrimeTime Live;* inducted into the Television Academy Hall of Fame, 1997; Crowning Glory Award, Role Models on the Web, 1997; *TV Guide*

Award nomination, news person of the year, 2001; Excellence in Media Award, GLAAD Media awards, Gay and Lesbian Alliance against Defamation (GLAAD), 2003; other awards include other Emmy Awards, another George Foster Peabody Broadcasting Award, grand prize from Investigative Reporters and Editors Association, duPont Award, Lifetime Achievement Award from International Radio and Television Society, Distinguished Achievement in Journalism Award from University of Southern California, and induction into the Broadcast Hall of Fame.

CREDITS

Television Appearances; Series:
Occasional correspondent, *Universe* (also known as *Walter Cronkite's Universe*), CBS, c. 1980–82.

Coanchor, *Morning with Charles Kuralt and Diane Sawyer,* CBS, 1981–82.

Coanchor, *CBS Morning News,* CBS, 1982–84.

CBS Evening News (also known as *CBS Evening News with Dan Rather*), CBS, 1983.

Correspondent, *60 Minutes,* CBS, c. 1983–89.

Occasional correspondent, *The American Parade* (also known as *Crossroads*), CBS, 1984.

Coanchor, *PrimeTime Live* (also known as *PrimeTime Live Wednesday, PrimeTime Live Thursday,* and *PrimeTime Thursday*), ABC, beginning 1989.

The Class of the 20th Century, Arts and Entertainment, 1992.

Correspondent, *Day One,* ABC, c. 1993–95, coanchor, 1995.

Coanchor and correspondent, *Turning Point* (also known as *Moment of Crisis*), ABC, c. 1993–97.

Coanchor, *20/20* (also known as *ABC News 20/20*), ABC, beginning 1998.

Anchor, *Vanished,* ABC, beginning 1999.

Cohost, *Good Morning America* (also known as *GMA*), ABC, 1999—.

Anchor, *America.01,* ABC, beginning 2001.

Occasional anchor for *ABC News Nightline, ABC Nightly News,* and *ABC World News Tonight* (also known as *ABC World News Tonight with Peter Jennings*), all ABC.

Television Appearances; Specials:
Correspondent, *48 Hours on Crack Street,* CBS, 1986.

David Letterman's Second Annual Holiday Film Festival (also known as *David Letterman's Second Annual Holiday Film Festival*), NBC, 1986.

Correspondent, *The Soviet Union—Seven Days in May,* CBS, 1987.

Correspondent, *Campaign '88: The Democratic Convention,* CBS, 1988.

Correspondent, *Campaign '88: The Republican Convention,* CBS, 1988.

Reporter, *Campaign '88: Election Night,* CBS, 1988.

(Uncredited) Herself, *Saturday Night Live: 15th Anniversary,* NBC, 1989.

Edward R. Murrow: This Reporter, PBS, 1990.

Donahue: The 25th Anniversary, NBC, 1992.

Anchor, *Murder in Beverly Hills: The Menendez Trial,* ABC, 1993.

Host, *James Reston: The Man Millions Read,* PBS, 1993.

Kathie Lee Gifford's Celebration of Motherhood, ABC, 1993.

60 Minutes ... 25 Years (also known as *60 Minutes Turns 25*), CBS, 1993.

Barbara Walters Presents "The Ten Most Fascinating People of 1994," ABC, 1994.

Correspondent, "Baby, Oh Baby: The Six Pack Turns Two," *Turning Point,* ABC, 1995.

Herself, *The NFL at 75: An All–Star Celebration* (also known as *NFL 75th Anniversary Special*), ABC, 1995.

Herself, "The Rosemary Clooney Golden Anniversary Celebration" (also known as "Golden Anniversary" and "Rosemary Clooney's Demi–Centennial"), *A & E Stage,* Arts and Entertainment, 1995.

Correspondent, "Baby, Oh Baby: The Six Pack Is Back," *Turning Point,* ABC, 1996.

Host, "Deadly Game: The Mark and Delia Owens Story," *Turning Point,* ABC, 1996.

Host, *Domestic Violence: Faces of Fear,* PBS, 1996.

Anchor, "Heroin: The New High School High," *Turning Point,* ABC, 1997.

Correspondent, "Baby, Oh Baby: The Six Pack Talks Back," *Turning Point,* ABC, 1997.

Host, *Town Meeting with Diane Sawyer: Celebrities vs. the Press,* ABC, 1997.

50 Years of Television: A Celebration of the Academy of Television Arts and Sciences Golden Anniversary, HBO, 1997.

Hollywood and the News, American Movie Classics, 1997.

Anchor, *The Whole World Was Watching,* ABC, 1998.

Herself, *The Real Ellen Story* (documentary), Bravo, PBS, and Channel 4 (England), 1998.

New York correspondent, *ABC 2000,* ABC, 1999.

The Great American History Quiz, History Channel, 1999.

Herself, *Lucille Ball: Finding Lucy,* CBS, 2000.

The Great American History Quiz: Heroes and Villains, History Channel, 2000.

Kids Pick the Issues, Nickelodeon, 2000.

Anchor, *Independence Day 2001,* ABC, 2001.

Herself, *Who Does She Think She Is?,* Oxygen, 2001.

Host, *Icebound: The Fight of Her Life,* Lifetime, 2001.

Host, *PrimeTime Special Edition: The Dilley Six–Pack's Happy New Year,* ABC, 2002.

Host, *PrimeTime Special Edition: Jennifer Lopez,* ABC, 2002.

Host, *PrimeTime Special Edition: Whitney Houston,* ABC, 2002.

Reporter from *PrimeTime Live, Inside the Philadelphia Police Department,* Arts and Entertainment, 2002.

Host, *A Life of Laughter: Remembering John Ritter,* ABC, 2003.

Host, *My Big Wild You're–Not–Gonna–Believe This Wedding,* ABC, 2003.

Host, *Oprah in Africa: A Personal Journey, a Global Challenge,* ABC, 2003.

Host, *President George W. Bush: The Interview,* ABC, 2003.

ABC's 50th Anniversary Celebration, ABC, 2003.

(In archive footage) Herself, *101 Biggest Celebrity Oops,* E! Entertainment Television, 2004.

Host, *Weddings Gone Wacky, Wonderful, and Wild: Anything for Love,* ABC, 2004.

Television Appearances; Awards Presentations:

The Television Academy Hall of Fame, NBC, 1986.

The Television Academy Hall of Fame, Fox, 1990.

Academy of Television Arts and Sciences (ATAS) 13th Annual Hall of Fame, Showtime, 1998.

Herself, *Lifetime's Achievement Awards: Women Changing the World,* Lifetime, 2003.

Presenter, *25th Annual News and Documentary Emmy Awards,* The Discovery Channel, 2004.

The 31st Annual Daytime Emmy Awards, NBC, 2004.

The 62nd Annual Golden Globe Awards, NBC, 2005.

Television Appearances; Episodic:

Late Night with David Letterman, NBC, 1986.

The Tonight Show Starring Johnny Carson, NBC, 1989.

The Howard Stern Show, syndicated, 1992.

The Late Show with David Letterman (also known as *The Late Show*), CBS, 1994, 2002, 2004.

Herself, "Wolfgang Puck: Recipe for Success," *Biography* (also known as *A&E Biography: Wolfgang Puck*), Arts and Entertainment, 2001.

Herself, *Intimate Portrait: Diane Sawyer,* Lifetime, 2001.

Entertainment Tonight (also known as *ET*), syndicated, 2003.

Extra (also known as *Extra: The Entertainment Magazine*), syndicated, 2003.

Live with Regis and Kelly, syndicated, 2003, 2005.

The View, ABC, 2003, 2005.

"Chasing Saddam's Weapons," *Frontline,* PBS, 2004.

Herself, *The Oprah Winfrey Show* (also known as *Oprah*), syndicated, 2004.

Herself, *Jimmy Kimmel Live,* ABC, 2004, 2005.

Herself, *Ellen: The Ellen DeGeneres Show* (also known as *Ellen* and *The Ellen DeGeneres Show*), syndicated, 2005.

Herself, *The Tony Danza Show,* syndicated, 2005.

Television Work; Series:

Coeditor of news, *PrimeTime Live* (also known as *PrimeTime Live Wednesday, PrimeTime Live Thursday,* and *PrimeTime Thursday*), ABC, beginning 1989.

WRITINGS

Teleplays; Series:
PrimeTime Live (also known as *PrimeTime Live Wednesday, PrimeTime Live Thursday,* and *PrimeTime Thursday*), ABC, beginning 1989.

Teleplays; Specials:
The Whole World Was Watching, ABC, 1998.
PrimeTime Special Edition: Jennifer Lopez, ABC, 2002.
PrimeTime Special Edition: Whitney Houston, ABC, 2002.
My Big Wild You're–Not–Gonna–Believe This Wedding, ABC, 2003.
Weddings Gone Wacky, Wonderful, and Wild: Anything for Love, ABC, 2004.

OTHER SOURCES

Books:
Contemporary Authors, Volume 115, Gale, 1985.
Newsmakers, 1994 Cumulation, Gale, 1994, pp. 438–41.

Periodicals:
Entertainment Weekly, March 4, 1994, p. 9; July 28, 1995, pp. 50–51; November 8, 1996, pp. 34–38.
Esquire, January, 1995, pp. 76–83.
Forbes, March 22, 1999, p. 248.
Harper's Bazaar, November, 1984, p. 232; December, 1999, p. 204.
Interview, September, 1984, p. 100.
Ladies Home Journal, October, 1999, p. 196.
Life, August, 1989, p. 72.
New Leader, March 14, 1994, pp. 20–21.
Newsweek, February 28, 1994, p. 58; January 18, 1999, p. 55.
New Yorker, February 14, 1994, pp. 61–63.
New York Times, September 30, 1981; April 1, 1997, p. B3.
People Weekly, November 5, 1984, p. 78; May 13, 2002, p. 117.
Television Quarterly, spring, 1992.
Time, February 28, 1994, p. 69; September 26, 1994, p. 10; January 18, 1999, p. 8.
TV Guide, March 26, 1994, pp. 8–14; November 5, 1994, p. 43; January 2, 1999, pp. 19–21; July 5, 2003, pp. 37–38.
Variety, February 21, 1994, pp. 171–72.
Vogue, August, 2002, pp. 210–15.
Wall Street Journal, April 1, 1997, p. B7.

Electronic:
ABC News Web Site, http://abcnews.go.com, March 29, 2005.

SCALIA, Jack 1951(?)–

PERSONAL

Born November 10, 1951 (some sources cite 1950), in Brooklyn, New York, NY; father, a baseball player; married Joan Rankin (a model; divorced); married Karen Baldwin (divorced, 1996); children: (second marriage) Olivia, Jacqueline. *Education:* Attended Ottawa University, Ottawa, KS. *Religion:* Roman Catholicism.

Addresses: *Agent*—Alan B. Ellsweig, Ellsweig Management, 8840 Wilshire Blvd., Second Floor, Beverly Hills, CA 90211. *Publicist*—Jonas Public Relations, 240 26th St., Suite 3, Santa Monica, CA 90402; Liza Anderson, Warren Cowan and Associates, 8899 Beverly Blvd., Suite 919, Los Angeles, CA 90048.

Career: Actor, producer, and director. Montreal Expos, professional baseball player; Ford Modeling Agency, professional model, including work for Jordache jeans; also a construction worker and food packager. Child Health USA (child abuse prevention organization), national ambassador, 1990; member of Mothers against Drunk Driving and Celebrities against Drunk Driving.

Awards, Honors: *Soap Opera Digest* Award nomination, outstanding actor in a supporting role, primetime category, 1989, for *Dallas;* Daytime Emmy Award nomination, outstanding lead actor in a drama series, 2002, for *All My Children.*

CREDITS

Television Appearances; Series:
Nick Corsello, *The Devlin Connection,* NBC, 1982.
Blue Stratton, *High Performance,* ABC, 1983.
Danny Krucek/Tony Rinaldi, *Berrenger's,* NBC, 1985.
Detective Nick McCarren, *Hollywood Beat,* ABC, 1985.
Nicholas Pearce/Joey Lombardi, *Dallas,* CBS, 1987–88.
Tony Wolf (title role), *Wolf,* CBS, 1989–91.
Cohost, *Stuntmasters* (documentary), syndicated, 1991–92.
Detective Nico "Nick" Bonetti, *Tequila and Bonetti,* CBS, 1992.
Constantine "Connie" Harper, *Pointman,* syndicated, 1994–95.
Detective Nico "Nick" Bonetti, *Tequila & Bonetti,* [Italy], beginning 2000.
Christopher "Chris" Stamp, *All My Children* (also known as *All My Children: The Summer of Seduction*), ABC, 2001–2003.

Television Appearances; Miniseries:
Vince Martino, *The Star Maker*, NBC, 1981.
Rocco Cipriani, *I'll Take Manhattan*, CBS, 1987.
Lennie Golden, *Lady Boss* (also known as *Jackie Collins's "Lady Boss"*), NBC, 1992.

Television Appearances; Movies:
Lieutenant Tony Monaco, *Amazons*, ABC, 1984.
Jack Hollander, *The Other Lover*, CBS, 1985.
O'Shea, *Club Med*, ABC, 1986.
Tony Roselli, *Remington Steele: The Steele That Wouldn't Die*, NBC, 1987.
Dr. Eugene Kesselman, *Donor*, CBS, 1990.
Jack Thompson, *After the Shock* (also known as *To the Heroes: The San Francisco Earthquake, October 17, 1989*), USA Network, 1990.
Richard Devereaux, *The Ring of Scorpio*, NBC and BBC, 1990.
Frank Decker, *Deadly Desire*, USA Network, 1991.
John Payton (some sources cite Tommy Griffin), *Runaway Father*, CBS, 1991.
Mike Barcetti, *With a Vengeance* (also known as *Undesirable*), CBS, 1992.
Joseph "Joey" Buttafuoco, *Casualties of Love: The "Long Island Lolita" Story* (also known as *The Buttafuoco Story* and *Casualty of Love*), CBS, 1993.
Mike Lanahan, *Torch Song* (also known as *Judith Krantz's "Torch Song"*), ABC, 1993.
Brian Dillon, *Shattered Image*, USA Network, 1994.
Detective sergeant Vince Morgan, *Beyond Suspicion*, 1994.
Michael Carvella, *Shadow of Obsession* (also known as *Unwanted Attentions*), NBC, 1994.
Roy Calvin, *Tall, Dark and Deadly* (also known as *The Charmer*), USA Network, 1995.
Michael DeMarco (some sources cite Detective Nick DeMarco), *Barbara Taylor Bradford's "Everything to Gain"* (also known as *Barbara Taylor Bradford Trilogy: Everything to Gain* and *Everything to Gain*), CBS, 1996.
Brett Newcomb, *Sweet Deception* (also known as *Sweet Lies*), Fox Family Channel, 1998.
Bailey Silverwood, *Mel*, HBO, 1999.
Max Farrington, *Silent Predators*, TBS, 1999.

Television Appearances; Specials:
CBS team member, *Battle of the Network Stars XIX*, ABC, 1988.
The Hollywood Christmas Parade, syndicated, 1988, 1989.
New York parade host, *The CBS All–American Thanksgiving Day Parade*, CBS, 1989.
The 61st Annual Hollywood Christmas Parade, syndicated, 1992.
The Art of the Cigar, 1996.
Himself, *Our Contributions: The Italians in America*, PBS, 1999.

Himself, *TV Movie Superstars: Women You Love*, Lifetime, 2004.
(Uncredited; in archive footage) Nicholas Pearce/Joey Lombardi, *Dallas Reunion: Return to Southfork*, CBS, 2004.

Television Appearances; Awards Presentations:
The 29th Annual Daytime Emmy Awards, CBS, 2002.

Television Appearances; Episodic:
Guest, *The Oprah Winfrey Show* (also known as *Oprah*), syndicated, 1987.
Nicholas Pearce, "Conundrum," *Dallas*, CBS, 1991.
Max Chamberlain, "The Big Bang," *Touched by an Angel*, CBS, 1995.
Frank Reynolds, "Total Recall," *Fired Up* (also known as *Fired*), NBC, 1997.
Himself, "Rock Hudson: Acting the Part," *Biography* (also known as *A&E Biography: Rock Hudson*), Arts and Entertainment, 1999.
Himself, *Celebrity Profile: Alyssa Milano* (also known as *Celebrity Profile* and *E! Celebrity Profile*), E! Entertainment Television, 1999.
Himself and Christopher "Chris" Stamp in archive footage, "All My Children," *Biography* (also known as *A&E Biography: All My Children*), Arts and Entertainment, 2003.
Himself, *Intimate Portrait: Susan Lucci*, Lifetime, 2003.

Television Appearances; Pilots:
Nick Corsello, *The Devlin Connection III*, NBC, 1982.
Tony Wolf (title role), *Wolf*, CBS, 1989.
Constantine "Connie" Harper, *Pointman*, syndicated, 1994.

Television Appearances; Other:
Tommy, *Un cane e un poliziotto*, [Italy], 1999.

Television Director; Movies:
Shattered Image, USA Network, 1994.

Film Appearances:
Nicky Piacenza, *Fear City* (also known as *Border* and *Ripper*), Chevy Chase Distribution, 1984.
Wick Hayes, *The Rift* (also known as *Endless Descent* and *La grieta*), Columbia, 1989.
Mike Yarnell, *Illicit Behavior* (also known as *Criminal Intent*), Prism Pictures, 1992.
Saul Schwartz, *Amore!*, PM Entertainment Group/Sunland Entertainment, 1993.
Brandon's father, *Storybook*, PM Entertainment Group, 1995.
Chuck Rafferty, *The Silencers*, PM Entertainment Group, 1995.
Daniel, *P.C.H.* (also known as *Kill Shot*), Ajax Home Entertainment, 1995.

Jack Floyd, *T–Force,* PM Entertainment Group, 1995.

Nicholas "Nick" Saxon, *Dark Breed,* PM Entertainment Group, 1996.

Nick Hollit, *Under Oath* (also known as *Blood Money* and *Urban Justice*), Concorde–New Horizons, 1997.

Scott Thompson, *Follow Your Heart,* Republic Pictures, 1997.

Barry, *Charades* (also known as *Felons* and *First Degree*), Fries Film Group/York Entertainment, 1998.

Garrett, *Hell Mountain* (also known as *Chained Heat: The Horror of Hell Mountain, Chained Heat 3,* and *Chained Heat 3: The Horror of Hell Mountain*), New Films International, 1998.

Henry Barridge, *The Last Leprechaun,* Peakviewing Transatlantic, 1998.

Jack Gracy, *Act of War,* North American Pictures, 1998.

An American Affair, 1999.

Michael Brandeis, *Ground Zero,* Euro Video, 2000.

Captain Sterling, *Shattered Lies,* F.T.L. Films, 2002.

Jack, *Exit* (short film), Friends of Young Filmmakers/Spot Creative, 2005.

Mark, *R.I.P.,* Noble House Entertainment Pictures, 2005.

President, *End Game,* Metro–Goldwyn–Mayer/Millennium Films, 2005.

William Keefe, *Red Eye,* DreamWorks, 2005.

Some sources cite an appearance as Rick Giordano in *Sudden Fears.*

Film Associate Producer:

The Silencers, PM Entertainment Group, 1995.
T–Force, PM Entertainment Group, 1995.
Dark Breed, PM Entertainment Group, 1996.
Follow Your Heart, Republic Pictures, 1997.

Stage Appearances:

Red River Rats, Burbage Theatre, Los Angeles, 1994.

OTHER SOURCES

Periodicals:

Good Housekeeping, April, 1990, pp. 56, 58.

SCHELL, Maximilian 1930–
(Maximillian Schell)

PERSONAL

Born December 8, 1930, in Vienna, Austria; raised in Switzerland; son of Hermann Ferdinand (a pharmacy owner, writer, and poet) and Margarethe (an actress; maiden name, Noe von Nordberg) Schell; brother of Maria Schell and Immy Schell (both actresses), and Karl Schell (an actor); married Natasha Andreichenko (an actress; name sometimes cited as Natalya Andrejchenko or Natalia Andreichenko), 1985; children: Nastia (daughter). *Education:* Attended the universities of Zurich, Basel, and Munich. *Avocational Interests:* Playing the piano, conducting.

Addresses: *Agent*—The Blake Agency, 1327 Ocean Ave., Suite J, Santa Monica, CA 90401.

Career: Actor, director, producer, and writer. Volkstheater, Munich, West Germany (now Germany), director, beginning 1981. *Military service:* Swiss Army, 1948–49, became corporal.

Awards, Honors: New York Film Critics Circle Award, best actor, 1961, Academy Award, best actor, Golden Globe Award, best motion picture actor—drama, Film Award nomination, best foreign actor, British Academy of Film and Television Arts, and nomination for Golden Laurel Award, top male dramatic performance, Laurel awards, Producers Guild of America, all 1962, all for *Judgment at Nuremberg;* Golden Laurel Award, top male new personality, 1962; Ondas Award, best international television actor, 1965; Silver Seashell, San Sebastian International Film Festival, 1970, Filmband in Gold, best picture, Swiss Film Award, best picture, Panama Film Festival Award, best director, special award of the jury, Cartagena Film Festival, and Academy Award nomination, best foreign film, all 1971, all for *Erste Liebe;* Chicago Film Critics Award, best foreign film, and Silver Sirene Award, best picture, Sorrento and Naples Film Festival, both 1973, Golden Globe Award, best foreign film, Golden Cup (Germany), best picture, and Academy Award nomination, best foreign film, all 1974, and other international awards, all for *Der Fussgaenger;* Silver Seashell, 1975, and Filmband in Silver, best picture, 1979, both for *Der Richter und sein Henker;* Academy Award nomination, best actor, and Golden Globe Award nomination, best actor in a motion picture—drama, both 1976, for *The Man in the Glass Booth;* New York Film Critics Circle Award, best supporting actor, 1977, Academy Award nomination, best supporting actor, 1978, and Golden Globe Award nomination, best motion picture actor in a supporting role, 1978, all for *Julia;* Golden Hugo Award, best foreign film, Chicago Film Festival, 1979, Filmband in Silver, best picture, 1980, and Oxford Film Festival Award, best screenplay, 1980, all for *Geschichten aus dem Wienerwald;* Silver Bear, best picture, Berlin Film Festival, and Golden Federation Award of Germany, best actor, both 1984, for *Morgen in Alabama;* New York Film Critics Circle Award, National Board of Review Award, and Academy Award nomination, best documentary, all 1984, for *Marlene;* honorary German Film Award, outstanding individual contributions to German film, 1990; Emmy Award nomination, outstanding lead actor in a miniseries or special, 1992, for "Miss Rose White," *Hallmark Hall of Fame;* honorary doctorate, University of Chicago, 1992; Golden Globe Award, best performance by an actor in a supporting role in a series, miniseries, or movie made for television, Annual CableACE Award, best supporting actor in a movie or miniseries, National Cable Television Association, and Emmy Award nomination, outstanding supporting actor in a miniseries or special, all 1993, for *Stalin;* Silver Lion, Venice Film Festival, 1994, for *Little Odessa;* Akira Kurosawa Award, outstanding contribution to the entertainment industry, International Press Academy, 1999; Lifetime Achievement Award, Method Fest, 1999; Platin Romy, Romy Gala, 1999; Mary Pickford Award, Golden Satellite awards, International Press Academy, 2000; Actor of the Millennium Award, Baltic Pearl Film Festival, 2000; Lifetime Achievement Award, Bambi awards, 2002.

CREDITS

Film Appearances:

Deserter, *Kinder, Muetter und ein General* (also known as *Children, Mother, and the General*), 1955.

Mitglied des Kreisauer Kreises, *Der 20. Juli* (also known as *The Plot to Assassinate Hitler*), 1955.

Reifende Jugend (also known as *Ripening Youth*), 1955.

Dr. Hauser, *Die Ehe des Dr. med. Danwitz* (also known as *Marriage of Dr. Danwitz*), 1956.

Wolfgang Thomas, *Ein Herz kehrt heim,* 1956.

Lieutenant Alexander "Alex" Haller, *Ein Maedchen aus Flandern* (also known as *The Girl from Flanders*), 1956, released in United States, 1963.

Lorenz Darrandt, *Die Letzten werden die Ersten sein* (also known as *The Last Ones Shall Be First*), 1957.

Toni Schellenberg, *Taxichauffeur Baenz* (also known as *Taxi Driver Baenz*), 1957.

Der Meisterdieb, 1957.

Captain Hardenberg, *The Young Lions,* Twentieth Century–Fox, 1958.

Josef Ospel, *Kinder der Berge* (also known as *Ein Wunderbarer Sommer*), 1958.

Die Sechste Frau, 1958.

Eine Dummheit macht Auch der Gescheiteste, 1959.

Hans Rolfe, *Judgment at Nuremberg,* United Artists, 1961.

Walter, *Five Finger Exercise,* Columbia, 1961.

Giuseppe Desa, *The Reluctant Saint* (also known as *Joseph Desa* and *Cronache di un convento*), Columbia, 1962.

Franz, *I sequestrati di Altona* (also known as *The Condemned of Altona* and *Les sequestres d'Altona*), Twentieth Century–Fox, 1963.

Walter Harper, *Topkapi,* United Artists, 1964.

Letters of Mozart, 1964.

Stanislaus Pilgrin, *Return from the Ashes,* United Artists, 1965.

Dieter Freey, *The Deadly Affair,* Columbia, 1967.

General Schiller, *Counterpoint,* Universal, 1968.

Himself, *Flash 14* (short documentary film), Television Espanola, 1968.

Captain Chris Hanson, *Krakatoa, East of Java* (also known as *Volcano*), Cinerama, 1969.

"K," *Das Schloss* (also known as *The Castle*), Continental, 1969.

Marek, *The Desperate Ones* (also known as *Beyond the Mountains* and *Mas alla de las montanas*), Commonwealth United, 1969.

L'assoluto naturale, 1969.

Simon Bolivar (also known as *La epopeya de Bolivar*), 1969.

Father, *Erste Liebe* (also known as *First Love* and *First Love—Die Geschichte einer Liebe*), UMC Pictures, 1970.

Brother Adrian, *Pope Joan* (also known as *The Devil's Imposter*), Columbia, 1972.

Count Michel Cantarini, *Paulina 1880,* 1972.

Trotta (also known as *Trotta—Die Kapuzinergruft*), 1972.

Andreas Giese, *Der Fussgaenger* (also known as *The Pedestrian*), Cinerama, 1973.

The Rehearsal (also known as *I Dokimi*), 1974.

Arthur Goldman, *The Man in the Glass Booth,* American Film Theatre, 1975.

Djuro Sarac (some sources cite Shastar), *Sarajevski atentat* (also known as *Assassination in Sarajevo, The Day That Shook the World, Atentat u Sarajevu, Der Tag, der die Welt veraenderte,* and *Sarajevsky atentat*), 1975.

Eduard Roschmann, *The Odessa File* (also known as *Der Fall Odessa* and *Die Akte Odessa*), Columbia, 1975.

Dr. John Constable, *St. Ives,* Warner Bros., 1976.

Hauptmann Stransky, *Cross of Iron* (also known as *Steiner—Das Eiserne Kreuz*), Avco–Embassy, 1977.

Johann, *Julia,* Twentieth Century–Fox, 1977.

Lieutenant general Wilhelm Bittrich, *A Bridge Too Far,* United Artists, 1977.

Nikolai Bunin, *Avalanche Express,* Twentieth Century–Fox, 1978.

Gesprache mit Jedermann, 1978.

Dr. Hans Reinhardt, *The Black Hole,* Buena Vista, 1979.

Giovanni, *Amo non amo* (also known as *I Love You, I Love You Not* and *Together?*), New Line Cinema, 1979.

Marco, *Players,* Paramount, 1979.

Geschichten aus dem Wienerwald (also known as *Tales from the Vienna Woods*), 1979, subtitled version released in the United States by Cinema 5 Distributing.

Fabrice, *Les iles* (also known as *The Islands*), 1982.

Professor David Malter, *The Chosen,* Twentieth Century–Fox, 1982.

The Great Hamlets, 1983.

David Landau, *Morgen in Alabama* (also known as *Man under Suspicion* and *Tomorrow in Alabama*), Futura Film, c. 1983, subtitled version released in the United States by International Spectrafilm, c. 1984.

Himself, *Marlene* (documentary; also known as *Marlene Dietrich—Portraet eines Mythos*), Futura Film, 1984, subtitled version, Alive Films, 1986.

Colonel Mueller, *The Assisi Underground,* Metro–Goldwyn–Mayer/United Artists, 1985.

Aaron Reichenbacher, *The Rose Garden* (also known as *Der Rosengarten*), Cannon, 1989.

Larry London, *The Freshman,* TriStar, 1990.

Himself, *Labyrinth,* 1991.

Colonel Mopani Theron, *A Far Off Place,* Buena Vista, 1993.

Isaak Kohler, *Justiz* (also known as *Justice*), 1993.

Arkady Shapira, *Little Odessa,* Fine Line Features, 1995.

Rodan, *The Vampyre Wars,* 1996.

Carl Stern, *Zwischen Rosen,* 1997.

Dr. Istvan Jonas, *Telling Lies in America,* Banner Entertainment, 1997.

Father Simeon, *The Eighteenth Angel,* Rysher Entertainment, 1997.

Mr. Silberschmidt, *Left Luggage* (also known as *2 koffers vol*), 1997, Castle Hill Productions, 2000.

Cardinal Alba, *Vampires* (also known as *John Carpenter's "Vampires"* and *Vampire$*), Sony Pictures Releasing, 1998.

Jason Lerner, *Deep Impact,* Paramount, 1998.

Hochberg, *Wer liebt, dem wachsen Fluegel...* (also known as *On the Wings of Love*), Concorde Filmverleih, 1999.

Himself, *Mein liebster Feind–Klaus Kinski* (documentary; also known as *My Best Fiend, Mein liebster Feind,* and *25. tunti: Klaus Kinski*), 1999, subtitled version released in the United States by New Yorker Films.

Himself, *Hamlet in Hollywood* (documentary), 2000.

Poser, *Fisimatenten* (also known as *Just Messing About*), Next Film/Saarlaendischer Rundfunk, 2000.

Walter Ekland, *I Love You Baby,* Warner Bros., 2000.

Viktor Kovner, *Festival in Cannes,* Paramount Classics, 2001.

Himself, *Meine Schwester Maria* (documentary; also known as *My Sister Maria*), 2002, subtitled version, Rainbow Releasing/Kirchmedia Entertainment, 2004.

Himself, *Ninth November Night* (short documentary film), Lohneranger, 2004.

(In archive footage) *Imaginary Witness: Hollywood and the Holocaust* (documentary), Anker Productions, 2004.

Film Director:

Erste Liebe (also known as *First Love* and *First Love—Die Geschichte einer Liebe*), UMC Pictures, 1970.

Der Fussgaenger (also known as *The Pedestrian*), Cinerama, 1973.

The Clown (also known as *Ansichten eines Clowns*), 1975.

Der Richter und sein Henker (also known as *Deception, The End of the Game, Getting Away with Murder, Murder on the Bridge,* and *Assassinio sul ponte*), Twentieth Century–Fox, 1976.

Geschichten aus dem Wienerwald (also known as *Tales from the Vienna Woods*), 1979, subtitled version released in the United States by Cinema 5 Distributing.

Marlene (documentary; also known as *Marlene Dietrich—Portraet eines Mythos*), Futura Film, 1984, subtitled version, Alive Films, 1986.

Meine Schwester Maria (documentary; also known as *My Sister Maria*), 2002, subtitled version, Rainbow Releasing/Kirchmedia Entertainment, 2004.

Film Producer:

(With Rudolf Noelte) *Das Schloss* (also known as *The Castle*), Continental, 1969.

Erste Liebe (also known as *First Love* and *First Love—Die Geschichte einer Liebe*), UMC Pictures, 1970.

Der Fussgaenger (also known as *The Pedestrian*), Cinerama, 1973.

The Clown (also known as *Ansichten eines Clowns*), 1975.

(With Arlene Sellers) *Der Richter und sein Henker* (also known as *Deception, The End of the Game, Getting Away with Murder, Murder on the Bridge,* and *Assassinio sul ponte*), Twentieth Century–Fox, 1976.

Geschichten aus dem Wienerwald (also known as *Tales from the Vienna Woods*), 1979, subtitled version released in the United States by Cinema 5 Distributing.

Morgen in Alabama (also known as *Man under Suspicion* and *Tomorrow in Alabama*), Futura Film, c. 1983, subtitled version released in the United States by International Spectrafilm, c. 1984.

Marlene (documentary; also known as *Marlene Dietrich—Portraet eines Mythos*), Futura Film, 1984, subtitled version, Alive Films, 1986.

Executive producer, *Meine Schwester Maria* (documentary; also known as *My Sister Maria*), 2002, subtitled version, Rainbow Releasing/Kirchmedia Entertainment, 2004.

Television Appearances; Series:

Amado Guzman, *Wiseguy,* CBS, 1990.

Fuerst Thorwald, *Der Fuerst und das Maedchen,* [Germany], beginning 2003.

Television Appearances; Miniseries:

Don Rodrigo, *Der Seidene Schuh,* 1965.

Commentator, *Bernstein/Beethoven,* PBS, 1981.

Title role, *Peter the Great,* NBC, 1986.

Frederick the Great, *Young Catherine,* TNT, 1991.

Vladimir Lenin, *Stalin* (also known as *Sztalin*), HBO, 1992.

Pharaoh, *Abraham* (also known as *The Bible: Abraham, Die Bibel—Abraham,* and *La Bible: Abraham*), TNT, 1994.

Cardinal Vittorio, *The Thorn Birds: The Missing Years,* CBS, 1996.

Narrator, *Sex and the Silver Screen,* Showtime, 1996.

Brother John Le'Maitre, *Joan of Arc* (also known as *Jeanne d'Arc*), CBS, 1999.

Franz Steininger, *Liebe, Luegen, Leidenschaft* (also known as *Love, Lies, Passions*), 2002.

Television Appearances; Movies:

Herzog Albrecht von Bayern, *Die Bernauerin,* 1958.

The Fifth Column, 1959.

Herr Richard Sessemann, *Heidi* (also known as *Heide kehrt heim*), 1968.

Sandor Korvin (title role), *The Phantom of the Opera,* CBS, 1983.

Colonel Arkush, *Candles in the Dark,* The Family Channel, 1993.

Wunsch, "The Song of the Lark," *Masterpiece Theatre,* PBS, 2000.

Casimir Michaelstadt, *Coast to Coast,* Showtime, 2004.

Pater Christoph, *Die Liebe eines Priesters,* ARD (Germany), 2005.

Television Appearances; Specials:

D'Artagnan, *The Three Musketeers,* 1960.

Title role, *Hamlet* (also known as *Hamlet, Prinz von Daenemark*), Germany, 1960, then United States, 1962.

Narrator, *The Beautiful Blue and Red Danube* (documentary), ABC, 1967.

Hamlet, 1970.

Otto Frank, *The Diary of Anne Frank,* NBC, 1980.

Mordecai Weiss, "Miss Rose White," *Hallmark Hall of Fame,* NBC, 1992.

Claudio Abbado: The Silence That Follows the Music, 1996.

Television Appearances; Awards Presentations:

The 34th Annual Academy Awards, ABC, 1962.

Presenter, *The 35th Annual Academy Awards,* ABC, 1963.

50th Annual Golden Globe Awards, TBS, 1993.

51st Annual Golden Globe Awards, TBS, 1994.

The 70th Annual Academy Awards, ABC, 1998.

The 75th Annual Academy Awards, ABC, 2003.

Television Appearances; Episodic:

Hans Rolfe, "Judgment at Nuremberg," *Playhouse 90,* CBS, 1959.

Hans, "Perilous," *Desilu Playhouse* (also known as *Westinghouse Desilu Playhouse*), CBS, 1959.

"Child of Our Time," *Playhouse 90,* CBS, 1959.

Peter Gerard, "Turn the Key Deftly," *Sunday Showcase,* NBC, 1960.

Sarrail, "The Observer," *Alcoa Theatre,* NBC, 1960.

Himself, *Here's Hollywood,* NBC, 1961, 1962.

Hans Rolfe, scene from *Judgment at Nuremberg, The Ed Sullivan Show* (also known as *Toast of the Town*), CBS, 1962.

August Holland, "A Time to Love," *Bob Hope Presents the Chrysler Theater,* NBC, 1967.

Guest, *The Tonight Show Starring Johnny Carson,* NBC, 1970.

Himself, *V.I.P.—Schaukel,* 1978.

Himself, "Festival de Berlin 1984," *Etoiles et toiles,* 1984.

Guest, "Wetten, dass ... ? aus Dresden," *Wetten, dass ... ?,* 2001.

Himself, "An Interview with Maximilian Schell," *Leute heute,* 2002.

Himself, "Aus Cannes," *Leute heute,* 2002.

Himself, "Premiere: Meine Schwester Maria," *Seitenblicke,* 2002.

Himself, *Beckmann,* 2003.

Himself, *Die Johannes B. Kerner Show,* 2003.

Himself, *Menschen bei Maischberger,* 2004.

Himself, *Tavis Smiley,* PBS, 2005.

Also appeared in *Willemsens Woche,* Zweites Deutsches Fernsehen.

Television Appearances; Other:

Karl Steingraf, *Der Bestseller—Mord auf italienisch,* [Austria and Germany], 2002.

Xaver Schoenborn, *Alles Glueck dieser Erde,* [Austria], 2003.

Fernando Hereira, *The Return of the Dancing Master* (also known as *Die Rueckkehr des Tanzlehrers*), [Austria and Germany], 2004.

Television Director; Movies:

Candles in the Dark, The Family Channel, 1993.

Stage Appearances:

Leonce, Berlin Theatre am Kurfurstendamn, Berlin, Germany, 1957.

Philotas, Berlin Theatre am Kurfurstendamn, 1957.

Paul, *Interlock,* American National Theatre and Academy, New York City, 1958.

Der Turn, Salzburg Festival, Salzburg, Austria, 1959.

Sappho, Hamburg, West Germany (now Germany), 1959.

Hamlet, 1961.

A Patriot for Me, Royal Court Theatre, London, 1965, then Bremen, West Germany (now Germany), 1966.

Herostrat, Bochum, West Germany (now Germany), 1966.

The Venetian Twins, Josefstadt, Vienna, Austria, 1966.

Title role, *Hamlet,* Munich, West Germany (now Germany), 1968.

Alfred Redl, *A Patriot for Me,* Imperial Theatre, New York City, 1969.

Old Times, Vienna, Austria, 1973.

Everyman, Salzburg Festival, 1978, 1979, 1980, 1981, and 1982.

Der seidene Schuh, 1982.

Poor Murderer, Berlin, Germany, 1982.

Ernst Janning, *Judgment at Nuremberg,* Longacre Theatre, New York City, 2001.

Appeared in productions of *Don Carlos, Mannerhouse,* and *The Prince of Homburg.*

Stage Director:

All the Best, Bremen, West Germany (now Germany), then Vienna, Austria, both 1966.

Hamlet, Munich, West Germany (now Germany), 1968.

Pygmalion, Dusseldorf, West Germany (now Germany), 1970.

La Traviata (opera), 1975.

Tales from the Vienna Woods, National Theatre, Olivier Theatre, London, 1977.

The Undiscovered Country, Salzburg Festival, Salzburg, Austria, 1979 and 1980.

Coronet, Deutsche Opera, Berlin, Germany, 1985.

Der seidene Schuh, Salzburg Festival, 1985.

Lohengrin (opera), Los Angeles Opera, Los Angeles Music Center, Los Angeles, 2001.

Der Rosenkavalier (opera), Los Angeles Opera, Los Angeles Music Center, Dorothy Chandler Pavilion, Los Angeles, 2005.

RECORDINGS

Videos:

(As Maximillian Schell) Himself, *In Conversation: Abby Mann and Maximillian Schell* (short documentary), Metro–Goldwyn–Mayer Home Entertainment, 2004.

WRITINGS

Screenplays:

Das Schloss (also known as *The Castle*), Continental, 1969.

(With John Gould) *Erste Liebe* (also known as *First Love* and *First Love—Die Geschichte einer Liebe*), UMC Pictures, 1970.

Trotta (also known as *Trotta–Die Kapuzinergruft*), 1972.

Der Fussgaenger (also known as *The Pedestrian*), Cinerama, 1973.

(With Friedrich Duerrenmatt) *Der Richter und sein Henker* (also known as *Deception, The End of the Game, Getting Away with Murder, Murder on the Bridge,* and *Assassinio sul ponte*), Twentieth Century–Fox, 1976.

Geschichten aus dem Wienerwald (also known as *Tales from the Vienna Woods*), 1979, subtitled version released in the United States by Cinema 5 Distributing.

Marlene (documentary; also known as *Marlene Dietrich—Portraet eines Mythos*), Futura Film, 1984, subtitled version, Alive Films, 1986.

Meine Schwester Maria (documentary; also known as *My Sister Maria*), 2002, subtitled version, Rainbow Releasing/Kirchmedia Entertainment, 2004.

Writings for the Stage:

Murder on the Bridge, 1975.

(With Christopher Hampton) *Tales from the Vienna Woods,* National Theatre, Olivier Theatre, London, 1977.

Nonfiction:

Anni und Josef Albers: Eine Retrospektive, Stuck–Jugendstil–Verein, 1989.

OTHER SOURCES

Books:

Contemporary Authors, Volume 116, Gale, 1986.

International Dictionary of Films and Filmmakers, Volume 3: *Actors and Actresses,* fourth edition, St. James Press, 2000.

Periodicals:

Starlog, April, 1980, pp. 43–47.

Electronic:

Playbill Online, http://www.playbill.com, August 31, 2000; March 1, 2001.

SCHIFF, Richard 1955–

PERSONAL

Born May 27, 1955, in Bethesda, MD; son of Edward (a real estate lawyer) and Charlotte (a television and publishing executive) Schiff; married Sheryl Noeth (a poet; marriage ended); married Sheila Kelley (an actress), 1996; children: (second marriage) Gus, Ruby Christine. *Education:* Attended City College of the City University of New York.

Addresses: *Agent*—Scott Melrose, Endeavor, 9601 Wilshire Blvd., Third Floor, Beverly Hills, CA 90210.

Manager—Leverage Management, 3030 Pennsylvania Ave., Santa Monica, CA 90404. *Publicist*—David Lust, Patricola/Lust Public Relations, 8383 Wilshire Blvd., Suite 530, Beverly Hills, CA 90211.

Career: Actor and director. Manhattan Repertory Theatre, New York City, founder, 1982, and artistic director; also worked as a stage manager.

Awards, Honors: Townsend Harris Medal, City College of the City University of New York, 2000; Emmy Award, 2000, and Emmy Award nominations, 2001 and 2002, all outstanding supporting actor in a drama series, Screen Actors Guild awards (with others), 2001 and 2002, and Screen Actors Guild Award nominations (with others), 2003, 2004, and 2005, all outstanding ensemble in a drama series, all for *The West Wing;* Drama-Logue Award, best actor, for *Goose and Tom Tom;* L.A. Ovation Award, for *Urban Folktales.*

CREDITS

Television Appearances; Series:
Barry Roth, *Relativity,* ABC, 1996–97.
Tobias Zachary "Toby" Ziegler, *The West Wing,* NBC, 1999—.

Television Appearances; Miniseries:
Cruel Doubt, NBC, 1992.

Television Appearances; Movies:
Mole, *Trenchcoat in Paradise,* CBS, 1989.
Jack Wells, *Till Death Do Us Part* (also known as *Married for Murder*), NBC, 1992.
Life photographer, *The Positively True Adventures of the Alleged Texas Cheerleader–Murdering Mom,* HBO, 1993.
Deputy Dano, *Saved by the Bell: Wedding in Las Vegas,* NBC, 1994.
Movietone news director, *Amelia Earhart: The Final Flight,* TNT, 1994.
Eric Altman, *Special Report: Journey to Mars,* CBS, 1996.
Mr. Green, *The Taking of Pelham One Two Three,* 1998.
Robert Laurel Smith, *The Pentagon Wars,* HBO, 1998.
Forever Lulu (also known as *Along for the Ride*), Starz!, 2000.

Television Appearances; Specials:
Presenter, *Sports Illustrated's Night of Champions,* NBC, 2001.
The West Wing Documentary Special, NBC, 2002.
Himself, *Happy Birthday Oscar Wilde,* BBC, 2004.

Television Appearances; Awards Presentations:
The 54th Annual Primetime Emmy Awards, NBC, 2002.

Television Appearances; Episodic:
Lester Middleton, "Korman's Kalamity," *Tales from the Crypt* (also known as *HBO's "Tales from the Crypt"*), HBO, 1990.
Dog pound operator, "Helter Shelter," *L.A. Law,* NBC, 1992.
Lester Michaels, "The Bum," *Love and War,* CBS, 1994.
Mel Woodworthy, "Anything but Cured," *Murphy Brown,* CBS, 1994.
Pat Perkins, "Bloodsuckers," *Thunder Alley,* ABC, 1994.
Wilson, "Don't Drink and Drive Nuclear Waste," *The John Larroquette Show,* NBC, 1994.
Perlman, "Snitch Doggy–Dogg," *Maybe This Time,* ABC, 1995.
Professor Stanley Fletcher, "Chapter Nine," *Murder One,* ABC, 1995.
Vartan Illiescu, "Bombs Away," *NYPD Blue,* ABC, 1995.
Ed Ossip (some sources cite Dominic), "Coroner's Day Off," *High Incident,* ABC, 1996.
Mark Sarison, "Quiet Riot," *Chicago Hope,* CBS, 1996.
Mr. Bartoli, "The Match Game," *ER* (also known as *Emergency Room*), NBC, 1996.
Steve Cameron, "Is Paris Burning?," *NYPD Blue,* ABC, 1997.
Bernie Gilson, "These Are the Days," *Ally McBeal,* Fox, 1998.
Bobby Snow (some sources cite Bob Show), "Trees in the Forest," *The Practice,* ABC, 1998.
Chris McIntrick, "Cinnamon Buns," *Brooklyn South,* CBS, 1998.
Agent Stevens, "The Morning After," *Roswell* (also known as *Roswell High*), The WB, 1999.
Agent Stevens, "River Dog," *Roswell* (also known as *Roswell High*), The WB, 1999.
Berry, "Truth and Consequences," *Becker,* CBS, 1999.
Guest, *Mad TV,* Fox, 2000.
Guest, "Tobacco," *Dennis Miller Live,* HBO, 2001.
Himself, *Intimate Portrait: Allison Janney,* Lifetime, 2001.
Guest, *The View,* ABC, 2002.
(Uncredited) *Saturday Night Live* (also known as *NBC's "Saturday Night," Saturday Night,* and *SNL*), NBC, 2002.
Contestant, "Tournament 1, Game 2," *Celebrity Poker Showdown,* Bravo, 2003.
Contestant, "Tournament 1 Championship," *Celebrity Poker Showdown,* Bravo, 2003.
Guest, *The Best Damn Sports Show Period,* Fox Sports Network, 2003.
Guest, *Last Call with Carson Daly,* NBC, 2004.
Guest, *On–Air with Ryan Seacrest,* syndicated, 2004.
Entourage, HBO, 2005.
The Richard and Judy Show, Channel 4 (England), 2005.

Appeared as Billy Tischler, *Doogie Howser, M.D.*, ABC; as Bobby Bruck, *South of Sunset*, CBS; and as a panelist, *The List*, VH1.

Television Appearances; Pilots:
Joey Fero, *Picket Fences*, CBS, 1992.
In Security, NBC, 1992.
(Uncredited) Agent Stevens, *Roswell* (also known as *Roswell High*), The WB, 1999.

Appeared as Chernikov in *If Not for You*, CBS.

Television Director; Episodic:
"A Good Day," *The West Wing*, NBC, 2004.
"Talking Points," *The West Wing*, NBC, 2004.

Film Appearances:
Deli clerk, *Arena Brains* (short film), 1988.
Joey Mannucci (some sources cite Pat Harding), *Medium Straight*, New Films International, 1989.
Rat Bag, *Young Guns II* (also known as *Hell Bent for Leather* and *Young Guns II: Blaze of Glory*), Twentieth Century–Fox, 1990.
Art teacher, *Rapid Fire*, Twentieth Century–Fox, 1992.
Government attorney, *Hoffa*, Twentieth Century–Fox, 1992.
Gun shop clerk, *Stop! Or My Mom Will Shoot*, Universal, 1992.
JFK reporter, *Malcolm X* (also known as *X*), Warner Bros., 1992.
Skip Thomas, *The Bodyguard*, Warner Bros., 1992.
Thompson Street photographer, *The Public Eye*, Universal, 1992.
Scanner technician, *Ghost in the Machine* (also known as *Deadly Terror*), Twentieth Century–Fox, 1993.
Young Bill, *My Life*, Columbia, 1993.
Director, *Major League II* (also known as *Wild Thing II*), Warner Bros., 1994.
Mailroom screamer, *The Hudsucker Proxy* (also known as *Hudsucker—Der grosse Sprung*), Warner Bros., 1994.
Sound technician, *Speechless*, Metro–Goldwyn–Mayer, 1994.
Train driver, *Speed*, Twentieth Century–Fox, 1994.
Eddie, *Skinner*, A–pix Entertainment, 1995.
Mark Swarr, *Se7en* (also known as *Seven*), New Line Cinema, 1995.
Trooper in trench, *Tank Girl*, United Artists, 1995.
Wiggins, *Rough Magic* (also known as *Miss Shumway jette un sort*), Samuel Goldwyn, 1995.
Audition record producer, *Grace of My Heart*, Gramercy Pictures, 1996.
Calvin, *The Arrival* (also known as *Shockwave*), Orion, 1996.
Gun shop clerk, *The Trigger Effect*, Gramercy Pictures, 1996.
Italian waiter, *Michael*, New Line Cinema, 1996.

Larry Schwartz, *City Hall*, Columbia, 1996.
Alex, *Santa Fe*, Absolute Unequivocal Productions, 1997.
District attorney Steve Waters, *Loved*, Imperial Entertainment, 1997.
Eddie Carr, *The Lost World: Jurassic Park* (also known as *Jurassic Park: The Lost World*, *Jurassic Park 2*, *The Lost World*, and *The Lost World Jurassic Park 2*), Universal, 1997.
Haskins, *Volcano*, Twentieth Century–Fox, 1997.
Jerry, *Touch*, Metro–Goldwyn–Mayer, 1997.
Dr. Gene "Geno" Reiss, *Doctor Dolittle* (also known as *Dr. Dolittle*), Twentieth Century–Fox, 1998.
Don Beiderman, *Deep Impact*, Paramount, 1998.
Phil "Philly" Francato, *Living Out Loud*, New Line Cinema, 1998.
Joe, *Forces of Nature*, DreamWorks, 1999.
Norman, *Crazy in Alabama*, Columbia, 1999.
Stanner, *Heaven*, Miramax, 1999.
Elliott, *Gun Shy*, Buena Vista, 2000.
Jerry Green, *Lucky Numbers* (also known as *Le bon numero*), Paramount, 2000.
Physical education teacher, *Whatever It Takes* (also known as *I'll Be You*), Columbia, 2000.
Turner, *I Am Sam*, New Line Cinema, 2001.
Walter Greenbaum, *What's the Worst That Could Happen?*, Metro–Goldwyn–Mayer, 2001.
Elliot Sharansky, *People I Know* (also known as *Der Innere Kreis* and *Im inneren Kreis*), Miramax, 2003.
Jerry Wexler, *Ray*, Universal, 2004.
Virgil LaRocca, *With It* (short film), MainPix, 2004.

Stage Appearances:
The Exonerated, Forty–Five Bleecker Street Theatre, New York City, between 2002 and 2004.

Appeared as Goose, *Goose and Tom Tom*, West Coast production; appeared in *Urban Folktales*, Los Angeles area production; appeared in productions as a member of the Actors' Gang.

Stage Director:
Assistant director, *SIM; or, One Night with a Lady Undertaker from Texas*, American Place Theatre, New York City, 1980.
Antigone, off–Broadway production, 1983.

RECORDINGS

Videos:
Himself, *Becoming Sam* (short documentary film), New Line Home Video, 2002.

OTHER SOURCES

Periodicals:
People Weekly, April 23, 2001, p. 71.
TV Guide, December 9, 2000, pp. 34–36.

SCHILLER, Lawrence 1936–

PERSONAL

Full name, Lawrence Julian Schiller; born December 28, 1936, in New York, NY; son of Isidore (a merchant) and Jean (a department store buyer; maiden name, Liebowitz) Schiller; married Judith Holtzer, 1961 (some sources cite 1960; divorced, 1975 [some sources cite 1974]); married Stephanie Wolf, November 5, 1977 (divorced); married Ludmilla Peresvetova (a translator), 1991 (marriage ended); married Kathy Amerman, February 15, 1997; children: (first marriage) Suzanne, Marc, Howard; (second marriage) Anthony, Cameron. *Education:* Pepperdine College, B.A.; also trained as a photojournalist. *Politics:* Democrat. *Religion:* Judaism.

Addresses: *Agent*—International Creative Management, 8942 Wilshire Blvd., Beverly Hills, CA 90211.

Career: Director, producer, cinematographer, film editor, photographer, and writer. Photojournalist with *Sport,* 1956–60, *Sports Illustrated,* 1956–64, *Life,* 1958–70, *Saturday Evening Post,* 1958–70, *London Sun Times,* 1960–69, *Paris Match,* 1960–69, *Stern,* 1960–69, and *Look,* 1963–65; creator of special photographic montages and other sequences for use in films and television productions; consultant to NBC News. Moscow International Forum on Peace, American delegate, 1987; American–Soviet Film Initiative, chair of the board of directors, 1988; U.S.S.R.–U.S.A. Bi–Lateral Talks, member, 1988.

Member: Directors Guild of America, American Federation of Television and Radio Artists, Academy of Motion Picture Arts and Sciences, Screen Actors Guild, National Press Photographers Association, California Press Photographers Association, Broadcast Music Inc., American Society of Composers, Authors and Publishers.

Awards, Honors: National Press Photographers Association Award, 1975; Emmy Award, c. 1983, for *The Executioner's Song;* Emmy Award (with others), outstanding miniseries, 1986, for *Peter the Great;* Christopher Award; award from William R. Hearst Scholastic Sports Association; Graflex Award; California Press Photographers Award; other awards, including awards for photojournalism.

CREDITS

Television Work; Series:
Executive producer, director, and cinematographer, *Trace Evidence: The Case Files of Dr. Henry Lee,* Court TV, beginning 2004.

Television Work; Miniseries:
Associate producer, *The Trial of Lee Harvey Oswald,* ABC, 1977.
Producer and director, *The Executioner's Song,* NBC, 1982.
Executive producer and director (with Marvin J. Chomsky), *Peter the Great,* NBC, 1986.
Executive producer and director, *American Tragedy,* CBS, 2000.
Executive producer and director, *Perfect Murder, Perfect Town,* CBS, 2000.
Executive producer and director, *Master Spy: The Robert Hanssen Story,* CBS, 2002.

Television Work; Movies:
Producer and director (with L. M. Kit Carson), *Hey, I'm Alive!,* 1975.
Producer, *The Winds of Kitty Hawk,* 1978.
Producer and sequence director, *Marilyn: The Untold Story,* 1980.
Executive producer, *An Act of Love: The Patricia Neal Story* (also known as *The Patricia Neal Story*), 1981.
Producer, *Raid on Short Creek* (also known as *Child Bride of Short Creek*), 1981.
Executive producer, *Her Life as a Man,* 1984.
Producer, *Murder: By Reason of Insanity* (also known as *My Sweet Victim*), 1985.
Producer, director, and still photographer, *Margaret Bourke–White* (also known as *Double Exposure* and *Double Exposure: The Story of Margaret Bourke–White*), TNT, 1989.
Director, *The Plot to Kill Hitler,* CBS, 1990.
Producer and director, *Double Jeopardy,* Showtime, 1992.

Television Work; Specials:
Producer and director, *Come with Me—Lainie Kazan,* syndicated, 1971.
Photographs, *Marilyn Monroe: The Final Days* (documentary), American Movie Classics, 2001.

Television Appearances; Miniseries:
The Executioner's Song, NBC, 1982.
Wedding photographer, *Master Spy: The Robert Hanssen Story,* CBS, 2002.

Television Appearances; Specials:
Himself, *People v. Simpson: Unfinished Business,* Court TV, 1999.

Film Work:
Special still photographer, *Butch Cassidy and the Sundance Kid,* Twentieth Century–Fox, 1969.
Director and cinematographer, *The Lexington Experience,* Corda, 1971.
Director and editor, *The American Dreamer,* EYR, 1971.

Material supplier, *Lenny,* United Artists, 1974.
Codirector, *The Man Who Skied down Everest,* 1975.
Coproducer, *Quiet Days in Clichy,* 1990.

Affiliated with other films.

WRITINGS

Screenplays:
The American Dreamer, EYR, 1971.
The Lexington Experience, Corda, 1971.

Nonfiction:
(Photographer and author of foreword) Richard Alpert and Sidney Cohen, *LSD,* New American Library, 1966.
(With Susan Atkins) *Killing of Sharon Tate,* Signet, 1970.
(With James Willwerth) *American Tragedy: The Uncensored Story of the Simpson Defense,* Random House, 1996.
Perfect Murder, Perfect Town: JonBenet and the City of Boulder, HarperCollins, 1999.
Cape May Court House, HarperCollins, 2002.
(With Norman Mailer) *Into the Mirror: The Life of Master Spy Robert P. Hanssen,* HarperCollins, 2002.

Affiliated as investigator, compiler, or interviewer with *The Scavengers and Critics of the Warren Report: The Endless Paradox,* by Richard Warren Lewis, Delacorte, 1967; *Marilyn, a Biography,* by Norman Mailer, Grosset & Dunlap, 1973; *The Faith of Graffiti,* by Mailer, Praeger, 1974; *Ladies and Gentlemen—Lenny Bruce!,* by Albert Goldman, Random House, 1975; *Muhammad Ali: A Portrait in Words and Photographs,* by Wilfrid Sheed, Crowell, 1975; *Minamata: Words and Photographs,* by W. Eugene Smith and Aileen M. Smith, 1976; *The Executioner's Song,* by Mailer, Little, Brown, 1979; *I Want to Tell You: My Response to Your Letters, Your Messages, Your Questions* (also known as *I Want to Tell You*), by O. J. Simpson, Little, Brown, 1995; *Oswald's Tale: An American Mystery,* by Mailer, Random House, 1995; and *Boulder: JonBenet and the West,* by Charles Brennan, HarperCollins, 2000; also affiliated with the book *Sunshine,* by Norma Klein. Contributor to the book series Masters of Contemporary Photography. Contributor to periodicals, including *George* and *New Yorker.*

ADAPTATIONS

The television miniseries *Perfect Murder, Perfect Town,* broadcast by CBS in 2000, was based on Schiller's book *Perfect Murder, Perfect Town: JonBenet and the*

City of Boulder. The television miniseries *American Tragedy,* broadcast by CBS in 2000, was based on Schiller's book *American Tragedy: The Uncensored Story of the Simpson Defense.*

OTHER SOURCES

Periodicals:
Business Wire, October 17, 1997.
Playboy, February, 1997, p. 47.
Publishers Weekly, April 29, 2002, p. 58.
Time, May 6, 2002, p. 8.

Electronic:
Lawrence Schiller Official Site, http://www.lawrenceschiller.com, March 15, 2005.

SCHLAMME, Thomas 1950–
(Tommy Schlamme)

PERSONAL

Full name, Thomas David Schlamme; born May 22, 1950, in Houston, TX; married Christine Lahti (an actress), September 4, 1983; children: Wilson, Joseph, Emma. *Education:* Attended University of Texas.

Addresses: *Office*—Shoe Money Productions, 4000 Warner Blvd., Building 138, Room 1101, Burbank, CA 91522. *Agent*—Ariel Emanuel, Endeavor, 9601 Wilshire Blvd., Third Floor, Beverly Hills, CA 90210. *Manager*—Rosalie Swedlin, Industry Entertainment, 955 South Carrillo Dr., Suite 300, Los Angeles, CA 90048.

Career: Director and producer. Perpetual Motion (animation company), began as messenger, became editor, then director of live action television commercials; Schlamme Productions (producers of commercials for stage plays), founder, 1980; Berner/Schlamme Productions (producers of television specials), founder; Shoe Money Productions, Burbank, CA, president. Also known as Tommy Schlamme.

Member: Directors Guild of America.

Awards, Honors: Annual CableACE Award (with others), best variety special or series, National Cable Television Association, 1996, for *Tracey Takes On ... ;* Emmy Award nomination (with others), outstanding variety, music, or comedy special, 1996, for *The Best of Tracey Takes On ... ;* Emmy Award (with others), outstanding variety, music, or comedy series, 1997, for "Las Vegas," *Tracey Takes On ...* ; Directors Guild of America Award nomination, outstanding directorial achievement in a musical or variety program, 1997, for "Romance," *Tracey Takes On ...* ; Emmy Award nomination, outstanding individual achievement in directing for a variety or music program, 1997, and Directors Guild of America Award nomination, outstanding directorial achievement in a musical or variety program, 1998, both for "1976," *Tracey Takes On ...* ; Emmy Award nomination, outstanding directing for a drama series, 1998, for "Ambush," *ER;* Emmy Award, outstanding directing for a comedy series, and Directors Guild of America Award (with others), outstanding directorial achievement in a comedy series, both 1999, for the pilot of *Sports Night;* Golden Satellite awards, best television drama series, International Press Academy, 1999 and 2000, Golden Globe Award, best television drama series, 2000, Emmy awards, outstanding drama series, 2000, 2001, 2002, and 2003, nominations for Norman Felton Television Producer of the Year Award, episodic category, Golden Laurel awards, Producers Guild of America, 2000, 2003, and 2004, and Norman Felton Television Producer of the Year awards, episodic category, 2001 and 2002, all with others, all for *The West Wing;* Emmy Award, outstanding directing for a drama series, and Directors Guild of America Award nomination, outstanding directorial achievement in a nighttime dramatic series, both 2000, for the pilot of *The West Wing;* Directors Guild of America Award (with others), outstanding directing in a comedy series, 2000, for "Small Town," *Sports Night;* nomination for Norman Felton Television Producer of the Year Award (with others), episodic category, 2000, for *Sports Night;* Emmy Award nomination, outstanding directing for a comedy series, 2000, for "Quo Vadimus," *Sports Night;* Emmy Award, outstanding directing for a drama series, 2001, for "In the Shadow of Two Gunmen: Parts 1 & 2," *The West Wing;* Directors Guild of America Award (with others), outstanding directorial achievement in a nighttime dramatic series, 2001, for "Noel," *The West Wing;* Emmy Award (with others), outstanding special class program, 2002, for *The West Wing Documentary Special;* Directors Guild of America Award nomination, outstanding directing in a nighttime dramatic series, 2002, for "Two Cathedrals," *The West Wing.*

CREDITS

Television Executive Producer; Series:
Sports Night, ABC, 1998–2000.
The West Wing, NBC, 1999–2003.
Jack & Bobby, The WB, 2004–2005.
Invasion, ABC, beginning 2005.

Television Producer; Series:
(With others) *Tracey Takes On ... ,* HBO, beginning 1996.

Television Director; Series:
Mad about You (also known as *Loved by You*), NBC, multiple episodes, 1993–96.
Sports Night, ABC, multiple episodes, 1998–2000.
The West Wing, NBC, multiple episodes, 1999–2002.

Television Director; Movies:
Crazy from the Heart, TNT, 1991.
Kingfish: A Story of Huey P. Long, TNT, 1995.

Television Director; Specials:
Bette Midler: Art or Bust!, HBO, 1984.
Whoopi Goldberg—Direct from Broadway, HBO, 1985.
"Can a Guy Say No?," *ABC Afterschool Specials,* ABC, 1986.
"The Gift of Amazing Grace," *ABC Afterschool Specials,* ABC, 1986.
A Prairie Home Companion, PBS, 1986.
Robert Klein on Broadway, HBO, 1986.
Gilbert Gottfried ... Naturally, Cinemax, 1987.
High School Video Yearbook with Franken and Davis, Cinemax, 1987.
Carol Doesn't Leifer Anymore, Cinemax, 1988.
Spalding Gray: Terrors of Pleasure, HBO, 1988.
"Mambo Mouth," *HBO Comedy Theatre,* HBO, 1991.
Rowan Atkinson Live (also known as *Rowan Atkinson: Not Just a Pretty Face* and *Rowan Atkinson on Location in Boston*), HBO, 1992.
(And producer) "Charity," "Family," and "Romance," segments of *The Best of Tracey Takes On ... ,* HBO, 1996.

Television Executive Producer; Specials:
Bette Midler: Art or Bust!, HBO, 1984.
"The Gift of Amazing Grace," *ABC Afterschool Specials,* ABC, 1986.
The West Wing Documentary Special, NBC, 2002.

Television Director; Episodic:
"Sledgepoo," *Sledge Hammer!,* ABC, 1987.
Wish You Were Here, CBS, 1990.
"Soccer," *The Wonder Years,* ABC, 1991.
"Of Mastodons and Men," *The Wonder Years,* ABC, 1992.
"Road Test," *The Wonder Years,* ABC, 1992.
"Detour Ahead," *If Not for You,* CBS, 1995.
"Growth Pains," *Chicago Hope,* CBS, 1995.
"The Quarantine," *Chicago Hope,* CBS, 1995.
"The Secret Sharer," *ER* (also known as *Emergency Room*), NBC, 1995.
"Charity," *Tracey Takes On ... ,* HBO, 1996.
"Family," *Tracey Takes On ... ,* HBO, 1996.
"Getting over the Hump," *Ink,* CBS, 1996.
"The Match Game," *ER* (also known as *Emergency Room*), ABC, 1996.
"Mind Games," *Almost Perfect,* CBS, 1996.

"The One with Russ," *Friends,* NBC, 1996.
"The One with the Lesbian Wedding," *Friends,* NBC, 1996.
"Paper Cuts," *Ink,* CBS, 1996.
"Romance," *Tracey Takes On ... ,* HBO, 1996.
"Three Men and a Lady," *Chicago Hope,* CBS, 1996.
"Ambush," *ER* (also known as *Emergency Room*), NBC, 1997.
"Betrayal," *The Practice,* ABC, 1997.
"Boy to the World," *Ally McBeal,* Fox, 1997.
"Las Vegas," *Tracey Takes On ... ,* HBO, 1997.
"1976," *Tracey Takes On ... ,* HBO, 1997.
"Overtime," *Arsenio,* ABC, 1997.
Dellaventura, CBS, 1997.
"Another List," *The Larry Sanders Show,* HBO, 1998.
"Happy Birthday, Baby," *Ally McBeal,* Fox, 1998.
"Boy to the World," *Ally* (abridged version of *Ally McBeal*), Fox, 1999.
"An Innocent Man" (also known as "You're No Jack McCallister"), *Jack & Bobby,* The WB, 2004.

Director of episodes of other series, including *It's Garry Shandling's Show,* Showtime and Fox; and *Sessions,* HBO. Director of short film segments for such programs as *That Thing on ABC* (also known as *That Thing*), ABC; *Weekend,* NBC; and productions of NBC Sports.

Television Director; Pilots:
Bette Midler's "Mondo Beyondo" (also known as *Mondo Beyondo*), HBO, 1988.
What's Alan Watching? (also known as *What's Alan Watching Now?*), CBS, 1989.
Steel Magnolias, CBS, 1990.
Man of the People, NBC, 1991.
Pride & Joy, NBC, 1995.
"Above the Fold," *Ink,* CBS, 1996.
Spin City (also known as *Spin*), ABC, 1996.
Modern Man, ABC, 1997.
Sports Night, ABC, 1998.
The West Wing, NBC, 1999.
"Chapter One," *Boston Public,* Fox, 2000.
Invasion, ABC, 2005.
The Nice Guys, CBS, 2005.

Television Director; Other:
Wayside School (animated), ABC, 1986.

Television Appearances; Episodic:
Himself, *Intimate Portrait: Christine Lahti,* Lifetime, 1998.
The Best Damn Sports Show Period, Fox Sports Network, 2003.

Film Director:
Miss Firecracker, Corsair Pictures, 1989.
So I Married an Axe Murderer, TriStar, 1993.

You So Crazy (also known as *Martin Lawrence! You So Crazy*), Samuel Goldwyn, 1994.
(And co–executive producer) *The Farnsworth Invention,* New Line Cinema, 2005.

Stage Director:
Robert Klein on Broadway (solo show), Nederlander Theatre, New York City, beginning 1986.

Director of other productions, including *Signature.*

OTHER SOURCES

Periodicals:
Playboy, October, 2001, pp. 71–82, 153–54.

━━━━━━━━━━━━━━━━━━━━━━━━

SCHWARTZ, Michael
    See BLACK, Michael Ian

━━━━━━━━━━━━━━━━━━━━━━━━

SCOTT, Keith 1954–

PERSONAL

Born 1954, in Sydney, Australia.

Addresses: *Agent*—Kazarian Spencer & Associates, Inc., 11365 Ventura Blvd., Suite 100, Studio City, CA 91604.

Career: Actor and voice performer. Warner Bros. Consumer Producers, official voice recreater for all projects in the Southern Hemisphere, 1989—; official voice of Bullwinkle (a cartoon character), 1992—; provided voices for radio and television commercials; research associate/consultant on books, including Leonard Maltin's *The Great American Broadcast,* 1997, Jordan Young's *The Laugh Crafters,* 1998, and Graham Webb's *The Animated Film Encyclopedia,* 2000; also worked as a comedian and MC.

Awards, Honors: Screen Actors Guild, American Federation of Television and Radio Artists, MEAA (Australia), Author's Society, Australia.

CREDITS

Film Appearances:
Voice, *Around the World with Dot* (animated; also known as *Dot & Santa Claus*), Hoyts Distribution, 1982.

Voices, *Dot and the Koala* (animated), 1985.

Voice, *Dot and the Whale* (animated), 1985.

Voice of Keeto, *Dot and Keeto* (animated), 1986.

Voice of radio announcer, *Frenchman's Farm,* Malo Video 1987.

Voice, *Dot Goes to Hollywood* (animated; also known as *Dot in Concert*), 1987.

Voice, *Dot and the Smugglers* (animated; also known as *Dot and the Bunyip*), 1987.

Voice, *Black Tulip* (animated), 1988.

Voice of Mad Hatter, *Alice in Wonderland* (animated), 1988 of male characters, *The Magic Riddle,* 1991.

Voice, *Blinky Bill* (animated; also known as *Blinky Bill: The Mischievous Koala*), 1992.

Go to Hell! (animated), 1997.

Narrator, *George of the Jungle,* Buena Vista, 1997.

Voices of The Phox and The Lox, *Fractured Fairy Tales: The Phox, the Box & the Lox* (animated short film), 1999.

Voices of Bluto and Popeye, *Popeye's Bilgerat Barges* (animated), 1999.

Voices of Dudley Do–Right and Inspector Fenwick, *Dudley Do–Right's "Ripsaw Falls"* (animated), 1999.

Voices of Bullwinkle J. Moose, narrator, cartoon Fearless leader, and cartoon Boris Badenov, *The Adventures of Rocky & Bullwinkle,* Universal, 2000.

Narrator, *George of the Jungle 2,* Buena Vista Home Video, 2003.

Himself, *Behind the Tunes—Wagnerian Wabbit: The Making of "What's Opera, Doc?"* (documentary short film), 2004.

Himself, *Behind the Tunes: Looney Tunes Go Hollywood* (documentary short film), 2004.

Himself, *Behind the Tunes—It Hopped One Night: A Look at "One Froggy Evening"* (documentary short film), 2004.

Himself, *Behind the Tunes—Crash! Bang! Boom!: The Wild Sounds of Treg Brown* (documentary short film), 2004.

Television Appearances; Series:

Various voices, *The Adventures of Blinky Bill* (animated), Australian Broadcasting Corporation, 1993.

(English version) Voices, *Tabaluga,* 1994.

Voice, *Blinky Bill's Extraordinary Excursion,* 1995.

Skippy: Adventures in Bushtown, 1998.

Computer voice, *Paws,* HBO, 1999.

Voice of Old Tom, *Old Tom,* 2002.

Television Appearances; Specials:

Voice of Santa Claus, *The Adventures of Candy Claus* (animated), syndicated, 1987.

Radio Appearances:

Various voices, *How Green Was My Cactus,* Australian radio, 1986—.

RECORDINGS

Video Games:

Various voices, *Rocky & Bullwinkle's "Know–It–All Quiz Game,"* 1998.

WRITINGS

Books:

The Moose That Roared (nonfiction), 2000.

Contributor to *Animato Magazine.*

OTHER SOURCES

Periodicals:

Animation World Magazine, July 1, 2000.

Electronic:

Keith Scott Official Site, http://www.keithscott.com, July 1, 2005.

·

SEAGAL, Steven 1952(?)–

(Steve Seagal, Steven Slowhand Seagal, Steven Seagel, Steven Segal)

PERSONAL

Surname is pronounced Say–gal; born April 10, 1952 (some sources cite 1950 or 1951), in Lansing, MI; raised in Lansing and in Fullerton, CA; father, a high school math teacher; mother's name, Patrizia Seagal (a medical technician); married Miyako Fujitani (a dojo owner), 1975 (divorced, 1986); married Adrienne La Russa, 1984 (marriage annulled, 1984); married Kelly LeBrock (an actress and model), September 5, 1987 (divorced, 1996); companion of Arissa Wolf; children: (first marriage) Justice (also known as Kentaro), Ayako (an actress); (third marriage) Annaliza, Dominic San Rocco, Arissa; (with Arissa Wolf) Savannah. *Education:* Attended Orange Coast College; studied martial arts in Japan; also studied acupuncture and Tibetan Buddhism. *Religion:* Buddhism. *Avocational Interests:* Animal advocacy.

Addresses: *Office*—Steamroller Productions, 4117–1/2 Radford Ave., Studio City, CA 91604. *Agent*—Cassian Elwes, William Morris Agency, One William Morris

Place, Beverly Hills, CA 90212. *Manager*—Gerry Harrington, Brillstein–Grey Entertainment, 9150 Wilshire Blvd., Suite 350, Beverly Hills, CA 90212; Jason Barrett, Jason Barrett Entertainment, 1401 Ocean Ave., Suite 301, Santa Monica, CA 90401.

Career: Actor, producer, martial arts expert, writer, and songwriter. Steamroller Productions, Studio City, CA, partner. Fight scene choreographer for motion pictures; musical performer; appeared in commercials. Earned black belt in several martial arts disciplines, including karate and aikido; Aikido Tenshin Dojo (martial arts academy), Osaka, Japan, founder; worked in international security and personal protection; owner of Aikido Ten Shin Dojo, Los Angeles, and a martial arts academy in Taos, NM. Owner of Arroyo Perdido Winery, Los Olivos, CA; investor in restaurants in Russia; promoter of Steven Seagal Essential Oil product line and of energy bars; worked in a restaurant.

Member: Screen Actors Guild.

CREDITS

Film Appearances:

Nico Toscani, *Above the Law* (also known as *Nico* and *Nico: Above the Law*), Warner Bros., 1988.

Detective Mason Storm, *Hard to Kill* (also known as *Seven Year Storm*), Warner Bros., 1990.

John Hatcher, *Marked for Death* (also known as *Screwface*), Twentieth Century–Fox, 1990.

Detective Gino Felino, *Out for Justice* (also known as *The Night* and *The Price of Our Blood*), Warner Bros., 1991.

Casey Ryback, *Under Siege* (also known as *Piege en haute mer*), Warner Bros., 1992.

Himself, *Universal Cops* (documentary), Unia Films, 1992.

Forrest Taft, *On Deadly Ground* (also known as *Rainbow Warrior* and *Spirit Warrior*), Warner Bros., 1994.

Casey Ryback, *Under Siege 2: Dark Territory* (also known as *Dark Territory, End of the Line,* and *Under Siege 2*), Warner Bros., 1995.

Jack Cole, *The Glimmer Man* (also known as *Glimmerman*), Warner Bros., 1996.

Lieutenant colonel Austin Travis, *Executive Decision* (also known as *Critical Decision*), Warner Bros., 1996.

Jack Taggart, *Fire Down Below,* Warner Bros., 1997.

Himself, *My Giant,* Columbia, 1998.

Himself, *Get Bruce!* (documentary), Miramax, 1999.

(As Steven Slowhand Seagal) Frank Glass, *Ticker,* Artisan Entertainment, 2001.

Orin Boyd, *Exit Wounds,* Warner Bros., 2001.

Sasha Petrosevitch, *Half Past Dead* (also known as *Halb tot*), Screen Gems, 2002.

Jake Hopper, *Belly of the Beast,* Millennium Films, 2003.

Jonathan Cold, *The Foreigner,* TriStar, 2003.

Professor Robert Burns (some sources cite Travis Bidner), *Out for a Kill,* TriStar, 2003.

Himself, *Words of My Perfect Teacher* (documentary), ZIJI Film and Television, 2003.

Jack Miller, *Clementine,* Pulsar Pictures, 2004.

William "Billy–Ray" Lancing, *Out of Reach,* Screen Gems, 2004.

Chris Cody, *Submerged* (also known as *Enemy Within*), Nu Image, 2005.

Cock Puncher, *The Untitled Onion Movie,* Fox Searchlight Pictures, 2005.

John Seeger, *Mercenary,* Nu Image, 2005.

Jonathan Cold, *Black Dawn,* Screen Gems, 2005.

Max (some sources cite Ellis Hall), *Today You Die,* Nu Image, 2005.

Travis Hunter (some sources cite Ross Hunter), *Into the Sun* (also known as *Yakuza*), Screen Gems, 2005.

Shadows on the Sun, Screen Gems, 2006.

Film Executive Producer:

Out of Reach, Screen Gems, 2004.

Dragon Squad, Shankara Productions/Visualizer Film Productions/Mei Ah Entertainment, 2005.

Mercenary, Nu Image, 2005.

Submerged (also known as *Enemy Within*), Nu Image, 2005.

Film Producer:

(With Andrew Davis) *Above the Law* (also known as *Nico* and *Nico: Above the Law*), Warner Bros., 1988.

(With Michael Grais and Mark Victor) *Marked for Death* (also known as *Screwface*), Twentieth Century–Fox, 1990.

(With Arnold Kopelson) *Out for Justice* (also known as *The Night* and *The Price of Our Blood*), Warner Bros., 1991.

Under Siege (also known as *Piege en haute mer*), Warner Bros., 1992.

On Deadly Ground (also known as *Rainbow Warrior* and *Spirit Warrior*), Warner Bros., 1994.

Under Siege 2: Dark Territory (also known as *Dark Territory, End of the Line,* and *Under Siege 2*), Warner Bros., 1995.

My Giant, Columbia, 1998.

Prince of Central Park, Keystone Entertainment, 1999.

Half Past Dead (also known as *Halb tot*), Screen Gems, 2002.

Belly of the Beast, Millennium Films, 2003.

The Foreigner, TriStar, 2003.

Out for a Kill, TriStar, 2003.

Into the Sun (also known as *Yakuza*), Screen Gems, 2005.

Today You Die, Nu Image, 2005.

Some sources cite work on the film *Unleashed.*

Film Director:
On Deadly Ground (also known as *Rainbow Warrior* and *Spirit Warrior*), Warner Bros., 1994.

Film Martial Arts Choreographer or Coordinator:
(As Steve Seagal) *The Challenge* (also known as *Equals* and *Sword of the Ninja*), Rank Film Distributors, 1982.
(Uncredited) *Never Say Never Again* (also known as *James Bond 007—Sag niemals nie*), Orion/Warner Bros., 1983.
Above the Law (also known as *Nico* and *Nico: Above the Law*), Warner Bros., 1988.
Hard to Kill (also known as *Seven Year Storm*), Warner Bros., 1990.
Marked for Death (also known as *Screwface*), Twentieth Century–Fox, 1990.

Worked as a martial arts instructor for other films.

Film Song Producer:
Under Siege 2: Dark Territory (also known as *Dark Territory, End of the Line,* and *Under Siege 2*), Warner Bros., 1995.
The Glimmer Man (also known as *Glimmerman*), Warner Bros., 1996.
Fire Down Below, Warner Bros., 1997.

Television Appearances; Series:
Himself, *Dreams of Tibet* (documentary), PBS, beginning 1997.

Television Appearances; Movies:
Dr. Wesley McClaren, *The Patriot,* HBO, 1998.

Television Appearances; Specials:
"Naked Hollywood," *A & E Premieres,* Arts and Entertainment, 1991.
Happy Birthday Elizabeth—A Celebration of Life, ABC, 1997.
A Tribute to Muddy Waters, King of the Blues, PBS, 1999.
AFI's 100 Years, 100 Thrills: America's Most Heart–Pounding Movies, CBS, 2001.
(In archive footage) Himself, *Who Is Alan Smithee?,* American Movie Classics, 2002.

Television Appearances; Awards Presentations:
Presenter, *The 67th Annual Academy Awards,* ABC, 1995.
Presenter, *The 68th Annual Academy Awards,* ABC, 1996.
Presenter, *The 1998 World Music Awards,* ABC, 1998.

The 1998 VH1 Fashion Awards, VH1, 1998.
(As Steven Seagel) *2000 MTV Movie Awards,* MTV, 2000.

Television Appearances; Episodic:
Guest host, *Saturday Night Live* (also known as *NBC's "Saturday Night," Saturday Night,* and *SNL*), NBC, 1991.
Guest, *The Late Show with David Letterman* (also known as *The Late Show*), CBS, 1994, 1997.
Himself, "Roseambo," *Roseanne,* ABC, 1996.
Guest, *The Rosie O'Donnell Show,* syndicated, 1997.
Sin City Spectacular (also known as *Penn & Teller's "Sin City Spectacular"*), FX Channel, 1998.
Guest, *The Tonight Show with Jay Leno,* NBC, 2001.
Himself, *Stevan Seagal: The E! True Hollywood Story,* E! Entertainment Television, 2002.
Guest, *Tinseltown TV,* International Channel, 2003.
(As Steven Segal; in archive footage) *Celebrities Uncensored,* E! Entertainment Television, 2004.
Himself, *20h10 petantes,* 2004.
Himself, "Steven Seagal," *Biography* (also known as *A&E Biography: Steven Seagal*), Arts and Entertainment, 2005.

Television Work; Movies:
Producer, *The Patriot,* HBO, 1998.

RECORDINGS

Videos:
Celebrity Guide to Wine, Malofilm Distribution, 1990.
Narrator and executive producer, *The Path beyond Thought* (also known as *Aikido: The Path beyond Thought*), Steamroller Productions, 2001.
Himself, *The Art of Action: Martial Arts in Motion Picture,* Columbia/TriStar, 2002.

Albums:
(And producer) *Songs from the Crystal Cave,* Outwest Records, 2004.

WRITINGS

Screenplays:
Hard to Kill (also known as *Seven Year Storm*), Warner Bros., 1990.
Out for Justice (also known as *The Night* and *The Price of Our Blood*), Warner Bros., 1991.
Exit Wounds, Warner Bros., 2001.
Into the Sun (also known as *Yakuza*), Screen Gems, 2005.

Stories for Films:
(With Andrew Davis) *Above the Law* (also known as *Nico* and *Nico: Above the Law*), Warner Bros., 1988.
Belly of the Beast, Millennium Films, 2003.

Film Music; Songs:

Under Siege 2: Dark Territory (also known as *Dark Territory, End of the Line,* and *Under Siege 2*), Warner Bros., 1995.

The Glimmer Man (also known as *Glimmerman*), Warner Bros., 1996.

Fire Down Below, Warner Bros., 1997.

"Love Doctor," *Ticker,* Artisan Entertainment, 2001.

Into the Sun (also known as *Yakuza*), Screen Gems, 2005.

Albums:

Songs from the Crystal Cave, Outwest Records, 2004.

Nonfiction:

Contributor to Japanese magazines and newspapers.

OTHER SOURCES

Periodicals:

Entertainment Weekly, February 10, 1995, pp. 6–7; April 5, 1996, p. 14; May 17, 1996, p. 13; October 11, 1996, p. 19; November 15, 1996, p. 16; April 13, 2001, p. 80.

Esquire, July, 1995, pp. 124–25.

GQ, March, 1991, p. 231.

Movieline, April, 1991.

People Weekly, November 19, 1990, p. 163; December 9, 2002, p. 141.

Prevue, October, 1991, pp. 18–23.

Time, November 14, 1994, p. 39; March 18, 1996, p. 101; June 23, 1997, p. 85.

Vanity Fair, February, 1993, p. 100.

Electronic:

Steven Seagal Official Site, http://www.stevenseagal.com, March 15, 2004.

SEINFELD, Jerry 1954(?)–

PERSONAL

Full name, Jerome Seinfeld; born April 29, 1954 (some sources cite 1955), in Brooklyn, New York, NY; raised in Massapequa, Long Island, NY; son of Kalman (an owner of a sign company) and Betty Seinfeld; married Jessica Sklar (a public relations executive), December 25, 1999; children: Sascha, Julian Kal, Shepherd Kellen. *Education:* Queens College at City University of New York, B.A., 1976; attended State University of New York Oswego. *Avocational Interests:* Porsche automobiles, collecting sneakers, baseball.

Addresses: *Agent*—George Shapiro, Shapiro/West and Associates, 141 El Camino Dr., Suite 205, Beverly Hills, CA 90212.

Career: Comedian, actor, and writer. Toured regularly as a stand–up comedian; appeared at clubs, including Catch a Rising Star, New York City, 1976; Comic Strip, worked as the master of ceremonies. Appeared in commercials, public service announcements, and print advertisements. Featured in archive footage in the short documentary film *Disneyland: The First 50 Magical Years,* shown at Disneyland, 2005–06. Worked as a salesperson, street vendor, and waiter. Jerry Seinfeld Family and Scholarship Foundation, founder.

Awards, Honors: American Comedy Award, funniest comedy club male stand–up comic, 1988; Clio Award, best announcer of a radio commercial, 1988; Emmy Award nomination (with others), outstanding writing in a comedy series, 1991, American Comedy awards, funniest male performer in a leading role in a television series, 1992 and 1993, Emmy Award nominations, outstanding lead actor in a comedy series, 1992, 1993, 1994, 1995, and 1996, Emmy Award nominations (with others), outstanding comedy series, 1992, 1994, 1995, 1996, 1997, and 1998, Emmy Award (with others), outstanding comedy series, 1993, Q Award, best actor in a quality comedy series, Viewers for Quality Television, 1993, Golden Globe Award, best performance by an actor in a television series—comedy or musical, 1994, Nova Award (with Larry David), most promising producer in television, Golden Laurel awards, Producers Guild of America, 1994, Screen Actors Guild awards (with others), outstanding ensemble in a comedy series, 1994, 1996, 1997, and 1998, Golden Globe Award nominations, best performance by an actor in a television series—comedy or musical, 1995, 1996, and 1998, People's Choice Award, favorite television actor, 1996, American Comedy Award nomination, funniest male performer in a leading role in a television series, 1996, and People's Choice Award, favorite television comedy series, 1998, all for *Seinfeld;* honorary doctorate, Queens College, City University of New York, 1994; Emmy Award nomination (with others), outstanding variety, music, or comedy special, and American Comedy Award nomination, funniest male performer in a television special, both 1999, for *Jerry Seinfeld: "I'm Telling You for the Last Time";* American Film Institute Star Award, U.S. Comedy Arts Festival, 1999; named one of the "100 greatest entertainers," *Entertainment Weekly,* 1999; Aftonbladet TV prizes, best foreign male television personality, 1999 and 2000; Chairman's Award, National Association of Television Program Executives, 2001; named one of the "200 greatest pop culture icons," VH1, 2003; named one of the "100 greatest stand–ups of all time," Comedy Central, 2004.

CREDITS

Television Appearances; Series:

Frankie (the governor's joke writer), *Benson*, ABC, 1980–81.

Jerry Seinfeld (title role), *Seinfeld*, NBC, 1990–98.

Television Appearances; Miniseries:

Himself, *The Hamptons*, ABC, 2002.

(In archive footage) Himself, *200 Greatest Pop Culture Icons*, VH1, 2003.

(In archive footage) Himself, *Comedy Central Presents: 100 Greatest Stand–Ups of All Time*, Comedy Central, 2004.

Television Appearances; Movies:

Network representative, *The Rating Game* (also known as *The Mogul*), The Movie Channel, 1984.

Second prison man, *Pros and Cons*, Cinemax, 1999.

Television Appearances; Specials:

Sixth Annual Young Comedians (also known as *HBO's "Sixth Annual Young Comedians"*), HBO, 1981.

The Tonight Show Starring Johnny Carson 19th Anniversary Special, NBC, 1981.

Disneyland's Summer Vacation Party, NBC, 1986.

"*Rodney Dangerfield—It's Not Easy Bein' Me*," *On Location*, HBO, 1986.

The Tommy Chong Roast (also known as *Playboy Comedy Roast—Tommy Chong*), 1986.

The Tonight Show Starring Johnny Carson 24th Anniversary Special, NBC, 1986.

"*Jerry Seinfeld—Stand–Up Confidential*," *On Location*, HBO, 1987.

An All–Star Celebration: The '88 Vote, ABC, 1988.

Get Out the Vote, 1988.

Himself, *Late Night with David Letterman Seventh Anniversary Show*, NBC, 1989.

"*Montreal International Comedy Festival*," *HBO Comedy Hour*, HBO, 1989.

Host, *The Second Annual Aspen Comedy Festival*, Showtime, 1990.

Host, *Spy Magazine Presents How to Be Famous*, NBC, 1990.

Funny Business with Charlie Chase III, The Nashville Network, 1990.

Night of 100 Stars III (also known as *Night of One Hundred Stars*), NBC, 1990.

The Second Annual Valvoline National Driving Test, CBS, 1990.

Back to School '92, CBS, 1992.

The Barbara Walters Special, ABC, 1992.

Carol Leifer: Gaudy, Bawdy and Blue, Showtime, 1992.

Free to Laugh: A Comedy and Music Special for Amnesty International, Lifetime, 1992.

HBO's 20th Anniversary—We Hardly Believe It Ourselves, CBS and HBO, 1992.

Today at 40, NBC, 1992.

Himself, *The Barbara Walters Special with Kathie Lee and Frank Gifford, Al Pacino, Jerry Seinfeld, and Clint Eastwood*, ABC, 1993.

Baseball Relief: An All–Star Comedy Salute, Fox, 1993.

Laughing Matters (also known as *Funny Business*), Showtime, 1993.

The NBC Super Special All–Star Comedy Hour, NBC, 1993.

Rolling Stone '93: The Year in Review, Fox, 1993.

What Is This Thing Called Love? (also known as *The Barbara Walters Special*), ABC, 1993.

Host, *Abbott and Costello Meet Jerry Seinfeld*, NBC, 1994.

20 Years of Comedy on HBO, HBO, 1995.

Classic Stand–Up Comedy of Television, NBC, 1996.

Comedy Club Superstars (also known as *Comedy Club All–Stars*), ABC, 1996.

The Late Show with David Letterman Video Special 2 (also known as *The Late Show with David Letterman Primetime Video Special 2*), CBS, 1996.

MDA Jerry Lewis Telethon, syndicated, 1997.

Rodney Dangerfield's 75th Birthday Toast, HBO, 1997.

Himself, *Jerry Seinfeld: "I'm Telling You for the Last Time,"* HBO, 1998.

The Late Show with David Letterman Fifth Anniversary Special, CBS, 1998.

Seinfeld: The Chronicle, NBC, 1998.

Larry David: Curb Your Enthusiasm, HBO, 1999.

Saturday Night Live: Game Show Parodies, NBC, 1999.

Saturday Night Live: 25th Anniversary, NBC, 1999.

The Concert for New York City, VH1, 2001.

Mark Twain Prize—Celebrating the Humor of Carl Reiner, PBS, 2001.

Diet Coke with Lemon Celebrates 40 Years of Laughter: At the Improv, NBC, 2002.

(In archive footage) *Just for Laughs*, 2002.

NBC 75th Anniversary Special (also known as *NBC 75th Anniversary Celebration*), NBC, 2002.

TV Guide 50 Best Shows of All Time: A 50th Anniversary Celebration, ABC, 2002.

Host, *The Seinfeld Story*, NBC, 2004.

(In archive footage) *101 Most Unforgettable SNL Moments*, E! Entertainment Television, 2004.

Appeared in a tribute to Brandon Tartikoff, 1997. Some sources cite an appearance in *When Cameras Cross the Line*, Fox, c. 2000.

Television Appearances; Awards Presentations:

Presenter, *The 42nd Annual Primetime Emmy Awards Presentation*, Fox, 1990.

The Fourth Annual American Comedy Awards, ABC, 1990.

Cohost, *The 43rd Annual Primetime Emmy Awards Presentation* (also known as *The Emmys* and *The 43rd Annual Emmy Awards*), Fox, 1991.

Presenter, *The 44th Annual Primetime Emmy Awards,* Fox, 1992.

The Sixth Annual American Comedy Awards, ABC, 1992.

Presenter, *The 45th Annual Primetime Emmy Awards,* 1993.

The American Television Awards, ABC, 1993.

The Seventh Annual American Comedy Awards, ABC, 1993.

Presenter, *The 46th Annual Primetime Emmy Awards,* ABC, 1994.

Presenter, *The 47th Annual Primetime Emmy Awards,* Fox, 1995.

Presenter, *The Ninth Annual American Comedy Awards,* ABC, 1995.

Presenter, *The Second Annual Screen Actors Guild Awards,* NBC, 1996.

Presenter, *The 49th Annual Primetime Emmy Awards,* CBS, 1997.

The 24th Annual People's Choice Awards, CBS, 1998.

Presenter, *The 41st Annual Grammy Awards,* CBS, 1999.

The 51st Annual Primetime Emmy Awards, Fox, 1999.

The British Comedy Awards 2001, Independent Television, 2001.

The 34th Annual Songwriters Hall of Fame Awards, Bravo, 2003.

Television Appearances; Episodic:

Guest, *The John Davidson Show,* syndicated, 1981.

Himself, *The Tonight Show Starring Johnny Carson,* NBC, multiple episodes, 1981–91.

Himself, *Late Night with David Letterman,* NBC, multiple episodes, 1982–93.

Guest, *Just Men!,* NBC, 1983.

Himself, *Our Time,* NBC, 1985.

Guest, *The Howard Stern Show,* syndicated, 1991.

Alan King: Inside the Comedy Mind, 1991.

Guest host, *Saturday Night Live* (also known as *NBC's "Saturday Night," Saturday Night,* and *SNL*), NBC, 1992, 1999.

Himself, "The Grand Opening," *The Larry Sanders Show,* HBO, 1993.

Himself, "Johnny Goes Hollywood," *The New WKRP in Cincinnati,* syndicated, 1993.

Guest, "American Inefficiency," *Dennis Miller Live,* HBO, 1994.

Guest, *The Late Show with David Letterman* (also known as *The Late Show*), CBS, multiple appearances, beginning 1994.

Guest, "Driving," *Dennis Miller Live,* HBO, 1997.

Himself, "The Raw Deal," *NewsRadio* (also known as *News Radio* and *The Station*), NBC, 1997.

Himself, "Flip," *The Larry Sanders Show,* HBO, 1998.

Himself, "Jerry Seinfeld: Master of His Domain," *Biography* (also known as *A&E Biography: Jerry Seinfeld: Master of His Domain*), Arts and Entertainment, 1998.

Himself, "Season Opener," *Mad about You* (also known as *Loved by You*), NBC, 1998.

Guest, *The Howard Stern Show,* E! Entertainment Television, 1998.

Voice of Comp–u–Comp, "The Return," *Dilbert* (animated), UPN, 2000.

Guest, "Dennis Miller/Jerry Seinfeld," *Primetime Glick,* Comedy Central, 2001.

Guest, *The Tonight Show with Jay Leno,* NBC, 2002, 2003, 2004.

Guest, "New York Yankees: Part 1," *SportsCentury,* ESPN, 2003.

(In archive footage) Himself, *Celebrities Uncensored,* E! Entertainment Television, multiple episodes in 2003.

(Uncredited) Himself, "Opening Night," *Curb Your Enthusiasm,* HBO, 2004.

Guest, *The Daily Show* (also known as *The Daily Show with Jon Stewart* and *The Daily Show with Jon Stewart Global Edition*), Comedy Central, 2004.

Guest, *The Oprah Winfrey Show* (also known as *Oprah*), syndicated, 2004.

Guest, *Live with Regis and Kelly,* syndicated, 2004, 2005.

Appeared in episodes of *Celebrity Profile* (also known as *E! Celebrity Profile*), E! Entertainment Television; *An Evening at the Improv,* syndicated and Arts and Entertainment; *Love and War,* CBS; *The Merv Griffin Show,* NBC, syndicated, and CBS; *Stand Up America,* BBC; and *Tough Crowd with Colin Quinn* (also known as *Tough Crowd*), Comedy Central.

Television Appearances; Pilots:

Jerry Seinfeld (title role), *Seinfeld* (also known as *Good News, Bad News* and *The Seinfeld Chronicles*), NBC, 1989.

Television Work; Series:

Creator, *Seinfeld,* NBC, 1990–98.

Producer, *Seinfeld,* NBC, 1991–96.

Executive producer, *Seinfeld,* NBC, 1996–98.

Television Work; Specials:

Creator and executive producer, *Seinfeld: The Chronicle,* NBC, 1998.

Executive producer, *Jerry Seinfeld: "I'm Telling You for the Last Time,"* HBO, 1998.

Segment director, *The Concert for New York City,* VH1, 2001.

Executive producer, *The Seinfeld Story,* NBC, 2004.

Television Work; Pilots:

(With Larry David) Creator, *Seinfeld* (also known as *Good News, Bad News* and *The Seinfeld Chronicles*), NBC, 1989.

Film Appearances:

Himself, *Good Money*, Pfquad Group, 1995.
(In archive footage) *Full Mountie*, 2000.
Himself, *Comedian* (documentary), Miramax, 2002.
Himself, *Hindsight Is 20/20* (short film), 2004.
Himself, *A Uniform Used to Mean Something* (short film), 2004.
Voice of Barry B. Benson, *Bee Movie* (animated), DreamWorks, 2006.

Film Work:

Executive producer, *Comedian* (documentary), Miramax, 2002.
Producer, *Bee Movie* (animated), DreamWorks, 2006.

Stage Appearances:

Night of 100 Stars III (also known as *Night of One Hundred Stars*), Radio City Music Hall, New York City, 1990.
I'm Telling You for the Last Time (solo show; also known as *Jerry Seinfeld, Live on Broadway: "I'm Telling You for the Last Time"*), Broadhurst Theatre, New York City, beginning 1998.

Major Tours:

I'm Telling You for the Last Time (solo show; also known as *Jerry Seinfeld, Live on Broadway: "I'm Telling You for the Last Time"*), international cities, 1998.

Radio Appearances:

Guest, *The Howard Stern Radio Show*, 1998.

RECORDINGS

Videos:

Himself, *Doctor Duck's Super Secret All–Purpose Sauce*, Music Video Distributors, 1985.
Johnny Carson: The Comedians—"Good Stuff"—Stand–Up Debuts from "The Tonight Show Starring Johnny Carson," Buena Vista Home Video, 1996.

Albums:

I'm Telling You for the Last Time (also known as *Jerry Seinfeld: "I'm Telling You for the Last Time"* and *Jerry Seinfeld Live on Broadway: "I'm Telling You for the Last Time"*), Universal, 1998.

CD ROMS:

Appeared in *The Seinfeld CD–ROM* (based on the television show *Seinfeld*), Arts and Commerce.

Audiobooks:

Jerry Seinfeld, *Halloween*, Little, Brown/Byron Preiss, 2002.

WRITINGS

Teleplays with Others; Series:

Seinfeld, NBC, 1990–96, some teleplays published as *The Seinfeld Scripts: The First and Second Seasons*, Harper, 1998.

Teleplays; Specials:

"Jerry Seinfeld—Stand–Up Confidential," *On Location*, HBO, 1987.
Jerry Seinfeld: "I'm Telling You for the Last Time," HBO, 1998.
(With others) *The Seinfeld Story*, NBC, 2004.

Author of material appearing in various specials.

Teleplays with Others; Episodic:

Writer for *An Evening at the Improv*, syndicated and Arts and Entertainment.

Teleplays; Pilots:

Seinfeld (also known as *Good News, Bad News* and *The Seinfeld Chronicles*), NBC, 1989.

Screenplays:

Author of material, *Comedian* (documentary), Miramax, 2002.
Hindsight Is 20/20 (short film), 2004.
A Uniform Used to Mean Something (short film), 2004.
Bee Movie (animated), DreamWorks, 2006.

Writings for the Stage:

I'm Telling You for the Last Time (solo show; also known as *Jerry Seinfeld, Live on Broadway: "I'm Telling You for the Last Time"*), international cities, 1998, Broadhurst Theatre, New York City, beginning 1998.

Humor:

SeinLanguage, Bantam, 1993.

Author of the introduction (some sources cite the anonymous author) of *Letters from a Nut*, by Ted L. Nancy, William Morrow, 1997; *More Letters from a Nut*, by Ted L. Nancy, Bantam, 1998; and *The Moron Stories of Ed Broth*, by Ed Broth, St. Martin's Press, 2003. Author of the "backword" (some sources cite the anonymous author) of *Extra Nutty! Even More Letters from a Nut!*, by Ted L. Nancy, St. Martin's Press, 2000.

Nonfiction:

Sein Off: The Final Days of Seinfeld, HarperEntertainment, 1998.

Writings for Children:

Halloween, Little, Brown, 2002.

OTHER SOURCES

Books:

Authors and Artists for Young Adults, Volume 11, Gale, 1993.

Contemporary Authors, Volume 140, Gale, 1993.

Costanza, Mike, and Greg Lawrence, *The Real Seinfeld—As Told by the Real Costanza,* WorldWise Books, 1998.

Newsmakers 1992 Cumulation, Gale, 1992.

Oppenheimer, Jerry, *Seinfeld: The Making of an American Icon,* HarperCollins, 2002.

Tracy, Kathleen, *Jerry Seinfeld: The Entire Domain,* Birch Lane Press, 1998.

Periodicals:

Cable TV, August, 1998, p. 31.

Entertainment Weekly, March 1, 1991, pp. 29–30; September 11, 1992, p. 35; November 7, 1997, pp. 8–9; November 1, 1999, p. 115; April 28, 2000, p. 11.

Forbes, March 22, 1999, p. 180.

Hollywood Reporter, July 16, 1991.

Newsweek, November 22, 1999, p. 71; April 17, 2000, p. 69; October 21, 2002, p. 79.

New York, February 20, 1995, p. 45.

New York Times, September 29, 1991, pp. H33–H34; January 29, 1998; March 24, 2002, p. 8; May 19, 2002, p. AR34; May 11, 2003.

People Weekly, June 4, 1990, p. 14; December 2, 1991, pp. 87–88; January 12, 1998, p. 118; May 18, 1998, p. 124; November 2, 1998, p. 11; November 22, 1999, pp. 178–82, 184; January 1, 2000, p. 56; April 24, 2000, p. 17; July 3, 2000, p. 17; November 20, 2000, p. 91; October 21, 2002, p. 86.

Rolling Stone, September 22, 1994, pp. 47–50, 112–14; May 28, 1998, pp. 64–75, 200–206.

Time, January 12, 1998, p. 76; April 24, 2000, p. 94; November 4, 2002, p. 74.

TV Guide, May 23, 1992, pp. 11–15; August 8, 1998, pp. 37–39; November 21, 1998, pp. 34–38; January 22, 2000, pp. 52–54; June 30, 2001, pp. 12–19; July 18, 2004, pp. 26–27.

USA Today, October 2, 1991, p. D1.

US Weekly, April 4, 1991, pp. 16–19; March 18, 2002, pp. 24–25; October 7, 2002.

Vanity Fair, May, 1998.

Variety, July 21, 2003, p. 5.

Washington Post, October 20, 2002, pp. G1, G7.

SEVIGNY, Chloe 1974–

PERSONAL

Born November 18, 1974, in Springfield, MA; raised in Darien, CT; father, in insurance sales and a interior painter (some sources cite original occupation as accountant); mother's name, Janine Sevigny; sister of Paul Sevigny (a disc jockey). *Avocational Interests:* Sewing.

Addresses: *Agent*—Endeavor, 9601 Wilshire Blvd., Beverly Hills, CA 90210. *Manager*—Danny Sussman, Brillstein–Grey Entertainment, 9150 Wilshire Blvd., Suite 350, Beverly Hills, CA 90212. *Publicist*—Amanda Horton, ALH Public Relations, 686 South Arroyo Blvd., Pasadena, CA 91105.

Career: Actress. *Sassy* (magazine), intern, beginning c. 1993; Liquid Sky (clothing and music store), Brooklyn Heights, New York, NY, salesclerk, beginning 1993; salesclerk at other stores. Appeared in television commercials and print advertisements; worked as a model; spokesperson for MAC Cosmetics, beginning 2004; Imitation of Christ (fashion label), model and creative director.

Awards, Honors: Independent Spirit Award nomination, best supporting female, Independent Features Project/West, 1996, for *Kids;* Los Angeles Film Critics Association Award and Boston Society of Film Critics Award, both best supporting actress, 1999, Independent Spirit Award, National Society of Film Critics Award, Chicago Film Critics Association Award, Sierra Award, Las Vegas Film Critics Society, Golden Satellite Award, International Press Academy, Academy Award nomination, Golden Globe Award nomination, Screen Actors Guild Award nomination, Chlotrudis Award nomination, and Online Film Critics Society Award nomination, all best supporting actress, 2000, and MTV Movie Award nomination (with Hilary Swank), best kiss, 2000, all for *Boys Don't Cry.*

CREDITS

Film Appearances:

Jennie, *Kids,* Miramax, 1995.

Debbie, *Trees Lounge,* LIVE Entertainment, 1996.

Dot, *Gummo,* Fine Line Features, 1997.

Alice Kinnon, *The Last Days of Disco,* Gramercy Pictures, 1998.

Odette Malroux, *Palmetto* (also known as *Dumme sterben nicht aus*), Columbia, 1998.

Carole Mackessy, *A Map of the World* (also known as *Unschuldig verfolgt*), USA Films, 1999.
Lana Tisdel, *Boys Don't Cry* (also known as *Take It Like a Man*), Twentieth Century–Fox/Fox Searchlight Pictures, 1999.
Pearl, *Julien Donkey–Boy* (also known as *julien donkey–boy* and *Dogme #6—Julien Donkey–Boy*), Fine Line Features, 1999.
Jean, *American Psycho,* Lions Gate Films, 2000.
"Int. Trailer Night," *Ten Minutes Older: The Trumpet,* Blue Dolphin Film Distribution, 2002.
Caitlin Avey, *Shattered Glass,* Lions Gate Films, 2003.
Herself, *Dogville Confessions,* Trust Film Sales, 2003.
Elise Lipsky, *Demonlover,* Palm Pictures, 2003.
Gitsie, *Party Monster,* Strand Releasing/ContentFilm, 2003.
Herself, *Death of a Dynasty,* TLA Releasing, 2004.
Herself, *The Making of "Invasion of the Freedom Snatchers,"* Behind the Scenes Productions, 2004.
Daisy, *The Brown Bunny,* Wellspring Media, 2004.
Laurel, *Melinda and Melinda,* Twentieth Century–Fox, 2004.
Liz Henson, *Dogville* (also known as *U—Der Film "Dogville" erzaehlt in neun Kapiteln und einem Prolog.*), Lions Gate Films, 2004.
Clara, *3 Needles,* ThinkFilm, 2005.
Philomena, *Manderlay,* Trust Film Sales, 2005.
Zodiac, Paramount, 2006.

Some sources cite an appearance in *The Assumption.*

Film Work:
Costume designer, *Gummo,* Fine Line Features, 1997.

Television Appearances; Series:
Nicki Henderson, *Big Love,* HBO, beginning 2006.

Television Appearances; Movies:
Amy, "1972," *If These Walls Could Talk 2,* HBO, 2000.
Nurse, *Mrs. Harris,* HBO, 2005.

Television Appearances; Specials:
Herself, *The Road to Manderlay* (documentary), [Denmark], 2005.

Television Appearances; Awards Presentations:
The 15th Annual IFP/West Independent Spirit Awards, Bravo and Independent Film Channel, 2000.
The 72nd Annual Academy Awards, ABC, 2000.
The VH1/Vogue Fashion Awards, VH1, 2000.
Presenter, *The 2001 IFP/West Independent Spirit Awards* (also known as *The 16th Annual IFP/West Independent Spirit Awards*), Independent Film Channel, 2001.
Herself, *Ceremonia de apertura del festival de cine de San Sebastian,* Canal+ Espana (Spain), 2004.

Television Appearances; Episodic:
Guest, *The Late Show with David Letterman* (also known as *The Late Show*), CBS, 1998, 2003.
Guest, *Late Night with Conan O'Brien,* NBC, 2003.
Monet, "East Side Story," *Will & Grace,* NBC, 2004.
Herself, *Silenci?,* Televisio de Catalunya (Spain), 2005.

Television Appearances; Pilots:
Nicki Henderson, *Big Love,* HBO, 2006.

Stage Appearances:
Hazelwood Jr. High, New Group, New York City, 1998.
Miss Geraldine Barclay, *What the Butler Saw,* New Group Theatre at St. Clement's Theatre, New York City, 2000.

Appeared in summer theatre productions.

RECORDINGS

Videos:
Herself, *The Making of "American Psycho,"* Lions Gate Films, 2000.
(In archive footage) *Sex at 24 Frames per Second* (documentary; also known as *Playboy Presents "Sex at 24 Frames per Second: The Ultimate Journey through Sex in Cinema"*), Playboy Entertainment Group, 2003.

Music Videos:
Sonic Youth, "Sugar Kane," 1993.
The Lemonheads, "Big Gay Heart," 1994.

OTHER SOURCES

Books:
Newsmakers, Issue 4, Gale, 2001.

Periodicals:
Current Biography, August, 2000.
Empire, October, 1998, pp. 58–59.
Entertainment Weekly, October 11, 1996, p. 69; March 1, 2000, p. 57.
Interview, August, 1995, pp. 62–66; November, 1999, p. 66; September, 2000, pp. 150, 183.
People Weekly, August 7, 1995, p. 12; October 14, 1996, p. 29; June 8, 1998, p. 37.
Premiere, March, 2004, pp. 84–87, 119.
Psychology Today, September/October, 2003, pp. 30–36.
Rolling Stone, November 13, 2003, pp. 49–50.
Sweater, October, 1997, pp. 40–43.
Vogue, July, 2000, pp. 30–32; August, 2002, pp. 230–33.

SEXTON Brendan III 1980–
(Brendan Sexton, Brendan Sexton, Jr.)

PERSONAL

Full name, Brendan Eugene Sexton III; born February 21, 1980, in Staten Island, New York, NY. *Education:* Attended High School for the Humanities, New York City.

Addresses: *Agent*—Sally Ware, The Gersh Agency, 232 North Canon Dr., Beverly Hills, CA 90210.

Career: Actor.

Awards, Honors: Independent Spirit Award nomination, best debut performance, Independent Features Project/West, 1997, for *Welcome to the Dollhouse.*

CREDITS

Film Appearances:
(As Brendan Sexton, Jr.) Brandon McCarthy, *Welcome to the Dollhouse* (also known as *Middle Child*), Sony Pictures Classics, 1995.
(As Brendan Sexton) Shoplifter Warren Beatty, *Empire Records* (also known as *Empire* and *Rock & Fun*), Warner Bros., 1995.
Boom (short film), 1996.
Bob, *A, B, C ... Manhattan,* Alphaville Films/Open City Films, 1997.
(As Brendan Sexton, Jr.) Soldier, *Arresting Gena,* Fuel Films, 1997.
Blue Baxter, *Desert Blue,* Samuel Goldwyn, 1998.
Marcus, *Hurricane Streets* (also known as *Hurricane* and *Hurricane Club*), Metro–Goldwyn–Mayer, 1998.
Matt, *Pecker* (also known as *I Love Pecker*), Fine Line Features, 1998.
Mooney, *Spark,* Rosefunk Pictures, 1998.
Myth America, 1998.
Tom Nissen, *Boys Don't Cry* (also known as *Take It Like a Man*), Twentieth Century–Fox/Fox Searchlight Pictures, 1999.
Dez, *Muse 6,* 2000.
Voice of Herschel, *Herschel Hopper: New York Rabbit* (animated short film), Rumpus Toys, 2000.
Jeff, *Session 9,* USA Films, 2001.
Private first class Richard "Alphabet" Kowalewski, *Black Hawk Down,* Columbia, 2001.
Robbie, *Winter Solstice,* Paramount, 2004.
Daniel Symptom, *This Revolution,* Artists/Media Co–Operative/Guerrilla News Network, 2005.
Ludlow, *Love, Ludlow,* Washington Square Films, 2005.

(Uncredited) Store clerk, *Hide and Seek,* Twentieth Century–Fox, 2005.
Little Fugitive, Ruby Slipper Productions, 2005.
Ethan, *The Secret,* EuropaCorp Distribution, 2006.
Grant, *Just Like the Son,* 2006.

Stage Appearances:
Oliver (musical), c. 1988.
Joshua, *The Moonlight Room,* Worth Street Theatre Company, Samuel Beckett Theatre, New York City, 2004.

RECORDINGS

Videos:
Himself, *The Essence of Combat: Making "Black Hawk Down,"* Columbia/TriStar Home Entertainment, 2003.

OTHER SOURCES

Periodicals:
Time Out New York, September 11, 1996.

SHAW, Joe Norman 1957–
(Joe–Norman Shaw)

PERSONAL

Full name, Joseph Norman Shaw; born 1957, in Anderson, IN; son of Norman and Mary Shaw; married Christianne Hart (an actress); children: one daughter. *Education:* University of Guelph, B.A. (honors), drama, 1981; University of Calgary, M.F.A., directing; studied acting in Toronto, Ontario, Canada, with George Luscombe, Michelle George, Marti Maraden, Bernadette Jones, Tom Bentley Fisher; studied film acting with David Rotenberg and Christianne Hart; studied voice with Janine Pearson, Lloyd Coutts, and Ann Skinner. *Avocational Interests:* Ashtanga yoga and playing the guitar.

Addresses: *Office*—c/o Company of Rogues, 2nd Floor, 1232–17th Ave. SW, Calgary, Alberta T2T 0B8, Canada; c/o Mount Royal College, Department of Theatre, Speech & Music Performance, 4825 Mount Royal Gate SW, Calgary, Alberta T3E 6K6, Canada. *Agent*—Lucas Talent, Inc., Sun Tower, 7th Floor, 100 West Pender St., Vancouver, British Columbia V6B 1R8, Canada.

Career: Actor and director. The Shaw Festival, apprentice, 1985; Stratford Festival, apprentice, 1987 and 1990; Gastown Actors Studio, Vancouver, British

Columbia, Canada, resident acting instructor, 1991–93; The Alberta Centre of Acting Studios, resident acting instructor, 1994–96; Company of Rogue Actors Studio, cofounder, 1993, then studio director and acting teacher; Rogues Theatre, artistic director; University of Calgary, instructor; Mount Royal College, department of theatre, instructor.

Awards, Honors: Association of Canadian Television and Radio Artists, Canadian Actors' Equity Association.

CREDITS

Film Appearances:

Jim, *No Sad Songs,* 1985.

30 Something to Life, *Stay Tuned,* Warner Bros., 1992.

Boy Meets Girl, 1993.

Detective Edwards, *Exquisite Tenderness* (also known as *Die Bestie im weissen Kittel* (also known as *Exquisite Tenderness—Hollische Qualen*), A–Pix Entertainment, 1995.

Paul, *Claire* (short film), 1996.

The senator, *One of Our Own* (also known as *Denver P.D.: One of Our Own*), 1997.

Soloman's aide, *Bad Faith* (also known as *Cold Blooded* and *Le delateur*), Oasis International, 2000.

Nathan's first pick–up, *Jet Boy,* 2001.

Television Appearances; Series:

(As Joe–Norman Shaw) Ron Ackerman, *Tom Stone,* CBC, 2002.

Television Appearances; Miniseries:

New York newsman, *In Cold Blood,* CBS, 1996.

Bobby, *Johnson County War,* The Hallmark Channel, 2002.

Television Appearances; Movies:

Larry, *Posing: Inspired by Three Real Stories* (also known as *I Posed for Playboy*), CBS, 1991.

Aris, *Noah,* ABC, 1998.

Fireman, *Oklahoma City: A Survivor's Story,* Lifetime, 1998.

Dave Cleaver, *High Noon,* 2000.

Kallen, *A Father's Choice,* CBS, 2000.

Walt, *For All Time,* CBS, 2000.

Loren Smith, *Children of Fortune,* CBS, 2000.

Jack Crosbie, *The Investigation,* CTV, 2002.

Coach, *Wasted,* MTV, 2002.

Buddy, *Sightings: Heartland Ghost,* Showtime, 2002.

Vince Tiso, *Undercover Christmas* (also known as *Undercover Lover*), CBS, 2003.

(As Joe–Norman Shaw) Colin Lund, *Crazy Canucks,* CTV, 2004.

Heidi's lawyer, *Call Me: The Rise and Fall of Heidi Fleiss,* USA Network, 2004.

Ed Samuels, *Lies My Mother Told Me,* Lifetime, 2005.

Television Appearances; Episodic:

(As Joe–Norman Shaw) Steve, "VCR–Very Careful Rape," *Alfred Hitchcock Presents,* USA Network, 1988.

Tommy Paul, "Cops and Robbers," *Katts and Dog,* CTV and The Family Channel, 1990.

(As Joe–Norman Shaw) Mr. Samuels, "Trail of Tears," *MacGyver,* ABC, 1991.

(As Joe–Norman Shaw) Eddie, "The Long Way Home," *Street Justice,* syndicated, 1992.

Officer Shelton, "Winner Take All," *Viper,* syndicated, 1996.

Customer #1, "Vantage Point," *North of 60,* 1996.

Dennis James, "A Sparrow Falls," *North of 60,* 1997.

"Honey, I'm Dreaming, But Am I?," *Honey, I Shrunk the Kids: The TV Show,* syndicated, 1998.

Staff Sergeant Boulanger, "Trial by Fire," *North of 60,* 2000.

David Seeger, "The Promise: Parts 1 & 2," *Caitlin's Way,* Nickelodeon and YTV, 2002.

Also appeared as Dr. Bradshaw, *The Commish,* ABC; Dr. Robert Davis, *The Commish,* ABC.

Stage Appearances:

Ron Bloom, *Taking Liberties,* Vancouver Fringe Festival, Vancouver, British Columbia, Canada, 1992.

Also appeared as Tommy Paul, *One Tiger to a Hill,* Stratford Festival, Stratford, Ontario, Canada; Rick, *I Slept with Tony Trouble: The Confessions of a Hollywood Hustler* (one–man show), Toronto Fringe Festival, London, Petameters and Old Red Lion, Edinburgh Festival, Stratford Fringe, and Vancouver Little Theatre; Ross, *Zero Hour,* Theatre New Brunswick; Paris, *Romeo and Juliet,* Toronto Free Theatre, High Park; Murder and Porter, *Macbeth,* Stratford Festival; Lennox, *Macbeth,* Vancouver Playhouse; second murderer, *Richard III,* The Citadel, Edmonton, Alberta, Canada; John Wheeler, *Night Watch,* Pleiades Theatre, Calgary, Alberta; Lysander, *A Mid Summer's Night Dream,* Western Canada Theatre, Kamloops, British Columbia; Robert, *Unidentified Remains and the True Nature of Love Crows,* Theatre Toronto, National Arts Centre, Montreal, and Mexico City; Charlie, *The Collected Works of Billy the Kid,* Alberta Theatre Projects, Calgary; Joe, *Angels in America,* Phoenix Theatre, Edmonton; Jude, *Whale Riding Weather,* Touchstone Theatre, Vancouver; Williamson, *Glengarry Glen Ross Theatre,* Junction, Calgary; Charlie Bowdrie, *The Collected Works of Billy the Kid,* A.T.P.; Old Ed, *Ed & Ed: The Fisherman's Trap/Ed & Ed: Go to Jail,* Lunchbox Theatre; in *As Is,* Toronto Free Theatre, National Arts Centre, and Bathurst Street Theatre.

Stage Director:
Selling Mr. Rushdie, Vertigo Studio, Tower Centre, Calgary, Alberta, Canada, 2004.

Also directed *The Zoo Story,* Vancouver Fringe, Vancouver, British Columbia, Canada; *Danny and the Deep Blue Sea, The Melville Boys, Selling Mr. Rushdie, Criminal Genius, Savage in Limbo,* and *Italian American Reconciliation,* all Rogues Theatre, Calgary; *The Diviners,* Theatre MRC; *Rocket to the Moon,* University of Calgary; *Becoming Memories, The Bar Off Melrose, Bury the Dead, Truckline Cafe, Scenes from American Life, The Dining Room, The Rimers of Eldritch, Barbarians, Metastasis, LaRonde, Lysistrata, Call of the Land,* and *Beyond Spoon River,* all Company of Rogues; *Bobby Fell in Love,* Art Ranch; *D.I.N.K.S.,* Lunchbox Theatre workshop.

SHELTON, Ron 1945–

PERSONAL

Full name, Ronald W. Shelton; born September 15, 1945, in Whittier, CA; married Lolita Davidovich (an actress; also known as Lolita David); children: Valentina. *Education:* Westmont College, B.A., 1967; University of Arizona, Tucson, M.F.A., 1974.

Addresses: *Agent*—William Morris Agency, One William Morris Place, Beverly Hills, CA 90212. *Publicist*—David Lust, Patricola/Lust Public Relations, 8383 Wilshire Blvd., Suite 530, Beverly Hills, CA 90211.

Career: Writer, director, and producer. Bordertown Pictures, principal. Played for several minor league baseball teams, including the Baltimore Orioles farm team, 1967–71, and Rochester Red Wings; worked in various other fields, including landscaping, carpentry, and substitute teaching. As a sculptor, exhibitions included a solo show at the Space Gallery.

Member: Directors Guild of America, Writers Guild of America.

Awards, Honors: New York Film Critics Circle Award and Los Angeles Film Critics Award, both 1988, Writers Guild of America Award, National Society of Film Critics Award, and Academy Award nomination, all 1989, all best original screenplay, all with Daniel Yost, for *Bull Durham;* Maverick Tribute Award, Cinequest San Jose Film Festival, 2001.

CREDITS

Film Director:
Bull Durham, Orion, 1988.
Blaze, Buena Vista, 1990.

White Men Can't Jump, Twentieth Century–Fox, 1992.
Cobb, Warner Bros., 1994.
Tin Cup, Warner Bros., 1996.
Play It to the Bone (also known as *Play It*), Buena Vista, 1999.
Dark Blue, Metro–Goldwyn–Mayer, 2003.
Hollywood Homicide, Columbia/Revolution Studios, 2003.

Film Executive Producer:
Sharkskin (short film), 1991.
Blue Chips, Paramount, 1994.
Open Season, Legacy Releasing, 1996.
No Vacancy, Highlight Film, 1999.

Film Producer:
Associate producer, *The Pursuit of D. B. Cooper* (also known as *Pursuit*), Universal, 1981.
Hollywood Homicide, Columbia/Revolution Studios, 2003.

Film Second Unit Director:
Under Fire, Orion, 1983.
The Best of Times, Universal, 1986.

Film Creative Consultant:
The Pursuit of D. B. Cooper (also known as *Pursuit*), Universal, 1981.

Film Appearances:
Himself, *Looking for Oscar* (documentary), Lesser/Montague Productions, 1998.
Himself, *Welcome to Hollywood,* PM Entertainment Group, 1998.

Television Appearances; Specials:
Himself, *Diamonds on the Silver Screen,* American Movie Classics, 1992.
Himself, *Sports on the Silver Screen,* HBO, 1997.
Himself, *Billy Wilder: The Human Comedy,* PBS, 1998.
Himself, *The N–Word,* Trio, 2004.

Television Appearances; Episodic:
Himself, "His Name Is Arliss Michaels," *Arli$$,* HBO, 1998.
Himself, *Intimate Portrait: Gladys Knight,* Lifetime, 2003.

Appeared in episodes of other series, including an appearance as a guest, *On the Record with Bob Costas,* HBO.

RECORDINGS

Videos:
Himself, *Between the Lines: The Making of "Bull Durham"* (short documentary), Metro–Goldwyn–Mayer Home Entertainment, 2001.
Himself, *Blue Code* (short documentary), Metro–Goldwyn–Mayer Home Entertainment, 2003.

WRITINGS

Screenplays:
(With Clayton Frohman) *Under Fire,* Orion, 1983.
The Best of Times, Universal, 1986.
Bull Durham, Orion, 1988.
Blaze, Buena Vista, 1990.
(And songs "Gloria" and "If I Lose") *White Men Can't Jump,* Twentieth Century–Fox, 1992.
Blue Chips, Paramount, 1994.
Cobb, Warner Bros., 1994.
The Great White Hype, Twentieth Century–Fox, 1996.
Tin Cup, Warner Bros., 1996.
Play It to the Bone (also known as *Play It*), Buena Vista, 1999.
(With others) *Bad Boys II* (also based on a story by Shelton; also known as *Good Cops: Bad Boys II*), Columbia, 2003.
Hollywood Homicide, Columbia/Revolution Studios, 2003.

OTHER SOURCES

Periodicals:
Los Angeles Times Magazine, January 16, 2000, pp.14–17, 36.
Saturday Night, June, 1996, p. S12.
Sport, December, 1994, p. 66.
Sporting News, January 30, 1995, p. 8.
Sports Illustrated, November 28, 1994, p. 7.
Variety, May 21, 2001, p. S43.

SIGEL, Newton Thomas 1960–
(Thomas Sigel, Tom Sigel)

PERSONAL

Born 1960. *Education:* Studied painting in Detroit and at the Whitney Museum, New York.

Addresses: *Agent*—International Creative Management, 8942 Wilshire Blvd., Beverly Hills, CA 90211–1934; Dattner Dispoto and Associates, 10635 Santa Monica Blvd., Suite 165, Los Angeles, CA 90025.

Career: Cinematographer, director, and writer. Worked on television commercials for Mercedes, BMW, Toyota, Budweiser, and Coca–Cola; also worked as a painter and experimental filmmaker.

Member: American Society of Cinematographers.

Awards, Honors: CableACE Award nomination, direction of photography and/or lighting direction for a dramatic or theatrical special/movie or miniseries, 1988, for *Home Fries;* Independent Spirit Award nomination, best cinematography, 1996, for *The Usual Suspects;* Online Film Critics Society Award nomination, best cinematography, 2000, for *Three Kings;* Apex Award, cinematography—fantasy/science fiction/horror, 2000, for *X–Men;* Apex Award nomination, cinematography—fantasy/science fiction/horror, for *X2;* Audience Award (with Lisa Chang), best live–action short film, Malibu Film Festival, 2005, for *The Big Empty;* Fennecus Award nomination, cinematography—lighting.

CREDITS

Film Cinematographer:
(As Thomas Sigel) *Resurgence: The Movement for Equality vs. the Klu Klux Klan,* 1981.
(As Thomas Sigel) *El Salvador: Another Vietnam,* Icarus Films, 1981.
(As Thomas Sigel) *When the Mountains Tremble,* New Yorker Films, 1983.
Atomic Artist (documentary short film), 1983.
(As Thomas Sigel) *In Our Hands* (documentary), Libra Cinema 5, 1984.
(As Thomas Sigel) *Latino,* CBS/Fox, 1985.
(As Tom Sigel; second unit) *Platoon,* Orion, 1986.
(Second unit) *Dead of Winter,* Metro–Goldwyn–Mayer, 1987.
(Second unit) *Matewan,* Cinecom, 1987.
(As Tom Sigel; second unit) *Wall Street,* Twentieth Century Fox, 1987.
(As Tom Sigel) *Machito: A Latin Jazz Legacy,* First Run/Icarus Films, 1987.
(As Tom Sigel) *Inheritance,* 1988.
(As Tom Sigel) *Teatro!,* 1989.
Rude Awakening, Orion, 1989.
(As Tom Sigel) *No More Disguises,* 1989.
(As Tom Sigel; Kansas) *Wild Orchid,* Triumph Releasing, 1990.
(As Tom Sigel) *H–2 Worker,* First Run Features, 1990.
(As Tom Sigel; second unit) *The Doors,* TriStar, 1991.
Salmonberries (also known as *Percy Adlon's "Salmonberries"*), Roxie Releasing, 1991.
Oliver Stone (documentary), 1992.
(As Tom Sigel) *Into the West,* Miramax, 1992.
(As Tom Sigel) *Crossing the Bridge,* Buena Vista, 1992.

Indian Summer (also known as *L'ete indien*), Buena Vista, 1993.

(As Tom Sigel) *Money for Nothing,* Buena Vista, 1993.

Suspicious (short film), 1994.

Blankman, Columbia, 1994.

The Usual Suspects (also known as *Die Ublichen Verdachtigen*), Gramercy, 1995.

(As Tom Sigel; second unit) *Casino,* Universal, 1995.

Foxfire, Samuel Goldwyn Company, 1996.

The Trigger Effect, Gramercy, 1996.

Blood and Wine (also known as *Blood & Wine*), Fox Searchlight Pictures, 1996.

Fallen, Warner Bros., 1998.

Apt Pupil (also known as *L'eleve doue* and *Un eleve doue—Ete de corruption*), Sony Pictures Entertainment, 1998.

Brokedown Palace, Twentieth Century–Fox, 1999.

Three Kings, Warner Bros., 1999.

X–Men (also known as *X–Men 1.5*), Twentieth Century–Fox, 2000.

Confessions of a Hotroddin', Pinstripin', Kustomizin' Teenage Icon, Lions Gate Releasing, 2000.

Confessions of a Dangerous Mind (also known as *Confessions d'un homme dangereux*), Miramax, 2002.

X2 (also known as *X–Men 2, X–2, X–Men 2: X–Men United,* and *X2: X–Men United*), Twentieth Century–Fox, 2003.

When the Mountains Trembled, New Video, 2004.

The Big Empty (short film), 2005.

The Brothers Grimm, Dimension Films, 2005.

Superman Returns, Warner Bros., 2006.

Logan's Run, Warner Bros., 2006.

Film Additional Photographer:

(As Thomas Sigel) *We Are the Guinea Pigs,* 1980.

The Thin Blue Line (documentary), Miramax, 1988.

(As Tom Sigel) *Exquisite Corpses,* Upfront Films, 1988.

(As Tom Sigel) *Comic Book Confidential,* Cinecom International Films, 1988.

(As Tom Sigel) *Heart of Dixie,* 1989.

(As Tom Sigel) *Pump Up the Volume,* New Line Cinema, 1990.

Wild Orchid, Triumph Releasing, 1990.

No Secrets, IRS Media, 1991.

Film Camera Operator:

(As Thomas Sigel) *In Our Hands,* Richter Productions, 1984.

(As Tom Sigel; second unit) *True Stories,* Warner Bros., 1986.

(As Tom Sigel) *Matewan,* First Run/Icarus Films, 1987.

(As Tom Sigel; second unit) *Dead of Winter,* Metro–Goldwyn–Mayer, 1987.

Film Director:

(As Thomas Sigel) *Resurgence: The Movement for Equality vs. the Klu Klux Klan,* 1981.

(As Tom Sigel) *No More Disguises,* 1989.

(As Thomas Sigel) *When the Mountains Tremble,* 2004.

The Big Empty, 2005.

Film Appearances:

Himself, *On the Set of Three Kings* (documentary short film), Warner Home Video, 2000.

(As Tom Sigel) Himself, *X–Men Production Scrapbook* (documentary), Twentieth Century Fox Home Entertainment, 2003.

(As Tom Sigel) Himself, *The Second Uncanny Issue of X–Men! Making "X2"* (documentary), Twentieth Century Fox Home Entertainment, 2003.

(Uncredited) Police officer, *X2* (also known as *X–Men 2, X–2, X–Men 2: X–Men United,* and *X2: X–Men United*), Twentieth Century–Fox, 2003.

Television Cinematographer; Series:

The Wonder Years, ABC, 1988—.

Cop Rock, ABC, 1990.

House, M.D. (also known as *House*), Fox, 2004.

Television Camera; Series:

TV Nation, Fox, 1994–95.

Television Cinematographer; Miniseries:

(As Thomas Sigel) *Home Fires,* NBC, 1987.

Television Cinematographer; Movies:

(As Thomas Sigel) *Perfect People,* ABC, 1988.

(As Thomas Sigel) *Roe vs. Wade,* NBC, 1989.

(As Tom Sigel) *Rock Hudson,* ABC, 1990.

(As Tom Sigel) *Challenger,* ABC, 1990.

(As Tom Sigel) *A Promise to Keep,* NBC, 1990.

(As Tom Sigel) *Daybreak,* HBO, 1993.

(As Tom Sigel) *A Time to Heal* (also known as *Jenny's Story*), NBC, 1994.

Television Work; Movies:

Camera operator, *A Time to Heal* (also known as *Jenny's Story*), NBC, 1994.

Director, *Point of Origin* (also known as *In the Heat of Fire*), HBO, 2002.

Television Cinematographer; Pilots:

(As Tom Sigel) *Turner and Hooch,* NBC, 1990.

(As Tom Sigel) *Murder in High Places,* NBC, 1991.

Television Cinematographer; Specials:

Tales from the Hollywood Hills: Pat Hobby Teamed with Genius (also known as *Pat Hobby Teamed with Genius*), PBS, 1987.

Tales from the Hollywood Hills: Natica Jackson (also known as *Natica Jackson* and *Power, Passion and Murder*), PBS, 1987.

Tales from the Hollywood Hills: A Table at Ciro's (also known as *A Table at Ciro's*), PBS, 1987.

(As Tom Sigel) *Oliver Stone: Inside Out* (documentary), Showtime, 1992.

Television Work; Specials:

(As Tom Sigel) Codirector, *Vandemonium Plus* (also known as *Ann Magnuson's "Vandemonium Plus"*), HBO, 1987.

(As Tom Sigel) Camera operator, *Martin Scorsese Directs* (documentary), PBS, 1990.

(As Tom Sigel) Camera operator, *A Comedy Salute to Michael Jordan,* NBC, 1991.

(As Tom Sigel) Editor and photography, *In the Beginning ... The Creationist Controversy* (documentary), PBS, 1995.

Television Director; Episodic:

"Maternity," *House, M.D.* (also known as *House*), Fox, 2004.

Television Work:

Also worked on *Central America in Crisis* (documentary), CBS; *Guatemala* (documentary), CBS; "El Salvador" (documentary), *Frontline,* PBS; "The Other England" (documentary), *Frontline,* PBS; "Our Aging Parents" (documentary), *Frontline,* PBS.

RECORDINGS

Music Videos; as Cinematographer:

K. D. Lang, "So In Love," 1991.

K. D. Lang, "Barefoot," 1991.

Nine Inch Nails, "Burn," 1994.

Also worked as cinematographer on Talking Heads, "Burning Down the House"; UB40, "I Got You, Babe."

WRITINGS

Screenplays; Adapter:

The Big Empty, 2005.

SKYE, Ione 1970(?)–
    (Ione Skye Leitch)

PERSONAL

Given name is pronounced Eye–oh–nee; born September 4, 1970 (some sources cite 1971), in London (some sources cite Hertfordshire), England; raised in Los Angeles, San Francisco, CA, and Connecticut; daughter of Donovan Leitch (a folksinger and songwriter) and Enid Karl (a model); sister of Donovan Leitch (an actor and producer); married Adam Horovitz (a musician, member of the band Beastie Boys, and actor), July, 1992 (divorced, 2000); married David Netto (an architectural designer), March, 2001; children: (second marriage) Kate. *Education:* Attended high school in Hollywood, CA.

Addresses: *Agent*—Steven Muller, Innovative Artists, 1505 10th St., Santa Monica, CA 90401. *Manager*—Art/Work Entertainment, 260 South Beverly Dr., Suite 205, Beverly Hills, CA 90210.

Career: Actress and director. Worked as a model.

Awards, Honors: Young Artist Award nomination, best young actress in a motion picture drama, Young Artist Foundation, 1988, for *River's Edge.*

CREDITS

Film Appearances:

(As Ione Skye Leitch) Clarissa, *River's Edge,* Hemdale Releasing, 1987.

Deirdre Clark, *Stranded,* New Line Cinema, 1987.

Denise Hunter, *A Night in the Life of Jimmy Reardon,* Twentieth Century–Fox, 1988.

Diane Court, *Say Anything ... ,* Twentieth Century–Fox, 1990.

Kit Hoffman, *Mindwalk,* Overseas Filmgroup, 1990.

Rachel Seth–Smith (some sources cite Rachel Noyce), *The Rachel Papers,* United Artists, 1990.

Halys Smith, *The Color of Evening,* 1991, York Home Video, 1995.

Elaine, *Samantha,* Academy Entertainment, 1992.

Elyse, *Wayne's World,* Paramount, 1992.

Trudi, *Gas Food Lodging,* IRS Releasing, 1992.

Eva, *Four Rooms,* Miramax, 1995.

Frankie, *Dream for an Insomniac,* Tritone Productions, 1996.

Gabby, *Went to Coney Island on a Mission from God ... Be Back by Five,* Evenmore Entertainment, 1996.

Maggie, *The Size of Watermelons* (also known as *Chicken Blood and Other Fables*), Norstar Entertainment, 1996.

Young woman, *Cityscrapes: Los Angeles* (also known as *CITYSCRAPES los angeles*), High Octane Productions/Centre Films/FilmTribe Moving Pictures, 1996.

Jenny, *One Night Stand,* New Line Cinema, 1997.

Rebecca, *Mascara,* Phaedra Cinema, 1999.

Stephanie, *Jump,* Arrow Releasing, 1999.

(Uncredited) Kelly, *But I'm a Cheerleader,* Lions Gate Films, 2000.

Contemporary Theatre, Film and Television • Volume 66

Nadia Wickham, *The Good Doctor* (short film), Chesterfield Motion Pictures, 2000.
Men Make Women Crazy Theory, 2000.
Moonglow, Latitude 20 Pictures, 2000.
Catherine, *Free,* 2001.
Mama, *Chicken Night* (short film), Power Up Films, 2001.
Miss Highrise, *Southlander,* Propaganda Films, 2001.
Angryman, Blue Mutt Productions, 2001.
Jolynn, *Dry Cycle* (also known as *Spin, Shoot & Run*), Quantum Entertainment, 2003.
Virginia Rappe, *Return to Babylon* (also known as *Babylon Revisited*), Ambyth Productions/Babylon Productions, 2004.
Molly, *Fever Pitch,* Twentieth Century–Fox, 2005.

Some sources cite appearances in *Forever Love,* c. 1994 and *Das Geheimnis in der Wueste,* c. 1998.

Film Director:
Bed, Bath and Beyond (short film), Hi–8 Productions, 1996.

Television Appearances; Series:
Eleanor Gray, *Covington Cross* (also known as *Charing Cross*), ABC, 1992.

Television Appearances; Miniseries:
Pauline, *Napoleon and Josephine: A Love Story,* ABC, 1987.
Herself, *E! 101 Most Awesome Moments in Entertainment,* E! Entertainment Television, 2004.

Television Appearances; Movies:
Joy, *Guncrazy,* Showtime, 1992.
Carol Madison, *Girls in Prison* (also known as *Rebel Highway*), Showtime, 1994.
Kathryn Mitrou Podaras, *The Perfect Mother* (also known as *Kathryn Alexandra* and *The Mother–in–Law*), CBS, 1997.
Diane Shannon, *I guardini del cielo* (also known as *The Sands of Time, Tower of the Firstborn, Il cielo sotto il deserto,* and *La tour secrete*), Radiotelevisione Italiana, 1998.
Emma Matthews, *The Clinic,* Animal Planet, 2004.

Television Appearances; Specials:
Marie, "Carmilla," *Nightmare Classics,* Showtime, 1989.
Joanna Dibble, "It's Called the Sugar Plum," *General Motors Playwrights Theatre,* Arts and Entertainment, 1991.
Minerva "Min" Foo, "Back When We Were Grownups," *Hallmark Hall of Fame,* CBS, 2004.

Television Appearances; Episodic:
Guest, *Howard Stern,* E! Entertainment Television, 1999.

Melina Kroner, "Night Route," *The Twilight Zone,* UPN, 2002.
Madeleine Wey, "Visions," *The Dead Zone* (also known as *Stephen King's "Dead Zone"*), USA Network, 2003.
Guest judge, "South West," *Ultimate Film Fanatic,* Independent Film Channel, 2005.
Mrs. Veal, "Meet the Veals," *Arrested Development,* Fox, 2005.

Appeared as Irene, "Gentleman Caller," *The Fearing Mind,* Fox Family Channel.

Stage Appearances:
Gina Bello, *Evolution,* Bleecker Street Theatre, New York City, 2002.

Radio Appearances:
Guest, *The Howard Stern Radio Show,* 1999.

RECORDINGS

Music Videos:
Guster, "Fa Fa," 2000.

WRITINGS

Screenplays:
Bed, Bath and Beyond (short film), Hi–8 Productions, 1996.

OTHER SOURCES

Periodicals:
Movieline, June, 1999, p. 13.
People Weekly, August 3, 1987.
Premiere, December, 1987.
Us, October 2, 1989.
Vogue, February, 2003, pp. 270–77, 300–301.

SMITH, Cedric 1943–

PERSONAL

Born 1943, in Bournemouth, England; citizenship, Canadian; married Catherine Disher (an actress).

Addresses: *Agent*—Premier Artists Management, 671 Danforth Ave., Suite 305, Toronto, Ontario M4J 1L3, Canada; (commercials) Bobby Ball Talent Agency, 4342 Lankershim Blvd., Universal City, CA 91602.

Career: Actor, director, writer, and composer. Perth County Conspiracy (folk music group), Stratford, Ontario, Canada, founder, concert performer, and recording artist.

Awards, Honors: Gemini Award, 1993, and Gemini Award nominations, 1995 and 1997, all best performance by an actor in a continuing leading role in a dramatic series, Academy of Canadian Cinema and Television, for *Road to Avonlea;* Best Actor Award, Yorkton Film Festival, for *In the Falls.*

CREDITS

Television Appearances; Series:
Luke, *Teleplay,* CBC, beginning 1976.
Captain Thomas Sims, *The Campbells,* Canadian television, Family Channel, and syndicated, 1986–89.
Alec King, *Road to Avonlea* (also known as *Avonlea* and *Tales from Avonlea*), CBC, 1989–97, The Disney Channel, 1990–97.
Voice of Count Geoffrey, *Blazing Dragons* (animated), beginning c. 1992.
Voice of Mentor, *Silver Surfer* (animated), Fox, 1998–99.

Television Appearances; Miniseries:
Reverend Allan, *Anne of Green Gables,* PBS, 1985.
Tony Wilson, *Love and Hate: The Story of Colin and Joanne Thatcher* (also known as *Love and Hate: A Marriage Made in Hell*), CBC, 1989, NBC, 1990.
Professor Bruce Hopper, *JFK: Reckless Youth,* NBC, 1993.
Lowell Thomas, *Million Dollar Babies* (also known as *Les jumelles Dionne*), CBS, 1994.
General Curtis Lemay, *Hiroshima,* Showtime, 1995.

Television Appearances; Movies:
Mr. Macdonald, *Heaven on Earth,* CBC and BBC, 1987, broadcast on *Masterpiece Theatre,* PBS, 1988.
Commissioner Warner, *The Penthouse,* ABC, 1989.
Inspector Frost, *Dick Francis: In the Frame* (also known as *In the Frame*), syndicated, 1989.
Lieutenant Colonel Hatfield, *Le peloton d'execution* (also known as *Firing Squad*), CTV, 1991.
Shane O'Connolly, *Lost in the Barrens II: The Curse of the Viking Grave* (also known as *Curse of the Viking Grave*), Canadian television and The Disney Channel, 1991.
Dr. Frank Davis, *Butterbox Babies* (also known as *Les nourrissons de la misere*), Arts and Entertainment, 1996.
Edward Jordan, *Barbara Taylor Bradford's "Everything to Gain"* (also known as *Barbara Taylor Bradford Trilogy: Everything to Gain* and *Everything to Gain*), CBS, 1996.
Mike Spracklen, *Golden Will: The Silken Laumann Story,* The Disney Channel, 1996.

Alec King, *Happy Christmas, Miss King* (also known as *An Avonlea Christmas* and *Joyeux Noel Mademoiselle King*), CBC, 1998.
Henry Baker, *Thunder Point* (also known as *Jack Higgins' "Thunder Point"*), Showtime, 1998.
Tim Bobek, *The Long Island Incident,* NBC, 1998.
Samuel "Sam" Casey, *Sea People,* Showtime, 1999.
Dr. Richards, *Jenifer* (also known as *The Jenifer Estess Story*), CBS, 2001.
Three Days, ABC Family Channel, 2001.
Dr. Jaffe, *Heart of a Stranger,* Lifetime, 2002.
President Harry S Truman, *Keep the Faith, Baby,* Showtime, 2002.
Thompson, *Power and Beauty,* Showtime, 2002.
More Than Meets the Eye: The Joan Brock Story, Lifetime, 2003.
Pope's cardinal, *Our Fathers,* Showtime, 2005.

Television Appearances; Specials:
Michael Wellborne/Vincent McCarthy, *In This Corner,* CBC, 1985.
Duke of Milan (Il Moro), *Leonardo: A Dream of Flight,* HBO, 1997.
Francisco Goya, *Goya: Awakened in a Dream,* HBO, 1999.
Narrator, *Turning Points of History,* 2001.

Television Appearances; Episodic:
Terry, "Rabies," *The Littlest Hobo,* syndicated, 1982.
Agent Jack Deacon, "The Fifth Man," *Night Heat,* CBS, 1985.
Max, "Matter of Honour," *Street Legal,* CBC, 1986.
Andrew Demarus, "The Privilege of Freedom," *Night Heat,* CBS, 1988.
Jeremy Sinclair, "The Curious Case of Edgar Witherspoon," *The Twilight Zone,* syndicated, 1988.
Joe Fenton, "The Pirates Promise," *Friday the 13th* (also known as *Friday's Curse* and *Friday the 13th: The Series*), syndicated, 1988.
Paul Stevens, "VCR—Very Careful Rape," *Alfred Hitchcock Presents,* USA Network, 1988.
"Exposure," *Diamonds,* CBS, 1988.
Adrian Bouchard, "Among the Philistines," *War of the Worlds,* syndicated, 1989.
Van Dorn, "South by Southeast," *Alfred Hitchcock Presents,* USA Network, 1989.
Cantrell, "The Dealbreaker," *Counterstrike,* CTV, 1990.
Commissioner Geoffrey Osborne, "Two Moons," *Bordertown,* Family Channel and CanWest Global Television, 1990.
Dr. Fellows, "The Murderer," *The Ray Bradbury Theater,* USA Network, 1990.
Michael Marloe, "Cinema Verite," *Counterstrike,* CTV, 1990.
Bill Bowen, "Miracle Worker," *Beyond Reality,* USA Network, 1991.
Dr. Dawson, "Heart of the Matter," *E.N.G.,* CTV and Lifetime, 1992.

Dr. Mims, "Straightjacket," *Kung Fu: The Legend Continues,* syndicated, 1993.

Henry Sutton, "But Not Forgotten," *Street Legal,* CBC, 1993.

Liam O'Neal, "Bad Blood," *Forever Knight,* CBS and syndicated, 1994.

Voice of Professor Charles F. Xavier/Professor X, "Neogenic Nightmare Chapter 4: The Mutant Agenda," *Spider–Man* (animated), Fox, 1995.

Voice of Professor Charles F. Xavier/Professor X, "Neogenic Nightmare Chapter 5: Mutants Revenge," *Spider–Man* (animated), Fox, 1995.

Mickey O'Brian, "Shooting Mickey," *F/X: The Series,* CTV and syndicated, 1997.

Senior officer of the Royal Canadian Mounted Police, "Perfect Strangers," *Due South* (also known as *Due South: The Series, Direction: Sud,* and *Tandem de choc*), CTV and CBS, 1997.

King Polydectes, "Perseus: The Search for Medusa," *Mythic Warriors* (animated), CBS, 1998.

Morgan Kenworth, "Bloodlines," *Highlander: The Raven,* syndicated, 1998.

Dr. Eldrige Hawke, "School's Out," *Twice in a Lifetime,* PAX TV, 1999.

Dr. Paul Breedlove, "The Shock of the New," *Mutant X,* syndicated, 2001.

Michael Hamori, "Dr. Tara," *Blue Murder,* CanWest Global Television, 2001.

Alderman Glickman, "Out with the Old ... ," *Soul Food,* Showtime, 2002.

Hightower, "Grave Danger," *Earth: Final Conflict* (also known as *EFC, Gene Roddenberry's "Battleground Earth," Gene Roddenberry's "Earth: Final Conflict," Invasion planete Terre,* and *Mission Erde: Sie sind unter uns*), syndicated, 2002.

Lawyer, "Pandora's Box," *Relic Hunter* (also known as *Relic Hunter—Die Schatzjaegerin* and *Sydney Fox l'aventuriere*), syndicated, 2002.

Elliot Winthrop, "Follow the Money," *Street Time,* Showtime, 2003.

Martin Wainwright, "Smoke Gets in Your Eyes," *Doc,* PAX TV, 2003.

Voice of Professor Link, "Head Shrinker Much?," *Totally Spies* (animated), TeleToon and Cartoon Network, 2005.

Appeared as Willie Anderson, "Sangraal," *Veritas: The Quest,* ABC.

Television Director; Episodic:

The Campbells, Canadian television, Family Channel, and syndicated, 1988.

Film Appearances:

Dr. Svarich, *Who Has Seen the Wind?,* Souris River/ Cinema World, 1977.

Narrator, *Boomer* (short documentary), National Film Board of Canada, 1978.

Gary "The Blacksmith" Black, *Fast Company,* Admit One Presentations, 1979.

Narrator, *Never a Dull Moment* (documentary), National Film Board of Canada, 1979.

Narrator, *Pamiat, Memory of Ancestors* (short documentary), National Film Board of Canada, 1981.

Voice of bartender, "Taarna," *Heavy Metal* (animated), Columbia, 1981.

Squid Hayman, *Bayo,* Bayo Film Productions, 1985.

William Lyon Mackenzie, *Samuel Lount,* Utopia Pictures, 1985.

Discussions in Bioethics: Family Tree (documentary; also known as *La bioethique; une question de choix—Me steriliser? ... Jamais!*), 1985.

The Sight, 1985.

Narrator, *Juju Music* (documentary), Jacques Holender Films, 1987.

Narrator, *Where Is Here?* (documentary), National Film Board of Canada, 1987.

Farmers Helping Farmers (short film), National Film Board of Canada, 1987.

Wednesday's Children: Robert (short film; also known as *Les enfants du desarroi: Robert*), National Film Board of Canada, 1987.

A Wake for Milton, National Film Board of Canada, 1988.

Eli Seibel, *Millennium,* Twentieth Century–Fox, 1989.

Narrator, *Children for Hire* (documentary), National Film Board of Canada, 1994.

Francis Redmund, *Witchboard III: The Possession* (also known as *Witchboard: The Possession*), Telescene Film Group Productions/Vista Street Entertainment, 1995.

Narrator, *The Barrens Quest* (documentary), National Film Board of Canada/Bar Harbour Films, 1997.

J. J. Gallagher, *Sleeping Dogs Lie* (also known as *Le mystere d'Ambrose Small*), 1998.

Voice of Mentor, *The Silver Surfer* (animated), Fox Family Films, 1999.

Grey Owl, Allied Filmmakers/Largo Entertainment, 1999.

Pediatric doctor, *Bless the Child* (also known as *Die Prophezeiung*), Paramount, 2000.

Caiaphas, *The Gospel of John,* ThinkFilm, 2003.

Frederick Radcliffe, *Raymond Radcliffe* (short film), Honey Wagon Films, 2004.

Some sources cite an appearance in *In the Falls.*

Film Director:

Wednesday's Children: Robert (short film; also known as *Les enfants du desarroi: Robert*), National Film Board of Canada, 1987.

Stage Appearances:

Singer, *Le bourgeois gentilhomme,* Stratford Festival of Canada, Stratford, Ontario, Canada, 1964.

The Country Wife, Stratford Festival of Canada, 1964.

King Lear, Stratford Festival of Canada, 1964.

Richard II, Stratford Festival of Canada, 1964.

One of Antony's soldiers, *Antony and Cleopatra,* Festival Theatre, Stratford Festival of Canada, 1967.

Pursuivant, *Richard III,* Festival Theatre, Stratford Festival of Canada, 1967.

Twelfth Night, Manitoba Theatre Centre, Winnipeg, Manitoba, Canada, 1976–77.

The Contractor, Manitoba Theatre Centre, 1977–78.

Billy Bishop, *Billy Bishop Goes to War,* Morosco Theatre, then Theatre de Lys (now Lucille Lortel Theatre), both New York City, 1980, later Manitoba Theatre Centre, 1980–81.

A Wake for Milton, 1986, released as a feature film, National Film Board of Canada, 1988.

Appeared as Salieri, *Amadeus,* Vancouver Playhouse, Vancouver, British Columbia, Canada; and in the title role, *Richard III,* Manitoba Theatre Centre; appeared in productions of the Stratford Festival, 1979; performed at the Scream in High Park, Toronto, Ontario, Canada, 1997.

WRITINGS

Teleplays; Episodic:

Author of "The Hunting Party" and "Live by the Sword," episodes of *The Campbells,* Canadian television, Family Channel, and syndicated.

Stage Plays:

(With Milton Acorn; and music composer) *Road to Charlottetown,* 1977.

Adaptor (with others) and music composer, *Ten Lost Years* (based on the work of Barry Broadfoot).

SMITH, Lewis 1958–
(Lewis C. Smith)

PERSONAL

Born 1958, in Chattanooga, TN. *Education:* Graduated from Lookout Valley High School, Chattanooga, TN; studied acting with Stella Adler, Lee Strasberg, Sanford Meisner, and Roy London.

Addresses: *Manager*—Incognito Entertainment, 9440 Santa Monica Blvd., #302, Beverly Hills, CA 90210.

Career: Actor. Donna Reed Festival for the Performing Arts, Denison, IA, presenter and/or friend, 2005. Sometimes credited as Lewis C. Smith.

CREDITS

Film Appearances:

Rifleman Earl Stuckey, *Southern Comfort,* Twentieth Century–Fox, 1981.

Soldier, *I Ought to Be In Pictures,* Twentieth Century–Fox, 1982.

Jesse Chaney, *Love Child,* Warner Bros., 1982.

Boone, *The Final Terror* (also known as *Bump in the Night, Campsite Massacre, Carnivore,* and *The Forest Primeval*), Vestron Video, 1983.

Perfect Tommy, *The Adventures of Buckaroo Banzai across the 8th Dimension,* Twentieth Century–Fox, 1984.

Bobby Fantana, *The Heavenly Kid* (also known as *Heavenly Kid*), Orion, 1985.

Al Zidyck, *Diary of a Hitman,* Vision International, 1991.

Curly Bill Brocius, *Wyatt Earp,* Warner Bros., 1994.

Himself, *Buckaroo Banzai Declassified* (documentary), Metro–Goldwyn–Mayer/United Artists Home Entertainment, 2002.

Seventh Veil, 2003.

Film Work:

Executive producer, *Seventh Veil,* 2003.

Television Appearances; Series:

Steven Foreman, *Karen's Song,* Fox, 1987.

Mark, *Beauty and the Beast,* CBS, 1989–90.

Television Appearances; Miniseries:

Charles Main, *North and South,* ABC, 1985.

Charles Main, *North and South II,* ABC, 1986.

Dennis Church, *Texas Justice,* CBS, 1995.

Television Appearances; Movies:

Spinner Limbaugh, *Kentucky Woman,* CBS, 1983.

Aaron Gray, *The Fulfillment of Mary Gray* (also known as *Fulfillment*), CBS, 1989.

Robert Williams, *In the Line of Duty: Ambush in Waco,* NBC, 1993.

Young hot guy, *Toothless,* ABC, 1997.

Commander Frank Stein, *Avalon: Beyond the Abyss,* UPN, 1999.

Television Appearances; Pilots:

Ranger Ben McCollum, *Lone Star,* NBC, 1983.

John Dory, *The Man Who Fell To Earth,* ABC, 1987.

Garson MacBeth, *Badlands 2005,* ABC, 1988.

Television Appearances; Episodic:

David Saxton, "Black Diamond Run," *Booker,* Fox, 1990.

Louis Paloma, "The Mole," *Murder, She Wrote,* CBS, 1992.

Michael Davis, "Lily," *Diagnosis Murder,* CBS, 1994.

Tom Riley, "Simply Shocking," *Melrose Place,* Fox, 1995.

Tom Riley, "The Jane Mutiny," *Melrose Place,* Fox, 1995.

James Sloan, "Sins of the Father: Parts 1 & 2," *Diagnosis Murder,* CBS, 2001.

SOFER, Rena 1968–

PERSONAL

Full name, Rena S. Sofer; born December 2, 1968, in Arcadia, CA; daughter of Martin (an Orthodox Jewish rabbi) and Susan (a professor of psychology) Sofer; married Wallace Kurth (an actor and musician), March 31, 1995 (divorced, 1997); married Sanford Bookstaver (a director, producer, and writer), May 18, 2003; children: (first marriage) Rosabel Rosalind; (second marriage) Avalon Leone; Meghann (stepdaughter). *Education:* Attended Montclair State College; studied acting in New York City. *Avocational Interests:* Running, watching films.

Addresses: *Agent*—Metropolitan Talent Agency, 4526 Wilshire Blvd., Los Angeles, CA 90010; Karen Forman, Agency for the Performing Arts, 9200 Sunset Blvd., Suite 900, Los Angeles, CA 90069. *Publicist*—Nancy Iannios, Nancy Iannios Public Relations, 8271 Melrose Ave., Suite 102, Los Angeles, CA 90046 (some sources cite 8225 Santa Monica Blvd., West Hollywood, CA 90046).

Career: Actress. Worked as a model; appeared in industrial films, commercials, and music videos.

Awards, Honors: Daytime Emmy Award, outstanding supporting actress in a drama series, and *Soap Opera Digest* Award, outstanding younger actress, both 1995, for *General Hospital.*

CREDITS

Television Appearances; Series:
Joyce Abernathy, *Another World* (also known as *Another World: Bay City*), NBC, 1987.

Amelia "Rocky" McKenzie Domecq, *Loving* (also known as *The City*), ABC, 1988–91.

Lois Cerullo Ashton Ashton, *General Hospital,* ABC, 1993–97, 1998.

Eve Cleary Burns, a recurring role, *Melrose Place,* Fox, 1998–99.

Suzanne Vandermeer, *Oh Grow Up,* ABC, 1999.

Ms. Gibson, *Opposite Sex,* Fox, 2000.

Bonnie Hane, a recurring role, *Ed* (also known as *Stuckeyville*), NBC, 2001.

Grace Hall, *The Chronicle* (also known as *News from the Edge*), Sci–Fi Channel, 2001–2002.

Vicki Costa, *Just Shoot Me!,* NBC, 2002–2003.

Susan Walker (some sources cite Susan Freeman), *Coupling,* NBC, 2003.

Christie Dunbar, *Blind Justice,* ABC, 2005.

Television Appearances; Miniseries:
Herself, *I Love the '80s Strikes Back,* VH1, 2003.

Television Appearances; Movies:
Andrea Larson, *Saved by the Bell—Hawaiian Style,* NBC, 1992.

Kerry Ellison, *Hostile Advances: The Kerry Ellison Story,* Lifetime, 1996.

Darcy Canfield, *The Stepsister,* USA Network, 1997.

Penny Randolph, *Nightmare Street,* ABC, 1998.

Miss Desjarden, *Carrie,* NBC, 2002.

Television Appearances; Specials:
The General Hospital 35th Anniversary Show, ABC, 1998.

Member of blue team, *Battle of the Network Stars,* NBC, 2003.

(In archive footage) *101 Biggest Celebrity Oops,* E! Entertainment Television, 2004.

Television Appearances; Awards Presentations:
Presenter, *The 21st Annual Daytime Emmy Awards,* ABC, 1994.

The 12th Annual Soap Opera Awards, NBC, 1996.

Television Appearances; Episodic:
Veronica, "The Last Sonnet," *Freshman Dorm,* CBS, 1992.

Veronica, "Sex, Truth, and Theatre," *Freshman Dorm,* CBS, 1992.

Stephanie, "When Hermie Met Crawford's Girlfriend," *Herman's Head,* Fox, 1993.

Risa Glickman, "Caroline and the Nice Jewish Boy," *Caroline in the City* (also known as *Caroline*), NBC, 1996.

Mary Anne, "The Muffin Tops," *Seinfeld,* NBC, 1997.

Dr. Carrie Ann Trent, "D.O.A.," *Timecop,* ABC, 1998.

Jean Kelly, "Womyn Fest," *Ellen* (also known as *These Friends of Mine*), ABC, 1998.

Lauren Henderson, "Two Guys, a Girl and a Recovery," *Two Guys, a Girl and a Pizza Place* (also known as *Two Guys and a Girl*), ABC, 1998.

Sam, "Lost and Found," *Spin City* (also known as *Spin*), ABC, 2000.

Dawn Cheswick, "Dog Eat Dog," *Cursed* (also known as *The Weber Show*), NBC, 2001.
Guest, *The Late Late Show with Craig Kilborn*, CBS, 2001.
Katie, "The One with the Cooking Class," *Friends*, NBC, 2002.
Alison Roufow, "Grave Young Men," *CSI: Miami*, CBS, 2003.
Herself, "A Funny Business," *Imagine ...* , BBC, 2003.
Guest, *Howard Stern*, E! Entertainment Television, 2003.
Guest, *Last Call with Carson Daly*, NBC, 2003.
Melrose Place: The E! True Hollywood Story, E! Entertainment Television, 2003.
Herself, *The E! True Hollywood Story: Heather Locklear*, E! Entertainment Television, 2004.

Television Appearances; Pilots:
Elizabeth Hopewell, *Glory, Glory*, CBS, 1998.
Suzanne Vandermeer, *Oh Grow Up*, ABC, 1999.
Ms. Gibson, *Opposite Sex*, Fox, 2000.
Grace Hall, *The Chronicle* (also known as *News from the Edge*), Sci–Fi Channel, 2001.
Christie Dunbar, *Blind Justice*, ABC, 2005.

Film Appearances:
Shayna, *A Stranger among Us* (also known as *Close to Eden*), Buena Vista, 1992.
Judy, *Twin Sitters* (also known as *The Babysitters*), Columbia/TriStar Home Video, 1994.
Rachel Rose, *Keeping the Faith*, Buena Vista, 2000.
Hedy Pullman, *March*, Kanan/Hammerschlag, c. 2000.
Helena's friend, *Traffic* (also known as *Traffic—Die Macht des Kartells*), USA Films, 2001.

Appeared in the student film *Theresa*.

RECORDINGS

Audiobooks:
Christina Skye, *Enchantment*, Renaissance Productions, 1998.

OTHER SOURCES

Periodicals:
InStyle, February, 2004, p. 264.
People Weekly, October 31, 1994, pp. 117–18; June 16, 2003, p. 104.
TV Guide, October 12, 2002, p. 14.

SORKIN, Aaron 1961–

PERSONAL

Full name, Aaron Benjamin Sorkin; born June 9, 1961, in New York, NY; father, a lawyer; married Megan Gal-lagher (an actress; divorced); married Julia Bingham (an entertainment lawyer and studio executive), April 13, 1996 (separated); children: (second marriage) Roxy. *Education:* Syracuse University, B.F.A.; some sources cite attendance at College at Purchase State University of New York.

Addresses: *Agent*—Ariel Emanuel, Endeavor, 9601 Wilshire Blvd., Third Floor, Beverly Hills, CA 90210. *Publicist*—PMK/HBH Public Relations, 700 San Vicente Blvd., Suite G910, West Hollywood, CA 90069 (some sources cite 8500 Wilshire Blvd., Suite 700, Beverly Hills, CA 90211).

Career: Writer and producer. Founder of the Playwrights Unit of Playwrights Horizons. Traveling Playhouse, toured southern American cities as an actor; appeared in print advertisements. Worked as a bartender.

Member: Writers Guild of America.

Awards, Honors: Outer Critics Circle Award, outstanding American playwright, 1989, for *A Few Good Men*; Golden Globe Award nomination, best screenplay for a motion picture, and Edgar Allan Poe Award nomination, best motion picture, Mystery Writers of America, both 1993, for *A Few Good Men*; Edgar Allan Poe Award nomination, best motion picture, 1994, for *Malice*; Golden Globe Award nomination, best screenplay for a motion picture, and Writers Guild of America Screen Award nomination, best screenplay written directly for the screen, both 1996, for *The American President*; Emmy Award nomination, outstanding writing for a comedy series, 1999, for "The Apology," *Sports Night*; Humanitas Prize, thirty–minute category, Human Family Educational and Cultural Institute, 1999, *TV Guide* Award, "the best show you're not watching," 2000, and nomination for Norman Felton Television Producer of the Year Award, episodic category, Golden Laurel awards, Producers Guild of America, 2000, all with others, for *Sports Night*; Golden Satellite awards, best television drama series, International Press Academy, 1999 and 2000, *TV Guide* Award nomination, favorite new series, 2000, Television Critics Association Award nomination, individual achievement in writing, 2000, Emmy awards, outstanding drama series, 2000, 2001, 2002, and 2003, nominations for Norman Felton Television Producer of the Year Award, episodic category, 2000, 2003, and 2004, and Norman Felton Television Producer of the Year Award, episodic category, 2001 and 2002, all with others, all for *The West Wing*; Nova Award, most promising producer in television, Golden Laurel awards, 2000, for *Sports Night* and *The West Wing*; Prism Award, 2000; Emmy Award, outstanding writing for a drama series, 2000, and Writers Guild of America Television Award, episodic drama, 2001, both with Rick Cleveland, for

"Excelsis Deo," *The West Wing;* Humanitas Prize, sixty–minute category, 2000, and Writers Guild of America Television Award nomination, episodic drama, 2001, both with others, for "Take This Sabbath Day," *The West Wing;* Emmy Award nominations, outstanding writing for a drama series, 2000, for the pilot episode, 2001, for "In the Shadow of Two Gunmen: Parts 1 & 2," 2002, for "Posse Comitatus," and 2003, for "Twenty Five," all episodes of *The West Wing;* Emmy Award (with others), outstanding special class program, 2002, for *The West Wing Documentary Special;* Humanitas Prize, sixty–minute category, and Writers Guild of America Television Award nomination, episodic category, both with others, 2002, for "Two Cathedrals," *The West Wing;* Writers Guild of America Television Award nomination (with Paul Redford), episodic drama, 2002, for "Somebody's Going to Emergency, Somebody's Going to Jail," *The West Wing;* Writers Guild of America Television Award nomination (with Redford), episodic drama, 2003, for "Game On," *The West Wing.*

CREDITS

Television Work; Series:
Cocreator and executive producer, *Sports Night,* ABC, 1998–2000.
Creator and executive producer, *The West Wing,* NBC, 1999–2003.

Television Work; Specials:
Executive producer, *The West Wing Documentary Special,* NBC, 2002.

Television Appearances; Specials:
AFI's 100 Years ... 100 Passions, CBS, 2002.
Emmy's Greatest Moments, TV Land, 2004.

Television Appearances; Awards Presentations:
Prism Awards 2000, syndicated, 2000.
Himself, *The 54th Annual Primetime Emmy Awards,* NBC, 2002.

Television Appearances; Episodic:
Man at bar, "Small Town," *Sports Night,* ABC, 1999.
Himself, *The Charlie Rose Show,* PBS, 2003.

Film Co–Executive Producer:
The Farnsworth Invention, New Line Cinema, 2005.

Film Appearances:
Man in bar, *A Few Good Men,* Columbia, 1992.
Aide in bar, *The American President,* Columbia, 1995.

Stage Appearances:
"Hidden in This Picture" (one–act), *Uncounted Blessings,* St. Clement's Theatre, New York City, 1988.

RECORDINGS

Videos:
Code of Conduct (short documentary), 2001.
A Few Good Men: From Stage to Screen (short documentary), 2001.

WRITINGS

Teleplays; Series:
Sports Night, ABC, 1998–2000.
The West Wing (based on his screenplay *The American President*), NBC, 1999–2003, some teleplays published in *The West Wing Script Book,* Newmarket Press, 2002.

Teleplays; Pilots:
Sports Night, ABC, 1998.
The West Wing (based on his screenplay *The American President*), NBC, 1999.

Screenplays:
A Few Good Men (based on his play), Columbia, 1992.
(And story) *Malice,* Columbia, 1993.
The American President, Columbia, 1995.
The Farnsworth Invention, New Line Cinema, 2005.
Charlie Wilson's War, Universal, 2006.

Screenplays with Others; Uncredited Author of Revisions:
Schindler's List, Universal, 1993.
The Rock, Buena Vista, 1996.
Excess Baggage, Sony Pictures Entertainment, 1997.
Bulworth (also known as *Tribulations*), Twentieth Century–Fox, 1998.
Enemy of the State, Buena Vista, 1998.

Stage Plays:
Removing All Doubt (also known as *Removing Doubt*), 1984.
"Hidden in This Picture" (one–act), *Uncounted Blessings,* St. Clement's Theatre, New York City, 1988, expanded version produced as *Making Movies,* Promenade Theatre, New York City, 1990.
A Few Good Men, Music Box Theatre, New York City, 1989, and other productions.

Nonfiction:
Contributor to periodicals, including *Rolling Stone.*

OTHER SOURCES

Books:
Authors and Artists for Young Adults, Volume 55, Gale, 2004.

Fahy, Thomas, editor, *Considering Aaron Sorkin,* McFarland and Co., 2005.
Newsmakers, Issue 2, Gale, 2003.

Periodicals:
Newsweek, October 11, 1999, p. 80; May 12, 2003, p. 67.
New York Post, August 1, 2001.
TV Guide, August 11, 2001, pp. 19, 44–46.

SOVA, Peter

PERSONAL

Addresses: *Office*—c/o Peter Sova Productions, 1492 Roses Brook Rd., South Kortright, NY 13842. *Agent*—Innovative Artists, 1505 Tenth St., Santa Monica, CA 90401.

Career: Cinematographer.

Awards, Honors: Vision Award in Cinematography, AFI Fest, 2000, for *Gangster No. 1.*

CREDITS

Film Cinematographer:
Short Eyes (also known as *Slammer*), Film League, 1977.
(And camera operator) *Samba da criacao do mundo* (documentary; also known as *Samba of the Creation of the World*), 1978.
Rockers, New Yorker Films, 1978.
Diner, Metro–Goldwyn–Mayer, 1982.
Tin Men, Buena Vista, 1987.
Good Morning, Vietnam, Buena Vista, 1987.
Sing, TriStar, 1989.
Late for Dinner, Columbia, 1991.
Straight Talk, Buena Vista, 1992.
Bed & Breakfast, Hemdale Picture Corp., 1992.
Jimmy Hollywood, Paramount, 1995.
Feast of July, Buena Vista, 1995.
Sgt. Bilko (also known as *Sergeant Bilko*), Universal, 1996.
Donnie Brasco, TriStar, 1997.
The Proposition, PolyGram Filmed Entertainment, 1998.
Gangster No. 1 (also known as *Gangster Nr. 1*), IFC Films, 2000.
Doctor Sleep (also known as *Close Your Eyes* and *Hypnotic*), First Look Pictures Releasing, 2002.
The Reckoning (also known as *El misterio de wells* and *Morality Play*), Paramount Classics, 2003.

Wicker Park, Metro–Goldwyn–Mayer, 2004.
Lucky Number Slevin (also known as *Lucky Slevin*), New Line Cinema, 2005.

Film Work:
Additional photographer, *The Thin Blue Line* (documentary), Miramax, 1988.
Interrotron photography, *Fast, Cheap & Out of Control* (documentary), Sony Pictures Classics, 1997.
Photographer: Leuchter interview, *Mr. Death: The Rise and Fall of Fred J. Leuchter, Jr.* (documentary; also known as *Mr. Death*), Lions Gate Films, 1999.

Film Appearances:
Cabbie, *Straight Talk,* Buena Vista, 1992.

Television Cinematographer; Series:
Baker's Dozen, CBS, 1982.
The Equalizer, CBS, 1985.
Thief, F/X, 2005.

Television Cinematographer; Miniseries:
Story of a Marriage, PBS, 1987.
Perfect Murder, Perfect Town: JonBenet and the City of Boulder, CBS, 2000.

Television Cinematographer; Movies:
Summer of My German Soldier, NBC, 1978.
A Doctor's Story, NBC, 1984.
Double Jeopardy, Showtime, 1992.
Fatherland, HBO, 1994.

Television Cinematographer; Pilots:
Nurse, CBS, 1980.
Adam's Apple, CBS, 1986.

Television Cinematographer; Specials:
"The Jolly Corner," *American Short Story,* PBS, 1975.
"Soldier's Home," *American Short Story,* PBS, 1977.
The Halloween That Almost Wasn't (also known as *The Night Dracula Saved the World*), ABC and HBO, 1979.
Barn Burning (also known as *The American Short Story Collection: "Barn Burning"*), Showtime, 1980.
Women of Russia (documentary), syndicated, 1981.

SPALL, Timothy 1957–
(Tim Spall)

PERSONAL

Full name, Timothy Leonard Spall; born February 27, 1957, in Battersea, London, England; father, a postal worker; mother, a hairdresser; married Shane (some sources cite Mary–Jane), 1981; children: Pascale, Rafe (an actor), Mercedes. *Education:* Royal Academy of Dramatic Art, graduated.

Addresses: *Agent*—Pippa Markham, Markham and Froggatt Agency, 4 Windmill St., London W1T 2H2, England (some sources cite 4 Windmill St., London W1P 1HF). *Manager*—Hofflund/Polone, 9465 Wilshire Blvd., Suite 890, Beverly Hills, CA 90212.

Career: Actor. Royal Academy of Dramatic Art, London, associate member; Royal Shakespeare Company, Stratford–upon–Avon, England, member of company, c. 1979–81; former member of National Youth Theatre, London. Appeared in commercials. Archie and Gwen Smith Memorial Trust Fund, honorary vice chair.

Member: Royal Society of Arts (fellow), Colony Club, Dean Street Soho Club.

Awards, Honors: British Comedy Award, 1994, for *Outside Edge;* London Critics Circle Film Award nomination, British actor of the year, 1997, for *Secrets & Lies;* Broadcasting Press Guild Award, and Television Award nomination, British Academy of Film and Television Arts, both best actor, 1999, for *Our Mutual Friend;* decorated officer, Order of the British Empire, 1999; Television Award nomination, best actor, British Academy of Film and Television Arts, 2000, *Shooting the Past;* Film Award nomination, best supporting actor, British Academy of Film and Television Arts, 2000, and London Critics Circle Film Award nomination, British supporting actor of the year, 2001, both for *Topsy–Turvy;* British Independent Film Award nomination, best actor, 2001, for *Lucky Break;* National Board of Review Award (with others), best acting by an ensemble, 2002, for *Nicholas Nickleby;* Television Award nomination, best actor, British Academy of Film and Television Arts, 2002, for *Vacuuming Completely Nude in Paradise;* British Independent Film Award nomination and European Film Award nomination, both best actor, 2002, for *All or Nothing;* Australian Film Institute Award nomination, best actor in a leading role, 2003, for *Gettin' Square.*

CREDITS

Film Appearances:
Lupu, *The Life Story of Baal,* 1978.
Harry, *Quadrophenia* (also known as *Quadrophenia: A Way of Life*), World Northal, 1979.
Douglas, *Remembrance,* Mainline Releasing, 1982.
Parswell, *The Missionary,* Columbia, 1982.
Paulus (Tim), *The Bride,* Columbia, 1985.
Dr. John Polidori, *Gothic,* Vestron Pictures, 1986.

Igor, *To Kill a Priest* (also known as *Le complot, Popieluszko,* and *Zabic ksiedza*), Columbia, 1988.
Peck, *Dream Demon,* Spectrafilm, 1988.
(As Tim Spall) Reverend Milne, *Crusoe,* Island Films, 1988.
Aubrey, *Life Is Sweet,* October Films, 1990.
Eric Lyle, *The Sheltering Sky* (also known as *Il te nel deserto*), Warner Bros., 1990.
Hodkins, *White Hunter, Black Heart,* Warner Bros., 1990.
Ramborde, *1871,* 1990.
Maurice Purley, *Secrets & Lies* (also known as *Secrets et mensonges*), October Films, 1996.
Rosencrantz, *Hamlet* (also known as *William Shakespeare's "Hamlet"*), Columbia, 1996.
(In archive footage) *Whatever Happened to ... Clement and La Frenais?,* 1997.
David "Beano" Baggot, *Still Crazy,* Columbia, 1998.
Inspector Healey, *The Wisdom of Crocodiles* (also known as *Immortality*), Miramax, 1998.
Richard "Dickie" Temple (*The Mikado*), *Topsy–Turvy,* October Films/USA Films, 1999.
Sterling, *The Clandestine Marriage,* United International Pictures, 1999.
Don Armado, *Love's Labour's Lost* (also known as *Peines d'amour perdues*), Miramax, 2000.
Gourville, *Vatel,* Miramax, 2000.
Voice of Nick, *Chicken Run* (animated; also known as *C:R–1*), DreamWorks, 2000.
Andy, *Intimacy* (also known as *Intimidad* and *Intimite*), Empire Pictures, 2001.
Luis Agalla, *The Old Man Who Read Love Stories* (also known as *El viejo que leia novelas de amor* and *Le vieux qui lisait des romans d'amour*), Pandora Films, 2001.
Mats, *Rock Star* (also known as *Metal God*), Warner Bros., 2001.
Thomas Tipp, *Vanilla Sky,* Paramount, 2001.
Cliff Gumbell, *Lucky Break* (also known as *Rein oder raus*), Paramount, c. 2001.
Charles Cheeryble, *Nicholas Nickleby,* Metro–Goldwyn–Mayer, 2002.
Phil Bassett, *All or Nothing,* United Artists, 2002.
Victor Monroe, *In the Eyes of Kyana,* 2002.
Darren "Dabba" Barrington, *Gettin' Square,* Universal, 2003.
Frederico Formaggio, *Last Rumble in Rochdale* (short film), 2003.
Simon Graham, *The Last Samurai* (also known as *The Last Samurai: Bushido*), Warner Bros., 2003.
Mr. Poe, *Lemony Snicket's "A Series of Unfortunate Events"* (also known as *Lemony Snicket* and *Lemony Snicket—Raetselhafte Ereignisse*), Paramount, 2004.
Peter Pettigrew, *Harry Potter and the Prisoner of Azkaban,* Warner Bros., 2004, also released as *Harry Potter and the Prisoner of Azkaban: The IMAX Experience.*.
Peter Pettigrew, *Harry Potter and the Goblet of Fire* (also known as *Wormtail*), Warner Bros., 2005.

Television Appearances; Series:

Barry Taylor, *Auf Wiedersehen, Pet,* Central Television, 1983–84 and 1986.

Robert Cunningham, *Spender,* BBC, 1991–93.

Frank Stubbs, *Frank Stubbs Promotes,* Carlton Television, 1993.

Title role, *Frank Stubbs,* Carlton Television, 1994.

Phil Bachelor, *Nice Day at the Office,* BBC, beginning 1994.

Kevin Costello, *Outside Edge,* Central Independent Television, 1994, Central Independent Television and Carlton Television, 1995.

Television Appearances; Miniseries:

Mr. Venus, *Our Mutual Friend* (also known as *Our Mutual Friend—by Charles Dickens*), BBC, 1998, broadcast on *Masterpiece Theatre,* PBS, 1999.

Oswald Bates, *Shooting the Past,* BBC, 1999, broadcast on *Masterpiece Theatre,* PBS, 1999.

Vince Skinner, *The Thing about Vince,* Carlton Television, 2000.

Irving, *Perfect Strangers* (also known as *Almost Strangers*), BBC, 2001.

Mitchel Greenfield, *Bodily Harm,* [Great Britain], 2002.

Voice, *Bosom Pals* (animated), BBC, 2004.

Narrator, *Jamie's School Dinners,* Channel 4 (England) and Food Network Canada, 2005.

Television Appearances; Movies:

Jim, *SOS Titanic,* ABC, 1979.

First constable, *Oliver Twist,* CBS, 1982.

Lyndon, *Dutch Girls,* London Weekend Television, 1985.

Paul, *Body Contact,* BBC, 1987.

Francis Meakes, *Broke,* BBC, 1990.

Nona, BBC, 1991.

B, *Rough for Theatre II,* RTE (Ireland), then PBS, 2000.

Tommy Rag, *Vacuuming Completely Nude in Paradise,* BBC, 2001, BBC America, 2002.

Quinty, *My House in Umbria,* HBO, 2003.

Albert Pierrepont, *The Last Hangman* (also known as *Pierrepont*), Granada Television, 2005.

Mr. Harvey, *Mr. Harvey Lights a Candle,* BBC, 2005.

Terry Cannings, *Cherished,* BBC, 2005.

Television Appearances; Specials:

Wainwright, "The Vanishing Army," *Play for Today* (also known as *Play for Today: The Vanishing Army*), BBC, 1980.

Gordon Leach, "Home Sweet Home," *Play for Today* (also known as *Play for Today: Home Sweet Home*), BBC, 1982.

Sergeant Baxter, "A Cotswold Death," *Play for Today* (also known as *Play for Today: A Cotswold Death*), BBC, 1982.

Lieutenant Hibbert, *Journey's End,* 1988.

Donald Caudell, *Stolen,* London Weekend Television, 1990.

Gordon, *Neville's Island,* Yorkshire Television, 1998.

Appeared as Yepikhodov, *The Cherry Orchard,* BBC; as Hawkins, *Guest of the Nation,* BBC; and as Andrei, *Three Sisters.*

Television Appearances; Awards Presentations:

The Evening Standard British Film Awards, ITV-3 (England), 2005.

Television Appearances; Episodic:

Title role, "John Burnett," *The South Bank Show,* London Weekend Television, 1989.

Pathologist, "The Case of the Missing," *Murder Most Horrid,* BBC-2, 1991.

Andy, "Back to Reality," *Red Dwarf,* BBC-2, 1992.

Bill Webster, "Pillow Talk," *Boon,* Central Television, 1992.

Cunningham, "Barcelona, May 1917," *The Young Indiana Jones Chronicles,* ABC, 1992.

Pilot, *Tracey Ullman: A Class Act,* [Great Britain], c. 1992, HBO, 1993.

Cell mate, "Cell," *Rab C. Nesbitt,* BBC, 1993.

Guest, *The Danny Baker Show,* BBC, 1994.

Salesperson, "The Swords," *The Hunger,* Showtime, 1997.

Himself, "A Man for All Stages: The Life and Times of Christopher Plummer," *Life and Times,* CBC, 2002.

Guest, *Parkinson,* BBC, 2002.

Himself, *Top Gear* (also known as *Top Gear Xtra*), BBC, 2005.

Appeared as Clevor Trevor, "Night Moves," *Arena* (also known as *Arena—Night Moves*), BBC-2.

Television Appearances; Other:

Appeared as Shorty, *The Brylcreem Boys,* BBC; as Porfiry, *Great Writers—Dostoevsky;* as Chico, *La Nona,* BBC; as Nick Watt, *The Nihilist's Double Vision;* as Jimmy Beales, *Roots,* BBC; and as Little Pig Robinson, *The Tale of Little Pig Robinson.* Also appeared in *Dread Poets Society,* BBC; and *African Footsteps.*

Stage Appearances:

Vic Maggot, *Smelling a Rat,* Hampstead Theatre Club, London, 1988.

Appeared as Andrei, *Three Sisters,* as Mech, *Baal,* as Rafe, *Knight of the Burning Pestle,* as Simple, *The Merry Wives of Windsor,* as Wackford Spears and Mr. Folair, *Nicholas Nickleby,* and in *Cymbeline,* all Royal Shakespeare Company, Stratford–upon–Avon, England; as Bottom, *A Midsummer Night's Dream,* as the dauphin,

Saint Joan, as Ligurio, *Mandragola,* and in *Le bourgeois gentilhomme,* all Royal National Theatre, London; as Boucicault, *Heavenly Bodies,* as Gratiano, *The Merchant of Venice,* and as Harry Trevor and Baptista, *Kiss Me Kate,* all Birmingham Repertory Theatre, Birmingham, England; as Lawrence, *Mary Barns,* Birmingham Repertory Theatre and Royal Court Theatre, London; as Martin, *Aunt Mary,* Warehouse Theatre, London; as Khelstakov, *The Government Inspector,* Greenwich Theatre, London; as Derek, *Screamers,* Playhouse Studio Theatre, Edinburgh, Scotland; and as Ivan, *Suicide.*

RECORDINGS

Videos:
Robin, *Coaching Skills* (corporate video), late 1990s.

OTHER SOURCES

Periodicals:
Daily Telegraph, January 5, 2004, p. 13.
Radio Times, July 6, 1991, p. 5; March 11, 1995, p. 8; January 6, 1996, pp. 14–17; October 12, 2002, pp. 30–32.

SPINELLA, Stephen 1956–

PERSONAL

Born October 11, 1956, in Naples, Italy; raised in Glendale, AZ; father, a naval airplane mechanic. *Education:* University of Arizona, B.F.A., 1978; graduate study at New York University.

Addresses: *Agent*—Gary Gersh, Innovative Artists, 1505 10th St., Santa Monica, CA 90401. *Manager*—Maryellen Mulcahy, Framework Entertainment, 9057 Nemo St., Suite C, West Hollywood, CA 90069.

Career: Actor. Arizona Theatre Company, actor, 1978–79.

Awards, Honors: Marion Scott Actor Achievement Award; Antoinette Perry Award, best featured actor in a play, *Theatre World* Award, and Drama Desk Award, outstanding featured actor in a play, all 1993, for *Angels in America: Part One: Millennium Approaches;* Antoinette Perry Award, best featured actor in a play, and Drama Desk Award, outstanding actor in a play, both 1994, for *Angels in America: Part Two: Perestroika;* Obie Award, *Village Voice,* outstanding ensemble

performance (with others), 1995, for *Love! Valour! Compassion!;* Annual Shakespeare Award, Artists' Equity Association, 1995, for *Troilus and Cressida;* Antoinette Perry Award nomination, Outer Critics Circle Award, and Drama Desk Award, all best featured actor in a musical, 2000, for *James Joyce's "The Dead."*

CREDITS

Stage Appearances:
The Taming of the Shrew, Colonnades Theatre, New York City, 1985.
7 by Beckett, Syracuse Stage, Syracuse, NY, 1987–88.
The Amanuensis, *L'illusion,* New York Theatre Workshop, Perry Street Theatre, New York City, 1988–89.
Prior Walter, *Millennium Approaches,* Center Theatre Group, Mark Taper Forum, Los Angeles, 1989–90.
Prior Walter, *Angels in America: Part One: Millenium Approaches,* Center Theatre Group, Mark Taper Forum, 1992–93.
Prior Walter, *Angels in America: Part Two: Perestroika,* Center Theatre Group, Mark Taper Forum, 1992–93.
Prior Walter and man in park, *Angels in America: Part One: Millennium Approaches,* Walter Kerr Theatre, New York City, 1993–94.
Prior Walter, *Angels in America: Part Two: Perestroika,* Walter Kerr Theatre, 1993–94.
Love! Valour! Compassion!, Manhattan Theatre Club Stage I, New York City, 1994–95.
Pandarus, *Troilus and Cressida,* New York Shakespeare Festival, Delacorte Theatre, Public Theatre, New York City, 1995.
Waiting for Godot, Seattle Repertory Theatre, Seattle, WA, 1996.
Thomas, *A Question of Mercy,* New York Theatre Workshop, 1997.
Alfieri, *A View from the Bridge,* Roundabout Theatre Company, Criterion Center Stage Right Theatre, New York City, 1997–98.
Servant to Orestes, *Electra,* McCarter Theatre, Princeton, NJ, then Ethel Barrymore Theatre, New York City, 1998–99.
Sherlock Holmes, *Crucifer of Blood,* Berkshire Theatre Festival, MA, 1999.
Freddy Malins, *James Joyce's "The Dead"* (musical), Playwrights Horizons, Belasco Theatre, New York City, 1999–2000, then Ahmanson Theatre, Los Angeles, 2000.
Semyon Semyonovich Medvedenko, *The Seagull,* New York Shakespeare Festival, Delacorte Theatre, 2001.
Elle, Zipper Theatre, New York City, 2002.
Simon Stimson, *Our Town,* Westport Country Playhouse, Westport, CT, 2002, then Booth Theatre, New York City, 2002.
James Joyce, *Travesties,* Williamstown Theatre Festival, Williamstown, MA, 2003.

Title role, *Svejk,* Theatre for a New Audience, Duke Theatre on Forty–Second Street, New York City, 2004.

The Singing Forest, Pacific Playwrights Festival, Segerstrom Stage, South Coast Repertory, Costa Mesa, CA, 2004.

Dominique de Villepin, *Stuff Happens,* Mark Taper Forum, Los Angeles, 2005.

Also appeared in *The Age of Assassins, Bremen Coffee, A Bright Room Called Day, Burrhead, Dance for Me Rosetta, La fin de la baleine, Heavenly Theatre, Hydriota, King Lear, Major Barbara, Serious Money, Tartuffe,* and *The Virgin Molly.*

Television Appearances; Series:

Rex Pinsker, a recurring role, *The Education of Max Bickford,* CBS, 2001–2002.

Television Appearances; Specials:

In the Wings: Angels in America on Broadway, PBS, 1993.

Voice of Michael Wigglesworth, *Out of the Past,* PBS, 1998.

Simon Stimson, *Our Town,* Showtime, 2003.

Television Appearances; Movies:

Brandy Alexander, *And the Band Played On,* HBO, 1993.

Percy, "What the Deaf Man Heard," *Hallmark Hall of Fame,* CBS, 1997.

Television Appearances; Miniseries:

Voice, *Broadway: The American Musical,* PBS, 2004.

Television Appearances; Episodic:

Andy Polone, "High & Low," *Law & Order,* NBC, 2000.

Bob McCarthy, "Ends and Means," *Ed,* NBC, 2002.

Mr. Kishell, "Snowman," *Alias,* ABC, 2002.

Randall Schoonover, "Sea Bee Jeebies," *Frasier,* NBC, 2003.

Mr. Kishell, "The Frame," *Alias,* ABC, 2004.

Guest, *Larry King Live,* Cable News Network, 2004.

Joel Kemper, "Shadows," *Without a Trace,* CBS, 2004.

Mr. Heard, "Lipstick on Your Panties," *Huff,* Showtime, 2004.

Mr. Heard, "Control," *Huff,* Showtime, 2004.

Appeared as Kenneth Croft in an episode of *Sirens.*

Television Appearances; Awards Presentations:

The 47th Annual Tony Awards, CBS, 1993.

The 50th Annual Tony Awards, CBS, 1996.

Film Appearances:

Frank, *Tarantella,* Tara Releasing, 1995.

Dr. Darrel Lindenmeyer, *Virtuosity,* Paramount, 1995.

Young man at Rolls, *Faithful,* New Line Cinema, 1996.

Perry Sellars, *Love! Valour! Compassion!,* Fine Line, 1997.

RECORDINGS

Audio Books:

Reader, *A Few Short Notes on Tropical Butterflies: Stories,* by John Murray, Harper Audio, 2003.

OTHER SOURCES

Periodicals:

New York Times, June 5, 1993.

SPYBEY, Dina 1965(?)–
(Dina Waters)

PERSONAL

Born August 29, 1965 (some sources cite August 28 or 1966), in Columbus, OH; married Mark S. Waters (a director), November 10, 2000. *Education:* Ohio State University, B.F.A.; Rutgers University, M.F.A. *Avocational Interests:* Dancing.

Addresses: *Agent*—Jennifer Craig, The Gersh Agency, 232 North Canon Dr., Beverly Hills, CA 90210; William Morris Agency, One William Morris Place, Beverly Hills, CA 90212. *Manager*—Peter Principato, Principato Young Entertainment, 9465 Wilshire Blvd., Suite 430, Beverly Hills, CA 90212.

Career: Actress. Drama Department, New York City, cofounder.

Awards, Honors: *Theatre World* Award, outstanding new performer, 1993, for *Five Women Wearing the Same Dress;* Daytime Emmy Award, outstanding performer in a children's special, 1993, for "Public Law 106: The Becky Bell Story," *Lifestories: Families in Crisis;* Screen Actors Guild Award nomination (with others), outstanding ensemble in a comedy series, 1997, for *Remember WENN;* silver medallist in gymnastics, Junior Olympics.

CREDITS

Film Appearances:

Monique, Jr., *Striptease,* Columbia, 1996.

Natalie, *Big Night,* Samuel Goldwyn, 1996.

Young Elise, *The First Wives Club,* Paramount, 1996.

Allessandra, *Burn, Hollywood, Burn* (also known as *An Alan Smithee Film: Burn Hollywood Burn*), Buena Vista, 1997.

Bee–Bee, *SubUrbia* (also known as *subUrbi@*), Sony Pictures Classics, 1997.

Dee, *Julian Po* (also known as *The Tears of Julian Po*), Fine Line Features, 1997.

Liz Carderelli, *Getting Personal* (also known as *The Mysterious Death of Kelly Lawman*), Lakeshore Entertainment, 1999.

Young woman, *Advice from a Caterpillar*, Keystone Entertainment, 1999.

Bambi Madison, *Isn't She Great* (also known as *Ist sie nicht grossartig?*), MCA/Universal, 2000.

Some sources cite an appearance as Colleen in *Surprise!*

Film Appearances; As Dina Waters:

Debby Utley, *John Q* (also known as *John Q.*), New Line Cinema, 2002.

Third fired employee, *Full Frontal*, Miramax, 2002.

Dottie Robertson, *Freaky Friday*, Buena Vista, 2003.

Emma, *The Haunted Mansion* (also known as *Disney's "The Haunted Mansion"*), Buena Vista, 2003.

Abby Brody, *Just Like Heaven* (also known as *If Only It Were True*), DreamWorks, 2005.

Television Appearances; Series:

Brenda Mikowski, *Men Behaving Badly* (also known as *It's a Man's World*), NBC, 1996–97.

Celia Mellon, *Remember WENN*, American Movie Classics, 1996–98.

Nina Bloom, *Conrad Bloom*, NBC, 1998.

Shelley, *Oh Baby*, Lifetime, 1998–2000.

Jenny Lombardi, *Cold Feet*, NBC, beginning 1999.

(As Dina Waters) Tracy Montrose Blair, a recurring role, *Six Feet Under*, HBO, 2001.

(As Waters) Dottie Sunshine, *Greg the Bunny*, Fox, 2002.

Television Appearances; Movies:

(As Dina Waters) Receptionist, *Warning: Parental Advisory*, VH1, 2002.

Television Appearances; Specials:

Becky Bell, "Public Law 106: The Becky Bell Story," *Lifestories: Families in Crisis*, HBO, 1992.

Leanne Strauss, "If I Die before I Wake," *CBS Schoolbreak Specials*, CBS, 1994.

Television Appearances; Episodic:

Genny, "All the President's Women," *Gun* (also known as *Robert Altman's "Gun"*), ABC, 1997.

Gina, "Don't Tell," *Suddenly Susan*, NBC, 1998.

Tina Schadowski, "Let's Go," *Fantasy Island*, ABC, 1998.

(As Dina Waters) Megan, "Hostess to Murder," *Just Shoot Me!*, NBC, 1999.

Katherine Yates, "The Crush," *Stark Raving Mad*, NBC, 2000.

Katherine Yates, "The Grade," *Stark Raving Mad*, NBC, 2000.

(As Waters) Nanette "Nanny G" Guzman, "Don Juan in Hell: Part 2," *Frasier*, NBC, 2001.

Judy, "Joey and the Valentine's Date," *Joey*, NBC, 2005.

Television Appearances; Pilots:

Jenny Lombardi, *Cold Feet* (first version), NBC, 1999.

Jenny Lombardi, *Cold Feet* (second version), NBC, 1999.

(As Dina Waters) Tracy Montrose Blair, *Six Feet Under*, HBO, 2001.

Stage Appearances:

Renee and magazine girl, *M. Butterfly*, Repertory Theatre of St. Louis, St. Louis, MO, 1992–93.

Frances, *Five Women Wearing the Same Dress*, Manhattan Class Company, New York City, 1993.

Kim, *The Perfectionist*, McCarter Theatre, Princeton, NJ, 1993–94.

Baby June and second dancer, *Girl Gone*, Manhattan Class Company, 1994.

Hortense, *Blue Light*, Bay Street Theatre, New York City, 1994, revised version produced as *The Shawl*, Playhouse 91, New York City, 1996.

Mary, *Dates and Nuts*, Theatre Off Park, New York City, 1995.

Zoey, *Don Juan in Chicago*, Primary Stages, New York City, 1995.

Pearl, *The Iceman Cometh*, Brooks Atkinson Theatre, New York City, 1999.

STARKE, Anthony 1963–

PERSONAL

Born June 6, 1963, in Syracuse, NY; raised in California and Illinois; married; wife's name, Lolly; children: Garrett. *Education:* Marquette University, theatre arts, B.A. *Avocational Interests:* Boxing, tae kwon do.

Addresses: *Agent*—Paradigm, 360 North Crescent Dr., North Building, Beverly Hills, CA 90210; Doug Segers, Metropolitan Talent Agency, 4526 Wilshire Blvd., Los Angeles, CA 90010; Mark Scroggs, Don Buchwald and Associates, 6500 Wilshire Blvd., Suite 2200, Los Angeles, CA 90048. *Manager*—Tony Chargin, Compass Entertainment, 9255 Sunset Blvd., Suite 727, Los Angeles, CA 90069.

Career: Actor.

Awards, Honors: Quarterfinalist, Texas Film Institute Screenwriting Competition, 2003, for *Blind Eye.*

CREDITS

Television Appearances; Series:
Don Hattan, *One Big Family,* syndicated, 1986.
Jack Donahue, *The George Carlin Show,* Fox, 1994–95.
Billy McPherson, *The Last Frontier,* Fox, 1996.
Ezra Standish, *The Magnificent Seven,* CBS, 1998–99.
David Chandler, *Cold Feet,* NBC, beginning 1999.

Television Appearances; Movies:
Dean Conroy, *First Steps,* CBS, 1985.
Heatwave!, ABC, 1990.
Star Witness, 1995.
Will Dezmond, *Inferno,* UPN, 1998.

Television Appearances; Episodic:
Donnie Dibiase, "Romero and Juliet," *Lady Blue,* ABC, 1985.
"Fear and Loathing with Russell Buckins" (also known as "Doin' the Quarter Mile in a Lifetime"), *21 Jump Street,* Fox, 1987.
Russell the ghost, "Ghost in the Machine," *The Flash,* CBS, 1990.
Dale Evans, "Halloween," *Beverly Hills 90210,* Fox, 1991.
Slim, "Take Me out of the Ballgame," *Cheers,* NBC, 1992.
Vaughan, *Down the Shore,* Fox, 1992.
Olaf Brackman, "Showdown," *The Adventures of Brisco County, Jr.* (also known as *Brisco County, Jr.*), Fox, 1993.
Jimmy, "The Jimmy," *Seinfeld,* NBC, 1995.
Kip Richmond, "First Episode," *Suddenly Susan,* NBC, 1996.
Kip Richmond, "A Boy Like That," *Suddenly Susan,* NBC, 1997.
Kip Richmond, "The Ways and Means," *Suddenly Susan,* NBC, 1997.
Kip Richmond, "What a Card," *Suddenly Susan,* NBC, 1997.
Michael Patrick, "The Better Part of Valor," *The Pretender,* NBC, 1997.
Devlin, "Muse to My Ears," *Charmed,* The WB, 2001.
Joey Miller, "Chapter Eleven," *Boston Public,* Fox, 2001.
Matt Hudson, "Anatomy of a Lye," *CSI: Crime Scene Investigation* (also known as *CSI*), CBS, 2002.
Tyke, "A New World," *Angel,* The WB, 2002.
Sean Parnell, "Leggo My Ego," *Abby,* UPN, 2003.
Brad Halford, "Dead or Alive," *Crossing Jordan,* NBC, 2004.
Sebastian, "Allen," *Prison Break,* Fox, 2005.
Sebastian, "Cell Test," *Prison Break,* Fox, 2005.

Television Appearances; Pilots:
Don Hattan, *One Big Family,* syndicated, 1986.
Tommy Byrd, *Smart Guys,* NBC, 1988.
Jack Donahue, *The George Carlin Show,* Fox, 1994.
Billy McPherson, *The Last Frontier,* Fox, 1996.
Max, NBC, 1996.
Ezra Standish, *The Magnificent Seven,* CBS, 1998.
David Chandler, *Cold Feet* (first version), NBC, 1999.
David Chandler, *Cold Feet* (second version), NBC, 1999.
Sebastian, *Prison Break,* Fox, 2005.

Film Appearances:
Cameron, *Nothing in Common,* TriStar, 1986.
Chad Finletter, *Return of the Killer Tomatoes!* (also known as *Return of the Killer Tomatoes: The Sequel*), New World Pictures, 1988.
Russ Deacon, *18 Again!* (also known as *Eighteen Again*), New World Pictures, 1988.
Truman–Lodge, *License to Kill* (also known as *Albert R. Broccoli's "Licence to Kill"* and *Licence to Kill*), Metro–Goldwyn–Mayer/United Artists, 1989.
Father Luke Brophy, *Repossessed,* New Line Cinema, 1990.
The ghost, *Flash III: Deadly Nightshade,* 1992.
Billy, *Nowhere to Run,* Columbia, 1993.

Stage Appearances:
Buried Child, South Coast Repertory Theatre, Costa Mesa, CA, 1985–86.
Macduff and messenger, *Kabuki Lady Macbeth,* Chicago Shakespeare Upstairs Theatre, Chicago, IL, 2005.

WRITINGS

Screenplays:
Blind Eye, c. 2002.

Some sources cite Starke as the author of *Blood Chemistry.*

Novels:
Author of *A Coal to His Lips,* 1stBooks Library.

STING, 1951–

PERSONAL

Full name, Gordon Matthew Sumner; born October 2, 1951, in Wallsend, Newcastle upon Tyne, England; son of Ernest Matthew (a milkman and engineer) and Audrey (a hairdresser; maiden name, Cowell) Sumner; married Frances Eleanor Tomelty (an actress), May 1, 1976 (divorced, March, 1984); married Trudie Styler (a director, producer, actress, and model), August 22 (some sources cite August 20), 1992; children: (first marriage) Joseph (Joe), Fuschia Katherine (Kate); (second marriage) Brigette Michael (Mickey), Jake, Eliot Paulina (Coco), Giacomo Luke. *Education:* Attended the University of Warwick. *Avocational Interests:* Yoga.

Addresses: *Agent*—Creative Artists Agency, 9830 Wilshire Blvd., Beverly Hills, CA 90212; Markham and Froggatt, Ltd., 4 Windmill St., London W1T 2HZ, England; Intellectual Property Group, 9200 Sunset Blvd., Suite 520, Los Angeles, CA 90069. *Manager*—KSM, Inc., 826 Broadway, Suite 411, New York, NY 10003. *Publicist*—Keith Sherman and Associates, 1776 Broadway, Suite 1200, New York, NY 10019.

Career: Singer, bass player, songwriter, composer, and actor. Performer with Earthrise, the Phoenix Jazz Band (some sources cite the Phoenix Jazzmen), and the River City Jazz Band in the 1970s, with the Newcastle Big Band, 1972, and with Last Exit; the Police (musical group), singer, bass player, and songwriter, c. 1977–83; solo performer; Blue Turtles (jazz group), founder and performer; musician on other instruments; affiliated with Strontium Ninety (a rock band); appeared in commercials and print advertisements. English teacher at a school in Newcastle upon Tyne, England, 1975–77; Kaleidoscope Cameras, London, managing director, beginning 1982; worked as a musical performer on a cruise ship (with the Ronnie Pierson Trio), an income tax clerk, a construction worker, ditch digger, and a soccer coach. Rainforest Foundation International, cofounder, 1989, member of the board of trustees, beginning 1989, and concert performer; affiliated with other charities and fund–raising activities.

Member: Performing Rights Society, Amnesty International.

Awards, Honors: As a member of the Police, named best new artist, *Rolling Stone,* 1979; Grammy Award (with the Police), best rock instrumental performance, National Academy of Recording Arts and Sciences, c. 1980; Grammy Award (with the Police), best rock instrumental performance, 1981, for "Behind My Camel"; Grammy Award (with the Police), best rock vocal performance by a duo or group, 1981, for "Don't Stand So Close to Me"; as a member of the Police, named best band, *Rolling Stone,* 1981; named best male singer, *Rolling Stone,* 1981; BRIT Award, best British rock group, 1982; Grammy Award (with the Police), best rock vocal performance by a duo or group, 1983, for *Synchronicity;* Grammy Award, best rock instrumental performance, 1983, for *Brimstone and Treacle;* Grammy awards, pop song of the year and best vocal

performance by a duo or group, and best single, *Rolling Stone,* both 1983, and American Video Award, best group video, 1984, all with the Police, all for "Every Breath You Take"; BRIT Award, outstanding contribution to British music, 1985; Grammy Award (with Michael Apted), best long form music video, 1987, for *Bring on the Night;* Grammy Award, best pop vocal performance, male, 1987, for *Bring on the Night;* Grammy Award (with others), best performance music video, 1988, for *The Prince's Trust All–Star Rock Concert;* Readers' Poll awards, pop/rock musician of the year and best pop/rock group, *Downbeat,* 1989; Grammy Award, best rock song, 1991, for "The Soul Cages"; International Rock Award, video legend, 1991; honorary doctorate of music degree, University of Northumbria, 1992; Grammy Award, best pop vocal performance—male, 1993, for "If I Ever Lose My Faith in You"; Grammy Award nomination (with Eric Clapton and Michael Kamen), best song written specifically for a motion picture or for television, and MTV Movie Award nomination (with Eric Clapton), best movie song, both 1993, for "It's Probably Me," from *Lethal Weapon 3;* Grammy Award (with others), best music video long form, 1993, for *Ten Summoner's Tales;* MTV Movie Award nomination (with Bryan Adams and Rod Stewart), best movie song, 1994, for "All for Love," from *The Three Musketeers;* honorary doctorate of music degree, Berklee College of Music, 1994; Grammy Award nomination (with others), 1995, for "Peter and the Wolf: A Prokofiev Fantasy," *A&E Stage;* Sierra Award, best original song, Las Vegas Film Critics Society, 1998, and Golden Globe Award nomination (with Trevor Jones), best original song—motion picture, 1999, both for "The Mighty," from *The Mighty;* Grammy Award, best pop album, 2000, for *Brand New Day;* Grammy Award, best male pop performance, 2000, for "Brand New Day"; Phoenix Film Critics Society Award, best original song, and Sierra Award nomination, best song, both 2000, Academy Award nomination, best music—original song, Golden Globe Award nomination, best original song—motion picture, Golden Satellite Award nomination, best original song, International Press Academy, Broadcast Film Critics Association Award, best song, and Annie Award, outstanding individual achievement for a song in an animated production, International Animated Film Society, all 2001, and Grammy Award nomination, best song written for a motion picture, television, or other visual media, 2002, all with David Hartley, all for "My Funny Friend and Me," from *The Emperor's New Groove;* Grammy Award, best male pop vocal performance, 2001, for "She Walks This Earth (Soberana Rosa)"; Emmy Award, outstanding individual performance in a variety or music program, 2002, for *Sting ... All This Time;* Golden Globe Award, best original song—motion picture, Academy Award nomination, best music—original song, Broadcast Film Critics Association Award nomination, best song, and World Soundtrack Award nomination, best original song written for a film, all 2002, for "Until," from *Kate & Leopold;* with the Police, inducted into the Rock and Roll Hall of Fame, 2003;

named a Commander of the Order of the British Empire, 2003; Grammy Award (with Mary J. Blige), best pop collaboration with vocals, 2004, for "Whenever I Say Your Name"; named person of the year, for music and charitable work, MusiCares, 2004; World Soundtrack Award (with Alison Krauss), best original song written for a film, Academy Award nomination, best music—original song, and Golden Globe Award nomination, best original song—motion picture, all 2004, and Grammy Award nomination, best song written for a motion picture, television or other visual media, 2005, all for "You Will Be My Ain True Love," from *Cold Mountain;* the Police were named one of the best rock and roll artists of all time by *Rolling Stone;* David Angell Humanitarian Award, American Screenwriters Association, c. 2005; other awards and designations as a member of the Police and as a solo artist.

CREDITS

Film Appearances:

Ace Face, *Quadrophenia* (also known as *Quadrophenia: A Way of Life*), Rhino Releasing/World Northal, 1979.

Just Like Eddie, *Radio On,* Unifilm, 1979.

(With the Police) Himself, *Punk and Its Aftershocks* (documentary; also known as *British Rock* and *British Rock—Ready for the 80s*), Stein Film, 1980.

Himself, *The Secret Policeman's Other Ball,* Miramax, 1981.

Himself, *Urgh! A Music War* (concert film), Lorimar, 1981.

Martin Taylor, *Brimstone and Treacle,* United Artists, 1982.

Feyd–Rautha, *Dune,* Universal, 1984.

Mick, *Plenty,* Twentieth Century–Fox, 1985.

Himself, *Bring on the Night* (concert film; also known as *Sting: Bring on the Night*), Samuel Goldwyn/A&M, 1985.

Victor Frankenstein, *The Bride,* Columbia, 1985.

Daniel Osler, *Julia and Julia* (also known as *Giulia e Giulia*), Cinecom International, 1987.

Finney, *Stormy Monday,* Atlantic Releasing, 1988.

Heroic officer, *The Adventures of Baron Munchausen* (also known as *Die Abenteuer des Baron von Muenchhausen*), TriStar/Columbia, 1988.

Himself, *Dance of Hope* (documentary), First Run Features, c. 1989.

Himself, *Resident Alien* (documentary; also known as *Resident Alien: Quentin Crisp in America*), Greycat Films, 1991.

Himself, *Branford Marsalis: The Music Tells You* (documentary; also known as *The Music Tells You*), Pennebaker Associates, 1992.

Reader of Pablo Neruda's sonnet "Morning," *Il Postino* (also known as *The Postman*), Miramax, 1994.

Fledge, *Gentlemen Don't Eat Poets* (also known as *Grave Indiscretion* and *The Grotesque*), LIVE Entertainment/Ster–Kinekor Pictures, 1995.

J. D., *Lock, Stock, and Two Smoking Barrels* (also known as *Two Smoking Barrels*), Gramercy Pictures, 1999.

Himself, *The Filth and the Fury* (documentary), Fine Line Features, 2000.

Himself, *All Access: Front Row. Backstage. Live!* (documentary; also known as *All Access* and *All Access: Front Row. Backstage. Live! Presented by Certs*), IMAX Corporation, 2001.

Himself, *The Sweatbox* (documentary), Buena Vista, 2002.

Himself, *George Michael: A Different Story* (documentary), Gorilla Entertainment, 2005.

Film Song Performer:

(With Eric Clapton and Michael Kamen) "It's Probably Me," *Lethal Weapon 3,* Warner Bros., 1992.

(With Bryan Adams and Rod Stewart) "All for Love," *The Three Musketeers,* Buena Vista, 1993.

"Demolition Man," *Demolition Man,* Warner Bros., 1993.

"The Secret Marriage," *Four Weddings and a Funeral,* Gramercy Pictures, 1994.

"Angel Eyes," "It's a Lonesome Town," and "My One and Only Love," *Leaving Las Vegas,* Metro–Goldwyn–Mayer/United Artists, 1995.

"Moonlight," *Sabrina,* Paramount, 1995.

"This Was Never Meant To Be," *Gentlemen Don't Eat Poets* (also known as *Grave Indiscretion* and *The Grotesque*), LIVE Entertainment/Ster–Kinekor Pictures, 1995.

The Living Sea (documentary), MacGillivray Freeman Films, 1995.

Title song, *The Mighty,* Miramax, 1998.

"My Funny Friend and Me" and other songs, *The Emperor's New Groove* (animated), Buena Vista, 2000.

"A Thousand Years" and "When the World Is Running Down, You Can't Go Wrong," *Red Planet* (also known as *Mars*), Warner Bros., 2000.

Dolphins (short documentary film), MacGillivray Freeman Films, 2000.

Videoflashback (short film), kientopp production, 2000.

"Until," *Kate & Leopold,* Miramax, 2001.

(With Alison Krauss) "You Will Be My Ain True Love," *Cold Mountain,* Miramax, 2003.

Performer of songs that have been featured in other films, television broadcasts, stage productions, and video collections.

Television Appearances; Series:

Voice of Zarm, *Captain Planet and the Planeteers* (animated; also known as and *Captain Planet's Mission to Save Earth*), TBS and syndicated, 1990–92.

Television Appearances; Miniseries:

The North Face Expeditions, NBC, 1999–2000.

Himself, *Unsere Besten—Wer ist der grosste Deutsche?* (documentary), Zweites Deutsches Fernsehen, 2003.

Television Appearances; Movies:
Helith, *Artemis 81,* BBC, 1981.

Television Appearances; Specials:
Ligmalion (musical; also known as *Ligmalion: A Musical for the 80s*), [Great Britain], 1985.

Live Aid, BBC and other networks, 1985.

The Flintstones 25th Anniversary Celebration, 1986.

The Prince's Trust All–Star Rock Concert (also known as *The Prince's Trust Rock Gala: 10th Birthday*), HBO, 1986.

Rolling Stone Magazine's 20 Years of Rock 'n' Roll (documentary), ABC, 1987.

Top of the Pops: A Very Special Christmas, CBS, 1987.

Himself, *Nelson Mandela 70th Birthday Tribute* (also known as *Freedomfest: Nelson Mandela's 70th Birthday Celebration*), Fox, 1988.

"Human Rights Now Tour," *HBO World Stage,* HBO, 1988.

Our Common Future, Arts and Entertainment and syndicated, 1989.

"Sting in Tokyo," *HBO World Stage,* HBO, 1989.

Late Night with David Letterman Eighth Anniversary Special, NBC, 1990.

Coca–Cola Pop Music "Backstage Pass to Summer," Fox, 1991.

Hard Rock Cafe New Year's Eve Special, CBS, 1991.

Spaceship Earth: Our Global Environment, The Disney Channel, 1991.

"Two Rooms: Tribute to Elton John and Bernie Taupin," *ABC in Concert '91* (also known as *ABC in Concert*), ABC, 1991.

Himself, *Sting at the Hollywood Bowl: A Birthday Celebration* (also known as *Sting at the Hollywood Bowl*), The Disney Channel, 1992.

Rolling Stone 25: The MTV Special (documentary), MTV, 1992.

The 25th Montreux Music Festival, The Disney Channel, 1992.

Music in Movies '93, ABC, 1993.

Pavarotti and Friends, PBS, 1993.

"Sting: Summoner's Travels" (also known as "Sting: A Musical Voyage"), *In the Spotlight,* PBS, 1993.

Narrator, "Peter and the Wolf: A Prokofiev Fantasy," *A&E Stage,* Arts and Entertainment, 1994.

Himself, *The State's 43rd Annual Halloween Special,* CBS, 1995.

Himself, *Sting in Vietnam,* 1996.

Sounds of Summer Preview '96, ABC, 1996.

Himself, *An Audience with Elton John,* Independent Television, 1997.

Himself, *Music for Montserrat* (also known as *All–Star Concert for Motserrat*), pay–per–view, 1997.

Independence Day Concert from the Glastonbury Festival, ABC, 1997.

Billy Idol, *Saturday Night Live: The Best of Phil Hartman,* NBC, 1998.

Himself, *Divas Live: An Honors Concert for VH1 Save the Children* (also known as *VH1 "Divas Live"*), VH1, 1998.

Himself, *The X–Files Movie Special* (documentary), Fox, 1998.

Tony Bennett: An All–Star Tribute–Live by Request, Arts and Entertainment, 1998.

Billy Idol, *Saturday Night Live: The Best of Chris Rock,* NBC, 1999.

Performer of song "Brand New Day," *Radio City Music Hall's Grand Re–Opening Gala,* NBC, 1999.

Himself, *Saturday Night Live: 25th Anniversary Primetime Special* (also known as *Saturday Night Live: 25th Anniversary*), NBC, 1999.

NetAid, VH1, 1999.

NetAid: A Concert Special, TNT, 1999.

The Nobel Peace Concert 1999, Fox Family Channel, 1999.

Performer, *VH1: Men Strike Back* (also known as *Men Strike Back*), VH1, 2000.

Himself, *The Beatles Revolution* (documentary), ABC, 2000.

Himself, *Stand and Be Counted* (documentary), The Learning Channel, 2000.

New Orleans Jazz & Heritage Special, VH1, 2000.

Himself, *ABC 2002* (documentary; also known as *2002*), ABC, 2001.

Himself, *America: A Tribute to Heroes,* multiple networks, 2001.

Himself, *Being Mick* (documentary), ABC, 2001.

Himself, *Eric Clapton: Standing at the Crossroads* (documentary), The Learning Channel, 2001.

Himself, *From the Waist Down: Men, Women & Music* (documentary), VH1, 2001.

Himself, *Rock and Roll Moments: Super Star Artists and Groups* (documentary), The Learning Channel, 2001.

Himself, *Sting in Tuscany: All This Time* (documentary), Arts and Entertainment, 2001.

Himself, *Super Bowl XXXV,* CBS, 2001.

Himself, *VH1 News Special: Islamabad Rock City,* VH1, 2001.

Guest performer, *Pavarotti & Friends 2002 for Angola* (also known as *Pavarotti & Friends for Angola, from the Parco Novi Sad in Modena*), 2002.

Performer, *2002 Olympic Winter Games* (also known as *XIX Winter Olympics Opening Ceremony*), CBS, 2002.

Friday Night Super Bowl Bash, CBS, 2002.

Halftime performer, *Super Bowl XXXVII,* ABC, 2003.

Himself, *Children in Need,* BBC, 2003.

Himself, *A Journey to "Cold Mountain"* (documentary), 2003.

Himself, *The Victoria's Secret Fashion Show,* CBS, 2003.

Himself, *The Words and Music of "Cold Mountain,"* 2003.

Sting: Sacred Love (documentary), Arts and Entertainment, 2003.

Billy Idol, *101 Most Unforgettable SNL Moments,* E! Entertainment Television, 2004.

Bob Geldof: Saint or Singer? (documentary), BBC, 2004.

Himself, *All I Want: A Portrait of Rufus Wainwright,* 2005.

MTV Asia Aid, MTV, 2005.

Himself, *Live 8,* multiple networks, 2005.

Appeared in other specials, including a concert broadcast on DirecTV.

Television Appearances; Awards Presentations:

MTV Video Music Awards 1985, MTV, 1985.

The 28th Annual Grammy Awards, CBS, 1986.

Grammy Lifetime Achievement Award Show, CBS, 1987.

The 32nd Annual Grammy Awards, CBS, 1990.

The Third Annual International Rock Awards, ABC, 1991.

The 33rd Annual Grammy Awards, CBS, 1991.

The 1993 MTV Music Video Awards, MTV, 1993.

Himself, *41 edicion de los premios Ondas,* 1994.

The 36th Annual Grammy Awards, CBS, 1994.

The 1995 BRIT Awards, 1995.

The BRIT Awards '96, 1996.

Performer, *The MTV Video Music Awards,* MTV, 1997.

The 31st Annual Country Music Association Awards, CBS, 1997.

The 39th Grammy Awards, CBS, 1997.

Presenter, *The 40th Annual Grammy Awards,* CBS, 1998.

The 1998 VH1 Fashion Awards, VH1, 1998.

Presenter, *The 41st Annual Grammy Awards,* CBS, 1999.

Himself, *MTV Video Music Awards 2000* (also known as *The 2000 MTV Video Music Awards*), MTV, 2000.

The 42nd Annual Grammy Awards, CBS, 2000.

Himself, *My VH1 Music Awards,* VH1, 2001.

Himself, *The 73rd Annual Academy Awards,* ABC, 2001.

The 2001 Billboard Music Awards, Fox, 2001.

Performer, *BRIT Awards 2002,* Independent Television, 2002.

Performer, *The 74th Annual Academy Awards,* ABC, 2002.

Presenter, *The 59th Annual Golden Globe Awards,* NBC, 2002.

Presenter, *The Mirror's Pride of Britain Awards 2002,* Independent Television, 2002.

Himself, *The Orange British Academy Film Awards,* E! Entertainment Television, 2002.

Performer, *The 2003 Billboard Music Awards,* Fox, 2003.

Himself, *50 edicion de los premios Ondas,* 2003.

Himself, *MTV Europe Movie Awards 2003,* MTV, 2003.

Performer, *The 46th Annual Grammy Awards,* CBS, 2004.

Performer and presenter, *The 76th Annual Academy Awards,* ABC, 2004.

Himself, *BRIT Awards 2005,* Independent Television and BBC America, 2005.

Television Appearances; Episodic:

(With the Police) Himself, *Top of the Pops* (also known as *All New Top of the Pops* and *TOTP*), BBC, 1979, 1981, 1983, 2002, 2003.

(With the Police) Himself, *Aplauso,* 1980.

(With the Police) *Musikladen,* 1980.

Himself, *Late Night with David Letterman,* NBC, 1982, 1985, 1991.

Himself, *Soul Train,* syndicated, 1987.

Musical guest, *Saturday Night Live* (also known as *NBC's "Saturday Night," Saturday Night,* and *SNL*), NBC, 1987, 1993, 1996, 1997, 1999.

Himself, *Programa piloto,* 1988.

Himself, *Famous Last Words,* MTV, 1990.

Himself, *Unplugged* (also known as *MTV's "Unplugged"*), MTV, 1991.

Voice of himself, "Radio Bart," *The Simpsons* (animated), Fox, 1991.

Saturday Night Live (also known as *NBC's "Saturday Night," Saturday Night,* and *SNL*), NBC, 1991.

Himself, *The Late Show with David Letterman,* CBS, 1994, 1996, 1998, 1999, 2004, 2005.

Himself, "Muscle Chemicals," *The Smell of Reeves and Mortimer,* 1995.

Himself, "Punk," *The History of Rock 'n' Roll Vol. 9* (documentary), syndicated, 1995.

Himself, "Sting" (documentary), *The South Bank Show,* Independent Television and Bravo, 1996.

Himself, "Where Is the Love?," *The Larry Sanders Show,* HBO, 1996.

Himself, *Clive Anderson Talks Back,* Channel 4 (England), 1996.

Himself, *Lo mas plus* (also known as *Lo + plus*), 1996.

Himself, *TFI Friday,* Channel 4, 1996.

Host, *Saturday Night Live* (also known as *NBC's "Saturday Night," Saturday Night,* and *SNL*), NBC, 1997.

Himself, *On Tour,* PBS, 1997.

Himself, *The Rosie O'Donnell Show,* syndicated, 1997.

Himself, *Howard Stern,* E! Entertainment Television, 1997, 2000.

Himself, "Sting: Behind the Music" (also known as "Sting"), *Behind the Music* (also known as *BtM* and *VH1's "Behind the Music"*), VH1, 1999.

Himself, *Des O'Connor Tonight,* Independent Television, 1999.

Himself, *Late Night with Conan O'Brien,* NBC, 1999.

Himself, *Parkinson,* BBC, 1999, 2003.

Himself, *Dale's All Stars*, BBC, 2000.

Himself, *Good Morning Australia*, Ten Network (Australia), 2000.

Himself, *The Late Late Show with Craig Kilborn*, CBS, 2000.

Himself, *Rove Live*, Ten Network, 2000.

HermanSIC, multiple episodes in 2000.

Himself, "Cloudy Skies, Chance of Parade," *Ally McBeal*, Fox, 2001.

Himself, "Tangled Web," *The Nightmare Room*, The WB, 2001.

Himself, "Wetten, dass ... ? aus Boblingen," *Wetten, dass ... ?*, 2001.

Himself, *CD:UK*, Independent Television, 2001.

Himself, *Mad TV*, Fox, 2001.

Herself, *Operacion triunfo*, 2001.

Himself, *Today* (also known as *NBC News Today* and *The Today Show*), NBC, 2001.

Himself, *The Tonight Show with Jay Leno*, NBC, 2001, 2003.

Himself, *Musikbutikken*, 2002.

Himself, *Ellen: The Ellen DeGeneres Show* (also known as *Ellen* and *The Ellen DeGeneres Show*), syndicated, 2003.

Himself, *Friday Night with Jonathan Ross*, BBC, 2003.

Himself, *God kveld Norge*, 2003.

Himself, *The Oprah Winfrey Show* (also known as *Oprah*), syndicated, 2003.

Himself, *Top of the Pops 2*, BBC, 2003.

Himself, *TROS TV Show*, 2003.

Himself, "John Lennon's Jukebox," *The South Bank Show*, Independent Television and Bravo, 2004.

Himself, *Anke Late Night*, 2004.

Himself, *Jeremy Vine Meets ...* , BBC, 2004.

Himself, *McEnroe*, CNBC, 2004.

Himself, *Pepsi Smash*, The WB, 2004.

Himself, *Richard & Judy*, Channel 4, 2004.

Himself, *This Morning*, Independent Television, 2004.

Himself, *Tout le monde en parle*, 2004.

On–Air with Ryan Seacrest, syndicated, 2004.

TV total, 2004.

Himself, *Jimmy Kimmel Live*, ABC, 2005.

Appeared as himself, *Movie Surfers* (also known as *Disney's "The Movie Surfers"*), The Disney Channel; appeared as himself, *Storytellers* (also known as *VH1 Storytellers*), VH1.

Television Work; Specials:

Executive producer and music producer, *Sting: Sacred Love* (documentary), Arts and Entertainment, 2003.

Stage Appearances:

Macheath, *Threepenny Opera* (opera; also known as *3 Penny Opera*), Lunt–Fontanne Theatre, New York City, 1989.

Radio Appearances:

Himself, *The Howard Stern Radio Show*, 1997, 2000.

Appeared in other radio productions.

RECORDINGS

Albums:

Brimstone and Treacle (original soundtrack), A&M, 1982.

The Dream of the Blue Turtles, A&M, 1985.

Bring on the Night, A&M, 1986.

Nothing Like the Sun, A&M, 1987, five songs translated into Spanish and released as *Nada como el sol ...* , A&M, 1988.

Live in Newcastle, Alex, 1991.

The Soul Cages (includes "The Soul Cages"), A&M, 1991.

Ten Summoner's Tales, A&M, 1993.

Fields of Gold: The Best of Sting, 1984–1994 (compilation), A&M, 1994.

Mercury Falling, A&M, 1996.

(With Strontium Ninety) *Police Academy* (recordings from 1970, Ark 21/Pangea, 1997.

Sting at the Movies (compilation), A&M, 1997.

The Very Best of Sting and the Police (compilation), A&M, 1997.

Brand New Day, A&M/Interscope, 1999.

Desert Rose, Interscope, 2000.

All This Time (song compilation), A&M, 2001.

Sacred Love, A&M, 2003.

Singles:

"I Burn for You," A&M, c. 1982.

"Spread a Little Happiness," A&M, 1982.

(With Band Aid) "Do They Know It's Christmas," 1984.

(With Dire Straits) "Money for Nothing," c. 1984.

"Fortress around Your Heart," A&M, 1985.

"If You Love Somebody Set Them Free," A&M, 1985.

"Love Is the Seventh Wave," A&M, 1985.

"Russians," A&M, 1985.

"Bring on the Night," 1986.

"Moon over Bourbon Street," 1986.

"Be Still My Beating Heart," A&M, 1987.

"Englishman in New York," A&M, 1987.

"Fragile," A&M, 1987.

"Gabriel's Message," 1987.

"They Dance Alone (Gueca solo)," A&M, 1987.

"We'll Be Together," A&M, 1987.

"All This Time," A&M, 1991.

"Mad about You," 1991.

"Muoio per te," 1991.

"The Soul Cages," 1991.

"Why Should I Cry for You?," A&M, 1991.

"Epilogue (Nothing 'bout Me)," 1992.

(With Eric Clapton) "It's Probably Me," 1992.

(With Bryan Adams) "All for Love," A&M, 1993.

"Demolition Man," A&M, 1993.
"Fields of Gold," A&M, 1993.
"If I Ever Lose My Faith in You," A&M, 1993.
"Love Is Stronger Than Justice," 1993.
"Seven Days," 1993.
"Shape of My Heart," 1993.
"Fortress," Angel, 1994.
(With Julio Iglesias) "Fragile," 1994.
"This Cowboy Song," Phantom, 1994.
"When We Dance," A&M, 1994.
"Moonlight," 1995.
(With Pato Banton) "Spirits in the Material World," MCA, 1995.
"I'm So Happy I Can't Stop Crying," A&M, 1996.
"Let Your Soul Be Your Pilot," A&M, 1996.
"You Still Touch Me," A&M, 1996.
"Morning (Love Sonnet XXVII)," 1997.
(With Puff Daddy) "Roxanne '97: Puff Daddy Remix," A&M, 1997.
(With Ziggy Marley) "One World (Not Three)," c. 1997.
(With Toby Keith) "I'm So Happy I Can't Stop Crying," 1998.
"Brand New Day," 1999.
"The Mighty," 1999.
"After the Rain Has Fallen," 2000.
"After the Rain Has Fallen (Part 2)," 2000.
(Featuring Cheb Mami) "Desert Rose," 2000.
"My Funny Friend and Me," 2000.
"Until," 2001.
(With Craig David) "Rise & Fall," 2003.
"Send Your Love," 2003.
(With Twista) "Stolen Car," 2004.

Recorded other singles.

Albums with the Police:
Outlandos d'Amour, A&M, 1978.
Regatta de Blanc, A&M, 1979.
Zenyatta Mondatta (includes "Behind My Camel"), A&M, 1980.
Ghost in the Machine, A&M, 1981.
Synchronicity, A&M, 1983.
Live! (also known as *Police: Live!*), A&M, 1985.
Every Breath You Take: The Singles (compilation), A&M, 1986.
Message in a Box: Complete Recordings (compilation; boxed set of four compact discs), A&M, 1993.
Every Breath You Take: The Classics (compilation), A&M, 1995.
The Very Best of Sting & the Police, A&M, 1997, Universal, 2002.

Singles with the Police:
"Born in the 50s," 1978.
"Bring on the Night," 1978.
"Can't Stand Losing You," 1978.
"Hole in My Life," 1978.
"Peanuts," 1978.

"Roxanne," 1978.
"So Lonely," 1978.
"Truth Hits Everybody," 1978.
"Fall Out," 1979.
"Landlord," 1979.
"Message in a Bottle," 1979.
"Walking on the Moon," 1979.
"De Do Do Do, De Da Da Da," 1980.
"Don't Stand So Close to Me," 1980.
"Voices inside My Head," 1980.
"Every Little Thing She Does Is Magic," 1981.
"Invisible Sun," 1981.
"Spirits in the Material World," 1981.
"When the World Is Running Down, You Make the Best of What's Still Around," 1981.
"Demolition Man," 1982.
"One World (Not Three)," 1982.
"Synchronicity II," 1982.
"Every Breath You Take," 1983.
"King of Pain," 1983.
"Wrapped around Your Finger," 1983.
"Don't Stand So Close to Me '86," 1986.
"Tea in the Sahara," 1998.

Recorded other singles with the Police.

Albums; Contributing Vocals:
Eberhard Schoener, *Video Flashback,* Harvest, 1979.
Eberhard Schoener, *Video Magic,* Harvest, 1981.
Phil Collins, *Hello, I Must Be Going,* Atlantic, 1982.
Dire Straits, *Brothers in Arms,* Warner Bros., 1985.
Phil Collins, *No Jacket Required,* Virgin, 1985.
Various artists, *Tribute to Kurt Weill: Lost in the Stars,* A&M, 1985.
Red Hot & Rio, *Red Hot & Rio,* Antilles/Verve, 1986.
Dire Straits, *Money for Nothing,* Warner Bros., 1988.
Kip Hanrahan, *Tenderness,* American Clave, 1990.
Vinx, *Rooms in My Fatha's House,* IRS Releasing, 1991.
Luciano Pavarotti and various artists, *Pavarotti and Friends,* Decca, 1993.
Plus from Us, *Plus from Us,* Realworld, 1993.
Julio Iglesias, *Crazy,* Columbia, 1994.
Tammy Wynette, *Without Walls,* Epic, 1994.
Chieftains, *Long Black Veil,* RCA, 1995.
Vanessa Williams, *Sweetest Days,* Mercury, 1995.
Tina Turner, *Wildest Dreams,* Virgin, 1996.
James Taylor, *Hour Glass,* Sony, 1997.
Joe Henderson, *Porgy & Bess,* PolyGram, 1997.
Various artists, *Carnival: Rainforest Foundation Concert,* RCA, 1997.
Various artists, "She Walks This Earth (Soberana Rosa)," *A Love Affair—The Music of Ivan Lins,* Telarc Records, 2000.
Various artists, *Unity: The Official Athens 2004 Olympic Games Album,* 2004.

Contributor to albums by other recording artists.

Albums; Bass Player:
Eberhard Schoener, *Video Flashback,* Harvest, 1979.
Eberhard Schoener, *Video Magic,* Harvest, 1981.
Andy Summers, *Charming Snakes,* Private Music, 1990.
Kip Hanrahan, *Tenderness,* American Clave, 1990.
Vinx, *Rooms in My Fatha's House,* IRS Releasing, 1991.
Vinnie Colaiuta, *Vinnie Colaiuta,* Stretch, 1994.
John McLaughlin, *Promise,* Verve, 1995.

Albums; Producer:
Various artists, *Green Peace: Rainbow Warriors,* Geffen, 1989.
Various artists, *Very Special Christmas,* A&M, 1989.
Vinx, *Rooms in My Fatha's House,* IRS Releasing, 1991.
Various artists, *Four Weddings and a Funeral* (soundtrack), PolyGram, 1994.
Various artists, *The Truth about Cats and Dogs* (soundtrack), A&M, 1996.

Albums; Sound Engineer:
Various artists, *Tan–Yah Presents Mission,* Tan–Yah Records, 1992.
Various artists, *Mission,* Tan–Yah Records, 1995.
Red Fox, *Face the Fox,* VP Records, 1996.

Videos:
(With the Police) *Police: Around the World,* PolyGram, 1981.
(With the Police) *Synchronicity,* PolyGram, 1983.
Do They Know It's Christmas (documentary), 1984.
(With the Police) *Synchronicity Concert: The Police,* IRS Releasing, 1985.
(With the Police) *The Police: Every Breath You Take,* PolyGram, 1986.
Nothing Like the Sun: The Videos, 1987.
(With Branford Marsalis) *Steep,* Sony Music Video, 1988.
Soul Cages Concert, PolyGram, 1991.
Soul Cages Videos, PolyGram, 1991.
Ten Summoner's Tales (compilation of music videos; also known as *Sting: Ten Summoners Tales*), A&M/ PolyGram, 1993.
Performer, *Grammy's Greatest Moments Volume I,* 1994.
The Police: Outlandos to Synchronicities, PolyGram, 1995.
Sting: Fields of Gold, PolyGram, 1995.
I Want My MTV, MTV Home Video/Sony Music Video Enterprises, 1996.
Twentieth Century Blues: The Songs of Noel Coward (documentary), 1998.
Tina Turner: Celebrate Live 1999 (documentary; also known as *Happy Birthday Tina!*), 1999.
Himself, *Sting: The Brand New Day Tour—Live from the Universal Amphitheatre* (documentary), A&M, 2000.
Himself, *Sting ... All This Time* (documentary), IMAX Corporation, 2001.

Himself, *Chris Botti & Friends: Night Sessions Live in Concert* (documentary), Columbia Music Video, 2002.
Host, *Everest: The Mountain at the Millennium, Vol. 1* (short documentary film), North American Adventures, 2003.
Himself, *Sting: Inside—The Songs of Sacred Love,* Universal Music, 2003.
(With others) Nas, *Nas: Video Anthology Vol. 1,* Sony Music, 2004.

Videos; Art Director:
Ten Summoner's Tales (compilation of music videos; also known as *Sting: Ten Summoners Tales*), A&M/ PolyGram, 1993.

Music Videos:
"I Burn for You," A&M, c. 1982.
"Spread a Little Happiness," A&M, 1982.
(With Band Aid) "Do They Know It's Christmas," 1984.
(With Dire Straits) "Money for Nothing" (version one), 1984.
"Fortress around Your Heart," A&M, 1985.
"If You Love Somebody Set Them Free," A&M, 1985.
"Love Is the Seventh Wave," A&M, 1985.
(With Dire Straits) "Money for Nothing" (version two), 1985.
"Russians," A&M, 1985.
"Bring on the Night," 1986.
"Moon over Bourbon Street," 1986.
"Be Still My Beating Heart," A&M, 1987.
"Englishman in New York," A&M, 1987.
"Fragile" (version one), A&M, 1987.
"Gabriel's Message," 1987.
"They Dance Alone (Gueca solo)," A&M, 1987.
"We'll Be Together," A&M, 1987.
"All This Time," A&M, 1991.
"Mad about You" (two versions), 1991.
"Muoio per te," 1991.
"The Soul Cages," 1991.
"Why Should I Cry for You?," A&M, 1991.
"Epilogue (Nothing 'bout Me)," 1992.
(With Eric Clapton) "It's Probably Me," 1992.
(With Bryan Adams) "All for Love," A&M, 1993.
"Demolition Man," A&M, 1993.
"Fields of Gold," A&M, 1993.
"If I Ever Lose My Faith in You" (two versions), A&M, 1993.
"Love Is Stronger Than Justice," 1993.
"Seven Days," 1993.
"Shape of My Heart," 1993.
"Fortress," Angel, 1994.
(With Julio Iglesias) "Fragile," 1994.
"This Cowboy Song," Phantom, 1994.
"When We Dance," A&M, 1994.
"Moonlight," 1995.
(With Pato Banton) "Spirits in the Material World," MCA, 1995.

"I'm So Happy I Can't Stop Crying," A&M, 1996.
"Let Your Soul Be Your Pilot," A&M, 1996.
"You Still Touch Me," A&M, 1996.
"Morning (Love Sonnet XXVII)," 1997.
(With Puff Daddy) "Roxanne '97: Puff Daddy Remix," A&M, 1997.
(With Ziggy Marley) "One World (Not Three)," c. 1997.
(With Toby Keith) "I'm So Happy I Can't Stop Crying," 1998.
"Brand New Day," 1999.
"The Mighty," 1999.
"After the Rain Has Fallen," 2000.
"After the Rain Has Fallen (Part 2)," 2000.
(Featuring Cheb Mami) "Desert Rose," 2000.
"My Funny Friend and Me," 2000.
"Fragile" (version two), A&M, 2001.
"Until," 2001.
(With Craig David) "Rise & Fall," 2003.
"Send Your Love," 2003.
(With Twista) "Stolen Car," 2004.

Music Videos with the Police:

"Born in the 50s," 1978.
"Bring on the Night," 1978.
"Can't Stand Losing You" (version one: Great Britain/ liver version), 1978.
"Hole in My Life," 1978.
"Peanuts," 1978.
"Roxanne" (version one: United States/red background), 1978.
"Roxanne" (version two: Great Britain/live version), 1978.
"So Lonely," 1978.
"Truth Hits Everybody," 1978.
"Can't Stand Losing You" (version two: United States), 1979.
"Fall Out," 1979.
"Landlord," 1979.
"Message in a Bottle," 1979.
"Walking on the Moon," 1979.
"De Do Do Do, De Da Da Da," 1980.
"Don't Stand So Close to Me" (two versions), 1980.
"Voices inside My Head," 1980.
"Every Little Thing She Does Is Magic," 1981.
"Invisible Sun," 1981.
"Spirits in the Material World," 1981.
"When the World Is Running Down, You Make the Best of What's Still Around," 1981.
"Demolition Man," 1982.
"One World (Not Three)," 1982.
"Synchronicity II," 1982.
"Every Breath You Take," 1983.
"King of Pain" (version one: live in Montreal), 1983.
"Wrapped around Your Finger," 1983.
"Don't Stand So Close to Me '86," 1986.
"Can't Stand Losing You" (version three: live), 1995.
"King of Pain" (version two: live in Atlanta), 1998.
"Tea in the Sahara," 1998.

CD ROMs:
All This Time, 1995.

WRITINGS

Film Music; Scores:
Radio On, Unifilm, 1979.
Brimstone and Treacle, United Artists, 1982.
The Panama Deception (documentary), Empowerment Project, 1992.
The Living Sea (documentary), A&M, 1995.

Film Music; Songs:
(With Eric Clapton and Michael Kamen) "It's Probably Me," *Lethal Weapon 3*, Warner Bros., 1992.
(With Bryan Adams and Rod Stewart) "All for Love," *The Three Musketeers*, Buena Vista, 1993.
"Demolition Man," *Demolition Man*, Warner Bros., 1993.
"The Secret Marriage," *Four Weddings and a Funeral*, Gramercy Pictures, 1994.
"Angel Eyes," "It's a Lonesome Town," and "My One and Only Love," *Leaving Las Vegas*, Metro–Goldwyn–Mayer/United Artists, 1995.
"Moonlight," *Sabrina*, Paramount, 1995.
"This Was Never Meant To Be," *Gentlemen Don't Eat Poets* (also known as *Grave Indiscretion* and *The Grotesque*), LIVE Entertainment/Ster–Kinekor Pictures, 1995.
The Living Sea (documentary), MacGillivray Freeman Films, 1995.
Title song, *The Mighty*, Miramax, 1998.
"My Funny Friend and Me" and other songs, *The Emperor's New Groove* (animated), Buena Vista, 2000.
"A Thousand Years" and "When the World Is Running Down, You Can't Go Wrong," *Red Planet* (also known as *Mars*), Warner Bros., 2000.
Dolphins (short documentary film), MacGillivray Freeman Films, 2000.
Videoflashback (short film), kientopp production, 2000.
"Until," *Kate & Leopold*, Miramax, 2001.
"You Will Be My Ain True Love," *Cold Mountain*, Miramax, 2003.

Sting's songs and music has been featured in other films, television broadcasts, stage productions, and video collections. Songwriter for the unfinished and unreleased film *Kingdom of the Sun* (animated; also known as *Kingdom in the Sun*), Buena Vista.

Albums:
Brimstone and Treacle (original soundtrack), A&M, 1982.
The Dream of the Blue Turtles, A&M, 1985.
Bring on the Night, A&M, 1986.

Nothing Like the Sun, A&M, 1987, five songs translated into Spanish and released as *Nada como el sol ... ,* A&M, 1988.

Live in Newcastle, Alex, 1991.

The Soul Cages (includes "The Soul Cages"), A&M, 1991.

Ten Summoner's Tales, A&M, 1993.

Fields of Gold: The Best of Sting, 1984–1994 (compilation), A&M, 1994.

Mercury Falling, A&M, 1996.

(With Strontium Ninety) *Police Academy* (recordings from 1970, Ark 21/Pangea, 1997.

Sting at the Movies (compilation), A&M, 1997.

The Very Best of Sting and the Police (compilation), A&M, 1997.

Brand New Day, A&M/Interscope, 1999.

Desert Rose, Interscope, 2000.

All This Time (song compilation), A&M, 2001.

Sacred Love, A&M, 2003.

Singles:

"I Burn for You," A&M, c. 1982.

"Spread a Little Happiness," A&M, 1982.

(With Band Aid) "Do They Know It's Christmas," 1984.

(With Dire Straits) "Money for Nothing," c. 1984.

"Fortress around Your Heart," A&M, 1985.

"If You Love Somebody Set Them Free," A&M, 1985.

"Love Is the Seventh Wave," A&M, 1985.

"Russians," A&M, 1985.

"Bring on the Night," 1986.

"Moon over Bourbon Street," 1986.

"Be Still My Beating Heart," A&M, 1987.

"Englishman in New York," A&M, 1987.

"Fragile," A&M, 1987.

"Gabriel's Message," 1987.

"They Dance Alone (Gueca solo)," A&M, 1987.

"We'll Be Together," A&M, 1987.

"All This Time," A&M, 1991.

"Mad about You," 1991.

"Muoio per te," 1991.

"The Soul Cages," 1991.

"Why Should I Cry for You?," A&M, 1991.

"Epilogue (Nothing 'bout Me)," 1992.

(With Eric Clapton) "It's Probably Me," 1992.

(With Bryan Adams) "All for Love," A&M, 1993.

"Demolition Man," A&M, 1993.

"Fields of Gold," A&M, 1993.

"If I Ever Lose My Faith in You," A&M, 1993.

"Love Is Stronger Than Justice," 1993.

"Seven Days," 1993.

"Shape of My Heart," 1993.

"Fortress," Angel, 1994.

(With Julio Iglesias) "Fragile," 1994.

"This Cowboy Song," Phantom, 1994.

"When We Dance," A&M, 1994.

"Moonlight," 1995.

(With Pato Banton) "Spirits in the Material World," MCA, 1995.

"I'm So Happy I Can't Stop Crying," A&M, 1996.

"Let Your Soul Be Your Pilot," A&M, 1996.

"You Still Touch Me," A&M, 1996.

"Morning (Love Sonnet XXVII)," 1997.

(With Puff Daddy) "Roxanne '97: Puff Daddy Remix," A&M, 1997.

(With Ziggy Marley) "One World (Not Three)," c. 1997.

(With Toby Keith) "I'm So Happy I Can't Stop Crying," 1998.

"Brand New Day," 1999.

"The Mighty," 1999.

"After the Rain Has Fallen," 2000.

"After the Rain Has Fallen (Part 2)," 2000.

(Featuring Cheb Mami) "Desert Rose," 2000.

"My Funny Friend and Me," 2000.

"Until," 2001.

(With Craig David) "Rise & Fall," 2003.

"Send Your Love," 2003.

(With Twista) "Stolen Car," 2004.

Albums with the Police:

Outlandos d'Amour, A&M, 1978.

Regatta de Blanc, A&M, 1979.

Zenyatta Mondatta (includes "Behind My Camel"), A&M, 1980.

Ghost in the Machine, A&M, 1981.

Synchronicity, A&M, 1983.

Live! (also known as *Police: Live!*), A&M, 1985.

Every Breath You Take: The Singles (compilation), A&M, 1986.

Message in a Box: Complete Recordings (compilation; boxed set of four compact discs), A&M, 1993.

Every Breath You Take: The Classics (compilation), A&M, 1995.

The Very Best of Sting & the Police, A&M, 1997, Universal, 2002.

Singles with the Police:

"Born in the 50s," 1978.

"Bring on the Night," 1978.

"Can't Stand Losing You," 1978.

"Hole in My Life," 1978.

"Peanuts," 1978.

"Roxanne," 1978.

"So Lonely," 1978.

"Truth Hits Everybody," 1978.

"Fall Out," 1979.

"Landlord," 1979.

"Message in a Bottle," 1979.

"Walking on the Moon," 1979.

"De Do Do Do, De Da Da Da," 1980.

"Don't Stand So Close to Me," 1980.

"Voices inside My Head," 1980.

"Every Little Thing She Does Is Magic," 1981.

"Invisible Sun," 1981.

"Spirits in the Material World," 1981.

"When the World Is Running Down, You Make the Best of What's Still Around," 1981.

"Demolition Man," 1982.

"One World (Not Three)," 1982.
"Synchronicity II," 1982.
"Every Breath You Take," 1983.
"King of Pain," 1983.
"Wrapped around Your Finger," 1983.
"Don't Stand So Close to Me '86," 1986.
"Tea in the Sahara," 1998.

Recorded other singles with the Police.

Album Song Contributor:

"Gabriel's Message," *A Very Special Christmas,* A&M, 1989.
"Love Is the Seventh Wave," *Green Peace: Rainbow Warriors,* Geffen, 1989.
"Cushie Butterfield," *For Our Children,* Disney, 1991.
Luciano Pavarotti and various artists, *Pavarotti and Friends,* Decca, 1993.
Jimi Hendrix, "The Wind Cries Mary," *In from the Storm: A Tribute to Jimi Hendrix,* BMG, 1995.
(With the Police) *Regatta Mondatta: The Police Reggae Tribute,* Pangea/Ark 21, 1997.
(With the Police) *Regatta Mondatta, Vol. 2: Police Reggae Tribute,* Ark 21, 1998.
Various artists, *Unity: The Official Athens 2004 Olympic Games Album,* 2004.

Contributor to albums by other recording artists.

Video Music:

(With the Police) *Police: Around the World,* PolyGram, 1981.
(With the Police) *Synchronicity,* PolyGram, 1983.
(With the Police) *Synchronicity Concert: The Police,* IRS Releasing, 1985.
(With the Police) *The Police: Every Breath You Take,* PolyGram, 1986.
Nothing Like the Sun: The Videos, 1987.
(With Branford Marsalis) *Steep,* Sony Music Video, 1988.
Soul Cages Concert, PolyGram, 1991.
Soul Cages Videos, PolyGram, 1991.
Ten Summoner's Tales (compilation of music videos; also known as *Sting: Ten Summoners Tales*), A&M/PolyGram, 1993.
(With others) *Grammy's Greatest Moments Volume I,* 1994.
The Police: Outlandos to Synchronicities, PolyGram, 1995.
Sting: Fields of Gold, PolyGram, 1995.
Himself, *Sting: The Brand New Day Tour—Live from the Universal Amphitheatre* (documentary), A&M, 2000.
Himself, *Sting ... All This Time* (documentary), IMAX Corporation, 2001.

Himself, *Sting: Inside—The Songs of Sacred Love,* Universal Music, 2003.
(With others) Nas, *Nas: Video Anthology Vol. 1,* Sony Music, 2004.

Nonfiction:

(With Jean–Pierre Dutilleux) *Jungle Stories: The Fight for the Amazon,* Barrien & Jenkins, 1989, St. Martin's, 1996.
Broken Music (autobiography; also known as *Sting: Broken Music*), Bantam/Dell, 2003.

Poetry:

Shape of My Heart: Poem by Sting; Art by Picasso, edited by Linda Sunshine, Stewart, Tabori & Chang, 1998.

Juvenile:

Rock Steady: A Story of Noah's Ark, illustrated by Hugh Whyte, HarperCollins, 2001.

ADAPTATIONS

Ten of Sting's songs were adapted by Darryl Way for performance by the London Symphony Orchestra, released as *Fortress: The London Symphony Orchestra Performs the Music of Sting,* Capitol, 1995.

OTHER SOURCES

Books:

Clarkson, Wensley, *Sting: the Secret Life of Gordon Sumner,* Blake, 1996, Thunder's Mouth, 1999.
Cohen, Barney, *Sting: Every Breath He Takes,* Berkley Publishing, 1984.
Contemporary Literary Criticism, Volume 26, Gale, 1983.
Contemporary Musicians, Gale, Volume 2, 1990, Volume 20, 1997, Volume 41, 2003.
Sanford, Christopher, *Sting: Demolition Man,* Carroll & Graf, 1998.
Sellers, Robert, *Sting: A Biography,* Omnibus Press, 1988.
Sutcliffe, Phil and Hugh Fielder, *L'historia bandido,* Proteus, 1981.
Toler, John and Miles, *The Police: A Visual Documentary,* Omnibus Press, 1981.

Periodicals:

Architectural Digest, January, 1996, p. 56.
Billboard, September 18, 1991, p. 1.
Brandweek, December 6, 1999, p. 10.
Details, February, 1994, p. 114.
Entertainment Weekly, August 9, 1996, p. 30; November 7, 2003, p. 72.

Esquire, September, 1999, p. 103.
Harper's Bazaar, February, 2002, pp. 112–14.
Hello!, November 13, 2001, pp. 4–12.
Interview, July, 1996, p. 90; August, 2003, pp. 134–35.
New Media Age, June 7, 2001, p. 64.
Newsweek, September 30, 1985, p. 68.
New Yorker, December 24, 1984, p. 74.
Parade, August 10, 2003, pp. 4–6.
People Weekly, November 20, 1989, p. 77; October 6, 2003, p. 47; November 24, 2003, p. 49; December 1, 2003, p. 116; December 15, 2003, p. 87.
Rolling Stone, November 5, 1987, pp. 297–98.
Spin, July, 1985.
TV Guide, September 27, 2003, p. 18.
US Weekly, October 2, 2000, p. 12.

Electronic:

Sting, http://www.sting.com, August 9, 2005.

STOPPELMOOR, Cheryl Jean
See LADD, Cheryl

STRACZYNSKI, J. Michael 1954–
(Fettes Grey)

PERSONAL

Full name, Joseph Michael Straczynski; born July 17, 1954, in Paterson, NJ; son of Charles (a manual laborer) and Evelyn (maiden name, Pate) Straczynski; married Kathryn May Drennan (a writer), 1983. *Education:* Attended Kankakee Community College, 1972–73, and Richland College, 1973; Southwestern College, A.A., 1975; San Diego State University, B.A. (clinical psychology), 1976, B.A. (sociology), 1978. *Politics:* Democrat. *Religion:* "Atheist."

Addresses: *Agent*—Joel Begleiter, United Talent Agency, 9560 Wilshire Blvd., Suite 500, Beverly Hills, CA 90212.

Career: Writer, producer, journalist, critic, story editor, and educator. KSDO–AM Radio, San Diego, CA, entertainment editor and theatre and film reviewer, 1979–81; Airstage Radiodrama Productions, artistic director, resident writer, producer, director, workshop instructor, and facilitator, 1980–81; Filmation Studios, Reseda, CA, staff writer, 1984–85; story editor for DIC Enterprises, 1985–86, Landmark Entertainment, 1986–87, and London Films, 1987–88; development writer for TMS Enterprises, 1985–87, Nelvana Entertainment, 1988, and Warner Bros., beginning 1988; Scifi.

com (Internet Web site), creator, executive producer, and writer for the Internet series *The City of Dreams,* broadcast as part of *Seeing Ear Theatre;* also works as title designer for some of his own films. San Diego State University, personal and academic counselor, 1975–77, instructor, 1979; Grossmont Junior College, instructor, 1978; guest speaker at other institutions and at workshops, science fiction conventions, and seminars. *Racquetball News,* El Cajon, CA, editor, 1975–77, editor in chief, 1978; *Los Angeles Times,* San Diego Bureau, special correspondent, 1977–79; *Daily Californian,* special correspondent and reviewer, 1978–79; *TV Cable Week,* affiliate, 1981–82; Top Cow/Image (comic book publisher), writer and publisher of the imprint Joe's Comics.

Member: Writers Guild of America West, Horror Writers of America, People for the American Way, Psi Chi (life member).

Awards, Honors: Gemini Award nomination, Academy of Canadian Cinema and Television, best writing in a drama series, for *Captain Power and the Soldiers of the Future;* Bram Stoker Award nomination, Horror Writers of America, best first novel, c. 1988, for *Demon Knight;* Annual CableACE Award nomination, National Cable Television Association, c. 1989, and Writers Guild of America Award nomination, best anthology episode or single program, 1991, both for "The Strange Case of Dr. Jekyll and Mr. Hyde," *Nightmare Classics;* San Diego International Comic Arts Exposition, Inkpot Award, 1993, Eisner Award, 2002; Hugo Awards, World Science Fiction Society, best dramatic presentation, 1996, for "The Coming of Shadows," and 1997, for "Severed Dreams" (with others), both episodes of *Babylon 5;* Bradbury Award, Science Fiction and Fantasy Writers of America, 1999, for *Babylon 5.*

CREDITS

Television Work; Series:
Coproducer, *Murder, She Wrote,* CBS, 1991–93.
(Uncredited) Supervising producer, *Walker, Texas Ranger,* CBS, 1993.
Creator and executive producer, *Babylon 5* (also known as *B5*), syndicated, 1994–97, TNT, 1998.
Creator and executive producer, *Crusade,* TNT, 1999.
Creator and executive producer, *Jeremiah,* Showtime, 2002–2004.

Creator of *Aragon and the Wuff,* ABC. Also producer of *Jake and the Fatman,* CBS.

Television Work; Movies:
Creator and executive producer, *Babylon 5: In the Beginning* (also known as *In the Beginning*), TNT, 1998.

Creator and executive producer, *Babylon 5: Thirdspace* (also known as *Thirdspace* and *Thirdspace: A Babylon 5 Adventure*), TNT, 1998.

Creator and executive producer, *Babylon 5: The River of Souls* (also known as *The River of Souls*), TNT, 1998.

Producer, *Murder She Wrote: A Story to Die For*, CBS, 2000.

Television Work; Pilots:
Creator and co–executive producer, *Babylon 5: The Gathering* (also known as *Babylon 5* and *B5*), syndicated, 1993.

Creator and executive producer, *Babylon 5: A Call to Arms* (also known as *A Call to Arms*), TNT, 1999.

Executive producer, *Babylon 5: The Legend of the Rangers—To Live and Die in Starlight* (also known as *Legend of the Rangers: Babylon 5*), Sci–Fi Channel, 2002.

Television Director; Episodic:
"Sleeping in Light," *Babylon 5* (also known as *B5*), TNT, 1998.

Television Appearances; Specials:
The Guide to Babylon 5, TNT, 1997.

Television Appearances; Episodic:
(Uncredited) Maintenance worker, "Sleeping in Light," *Babylon 5* (also known as *B5*), TNT, 1998.

Radio Appearances; Series:
Host, *Hour 25*, KPFK–FM (Los Angeles), 1987–92.

RECORDINGS

Video Appearances:
Hero in Crisis, Columbia TriStar Home Entertainment, 2004.

WRITINGS

Television Series:
He–Man and the Masters of the Universe (also known as *He–Man*), syndicated, 1984.

She–Ra, Princess of Power, syndicated, 1985.

Jayce and the Wheeled Warriors (also known as *Jayce et les conquerants de la lumiere*), CBS, 1986.

Elfquest, CBS, 1986.

Captain Power and the Soldiers of the Future, syndicated, 1986–87.

The Real Ghostbusters, ABC, between 1986 and 1989.

Batman, ABC, 1988.

The Twilight Zone, syndicated, 1988–89.

(As Fettes Grey) *Spiral Zone*, syndicated, 1989.

V: The Next Chapter, The WB, 1989–91.

Jake and the Fatman, CBS, multiple episodes, 1990.

Murder, She Wrote, CBS, between 1991 and 1993.

Babylon 5 (also known as *B5*), syndicated, 1994–97, TNT, 1997–99.

Crusade, TNT, 1999.

Jeremiah, Showtime, 2002–2004.

Television Movies:
Babylon 5: In the Beginning (also known as *In the Beginning*), TNT, 1998.

Babylon 5: Thirdspace (also known as *Thirdspace* and *Thirdspace: A Babylon 5 Adventure*), TNT, 1998.

Babylon 5: The River of Souls (also known as *The River of Souls*), TNT, 1998.

Murder, She Wrote: A Story to Die For, CBS, 2000.

Television Specials:
"The Shy Stegosaurus of Cricket Creek," *CBS Storybreak*, CBS, 1985.

(Including songs "Boogaloo's Back in Town" and "Touching Old Magic") *The Halloween Door*, ABC, 1989.

"The Strange Case of Dr. Jekyll and Mr. Hyde" (also based on a story by Straczynski), *Nightmare Classics*, Showtime, 1989.

The Strange Case of Dr. Jekyll and Mr. Hyde, ABC, 1989.

Television Pilots:
Babylon 5: The Gathering (also known as *Babylon 5* and *B5*), syndicated, 1993.

Guardians, 1995.

Babylon 5: A Call to Arms (also known as *A Call to Arms*), TNT, 1999.

Babylon 5: The Legend of the Rangers—To Live and Die in Starlight (also known as *Legend of the Rangers: Babylon 5*), Sci–Fi Channel, 2002.

Jeremiah, Showtime, 2002.

Television Episodes:
"A Shadow in the Night," *Walker, Texas Ranger*, CBS, 1993.

Composer and lyricist (uncredited), "Untitled Telepath Song," for various episodes of *Babylon 5* (also known as *B5*).

Television Scripts; Other:
Captain Power: The Beginning (also known as *Captain Power: Against the New Order*), 1989.

Stage Plays:
The Apprenticeship, Marquis Public Theater, San Diego, CA, 1980.

Author of more than twelve produced stage plays, including one published by Baker's Plays.

Radio Series:

Writer for the series *Alien Worlds* and *Mutual Radio Theater.*

Comic Books:

(With Mark Moretti) *Babylon 5: The Price of Peace,* DC Comics, 1998.

Rising Stars (series; includes *Power,* 2002, *Visitations,* 2003, and *Born in Fire,* 2003, Joe's Comics, 1999–2004, hard–cover compilation, illustrated by Keu Cha and Brent Anderson, Diamond Comic Distributors, 2005.

The Amazing Spider–Man (series; includes *Coming Home,* illustrated by John Romita and John Hanna, 2001, *Revelations,* 2002, *Until the Stars Turn Cold,* illustrated by Romita and Hanna, 2002, *The Life & Death of Spiders,* illustrated by Romita and Hanna, 2003, *Unintended Consequences,* illustrated by Romita, Hanna, and Fiona Avery, 2003, *Skin Deep,* illustrated by Mike Deodato, Jr. and Mark Brooks, 2005, *Sins Past,* illustrated by Deodato and Joe Pimentel, 2005, Marvel Comics, beginning 2001.

Delicate Creatures, illustrated by Michael Zulli, Image Comics, 2002.

Midnight Nation (series), Joe's Comics, 2003.

Supreme Power (series; includes *Powers and Principalities;* based on an earlier Marvel series titled *Squadron Supreme*), Marvel Comics, beginning 2003.

No Surrender, No Retreat: Babylon 5, illustrated by Shannon Kalvar, Diamond Comic Distributors, 2004.

The Book of Lost Souls (series), Marvel Comics, beginning 2005.

The Fantastic Four (series), Marvel Comics, beginning 2005.

Dream Police, Marvel Comics, 2005.

Strange: Beginnings and Endings, illustrated by Gary Frank and Jonathan Sibal, Marvel Enterprises, 2005.

Author of, or contributor to, other comic books, including *Star Trek 16: Worldsinger,* DC Comics; *Teen Titans Spotlight;* and *Twilight Zone.*

Other:

The Complete Book of Scriptwriting: Television, Radio, Motion Pictures, the Stage Play, Writer's Digest Books, 1982, expanded edition published as *The (Even More!) Complete Book of Scriptwriting,* 1996.

Demon Night (novel), E. P. Dutton, 1988, reprinted, Simon & Schuster, 2005.

Tales from The New Twilight Zone (short stories based on his own scripts), Bantam/Spectra, 1989.

(With David Bassom) *Creating Babylon 5: Behind the Scenes of Warner Bros. Revolutionary Deep Space TV Drama,* Del Rey, 1997.

(With Jim Mortimore, Allan Adams, and Roger Clark) *Babylon 5 Security Manual,* Del Rey, 1998.

OtherSyde (novel), E. P. Dutton, 1990, reprinted, Simon & Schuster, 2005.

Straczynski Unplugged (short stories), Pocket Books, 2004.

(With August Hahn) *The Centauri Republic Fact Book,* Mongoose Publishing, 2004.

Tribulations (novel), Simon & Schuster, 2005.

But in Purple, I'm Stunning ... : The Babylon 5 Quote Book, Pocket Books, 2005.

(Editor, with Greg Rucka, Peter Milligan, and others) *Best of Spider–Man,* edited by Romita and Deodato, Marvel Enterprises, 2005.

Author of "Scripts," a column in *Writer's Digest,* 1982. Work represented in fiction anthologies, including *Shadows 6.* Contributor of more than 500 short stories and articles to periodicals, including *Amazing Stories, Los Angeles Herald Examiner, Los Angeles Reader, Los Angeles Times, Penthouse, Pulphouse, San Diego, San Diego Reader, Time,* and *Video Review.* Contributing editor, *Writer's Digest,* beginning 1981, and *Twilight Zone,* 1983—.

ADAPTATIONS

The television series *Crusade* was adapted as a book by Christopher Blackmoor and published by Mongoose Publishing in 2005.

OTHER SOURCES

Periodicals:

Babylon 5, August, 1997, pp. 32–37; November, 1997, p. 57; January, 1998, pp. 4–5; June, 1998, pp. 16–19; fall, 1998, pp. 24–25, 42, 44–45; June, 1999, pp. 11–13.

Dream Watch, July, 1997, pp. 12–17.

Starlog, April, 1998.

Universe Today, fall, 1997, pp. 10–11.

STRAND, Chantal 1987–

PERSONAL

Born October 15, 1987, in Vancouver, British Columbia, Canada. *Avocational Interests:* Horseback riding, singing, and dancing.

Addresses: Agent—Robert Carrier Talent, 1260 Hornby St., Vancouver, British Columbia V6Z 1W2, Canada.

Career: Actress and voice performer.

CREDITS

Film Appearances:
(English version) Voice of Kazuko, *Junkers Come Here* (animated), Bandai Entertainment, 1995.
(English version) Voice of Angela, *Merutiransa* (animated; also known as *Melty Lancer*), 1999.
Tammy, *Air Bud: World Pup* (also known as *Air Bud 3* and *Tobby III: Le chien etoile*), Miramax Home Entertainment, 2000.
Tammy, *Air Bud: Seventh Inning Fetch* (also known as *Tobby, le frappeur etoile*), Miramax Home Entertainment, 2002.
Voices of Kelly and Katrina, *Barbie as Rapunzel* (animated), Cartoon Network, 2002.
Tammy, *Air Bud: Spikes Back* (also known as *Tobby 5: L'as du volley–ball*), Miramax, 2003.
Voice of Kelly, *Barbie of Swan Lake* (animated), Universal Home Video, 2003.

Film Work:
Stunts, *Look Who's Talking Now,* TriStar, 1993.

Television Appearances; Series:
Suzy, *Super Dave's All Stars,* YTV and syndicated, 1997.
(English version) Voice of Young Nami, *Silent Mobius* (animated), 1998.
(English version) Voice of Flora, *Master Keaton* (animated), 1998, 2003.
Holly, *The Charlie Horse Music Pizza,* PBS, 1998.
(English version) Voice of Akari Comodo, *Brain Powered* (animated), 1998.
(English version) Voice of Neya, *Mugen no Ryvius* (animated; also known as *Infinite Ryvius*), 1999.
Cassie, *Dragon Tales,* PBS, 1999.
Voices of Gemeni "Gem" Stone, Pi, and Bernard, *Sabrina the Animated Series* (animated; also known as *Sabrina*), ABC, 1999.
Voice of Molly O!, *Generation O!* (animated), The WB and YTV, 2000.
(English version) Voice of Mayu, *Inuyasha* (animated), Cartoon Network and YTV, 2000—.
Voice, *Make Way for Noddy* (animated), 2001.
(English version) Voice of Yuko, *The SoulTaker* (animated), 2001.
(Uncredited) Voice, *Sitting Ducks* (animated), 2001.
Anne, *Los Luchadores,* Fox, 2001.
Voice of Prima, *Super Duper Sumos* (animated), YTV, 2001.

Voice of Bijou, *Hamtaro* (animated; also known as *Tottoko Hamutaro* and *Trotting Hamtaro*), Cartoon Network and YTV, 2002.
(English version) Voice of Lacus Clyne, *Kido senshi Gundam Seed* (animated; also known as *Gundam Seed* and *Mobile Suit Gundam Seed*), Cartoon Network, 2002, 2004.
Voice of Sophie, *ToddWorld,* 2004.

Also appeared as voices of Danielle and Yvette, *Madeline* (animated); voice of Alex Mills, *Cardcaptors* (animated).

Television Appearances; Miniseries:
Girl in street, *Aftershock: Earthquake in New York* (also known as *Aftershock—Das grosse Beben* and *Erdbeben–Inferno: Wenn die Welt untergeht*), CBS, 1999.

Television Appearances; Movies:
Young girl, *Beauty's Revenge* (also known as *Midwest Obsession*), NBC, 1995.
Margo Raphael, *The Commish: Redemption,* ABC, 1996.
Sarah's sister, *Life–Size,* ABC, 2000.
Voice of Mariemaia Kushrenada, *Mobile Suit Gundam Wing: The Movie—Endless Waltz* (animated; also known as *Endless Waltz* and *Gundam Wing: The Movie—Endless Waltz*), Cartoon Network, 2000.
Voice of Madeline, *Madeline: My Fair Madeline* (animated), 2002.
Nancy Nut–What, *It's A Very Merry Muppet Christmas Movie,* NBC, 2002.

Television Appearances; Specials:
Voice of Kelly, *Barbie in "The Nutcracker"* (animated), CBS, 2001.

Television Appearances; Episodic:
Vickie, "Revelations," *Poltergeist: The Legacy,* 1996.
Young girl, "Nightmare," *The Outer Limits,* Showtime and syndicated, 1998.
Voice of Wolfsbane/Rahne Sinclair, "Growing Pains," *X–Men: Evolution* (animated), The WB, 2001.
Voice of Wolfsbane/Rahne Sinclair, "Joyride," *X–Men: Evolution* (animated), The WB, 2001.
Voice of Wolfsbane/Rahne Sinclair, "On Angel's Wings," *X–Men: Evolution* (animated), The WB, 2001.
Voice of Wolfsbane/Rahne Sinclair, "Retreat," *X–Men: Evolution* (animated), The WB, 2002.
Voice of King Lili, "The King and Jade," *Jackie Chan Adventures* (animated), 2002.

Also appeared in *Alienators: Evolution Continues.*

Television Work; Series:
Additional voices, *Cybersix* (animated), Fox, 1999.
Supporting voices, *Project Arms,* 2001.

RECORDINGS

Video Games:
Appeared as voice of Lacus Clyne, *Battle Assault 3 Featuring Gundam Seed.*

STREEP, Meryl 1949–

PERSONAL

Born Mary Louise Streep, June 22, 1949, in Madison (some sources cite Summit), NJ; daughter of Harry, Jr. (a pharmaceutical company executive) and Mary W. (a commercial artist) Streep; sister of Harry Streep III (a choreographer and dancer); married Donald J. Gummer (a sculptor), September 15, 1978; children: Henry "Harry"/"Hank", Mary Willa "Mamie", Grace Jane, Louisa Jackson. *Education:* Vassar College, B.A., 1971; Yale University, M.F.A., 1975; also attended Dartmouth College; studied singing with Estelle Liebling. *Avocational Interests:* Gardening, skiing, art and museums, family activities.

Addresses: *Agent*—Kevin Huvane, Creative Artists Agency, 9830 Wilshire Blvd., Beverly Hills, CA 90212. *Publicist*—PMK/HBH Public Relations, 8500 Wilshire Blvd., Suite 700, Beverly Hills, CA 90211.

Career: Actress and producer. Appeared in productions with Green Mountain Guild, Woodstock, VT; O'Neill Playwrights Conference, actress, summer, 1975. Mothers and Others for a Livable Planet, cofounder; Mothers and Others for Pesticide Limits, campaign chair; narrator of public service announcements on behalf of American forests; supporter of Poetry and the Creative Mind (honorary benefit for Academy of American Poets), Connecticut Farmland Trust/Hartford Food System, Equality Now, Harvard Center for Health and the Global Environment, and Scenic Hudson. Once performed as a singer with a group called the Night Owls; also worked as a waitress at Hotel Somerset, Somerville, NJ.

Awards, Honors: Outer Critics' Circle Award, 1975, *Theatre World* Award, 1976, and Antoinette Perry Award nomination, best featured actress in a play, 1976, all for *27 Wagons Full of Cotton; Theatre World Award,* 1976, for *Secret Service; Mademoiselle* Award, 1976; Emmy Award, outstanding lead actress in a

limited series, 1978, for *Holocaust;* Academy Award nomination, best supporting actress, 1979, National Society of Film Critics' Award, best supporting actress, 1979, Golden Globe Award nomination, best supporting actress in a motion picture, 1979, Marquee Award, American Movie Awards, best supporting actress, 1980, and Film Award nomination, British Academy of Film and Television Arts, best actress, 1980, all for *The Deer Hunter;* Woman of the Year Award, B'nai Brith, 1979; Academy Award, best supporting actress, 1979, Golden Globe Award, best supporting actress in a motion picture, 1980, Kansas City Film Critics Circle Award, best supporting actress, 1980, and Film Award nomination, British Academy of Film and Television Arts, best actress, 1981, all for *Kramer vs. Kramer;* New York Film Critics Circle Award, best supporting actress, 1979, for *Kramer vs. Kramer* and *The Seduction of Joe Tynan;* Los Angeles Film Critics Association Award, best supporting actress, 1979, National Board of Review Award, 1979, and National Society of Film Critics Award, 1980, all for *Kramer vs. Kramer, Manhattan,* and *The Seduction of Joe Tynan.* Film Award nomination, British Academy of Film and Television Arts, best supporting actress, 1980, for *Manhattan;* named Hasty Pudding Woman of the Year, Hasty Pudding Theatricals, Harvard University, 1980; Los Angeles Film Critics Association Award, best actress, 1981, Academy Award nomination, best actress, 1982, Film Award, British Academy of Film and Television Arts, best actress, 1982, and Golden Globe Award, best actress in a motion picture drama, 1982, all for *The French Lieutenant's Woman;* Obie Award, *Village Voice,* 1981, for *Alice in Concert;* honorary D.F.A., Dartmouth College, 1981; Star of the Year Award, National Association of Theatre Owners, 1982; honorary D.F.A., Yale University and Vassar College, both 1983; New York Film Critics Circle Award, best actress, 1982, Academy Award, Boston Society of Film Critics Award, Los Angeles Film Critics Association Award, National Society of Film Critics Award, National Board of Review Award, and Kansas City Film Critics Circle Award, all best actress, 1983, Golden Globe Award, best actress in a motion picture drama, 1983, and Film Award nomination, British Academy of Film and Television Arts, best actress, 1984, all for *Sophie's Choice;* Academy Award nomination, best actress, 1984, Golden Globe Award nomination, best actress in a motion picture drama, 1984, and Film Award nomination, British Academy of Film and Television Arts, best actress, 1985, all for *Silkwood;* People's Choice Awards, Proctor & Gamble Productions, favorite motion picture actress, 1984–87; David Award, David di Donatello Awards, best foreign actress, 1985, for *Falling in Love;* Los Angeles Film Critics Association Award, best actress, 1985, Golden Globe Award nomination, best actress in a motion picture drama, 1986, David Award, best foreign actress, 1986, Academy Award nomination and Kansas City Film Critics Circle Award, both best actress, 1986, and Film Award nomination, British Academy of Film and Television Arts, best actress, 1987, all for *Out of Africa;* Best Actress Award, Valladolid International Film Festival,

1986, for *Heartburn;* TV Prize, Aftonbladet TV Prize, best female foreign television personality, 1987; Academy Award nomination and New York Film Critics Circle Award, both best actress, 1988, for *Ironweed;* New York Film Critics Circle Award, best actress, 1988, Academy Award nomination, Cannes Film Festival Award, and Australian Film Institute Award, all best actress, and Golden Globe Award nomination, best actress in a motion picture drama, all 1989, all for *A Cry in the Dark;* People's Choice Awards, favorite dramatic motion picture actress, 1989, and world–favorite motion picture actress, 1990. Golden Globe Award nomination, best actress in a motion picture comedy or musical, 1990, for *She–Devil;* Academy Award nomination, best actress, Golden Globe Award nomination, best actress in a motion picture comedy or musical, and American Comedy Award, funniest leading actress in a motion picture, all 1991, for *Postcards from the Edge;* Saturn Award nomination, Academy of Science Fiction, Fantasy, and Horror Films, best actress, 1992, for *Defending Your Life;* Golden Globe Award nomination, best actress in a motion picture comedy or musical, and Saturn Award nomination, best actress, both 1993, for *Death Becomes Her;* Golden Globe Award nomination, best actress in a motion picture drama, and Screen Actors Guild Award nomination, outstanding performance by an actress in a leading role, both 1995, for *The River Wild;* Academy Award nomination, best actress, Screen Actors Guild Award nomination, outstanding performance by an actress in a leading role, and Golden Globe Award nomination, best actress in a motion picture drama, all 1996, for *The Bridges of Madison County;* Golden Globe Award nomination, best actress in a motion picture drama, Chlotrudis Award nomination, best supporting actress, and Screen Actors Guild Award nomination, outstanding cast performance (with others), all 1997, for *Marvin's Room;* Crystal Award, Women in Film, 1998; Emmy Award nomination, outstanding lead actress in a miniseries or special, 1997, and Golden Globe Award nomination and Golden Satellite Award nomination, International Press Academy, both best actress in a miniseries or television movie, 1998, all for *... First Do No Harm;* received star on Hollywood Walk of Fame, 1998; Academy Award nomination, best actress, Screen Actors Guild Award nomination, outstanding performance by an actress in a leading role, Golden Globe Award nomination, best actress in a motion picture drama, Golden Satellite Award nomination, best actress in a motion picture drama, all 1999, for *One True Thing;* Lifetime Achievement Award, Gotham Awards, Independent Features Project, 1999; People's Choice Award nomination, favorite motion picture actress, 1999; Berlinale Camera, Berlin International Film Festival, 1999. Decorated officer, French Order of Arts and Letters, 2000; Academy Award nomination, best actress, Golden Globe Award nomination, best actress in a motion picture drama, and Screen Actors Guild Award nomination, best actress, all 2000, for *Music of the Heart;* Drama Desk Award nomination, outstanding actress in a play, 2002, for *The Seagull;* Southeastern

Film Critics Association Award, best supporting actress, 2002, Academy Award nomination, Film Award nomination, British Academy of Film and Television Arts, Chicago Film Critics Association Award, Florida Film Critics Circle Award, Broadcast Film Critics Association Award nomination, and Online Film Critics Society Award nomination, all best supporting actress, Golden Globe Award and Golden Satellite Award nomination, both best supporting actress in a motion picture, Phoenix Film Critics Society Award nominations, best supporting actress and best acting ensemble (with others), and Screen Actors Guild Award nomination, outstanding cast performance in a theatrical motion picture (with others), all 2003, for *Adaptation;* Golden Globe Award nomination and Golden Satellite Award nomination, both best actress in a motion picture drama, Film Award nomination, British Academy of Film and Television Arts, best actress, Silver Berlin Bear, best actress (with others), Screen Idol Award, L.A. Outfest, best actress, Screen Actors Guild Award nomination, outstanding cast in a theatrical motion picture (with others), and Phoenix Film Critics Society Award nomination, best acting ensemble (with others), all 2003, for *The Hours;* honorary Cesar Award, Academie des Arts et Techniques du Cinema, 2003; Lee Strasberg Artistic Achievement Award, Actors' Fund of America, 2003; Golden Globe Award, Golden Satellite Award, and Screen Actors Guild Award, all best actress in a television miniseries or movie, and Emmy Award, outstanding actress in a miniseries or movie, all 2004, and Gracie Allen award, outstanding female lead in a drama special, 2005, all for *Angels in America;* Lifetime Achievement Award, American Film Institute, 2004; Career Achievement Award, New Dramatists, 2004; Stanislavsky Prize, Moscow International Film Festival, 2004; Common Wealth Award, PNC Financial Services Group, 2004; Saturn Award nomination and Film Award nomination, British Academy of Film and Television Arts, both best supporting actress, and Golden Globe Award nomination, best supporting actress in a motion picture, all 2005, for *The Manchurian Candidate;* Emmy Award, best children's recording, for *The Velveteen Rabbit.*

CREDITS

Film Appearances:

Voice from Stage 6, *Everybody Rides the Carousel,* 1975.

Anne Marie, *Julia,* Twentieth Century–Fox, 1977.

Linda, *The Deer Hunter,* Universal, 1978.

Jill, *Manhattan,* United Artists, 1979.

Karen Traynor, *The Seduction of Joe Tynan,* Universal, 1979.

Joanna Kramer, *Kramer vs. Kramer,* Columbia, 1979.

Sarah Woodruff and Anna, *The French Lieutenant's Woman,* United Artists, 1981.

Brooke Reynolds, *Still of the Night,* Metro–Goldwyn–Mayer/United Artists, 1982.

Sophie Zawistowska, *Sophie's Choice,* Universal, 1982.

Karen Silkwood, *Silkwood,* Twentieth Century–Fox, 1983.

Narrator, *In Our Hands* (documentary), Libra Cinema 5, 1983.

Molly Gilmore, *Falling in Love,* Paramount, 1984.

Susan Traherne, *Plenty,* Twentieth Century–Fox, 1985.

Karen Blixen–Finecke, *Out of Africa,* Universal, 1985.

Rachel Louise Samstat/Forman, *Heartburn,* Paramount, 1986.

Helen Archer, *Ironweed,* TriStar, 1988.

Lindy Chamberlain, *A Cry in the Dark* (also known as *Evil Angels*), Warner Bros., 1988.

Mary Fisher, *She–Devil,* Orion, 1989.

Suzanne Vale, *Postcards from the Edge,* Columbia, 1990.

Julia, *Defending Your Life,* Warner Bros., 1991.

Madeline Ashton, *Death Becomes Her,* Universal, 1992.

Clara Del Valle Trueba, *The House of the Spirits* (also known as *Aandernes hus, A casa dos espiritos,* and *Das geisterhaus*), Miramax, 1994.

Gail Hartman, *The River Wild,* Universal, 1994.

Francesca Johnson, *The Bridges of Madison County,* Warner Bros., 1995.

Narrator, *The Living Sea* (documentary), MacGillivray Freeman Films, 1995.

Carolyn Ryan, *Before and After,* Buena Vista, 1996.

Lee, *Marvin's Room,* Miramax, 1996.

Narrator, *Assignment: Rescue* (documentary; also known as *The Story of Varian Fry and the Emergency Rescue Committee*), 1997.

Kate "Kit" Mundy, *Dancing at Lughnasa,* Sony Pictures Classics, 1998.

Kate Gulden, *One True Thing,* Universal, 1998.

Narrator, *Eternal Memory: Voices from the Great Terror* (documentary), Cinema Guild, 1998.

Narrator, *Chrysanthemum* (short film), 1999.

Roberta Guaspari–Tzavaras, *Music of the Heart* (also known as *Fifty Violins*), Miramax, 1999.

Voice of Blue Mecha, *Artificial Intelligence: AI* (also known as *A.I.: Artificial Intelligence*), Warner Bros., 2001.

Herself, *The Papp Project* (documentary), American Masters, 2001.

Susan Orlean, *Adaptation,* Columbia, 2002.

Clarissa Vaughan, *The Hours,* Paramount, 2002.

(Uncredited) Herself, *Stuck on You,* Twentieth Century–Fox, 2003.

Narrator, *Monet's Palate: A Gastronomic View from the Gardens of Giverny* (documentary), AFB Productions/Renaissance Films, 2003.

Eleanor Prentiss Shaw, *The Manchurian Candidate,* Paramount, 2004.

Aunt Josephine, *Lemony Snicket's A Series of Unfortunate Events,* Paramount, 2004.

Lisa Metzger, *Prime,* Universal/Focus Features, 2005.

Narrator, *Stolen Childhoods* (documentary), Balcony Releasing, 2005.

Television Appearances; Miniseries:

Inga Helms Weiss, *Holocaust* (also known as *Holocaust—The Story of the Family Weiss*), NBC, 1978.

Voice of Margaret Sanger, *A Century of Women* (also known as *A Family of Women*), TBS, 1994.

A Century of Women, Cable News Network, 1998.

Narrator, *School* (also known as *School: The Story of American Public Education*), PBS, 2001.

Rabbi Isidor Chemelwitz, Hannah Porter Pitt, Ethel Greenglass Rosenberg, and the Angel Australia, *Angels in America,* HBO, 2003.

Voices of Abigail Adams, Mother Jones, and Margaret Chase Smith, *Freedom: A History of the U.S.,* PBS.

Television Appearances; Specials:

Edith Varney, *Secret Service,* PBS, 1977.

Leilah, "Uncommon Women ... and Others," *Great Performances,* PBS, 1978.

Katherine, *Kiss Me, Petruchio,* PBS, 1981.

The Kennedy Center Honors: A Celebration of the Performing Arts, CBS, 1981.

(In archive footage) *Sixty Years of Seduction,* ABC, 1981.

Narrator, "Little Ears: The Velveteen Rabbit," *Children's Storybook Classics,* PBS, 1985.

Host and narrator, *Power Struggle* (distributed to schools in two parts: *Energy Supply* and *Energy Efficiency*), PBS, 1985.

Narrator, "Harold Clurman: A Life of Theatre," *American Masters,* PBS, 1989.

Premiere Presents: Christmas Movies '89, Fox, 1989.

The 3rd Annual Hollywood Insider Academy Awards Special, USA Network, 1989.

Host and narrator, "Arctic Refuge: A Vanishing Wilderness?," *World of Audubon Specials* (also known as *National Audubon Society Specials*), PBS and TBS, 1990.

An Evening with Bette, Cher, Goldie, Meryl, Olivia, Lily and Robin, ABC, 1990.

Time Warner Presents the Earth Day Special, ABC, 1990.

Member of choir, *Voices that Care,* Fox, 1991.

Host and narrator, *Age Seven in America* (documentary; also known as *7–Up in America*), CBS, 1992.

Host, *Great Performances 20th Anniversary Special,* PBS, 1992.

Oprah: Behind the Scenes, ABC, 1992.

Narrator, "The Night before Christmas," *We All Have Tales* (animated), Showtime, 1992.

Hollywood Stars: A Century of Cinema, The Disney Channel, 1995.

Interviewee, *The Siskel and Ebert Interviews,* CBS, 1996.

Interviewee, "Roseanne: Tabloids, Trash & Truth," *Biography,* Arts and Entertainment, 1996.

Interviewee, "William Styron: The Way of the Writer," *American Masters,* PBS, 1997.

Christopher Reeve: A Celebration of Hope, ABC, 1998.

Host, *Defending Our Daughters: The Rights of Women in the World*, Lifetime, 1998.

Narrator, *Intimate Portrait: Vanessa Redgrave*, Lifetime, 1998.

Rings of Passion: Five Emotions in World Art, PBS and Ovation, 1998.

From Star Wars to Star Wars: The Story of Industrial Light & Magic, Fox, 1999.

Netaid: A Concert Special, TNT, 1999.

Netaid, VH1, 1999.

Interviewee, *Kurt Russell: Hollywood's Heavy Hitter*, Arts and Entertainment, 1999.

Host, *The Concert of the Century for VH1 Save the Music*, VH1, 1999.

Interviewee, "Clint Eastwood: Out of the Shadows," *American Masters*, PBS, 2000.

Narrator, *Isaac Stern: Life's Virtuoso*, PBS, 2000.

Narrator, *Ginevra's Story: Solving the Mysteries of Leonardo da Vinci's First Known Portrait*, PBS, 2000.

Interviewee, *Intimate Portrait: Diane Keaton*, Lifetime, 2001.

Host, *Nobel Peace Prize Concert* (also known as *The Nobel Peace Prize 100th Anniversary Concert*), USA Network and Trio, 2001.

Narrator, *New York at the Movies*, Arts and Entertainment, 2002.

There's Only One Paul McCartney, BBC (England), 2002.

Hollywood Salutes Nicolas Cage: An American Cinematheque Tribute, TNT, 2002.

Narrator, *Vermeer: Master of Light*, PBS, 2002.

Interviewee, *Kevin Bacon: Am I Me?*, Arts and Entertainment, 2002.

Interviewee, *What Not to Wear on the Red Carpet*, BBC, 2003.

Nicole Kidman: An American Cinematheque Tribute (also known as *The 18th Annual American Cinematheque Award*), AMC, 2003.

The 26th Annual Kennedy Center Honors: A Celebration of the Performing Arts, CBS, 2003.

AFI Lifetime Achievement Award: A Tribute to Meryl Streep, USA Network, 2004.

Jonathan Demme and the Making of "The Manchurian Candidate," 2004.

(In archive footage) *Imaginary Witness: Hollywood and the Holocaust* (documentary), Anker Productions, 2004.

Interviewee, "Bruce Willis," *Biography*, Arts and Entertainment, 2005.

Also narrator of a documentary special on Lyme disease, PBS, 1999.

Television Appearances; Movies:
Sharon Miller, *The Deadliest Season*, CBS, 1977.
Alice, *Alice at the Palace*, 1981.
Lori Reimuller, *... First Do No Harm*, ABC, 1997.

Television Appearances; Episodic:
Guest, *Omnibus*, BBC (England), 1980.
Voice of Jessica Lovejoy, "Bart's Girlfriend," *The Simpsons* (animated), Fox, 1994.
Guest, *Today*, NBC, 1994, 2004.
Guest, *CBS This Morning*, CBS, 1996.
Inside the Actors Studio, Bravo, 1998.
Guest, *The Rosie O'Donnell Show*, syndicated, 1999.
Voice of Aunt Esme Dauterive, "A Beer Can Named Desire," *King of the Hill* (animated), Fox, 1999.
Guest, *Late Show with David Letterman*, 1999.
"The Films of Wes Craven," *The Directors*, Encore!, 1999.
"The Films of Sydney Pollack," *The Directors*, Encore!, 2000.
"The Films of Clint Eastwood," *The Directors*, Encore!, 2000.
Guest, *The Oprah Winfrey Show*, syndicated, 2002.
Guest, *Tinseltown TV*, International Channel, 2003.
"Stuck on You," *HBO First Look*, HBO, 2003.
"Dustin Hoffman," *The Hollywood Greats*, BBC1 (England), 2004.
Guest, *Film '72*, BBC, 2004.
Guest, *The View*, ABC, 2004.
Guest, *Coming Attractions*, 2004.
Herself, *Unscripted*, HBO, 2005.
"The Films of Carl Franklin," *The Directors*, Encore!, 2005.

Television Appearances; Awards Presentations:
The 52nd Annual Academy Awards, ABC, 1980.
The 55th Annual Academy Awards, ABC, 1983.
The 56th Annual Academy Awards, ABC, 1984.
The 58th Annual Academy Awards, ABC, 1986.
The 60th Annual Academy Awards, ABC, 1988.
The 61st Annual Academy Awards, ABC, 1989.
Presenter, *The 32nd Annual Grammy Awards*, CBS, 1990.
Presenter, *The 63rd Annual Academy Awards Presentation*, ABC, 1991.
The 68th Annual Academy Awards, ABC, 1996.
The 71st Annual Academy Awards, ABC, 1999.
The 9th Annual Gotham Awards, Metroguide Network, 1999.
The 72nd Annual Academy Awards, ABC, 2000.
The 60th Annual Golden Globe Awards, NBC, 2003.
Presenter, *The 75th Annual Academy Awards*, ABC, 2003.
Presenter, *The 61st Annual Golden Globe Awards*, NBC, 2004.
Presenter, *The 10th Annual Screen Actors Guild Awards*, TNT, 2004.
The 56th Annual Primetime Emmy Awards, ABC, 2004.
Presenter, *The 62nd Annual Golden Globe Awards*, NBC, 2005.

Television Appearances; Others:
Herself, *The Best of Everything*, 1983.
Host, *Race to Save the Planet* (series; also known as *State of the World*), PBS, 1990.

Television Work; Movies:
Executive producer, ... *First Do No Harm,* ABC, 1997.

Stage Appearances:
The Playboy of Seville, Cubiculo Theatre, New York City, 1971.

Lieutenant Lillian Holliday, *Happy End* (musical), Yale Repertory Theatre, New Haven, CT, 1974.

(Broadway debut) Imogen Parrot, *Trelawny of the "Wells,"* New York Shakespeare Festival, Vivian Beaumont Theatre, Lincoln Center, New York City, 1975.

Flora Meighan, *27 Wagons Full of Cotton* and Patricia, *A Memory of Two Mondays* (double–bill), Phoenix Repertory Theatre, Playhouse Theatre, New York City, 1976.

Edith Varney, *Secret Service,* Phoenix Repertory Theatre, Playhouse Theatre, 1976.

Katherine, *Henry V,* New York Shakespeare Festival, Delacorte Theatre, Public Theatre, New York City, 1976.

Juliet and Isabella, *Measure for Measure,* New York Shakespeare Festival, Delacorte Theatre, Public Theatre, 1976.

Dunyasha, *The Cherry Orchard,* New York Shakespeare Festival, Vivian Beaumont Theatre, Lincoln Center, 1977.

Lieutenant Lillian Holliday, *Happy End* (musical), Chelsea Theatre Center, Brooklyn Academy of Music, Brooklyn, NY, then Martin Beck Theatre, New York City, both 1977.

Katharina, *The Taming of the Shrew,* New York Shakespeare Festival, Delacorte Theatre, Public Theatre, 1978.

Alice, *Wonderland in Concert,* New York Shakespeare Festival, Public Theatre, 1978.

Andrea, *Taken in Marriage,* New York Shakespeare Festival, Estelle R. Newman Public Theatre, New York City, 1979.

Alice, *Alice in Concert,* New York Shakespeare Festival, Estelle R. Newman Public Theatre, 1980.

Cynthia Peterson, *Isn't It Romantic?,* Playwrights Horizons Theatre, New York City, 1983, then Lucille Lortel Theatre, New York City, 1984.

Necessary Targets (staged reading), Helen Hayes Theatre, New York City, 1996.

An American Daughter (workshop reading), Seattle Repertory Theatre, Seattle, WA, 1996.

Arkadina, *The Seagull,* New York Shakespeare Festival, Delacorte Theatre, Public Theatre, 2001.

Poetry and the Creative Mind (benefit reading), Alice Tully Hall, Lincoln Center, New York City, 2004.

"Sawbones" and "Hope Leaves the Theatre," *Theatre of the New Ear* (reading), St. Ann's Warehouse Theatre, New York City, and Royal Festival Hall, London, both 2005.

Stage Work:
Coproducer, *Sarah Jones: Bridge and Tunnel,* Culture Project, Forty–Five Bleecker Street Theatre, New York City, 2004.

RECORDINGS

Videos:
Voice of storyteller, *Rabbit Ears: The Tale of Peter Rabbit,* 1987.

Voice of storyteller, *Rabbit Ears: The Tale of Mr. Jeremy Fisher,* 1987.

Narrator, *The Tailor of Gloucester,* 1988.

Voice of storyteller, *Rabbit Ears: The Fisherman and His Wife,* 1989.

(In archive footage) *Oscar's Greatest Moments,* Columbia TriStar Home Video, 1992.

A Song of Africa, Universal Studios Home Video, 1999.

Finding the Truth: The Making of "Kramer vs. Kramer," Columbia TriStar Home Video, 2001.

Reader for the videos *For Yourself: A Guide to Breast Self–Examination* and *What Should I Tell My Child about Drinking?* Appeared in choir for the music video "Voices that Care," Warner Bros., 1991.

Albums:
Reader, *I Will Sing Life: Voices from the Hole in the Wall Gang,* 1995.

Narrator, *Babar the Elephant: Mother Goose Suite,* 1996.

Reader, *Dance on a Moonbeam* (music and poetry for children), Telarc, 2000.

Recorded the albums *For Our Children* and *The Velveteen Rabbit;* also singer of the song "Nobody Understands Me" on the children's album *Philadelphia Chickens.*

Audio Books:
Narrator, "The Enormous Radio" and "The Sorrows of Gin," *The John Cheever Audio Collection,* 2003.

Also reader for *Fifty Poems of Emily Dickinson,* two volumes.

OTHER SOURCES

Books:
Encyclopedia of World Biography Supplement, Volume 23, Gale, 2005.

International Dictionary of Films and Filmmakers, Volume 3: *Actors and Actresses,* St. James Press, 2000.

Maychick, Diana, *Meryl Streep: The Reluctant Superstar,* 1984.

Pfaff, Eugene E., Jr., and Mark Emerson, *Meryl Streep: A Critical Biography,* McFarland and Co., 1987.

Smurthwaite, Nick, *The Meryl Streep Story,* 1984.

St. James Encyclopedia of Popular Culture, St. James Press, 2000.

Periodicals:

American Film, fall, 2004, pp. 10–11, 28–29.

Back Stage West, February 18, 1999, p. 6.

Daily Telegraph, September 3, 2004, p. 11.

Empire, October, 1997, p. 192.

Entertainment Weekly, February 11, 1994, pp. 17, 19, 21, 22, 24; February 23, 1996, pp. 42–43; August 15, 1997, p. 45; October 2, 1998, p. 44; November 27, 1998, p. 54; March 1, 1999, p. 41; March 24, 2000, pp. 50–55; February 21, 2003, p. 48.

Good Housekeeping, September, 1998, pp. 94–97.

Harper's Bazaar, January, 1999, p. 124.

Hollywood Reporter, June 6, 2004.

Interview, December, 1998, p. 66; December, 2002, p. 124.

Miami Herald, July 26, 2004.

Movieline, October, 1995, p. 77.

New York Times, July 25, 2004.

New York Times Magazine, September 18, 1994, pp. 42, 44, 45.

People Weekly, June 26, 1995, pp. 70–74, 76; February 3, 2003, p. 75.

Premiere (England), Volume 5, number 5, 1997, pp.62–67.

Premiere (United States), November, 2002, pp. 66–69.

Times (London), February 27, 2003; September 3, 2004, pp. 12–13.

USA Weekend, December 1, 2002.

Electronic:

Meryl Streep Online, http://www.merylstreeponline.net, July 21, 2005.

SUVARI, Mena 1979–
   (Mena A. Suvari)

PERSONAL

Name is pronounced Mee–na Soo–varr–ee; full name, Mena Adrienne Suvari; born February 9, 1979, in Newport, RI; daughter of Ando (a psychiatrist) and Candice (a nurse) Suvari; married Robert Brinkmann (a cinematographer), March 11 (some sources cite March 4), 2000 (separated May 10, 2005). *Religion:* Episcopalian. *Avocational Interests:* Photography, making jewelry, mountain biking, hiking.

Addresses: *Agent*—Chuck James, Gersh Agency, 232 North Canon Dr., Beverly Hills, CA 90210.

Career: Actress. Also worked as a model, beginning at age twelve; appeared in commercials, including print advertisements for Coach leather products, 2000, and Lancome cosmetics, 2004.

Awards, Honors: Film Award nomination, British Academy of Film and Television Arts, best supporting actress, Screen Actors Guild Award, outstanding cast performance (with others), and Online Film Critics Society Award, best ensemble cast (with others), all 2000, for *American Beauty;* Young Hollywood Award, *Movieline,* breakthrough female performance, and Blockbuster Entertainment Award nomination, Internet poll for favorite female newcomer, both 2000, for *American Beauty* and *American Pie;* Screen Actors Guild Award nomination, outstanding ensemble in a drama series (with others), 2005, for *Six Feet Under.*

CREDITS

Film Appearances:

Zoe, *Nowhere,* Fine Line, 1997.

(As Mena A. Suvari) Coty Pierce, *Kiss the Girls* (also known as *Collector*), Paramount, 1997.

Geli Raubal, *Snide and Prejudice,* Vine International Pictures, 1998.

Rachel Hoffman, *Slums of Beverly Hills,* Twentieth Century–Fox/Fox Searchlight Pictures, 1998.

Lisa Parker, *The Rage: Carrie 2* (also known as *Carrie 2* and *Carrie 2, Say You're Sorry*), United Artists, 1999.

Heather, *American Pie,* Universal, 1999.

Angela Hayes, *American Beauty,* DreamWorks, 1999.

Katrina Bartoloti, *American Virgin* (also known as *Live Virgin*), Granite Releasing, 2000.

Michelle "Kansas" Hill, *Sugar & Spice,* New Line Cinema, 2000.

Dora Diamond, *Loser,* Columbia, 2000.

Heather, *American Pie 2,* Universal, 2001.

Francesca bon Ansau, *The Musketeer,* Universal, 2001.

Carol, *Sonny,* Samuel Goldwyn Films, 2002.

Pony Ride, 2002.

Cookie, *Spun,* Newmarket Films, 2003.

Lana, *Standing Still,* Insomnia Entertainment/Rice–Walters Productions, 2004.

Charlotte, *Trauma,* Warner Bros., 2004.

Closing the Ring, 2004.

Light in the Sky, 2005.

Joanne, *Beauty Shop,* Metro–Goldwyn–Mayer, 2005.

Kimmie, *Domino,* New Line Cinema, 2005.

Brooklyn Rules, Lions Gate Films, 2005.

Whore, *Edmond,* First Independent Pictures, 2005.

Annie, *Rumor Has It,* Warner Bros., 2005.

Herself, *Stephen Tobolowsky's Birthday Party,* Brinkmann Company, 2005.

Television Appearances; Series:

Edie, a recurring role, *Six Feet Under,* HBO, 2004.

Television Appearances; Miniseries:
Grace Seger, *Atomic Train,* NBC, 1999.

Television Appearances; Episodic:
Laura, "Danger Bay," *Boy Meets World,* ABC, 1995.
Hilary, "The Grass Is Always Greener," *Boy Meets World,* ABC, 1996.
Emily, "A Fish Story," *Minor Adjustments,* NBC, 1996.
Laura Lee Armitage, "Last Call," *ER* (also known as *Emergency Room*), NBC, 1996.
Jill Marsh, "Nobody Walks in El Camino," *High Incident,* ABC, 1996.
Jill Marsh, "Camino High," *High Incident,* ABC, 1997.
Ivy Moore, "Sympathy for the Devil," *Chicago Hope,* CBS, 1997.
Crystal, "Thanksgiving," *413 Hope Street,* CBS, 1997.
Guest, *The Martin Short Show,* syndicated, 1999.
Guest host, *Saturday Night Live,* NBC, 2001.
Herself, "Finch in the Dogg House," *Just Shoot Me!,* NBC, 2001.
Guest, *The Late Late Show with Craig Kilborn,* CBS, 2001, 2003.
Guest, *The Tonight Show with Jay Leno,* 2001.
Guest, *The View,* ABC, 2001, 2004.
Guest, *The Early Show,* CBS, 2002.
"Tournament 2, Game 1," *Celebrity Poker Showdown,* Bravo, 2004.
Guest, *The Graham Norton Effect,* Comedy Central, 2004.
Guest, *Coming Attractions,* 2005.
Guest, *Live with Regis and Kelly,* syndicated, 2005.
Guest, *Last Call with Carson Daly,* NBC, 2005.

Television Appearances; Specials:
Spotlight on Location: American Pie (also known as *The Making of "American Pie"*), 1999.
Teen People's 25 Hottest Stars Under 25, ABC, 2000.
Interviewee, *Making the Movie: American Pie II,* MTV, 2001.

Television Appearances; Awards Presentations:
Presenter, *The 72nd Annual Academy Awards,* ABC, 2000.
Presenter, *The 2000 MTV Movie Awards,* MTV, 2000.
The 2001 MTV Movie Awards, MTV, 2001.
Young Hollywood Awards, 2004.

RECORDINGS

Videos:
American Beauty: Look Closer..., DreamWorks Home Entertainment, 2000.

Appeared in the music video "Teenage Dirtbag" by Wheatus, 2000.

OTHER SOURCES

Periodicals:
Entertainment Weekly, October 22, 1999, pp. 52–53.
Interview, March, 2000, p. 142.
Movieline, June, 2000, pp. 48–52, 98.
People Weekly, October 18, 1999, p. 164; December 31, 1999, p. 118.
Premiere, June, 2000, pp. 86–89.
Talk, August, 2000, pp. 32–33.
Teen People, June, 2000, p. 86.
TV Guide, January 10, 2004, p. 10.
Vanity Fair, April, 2000, p. 32.
Variety, January 3, 2000, p. 53.

SWANK, Hilary 1974–

PERSONAL

Full name, Hilary Ann Swank; born July 30, 1974, in Lincoln, NE; raised in Washington and California; daughter of Stephen (in the military and in sales) and Judy (a secretary and dancer) Swank; married Chad Lowe (an actor), September 28, 1997 (some sources cite October 2, 1997). *Education:* Attended Santa Monica College; studied martial arts with Pat Johnson. *Avocational Interests:* Outdoor activities, rafting, skiing, skydiving, animals.

Addresses: *Agent*—Creative Artists Agency, 9830 Wilshire Blvd., Beverly Hills, CA 90212. *Manager*—Untitled Entertainment, 331 North Maple Dr., Second Floor, Beverly Hills, CA 90210. *Publicist*—Baker Winokur Ryder, 9100 Wilshire Blvd., Sixth Floor West, Beverly Hills, CA 90212.

Career: Actress and producer. Appeared in television commercials and print advertisements; Harvey Milk School at the Hetrick–Martin Institute, New York City, spokesperson. Ranked gymnast as a teenager and a swimmer.

Awards, Honors: Young Artist Award nomination, best young actress in a new television series, Young Artist Foundation, 1993, for *Camp Wilder;* New York Film Critics Circle Award, Los Angeles Film Critics Association Award, Silver Hugo, Chicago International Film Festival, Boston Society of Film Critics Award, Stockholm Film Festival Award, and Gijon International Film Festival Award, all best actress, Toronto Film Critics Association Award, best performance, female, and National Board of Review Award, breakthrough performance—female, all 1999, Academy Award, best actress in a leading role, Golden Globe Award, best performance by an actress in a motion picture—drama, Chicago Film Critics Association Award, Dallas–Fort Worth Film Critics Association Award, Florida Film Critics Circle Award, Southeastern Film Critics Association Award, Broadcast Film Critics Association Award, and Chlotrudis Award, all best actress, Independent Spirit Award, best female lead, Independent Features Project/ West, Golden Satellite Award, best performance by an actress in a motion picture, drama, International Press Academy, Sierra awards, most promising actress and best actress, Las Vegas Film Critics Society, Santa Fe Film Critics Circle Award, best actress, Festival Diploma (with Kimberly Pierce), best full–length fiction film with special distinction for performance, Molodist International Film Festival, Screen Actors Guild Award nomination, outstanding performance by a female actor in a leading role, MTV Movie Award nomination, breakthrough female performance, Online Film Critics Society Award nomination, best actress, and MTV Movie Award nomination (with Chloe Sevigny), best kiss, all 2000, Film Award nomination, best performance by an actress in a leading role, British Academy of Film and Television Arts, ALFS Award nomination, actress of the year, London Critics Circle Film Award nomination, actress of the year, and Empire Award nomination, best actress, all 2001, all for *Boys Don't Cry;* ShoWest Award, female star of tomorrow, National Association of Theatre Owners, 2000; Saturn Award nomination, best supporting actress, Academy of Science Fiction, Fantasy & Horror Films, 2001, for *The Gift;* Empire Award nomination, best actress, 2003, for *Insomnia;* Boston Society of Film Critics Award and Florida Film Critics Circle Award, both best actress, and Phoenix Film Critics Society Award, best performance by an actress in a leading role, all 2004, Academy Award, best performance by an actress in a leading role, Golden Globe Award, best performance by an actress in a motion picture—drama, Screen Actors Guild Award, outstanding performance by a female actor in a leading role, National Society of Film Critics Award, Broadcast Film Critics Association Award, Dallas–Fort Worth Film Critics Association Award, and Kansas City Film Critics Circle Award, all best actress, Golden Satellite Award, best actress in a motion picture, drama, MTV Movie Award nomination, best female performance, Online Film Critics Society Award nomination, best actress, and Screen Actors Guild Award nomination (with Clint Eastwood and Morgan Freeman), outstanding performance by a cast in a motion picture, all 2005, all for *Million Dollar Baby;* Golden Globe Award nomination, best performance by an actress in a miniseries or a motion picture made for television, and Screen Actors Guild Award nomination, outstanding performance by a female actor in a television movie or miniseries, both 2005, for *Iron Jawed Angels.*

CREDITS

Film Appearances:

Kimberly Hannah, *Buffy the Vampire Slayer,* Twentieth Century–Fox, 1992.

Julie Pierce, *The Next Karate Kid,* Columbia, 1994.

Colleen, *Kounterfeit* (also known as *Money Crush*), LIVE Entertainment, 1996.

Michelle Porter, *Sometimes They Come Back ... Again* (also known as *Sometimes They Come Back 2*), Trimark Pictures, 1996.

Lolita, *The Way We Are* (also known as *Quiet Days in Hollywood*), Kick Film, 1997.

Brandon Teena/Teena Brandon, *Boys Don't Cry* (also known as *Take It Like a Man*), Twentieth Century–Fox, 1999.

Valerie Barksdale, *The Gift,* Paramount, 2000.

The Audition (short film), 2000.

Jeanne St. Remy de Valois, *The Affair of the Necklace,* Warner Bros., 2001.

Detective Ellie Burr, *Insomnia,* Warner Bros., 2002.

The Space Between (short film), 2002.

Buzzy, *11:14,* MDP Worldwide, 2003.

Major Rebecca "Beck" Childs, *The Core* (also known as *Core*), Paramount, 2003.

Maggie Fitzgerald, *Million Dollar Baby* (also known as *Rope Burns*), Warner Bros., 2004.

Sarah Barcant, *Red Dust,* BBC Films, 2004.

Madeleine Sprague, *The Black Dahlia,* Lions Gate Films, 2005.

Narrator, *On Native Soil* (documentary), Linda Ellman Productions, 2005.

Catherine, *The Reaping,* Warner Bros., 2006.

Teacher, *Freedom Writers,* Paramount, 2006.

Film Executive Producer:

11:14, MDP Worldwide, 2003.

Freedom Writers, Paramount, 2006.

Television Appearances; Series:

Aimee, *Evening Shade,* CBS, 1991–92.

Danielle, *Camp Wilder,* ABC, 1992–93.

Tiffany Roebuck, *Leaving L.A.,* ABC, 1997.

Carly Reynolds, *Beverly Hills 90210,* Fox, 1997–98.

Participant, *Celebrity Charades,* American Movie Classics, beginning 2005.

Television Appearances; Movies:

Patty, *Cries Unheard: The Donna Yaklich Story* (also known as *Victim of Rage*), CBS, 1994.

Deena Martin, *Terror in the Family,* Fox, 1996.

Lauren Schall, *The Sleepwalker Killings* (also known as *Crimes of Passion: Sleepwalker* and *From the Files of Unsolved Mysteries: "The Sleepwalker Killings"*), NBC, 1997.

Lisa Connors, *Dying to Belong,* NBC, 1997.

Sylvia Orsini, *Heartwood,* Family Channel, 1998.

Alice Paul, *Iron Jawed Angels,* HBO, 2004.

Television Appearances; Specials:

Narrator, *Reel Models: The First Women of Film* (documentary), American Movie Classics, 2000.

Herself, *The Concert for New York City,* multiple networks, 2001.

(In archive footage) Herself, "#63: Acceptance Speech Goofs," *101 Biggest Celebrity Oops,* E! Entertainment Television, 2004.

Herself, *Tsunami Aid: A Concert of Hope,* multiple networks, 2005.

Television Appearances; Awards Presentations:

Presenter, *Cybermania '94: The Ultimate Gamer Awards,* TBS, 1994.

Herself, *The 57th Annual Golden Globe Awards,* NBC, 2000.

Herself, *The 72nd Annual Academy Awards,* ABC, 2000.

Presenter, *VH1 Divas 2000: A Tribute to Diana Ross* (also known as *Divas 2000*), VH1, 2000.

Herself, *The Orange British Academy Film Awards,* 2001.

Presenter, *The 73rd Annual Academy Awards,* ABC, 2001.

Ladies' Home Journal's Most Fascinating Women to Watch, CBS, 2001.

(Uncredited) *The 2001 IFP/West Independent Spirit Awards,* Independent Film Channel, 2001.

Presenter, *The 2002 MTV Movie Awards,* MTV, 2002.

Presenter, *The 75th Annual Academy Awards,* ABC, 2003.

Presenter, *The 2004 IFP/West Independent Spirit Awards,* Independent Film Channel and Bravo, 2004.

Herself, *The 11th Annual Screen Actors Guild Awards,* TNT, 2005.

Herself, *The 77th Annual Academy Awards,* ABC, 2005.

Herself, *The 62nd Annual Golden Globe Awards,* NBC, 2005.

Herself, *The 10th Annual Critics' Choice Awards,* The WB, 2005.

Herself, *The 2005 MTV Movie Awards,* MTV, 2005.

Television Appearances; Episodic:

Sasha Serotsky, "There Must Be a Pony," *Growing Pains,* ABC, 1991.

"Harry Goes Ape," *Harry and the Hendersons,* syndicated, 1991.

Sasha Serotsky, "Menage a Luke," *Growing Pains,* ABC, 1992.

Herself, *Late Night with Conan O'Brien,* NBC, 1999.

Herself, *Today* (also known as *NBC News Today* and *The Today Show*), NBC, 2000, 2004.

Herself, *The View,* ABC, 2000, 2004.

Herself, "The Affair of the Necklace," *HBO First Look,* HBO, 2001.

Herself, *Beverly Hills 90210: The E! True Hollywood Story* (documentary), E! Entertainment Television, 2001.

Herself, *The Tonight Show with Jay Leno,* NBC, 2001, 2003, 2004.

Herself, *The Late Show with David Letterman,* CBS, 2002, 2003, 2004.

Herself, *The Daily Show* (also known as *The Daily Show with Jon Stewart* and *The Daily Show with Jon Stewart Global Edition*), Comedy Central, 2003.

Herself, *Ellen: The Ellen DeGeneres Show* (also known as *Ellen* and *The Ellen DeGeneres Show*), syndicated, 2004.

Coming Attractions, E! Entertainment Television, 2004.

Herself, *Late Night with Conan O'Brien,* NBC, 2005.

Herself, *The Oprah Winfrey Show* (also known as *Oprah*), syndicated, multiple appearances in 2005.

Host, *Saturday Night Live* (also known as *NBC's "Saturday Night," Saturday Night,* and *SNL*), NBC, 2005.

Herself, *Waratte iitomo,* [Japan], 2005.

Appeared as Danielle, *ABC TGIF* (also known as *TGIF*), ABC.

Television Appearances; Pilots:

Tiffany Roebuck, *Leaving L.A.,* ABC, 1997.

Appeared as Andi in the pilot *Reality Checks.*

Television Work; Series:

Executive producer, *Celebrity Charades,* American Movie Classics, beginning 2005.

Stage Appearances:

Gretel, *Hansel and Gretel,* Missoula Children's Theatre, Missoula, MT, 1987.

Cinderella, *Mad, Mad, Mad, Mad, Mad Cinderella,* Bellingham Theatre, Bellingham, WA, 1988.

Annie Sullivan, *The Miracle Worker,* Charlotte Repertory Theatre, Charlotte, NC, 2003.

RECORDINGS

Videos:

Herself, *The Gift: A Look Inside* (short documentary film), 2001.

Herself, *Day for Night: The Making of "Insomnia"* (short documentary film), Warner Home Video, 2002.

Herself, *Sex at 24 Frames per Second* (documentary; also known as *Playboy Presents "Sex at 24 Frames per Second: The Ultimate Journey through Sex in Cinema"*), Playboy Entertainment Group, 2003.

OTHER SOURCES

Books:

Newsmakers 2000, issue 3, Gale, 2000.

Periodicals:
Chicago Tribune, December 15, 2004.
Empire, issue 77, 1995, pp. 67–68.
Entertainment Weekly, October 29, 1999, p. 509; December 24, 2004, pp. 34–36; February 4, 2005, p. 35.
Femme Fatales, September 1, 2000, pp. 12–15.
Glamour (Great Britain), October, 2002, pp. 86–90, 92, 94.
Harpers & Queen, September, 2002, pp. 175–77.
InStyle, February, 1998, p. 203; September, 2002, pp. 490–91.
Interview, April, 2000, p. 136; June, 2000, p. 87; March, 2005, pp. 181–82.
Los Angeles Times, December 13, 2004.
Marie Claire, July, 2002, pp. 40–44, 46.
Newsweek, January 10, 2005, pp. 50–52.
Now, January 23, 2002, pp. 32–33.

Out, October, 1999.
Parade, August 7, 1994; November 18, 2001, pp. 26–27.
People Weekly, May 8, 2000, p. 192; April 14, 2003, p. 83.
Premiere, November, 1999, p. 46; September, 2001, pp. 68–71.
Seventeen, December, 2002, p. 174.
Talk, October, 1999.
Time, January 17, 2000, p. 88; April 18, 2005, p. 116.
Times (London), March 27, 2003.
USA Today, October 21, 1999.
US Weekly, April 10, 2000, pp. 62–63.
Washington Post, February 13, 2004, pp. C1, C8.

Electronic:
Hilary Swank Web Page, http://www.hilaryswank.com, August 31, 1999; April 11, 2000.

T

TAYLOR, Jeri 1938–

PERSONAL

Full name, Jeri Cecile Taylor; born June 30, 1938, in Evansville, IN; daughter of William Edward and Ruah Loraze (maiden name, Brackett) Suer; married Dick Enberg (a sportscaster), September 19, 1959 (divorced, 1977); married David Moessinger (a television writer), October 11, 1986; children: (first marriage) Jennifer, Andrew, Alexander (an actor). *Education:* Attended Stevens College, 1955–56; Indiana University, A.B., 1959; California State University, Northridge, M.A., 1967.

Career: Producer and writer. California State University, lecturer in English, 1967–69. Oxford Theatre, Los Angeles, director, 1972–78.

Member: Writers Guild of America, Directors Guild of America, American Federation of Television and Radio Artists.

Awards, Honors: Writers Guild of America Award, 1982; Emmy Award nomination, outstanding drama series (with others), 1994, for *Star Trek: The Next Generation.*

CREDITS

Television Producer; Series:
(With others) *Quincy, M.E.* (also known as *Quincy*), NBC, between 1976 and 1983.
(With Donald A. Baer) *Blue Thunder,* ABC, 1984.
Coproducer, *Magnum P.I.,* CBS, 1987–88.

Supervising producer, *In the Heat of the Night,* NBC, 1988–89.
Co–executive producer, *Jake and the Fatman,* CBS, 1989–90.
Supervising producer, *Star Trek: The Next Generation* (also known as *Star Trek: TNG*), syndicated, 1990–92.
Executive producer, *Star Trek: The Next Generation* (also known as *Star Trek: TNG*), syndicated, 1992–93.
Creator and executive producer, *Star Trek: Voyager* (also known as *Voyager*), UPN, 1995–98.

Also worked as story editor for *Quincy, M.E.* (also known as *Quincy*), NBC.

Television Work; Episodic:
Executive producer, "All Good Things..." (final episode), *Star Trek: The Next Generation* (also known as *Star Trek: TNG*), syndicated, 1992.

Directed episodes of *Jake and the Fatman,* CBS; and *Quincy, M.E.* (also known as *Quincy*), NBC.

Television Work; Other:
Supervising producer, *A Place to Call Home* (special), CBS, 1987.
Creator and executive producer, *Star Trek: Voyager—Caretaker* (pilot), UPN, 1995.

Television Appearances; Specials:
Journey's End: The Sage of Star Trek—The Next Generation, 1994.
Inside the New Adventure—Star Trek Voyager, syndicated, 1995.

Film Appearances:
Herself, *Trekkies,* Paramount Classics, 1999.

WRITINGS

Television Series:
Staff writer, *Star Trek: The Next Generation* (also known as *Star Trek: TNG;* also based on story by Taylor), syndicated, 1990–94.
Star Trek: Voyager (also known as *Voyager*), UPN, 1995–98.

Television Episodes:
Quincy, M.E. (also known as *Quincy*), NBC, c. 1982–83.
"Second Thunder," *Blue Thunder,* ABC, 1984.
Magnum P.I., CBS, three episodes, 1987–88.
In the Heat of the Night, NBC, between 1988 and 1989.
Author of "The Medical Mystery," an episode of *Father Dowling Mysteries* (also known as *Father Dowling Investigates*); "Gambini the Great" and "Wave of the Future," episodes of *Little House on the Prairie* (also known as *Little House: A New Beginning*), NBC; also wrote episodes of *The Incredible Hulk,* CBS; *Jake and the Fatman,* CBS; and *Salvage,* ABC.

Television Specials:
Please Don't Hit Me, Mom (also based on story by Taylor), ABC, 1981.
But It's Not My Fault! (also based on story by Taylor), ABC, 1983.

Television Scripts; Other:
A Place to Call Home (movie), CBS, 1987.
Star Trek: Voyager—Caretaker (pilot), UPN, 1995.

"Star Trek" Novels:
Unification, Pocket Books, 1991.
Mosaic, Pocket Books, 1996.
Pathways, Pocket Books, 1998.

Also author of *Day of Honor.*

ADAPTATIONS

The novels *Mosaic* and *Pathways* have been adapted as audio books. Episodes of the television series *Star Trek: Deep Space Nine* (also known as *Deep Space Nine, DS9,* and *Star Trek: DS9*), syndicated, beginning 1993, were created by Taylor. Video games based on Taylor's creations include *Star Trek Voyager: Elite Force,* released by Activision in 2000, and *Star Trek: Elite Force II,* released by Activision in 2003. The short film *Star Trek: The Experience—Borg Invasion 4D,* released by Paramount in 2004, was also based on Taylor's creations.

OTHER SOURCES

Periodicals:
Cult Times, July, 1997, pp. 26–29.
Starlog, February, 1995; October, 1996.

TAYLOR, Lili 1967–

PERSONAL

Born February 20, 1967, in Chicago (some sources cite Glencoe), IL; daughter of Park (an artist and hardware store operator) and Marie (a professional babysitter) Taylor. *Education:* Attended DePaul University and Piven Theatre Workshop.

Addresses: *Agent*—Michelle Stern–Bohan, Endeavor, 9601 Wilshire Blvd., 3rd Floor, Beverly Hills, CA 90210. *Manager*—Frank Frattaroli, Widescreen Management, 270 Lafayette St., Suite 402, New York, NY 10012. *Publicist*—I/D Public Relations, 8409 Santa Monica Blvd., West Hollywood, CA 90069.

Career: Actress and costume designer. Naked Angels (theatre company), former member of company; Machine Full (theatre company), founder, c. 1993; Humana Festival, participant; 52nd Street Project (theatre experience for children), affiliate; also worked with Actors Theatre of Louisville; appeared in commercials for Independent Film Channel, 1998, Tylenol pain relievers, and other products. Cultural Exchange Program, participant in Czechoslovakia, 1987.

Awards, Honors: Independent Spirit Award nomination, Independent Features Project West, best female lead, 1992, for *Bright Angel;* Volpi Cup, Venice Film Festival, 1993, and Golden Globe Award, 1994, both best ensemble cast (with others), for *Short Cuts;* Independent Spirit Award, best supporting actress, 1994, for *Household Saints;* National Board of Review Award, best ensemble (with others), 1994, for *Pret-a-Porter;* Best Actress Award, Thessaloniki Film Festival, 1996, for *Things I Never Told You;* Golden Space Needle Award, Seattle International Film Festival, best actress, 1996, for *Cold Fever, Girls Town,* and *I Shot Andy Warhol;* Independent Spirit Award nomination, best female lead, 1996, Best Actress Award, Malaga International Week of Fantastic Cinema, 1997, and Sant Jordi Award, best foreign actress, 1998, all for *The Addiction;* Special Recognition, Sundance Film Festival, acting category, 1996, Best Actress Award, Stockholm Film Festival, 1996, and Chlotrudis Award nomination, best actress, 1997, all for *I Shot Andy Warhol;* Independent Spirit Award nomination, best supporting female, 1997, for

Girls Town; Blockbuster Entertainment Award, favorite supporting actress in a suspense movie, 1997, for *Ransom;* Emmy Award nomination, outstanding guest actress in a drama series, 1998, for "Mind's Eye," *The X-Files;* Blockbuster Entertainment Award nomination, favorite supporting actress in a horror movie, 2000, for *The Haunting;* Emmy Award nomination, outstanding guest actress in a drama series, 2002, and Screen Actors Guild Award, outstanding ensemble performance (with others), 2004, both for *Six Feet Under;* Maverick Tribute Award, Cinequest San Jose Film Festival, 2002; Obie Award, *Village Voice,* outstanding performance, 2004, for *Aunt Dan and Lemon;* Special Jury Prize, Indianapolis International Film Festival, performance category (with Sara Rue), and Achievement Award, Newport Beach Film Festival, outstanding achievement in acting, both 2004, for *A Slipping-Down Life.*

CREDITS

Film Appearances:

Girl at medical lab, *She's Having a Baby,* Paramount, 1988.

Jojo Barboza, *Mystic Pizza,* Samuel Goldwyn Company, 1988.

Corey Flood, *Say ... Anything,* Twentieth Century-Fox, 1989.

Jamie Wilson, *Born on the Fourth of July,* Universal, 1989.

Lucy, *Bright Angel,* Hemdale, 1990.

Rose, *Dogfight,* Warner Bros., 1991.

Grace Stalker, *Arizona Dream* (also known as *The Arrowtooth Waltz*), 1992, Warner Bros., 1995.

Teresa Carmela Santangelo, *Household Saints,* Fine Line, 1993.

Sherry, *Rudy,* TriStar, 1993.

Honey Bush, *Short Cuts,* Fine Line, 1993.

Brenda, *Watch It,* Skouras, 1993.

Darcy Winningham, *Touch Base* (short film), Open City Films, 1994.

Edna Ferber, *Mrs. Parker and the Vicious Circle* (also known as *Mrs. Parker and the Round Table*), Fine Line, 1994.

Fiona Ulrich, *Pret-a-Porter* (also known as *Pret a Porter: Ready to Wear* and *Ready to Wear*), Miramax, 1994.

Jill, *Cold Fever* (also known as *A koeldum klaka*), Artistic License, 1996.

Woman in speakeasy, *Killer: A Journal of Murder* (also known as *The Killer*), Republic, 1995.

Raven, *Four Rooms,* Miramax, 1995.

Kathleen Conklin, *The Addiction,* October Films, 1995.

Ann, *Things I Never Told You* (also known as *Cosas que no et vaig dir mai* and *Cosas que nunca te dije*), Seventh Art Releasing, 1996.

Pattie Lucci, *Girls Town,* October Films, 1996.

Valerie Jean Solanas, *I Shot Andy Warhol,* Orion/Samuel Goldwyn Company, 1996.

Maris Connor, *Ransom,* Buena Vista, 1996.

Plain Pleasures, 1996.

Happy, *Kicked in the Head,* October Films, 1997.

Voice, *Letters Not About Love,* 1997.

Micky (some sources cite Suzanne), *Illtown,* Shooting Gallery, 1998.

Rachel, *O.K. Garage* (also known as *All Revved Up*), New City Releasing, 1998.

Lily "Lil", *The Imposters,* Twentieth Century-Fox, 1998.

Angela, *Come To* (short film), Janey Pictures, 1998.

Rorey Wheeler, *Pecker,* Fine Line, 1998.

Evie Decker, *A Slipping-Down Life,* 1999, Lions Gate Films, 2004.

Eleanor "Nell" Vance, *The Haunting* (also known as *La maldicion*), DreamWorks, 1999.

Sarah Kendrew, *High Fidelity,* Buena Vista, 2000.

Ben Harris, *Gaudi Afternoon* (also known as *Tardes de Gaudí*), First Look Home Entertainment, 2001.

Narrator, *The Weather Underground* (documentary), 2002.

Leslie, *Casa de los babys,* IFC Films, 2003.

Beyond Borders: John Sayles in Mexico (documentary), 2003.

Jan, *Factotum,* Mikado Films/Network Movie, 2005.

Paula Klaw, *The Notorious Bettie Page* (also known as *The Ballad of Bettie Page*), IFC Films, 2005.

Television Appearances; Series:

Hildy Baker, *Deadline,* NBC, 2000.

Lisa Kimmel Fisher, *Six Feet Under,* HBO, 2002–2003.

Television Appearances; Movies:

Marina, *Night of Courage,* ABC, 1987.

Belinda, "The Listeners," *Subway Stories: Tales from the Underground* (also known as *Subway*), HBO, 1997.

Title role, *Julie Johnson,* Here! TV, 2001.

Miep Gies, *Anne Frank: The Whole Story,* ABC, 2001.

Judy Parker, *Live from Baghdad,* HBO, 2002.

Television Appearances; Specials:

Younger Marianne, *Sensibility and Sense,* PBS, 1990.

Herself, *Luck, Trust and Ketchup: Robert Altman in Carver County* (also known as *Luck, Trust and Ketchup*), Bravo, 1994.

Interviewee, *In Bad Taste: The John Waters Story,* Independent Film Channel, 1999.

A Salute to Robert Altman, an American Maverick, 2002.

Voice of Doris Featherstone, *Penguins Behind Bars* (animated), Cartoon Network, 2003.

Women on Top: Hollywood and Power, AMC, 2003.

Interviewee, "John Waters," *Biography,* Arts and Entertainment, 2004.

Also affiliated with a local special, *No Laughing Matter.*

Television Appearances; Miniseries:
Third Laura Walker, *Family of Spies,* CBS, 1990.

Television Appearances; Episodic:
Waitress, "Hide and Go Thief," *Crime Story,* NBC, 1986.
"Habitat," *Monsters,* syndicated, 1990.
Arley, "The Magic Pants," *Mad About You,* NBC, 1997.
Guest, *The Rosie O'Donnell Show,* syndicated, 1998.
Marty Glenn, "Mind's Eye," *The X–Files,* Fox, 1998.
Arley, "Nat & Arley," *Mad About You,* NBC, 1998.
Guest, *Dinner for Five,* Independent Film Channel, 2003.

Also appeared in "The Haunting," *HBO First Look,* HBO.

Stage Appearances:
(Professional stage debut) *Bing and Walker,* Northlight Theatre, Chicago, IL, 1984.
Laurie, *Brighton Beach Memoirs,* New American Theater, Rockford, IL, 1986–87.
What Did He See?, New York Shakespeare Festival, Susan Stein Shiva Theatre, Public Theatre, New York City, 1988–89.
The Myth Project: A Festival of Competency, Mann Theatre, 1989.
Wendy, *Aven'U Boys,* John Houseman Theatre, New York City, 1993.
Irina, *Three Sisters,* Roundabout Theatre Company, Criterion Center Stage Right Theatre, New York City, 1997.
Shirley–Diane, *The Dead Eye Boy,* Manhattan Class Company Theatre, New York City, 2001.
Ophelia, *Hamlet,* New Jersey Shakespeare Festival, Madison, NJ, 2001.
Landscape of the Body, Williamstown Theatre Festival, Williamstown, MA, 2003.
Lemon, *Aunt Dan and Lemon,* Acorn Theatre, New York City, 2003–2004.
Emily, "Poem," *The 24 Hour Plays 2004* (benefit), American Airlines Theatre, New York City, 2004.
Psychos Never Dream (staged reading), Fine Arts Work Center, Provincetown, MA, 2005.

Also appeared in *Fun, The Love Talker,* and *Mud.*

Stage Work:
Costume designer, *A Candle in the Window,* 1995.

Director of *Halcyon Days,* Machine Full, WorkHouse Theatre; also director of *Collateral Damage.*

RECORDINGS

Videos:
The Making of "The Haunting," 1999.

Audio Books:
Reader, *Black and Blue,* by Anna Quindlen, Random Audio, 1998.
Reader, *The Princess Tales,* by Gail Carson Levine, Harper Children's Audio, 2002.

WRITINGS

(Coauthor) *Girls Town,* October Films, 1996.

OTHER SOURCES

Periodicals:
Entertainment Weekly, December 9, 1994, p. 47; October 18, 1996, p. 16; November–December, 1997, p. 54.
Interview, January, 1999, p. 44.
Ms., September–October, 1996, pp. 76–77.
Premiere, November, 1996, pp. 86–87.

TEMPLEMAN, Simon
(S. A. Templeman)

PERSONAL

Married Rosalind Chao (an actress).

Career: Actor and voice artist.

CREDITS

Film Appearances:
Psychoanalyst and Whitehall, *The Russia House,* Metro–Goldwyn–Mayer, 1990.
Bob, *Live Nude Girls,* 1995.
Voice of Sebastian Fox, *The Young Unknowns,* Indican Pictures, 2000.

Television Appearances; Series:
The Talisman, BBC, 1980.
Voice, *James Bond, Jr.,* syndicated, 1991.
Voice of Sir Mordred, *Legend of Prince Valiant* (animated), 1991–94.
Voice of Dr. Doom, *The Fantastic Four* (also known as *The Marvel Action Hour: The Fantastic Four*), syndicated, 1994.
Simon Leeds, *Just Shoot Me!,* NBC, 2002–2003.

Television Appearances; Movies:
Johnny Leighton, *Silent Cries,* NBC, 1993.

Harry Balfour, *Amelia Earhart: The Final Flight,* TNT, 1994.

Keith Bradshaw, *Don King: Only in America,* HBO, 1997.

Television Appearances; Pilots:
Fletcher Dichter, *Carly,* CBS, 1998.
Doug, *The Heart Department,* CBS, 2001.

Television Appearances; Episodic:
Neville Grant, "Cry Wolf," *The Professionals,* ITV, 1982.

(As S. A. Templeman) Bates, "The Defector," *Star Trek: The Next Generation,* syndicated, 1989.

Kurt (coffee shop manager), "For Love of Money," *Melrose Place,* Fox, 1992.

D. W. Ward, "Black River Bride," *Moon over Miami,* ABC, 1993.

Cal Ingram, "Mite Makes Right," *Northern Exposure,* CBS, 1994.

Martin, "Instant Karma," *Mad about You,* NBC, 1994.

Cal Ingram, "Lovers and Madmen," *Northern Exposure,* CBS, 1994.

Cal Ingram, "Horns," *Northern Exposure,* CBS, 1995.

Caledcott Ingram, "Let's Dance," *Northern Exposure,* CBS, 1995.

Voice of Sir Mordred, "Biker Knights of the Round Table: Parts 1 & 2," *Biker Mice From Mars* (animated), syndicated, 1995.

Nigel Davies, "Take My Wife, Please," *Ned and Stacey,* Fox, 1995.

Carl, "Can We Keep Her, Dad?," *Partners,* Fox, 1996.

The burglar, "The Family Jewels," *High Society,* CBS, 1996.

Lord Nor, "Lord of the Flys," *Lois & Clark: The New Adventures of Superman,* ABC, 1996.

Lord Nor, "Battleground Earth," *Lois & Clark: The New Adventures of Superman,* ABC, 1996.

The burglar, "Who's Afraid of Elizabeth Taylor?" (also known as "Liz Taylor Show"), *Can't Hurry Love,* 1996.

Voice of Dr. Doom/Dr. Victor von Doom, "Doomed," *The Incredible Hulk* (animated), UPN, 1996.

Laurence, "You Don't Know Jackal," *Murphy Brown,* CBS, 1997.

Ethan, "The Voice of Reason," *Temporarily Yours,* CBS, 1997.

Voice of Dr. Doom/Dr. Victor von Doom, "Hollywood Rocks," *The Incredible Hulk* (animated), UPN, 1997.

Darren Faxon, "Exposed," *The Pretender,* NBC, 1997.

Simon Downing–Chubb, "Taylor Got Game," *Home Improvement,* ABC, 1998.

Nigel Wiggans, "Tantric Turkey," *Chicago Hope,* CBS, 1998.

D'Art, "Hard Cheese on Zoe," *Zoe, Duncan, Jack & Jane,* The WB, 1999.

Andrew Conover, "Tea and Sympathy," *NYPD Blue,* ABC, 2000.

Angel of Death, "Death Takes a Halliwell," *Charmed,* The WB, 2001.

Henry Carto, "Thanks for the Mammaries," *Philly,* ABC, 2002.

Sebastian, "Brave New World," *The Division,* Lifetime, 2002.

Voice of Dr. Gilee, "Ice Man Cometh," *Totally Spies!,* ABC Family, 2002.

Karl Sebastion, "Mr. Monk Goes to the Theater," *Monk,* USA Network, 2003.

Matthias Pavayen, "Hell Bound," *Angel,* The WB, 2003.

Trevor Tomlinson, "Day 3: 5:00 a.m.–6 a.m.," *24,* Fox, 2004.

Angel of Death, "Styx Feet Under," *Charmed,* The WB, 2004.

Angel of Death, "Death Becomes Them," *Charmed,* The WB, 2005.

Also appeared as Roger Lacey, "Visit" and "Blood, Flopsweat and Tears," both episodes of *Bull,* TNT.

Television Work; Series:
Additional voices, *Tale Spin* (animated), syndicated, 1990–91.

Stage Appearances:
Captain Dumain, *All's Well That Ends Well,* Martin Beck Theatre, New York City, 1983.

Romeo, *Romeo and Juliet,* The Other Place, Stratford–upon–Avon, England, 1984.

Heinz Bayer, *Today,* The Other Place, 1984.

Jackson, Mr. Hetherington, Lord Frederick Verisopht, angry fellow, and Policeman, *The Life and Adventures of Nicholas Nickleby,* Broadhurst Theatre, New York City, 1986.

Becket or The Honor of God, Skirball Cultural Center, Los Angeles, 2004.

Radio Appearances:
The Man with the Scar, 2000.
Breaking the Code, L.A. Theatreworks, Los Angeles, 2003.

RECORDINGS

Video Games:
Voice of Kain, *Blood Omen: Legacy of Kain,* 1996.

Voices of Kain and Dumah, *Legacy of Kain: Soul Reaver,* 1999.

Voices of Prince James and MacDougall, *Gabriel Knight: Blood of the Sacred, Blood of the Damned,* Sierra OnLine, 1999.

Voice of Kain, *Legacy of Kain: Soul Reaver II* (also known as *The Legacy of Kain Series: Soul Reaver 2*), Crystal Dynamics, 2001.

Voice of Kain, *Blood Omen II: Legacy of Kain,* 2002.

Voice of Kain, *Legacy of Kain: Defiance* (also known as *Legacy of Kain: Soul Reaver III*), 2003.
Additional voices, *Star Wars: Knights of the Old Republic,* LucasArts Entertainment, 2003.
Additional voices, *The Bard's Tale,* InXile Entertainment, 2004.
Gondor soldier, narrator, and various characters, *The Lord of the Rings: The Battle for Middle–Earth,* 2004.
Jade Empire, Microsoft Game Studios, 2005.

Taped Readings:
The Doctor's Dilemma, L.A. Theatreworks, 1999.
(With others) *Betrayal,* L.A. Theatreworks, 2003.

Also read (with others) *Hay Fever, Thank You, Jeeves, Orson's Shadow,* and as Bertie, *Thank You, Jeeves,* all L.A. Theatreworks.

___

TENCH, John

PERSONAL

Born in Madison, WI. *Avocational Interests:* Painting, playing guitar, the outdoors, and canoeing.

Addresses: *Office*—c/o Victoria Target Theatre, 1728 Douglas St., Victoria, British Columbia V8W 2G7, Canada.

Career: Actor.

CREDITS

Film Appearances:
Sully, *The Darkside* (also known as *The Dark Side*), 1987.
Transit, *The Understudy: Graveyard Shift II* (also known as *Graveyard Shift II*), Virgin Vision, 1988.
MacLaughin, *Murder Blues* (also known as *Dead Certain*), Hemdale Home Video, 1990.
Cell guard, *If Looks Could Kill* (also known as *Teen Agent*), Warner Bros., 1991.
Dr. Susskind, *Landslide,* Samuel Goldwyn Company, 1992.
Carlos, *Power of Attorney,* Prism Pictures, 1995.
Schreck, *Cyberjack* (also known as *Virtual Assassin*), Prism Pictures, 1995.
Jerry, *Carpool,* Warner Bros., 1996.
The photographer, *Johnny Shortwave,* 1996.
Wes, *Grizzly Falls,* Providence Entertainment, 1999.
Guy, *Backroads* (also known as *Bearwalker*), 2000.

Norvid, *The Operative,* Studio Home Entertainment, 2000.
Kevin, *Black Point,* 2001.
Robert, *The Zero Sum* (also known as *Letters*), 2005.

Television Appearances; Series:
Leon, a recurring role, *Da Vinci's Inquest,* CBC, 1998–99.

Television Appearances; Miniseries:
(Uncredited) Fireman, *Titanic,* CBS, 1996.
General Doar, *Legend of Earthsea* (also known as *Earthsea*), Sci–Fi Channel, 2004.

Television Appearances; Movies:
Niagara Strip, 1989.
Mugger, *Home for Christmas,* Lifetime, 1990.
Grimes, *Christmas on Division Street,* CBS, 1991.
Sal, *Beyond Suspicion,* NBC, 1994.
Deadly Vows, Fox, 1994.
Leon, *Prisoner of Zenda, Inc.* (also known as *Double Play*), Showtime, 1996.
Anthony, *Dead Ahead,* USA Network, 1996.
Chuck Martin, *The Ticket,* USA Network, 1997.
Cap Clarke, *The Winning Season,* TNT, 2004.

Television Appearances; Specials:
First policeman, "The Real UFO Story," *Visitors from the Unknown,* CBS, 1992.
J. D., *Moment of Truth,* CBS, 1992.

Television Appearances; Episodic:
Worker, "The Raising of Lazarus," *War of the Worlds,* 1989.
Koslow, "Bad Penny," *Friday the 13th* (also known as *Friday the 13th: The Series*), syndicated, 1989.
First Gunsel, "Femme Fatale," *Friday the 13th* (also known as *Friday the 13th: The Series*), syndicated, 1989.
First gambler, "Totally Real," *War of the Worlds,* 1990.
Thurman, "Friendly Fire," *Street Justice,* syndicated, 1991.
"Justice," *Beyond Reality,* USA Network, 1992.
Reese, "The Sea Witch," *Highlander,* syndicated, 1992.
Smith, "Hello Again," *Street Justice,* 1993.
Artie Krause, "Accused," *The Commish,* 1995.
Max Jupe, "Song of the Executioner," *Highlander,* syndicated, 1995.
Steve, "F. Emasculata," *The X–Files,* Fox, 1995.
"I Hear You Calling," *The Outer Limits,* Showtime and syndicated, 1996.
"The Hideout," *Lonesome Dove: The Outlaw Years,* syndicated, 1996.
Sammie, "A.D.," *Two,* CBC and syndicated, 1996.
Jack, "True Crime," *The Sentinel,* UPN, 1996.
Harris, "Talk Is Cheap," *Viper,* syndicated, 1996.

Scarred Slave, "The Camp," *The Outer Limits,* Showtime and syndicated, 1997.

Joe Rule, "Death Warrant," *Dead Man's Gun,* Showtime, 1997.

Director, "The Girl Who Was Plugged In," *Welcome to Paradox,* Sci–Fi Channel, 1998.

T–Bird, "The Soul Can't Rest," *The Crow: Stairway to Heaven,* syndicated, 1998.

T–Bird, "It's a Wonderful Death," *The Crow: Stairway to Heaven,* syndicated, 1999.

Al King, "Safe House," *Viper,* syndicated, 1999.

Gerentex, "Under the Night," *Andromeda* (also known as *Gene Roddenberry's "Andromeda"*), syndicated, 2000.

Jim, "Skywatchers," *First Wave,* 2000.

Gerentex, "An Affirming Flame," *Andromeda* (also known as *Gene Roddenberry's "Andromeda"*), syndicated, 2000.

Mike Morrison, "Loose Ends: Part 2," *Cold Squad,* CTV, 2001.

Gerentex, "Fear and Loathing in the Milky Way," *Andromeda* (also known as *Gene Roddenberry's "Andromeda"*), syndicated, 2001.

Kane, "Wages of Sydney," *Relic Hunter,* syndicated, 2001.

Eliaures, "Sir Caradoc at the Round Table," *MythQuest,* PBS and CBC, 2001.

Double–Down, "Life on the Wire," *UC: Undercover,* NBC, 2001.

Andre, "The Shed," *Cold Squad,* CTV, 2002.

Mike Morrison, "Dead Letters," *Cold Squad,* CTV, 2002.

Andre, "Enough Is Enough," *Cold Squad,* CTV, 2002.

Mort, "Precipitate," *The Dead Zone,* USA Network, 2003.

Mal Oswald, "Puzzle Box," *Missing* (also known as *1–800–MISSING*), Lifetime, 2004.

Also appeared as Mickey Kennedy, *Secret Service,* NBC; in "Ties That Bind," *Lonesome Dove: The Series.*

Television Work; Series:

Additional voices, *The Adventures of Sonic the Hedgehog* (animated), syndicated, 1993.

Stage Appearances:

Appeared as juror No. 8, *Twelve Angry Men,* and in *Accidental Death of an Anarchist,* both Q Art Theatre, Montreal, Quebec, Canada.

Stage Director:

Directed *Accidental Death of an Anarchist,* Q Art Theatre, Montreal, Quebec, Canada.

WRITINGS

Plays:

Wrote *Alma; Best of Intentions; A Quiet Walk; I Don't Know You Anymore; Millicent Steps; A Quiet Day in the Country; The Bath; Father's Little Holiday; Of Mice and Money.*

THE WACHOWSKI BROTHERS
See WACHOWSKI, Andy/Larry

THOMPSON, Susanna 1958–

PERSONAL

Born January 27, 1958, in San Diego, CA. *Education:* San Diego State University, B.A.; also studied aikido.

Addresses: *Agent*—Alisa Adler, Paradigm, 360 North Crescent Dr., North Building, Beverly Hills, CA 90210. *Manager*—Craig Dorfman, Blueprint Artist Management, 1438 North Gower St., Building 15, Second Floor, Box 17, Los Angeles, CA 90028.

Career: Actress.

Awards, Honors: *DramaLogue* Award, for *A Shayna Maidel;* San Diego Critics Circle Award nomination, best actress, for *Agnes of God.*

CREDITS

Television Appearances; Series:

Karen Sammler, *Once and Again,* ABC, 1999–2002.

Judith Webster, *The Book of Daniel,* NBC, beginning c. 2005.

Television Appearances; Movies:

Christine, *Calendar Girl, Cop, Killer? The Bambi Bembenek Story* (also known as *The Heart of the Lie*), NBC, 1992.

Receptionist, *A Woman Scorned: The Betty Broderick Story* (also known as *Till Murder Do Us Part*), CBS, 1992.

Meg, *In the Line of Duty: Ambush in Waco,* NBC, 1993.

Burt–Hopkins, *In the Line of Duty: The Price of Vengeance,* NBC, 1994.

Connie Collins, *Slaughter of the Innocents,* HBO, 1994.

Janet, "MacShayne: Final Roll of the Dice" (also known as "MacShayne's Big Score"), *NBC Friday Night Mystery,* NBC, 1994.

Lorraine Clark, *Alien Nation: Dark Horizon,* Fox, 1994.

Marina Baiul, *A Promise Kept: The Oksana Baiul Story,* CBS, 1994.

Beth Ann, "The Reunion," *America's Dream,* TNT, 1996.

Grace Everman, *Bermuda Triangle,* 1996.

Sylvia Whitmire, *In the Line of Duty: Blaze of Glory* (also known as *Blaze of Glory*), NBC, 1997.
Denise Hydecker, *The Lake,* NBC, 1998.
Amy Kane, *High Noon,* TBS, 2000.

Television Appearances; Specials:
Florine Markland, *The Lemon Grove Incident,* PBS, 1986.

Television Appearances; Episodic:
Lorraine Dallek, "Oboe Phobia," *Civil Wars,* ABC, 1992.
Susan Phelan, "Denise and De Nuptials," *Civil Wars,* ABC, 1992.
Varel, "The Next Phase," *Star Trek: The Next Generation* (also known as *The Next Generation* and *Star Trek: TNG*), syndicated, 1992.
Elizabeth McCarty, "Flesh and Blood," *Bodies of Evidence,* CBS, 1993.
Inmate Jaya, "Frame of Mind," *Star Trek: The Next Generation* (also known as *The Next Generation* and *Star Trek: TNG*), syndicated, 1993.
Michelle Generoo, "Space," *The X–Files,* Fox, 1993.
Susan Allner, "Cold Cuts," *L.A. Law,* NBC, 1994.
Anna Marie Sheehan, "Fifi's First Christmas," *Dr. Quinn, Medicine Woman,* CBS, 1995.
Dr. Lenara Kahn, "Rejoined," *Star Trek: Deep Space Nine* (also known as *Deep Space Nine, DS9,* and *Star Trek: DS9*), syndicated, 1995.
Joyce Novak, "The Bookie and the Kooky Cookie," *NYPD Blue,* ABC, 1995.
Joyce Novak, "Dirty Socks," *NYPD Blue,* ABC, 1995.
Gweneth, "Daybreak," *Roar,* Fox, 1997.
Jane Daniels, "Origins," *Prey,* ABC, 1998.
Jane Daniels, "Veil," *Prey,* ABC, 1998.
Jean Cameron, "Conundrum," *Players,* NBC, 1998.
Mrs. Amanda Boland, "Devotion," *Michael Hayes,* CBS, 1998.
Borg queen, "Dark Frontier: Parts 1 & 2," *Star Trek: Voyager* (also known as *Voyager*), UPN, 1999.
Francesca Morgan, "From Here to Maternity," *Chicago Hope,* CBS, 1999.
Borg queen, "Unimatrix Zero: Parts 1 & 2," *Star Trek: Voyager* (also known as *Voyager*), UPN, 2000.
Annie MacIntosh, "Upgrade," *The Twilight Zone,* UPN, 2002.
Dr. Greta Heints, "Mother," *Law & Order: Special Victims Unit* (also known as *Law & Order: SVU* and *Special Victims Unit*), NBC, 2003.
Dr. Kate Ewing, "The Black Book," *Medical Investigation,* NBC, 2005.
Dr. Kate Ewing, "Mission La Roca: Parts 1 & 2," *Medical Investigation,* NBC, 2005.
Emma Taylor, "Happy Birthday," *Jake in Progress,* ABC, 2005.

Television Appearances; Pilots:
Silk Stalkings, CBS and USA Network, 1991.
Karen Sammler, *Once and Again,* ABC, 1999.

The Caseys, UPN, 1999.
Judith Webster, *The Book of Daniel,* NBC, c. 2005.

Film Appearances:
Janet, *When a Man Loves a Woman* (also known as *Significant Other* and *To Have and to Hold*), Buena Vista, 1994.
Patty Floyd, *Little Giants,* Warner Bros., 1994.
Peggy Lloyd, *Ghosts of Mississippi* (also known as *Ghosts from the Past*), Sony Pictures Entertainment, 1996.
Peyton Van Den Broeck, *Random Hearts,* Columbia, 1999.
Emily Darrow, *Dragonfly* (also known as *Im Zeichen der Libelle*), Universal, 2002.
Miriam Rance, *The Ballad of Jack and Rose* (also known as *Rose and the Snake*), IFC Films, 2005.
Rory, *Hello* (short film), 2005.

Stage Appearances:
Appeared as Agnes, *Agnes of God;* and as Luisa, *A Shayna Maidel.*

OTHER SOURCES

Periodicals:
TV Guide, February 16, 2002, pp. 30–33.
TV Zone Special, December, 1996, pp. 22–25.

TODOROFF, Tom 1957–

PERSONAL

Full name, Thomas Craig Todoroff; born May 17, 1957, in Buffalo, NY. *Education:* Attended Beloit College and Juilliard School; studied acting with Alan Schneider, Edith Skinner, Mary McDonnell, Harold Guskin, Michael Shurtleff, Cicely Berry, and Stella Adler, and at the American Center for the Alexander Technique; studied singing with Keith Davis; studied voice with Kristin Linklater, Robert Neff Williams, and Deena Kaye; also studied at the American Film Institute and the Kripalu Center. *Avocational Interests:* Surfing, cycling, the Beatles, Led Zeppelin, and drumming.

Addresses: *Office*—c/o Tom Todoroff Studio, The Hollywood Film Institute, 1223 Olympic Blvd., Santa Monica, CA 90404. *Manager*—Binder & Associates, 1465 Lindacrest Dr., Beverly Hills, CA 90210.

Career: Actor, producer, director, dialect coach, and acting coach. Tom Todoroff Studio, Santa Monica, CA, acting teacher; Malibu Actors Studio, Malibu, CA, founder and artistic director; American Conservatory Theatre, San Francisco, CA, voice and speech director and actor, 1988–89; artistic director of Jimmy Buffett's worldwide concert tours, 1988–94, and albums, 1989–94.

Member: Screen Actors Guild, American Federation of Television and Radio Artists, Actors Equity Association, Producers Guild, Creative Coalition, Academy of Television Arts and Sciences.

CREDITS

Film Appearances:
The running man, *Leap of Faith,* Paramount, 1992.
Second conductor, *Ethan Frome,* Miramax, 1993.
Hall of Fame announcer, *Cobb,* Warner Bros., 1994.
Second guy at bar, *Tin Cup,* Warner Bros., 1996.
Mr. Hollywood, *Turbulence,* Metro–Goldwyn–Mayer, 1997.
Steve, *No Vacancy,* 1999.
Croupier, *Play It to the Bone* (also known as *Play It*), Buena Vista, 1999.
The man, *Happy Holidaze from the Jonzes* (short film), 2001.
Police dispatcher, *Dark Blue,* Metro–Goldwyn–Mayer, 2002.
Internal Affairs detective Zino, *Hollywood Homicide,* Columbia, 2003.
Tom, the vegan S&M artist, *Easy,* Magic Lamp, 2003.
El padrino (also known as *El padrino—Mexican Godfather*), Laguna Productions, 2004.

Film Dialect Coach:
(Uncredited) *The Honorary Consul* (also known as *Beyond the Limit*), Paramount, 1983.
Leap of Faith, Paramount, 1992.
Ethan Frome, Miramax, 1993.
The Beans of Egypt, Maine (also known as *Forbidden Choices*), IRS Media, 1994.
Pooh's Great Adventure: The Search for Christopher Robin (animated; also known as *Winnie the Pooh's Most Grand Adventure*), Buena Vista Home Video, 1997.
Return to Never Land (animated), Buena Vista, 2002.
(For Brendan Gleeson) *Dark Blue,* United Artists, 2002.

Film Acting Coach:
(Uncredited) *The Honorary Consul* (also known as *Beyond the Limit*), Paramount, 1983.
(Uncredited; for Rene Russo) *Ransom,* Buena Vista, 1996.
(Uncredited; for Lolita Davidovich) *Jungle 2 Jungle* (also known as *Un indien a New York*), Buena Vista, 1997.

(Uncredited; for Robert Wagner) *Austin Powers: International Man of Mystery* (also known as *Austin Powers—Das Schaerfste, was Ihre Majestaet zu bieten hat*), New Line Cinema, 1997.
(Uncredited; for Robert Wagner) *Austin Powers in Goldmember* (also known as *Austin Powers: Goldmember*), New Line Cinema, 2002.

Film Work:
Associate producer, *Cobb,* Warner Bros., 1994.
(Uncredited) Vocal coach: Carmen Twillie, *The Lion King* (animated), Buena Vista, 1994.
Producer, *No Vacancy,* 1999.
Vocal coach: Robert Wagner, *Austin Powers: The Spy Who Shagged Me* (also known as *Austin Powers 2: The Spy Who Shagged Me*), New Line Cinema, 1999.
Director and producer, *RSC Meets USA: Working Shakespeare,* 2002.
Casting consultant, *Dark Blue,* United Artists, 2002.

Also worked as casting consultant, *Hollywood Homicide;* casting consultant, *Play It to the Bone;* casting consultant, *Tin Cup;* director, *DELGO: A Hero's Journey.*

Television Appearances; Series:
Doug O'Hara, *All My Children,* ABC, 1986–87.

Television Appearances; Miniseries:
Mr. Kenneth, a hairdresser (part II), *A Woman Named Jackie,* NBC, 1991.
Tuslow, *Heaven & Hell: North & South, Book III* (also known as *John Jakes' "Heaven & Hell: North & South, Book III"* and *North and South III*), ABC, 1994.

Television Appearances; Movies:
(Uncredited) Registrar, *Monday After the Miracle,* CBS, 1998.
The Swiss doctor and Nestor, *Noriega: God's Favorite,* Showtime, 2000.
The concierge, *Second Honeymoon,* CBS, 2001.

Television Appearances; Episodic:
Shamus/robber, "When Irish Eyes are Killing," *Lois & Clark: The New Adventures of Superman,* ABC, 1995.
Darod, "Resistance," *Star Trek: Voyager,* UPN, 1995.
Pastor Thompson, "Life Before Death," *Touched by an Angel,* CBS, 2000.
Blaine MacAllister, "Hard Choices," *Arli$$,* HBO, 2001.
The anger management consultant, "Profiles in Agenting," *Arli$$,* HBO, 2002.

Television Work; Miniseries:
(Uncredited) Acting coach and dialect coach, *A Woman Named Jackie,* NBC, 1991.

(Uncredited) Acting coach and dialect coach, *Heaven & Hell: North & South, Book III* (also known as *John Jakes' "Heaven & Hell: North & South, Book III"* and *North and South*), ABC, 1994.

Television Executive Producer; Movies:
Borrowed Hearts (also known as *Borrowed Hearts: A Holiday Romance*), CBS, 1997.
Monday After the Miracle, CBS, 1998.
A Test of Love, 1999.
A Secret Life (also known as *Breach of Trust*), 2000.
Second Honeymoon, CBS, 2001.
Sons of Mistletoe (also known as *Un Noel pas comme les autres*), CBS, 2001.
The Survivors Club, CBS, 2004.

Television Work; Movies:
(Uncredited) Acting coach: Lolita Davidovich, *Harvest of Fire,* CBS, 1996.
Coproducer, *Noriega: God's Favorite,* Showtime, 2000.

Television Work; Episodic:
Worked as dialect coach: Joel Grey, "The Last Immigrant," *Brooklyn Bridge,* CBS; vocal coach: Bai Ling, "The Spirit of Liberty Moon," *Touched by an Angel,* CBS.

Stage Appearances:
Appeared in *Oi! For England,* Yale Cabaret Theatre; *Savages,* Baltimore Center Stage, Baltimore, MD; *Godspell,* Edinburgh Fringe Festival, Edinburgh, Scotland.

Stage Work:
Dialect coach, *Seven Guitars,* Walter Kerr Theatre, New York City, 1996.

Also worked as director for Lolita Davidovich and Nell Carter, *The Vagina Monologues,* Westside Arts Theatre, New York City; dialect coach, *The Sum of Us,* Cherry Lane Theatre, New York City, and Williamstown Theatre Festival; voice, text, and acting coach, *Macbeth,* York Theatre, New York City; speech and acting coach, *Oi! For England,* Yale Cabaret Theatre; dialect coach, *Savages,* Baltimore Center Stage, Baltimore, MD; dialect coach, *Billy Bishop Goes to War,* Pennsylvania Stage Company; dialect coach, *The Foreigner,* Spoleto Festival, USA at the Charles St. Theatre; director, *Godspell,* Edinburgh Fringe Festival, Edinburgh, Scotland; resident acting, speech, and dialect coach, *Peer Gynt, Citizen Tom Paine, Daniela Frank, Tale of the Wolf,* and *Henry IV, parts I and II,* all Williamstown Theatre Festival; director, *Spring Awakening,* Williamstown Theatre Festival.

WRITINGS

Television Miniseries; With Others:
A Woman Named Jackie, NBC, 1991.

Heaven & Hell: North & South, Book III (also known as *John Jakes' "Heaven & Hell: North & South, Book III"* and *North and South*), ABC, 1994.

TYLO, Michael 1948–

PERSONAL

Born October 16, 1948, in Detroit, MI; son of Edward (a plumber) and Margaret Tylo; married Deborah Eckols, April 15, 1978 (divorced); married Hunter (original name, Deborah Jo Hunter; previously known as Deborah Morehart; an actress and model), July 7, 1987; children: (second marriage) Christopher (stepson); Michael, Jr., Izabella Grace, Katya Ariel. *Education:* Wayne State University, B.F.A., M.F.A., acting and directing; also attended The Oblates of St. Francis de Sales, University of Detroit, and Allentown College; studied acting with Uta Hagen and Ivana Chubbuck; studied acting in Ireland with Sir Tyrone Guthrie; studied theatrical fencing at the National Theatre of Hungary. *Avocational Interests:* Golf, reading, oldies rock 'n' roll, fencing, dancing, and collecting first editions of books.

Career: Actor. The Hilberry Theater Company, member for three years; Pennsylvania Shakespeare Festival, founding board member; Allentown College, head of television and film department, c. late 1990s; University of Nevada Las Vegas, instructor in acting. Previously worked as a U–Haul driver and a plumber.

CREDITS

Film Appearances:
Detroit 9000 (also known as *Call Detroit 9000* and *Detroit Heat*), Miramax, 1973.
Minister, *The Misery Brothers,* 1995.
CEO, *Longshot* (also known as *Jack of All Trades* and *Longshot: The Movie*), 2000.
Tony Hersh, *Intrepid* (also known as *Deep Water*), 2000.
Gustav, *Vegas, City of Dreams,* 2001.
Guidance technician, *Race to Space* (also known as *Race to Space—Mission ins Unbekannte*), Columbia TriStar, 2001.
Businessman in restaurant, *Mr. Deeds,* New Line Cinema, 2002.

Television Appearances; Series:
First Quinton "Quint" McCord Chamberlain (also known as Sean Ryan), *The Guiding Light* (also known as *Guiding Light*), CBS, 1981–85, 1996–97.

First Matthew "Matt" Connolly, *All My Children*, ABC, 1986–88.

Charlie Prince, *General Hospital*, ABC, 1989.

Alcalde Luis Ramone, *Zorro* (also known as *Les nouvelles aventures de Zorro, Zorro—The Legend Begins,* and *The New Zorro*), The Family Channel, 1990–91.

Alexander "Blade" Bladeson and Rick Bladeson, *The Young and the Restless* (also known as *Y&R*), CBS, 1993–95.

Television Appearances; Movies:

Dee Boot, *Lonesome Dove*, CBS, 1989.

Evan King, *Perry Mason: The Case of the Killer Kiss,* NBC, 1993.

Television Appearances; Episodic:

Daniel Kelly, "Kelly Green," *Gabriel's Fire*, ABC, 1991.

Daniel Kelly, "Belly of the Beast," *Gabriel's Fire*, ABC, 1991.

Sonny, "The Dark Side of the Door," *Murder, She Wrote,* CBS, 1996.

Craig Sanderson, "Body Odor," *Mike Hammer, Private Eye,* syndicated, 1997.

Dave Woods, "Duck Soup," *Even Stevens*, Disney, 2001.

Also appeared in *The Insiders; A Man Called Hawk; Tequila and Bonetti;* as Lord Peter Belton, *Another World;* Sherman Gale, *The Bold and the Beautiful.*

Stage Appearances:

John Watherstone, *The Winslow Boy,* Roundabout Theatre Stage II, New York City, 1980–81, then Theatre De Lys, New York City, 1981.

Iago, *Othello,* Pennsylvania Shakespeare Festival, Allentown College, 1996.

Title role, *Henry IV, Part 1,* Pennsylvania Shakespeare Festival, DeSales University, 2005.

The Duke of Norfolk, *A Man for All Seasons,* Nevada Conservatory Theatre, University of Nevada at Las Vegas, 2005.

Also appeared in *1776,* Dearborn Repertory, Dearborn, MI; *Arms and the Man* and *The Shadow Box,* both Alley Theatre; *Hamlet, The Taming of the Shrew, Death of a Salesman, The Lion in Winter, Tartuffe, The Good Doctor, As You Like It,* and *Othello,* all Hilberry Repertory Theatre; *Ring Round The Moon* and *Charley's Aunt,* both Meadowbrook Theatre; as Duke of Norfolk, *A Man For All Seasons;* Orlando, *As You Like It;* Regnault, *Becket;* Marko the Magnificent, *Carnival;* Cuigy, *Cyrano de Bergerac,* Long Wharf Theatre; Happy, *Death of a Salesman;* Mortimer, *Mary Stuart,* Missouri Repertory; Ham, *Noah;* Hugo, *Ring 'Round the Moon;* Damis, *Tartuffe;* Cherdyakov, Haband, and Young Cheko, *The Good Doctor;* Leslie, *The Hostage,* Missouri Repertory; Algernon, *The Importance of Being Ernest;* Richard, *The Lady's Not Burning;* Lieutenant Corignon, *The Lady From Maxim's;* Richard, *The Lion in Winter;* Clitandre, *The Misanthrope;* Young Rabbi, *The Tenth Man;* Tom, *The Time of Your Life;* Norman, *The Star Spangled Girl;* Mark, *The Shadow Box;* John, *The Winslow Boy,* Roundabout Theatre, New York City; Kolenkhov, *You Can't Take It with You.*

Stage Work:

Worked as producer, *Vikings,* Manhattan Theatre Club; producer, *Young Bucks.*

OTHER SOURCES

Periodicals:

Afternoon TV, June, 1982; October, 1984.

Daytime TV Magazine, May, 1982.

Soap Opera Digest, March 30, 1993.

Soap Opera's Greatest, January, 1983.

Soap Opera Magazine, May 19, 1992; August 17, 1993.

Soap Opera Weekly, September 8, 1992; November 21, 1995; February 13, 1996.

U-V

URBAN, Karl 1972–

PERSONAL

Original name, Karl–Heinz Urban; born June 7, 1972, in Wellington, New Zealand; father, a leather goods manufacturer; children: Hunter. *Education:* Attended Victoria University for one year. *Avocational Interests:* Horseback riding, fishing, surfing, golf, and gardening.

Addresses: *Agent*—Creative Artist Agency, 9830 Wilshire Blvd., Beverly Hills, CA 90212. *Manager*—Thruline Entertainment, 9250 Wilshire Blvd., Ground Floor, Beverly Hills, CA 90212. *Publicist*—Baker Winokur Ryder, 9100 Wilshire Blvd., 6th Floor West, Beverly Hills, CA 90212.

Career: Actor.

Awards, Honors: Film Award nomination, best actor, New Zealand Film and TV Awards, 2000, for *The Price of Milk;* DVDX Award nomination (with others), best audio commentary (new for DVD), 2003, for *The Lord of the Rings: The Two Towers;* National Board of Review Award (with others), best acting by an ensemble, 2003, Screen Actors Guild Award (with others), outstanding performance by a cast in a motion picture, Phoenix Film Critics Society Award nomination (with others), best ensemble acting, Broadcast Film Critics Association Award (with others), best acting ensemble, 2004, all for *The Lord of the Rings: The Return of the King.*

CREDITS

Film Appearances:
Wellington soldier, *Chunuk Bair* (also known as *Once in Chunuck*), 1992.
Sweeper, *Heaven*, Miramax, 1998.

Paul, Chrissy's boyfriend, *Via Satellite,* 1998.
Harry Ballard, *The Irrefutable Truth about Demons* (also known as *Truth about Demons*), 2000.
Rob, *The Price of Milk,* Lot 47 Films, 2000.
Munder, *Ghost Ship,* Warner Bros., 2002.
Eomer, *The Lord of the Rings: The Two Towers* (also known as *Der Herr der Ringe: Die zwei Tuerme* and *The Two Towers*), New Line Cinema, 2002.
Eomer, *The Lord of the Rings: The Return of the King* (also known as *Der Herr der Ringe: Die Rueckkeher des Koenigs* and *The Return of the King*), New Line Cinema, 2003.
Vaako, *The Chronicles of Riddick* (also known as *The Chronicles of Riddick: The Director's Cut*), Universal, 2004.
Kirill, *The Bourne Supremacy* (also known as *Die Bourne Verschwoerung*), Universal, 2004.
John Grimm, *Doom,* Universal, 2005.

Television Appearances; Series:
Tim Johnstone, *Homeward Bound,* 1992.
Paramedic Jamie Forrest, *Shortland Street,* TVNZ, 1993–94.
James Westwood, *Riding High,* WAM, 1995.

Television Appearances; Movies:
Captain Arn Dravyk, *The Privateers,* 2000.

Television Appearances; Pilots:
Kor, *Amazon High,* 1999.

Television Appearances; Specials:
The Chronicles of Riddick: The Lowdown (documentary), Sci–Fi Channel, 2004.

Television Appearances; Episodic:
Heroin addict, "Suffer Little Children," *Shark in the Park,* 1990.
Cupid, "The Green–Eyed Monster," *Hercules: The Legendary Journeys,* syndicated, 1996.

Mael, "Altared States," *Xena: Warrior Princess,* syndicated, 1996.

Julius Caesar, "Destiny," *Xena: Warrior Princess,* syndicated, 1997.

Cupid, "For Him the Bell Tolls," *Xena: Warrior Princess,* syndicated, 1997.

Cupid, "A Comedy of Eros," *Xena: Warrior Princess,* syndicated, 1997.

Julius Caesar, "The Deliverer," *Xena: Warrior Princess,* syndicated, 1997.

(Uncredited; in archive footage) Julius Caesar, "The Debt: Part 1," *Xena: Warrior Princess,* syndicated, 1997.

Julius Caesar, "The Bitter Suite," *Xena: Warrior Princess,* syndicated, 1998.

Julius Caesar, "When in Rome...," *Xena: Warrior Princess,* syndicated, 1998.

Julius Caesar, "A Good Day," *Xena: Warrior Princess,* syndicated, 1998.

Caius Julius Caesar, "Render Unto Caesar," *Hercules: The Legendary Journeys,* syndicated, 1998.

Julius Caesar, "Endgame," *Xena: Warrior Princess,* syndicated, 1999.

Julius Caesar, "The Ides of March," *Xena: Warrior Princess,* syndicated, 1999.

Kor, "Lifeblood," *Xena: Warrior Princess,* syndicated, 2000.

Julius Caesar, "When Fates Collide," *Xena: Warrior Princess,* syndicated, 2001.

Also appeared in *White Fang; Riding High.*

Stage Appearances:

Mark Antony, *Shakespeare's "Julius Caesar,"* Auckland Theatre Company, Auckland, New Zealand, 1998.

Jett Lane, *The Herbal Bed,* Maidment Theatre, Auckland, 1998.

Foreskin, *Foreskin's Lament,* Auckland, 1999.

VANCE, Courtney B. 1960(?)–
(Courtney Vance)

PERSONAL

Full name, Courtney Bernard Vance; born March 12, 1960 (some sources cite 1959), in Detroit (some sources cite Birmingham), MI; son of Conroy (a benefits administrator and grocery store manager) and Leslie (a librarian) Vance; married Angela Bassett (an actress), October 12, 1997. *Education:* Harvard University, B.A., 1982; Yale University, M.A., 1985. *Religion:* Baptist. *Avocational Interests:* Folk art.

Addresses: *Agent*—Adena Chawke, Innovative Artists, 1505 10th St., Santa Monica, CA 90401; Adam Venit, Endeavor Talent Agency, 9701 Wilshire Blvd., Third

Floor, Beverly Hills, CA 90212 (some sources cite 9601 Wilshire Blvd., Third Floor, Beverly Hills, CA 90210). *Manager*—Dolores Robinson, Dolores Robinson Entertainment, 112 South Almont Dr., Los Angeles, CA 90048. *Publicist*—Jessica Cohen, Bragman/Nyman/Cafarelli, 8687 Melrose Ave., Eighth Floor, Los Angeles, CA 90069.

Career: Actor and producer. Shakespeare and Company, Lenox, MA, company member, beginning 1981.

Awards, Honors: Clarence Derwent Award, 1987; *Theatre World* Award, outstanding newcomer, 1987; Antoinette Perry Award nomination, best featured actor in a play, 1987, for *Fences;* Obie Award, outstanding performance, *Village Voice,* 1990, for *My Children! My Africa!;* Antoinette Perry Award nomination, best lead actor, 1991, for *Six Degrees of Separation;* Independent Spirit Award nomination, best male lead, Independent Features Project/West, 1999, for *Blind Faith;* Video Premiere Award, best actor, DVD Exclusive awards, 2001, for *Love and Action in Chicago;* Image Award nomination, outstanding actor in a drama series, National Association for the Advancement of Colored People, 2002, for *Law & Order: Criminal Intent.*

CREDITS

Film Appearances:

Doc Johnson, *Hamburger Hill,* Paramount, 1987.

Sonar operator Jones, *The Hunt for Red October,* Paramount, 1990.

Jim, *The Adventures of Huck Finn* (also known as *The Adventures of Huckleberry Finn*), Buena Vista, 1993.

Journalist, *The Emperor's New Clothes,* 1993.

Cooper, *Holy Matrimony,* Buena Vista, 1994.

Bobby Seale, *Panther,* Gramercy Pictures, 1995.

George Grandey, *Dangerous Minds* (also known as *My Posse Don't Do Homework*), Buena Vista, 1995.

Luke, *The Last Supper,* Columbia, 1995.

Reverend Henry Biggs, *The Preacher's Wife,* Buena Vista, 1996.

Eddie Jones, *Love and Action in Chicago,* MTI Home Video, 1999.

Otis Tucker, *Cookie's Fortune,* October Films, 1999.

Himself, *The Acting Class,* 2000.

Roger Hines, *Space Cowboys,* Warner Bros., 2000.

Willie Jones, *D–Tox* (also known as *Eye See You* and *Im Auge der Angst*), DEJ Productions/Universal, 2002.

Film Work:

Coproducer, *Love and Action in Chicago,* MTI Home Video, 1999.

Television Appearances; Series:

Assistant district attorney Ron Carver, *Law & Order: Criminal Intent* (also known as *Law & Order: CI*), NBC, 2001—.

Television Appearances; Miniseries:

Martin Luther King, *Parting the Waters*, ABC, 2000.

Voice, *Jazz*, PBS, 2001.

Television Appearances; Movies:

Second male student, *First Affair*, CBS, 1983.

Justice Butler, *In the Line of Duty: Street War* (also known as *In the Line of Duty: The Two Tonys* and *Urban Crossfire*), NBC, 1992.

Wayne "Thunder" Carter, "Percy and Thunder," *TNT Screenworks*, TNT, 1993.

Conroy Price, *Beyond the Law* (also known as *Fixing the Shadow, Secret Investigation Division,* and *The Sid*), HBO, 1994.

Thomas, *Race to Freedom: The Underground Railroad* (also known as *Underground to Canada* and *Underground to Freedom*), syndicated, 1994.

(As Courtney Vance) Lieutenant Jeffrey Glenn, *The Tuskegee Airmen*, HBO, 1995.

Travis Holloway, *The Affair* (also known as *Black Tuesday*), HBO, 1995.

Jury foreman, *12 Angry Men*, Showtime, 1997.

Jerry Robinson, *Ambushed*, HBO, 1998.

John Williams, *Blind Faith*, Showtime, 1998.

Officer James "Jimmy" Halloran, *Naked City: Justice with a Bullet*, Showtime, 1998.

Officer James "Jimmy" Halloran, *Naked City: A Killer Christmas*, Showtime, 1998.

Clarence Brandley, *Whitewash: The Clarence Brandley Story*, Showtime, 2002.

Television Appearances; Specials:

Lymon, "The Piano Lesson," *Hallmark Hall of Fame*, CBS, 1995.

Lucien P. Singer, "The Boys Next Door," *Hallmark Hall of Fame*, CBS, 1996.

Narrator, "Born to Trouble: The Adventures of Huckleberry Finn," *Culture Shock*, PBS, 2000.

Voice, *The Tulsa Lynching of 1921: A Hidden Story* (documentary), Cinemax, 2000.

Reader, *Unchained Memories: Readings from the Slave Narratives* (documentary), HBO, 2003.

Voice, *War Letters* (documentary), PBS, 2003.

Narrator, "The Fight" (documentary), *The American Experience*, PBS, 2004.

Voices, *Unforgivable Blackness: The Rise and Fall of Jack Johnson* (documentary), PBS, 2005.

Television Appearances; Awards Presentations:

The 41st Annual Tony Awards, CBS, 1987.

Presenter, *The Ninth Annual Screen Actors Guild Awards*, TNT, 2003.

Television Appearances; Episodic:

Curtis Caldwell, "Trust Me," *thirtysomething*, ABC, 1989.

Voice of scribe, "The Emperor's New Clothes," *Long Ago and Far Away* (animated), PBS, 1989.

(Uncredited) Mr. McKee, "By Hooker, by Crook," *Law & Order*, NBC, 1990.

Benjamin "Bud" Greer, "Rage," *Law & Order*, NBC, 1995.

Warren Grier, "Final Judgment," *Picket Fences*, CBS, 1995.

Warren Grier, "Without Mercy," *Picket Fences*, CBS, 1995.

Guest, *The Rosie O'Donnell Show*, syndicated, 1996.

Walter Harrelson, "Chapter Five," *Boston Public*, Fox, 2000.

Television Appearances; Pilots:

(As Courtney Vance) Mr. James Jackson, "Unfinished Symphony," *Any Day Now*, Lifetime, 1998.

Walter Harrelson, "Chapter One," *Boston Public*, Fox, 2000.

Stage Appearances:

Attendant, *The Comedy of Errors*, Shakespeare and Company, Lenox, MA, 1982.

A Raisin in the Sun, Yale Repertory Theatre, New Haven, CT, 1983.

Fences, Yale Repertory Theatre, 1985.

Cory, *Fences*, Goodman Theatre, Chicago, IL, 1986, Forty-Sixth Street Theatre, New York City, 1987–88.

Mercutio, *Romeo and Juliet*, New York Shakespeare Festival, Public Theatre, Delacorte Theatre, New York City, 1988.

Thami Mbikwarna, *My Children! My Africa!*, New York Theatre Workshop, Perry Street Theatre, New York City, 1989–90.

Paul, *Six Degrees of Separation*, Lincoln Center Theater Company, Mitzi E. Newhouse Theater, New York City, 1990, then Lincoln Center, Vivian Beaumont Theater, New York City, 1990–92.

Walter Burns, *His Girl Friday*, Tyrone Guthrie Theater, Minneapolis, MN, 2005.

Also appeared in other productions, including *Butterfly, Geronimo Jones, Hamlet, Jazz Wives Jazz Lives, A Lesson from Aloes, Rosencrantz and Guildenstern Are Dead,* and *Temptation*.

RECORDINGS

Videos:

Nonesense and Lullabyes: Nursery Rhymes, 1992.

Nonesense and Lullabyes: Poems, 1992.

(In archive footage) Reverend Henry Biggs, *Whitney Houston: The Greatest Hits*, 2000.

Audiobooks:

Bo Jackson and Dick Schaap, *Bo Knows Bo,* Random House Audio, 1991.

Hank Aaron and Lonnie Wheeler, *I Had a Hammer: The Hank Aaron Story,* HarperAudio, 1991.

Anne Rice, *The Feast of All Saints,* Random House Audio, 1992.

Clancy Carlile, *Children of the Dust,* Publishing Mills, 1995.

Nuclear Waste Documentary Project, *Half Lives,* 1995.

E. Lynn Harris, *And This Too Shall Pass,* Random House Audio, 1996.

David Pesci, *Amistad,* Publishing Mills, 1999.

OTHER SOURCES

Books:

Contemporary Black Biography, Volume 15, Gale, 1997.

Periodicals:

Entertainment Weekly, October 24, 1997, p. 14.
InStyle, February, 1998, p. 205.
Jet, January 13, 1997, p. 33; October 27, 1997, p. 64.
People Weekly, January 20, 1997, pp. 96–97; October 6, 1997, p. 55.

VAUGHN, Robert 1932–

PERSONAL

Born Robert Francis Vaughn, November 22, 1932, in New York, NY; son of Gerald Walter (a radio actor) and Marcella Frances (a stage actress; maiden name, Gaudel) Vaughn; married Linda Staab (an actress), 1974; children: Caitlin, Cassidy. *Education:* Attended University of Minnesota, 1950–51; studied theatre arts at Los Angeles City College; Los Angeles State College of Applied Arts and Sciences (now California State University, Los Angeles), B.S., 1956; University of Southern California, M.A., 1960, Ph.D., 1970. *Politics:* Democrat. *Religion:* Roman Catholicism.

Addresses: *Agent*—Agency for the Performing Arts, 9200 Sunset Blvd., Suite 900, Los Angeles, CA 90069; International Creative Management, 8942 Wilshire Blvd., Beverly Hills, CA 90211.

Career: Actor, director, and writer. Radio actor in the 1940s; *Minneapolis Star Journal,* Minneapolis, MN, sports writer, early 1950s. Appeared in commercials. California Democratic Committee, member; Southern California Democratic Central Committee, former chairperson of registration and Speaker's Bureau. *Military service:* U.S. Army, 1956–57.

Member: Screen Actors Guild, American Federation of Television and Radio Artists, American Academy of Political and Social Science.

Awards, Honors: Nomination for Golden Laurel, top male new personality, Laurel awards, Producers Guild of America, 1960; Academy Award nomination, Golden Globe Award nomination, and nomination for Golden Laurel, all best supporting actor, 1960, for *The Young Philadelphians; Photoplay* Award, most popular male star, 1965; Golden Globe Award nominations, best male television star, 1965 and 1966, both for *The Man from U.N.C.L.E.;* Film Award nomination, best supporting actor, British Academy of Film and Television Arts, 1970, for *Bullitt;* Emmy Award, outstanding continuing performance by a supporting actor in a drama series, 1978, for *Washington: Behind Closed Doors;* Emmy Award nomination, outstanding supporting actor in a limited series or special, 1979, for *Backstairs at the White House;* received a star on the Hollywood walk of fame, 1998.

CREDITS

Television Appearances; Series:

Captain Ray Rambridge, *The Lieutenant,* NBC, 1963–64.

Napoleon Solo, *The Man from U.N.C.L.E.,* NBC, 1964–68.

Harry Rule, *The Protectors,* syndicated, 1972–74.

Harlan Adams, *Emerald Point, N.A.S.,* CBS, 1983–84.

Retired general Hunt Stockwell, *The A Team,* NBC, 1986–87.

Host and narrator, *Reaching for the Skies,* 1988–89.

Narrator, *America at War,* 1990.

Harry Winfield, *Love at First Sight,* BBC, beginning 1991.

Attorney general and narrator, *Danger Theatre,* Fox, 1993.

Rick Hamlin, *As the World Turns,* CBS, 1995.

Bishop Corrington, *One Life to Live,* ABC, 1996.

Judge Oren Travis, *The Magnificent Seven,* CBS, 1997–2000.

Albert Stroller, *Hustle,* BBC, beginning 2004.

Television Appearances; Miniseries:

Charles Desmond, *Captains and the Kings,* NBC, 1976.

Frank Flaherty, *Washington: Behind Closed Doors,* ABC, 1977.

Morgan Wendell, *Centennial,* NBC, 1978.

President Woodrow Wilson, *Backstairs at the White House,* NBC, 1979.

Seth McLean, *The Rebels,* Operation Prime Time, 1979.

Field marshal Erhard Milch, *Inside the Third Reich,* ABC, 1982.

Senator Reynolds, *The Blue and the Gray,* CBS, 1982.

General Douglas MacArthur, *The Last Bastion,* Ten Network (Australia) and PBS, 1984.

John Bradford, *Evergreen,* NBC, 1985.

Mr. Morris, *Tracks of Glory: The Major Taylor Story* (also known as *The Major Taylor Story*), The Disney Channel, 1992.

Television Appearances; Movies:

Jerry Hunter, *The Woman Hunter,* CBS, 1972.

Hayden Danziger, *Columbo: Troubled Waters,* NBC, 1975.

Charles Clay, *Columbo: Last Salute to the Commodore,* NBC, 1976.

Edward Fuller, *Kiss Me ... Kill Me,* ABC, 1976.

Mark Case, *The Gossip Columnist,* Operation Prime Time, 1979.

Michael Jacoby, *Mirror Mirror,* 1979.

Dr. Arno Franken, *Doctor Franken* (also known as *The Franken Project*), NBC, 1980.

Harrison Crawford III, *City in Fear* (also known as *Panic on Page One*), ABC, 1980.

Frederick Walker, *A Question of Honor,* CBS, 1982.

Girard, *Fantasies* (also known as *The Studio Murders*), ABC, 1982.

Richard Whitney, *The Day the Bubble Burst,* NBC, 1982.

Dave Fairmont, *Intimate Agony* (also known as *Doctor in Paradise*), ABC, 1983.

Napoleon Solo, *The Return of the Man from U.N.C.L.E.* (also known as *The Fifteen Years Later Affair*), CBS, 1983.

Captain Powell, *International Airport,* ABC, 1985.

Oliver Coles, *Private Sessions,* NBC, 1985.

Franklin Delano Roosevelt, *Murrow,* HBO, 1986.

Stanley Auerbach, *The Prince of Bel Air,* ABC, 1986.

Ray Melton, *Nightstick* (also known as *Calhoun*), 1987.

Sheriff John Whaley, *Desperado,* NBC, 1987.

Jay Corelli, *Perry Mason: The Case of the Defiant Daughter,* NBC, 1990.

Tatort–Camerone, [Germany], 1992.

W.S.H. (also known as *Weird Shit Happens*), 1994.

Dennis Forbes, *Dancing in the Dark,* Lifetime, 1995.

The devil, *Witch Academy* (also known as *Little Devils*), USA Network, 1995.

Edward Bolt, "Escape to Witch Mountain," *ABC Family Movie,* ABC, 1995.

Ron Fairfax, *The Sender,* HBO, 1997.

Adam Spring, *Virtual Obsession* (also known as *Host*), ABC, 1998.

Himself, *The Mystery of Natalie Wood,* ABC, 2004.

Television Appearances; Specials:

Guest, *Jimmy Durante Meets the Lively Arts,* ABC, 1965.

Franklin Delano Roosevelt (title role), *FDR* (also known as *FDR: That Man in the White House*), HBO, 1982.

Host and Charles Hemming, *You Are the Jury,* NBC, 1986.

Macy's Thanksgiving Day Parade, NBC, 1986, 1989.

NBC's 60th Anniversary Special, NBC, 1986.

Host, *Manhunt ... Update!,* syndicated, 1989.

Host, *Dangerous Game of Fame,* syndicated, 1992.

Voice of Isaac Arnold, *Lincoln,* ABC, 1992.

Host, *Classic Spy Movies,* TNT, 1996.

Himself, *Guns for Hire: The Making of "The Magnificent Seven"* (documentary), Channel 4 (England), 2000.

Himself, *Steve McQueen: The Essence of Cool* (documentary), TCM, 2005.

Television Appearances; Awards Presentations:

The 37th Annual Prime Time Emmy Awards, ABC, 1985.

Television Appearances; Episodic:

Dr. Charles A. Leale, "Black Friday," *Medic,* NBC, 1955.

Archibald Parker, "Bitter Waters," *Screen Directors Playhouse,* NBC, 1956.

Cowboy, "Cooter," *Gunsmoke,* CBS, 1956.

Jay Powers, "The Story of Jay Powers" (also known as "The Jay Powers Story"), *The Millionaire,* CBS, 1956.

Johnny Adler, "Courage Is a Gun," *Zane Grey Theater,* CBS, 1956.

Soldier, "The Heroism of Clara Barton," *You Are There,* CBS, 1956.

"Betty Goes Steady," *Father Knows Best,* NBC, 1956.

"Fake SOS," *Big Town,* NBC, 1956.

"The Marine Story," *Big Town,* NBC, 1956.

"The Operator and the Martinet," *West Point,* CBS, 1956.

"The Return of Jubal Dolan," *Frontier,* NBC, 1956.

Andy Bowers, "Romeo," *Gunsmoke,* CBS, 1957.

Billy Jack, "A Gun Is for Killing," *Zane Grey Theater,* CBS, 1957.

Title role, "Billy the Kid," *Tales of Wells Fargo* (also known as *Wells Fargo*), NBC, 1957.

Steve Sprock, "The Troublemakers," *Playhouse 90,* CBS, 1957.

"The Consort," *Telephone Time,* CBS, 1957.

"Double Identity," *Panic!,* NBC, 1957.

"The Twisted Road," *Frontier Doctor,* syndicated, 1957.

Dan Willard, "The Apprentice Sheriff," *The Rifleman,* ABC, 1958.

Roy Pelham, "The John Wilbot Story," *Wagon Train,* NBC, 1958.

Shelly Poe, "Return," *Jefferson Drum,* NBC, 1958.

"The Big Rat Pack," *Dragnet,* NBC, 1958.

"File #35," *Walter Winchell File,* ABC, 1958.

Art, "Dry Run," *Alfred Hitchcock Presents,* CBS, 1959.

Frank Warren, "Passage to the Enemy," *Wichita Town,* NBC, 1959.

Miguel Roverto, "Spark of Revenge," *Zorro,* ABC, 1959.

Roger Mowbray, "About Roger Mowbray," *Riverboat,* NBC, 1959.

Ross Drake, "The Innocents," *Law of the Plainsman,* NBC, 1959.

Sheriff Lloyd Stover, "Borrowed Glory," *Bronco,* ABC, 1959.

Stan Gray, "A Twisted Road," *Frontier Doctor,* syndicated, 1959.

Theodore Roosevelt, "The Dude," *Law of the Plainsman,* NBC, 1959.

"Made in Japan," *Playhouse 90,* CBS, 1959.

"Prelude to Violence," *The Lineup,* CBS, 1959.

Abner Benson, "Interrupted Honeymoon," *Checkmate,* CBS, 1960.

Asa, "Noblesse Oblige," *The Rebel,* ABC, 1960.

Dr. Collins, "Emergency," *The June Allyson Show* (also known as *The DuPont Show with June Allyson*), CBS, 1960.

Hayworth, "Remember Me Not," *The Man from Blackhawk,* ABC, 1960.

Lieutenant Dave Hutchins, "The Last Flight Out," *Alcoa Theatre,* NBC, 1960.

Perry Holcomb, "Moon Cloud," *Men into Space,* CBS, 1960.

Roger Bigelow, "The Roger Bigelow Show," *Wagon Train,* NBC, 1960.

Sandy Kale, "The Dark Trail," *Laramie,* NBC, 1960.

"The Awakening," *The Garlund Touch* (also known as *Mr. Garlund*), CBS, 1960.

"Death of a Dream," *Desilu Playhouse* (also known as *Westinghouse Desilu Playhouse*), CBS, 1960.

Albert, "The Far Side of Nowhere," *Follow the Sun,* ABC, 1961.

Beaumont Butler Buell, "Object: Patrimony," *Stagecoach West,* ABC, 1961.

Billy Brigode, "Treasure Coach," *Tales of Wells Fargo* (also known as *Wells Fargo*), NBC, 1961.

Billy Jack, "A Gun Is for Killing," *Frontier Justice,* CBS, 1961.

Dr. Frank Cordell, "The Ordeal of Dr. Cordell," *Thriller,* NBC, 1961.

Lace, "To Wear a Badge," *Target: The Corruptors,* ABC, 1961.

Ralph Borden, "A Rage for Justice," *Follow the Sun,* ABC, 1961.

Sordo, "The Heckler," *87th Precinct,* NBC, 1961.

Warren W. Scott, "The Scott Machine," *The Asphalt Jungle,* ABC, 1961.

Wes Grayson, "The Landslide Adventure," *Malibu Run,* CBS, 1961.

A. Dunster Lowell, "The Boston Terrier," *The Dick Powell Show,* NBC, 1962, broadcast as a pilot, ABC, 1963.

Luke Martin, "The Way Station," *Bonanza,* NBC, 1962.

Peter Warren, "The Blues My Babe Gave to Me," *The Eleventh Hour,* NBC, 1962.

Philip Colerane, "The Debasers," *Cain's Hundred,* NBC, 1962.

"Death of a Dream," *Kraft Mystery Theatre,* NBC, 1962.

Captain Paul Terman, "No Small Wars," *Empire,* NBC, 1963.

Charlie Argos, "The Charlie Argos Story," *The Untouchables,* ABC, 1963.

Clarence Darrow, "Defendant," *G.E. True,* CBS, 1963.

Douglas Milinder, "Your Fortune for a Penny," *77 Sunset Strip,* ABC, 1963.

Jim Darling, "It's a Shame She Married Me," *The Dick Van Dyke Show,* CBS, 1963.

St. Mark, "The Silence of Good Men," *The Eleventh Hour,* NBC, 1963.

Simon Clain, "If You Have Tears," *The Virginian,* NBC, 1963.

Host, *Hullabaloo,* NBC, 1965.

Guest, *The Red Skelton Comedy Hour* (also known as *The Red Skelton Hour* and *The Red Skelton Show*), CBS, 1965, 1966.

Napoleon Solo, "The Mother Muffin Affair," *The Girl from U.N.C.L.E.,* NBC, 1966.

Napoleon Solo, "Say U.N.C.L.E.," *Please Don't Eat the Daisies,* NBC, 1966.

Guest, *The Hollywood Palace,* ABC, 1968.

Guest, *Vergissmeinnicht,* 1968.

Himself, *Personality,* NBC, 1968.

Panelist, *Match Game '73,* CBS, 1973.

$10,000 Pyramid, 1973, 1974.

$20,000 Pyramid, 1974.

Andrew Simms, "Blast," *Police Woman,* NBC, 1975.

Panelist, *Match Game '75,* CBS, 1975.

Lou Malik, "Generation of Evil," *Police Woman,* NBC, 1976.

"Murder at F–Stop 11," *The Feather and Father Gang,* ABC, 1977.

Darius, "The Story of Daniel in the Lion's Den," *Greatest Heroes of the Bible,* 1978.

"Who Killed Charles Pendragon?," *Eddie Capra Mysteries,* NBC, 1978.

Sebastian Rolande, "The Spirit Is Willie," *Hawaii Five–O,* CBS, 1979.

T. K. Sheldon, "Girl under Glass: Parts 1 & 2" (also known as "The Sex Act: Parts 1 & 2"), *Trapper John, M.D.,* CBS, 1980.

"The Scream of Eagles," *Trapper John, M.D.,* CBS, 1980.

Charles Paris, "The Fashion Show: A Model Marriage/ This Year's Model/Original Sing/Vogue Rogue/Too Clothes for Comfort: Parts 1 & 2," *The Love Boat,* ABC, 1981.

Troy, "Charades," *Hotel,* ABC, 1983.

Dr. Christopher Hamilton, "Face to Face," *The Hitchhiker,* HBO, 1984.

Gideon Armstrong, "Murder Digs Deep," *Murder, She Wrote,* CBS, 1985.

Nameless master villain, "Abnormal Psych," *Stingray,* NBC, 1986.

"Trial By Fire," *The A Team,* NBC, 1986.

Guest, *Late Night with David Letterman,* NBC, 1987.

Huxley, "The Fruit at the Bottom of the Bowl," *The Ray Bradbury Theater,* USA Network, 1988.

Deputy chief Curtis Moorehead, "City under Siege: Parts 1–3," *Hunter,* NBC, 1989.

Edwin Chancellor, "The Grand Old Lady," *Murder, She Wrote,* CBS, 1989.

Guest, *The Howard Stern Show,* 1991.

Charles Winthrop, "The Witch's Curse," *Murder, She Wrote,* CBS, 1992.

Rykker, "Dragonswing," *Kung Fu: The Legend Continues,* syndicated, 1993.

Guest, *Later with Bob Costas* (also known as *Later*), NBC, 1993.

Ned Whelan, "Farewell to Arms," *Sirens,* syndicated, 1994.

Rykker, "Dragonswing II," *Kung Fu: The Legend Continues,* syndicated, 1994.

William Shane, "Who Killed the Movie Mogul?," *Burke's Law,* CBS, 1995.

Bill Stratton, "Murder, Murder," *Diagnosis Murder,* CBS, 1996.

Dr. Stewart Rizor, "Plague," *Walker, Texas Ranger,* CBS, 1996.

James Sheffield, "Me and Mrs. Joan," *The Nanny,* CBS, 1996.

Alexander Drake, "Discards," *Diagnosis Murder,* CBS, 1997.

Carl Anderton, "Burned," *Law & Order,* NBC, 1997.

Carl Anderton, "Bad Girl," *Law & Order,* NBC, 1998.

Carl Anderton, "Monster," *Law & Order,* NBC, 1998.

James Sheffield, "Immaculate Concepcion," *The Nanny,* CBS, 1998.

Himself, *Steve McQueen: The E! True Hollywood Story,* E! Entertainment Television, 1998.

Vince Deal, "The Real Deal," *The Sentinel,* UPN, 1999.

Voice of Mr. White, "The Story of Whomps," *Recess* (animated; also known as *Disney's "Recess"*), ABC, 1999.

Himself, "24–30 June, 1967," *That Was the Week We Watched,* BBC–2, 2003.

Himself, *Richard & Judy,* Channel 4 (England), 2004.

Appeared in episodes of other series, including *The Gordon Elliott Show,* syndicated.

Television Appearances; Pilots:

A. Dunster Lowell, *The Boston Terrier,* ABC, 1963, originally broadcast as a pilot on *The Dick Powell Show,* NBC, 1962.

Senator Gerald Stratton, *The Islander,* CBS, 1978.

Hart to Hart, ABC, 1979.

Commissioner Peter Kinghorn, *Dark Avenger,* CBS, 1990.

Television Director; Episodic:

"It Could Be Practically Anywhere on the Island," *The Protectors,* syndicated, 1973.

"The Melting Point of Ice," *Police Woman,* NBC, 1976.

Film Appearances:

Photographer, *I'll Cry Tomorrow,* Metro–Goldwyn–Mayer, 1955.

Spear carrier and Hebrew at golden calf, *The Ten Commandments,* Paramount, 1956.

Bob Ford, *Hell's Crossroads,* Republic, 1957.

Buddy Root, *No Time to Be Young* (also known as *The Big Day: Teenage Delinquents*), Columbia, 1957.

Don Bigelow, *Unwed Mother,* Allied Artists, 1958.

Symbol maker's teenage son, *Teenage Caveman* (also known as *Out of the Darkness* and *Prehistoric World*), American International Pictures, 1958.

Chester A. "Chet" Gwynn, *The Young Philadelphians* (also known as *The City Jungle*), Warner Bros., 1959.

Edward "Eddie"/"The Kid" Campbell, *Good Day for a Hanging,* Columbia, 1959.

Lee, *The Magnificent Seven,* United Artists, 1960.

Klaus Everard, *The Big Show,* Twentieth Century–Fox, 1961.

Jim Melford, *The Caretakers* (also known as *Borderlines*), United Artists, 1963.

(Uncredited) Napoleon Solo, *The Glass Bottom Boat* (also known as *The Spy in Lace Panties*), Metro–Goldwyn–Mayer, 1966.

Napoleon Solo, *One of Our Spies Is Missing,* Metro–Goldwyn–Mayer, 1966.

Napoleon Solo, *One Spy Too Many,* Metro–Goldwyn–Mayer, 1966.

Napoleon Solo, *The Spy in the Green Hat,* Metro–Goldwyn–Mayer, 1966.

Napoleon Solo, *The Spy with My Face,* Metro–Goldwyn–Mayer, 1966.

Napoleon Solo, *To Trap a Spy,* Metro–Goldwyn–Mayer, 1966.

Bill Fenner, *The Venetian Affair,* Metro–Goldwyn–Mayer, 1967.

Napoleon Solo, *The Karate Killers* (also known as *The Five Daughters Affair*), Metro–Goldwyn–Mayer, 1967.

(Uncredited) Himself, *Italy's in Season* (short documentary film), Metro–Goldwyn–Mayer, 1967.

Napoleon Solo, *The Helicopter Spies,* Metro–Goldwyn–Mayer, 1968.

Napoleon Solo, *How to Steal the World,* Metro–Goldwyn–Mayer, 1968.

Himself, *"Bullitt": Steve McQueen's Commitment to Reality* (short documentary film), Warner Bros., 1968.

Walter Chalmers, *Bullitt,* Warner Bros., 1968.

Antonio, *If It's Tuesday, This Must Be Belgium,* United Artists, 1969.

Major Paul Kreuger, *The Bridge at Remagen,* United Artists, 1969.

Casca, *Julius Caesar,* American International Pictures, 1970.

Dr. Michael Bergen, *The Mind of Mr. Soames,* Columbia, 1970.

Neilson, *The Clay Pigeon* (also known as *Trip to Kill*), Metro–Goldwyn–Mayer, 1971.

Ray, *The Statue,* Cinerama, 1971.

Harry S Truman, *The Man from Independence,* 1974.

Senator Gary Parker, *The Towering Inferno,* Twentieth Century–Fox, 1974.

Stuart "Star" Chase, *Wanted: Babysitter* (also known as *The Babysitter, L.A. Babysitter, The Raw Edge, Babysitter—Un maledetto pasticio, Das Ganz grosse Ding,* and *Jeune fille libre le soir*), SNC, 1975.

Atraco en la jungla (also known as *Blue Jeans and Dynamite, Double Cross,* and *Dynamite and Blue Jeans*), 1976.

(Uncredited) Voice of Proteus IV, *Demon Seed* (also known as *Proteus Generation*), United Artists, 1977.

Glenn Manning, *The Lucifer Complex,* Gold Key Entertainment, 1978.

Professor Allan Duncan, *Starship Invasions* (also known as *Alien Encounter, Project Genocide,* and *War of the Aliens*), Warner Bros., 1978.

Colonel Donald Rogers, *Brass Target,* United Artists, 1979.

Dr. Neal, *Good Luck, Miss Wyckoff* (also known as *Secret Yearnings, The Shaming,* and *The Sin*), Bel–Air/Gradison, 1979.

Barkley, *Virus* (also known as *The End, Day of Resurrection,* and *Fukkatsu no hi*), Media, 1980.

Gelt, *Battle beyond the Stars,* Orion, 1980.

Gordon Cain, *Hangar 18* (also known as *Invasion Force*), Sunn Classic, 1980.

Hud, *Cuba Crossing* (also known as *Assignment: Kill Castro, Key West Crossing, Kill Castro, The Mercenaries, Sweet Dirty Tony, Sweet Violent Tony,* and *Todeskommando Schweinebucht*), Key West, 1980.

David Blackman, *S.O.B.,* Paramount, 1981.

Lekar, *Veliki Transport* (also known as *Heroes*), 1983.

Ross Webster, *Superman III,* Warner Bros., 1983.

Ed Ryland, *Black Moon Rising,* New World, 1986.

General Woodbridge, *The Delta Force* (also known as *Mahatz Ha–Delta*), Cannon, 1986.

Dr. Fred Brown, *Killing Birds—uccelli assassini* (also known as *Dark Eyes of the Zombie, Raptors,* and *Zombie 5: Killing Birds*), 1987.

Sam Merrick, *Hour of the Assassin,* Concorde–New Horizons, 1987.

Eduard Delacorte, *Captive Rage* (also known as *Fair Trade*), Movie Group, 1988.

Lawson, *Renegade* (also known as *They Call Me Renegade, You Call Me Trinity, They Call Me Renegade,* and *Renegade, un osso troppo duro*), 1988.

Another Way (also known as *D Kikan Joho*), 1988.

Ambassador McKay, *The Emissary,* 1989.

Colonel Masters, *C.H.U.D. II: Bud the C.H.U.D.,* Vestron Pictures, 1989.

Colonel Schneider, *Skeleton Coast* (also known as *Coast of Skeletons*), Silvertree, 1989.

Dr. Gary, *Buried Alive* (also known as *Edgar Allen Poe's "Buried Alive"*), 21st Century Film Corporation, 1989.

Lord Byron Orlock, *Transylvania Twist,* Concorde/Aquarius Releasing, 1989.

Max, *Brutal Glory,* 1989.

Adolf Hitler, *That's Adequate,* Southgate Entertainment/Vidmark Entertainment, 1990.

Dr. Duncan, *Nobody's Perfect,* Moviestore Entertainment, 1990.

Wolfgang Manteuffil, *River of Death* (also known as *Alistair MacLean's "River of Death"*), Cannon, 1990.

Wedgewood, *Going Under* (also known as *Dive*), Warner Bros., 1991.

Mr. X, *Blind Vision,* Saban Entertainment, 1992.

Mayor Sampson Moses, *Dust to Dust,* 1994.

Agent Silvestri, *Visions,* 1996.

Senator Dougherty, *Joe's Apartment,* Warner Bros., 1996.

Senator Zachary Powell, *Menno's Mind* (also known as *Power.com*), 1996.

Uncle Andre, *Milk & Money,* 1996.

Baxter, *Vulcan* (also known as *Anak ng bulkan*), Premiere Entertainment, 1997.

Professor Michaels, *An American Affair,* TSC, 1997.

Baxter Cain, *BASEketball,* MCA/Universal, 1998.

Walter Denkins, *McCinsey's Island,* 1998.

Chief MacIntyre, *Motel Blue,* Bedford Entertainment, 1999.

Dick Lecter, *Pootie Tang,* Paramount, 2001.

Judge Mancini, *Cottonmouth* (also known as *Lethal Force* and *Silent Justice*), Madison Home Video, 2002.

Benny "The Bomb" Palladino, *Hoodlum & Son,* Peakviewing Transatlantic, 2003.

Tully, Sr., *Happy Hour,* Davis Entertainment Filmworks/O'Hara–Klein, 2003.

Braddock, *The Warrior Class,* Archer Entertainment/Talking Pictures, 2004.

Chief Hannigan, *Gang Warz,* Pittsburgh Pictures, 2004.

Dr. Gadsden Braden, *Scene Stealers,* 2004.

Nick, *2BPerfectly Honest* (also known as *2 B Perfectly Honest*), 2B Pictures, 2004.

Also appeared in *Twilight Blue* and *Rampage.*

Stage Appearances:
Title role, *Hamlet,* Pasadena Playhouse, Pasadena, CA, 1964.

Franklin Delano Roosevelt (title role), *FDR* (solo show; also known as *FDR: That Man in the White House*), 1978.

Henry Drummond, *Inherit the Wind,* Paper Mill Playhouse, Millburn, NJ, 1984–85.

Andrew Makepeace Ladd II, *Love Letters,* Edison Theatre, New York City, then Los Angeles, both 1990.

I Hate Hamlet, Jupiter Theatre, Jupiter, FL, 1992.

Reginald Paget, *Quartet,* Berkshire Theatre Festival, Stockbridge, MA, 2002.

The Exonerated, Forty–Five Bleecker Street Theatre, New York City, between 2002 and 2004.

Appeared in other plays, including *End as a Man,* California production.

RECORDINGS

Videos:

(In archive footage) *Hullabaloo Vol. 8,* MPI Home Video, 1996.

WRITINGS

Nonfiction:

Only Victims: A Study of Show Business Blacklisting (Ph.D. thesis), foreword by George McGovern, Putnam, 1972, reprinted, Limelight Editions, 1996.

Author of the autobiography *Christ, Shakespeare, Ho Chi Min: As I Knew Them.*

OTHER SOURCES

Books:

Contemporary Authors, Volumes 61–64, Gale, 1976.

Periodicals:

Radio Times, March 20, 2004, pp. 24, 25, 27.
TV Guide, November 8, 1997, pp. 24–27.

W

WACHOWSKI, Andy 1967–
(The Wachowski Brothers, Andrew Wachowski)

PERSONAL

Full name, Andrew Paul Wachowski; born December 29, 1967, in Chicago, IL; son of Ron (in business) and Lynne (a nurse and painter) Wachowski; brother of Larry Wachowski (a director, producer, and writer); married Alisa Blasingame, 1991; *Education:* Attended Whitney M. Young Magnet High School and Emerson College.

Addresses: *Agent*—William Morris Agency, One William Morris Place, Beverly Hills, CA 90212; Saville Productions, 468 North Camden Dr., Beverly Hills, CA 90210. *Manager*—Circle of Confusion, 8548 Washington Blvd., Culver City, CA 90232.

Career: Director, producer, and writer. Eon Entertainment (production company), principal. Worked as a house painter and carpenter. Also known as Andrew Wachowski.

Member: Directors Guild of America, Writers Guild of America West.

Awards, Honors: All with Larry Wachowski: Grand Jury Award—honorable mention, L.A. Outfest, outstanding American narrative feature, honorable mention, Stockholm Film Festival, and Grand Special Prize nomination, Deauville Film Festival, all 1996, International Fantasy Film Award, best film, Fantasporto, Saturn Award nomination, Academy of Science Fiction, Fantasy & Horror Films, best writer, and Chlotrudis Award nomination, best director, all 1997, all for *Bound;* honorable mention (also with Mehdi Benoufa),

Stockholm Film Festival, 1997, for *Assassin(s);* Saturn Award, best director, Reader's Choice Award, best foreign language film, Mainichi Film Concours, Saturn Award nomination, best writer, Sierra Award nomination, best screenplay, original, Las Vegas Film Critics Society, Nebula Award nomination, best script, Science Fiction and Fantasy Writers of America, and Amanda Award nomination, best foreign feature film, all 2000, for *The Matrix;* Andy and Larry Wachowski named to Power 100 List, *Premiere* magazine, 2002 and 2003.

CREDITS

Film Director with Larry Wachowski as the Wachowski Brothers:
Bound, Gramercy Pictures, 1996.
The Matrix, Warner Bros., 1999.
The Matrix Reloaded, Warner Bros., 2003, also released as *The Matrix Reloaded: The IMAX Experience,* IMAX Corporation, 2003.
The Matrix Revolutions, Warner Bros., 2003, also released as *The Matrix Revolutions: The IMAX Experience,* IMAX Corporation, 2003.
King Conan: Crown of Iron, Warner Bros., 2005.

Film Executive Producer with Larry Wachowski:
(And Barrie M. Osborne, Andrew Mason, Erwin Stoff, and Bruce Berman) *Bound,* Gramercy Pictures, 1996.
The Matrix, Warner Bros., 1999.
The Matrix Reloaded, Warner Bros., 2003, also released as *The Matrix Reloaded: The IMAX Experience,* IMAX Corporation, 2003.
The Matrix Revolutions, Warner Bros., 2003, also released as *The Matrix Revolutions: The IMAX Experience,* IMAX Corporation, 2003.

Film Producer with Larry Wachowski:
The Animatrix (animated short films), Warner Home Video, 2003.

King Conan: Crown of Iron, Warner Bros., 2005.
V for Vendetta, Warner Bros., 2005.

Film Appearances:
Independents' Days (short documentary film), Nomad Films International, 1997.
Window cleaner, *The Matrix,* Warner Bros., 1999.

Television Appearances; Specials:
Himself, *The Matrix: The Movie Special* (documentary), MTV, 1999.

Television Appearances; Episodic:
Himself, "Making The Matrix," *HBO First Look,* HBO, c. 1999.
Himself, "The Matrix Revolutions," *HBO First Look,* HBO, 2003.

RECORDINGS

Video Work:
Executive producer, *The Matrix Revisited,* Warner Home Video, 2001.

Video Appearances:
Himself, *The Matrix Revisited,* Warner Home Video, 2001.
Himself, *The Burly Man Chronicles* (documentary), Warner Home Video, 2004.

Video Game Director:
(With Larry Wachowski as the Wachowski Brothers; and production designer with Larry Wachowski) *Enter the Matrix,* Atari, 2003.
(With Larry Wachowski as the Wachowski Brothers) *The Matrix Online* (also known as *MxO*), Warner Bros. Interactive Entertainment, 2005.
The Matrix: Path of Neo, Atari, 2005.

WRITINGS

Screenplays with Larry Wachowski:
(And with Brian Helgeland) *Assassin(s)* (also known as *Day of Reckoning*), Warner Bros., 1995.
Bound, Gramercy Pictures, 1996.
The Matrix, Warner Bros., 1999.
The Matrix 2, Warner Bros., 2001.
The Matrix Reloaded, Warner Bros., 2003, also released as *The Matrix Reloaded: The IMAX Experience,* IMAX Corporation, 2003.
The Matrix Revolutions, Warner Bros., 2003, also released as *The Matrix Revolutions: The IMAX Experience,* IMAX Corporation, 2003.

(As the Wachowski Brothers) "The Second Renaissance Part 1" (also known as "The Animatrix: The Second Renaissance Part 1" and "The Animatrix: The Second Renaissance Part I"), "The Second Renaissance Part 2" (also known as "The Animatrix: The Second Renaissance Part 2"), "Kid's Story" (also known as "The Animatrix: Kid's Story"), and "Final Flight of the Osiris" (also known as "The Animatrix: Final Flight of the Osiris"), *The Animatrix* (animated short films), Warner Home Video, 2003.
V for Vendetta, Warner Bros., 2005.

Stories for Films with Larry Wachowski:
Assassin(s) (also known as *Day of Reckoning*), Warner Bros., 1995.
"Kid's Story" (also known as "The Animatrix: Kid's Story"), *The Animatrix* (animated short films), Warner Home Video, 2003.

Teleplays; Pilots:
Ecto–Kid, Nickelodeon, 2001.

Videos:
The Matrix Revisited, Warner Home Video, 2001.

Video Games:
(With Larry Wachowski as the Wachowski Brothers) *Enter the Matrix,* Atari, 2003.
The Matrix: Path of Neo, Atari, 2005.

Internet Comic Books:
(With Larry Wachowski) *The Matrix* (based on the film of the same name), illustrated by Geoff Darrow, beginning 1999.

Comic Books:
With Larry Wachowski, author of *Ecto–Kid,* illustrated by Steve Skroce, Razorline/Marvel Comics.

Nonfiction:
(With Larry Wachowski) *The Art of the Matrix,* Newmarket Press, 2000.

Short Fiction:
(With Clive Barker and others) *Clive Barker's "Hellraiser": Collected Best II,* Checker, 2003.

OTHER SOURCES

Books:
Authors and Artists for Young Adults, Gale Group, 2004.

Periodicals:

Entertainment Weekly, April 16, 1999, p. 7; April 18, 2003, p. 32.
Newsweek, December 30, 2002, pp. 80, 89.
NME, March 8, 1997, p. 26.
Publishers Weekly, October 4, 2004, p. 21.
Time, June 2, 2003, p. 87.
Variety, February 10, 2003, p. 8; May 26, 2003, pp. 6–7.

Electronic:

The Matrix, http://www.whatisthematrix.com/cmp/comix, April 14, 2000.

WACHOWSKI, Larry 1965–
(The Wachowski Brothers)

PERSONAL

Full name, Laurence Wachowski; born June 21, 1965, in Chicago, IL; son of Ron (in business) and Lynne (a nurse and painter) Wachowski; brother of Andy Wachowski (a director, producer, and writer); married Thea Bloom, October 30, 1993 (divorced, December, 2002). *Education:* Attended Whitney M. Young Magnet High School and Bard College.

Addresses: *Agent*—William Morris Agency, One William Morris Place, Beverly Hills, CA 90212; Saville Productions, 468 North Camden Dr., Beverly Hills, CA 90210. *Manager*—Circle of Confusion, 8548 Washington Blvd., Culver City, CA 90232.

Career: Director, producer, and writer. Eon Entertainment (production company), principal. Worked as a house painter and carpenter.

Member: Directors Guild of America, Writers Guild of America West.

Awards, Honors: All with Andy Wachowski: Grand Jury Award—honorable mention, L.A. Outfest, outstanding American narrative feature, honorable mention, Stockholm Film Festival, and Grand Special Prize nomination, Deauville Film Festival, all 1996, International Fantasy Film Award, best film, Fantasporto, Saturn Award nomination, Academy of Science Fiction, Fantasy & Horror Films, best writer, and Chlotrudis Award nomination, best director, all 1997, all for *Bound;* honorable mention (also with Mehdi Benoufa), Stockholm Film Festival, 1997, for *Assassin(s);* Saturn Award, best director, Reader's Choice Award, best foreign language film, Mainichi Film Concours, Saturn Award nomination, best writer, Sierra Award nomination, best screenplay, original, Las Vegas Film Critics Society, Nebula Award nomination, best script, Science Fiction and Fantasy Writers of America, and Amanda Award nomination, best foreign feature film, all 2000, for *The Matrix;* Larry and Andy Wachowski named to Power 100 List, *Premiere* magazine, 2002 and 2003.

CREDITS

Film Director with Andy Wachowski as the Wachowski Brothers:

Bound, Gramercy Pictures, 1996.
The Matrix, Warner Bros., 1999.
The Matrix Reloaded, Warner Bros., 2003, also released as *The Matrix Reloaded: The IMAX Experience,* IMAX Corporation, 2003.
The Matrix Revolutions, Warner Bros., 2003, also released as *The Matrix Revolutions: The IMAX Experience,* IMAX Corporation, 2003.
King Conan: Crown of Iron, Warner Bros., 2005.

Film Executive Producer with Andy Wachowski:

(And Barrie M. Osborne, Andrew Mason, Erwin Stoff, and Bruce Berman) *Bound,* Gramercy Pictures, 1996.
The Matrix, Warner Bros., 1999.
The Matrix Reloaded, Warner Bros., 2003, also released as *The Matrix Reloaded: The IMAX Experience,* IMAX Corporation, 2003.
The Matrix Revolutions, Warner Bros., 2003, also released as *The Matrix Revolutions: The IMAX Experience,* IMAX Corporation, 2003.

Film Producer with Andy Wachowski:

The Animatrix (animated short films), Warner Home Video, 2003.
King Conan: Crown of Iron, Warner Bros., 2005.
V for Vendetta, Warner Bros., 2005.

Film Appearances:

Independents' Days (short documentary film), Nomad Films International, 1997.
Window cleaner, *The Matrix,* Warner Bros., 1999.

Television Appearances; Specials:

Himself, *The Matrix: The Movie Special* (documentary), MTV, 1999.

Television Appearances; Episodic:

Himself, "Making The Matrix," *HBO First Look,* HBO, c. 1999.
Himself, "The Matrix Revolutions," *HBO First Look,* HBO, 2003.

RECORDINGS

Video Work:
Executive producer, *The Matrix Revisited,* Warner Home Video, 2001.

Video Appearances:
Himself, *The Matrix Revisited,* Warner Home Video, 2001.
Himself, *The Burly Man Chronicles* (documentary), Warner Home Video, 2004.

Video Game Director:
(With Andy Wachowski as the Wachowski Brothers; and production designer with Andy Wachowski) *Enter the Matrix,* Atari, 2003.
(With Andy Wachowski as the Wachowski Brothers) *The Matrix Online* (also known as *MxO*), Warner Bros. Interactive Entertainment, 2005.
The Matrix: Path of Neo, Atari, 2005.

WRITINGS

Screenplays with Andy Wachowski:
(And with Brian Helgeland) *Assassin(s)* (also known as *Day of Reckoning*), Warner Bros., 1995.
Bound, Gramercy Pictures, 1996.
The Matrix, Warner Bros., 1999.
The Matrix 2, Warner Bros., 2001.
The Matrix Reloaded, Warner Bros., 2003, also released as *The Matrix Reloaded: The IMAX Experience,* IMAX Corporation, 2003.
The Matrix Revolutions, Warner Bros., 2003, also released as *The Matrix Revolutions: The IMAX Experience,* IMAX Corporation, 2003.
(As the Wachowski Brothers) "The Second Renaissance Part 1" (also known as "The Animatrix: The Second Renaissance Part 1" and "The Animatrix: The Second Renaissance Part I"), "The Second Renaissance Part 2" (also known as "The Animatrix: The Second Renaissance Part 2"), "Kid's Story" (also known as "The Animatrix: Kid's Story"), and "Final Flight of the Osiris" (also known as "The Animatrix: Final Flight of the Osiris"), *The Animatrix* (animated short films), Warner Home Video, 2003.
V for Vendetta, Warner Bros., 2005.

Stories for Films with Andy Wachowski:
Assassin(s) (also known as *Day of Reckoning*), Warner Bros., 1995.
"Kid's Story" (also known as "The Animatrix: Kid's Story"), *The Animatrix* (animated short films), Warner Home Video, 2003.

Teleplays; Pilots:
Ecto–Kid, Nickelodeon, 2001.

Videos:
The Matrix Revisited, Warner Home Video, 2001.

Video Games:
(With Andy Wachowski as the Wachowski Brothers) *Enter the Matrix,* Atari, 2003.
The Matrix: Path of Neo, Atari, 2005.

Internet Comic Books:
(With Andy Wachowski) *The Matrix* (based on the film of the same name), illustrated by Geoff Darrow, beginning 1999.

Comic Books:
With Andy Wachowski, author of *Ecto–Kid,* illustrated by Steve Skroce, Razorline/Marvel Comics.

Nonfiction:
(With Andy Wachowski) *The Art of the Matrix,* Newmarket Press, 2000.

Short Fiction:
(With Clive Barker and others) *Clive Barker's "Hellraiser": Collected Best II,* Checker, 2003.

OTHER SOURCES

Books:
Authors and Artists for Young Adults, Gale Group, 2004.

Periodicals:
Entertainment Weekly, April 16, 1999, p. 7; April 18, 2003, p. 32.
Newsweek, December 30, 2002, pp. 80, 89.
NME, March 8, 1997, p. 26.
Publishers Weekly, October 4, 2004, p. 21.
Time, June 2, 2003, p. 87.
Variety, February 10, 2003, p. 8; May 26, 2003, pp.6–7.

Electronic:
The Matrix, http://www.whatisthematrix.com/cmp/comix, April 14, 2000.

WAIN, David 1969–

PERSONAL

Full name, David Benjamin Wain; born August 1, 1969, in Shaker Heights, OH.

Addresses: *Manager*—Principato Young Management, 9465 Wilshire Blvd., Suite 880, Beverly Hills, CA 90212. *Agent*—Creative Artists Agency, 9830 Wilshire Blvd., Beverly Hills, CA 90212.

Career: Actor, producer, writer, and director. Directed television commercials, including work for MTV.

Awards, Honors: Open Palm Award nomination, Gotham Awards, 2001, for *Wet Hot American Summer.*

CREDITS

Film Work:
Director and producer, *Aisle Six* (short film), 1991.
Director and coproducer, *Wet Hot American Summer,* USA Films, 2001.
Director and editor, *Stella Shorts 1998–2002,* 2002.

Film Appearances:
Steve Posner, *Keeping the Faith,* Buena Vista, 2000.
Bunning, *Bamboozled,* New Line Cinema, 2000.
(Uncredited) Paco, *Wet Hot American Summer,* USA Films, 2001.
David, *Stella Shorts 1998–2002,* 2002.
Ralphie, *The Third Date,* Iron, 2003.
(Uncredited) Wedding videographer, *Along Came Polly,* Universal, 2004.
The Baxter, IFC, 2005.

Television Work; Series:
Director, producer, and editor, *The State,* MTV, 1993–97.
Director and executive producer, *Stella,* 2005.

Television Appearances; Series:
You Wrote It, You Watch It, 1992.
The State, MTV, 1993–97.
Correspondent, *The Daily Show* (also known as *The Daily Show with Jon Stewart*), Comedy Central, 1996.
Random Play, VH1, 1999.
Host, *Late Friday,* NBC, 2001.
Panelist, *Best Week Ever,* 2004.
David, *Stella,* 2005.

Television Appearances; Episodic:
Voice of Al Foster, *Crank Yankers* (animated), Comedy Central, 2003.
Voice of David, *Crank Yankers* (animated), Comedy Central, 2003.
Sensual masseuse, "Dangle's Moving Day," *Reno 911!,* Comedy Central, 2003.
Jimmy Kimmel Live, ABC, 2004.
Interviewee, *My Coolest Years,* VH1, 2004.

Best Week Ever, 2004.
Brian Lewis, "High–School Cheerleading," *Cheap Seats,* 2004.

Also appeared as Jack, *Cosby,* CBS; in *Sheep In the City* (animated), Cartoon Network.

Television Appearances; Specials:
The State's 43rd Annual Halloween Special, CBS, 1995.

Television Appearances; Miniseries:
I Love the '70s (documentary), VH1, 2003.
I Love the '90s: Part Deux (documentary), VH1, 2005.

WRITINGS

Screenplays:
Aisle Six (short film), 1991.
Wet Hot American Summer, USA Films, 2001.
Stella Shorts 1998–2002, 2002.

Television Specials:
Two Rooms: Tribute to Elton John & Bernie Taupin, ABC, 1991.
The State's 43rd Annual Halloween Special, CBS, 1995.

Television Series:
You Wrote It, You Watch It, 1992.
The State, MTV, 1993–97.
Random Play, VH1, 1999.
Sheep in the Big City, Cartoon Network, 2000.
Mad TV, Fox, 2000–2001.
Stella, 2005.

Television Episodes:
"The Blank Page," *Strangers with Candy,* Comedy Central, 1999.

Stage Plays:
Sex a.k.a. Wieners and Boobs, 2005.

Also wrote *MOLT,* off–Broadway production; *Winter on Wheels; Assorted Cuts of Meat,* produced at Cleveland Public Theater.

OTHER SOURCES

Electronic:
David Wain Official Site, http://www.davidwain.com/, April 21, 2005.

WALLACH, Eli 1915–
(Ely Wallach)

PERSONAL

Born December 7, 1915, in Brooklyn, NY; son of Abraham and Bertha (maiden name, Schorr) Wallach; married Anne Jackson (an actress), March 5, 1948; children: Peter Douglas (a special effects director), Roberta Lee (an actress), Katherine Beatrice (an actress). *Education:* University of Texas at Austin, B.A., 1936; City College (now City University of New York), M.S., 1938; trained for the stage at Neighborhood Playhouse, 1938–40, and with Lee Strasberg at the Actors Studio; studied dance with Martha Graham. *Avocational Interests:* Woodworking, collecting antiques and clocks, tennis, baseball, architecture, photography, water–color painting, swimming.

Addresses: Agent—Elizabeth Fredericks, William Morris Agency, 1325 Avenue of the Americas, New York, NY 10019.

Career: Actor, voice artist, and writer. WLID–Radio, Brooklyn, NY, actor in radio plays, 1936–38; Actors Studio, New York City, original member of company, beginning 1947, vice president, 1980–81, and teacher; Jewish Repertory Theatre, New York City, member of advisory board, 1991–92; Neighborhood Playhouse School of the Theatre, corporate member and director; Arena Stage, Washington, DC, guest artist. Voice performer for commercials. Also worked as playground director, camp counselor, and hospital registrar. *Military service:* U.S. Army, Medical Administration Corps, served during World War II; became captain.

Member: Actors' Equity Association, Screen Actors Guild, American Federation of Television and Radio Artists.

Awards, Honors: Antoinette Perry Award, best featured actor, New York Drama Critics Poll, Donaldson Award, and *Theatre World* Award, all 1951, for *The Rose Tattoo;* Film Award, British Academy of Film and Television Arts, most promising newcomer, 1957, for *Baby Doll;* Drama League Award, distinguished performance, 1957; Obie Award, *Village Voice,* distinguished performance, 1963, for *The Tiger* and *The Typists;* Emmy Award, best supporting actor in a drama, 1967, for *Poppies Are Also Flowers;* Emmy Award nomination, outstanding supporting actor in a miniseries or special, 1987, for *Something in Common;* inducted into Theatre Hall of Fame, 1988; distinguished alumnus award, University of Texas at Austin, 1989; Helen Hayes Award, Washington Theatre Awards Society,

1991; honorary doctorate, School for the Visual Arts, 1991; Edith Oliver Award for Sustained Excellence, Lucille Lortel Awards, League of Off–Broadway Theatres and Producers, 1998; Life in Theatre Award, T. Schreiber Studio, 2000; Golden Boot Award, Motion Picture and Television Fund, 2001; Jury Award, Newport International Film Festival, best actor, 2004, for *King of the Corner;* honorary degree from Emerson College.

CREDITS

Stage Appearances:
Title role, *Liliom,* Curtain Club, University of Texas at Austin, Austin, TX, 1936.

The Bo Tree, Locust Valley, NY, 1939.

(Broadway debut) Crew chief, *Skydrift,* Belasco Theatre, 1945.

Cromwell, *King Henry VIII,* American Repertory Theatre, International Theatre, New York City, 1946–47.

Spintho, *Androcles and the Lion* (double–bill with *A Pound on Demand*), American Repertory Theatre, International Theatre, 1946–47.

Member of ensemble, *What Every Woman Knows,* American Repertory Theatre, International Theatre, 1946–47.

Busch, *Yellow Jack* (one–act), American Repertory Theatre, International Theatre, 1947.

The Duck, Two of Spades, and Leg of Mutton, *Alice in Wonderland,* American Repertory Theatre, International Theatre, 1947.

Diomedes and messenger, *Antony and Cleopatra,* Martin Beck Theatre, New York City, 1948.

Stefanowski, *Mister Roberts,* Alvin Theatre, New York City, 1949.

Alvarro Mangiacavallo, *The Rose Tattoo,* Martin Beck Theatre, 1951.

Kilroy, *Camino Real,* National Theatre, New York City, 1953.

Dickon, *Scarecrow,* Theatre De Lys (now Lucille Lortel Theatre), New York City, 1953.

Julien, *Mademoiselle Colombe,* Longacre Theatre, New York City, 1954.

(London debut) Sakini, *The Teahouse of the August Moon,* Her Majesty's Theatre, 1954, then Martin Beck Theatre, 1955.

Bill Walker, *Major Barbara,* Martin Beck Theatre, 1956.

Old Man Ionesos, "The Chairs" in *The Chairs* and *The Lesson* (double–bill), Phoenix Theatre, New York City, 1958.

Willie, *The Cold Wind and the Warm,* Morosco Theatre, New York City, 1958–59.

Berenger, *Rhinoceros,* Longacre Theatre, 1961.

Brecht on Brecht, Theatre De Lys, 1962–63.

Ben, *The Tiger,* and Paul XXX, *The Typists,* (double–bill), Orpheum Theatre, New York City, 1963, then Globe Theatre, London, 1964.

Milt Manville, *Luv,* Booth Theatre, New York City, 1964.

Charles Dyer, *Staircase,* Biltmore Theatre, New York City, 1967–68.

Ollie H. and Wesley, *Promenade All!,* Alvin Theatre, New York City, 1972.

General St. Pe, *The Waltz of the Toreadors,* Circle in the Square, New York City, then Eisenhower Theatre, John F. Kennedy Center for the Performing Arts, Washington, DC, 1973.

Peppino, *Saturday, Sunday, Monday,* Martin Beck Theatre, 1974.

Arthur Canfield, *The Sponsor,* Peachtree Playhouse, Atlanta, GA, 1975.

Colin, *Absent Friends,* Long Wharf Theatre, New Haven, CT, then Eisenhower Theatre, John F. Kennedy Center for the Performing Arts, later Royal Alexandra Theatre, Toronto, Ontario, Canada, all 1977.

Otto Frank, *The Diary of Anne Frank,* Theatre Four, New York City, 1978–79.

The Neighborhood Playhouse at Fifty: A Celebration, Shubert Theatre, New York City, 1978.

Alexander, *Every Good Boy Deserves Favour,* Metropolitan Opera House, New York City, then Concert Hall, John F. Kennedy Center for the Performing Arts, both 1979.

Leon Rose, "A Need for Brussels Sprouts," and Gus Frazier, "A Need for Less Expertise," in *Twice Around the Park* (double–bill), Syracuse Stage, Syracuse, NY, 1981, then Cort Theatre, New York City, 1982, later Edinburgh Festival, Edinburgh, Scotland, 1984.

Stephan Aleksey Sudakov, *The Nest of the Woodgrouse,* New York Shakespeare Festival, Estelle R. Newman Theatre, Public Theatre, New York City, 1984.

The Flowering Peach, Coconut Grove Playhouse, Coconut Grove, FL, 1986.

Monsieur Paul Vigneron, *Opera Comique,* Eisenhower Theatre, John F. Kennedy Center for the Performing Arts, 1987.

Waitin' in the Wings: The Night the Understudies Take Center Stage, Triplex International Theatre Festival, Triplex Theatre, New York City, 1988.

David Cole, *Cafe Crown,* New York Shakespeare Festival, Estelle R. Newman Theatre, Public Theatre, 1988, then Brooks Atkinson Theatre, New York City, 1989.

The Players Club Centennial Salute, Shubert Theatre, 1989.

Marley's ghost and Fezziwig, *A Christmas Carol,* Hudson Theatre, New York City, 1990.

Gregory Solomon, *The Price,* Roundabout Theatre Company, Criterion Center Stage Right Theatre, New York City, 1992.

In Persons, Kaufman Theatre, New York City, 1993.

Noah, *The Flowering Peach,* National Actors Theatre, Lyceum Theatre, New York City, 1994.

Mr. Green, *Visiting Mr. Green,* Stockbridge, MA, 1996, later Coconut Grove Playhouse, 1997, then Union Square Theatre, New York City, 1997.

Dear Heartsey (staged reading), Colden Auditorium, Queens College of the City University of New York, Flushing, NY, 1998.

Host and narrator, *Genius in Love,* Brooklyn Center for the Performing Arts, Brooklyn, NY, 1999.

Tennessee Williams Remembered, Arclight Theatre, New York City, 1999, then Bay Street Theatre, Sag Harbor, NY, 2003.

Sid Garden, *Down the Garden Paths,* George Street Theatre, New Brunswick, NJ, 1999, then Minetta Lane Theatre, New York City, 2000–2001.

A Shakespearean Tribute to the Late Sir John Gielgud, Kaye Playhouse, Hunter College of the City University of New York, New York City, 2000.

Brave New World, Town Hall Theatre, New York City, 2002.

An Evening with Eli Wallach, Martin E. Segal Theatre, Graduate Center of the City University of New York, New York City, 2003.

The Atrain Plays, Kaye Playhouse, Hunter College of the City University of New York, 2003.

Cohost, *My New York* (benefit performance), Lucille Lortel Theatre, 2004.

Remembering Anne Frank on Her 75th Birthday, Martin E. Segal Theatre, Graduate Center of the City University of New York, 2004.

In Persons, John Drew Theatre, Guild Hall, East Hampton, NY, 2005.

Love 'n Courage (benefit performance), Theatre for the New City, New York City, 2005.

Also appeared in *This Property Is Condemned,* Equity Library Theatre, New York City; and in *Lady from the Sea* and *What Every Woman Knows,* both New York City productions.

Stage Appearances; Major Tours:

Alvarro Mangiacavallo, *The Rose Tattoo,* U.S. cities, 1951.

Sakini, *The Teahouse of the August Moon,* U.S. cities, 1956.

Ben, *The Tiger,* and Paul XXX, *The Typists,* (double–bill), U.S. cities, 1966.

Ollie H. and Wesley, *Promenade All!,* U.S. cities, 1971.

General St. Pe, *Waltz of the Toreadors,* U.S. cities, 1973–74.

Colin, *Absent Friends,* U.S. cities, 1977.

Alexander, *Every Good Boy Deserves Favour,* U.S. cities, 1979.

Also toured in a production of *The House of Blue Leaves.*

Film Appearances:

Danger, 1952.

Silva Vacarro, *Baby Doll,* Warner Bros., 1956.

Dancer, *The Lineup,* Columbia, 1958.

Calvera, *The Magnificent Seven,* United Artists, 1960.

Poncho/Baron von Roelitz, *Seven Thieves,* Twentieth Century–Fox, 1960.

Guido, *The Misfits,* United Artists, 1961.

John, *Adventures of a Young Man* (also known as *Ernest Hemingway's "Adventures of a Young Man"* and *Hemingway's "Adventures of a Young Man"*), Twentieth Century–Fox, 1962.

Charlie Gant, *How the West Was Won,* Cinerama, 1962.

Sergeant Craig, *The Victors,* Columbia, 1963.

Warren Stone, *Act One,* Warner Bros., 1964.

Rodriguez Valdez, *Kisses for My President* (also known as *Kisses for the President*), Warner Bros., 1964.

Stratos, *The Moon–Spinners,* Buena Vista, 1964.

Shah of Khwarezm, *Genghis Khan* (also known as *Dschingis Khan* and *Dzingis–Kan*), Columbia, 1965.

The General, *Lord Jim,* Columbia, 1965.

David Leland, *How to Steal a Million* (also known as *How to Steal a Million Dollars and Live Happily Ever After*), Twentieth Century–Fox, 1966.

Tuco Benedito Pacifico Juan Maria Ramirez (The Ugly), *The Good, the Bad, and the Ugly* (also known as *The Good, the Ugly, and the Bad, El bo, el lleig I el dolent, El bueno, el feo y el malo,* and *Il buono, il brutto, il cattivo*), United Artists, 1967.

Ben Harris, *The Tiger Makes Out,* Columbia, 1967.

Harry Hunter, *How to Save a Marriage (and Ruin Your Life)* (also known as *Band of Gold*), Columbia, 1968.

Tennessee Fredericks, *A Lovely Way to Die* (also known as *A Lovely Way to Go*), Universal, 1968.

Cab driver, *New York City—The Most* (documentary), 1968.

Cacopoulos, *Revenge at El Paso* (also known as *Ace High, Four Gunmen of Ave Maria, Have Gun Will Travel, Revenge in El Paso,* and *Il quattro dell'ave Maria*), Paramount, 1969.

Frankie Scannapieco, *The Brain* (also known as *Le cerveau* and *Il cervello*), Paramount, 1969.

Ben Baker, *MacKenna's Gold,* Columbia, 1969.

Napoleon Bonaparte, *The Adventures of Gerard* (also known as *Adventures of Brigadier Gerard* and *Le avventure di Gerard*), United Artists, 1970.

Store clerk, *The Angel Levine,* United Artists, 1970.

Arthur Mason, *The People Next Door,* Avco Embassy, 1970.

Mario Gambretti, *Zigzag* (also known as *False Witness* and *Zig-Zag*), Metro–Goldwyn–Mayer, 1970.

Kifke, *Romance of a Horse Thief* (also known as *Le roman d'un voleur de chevaux*), Allied Artists, 1971.

Sotto a chi tocca! (also known as *Besos para Ella, Punetazos para todos* and *Vier Froehliche Rabauken*), 1972.

Lozoya, *Viva la muerte ... Tuya!* (also known as *Don't Turn the Other Cheek, The Killer from Yuma, Long Live Your Death, Viva le muerte ... Tua!,* and *Zwei wilde companeros*), 1972, International Amusement Corp., 1974.

Lynn Forshay, *Cinderella Liberty,* Twentieth Century–Fox, 1973.

Don Vittorio, *Crazy Joe,* Columbia, 1974.

Narrator, *L'Chaim–To Life!,* 1974.

Sheriff Edward Gideon (Blackjack), *Il bianco, il giallo, il nero* (also known as *Shoot First ... Ask Questions Later, Samurai, White, Yellow, Black, El blanco, el amarillo, y el negro,* and *Le blanc, le jaune et le noir*), CIDIF, 1975.

Ras (some sources cite Cesare), *Attenti al buffone!* (also known as *Eye of the Cat*), Medusa Distribuzione, 1975.

Monsignor, *Nasty Habits* (also known as *The Abbess*), Brut, 1976.

Benjamin Franklin, *Independence* (short film), Twentieth Century–Fox, 1976.

Joe, *Stateline Motel* (also known as *Last Chance, Last Chance for a Born Loser, Last Chance Motel, Motel of Fear,* and *L'ultima chance*), International Cinefilm–NMD, 1976.

Detective Pietro Riccio, *... E tanta paura* (also known as *Plot of Fear* and *Too Much Fear*), 1976.

Adam Coffin, *The Deep,* Columbia, 1977.

General Tom Reser, *The Domino Principle* (also known as *The Domino Killings* and *El domino principe*), Avco Embassy, 1977.

Detective Gatz, *The Sentinel,* Universal, 1977.

Rabbi Gold, *Girlfriends,* Warner Bros., 1978.

Vince Marlowe, "Dynamite Hands," and Pop, "Baxter's Beauties of 1933," *Movie Movie,* Warner Bros., 1978.

(As Ely Wallach) Gerolamo Giarra, *Squadra antimafia* (also known as *Little Italy*), 1978.

Man in oil, *Circle of Iron* (also known as *The Silent Flute*), Avco Embassy, 1979.

Sal Hyman, *Firepower,* Associated Film Distribution, 1979.

Joe Diamond, *Winter Kills,* Avco Embassy, 1979.

Ritchie Blumenthal, *The Hunter,* Paramount, 1980.

Himself, *Acting: Lee Strasberg and the Actors Studio* (documentary), Davada Enterprises, 1981.

Lieutenant General Leporello, *The Salamander* (also known as *La salamandra*), ITC, 1983.

Sam Orowitz, *Sam's Son,* Invictus, 1984.

Leon B. Little, *Tough Guys,* Buena Vista, 1986.

Himself, *Hello Actors Studio* (documentary), Actors Studio, 1987.

Dr. Herbert A. Morrison, *Nuts,* Warner Bros., 1987.

Hollywood Uncensored (documentary), Castle Hill, 1987.

"The Sahara Forest" and "Climbed up the Ladder and Had Her," *Funny,* Original Cinema, 1988.

Narrator, *Terezin Diary,* 1989.

Rosengarten (also known as *The Rose Garden*), 1989.

Smoke, 1990.

Cotton Weinberger, *The Two Jakes,* Paramount, 1990.

Don Altobello, *Mario Puzo's The Godfather, Part III* (also known as *The Godfather, Part III*), Paramount, 1990.

Sam Abrams, *Article 99,* Orion, 1992.

George Lieberhoff, *Mistress* (also known as *Hollywood Mistress*), Rainbow Releasing/Tribeca Productions, 1992.

Peck, *Night and the City,* Twentieth Century–Fox, 1992.

Don Siro, *Honey Sweet Love* (also known as *Caro dolce amore* and *Miele dolce amore*), 1994.

Sheldon Dodge, *Two Much* (also known as *Loco de amor*), Buena Vista, 1995.

Donald Fallon, *The Associate,* Buena Vista, 1996.

Strasser, *Uninvited* (also known as *L'escluso*), Vine International, 1999.

Rabbi Ben Lewis, *Keeping the Faith,* Touchstone, 2000.

The rebbe, *Advice and Dissent* (short film), Film Shack/Leibco Films, 2002.

Cinerama Adventure (documentary), Cinerama, 2002.

The Root, 2003.

(Uncredited) Mr. Loonie, *Mystic River,* Warner Bros., 2003.

Reader, *The Education of Gore Vidal* (documentary), 2003.

Broadway: The Golden Age, by the Legends Who Were There (documentary; also known as *Broadway, Broadway: The Golden Age,* and *Broadway: The Movie*), Dada Films, 2004.

Sol Spivak, *King of the Corner,* Elevation Filmworks/Ardustry Entertainment, 2004.

Voices, *Unforgivable Blackness: The Rise and Fall of Jack Johnson* (documentary), Paramount Home Video, 2004.

Voice of the father, *The Moon and the Son,* 2005.

Narrator, *The Easter Egg Adventure* (animated), First Look Home Entertainment, 2005.

Film Work:

(Uncredited) Producer, *The Tiger Makes Out,* Columbia, 1967.

Television Appearances; Series:

Narrator, *The Dream Factory,* 1975.

Vincent Danzig, *Our Family Honor,* ABC, 1985–86.

Cohost, *Character Studies,* PBS, 2005.

Also host of the series *Directions,* ABC.

Television Appearances; Miniseries:

Gus Farber, *Seventh Avenue,* NBC, 1977.

Ben Ezra, *Harold Robbins' "The Pirate"* (also known as *The Pirate*), CBS, 1978.

Uncle Vern Damico, *The Executioner's Song,* NBC, 1982.

Father Hernando DeTalavera, *Christopher Columbus* (also known as *Cristoforo Colombo*), CBS, 1985.

Frank Latella, *Vendetta: Secrets of a Mafia Bride* (also known as *Bride of Violence, A Family Matter, A Woman of Honor,* and *Dona d'onore,*), syndicated, 1991.

Frank Latella, *Vendetta II: The New Mafia* (also known as *Bride of Violence 2, Vendetta 2,* and *Dona d'onore 2*), syndicated, 1993.

Voice, *Baseball* (also known as *The History of Baseball*), PBS, 1994.

Narrator, "The Western," *American Cinema,* PBS, 1995.

Narrator, *Sex and the Silver Screen,* Showtime, 1996.

Voice, "New York: A Documentary Film," *American Experience,* PBS, 1999.

Television Appearances; Movies:

Dr. Frank Enari, *A Cold Night's Death* (also known as *The Chill Factor*), ABC, 1973.

DeWitt Foster, *Indict and Convict,* ABC, 1974.

Olan Vacio, *Fugitive Family,* CBS, 1980.

Sal Galucci, *The Pride of Jesse Hallam,* CBS, 1981.

Bert Silverman, *Skokie* (also known as *Once They Marched through a Thousand Towns*), CBS, 1981.

Mauritzi Apt, *The Wall,* CBS, 1982.

Dr. William Hitzig, *Anatomy of an Illness,* CBS, 1984.

Dr. Huffman, *Murder: By Reason of Insanity* (also known as *My Sweet Victim*), CBS, 1985.

Norman Voss, *Something in Common,* CBS, 1986.

Yacov, *The Impossible Spy,* HBO, 1987.

Moses Zelnick (some sources cite Moses Resnick), *Legacy of Lies,* USA Network, 1992.

Bill Presser, *Teamster Boss: The Jackie Presser Story* (also known as *Life on the High Wire* and *Teamster Boss*), HBO, 1992.

Deluca, *Naked City: Justice with a Bullet,* Showtime, 1998.

Erich, *The Bookfair Murders,* CTV (Canada), 2000.

Leonard Goldenson, *Monday Night Mayhem,* TNT, 2002.

Television Appearances; Episodic:

"The Beautiful Bequest," *The Philco Television Playhouse,* NBC, 1949.

"Rappaccini's Daughter," *Lights Out,* NBC, 1951.

"The System," *Danger,* CBS, 1952.

Maigret, "Stan, the Killer," *Summer Studio One* (also known as *Studio One*), CBS, 1952.

"Deadlock," *The Web,* CBS, 1952.

"The Portrait," *Armstrong Circle Theatre,* 1952.

"The Baby," *The Philco Television Playhouse,* NBC, 1953.

"The Brownstone," *Goodyear Playhouse,* NBC, 1954.

"Delicate Story," *Kraft Television Theatre,* 1954.

"Shadow of the Champ," *The Philco Television Playhouse,* NBC, 1955.

"Mr. Blue Ocean," *General Electric Theatre,* CBS, 1955.

Nacho, "The Outsiders," *The Philco Television Playhouse,* NBC, 1955.

Cristof, "A Fragile Affair," *The Kaiser Aluminum Hour,* NBC, 1956.

Guest, *Toast of the Town* (also known as *The Ed Sullivan Show*), 1956, 1970.

Peter Hendon, "The Man Who Wasn't Himself," *Studio One,* CBS, 1957.

"The World of Nick Adams," *The Seven Lively Arts,* CBS, 1957.

Albert Anastasia, "Albert Anastasia—His Life and Death," *Climax!,* CBS, 1958.

Poskrebyshev, "The Plot to Kill Stalin," *Playhouse 90,* CBS, 1958.

Raymond Perez, "My Father the Fool," *Desilu Playhouse* (also known as *Westinghouse Desilu Playhouse*), CBS, 1958.

Simon, "The Emperor's New Clothes," *Shirley Temple's Storybook,* NBC, 1958.

"The Death of Paul Dane," *Suspicion,* NBC, 1958.

Rafael, "For Whom the Bell Tolls: Parts 1 & 2," *Playhouse 90,* CBS, 1959.

"The Blue Men," *Playhouse 90,* CBS, 1959.

Sancho Panza, "I, Don Quixote," *The DuPont Show of the Month,* CBS, 1959.

"The Margaret Bourke–White Story," *Sunday Showcase,* NBC, 1960.

Joseph Lanowski, "Birthright," *Goodyear Theatre* (also known as *Alcoa/Goodyear Theatre*), NBC, 1960.

"Lullaby," *Play of the Week,* syndicated, 1960.

"Hope is the Thing with Feathers," *Robert Herridge Theatre,* CBS, 1960.

Detective Bane, "A Death of Princes," *Naked City,* ABC, 1960.

"A Bit of Glory," *Outlaws,* NBC, 1962.

George Manin, "A Run for the Money," *Naked City,* ABC, 1962.

Manny Jacobs, "Tomorrow, the Man," *The Dick Powell Show,* NBC, 1962.

Pantomime Quiz, 1963.

Mystery guest, *What's My Line?,* 1965.

"Carol Channing vs. Eli Wallach," *Password,* 1965.

Mr. Freeze, "Ice Spy," *Batman,* ABC, 1967.

Mr. Freeze, "The Duo Defy," *Batman,* ABC, 1967.

Doug Lambert, "Dear Friends," *CBS Playhouse,* CBS, 1967.

Personality, 1968.

Guest, *Rowan & Martin's Laugh–In,* 1969.

Guest, *The Tonight Show Starring Johnny Carson,* NBC, multiple appearances, 1970–72.

James Johnson Scott, "Legal Maneuver," *The Young Lawyers,* ABC, 1971.

"Paradise Lost," *N.E.T. Playhouse,* PBS, 1971.

"The Typists," *Hollywood Television Theatre,* PBS, 1971.

Fuzzy, "Compliments of the Season," *Orson Welles' "Great Mysteries"* (also known as *Great Mysteries*), syndicated, 1973.

Lee Curtin, "A Question of Answers," *Kojak,* CBS, 1975.

Gerry Williams (the target), "Shatterproof," *Tales of the Unexpected,* syndicated, 1981.

"Tommy Howell," *An American Portrait,* CBS, 1985.

"The Silver Maiden," *Shortstories,* Arts and Entertainment, 1986.

Tim Charles, "To Bind the Wounds," *Highway to Heaven,* NBC, 1986.

"The Black Tomb," *Worlds Beyond,* 1986.

Guest, *Late Night with David Letterman,* 1986, 1990.

Gene Malloy, "A Father's Faith," *Highway to Heaven,* NBC, 1987.

Salvatore Gambino, "A Very Good Year for Murder," *Murder, She Wrote,* CBS, 1988.

Yosef Kandinsky, "Kandinsky's Vault," *Alfred Hitchcock Presents,* USA Network, 1988.

Judge Adam Biel, "There Goes the Judge," *L.A. Law,* 1991.

Simon Vilanis, "The Working Stiff," *Law & Order,* NBC, 1992.

Narrator, "Once There Was a Tree," *Reading Rainbow,* 1994.

Inside the Actors Studio, Bravo, 1998.

Joe Franlangelo, "Kids: Part 1," *100 Centre Street,* Arts and Entertainment, 2001.

Jay Bickford, "I Never Schlunged My Father," *The Education of Max Bickford,* CBS, 2002.

Jay Bickford, "Genesis," *The Education of Max Bickford,* CBS, 2002.

Jay Bickford, "One More Time," *The Education of Max Bickford,* CBS, 2002.

Mr. Weiss, "Betrayal," *The Job,* ABC, 2002.

Mr. Langston, "A Boy Falling Out of the Sky" (also known as "Shifts Happen"), *ER,* NBC, 2003.

Norman, "American Woman," *Whoopi,* NBC, 2004.

Also appeared in the series *Backstory,* AMC.

Television Appearances; Specials:

Dauphin, "The Lark," *Hallmark Hall of Fame,* NBC, 1957.

Dan, "Where Is Thy Brother?," *Jewish Appeals Special,* NBC, 1958.

Narrator, *Gift of the Magi,* 1958.

"Happy" Locarno, *Poppies Are Also Flowers* (also known as *Danger Grows Wild, The Opium Connection, The Poppy Is Also a Flower,* and *Mohn ist auch eine blume*), ABC, 1966.

Presenter, *The 22nd Annual Tony Awards,* NBC, 1968.

Leo, "Paradise Lost," *Great Performances,* PBS, 1974.

Narrator, *Houston, We've Got a Problem,* 1974.

"Twenty Shades of Pink," *General Electric Theatre,* CBS, 1976.

"The Film Society of Lincoln Center: A Tribute to John Huston," *Live from Lincoln Center,* PBS, 1980.

The Kennedy Center Honors: A Celebration of the Performing Arts, CBS, 1984.

The ABC All–Star Spectacular, ABC, 1985.

Mr. Prince, "Rocket to the Moon," *American Playhouse,* PBS, 1986.

We the People 200: The Constitutional Gala, CBS, 1987.

Host and narrator, *Hollywood's Favorite Heavy: Businessmen on Primetime TV,* PBS, 1987.

The Typists, Arts and Entertainment, 1987.

Narrator, *It's Up to Us: The Giraffe Project,* PBS, 1988.

Ira Abrams, "A Matter of Conscience" (also known as "Silent Witness"), *CBS Schoolbreak Special,* CBS, 1989.

"Sanford Meisner: The American Theatre's Best Kept Secret," *American Masters,* PBS, 1990.

Himself, *The Godfather Family: A Look Inside,* HBO, 1990.

Voice, "Coney Island," *The American Experience,* PBS, 1991.

"Helen Hayes: First Lady of the American Theatre," *American Masters,* PBS, 1991.

Michael Landon: Memories with Laughter and Love, NBC, 1991.

"Miracle on 44th Street: A Portrait of the Actors Studio," *American Masters,* PBS, 1991.

World War II: A Personal Journey, The Disney Channel, 1991.

Voice of William H. Crook, *Lincoln,* ABC, 1992.

Street Scenes: New York on Film, AMC, 1992.

Voice, "The Donner Party," *The American Experience,* PBS, 1992.

Narrator, *It's Alive: The True Story of Frankenstein,* Arts and Entertainment, 1994.

Voice, *River of Steel,* PBS, 1994.

Narrator, *Elia Kazan: A Director's Journey,* AMC, 1995.

Voices of Horace Greeley and Henry Bergh, *P. T. Barnum: America's Greatest Showman,* The Discovery Channel, 1995.

Voice, "The Way West" (also known as "The West"), *The American Experience,* PBS, 1995.

(In archive footage) *Ennio Morricone,* BBC (England), 1995.

"Yul Brynner: The Man Who Was King," *Biography,* Arts and Entertainment, 1995.

"Marilyn Monroe: The Mortal Goddess," *Biography,* Arts and Entertainment, 1996.

Interviewee, *Clark Gable: Tall, Dark, and Handsome,* TNT, 1996.

Cronkite Remembers (also known as *Walter Cronkite Remembers*), CBS, 1996.

The 50th Annual Tony Awards, CBS, 1996.

Narrator, *The Man Who Drew Bug–Eyed Monsters,* PBS, 1996.

Narrator, *The Moviemakers: Arthur Penn* (also known as *Arthur Penn*), PBS, 1996.

Narrator, *The Moviemakers: Robert Wise* (also known as *Robert Wise*), PBS, 1996.

Narrator, *The Moviemakers: Stanley Donen* (also known as *Stanley Donen*), PBS, 1996.

Interviewee, *James Dean: A Portrait,* 1996.

Voice, *Mary Lincoln's Insanity File,* The Discovery Channel, 1996.

Interviewee, *Marilyn Monroe: The Mortal Goddess,* Arts and Entertainment, 1996.

Voices of Pinchas Freudiger and David Ben–Gurion, *The Trial of Adolf Eichmann,* PBS, 1997.

20th Century–Fox: The First 50 Years, AMC, 1997.

Interviewee, *Karl Malden: Workingman's Actor,* Arts and Entertainment, 1998.

Interviewee, *Lee Strasberg: The Method Man,* Arts and Entertainment, 1998.

Interviewee, *Steve McQueen: The E! True Hollywood Story,* E! Entertainment Network, 1998.

Interviewee, *Tennessee Williams,* Arts and Entertainment, 1998.

Narrator, *Jones Beach: An American Riviera,* PBS, 1999.

Narrator, *The Lives of Lillian Hellman,* PBS, 1999.

Interviewee, *Tony Randall: Center Stage,* Arts and Entertainment, 1999.

Guns for Hire: The Making of "The Magnificent Seven," Channel 4 (England), 2000.

Interviewee, "Clint Eastwood: Out of the Shadows," *American Masters,* PBS, 2000.

In Our City: New Yorkers Remember September 11th, PBS, 2002.

The 100 Greatest Movie Stars, Channel 4, 2003.

Voice, *Horatio's Drive: America's First Road Trip,* PBS, 2003.

"Making 'The Misfits'," *Great Performances,* PBS, 2003.

Steve McQueen: The Essence of Cool, TNT and TCM, 2005.

Television Appearances; Pilots:

Joe Verga, *Embassy,* ABC, 1985.

Vincent Danzig, *Our Family Honor,* ABC, 1985.

RECORDINGS

Videos:

Hollywood Remembers Marilyn Monroe, Amvest Video, 1989.

Nonsense and Lullabys: Poems, 1992.

Nonsense and Lullabys: Nursery Rhymes, 1992.

Leone's West, Metro–Goldwyn–Mayer/United Artists Home Entertainment, 2004.

The Leone Style, Metro–Goldwyn–Mayer/United Artists Home Entertainment, 2004.

WRITINGS

For Stage:

Compiler (with Anne Jackson) *Tennessee Williams Remembered,* Arclight Theatre, New York City, 1999, then Bay Street Theatre, Sag Harbor, NY, 2003.

Other:

(With David Black) *The Actor's Audition,* 1990.

The Good, the Bad, and Me: In My Anecdotage (memoir), Harcourt, 2005.

Contributor to periodicals, including *Films and Filming.*

ADAPTATIONS

Wallach's portrayal of Don Altobello in the film *Mario Puzo's The Godfather, Part III* was included in the compilation, *The Godfather Trilogy: 1901–1980* (also known as *The Godfather Trilogy*), 1992.

OTHER SOURCES

Books:

Thomas, Nicholas, editor, *The International Dictionary of Films and Filmmakers,* Volume 3: *Actors and Actresses,* 4th edition, St. James Press, 2000.

Wallace, Eli, *The Good, the Bad, and Me: In My Anecdotage,* Harcourt, 2005.

Periodicals:

Films in Review, August–September, 1983.

WALSH, Gwynyth
(Gwyneth Walsh, Gwynth Walsh)

PERSONAL

Born in Winnipeg, Manitoba, Canada. *Education:* University of Alberta, B.F.A., theatre.

Addresses: *Agent*—Lucas Talent, Sun Tower 100 West Pender St., 7th Floor, Vancouver V6B 1R8, Canada.

Career: Actor. Sometimes credited as Gwyneth Walsh.

Awards, Honors: DramaLogue Award, best actress, for *Much Ado about Nothing.*

CREDITS

Film Appearances:

Dr. Rachel Carson, *Blue Monkey* (also known as *Green Monkey, Insect,* and *Invasion of the Bodysuckers*), Winson Video, 1987.

Dr. Robert, *La bottega dell'orefice* (also known as *Der Laden des Goldschmieds, Bonds of Love, La boutique de l'orfevre* and *The Jeweller's Shop*), Alliance, 1988.

Helen Schroeder, *The Portrait,* 1992.

Liv Forrester, *The Crush,* Warner Bros., 1993.

Captain Brock, *Soft Deceit,* Le Monde, 1994.

B'Etor, *Star Trek: Generations* (also known as *Star Trek 7*), 1994.

Martine Quiller, *2103: The Deadly Wake* (also known as *Hydrosphere*), Cineplex–Odeon Home Video, 1997.

Jessica, *Crossing Fields,* Sterling, 1997.

Julie, *MXP: Most Xtreme Primat* (video; also known as *MVP 3* and *MXP: Mon xtreme primate*), Miramax, 2003.

Sarah, *Flush,* Base 9, 2004.

Television Appearances; Series:

Dr. Patricia Da Vinci, *Da Vinci's Inquest,* CBC, 1998–2002.

Television Appearances; Movies:

Phoebe, the wardrobe mistress, *Iolanthe,* 1984.

(Uncredited) Betty, *The Christmas Wife,* 1988.

Angie Daniels, *The Challengers* (also known as *Le defi de Marie* and *Le defis de Marie*), syndicated, 1989.

Maria Sorrento, *Perry Mason: The Case of the Maligned Mobster* (also known as *The Case of the Maligned Mobster*), NBC, 1991.

Stacey, *The Girl from Mars,* The Family Channel, 1991.

Janet David, *My Son Johnny* (also known as *Bad Seed*), CBS, 1991.

Sandra Guard, *Darkness before Dawn,* NBC, 1993.

Jenine, *Without a Kiss Goodbye* (also known as *Falsely Accused* and *The Laurie Samuels Story*), CBS, 1993.

(As Gwynth Walsh) *In the Heat of the Night: Give Me Your Life,* CBS, 1994.

Jake's mom, *Shock Treatment,* 1995.

Pearl Dion, *Falling from the Sky: Flight 174* (also known as *Freefall: Flight 174*), ABC, 1995.

Barbara, *The Other Mother: A Moment of Truth Movie,* Lifetime, 1995.

Lydia Sawyer, *Justice for Annie: A Moment of Truth Movie,* NBC, 1996.

Ann Lucca, *The Limbic Region,* Showtime, 1996.

Vicky Cooke, *Stand against Fear* (also known as *Moment of Truth: Stand against Fear* and *Unlikely Suspects*), NBC, 1996.

Joy Pigeon, *The Perfect Mother* (also known as *The Mother-In-Law*), CBS, 1997.

Patty, *Final Descent,* CBS, 1997.

Astrid Kar, *Zenon: Girl of the 21st Century,* The Disney Channel, 1999.

Lynn Young, *A Gift of Love: The Daniel Huffman Story,* Showtime, 1999.

Michelle Archer, *Our Guys: Outrage in Glen Ridge,* ABC, 1999.

Mrs. Bryan, *Ice Angel* (also known as *L'ange de la glace*), Fox Family, 2000.

Jo, *Stealing Christmas,* USA Network, 2003.

Television Appearances; Specials:

Mother in 1930, *A Child's Christmas in Wales,* PBS, 1987.

Linda Arndt, *Getting Away with Murder: The JonBenet Ramsey Story,* Fox, 2000.

Television Appearances; Miniseries:

Lee Kingsley, *Passion and Paradise,* 1988.

Doctor/abductee, *Taken* (also known as *Steven Spielberg Presents "Taken"*), Sci–Fi Channel, 2002.

Television Appearances; Pilots:

Rita Gillete, *The Return of Ben Casey,* syndicated, 1988.

Television Appearances; Episodic:

Jennifer Christie, "A Change of Mind," *Adderly,* CBS, 1986.

Val St. Clair, "Take My Jokes, Please," *Street Legal,* CBC, 1987.

April Morgan, "Equal Partners," *Street Legal,* CBC, 1988.

Lucy Morrison, "Ay, There's the Rib," *Diamonds,* USA Network and CBC, 1988.

Charlotte, "The Resurrection," *War of the Worlds,* syndicated, 1988.

"For Old Time's Sake," *My Secret Identity,* syndicated, 1988.

Christine, "Freedom One," *Captain Power and the Soldiers of the Future,* 1988.

Faith, *Starting from Scratch,* 1988.

Reatha Wilkerson, "13 O'Clock," *Friday the 13th* (also known as *Friday the 13th: The Series*), syndicated, 1989.

Anne Hathaway, "D.U.I." (also known as "Driving under the Influence"), *Alfred Hitchcock Presents,* USA Network, 1989.

Elaine, "Cat and Mouse," *The Twilight Zone,* syndicated, 1989.

Melanie Hayes, "Leave It to Geezer," *L.A. Law,* NBC, 1989.

(Uncredited) Melanie Hayes, "The Unbearable Lightness of Boring," *L.A. Law,* NBC, 1989.

Melanie Hayes, "His Suit Is Hersuit," *L.A. Law,* NBC, 1989.

Diane Elrea, "The Takeover," *Alien Nation,* Fox, 1989.

"Over the Edge," *Mom P.I.,* CBC, 1990.

Sandra Hopkins, "The Blackmailer," *Matlock,* NBC, 1990.

Joanna McKenney, "Not in My Back Yard," *E.A.R.T.H. Force,* 1990.

Miss Montana, parole agent, "High Control," *MacGyver,* ABC, 1991.

Marissa, "Marissa," *Sweating Bullets,* CBS, 1991.

B'Etor, "Redemption: Parts 1 & 2," *Star Trek: The Next Generation,* syndicated, 1991.

"Black Magic," *Beyond Reality,* 1991.

Rachael Rockwell, "Alive and Kicking," *Sweating Bullets,* CBS, 1992.

Pam Weldon, "Escape," *The Commish,* ABC, 1992.

B'Etor, "Past Prologue," *Star Trek: Deep Space Nine,* syndicated, 1993.

Kiki Rice, "Last Laugh," *Matlock,* ABC, 1993.

Tod's mother, "The Broken Record," *Eerie, Indiana,* NBC, 1993.

B'Etor, "Firstborn," *Star Trek: The Next Generation,* syndicated, 1994.

Lula Finch, "Give Me Your Life: Parts 1 & 2," *In the Heat of the Night,* CBS, 1994.

The hunter, "Hunted," *Forever Knight,* syndicated, 1994.

Tessa Stark, "Corporate Raiders," *Robocop,* syndicated, 1994.

Margaret Jeffers, "The Doctor Who Rocks the Cradle," *Melrose Place,* Fox, 1994.

Gina Powell, "Murder of the Month Club," *Murder, She Wrote,* CBS, 1994.

Joan Williams, "Holiday on Ice," *One West Waikiki,* syndicated, 1995.

Joan Williams, "Kingmare on Night Street," *One West Waikiki,* syndicated, 1996.

Detective L. Specateli, "Love Gods," *Sliders,* Fox, 1996.

"Till Death Do Us Part," *High Incident,* ABC, 1996.

"Hot Wire," *High Incident,* ABC, 1997.

"Meltdown," *The Newsroom,* 1997.

Chief Examiner Nimira, "Random Thoughts," *Star Trek: Voyager,* UPN, 1997.

Emma Shetterly, "Anamnesis," *Millennium,* Fox, 1998.

Madeline Strong, "Sixteen Candles," *Twice in a Lifetime,* PAX and CTV, 1999.

Barbara Knight, "Be Patient," *ER,* NBC, 2000.

Dr. Timmons, "Bats Off to Larry," *NYPD Blue,* ABC, 2000.

Dr. Timmons, "The Last Round Up," *NYPD Blue,* ABC, 2000.

Dr. Timmons, "Daveless in New York," *NYPD Blue,* ABC, 2001.

Dr. Timmons, "Waking up Is Hard to Do," *NYPD Blue,* ABC, 2001.

Kelmaa/Queen Egeria, "Cure," *Stargate SG–1,* Sci–Fi Channel and syndicated, 2002.

Mrs. Moore, "Nocturne," *Smallville,* The WB, 2002.

"Age of Reason," *Strange World,* ABC, 2002.

Also appeared in *The Round Table,* NBC; as Helen, *Marker,* UPN.

Stage Appearances:

Beatrice, *Much Ado about Nothing,* John Anson Ford Amphitheatre, Los Angeles, 1990.

Prospero, *The Tempest,* Mad Duck Equity Co–op, Jericho Arts Centre, Vancouver, British Columbia, Canada, 2004.

Also appeared as Cara, *Domino Heart,* Section 8, Pacific Theatre, Vancouver; in *Death of a Salesman; Diaries of Adam and Eve; King Lear; Henry IV.*

WARD, Wally
    See LANGHAM, Wallace

WATERS, Dina
    See SPYBEY, Dina

WEINBERG, Matt 1990–

PERSONAL

Full name, Matthew Phillip Weinberg; born July 13, 1990, in Los Angeles, CA; son of Larry (a public relations executive) and Dana Weinberg; brother of Mike Weinberg (an actor). *Education:* Studied acting with Marnie Cooper; studied dialect with Larry Moss. *Avocational Interests:* Playing baseball and with his dogs.

Addresses: *Agent*—Innovative Agents, 1505 Tenth St., Santa Monica, CA 90401. *Manager*—Reel Talent Management, P.O. Box 491035, Los Angeles, CA 90049.

Career: Actor. Appeared in television commercials for McDonald's, Digimon, and Loanworks.

Awards, Honors: Young Artist Award nomination, best performance in a TV comedy series—guest starring young performer, 2000, for *Friends;* CAMIE Award, Young Artist Award nomination, best performance in a TV movie (comedy or drama)—young actor ten or under, 2001, for *The Last Dance;* Young Artist Award nomination, best performance in a voice–over role—young artist, 2005, for *The Lion King 1 1/2;* Young Artist Award, for *An American Daughter.*

CREDITS

Film Appearances:
Max, *Spooky House,* Entertainment Highway, 2000.
Tommy, *X–Men* (also known as *X–Men 1.5*), Twentieth Century–Fox, 2000.
7–year–old Dawg, *Bad Boy* (also known as *Dawg*), Dawg LLC, 2002.
Booger Spencer, *The Hot Chick,* Touchstone, 2002.
8–year–old boy, *Who's Your Daddy?,* Premiere Marketing & Distribution Group, 2003.
Mike, *Haunted Lighthouse* (also known as *R. L. Stine's "Haunted Lighthouse"*), 2003.
Voice of Young Simba, *The Lion King 11/2* (animated; also known as *Lion King 3: Hakuna Matata!*), Walt Disney Home Video, 2004.

Television Appearances; Series:
Eli, *Eli's Theory,* 1999.
Mark O'Keefe, *The O'Keefes,* The WB, 2003.

Television Appearances; Movies:
Nicholas, *An American Daughter* (also known as *Trial by Media*), Lifetime, 2000.
Alex Cope, *The Last Dance,* CBS, 2000.

Television Appearances; Pilots:
Eli, *Eli's Theory,* 1999.
James Bishop, *The (mis)Adventures of Fiona Plum,* The WB, 2001.

Television Appearances; Episodic:
Jack, "Hospital," *Ellen,* ABC, 1998.
Raymond, "The One Where Rachel Smokes," *Friends,* NBC, 1999.
"From the Heart," *Chicken Soup for the Soul,* PAX, 1999.
Sam Lowe, "Subject: Me and My Shadow," *FreakyLinks,* Fox, 2001.
Mickey, "I Am an Angel," *Touched by an Angel,* CBS, 2001.
Sam Lowe, "Subject: The Final Word," *FreakyLinks,* Fox, 2001.
Douglas Leeman, "Beyond Repair," *ER,* NBC, 2002.

WILLIS, Jerome

PERSONAL

Career: Actor.

CREDITS

Film Appearances:
1st British Signals Sergeant, *Foxhole in Cairo,* Paramount, 1961.
The limping man, *Siege of the Saxons,* Columbia, 1963.
Armstrong, *A Jolly Bad Fellow* (also known as *They All Died Laughing*), Continental, 1964.
(Uncredited) Frank Power, *Khartoum,* United International, 1966.
"False" German officer, *The Magus,* Twentieth Century–Fox, 1968.
Lieutenant Commander Tavenar, *Doomwatch,* Embassy, 1972.
General Lord Fairfax, *Winstanley,* BFI, 1975.
Sir Frank Lockwood, *Forbidden Passion: Oscar Wilde,* 1976.
Pathologist, *Lifeforce* (also known as *Space Vampires*), TriStar, 1985.
Translator, *Orlando,* Concorde, 1992.
Moderator, *A Business Affair* (also known as *Astucias de mujer, D'une femme a l'autre* and *Liebe und andere Geschaefte*), Castle Hill, 1994.
Older board member, *The Sea Change* (also known as *Cambio de rumbo*), Europa, 1998.
Stevens, *Global Conspiracy,* BBC Worldwide, 2004.

Television Appearances; Movies:
Ryman, *Time in Advance* (also known as *Out of the Unknown: Time in Advance*), 1965.

Detective Sergeant Latcham, *The Portsmouth Defense,* 1966.

Daniel, *Toddler on the Run* (also known as *Wednesday Play: Toddler on the Run*), 1966.

Detective Inspector Latchem, *Little Master Mind* (also known as *Wednesday Play: Little Master Mind*), 1966.

Cyrano de Bergerac (also known as *Play of the Month: Cyrano de Bergerac*) 1968.

Ned Preston, *Episode* (also known as *W. Somerset Maugham: Episode*), 1969.

Delio, *The Duchess of Malfi* (also known as *Stage 2: The Duchess of Malfi*), BBC, 1972.

The sea captain, *Robinson Crusoe* (also known as *Play of the Month: Robinson Crusoe*), BBC and NBC, 1974.

Chorus, *Oedipus at Colonus* (also known as *Theban Plays: Oedipus at Colonus*), BBC, 1984.

First DPP official, *Death of a Son,* 1988.

Sir Henry Bryant, *March in Windy City,* YTV, 1998.

Otto Kemp, *Heaven on Earth,* BBC, 1998.

Judge, *Care,* 2000.

Magistrate, *Loving You* (also known as *The Rainbow Room*), 2003.

Stan Shaps, *Alibi,* 2003.

Television Appearances; Series:

Allan Woodcourt, *Bleak House,* 1959.

Oliver Cromwell, *Woodstock,* 1973.

Charles Radley, *Within These Walls,* ITV, 1974.

Matthew Peel, *The Sandbaggers,* ITV, 1978.

Captain Rexton Podly, *Space Precinct,* syndicated, 1994.

Television Appearances; Miniseries:

Richmond, *An Age of Kings,* BBC, 1960.

Pompey, *The Spread of the Eagle* (also known as *Antony and Cleopatra, Coriolanus,* and *Julius Caesar*), 1963.

Prince Lichtenstein, *War and Peace,* 1972.

Kessler, BBC, 1981.

Pym, *By the Sword Divided,* 1983.

T. F. Golding, *Tender Is the Night,* Showtime, 1985.

Kurt Vermehren, *Anastasia: The Mystery of Anna,* NBC, 1986.

Mycroft Holmes, *Incident at Victoria Falls* (also known as *Sherlock Holmes and the Incident at Victoria Falls, Sherlock Holmes: Incident at Victoria Falls, Sherlock Holmes: The Star of Africa,* and *The Star of Africa*), syndicated, 1991.

Mycroft Holmes, *Sherlock Holmes and the Leading Lady,* PBS and syndicated, 1992.

Baron Valdemar, *Scarlet Pimpernel* (also known as *The Scarlet Pimpernel and the Kidnapped King*), Arts and Entertainment, 1998.

Dr. Hans Troupman, *The Apocalypse Watch* (also known as *Robert Ludlum's "The Apocalypse Watch"*), ABC, 1997.

Kynaston, *A Certain Justice,* PBS, 1999.

Television Appearances; Specials:

Pathologist, *Unnatural Causes,* PBS, 1994.

Dr. Kynaston, *A Mind to Murder,* PBS, 1996.

Television Appearances; Episodic:

The prince, "The Prince of Limerick," *The Adventures of Sir Lancelot,* ITC, 1957.

"The Victorian Chaise Longue," *Studio Four,* 1962.

Mr. Garston, "Appearance in Court," *Z Cars,* BBC, 1962.

John Irvine, "The Dark Star," *Out of This World,* 1962.

"Comrade Jacob," *Studio Four,* 1962.

Lobb, "Intercrime," *The Avengers,* 1963.

Lieutenant Commander Johnson, "The Critical Moment," *R3,* BBC, 1965.

Pursuer, "The Mirror's New," *Danger Man,* ITV, 1965.

Official, "English Lady Takes Lodgers," *Danger Man,* ITV, 1965.

Ryman, "Time in Advance," *Out of the Unknown,* BBC, 1965.

Brian Logan, "But the Crying...," *Z Cars,* BBC, 1965.

Colonel Maturin, "Someone Is Liable to Get Hurt," *Danger Man,* ITV, 1966.

Joshua Rudge, "How to Succeed ... at Murder," *The Avengers,* ABC, 1966.

Dr. Newman, "The Bigger They Are," *The Troubleshooters,* 1966.

Melville, "Sing a Song of Murder," *Adam Adamant Lives!,* BBC, 1966.

"Defection! The Case of Colonel Petrov," *Play of the Month,* 1966.

Detective Inspector Thomson, "There's Someone Close behind You," *The Baron,* ITC, 1966.

Detective Inspector Pooley, "What Colour a Wolf?," *Softly, Softly,* BBC, 1967.

Mark Rutherford, "Man Running," *Champion House,* 1967.

Major Norman, "Lonely Road," *The Jazz Age,* 1968.

George, "The Rotters," *The Avengers,* ABC, 1969.

Flomard, "Death of a Friend," *Callan,* 1969.

Gilbey, "Kill or Cure," *Paul Temple,* BBC, 1970.

Superintendent Khan, "Influence: Parts 1 & 2," *Z Cars,* BBC, 1971.

"The Moses Basket," *Brett,* 1971.

Superintendent Richards, "Find," *Z Cars,* BBC, 1971.

"Death's Head," *Thirty–Minute Theatre,* BBC, 1971.

Detective Chief Superintendent Richards, "Operation Ascalon," *Z Cars,* BBC, 1972.

Detective Chief Superintendent Richards, "Miller," *Z Cars,* BBC, 1973.

Detective Chief Superintendent Richards, "Defection," *Z Cars,* BBC, 1973.

Stevens, "The Green Death," *Doctor Who,* BBC, 1973.

PPS, "Phase Two," *Scotch on the Rocks,* 1973.

PPS, "Phase Three," *Scotch on the Rocks,* 1973.

PPS, "Phase Four," *Scotch on the Rocks,* 1973.

PPS, "Phase Five," *Scotch on the Rocks,* 1973.

Ladbroke, "A Question of Research," *The Wilde Alliance,* 1978.

Jeremy Longmuir, "Golden Boy," *The Standard,* BBC, 1978.

Professor Henderson, "The Greasy Pole," *Yes, Minister,* BBC2, 1981.

Kessler, 1981.

Rupert Imison, "Low Profile," *Bergerac,* BBC1, 1985.

Roger Gary, "Friends," *King & Castle,* Thames, 1986.

Neil, the party chairman, "The National Education Service," *Yes, Prime Minister,* 1988.

Sir Austin Periam, "The Wapping Conspiracy," *The New Statesman,* 1989.

Sir Austin Periam, "Who Shot Alan B'Stard?," *The New Statesman,* 1989.

Edward Pengelley, "The Cornish Mystery," *Poirot,* ITV and Arts and Entertainment, 1990.

George Handley, "A List of Abuses," *This Is David Harper,* 1990.

Judge, "Shingle Beach," *Stay Lucky,* YTV, 1991.

Harry Enfield's Television Programme, 1992.

Doctor, "In the Mood," *Goodnight Sweetheart,* BBC, 1993.

Doctor, *Blue Heaven,* 1994.

Walker, "Private Lives," *A Touch of Frost,* ITV, 1999.

John Smith, "Blood Will Out," *Midsomer Murders,* ITV and Arts and Entertainment, 1999.

Arthur Clough, "House Rules," *Heartbeat,* ITV, 2003.

Mr. Parish, "The Long Bank Holiday," *The Last Detective,* ITV, 2004.

Ted Reeves, "Much Wants More," *Casualty,* BBC1, 2004.

Aurthur Peyton, "Family Secrets," *Doctors,* BBC, 2004.

Stage Appearances:

Abel, Where Is Your Brother?, Act–Inn Theatre Club, Piccadilly, London, 1974.

Mr. Hardcastle/Mr. Statelov, *The Break of Day,* Haymarket Theatre, Leicester, England, then Royal Court Theatre Downstairs, London, both 1995.

Gonzalo, *The Tempest,* Royal Shakespeare Company, 1999.

Octavius, *Caligula,* Donmar Warehouse, London, 2003.

Also appeared as fisherman, *Pericles,* Royal Shakespeare Company.

Z

ZACAPA, Daniel

PERSONAL

Born in Tegucigalpa, Honduras.

Addresses: *Agent*—House of Representatives, 400 S. Beverly Dr., Suite 101, Beverly Hills, CA 90212.

Career: Actor. Formerly a professional baseball player with the San Francisco Giants.

CREDITS

Film Appearances:

Detective Taylor, *Se7en,* New Line Cinema, 1995.

Harvey Harris, *Up Close & Personal,* Buena Vista, 1996.

Father at book fair, *Phenomenon,* Buena Vista, 1996.

Lead cop, *The Odd Couple II* (also known as *Neil Simon's "The Odd Couple"*), Paramount, 1998.

Hector Chavez, *The Bad Pack,* Lion Gate Films Home Entertainment, 1998.

Peter Vecino, *The Egg Plant Lady,* 2000.

Angel, *Broken* (short film), 2000.

Mexican bartender, *The Mexican,* DreamWorks, 2001.

Renda, *Confessions of a Dangerous Mind* (also known as *Confessions d'un homme dangereux*), Artisan Entertainment, 2002 Hawkins, *First Watch,* 2003.

Sancho, *Coronado,* Uncharted Territory, 2003.

Vice man, *Solomon's Turn,* 2004.

Television Appearances; Series:

Ruben Santiago, *Resurrection Blvd.,* Showtime, 2000.

Television Appearances; Movies:

Carlos, *Grand Avenue,* HBO, 1996.

Luis Flores, *Black Dawn* (also known as *Good Cop, Bad Cop*), Cinemax, 1997.

David Ramierez, *Witness Protection,* HBO, 1999.

Television Appearances; Specials:

The Fix, PBS, 1997.

Television Appearances; Episodic:

Henry Garcia, "Past Tense: Part 2," *Star Trek: Deep Space Nine,* syndicated, 1995.

Power guy, "The Cadillac: Parts 1 & 2," *Seinfeld,* NBC, 1996.

Cesar Fuente, "Hear No Evil," *The Sentinel,* UPN, 1997.

Detective Pate, "Child of the Night," *Beverly Hills, 90210,* Fox, 1997.

Detective Pate, "Deadline," *Beverly Hills, 90210,* Fox, 1997.

Mason, "Contamination," *Players,* NBC, 1998.

B, "The Art of War," *C–16: FBI,* ABC, 1998.

Priest, *Days of Our Lives,* 1999.

Waiter, "Gangland: Part 1," *Diagnosis Murder,* CBS, 1999.

Bernardo, "The Colonel's Wife," *JAG,* CBS, 1999.

Astronomer, "Blink of an Eye," *Star Trek: Voyager,* UPN, 2000.

"Checkmates," *The Practice,* ABC, 2000.

Detective Ben Saganey, "One for the Road," *Judging Amy,* CBS, 2001.

Mr. Suarez, Jr., "The Will," *Six Feet Under,* HBO, 2001.

Renaldo Molina, "Puppy Love," *NYPD Blue,* ABC, 2001.

"Heartless," *The Agency,* CBS, 2002.

Mr. Arintero, "Maple Street," *Without a Trace,* CBS, 2003.

"Blindsided," *The District,* CBS, 2003.

Detective Henry Gomez, "All That Glitters," *Dragnet* (also known as *L.A. Dragnet*), ABC, 2003.

Esteban "Steve" Hernandez, "Red Haven's on Fire," *The West Wing,* NBC, 2003.

Detective, "Redemption," *Dragnet* (also known as *L.A. Dragnet*), ABC, 2003.

Pepe, "Antonia Ramos," *Nip/Tuck,* F/X, 2003.

Pepe, "Escobar Gallardo," *Nip/Tuck,* F/X, 2003.

Warden Antista, "Crossed Out," *She Spies,* syndicated, 2003.

Carlos Ramirez, "Wannabe," *Boomtown,* NBC, 2003.

Also appeared as doctor, *First Time Out,* The WB.

Stage Appearances:

Guru, *Three Travelers,* Odyssey Theatre Ensemble, Los Angeles, 2005.

Cumulative Index

To provide continuity with *Who's Who in the Theatre*, this index interfiles references to *Who's Who in the Theatre*, 1st–17th Editions, and *Who Was Who in the Theatre* (Gale, 1978) with references to *Contemporary Theatre, Film and Television*, Volumes 1–66.

References in the index are identified as follows:

CTFT and volume number—*Contemporary Theatre, Film and Television*, Volumes 1–66
WWT and edition number—*Who's Who in the Theatre*, 1st–17th Editions
WWasWT—*Who Was Who in the Theatre*

Cumulative Index

Cumulative Index

Cumulative Index

H

Cumulative Index

L

M

Cumulative Index

Cumulative Index

U

V

Cumulative Index

X

Y

Cumulative Index

Z

Cumulative Index